Continental Philosophy

"This is a well-structured, informative and lively account of continental philosophy. It identifies and documents what are certainly some of the key problems for this philosophical tradition. The treatment is at once eminently accessible and thoughtful, never sacrificing complexity for the sake of clarity."

Brian Elliott, University College Dublin

Continental Philosophy: A contemporary introduction surveys the main trends of European philosophy from Kant to the present. It is clearly written and accessible to students. In a novel approach, Andrew Cutrofello looks at continental philosophy through the lens of four questions that derive from Kant:

- How is truth disclosed aesthetically?
- To what does the feeling of respect attest?
- Must we despair, or may we still hope?
- What is the meaning of philosophical humanism?

Cutrofello shows how these questions have been taken up by phenomenologists, continental ethicists, hermeneuticians and critical theorists, and existentialists and their critics. In the introduction and conclusion, he explains how the questions raised by continental philosophers differ from their analogues in the analytic tradition. With its frequent references to Shakespeare, Cutrofello's style is lively and engaging. His remarkably comprehensive book will be of interest not only to students but to anyone seeking a reliable overview of the continental tradition.

Andrew Cutrofello is Professor of Philosophy at Loyola University of Chicago.

Routledge Contemporary Introductions to Philosophy

Series editor:
Paul K. Moser
Loyola University of Chicago

This innovative, well-structured series is for students who have already done an introductory course in philosophy. Each book introduces a core general subject in contemporary philosophy and offers students an accessible but substantial transition from introductory to higher-level college work in that subject. The series is accessible to non-specialists and each book clearly motivates and expounds the problems and positions introduced. An orientating chapter briefly introduces its topic and reminds readers of any crucial material they need to have retained from a typical introductory course. Considerable attention is given to explaining the central philosophical problems of a subject and the main competing solutions and arguments for those solutions. The primary aim is to educate students in the main problems, positions and arguments of contemporary philosophy rather than to convince students of a single position.

Classical Philosophy
Christopher Shields

Epistemology
Second Edition
Robert Audi

Ethics
Harry Gensler

Metaphysics
Second Edition
Michael J. Loux

Philosophy of Art
Noël Carroll

Philosophy of Language
William G. Lycan

Philosophy of Mind
Second Edition
John Heil

Philosophy of Religion
Keith E. Yandell

Philosophy of Science
Second Edition
Alex Rosenberg

Social and Political Philosophy
John Christman

Philosophy of Psychology
José Luis Bermudez

Continental Philosophy
Andrew Cutrofello

Classical Modern Philosophy
Jeffrey Tlumak

Continental Philosophy
A contemporary introduction

Andrew Cutrofello

Routledge
Taylor & Francis Group

NEW YORK AND LONDON

First published 2005
by Routledge
711 Third Avenue, New York, NY 10017, USA

Simultaneously published in the UK
by Routledge
2 Park Square, Milton Park, Abingdon, Oxon OX14 4RN

Routledge is an imprint of the Taylor & Francis Group, an informa business

Typeset in Garamond by Wearset Ltd, Boldon, Tyne and Wear

Library of Congress Cataloging in Publication Data
Cutrofello, Andrew, 1961–
    Continental philosophy : a contemporary introduction /
Andew Cutrofello.
        p. cm. — (Routledge contemporary introductions to
    philosophy)
    Includes bibliographical references and index.
    1. Philosophy, Modern—Europe—20th century I. Title.
II. Series.
    B804.C88 2005
    190 dc22

                                                        2005000442

British Library Cataloguing in Publication Data
A catalogue record for this book is available from the British
Library

ISBN 0-415-24208-8 (hbk)
ISBN 0-415-24209-6 (pbk)
ISBN 978-04-415-24209-7 (pbk)

Contents

vi   Contents

Abbreviations

A	Derrida, *Aporias*
AC	Nietzsche, *The Anti-Christ*
AFPPV	Kant, *Anthropology from a Pragmatic Point of View*
AMAM	Beauvoir, *All Men are Mortal*
AME	Foucault, *Aesthetics, Method, and Epistemology*
AO	Deleuze and Guattari, *Anti-Oedipus*
AOK	Foucault, *The Archaeology of Knowledge*
AOR	Sartre, *The Age of Reason*
AP	Benjamin, *The Arcades Project*
AS	Bataille, *The Accursed Share* (three volumes)
AT	Adorno, *Aesthetic Theory*
B	Deleuze, *Bergsonism*
BAT	Heidegger, *Being and Time*
BBP	Freud, *Beyond the Pleasure Principle*
BCD	Deleuze, "Bergson's Conception of Difference"
BEP	Kristeva, "Bataille, Experience and Practice"
BGE	Nietzsche, *Beyond Good and Evil*
BN	Sartre, *Being and Nothingness*
BOT	Nietzsche, *The Birth of Tragedy*
BPAF	Arendt, *Between Past and Future*
BS	Kristeva, *Black Sun*
BSWM	Fanon, *Black Skin, White Masks*
BW	Heidegger, *Basic Writings* (revised edition)
C	Marx, *Capital Volume I*
CAC	Deleuze, *Coldness and Cruelty*
CAID	Freud, *Civilization and its Discontents*
CC	Ricoeur, *Critique and Conviction*
CDR	Sartre, *Critique of Dialectical Reason*
CE	Bergson, *Creative Evolution*
CES	Husserl, *Crisis of European Sciences and Transcendental Phenomenology*
CI	Ricoeur, *The Conflict of Interpretations*
CIS	Rorty, *Contingency, Irony, and Solidarity*
CM	Husserl, *Cartesian Meditations*
COF	Kant, *The Conflict of the Faculties*
COP	Rorty, *Consequences of Pragmatism*
COTR	Arendt, *Crises of the Republic*
CPJ	Kant, *Critique of the Power of Judgment*

CPR	Kant, *Critique of Pure Reason*
CPrR	Kant, *Critique of Practical Reason*
D	Nietzsche, *Daybreak*
DBBT	Irigaray, *Democracy Begins Between Two*
DD	Bachelard, *The Dialectic of Duration*
DIAE	Foucault, "Dream, Imagination, and Existence"
DOE	Adorno and Horkheimer, *Dialectic of Enlightenment*
DOSS	Kant, "Dreams of a Spirit-Seer"
DOT	Heidegger, *Discourse on Thinking*
DP	Foucault, *Discipline and Punish*
DPID	Lyotard, *The Differend: Phrases in Dispute*
DR	Deleuze, *Difference and Repetition*
DS	Bergson, *Duration and Simultaneity*
DSe	Blanchot, *Death Sentence*
DSST	Žižek, *Did Somebody Say Totalitarianism?*
E	Lacan, *Écrits*
EAE	Levinas, *Existence and Existents*
EAPM	Marx, *Economic and Philosophic Manuscripts of 1844*
EATI	Freud, *The Ego and the Id*
EC	Marcuse, *Eros and Civilization*
EH	Nietzsche, *Ecce Homo*
EHE	Sartre, *Existentialism and Human Emotions*
EIJ	Arendt, *Eichmann in Jerusalem*
EOA	Beauvoir, *The Ethics of Ambiguity*
EOAT	Kant, "The End of All Things"
EOHP	Heidegger, *Elucidations of Hölderlin's Poetry*
EOM	Adorno, *Essays on Music*
EOSD	Irigaray, *An Ethics of Sexual Difference*
EPM	Sellars, *Empiricism and the Philosophy of Mind*
ESK	Lévi-Strauss, *The Elementary Structures of Kinship*
F	Deleuze, *Foucault*
FA	Žižek, *The Fragile Absolute*
FAK	Hegel, *Faith and Knowledge*
FAMH	Irigaray, *The Forgetting of Air in Martin Heidegger*
FAP	Ricoeur, *Freud and Philosophy*
FBLOS	Deleuze, *Francis Bacon: the Logic of Sensation*
FLF	Althusser, *The Future Lasts Forever*
FM	Althusser, *For Marx*
FM-R	Ricoeur, *Fallible Man*
FOHN	Habermas, *The Future of Human Nature*
Fors	Derrida, "Fors"
FPF	Bachelard, *Fragments of a Poetics of Fire*
FR	Frege, *The Frege Reader*
Fr	Blanchot, *Friendship*
G	Kant, *Groundwork of the Metaphysics of Morals*

GI	Marx and Engels, *The German Ideology*
Gift	Mauss, *The Gift*
GLAPL	Žižek, "Georg Lukács as the Philosopher of Leninism"
GOC	Gadamer, *Gadamer on Celan*
GPAE	Freud, *Group Psychology and the Analysis of the Ego*
GPT	Freud, *General Psychological Theory*
GS	Nietzsche, *The Gay Science*
GT	Derrida, *Given Time I. Counterfeit Money*
HACC	Lukács, *History and Class Consciousness*
HC	Arendt, *The Human Condition*
HCOW	Althusser, *The Humanist Controversy and Other Writings*
HDWRS	Deleuze, "How Do We Recognize Structuralism?"
HOC	Nietzsche, "Homer on Competition"
HS	Foucault, *The History of Sexuality, Volume I*
I	Benjamin, *Illuminations*
IC	Blanchot, *The Infinite Conversation*
IM	Heidegger, *An Introduction to Metaphysics*
Imag	Sartre, *The Imaginary*
IOD	Freud, *The Interpretation of Dreams*
IOG	Derrida, *Edmund Husserl's Origin of Geometry: An Introduction*
IOMD	Blanchot, "The Instant of My Death"
IPOP	Merleau-Ponty, *In Praise of Philosophy*
IPTPP	Husserl, *Ideas Pertaining to a Pure Phenomenology and to a Phenomenological Philosophy*
IWMM	Lévi-Strauss, *Introduction to the Work of Marcel Mauss*
JKI	Kristeva, *Interviews*
JP	Lévi-Strauss, *The Jealous Potter*
JRU	Freud, *Jokes and their Relation to the Unconscious*
JTN	Irigaray, *Je, tu, nous*
KAH	Ricoeur, "Kant and Husserl"
KAPOM	Heidegger, *Kant and the Problem of Metaphysics* (Churchill)
KAPOM-T	Heidegger, *Kant and the Problem of Metaphysics* (Taft)
KCP	Deleuze, *Kant's Critical Philosophy*
KHI	Habermas, *Knowledge and Human Interests*
KMAR	Marx, *Karl Marx: a Reader*
L	Kant, *Logic*
LA	Žižek, *Looking Awry*
LAE	Bataille, *Literature and Evil*
LAP	Althusser, *Lenin and Philosophy*
LC	Bataille, *L'Abbé C*
LCMP	Foucault, *Language, Counter-Memory, Practice*
LE	Lyotard, *Libidinal Economy*
LI	Husserl, *Logical Investigations*
LKPP	Arendt, *Lectures on Kant's Political Philosophy*
LOAS	Lyotard, *Lessons on the Analytic of the Sublime*

LOM	Arendt, *The Life of the Mind* (two volumes)
LOM-K	Kant, *Lectures on Metaphysics*
LOS	Deleuze, *The Logic of Sense*
LPW	Marx, *Later Political Writings*
MAM	Bergson, *Matter and Memory*
MC	Foucault, *Madness and Civilization*
MFNS	Kant, *Metaphysical Foundations of Natural Science*
ML	Irigaray, *The Marine Lover of Friedrich Nietzsche*
MOE	Žižek, *The Metastases of Enjoyment*
MOM	Kant, *Metaphysics of Morals*
MOP	Derrida, *Margins of Philosophy*
MWTP	Heidegger, "My Way to Phenomenology"
N	Heidegger, *Nietzsche* (two volumes)
NAP	Deleuze, *Nietzsche and Philosophy*
Nau	Sartre, *Nausea*
NAVS	Klossowski, *Nietzsche and the Vicious Circle*
ND	Adorno, *Negative Dialectics*
Negations	Marcuse, *Negations*
NILOP	Freud, *New Introductory Lectures on Psycho-Analysis*
NSS	Bachelard, *The New Scientific Spirit*
NTL	Adorno, *Notes to Literature* (two volumes)
ODM	Marcuse, *One-Dimensional Man*
OFBS	Kant, *Observations on the Feeling of the Beautiful and Sublime*
OGOM	Nietzsche, *On the Genealogy of Morality*
OGTD	Benjamin, *The Origin of German Tragic Drama*
OKEW	Russell, *Our Knowledge of the External World*
OLSS	Habermas, *On the Logic of the Social Sciences*
ON	Bataille, *On Nietzsche*
OOG	Husserl, "The Origin of Geometry"
OOT	Arendt, *Origins of Totalitarianism*
OPCIT	Husserl, *On the Phenomenology of the Consciousness of Internal Time*
OR	Arendt, *On Revolution*
OT	Foucault, *The Order of Things*
OTAB	Heidegger, *On Time and Being*
OTB	Levinas, *Otherwise Than Being*
OTL	Nietzsche, "On Truth and Lying in a Non-Moral Sense"
P	Heidegger, *Pathmarks*
PARS	Husserl, "Philosophy as Rigorous Science"
PC	Lyotard, *The Postmodern Condition*
PDOM	Habermas, *The Philosophical Discourse of Modernity*
PE	Moore, *Principia Ethica*
Per	Lyotard, *Peregrinations*
PLT	Heidegger, *Poetry, Language, Thought*
PMN	Rorty, *Philosophy and the Mirror of Nature*
POH	Kristeva, *Powers of Horror*

POM	Russell, *The Principles of Mathematics*
POP	Merleau-Ponty, *Phenomenology of Perception*
POR	Bachelard, *The Poetics of Reverie*
POT	Foucault, *The Politics of Truth*
POTW	Friedman, *A Parting of the Ways*
P–PP	Habermas, *Philosophical–Political Profiles*
Prisms	Adorno, *Prisms*
PrOP	Merleau-Ponty, *Primacy of Perception*
PTAFM	Kant, *Prolegomena to Any Future Metaphysics*
PTPPP	Kant, "Proclamation of the Imminent Conclusion of a Treaty of Perpetual Peace in Philosophy"
PW	Kant, *Political Writings*
PW-L	Lyotard, *Political Writings*
QCT	Heidegger, *The Question Concerning Technology and Other Essays*
R	Sartre, *The Reprieve*
RBOE	Gadamer, *The Relevance of the Beautiful and Other Essays*
RC	Althusser, *Reading Capital*
RPL	Kristeva, *Revolution in Poetic Language*
RRT	Kant, *Religion and Rational Theology*
RWBMR	Kant, *Religion Within the Boundaries of Mere Reason*
S	Merleau-Ponty, *Signs*
S I	Lacan, *The Seminar of Jacques Lacan Book I*
S II	Lacan, *The Seminar of Jacques Lacan Book II*
S III	Lacan, *The Seminar of Jacques Lacan Book III*
S VII	Lacan, *The Seminar of Jacques Lacan Book VII*
S XI	Lacan, *The Four Fundamental Concepts of Psycho-Analysis*
S XX	Lacan, *The Seminar of Jacques Lacan Book XX*
SA	Lévi-Strauss, *Structural Anthropology*
SA II	Lévi-Strauss, *Structural Anthropology Volume II*
SAF	Lukács, *Soul and Form*
SAN	Merleau-Ponty, *Sense and Non-Sense*
SAP	Derrida, *Speech and Phenomena and Other Essays on Husserl's Theory of Signs*
SCTS	Beauvoir, *She Came to Stay*
SESMF	Kant, "Succinct Exposition of Some Meditations on Fire"
SFM	Sartre, *Search for a Method*
SM	Lévi-Strauss, *The Savage Mind*
SNB	Blanchot, *The Step Not Beyond*
SOE	Ricoeur, *The Symbolism of Evil*
SOI	Žižek, *The Sublime Object of Ideology*
SOL	Blanchot, *The Space of Literature*
SOM	Derrida, *Specters of Marx*
SOW	Irigaray, *Speculum of the Other Woman*
SPL	Lacan, "Seminar on 'The Purloined Letter'"
SS	Beauvoir, *The Second Sex*

SSB	Brentano, *On the Several Senses of Being in Aristotle*
STO	Kristeva, *Strangers to Ourselves*
SW	Benjamin, *Selected Writings* (four volumes)
T	Lévi-Strauss, *Totemism*
TAI	Levinas, *Totality and Infinity*
TAO	Levinas, *Time and the Other*
TAT	Freud, *Totem and Taboo*
TBT	Irigaray, *To Be Two*
TCA	Habermas, *The Theory of Communicative Action* (two volumes)
TCC	Adorno and Benjamin, *The Complete Correspondence*
TCM	Bergson, *The Creative Mind*
TFW	Bergson, *Time and Free Will*
THN	Lukács, *The Historical Novel*
TIHP	Levinas, *The Theory of Intuition in Husserl's Phenomenology*
TINAP	Foucault, *This is Not a Pipe*
TITD	McCumber, *Time in the Ditch*
TJ	Ricoeur, *The Just*
TLR	Lukács, *The Lukács Reader*
TM	Gadamer, *Truth and Method*
TOTE	Sartre, *The Transcendence of the Ego*
TOTI	Nietzsche, *Twilight of the Idols*
TOTN	Lukács, *The Theory of the Novel*
TP	Kant, *Theoretical Philosophy 1755–1770*
TPC	Derrida, *The Post Card*
TPON	Bachelard, *The Philosophy of No*
TRLAF	Derrida, "Text Read at Louis Althusser's Funeral"
TS	Sartre, *Troubled Sleep*
TWTN	Žižek, *Tarrying with the Negative*
UC	Blanchot, *The Unavowable Community*
VAI	Merleau-Ponty, *The Visible and the Invisible*
VED	Beauvoir, *A Very Easy Death*
VOE	Bataille, *Visions of Excess*
WAD	Derrida, *Writing and Difference*
WAOP	Derrida, *Who's Afraid of Philosophy?*
WAOS	Sartre, *The Wall and Other Stories*
WIL	Sartre, *What is Literature?*
WOE	Fanon, *The Wretched of the Earth*
WOP	Althusser, *Writings on Psychoanalysis*
WTDOR	Žižek, *Welcome to the Desert of the Real*
Z	Nietzsche, *Thus Spoke Zarathustra*

Preface

The aim of each of the books published as *Routledge Contemporary Introductions to Philosophy* is to introduce students and general readers to a "core general subject in contemporary philosophy." The same is true of this book. For reasons that will become clear, however, I felt that I could not adequately address my own topic – continental philosophy – without relating it to another of the "core general subjects" in the series, namely, analytic or "Anglo-American" philosophy. The reason for this has to do with the nature of the analytic/continental distinction, which I discuss in the introduction and concluding chapter of this book. For now, suffice it to say that the distinction operates on both sides of the divide (at least for those invested in it) as an "us versus them" principle.

In the introduction, I represent the long-standing rivalry between analytic and continental philosophers as a struggle over the legacy of Kant. Kant's critical philosophy presupposes a set of interrelated dualisms which his immediate successors found problematic. They tried to resolve them, but they did so in two diametrically opposed ways. Ever since, the academic discipline of philosophy has repeatedly divided itself into two competing factions, each of which accentuates one facet of the Kantian legacy. This division has taken a number of different forms, but since the 1950s it has been characterized in English-speaking philosophy departments as the difference between analytic and continental philosophy.

Kant identified four questions which he took to circumscribe the main divisions (i.e., the "core general subjects") of philosophy. In abandoning his dualisms, his successors implicitly modified these questions in divergent ways. After specifying the basic differences between the two versions, I go on to use the continental variants of Kant's questions to frame the overview of continental philosophy that I present in Chapters 1–4. In Chapter 5, I return to the analytic/continental division, which I take to represent a displacement of a common problem that all post-Kantian philosophers have had to face. This is the problem of how to live up to what Kant identifies in the *Critique of Pure Reason* as the cosmopolitan ideal of the philosopher.

While writing this book, as the reader will quickly see, Shakespeare has been my constant guide. Besides prefiguring many of the vicissitudes of the analytic/continental division (as I show in the introduction), Shakespeare often seems to have read, carefully, both Kant and his successors. To signal this fact, and to help the reader, I begin each section of the book with one or two relevant quotations from his plays. In a few places, I also show how the ideas of a particular philosopher lend themselves to a reading of one of Shakespeare's lines, scenes, or themes.

Throughout the book, I have tried to address a reader with little, if any, familiarity with either continental or analytic philosophy (or Kant or Shakespeare). My expectation is that the book will be used as a guide or accompaniment to further reading of the philosophers (or playwright) whose works I canvass in these pages.

At the beginning of the book is a list of the abbreviations that I use for most of the quotations. Full bibliographic information can be found at the back. Whenever I first mention a particular book or article that has been translated into English, I give its original title and year of publication in parentheses in the main body of the text.

Acknowledgments

My first debt of gratitude is to Paul Moser, who asked if I would be interested in writing this book for his series and helped me think about its overall shape at a crucial early stage. I am also grateful to Tony Bruce, who launched the project at Routledge and remained steadfastly committed to it over a period of almost five years. At different stages of the writing process, Siobhan Pattinson, Zoe Drayson, and Priyanka Pathak were all patient and supportive editors, as were Anne Robertson, Gail Welsh and Carl Gillingham during the production process. Two anonymous reviewers gave me constructive feedback on an earlier draft of the manuscript, as did Dan Price, the depth of whose comments frequently exceeded my ability to respond as carefully as I would have liked. Jean Tan also read through a complete draft, and her thoughtful comments saved me from numerous infelicities. Others who read sections of the manuscript and made valuable suggestions for revision include Brent Adkins, Emilia Angelova, Alison Brown, Michael Burke, Angela Capodivacca, Erik Gardner, Craig Greenman, Laura Hengehold, Burt Hopkins, Noah Horwitz, Patricia Huntington, Tom McCarthy, Michael McGettigan, Darin McGinnis, Ed McGushin, Kelly Oliver, Adriaan Peperzak, Josh Rayman, Richard Rorty, Dianne Rothleder, David Schweickart, Hans Seigfried, Adrian Switzer, J.D. Trout, Vicki Wike, Shannon Winnubst, and Tom Wren. For conversation, correspondence, and general encouragement, I also thank Paul Abela, Karl Ameriks, Chris Anderson, Jason Barrett, Stacy Bautista, Jim Bernauer, Jim Blachowicz, Paul Bryant, Ed Casey, Jeff Courtright, Steve Crowell, Blake Dutton, Ellen Feder, John Fehr, Domenic Ferri, Bob Gooding-Williams, Jürgen Habermas, David Ingram, Lori Kingen, Jeff Librett, Brian Lisle, Bill Martin, Noëlle McAfee, John McCumber, Heather McGee, Renee McGurk, Will McNeill, Elaine Miller, Hugh Miller, Tracy Murray, Serena Parekh, Jennifer Parks, Mark Rockwell, Paul Saurrette, Jacqueline Scott, Tom Sheehan, Kristi Sweet, Dianna Taylor, Masanori Tohara, Arnie vander Nat, Andrew Wall, and Dave Yandell. To those of my colleagues and students in the

Philosophy Department at Loyola University Chicago whom I have not already mentioned by name, I thank all of you for the truly cosmopolitan atmosphere in which this book was written. I thank David Pellauer, the editor of *Philosophy Today*, for permission to include revised excerpts of "Frege, Nietzsche, and the Origins of the Analytic/Continental Polemic," the published version of a paper that I presented at the Society for Phenomenology and Existential Philosophy in October 2002, in the Introduction. I also thank Elizabeth Hoppe both for inviting me to present an earlier draft of this paper at a conference on Nietzsche held at Lewis University in February 2002 and for her hospitality in Romeoville, Illinois. An excerpt from Chapter 3 was presented at the Eastern Division meeting of the American Philosophical Association in December 2003 as "Habermas, Žižek and the Legacy of the Frankfurt School;" and an excerpt from Chapter 2 was presented at the Central Division meeting of the APA in April 2004 as "Levinas, Lacan, and Moral Skepticism." I thank Shannon Winnubst and Jeff Kosky for their illuminating responses to these papers. Part of Chapter 2 was presented as "What is Transcendental Philosophy? Reflections on Kant, Lacan, and Deleuze" at a conference on Deleuze held at Trent University in February 2004. I am grateful to Constantin Boundas, Emilia Angelova, and David Morris for their hospitality in Peterborough, Ottawa. Finally, I would like to thank Dianne Rothleder, my wife, and my children, Megan Cutrofello and Quinn Cutrofello, for their love and shared love of Shakespeare. Needless to say – but it is a noble tradition to say it – in thanking all these people for helping to shape what I have rough-hewn, I claim sole responsibility for its unfinished surface. Such as it is, I dedicate the book, with love, to my parents, Paul Cutrofello and Rita Carroll Cutrofello, and to my siblings, Mary Cushing, Tom Cutrofello, and Susan Miele.

Introduction: what is continental philosophy?

I.1   The Wars of the Roses

> Great lords and gentlemen, what means this silence?
> Dare no man answer in a case of truth?
> 　　　　　(*The First Part of Henry the Sixth*, II, iv, 1–2)

> Allow me to return once again to Shakespeare, in whom I have overindulged in the course of these lectures. But it sometimes seems to me that the whole of philosophy is only a meditation of Shakespeare.
> 　　　　　(Levinas, *Time and the Other*, 72)

This book is a "contemporary introduction" to "continental philosophy." Another book to be published in the same series will be a "contemporary introduction" to "Anglo-American philosophy." The separation of these two topics accurately reflects a long-standing division between rival factions in philosophy departments in the US and UK. Originally, the Anglo-American/continental distinction was simply geographical, the term "continental" referring to contemporary or recent philosophical happenings on the European continent. But over the years the distinction has acquired metaphilosophical connotations, that is, it has come to be thought of as a distinction between competing conceptions of the philosophical enterprise itself. Today, *Anglo-American* philosophy is typically equated with *analytic* philosophy, since a majority of the members of Anglo-American philosophy departments describe themselves as working within the analytic "tradition." Conversely, the label "continental" is applied not only to European philosophers, but to the significant minority of Anglo-American philosophers who see themselves as continuing the continental "tradition." Each of these traditions has its own legacy: analytic philosophers address problems that have been bequeathed to them by thinkers such as Mill, Frege, Russell, Wittgenstein, Carnap, Quine, and Davidson; while continental philosophers take up the inheritance of Hegel, Nietzsche, Bergson, Husserl, Heidegger, Foucault, and Derrida. To identify oneself as a member of the House of Analytic or the House of Continental is to ally oneself with one of these two branches of a common family tree. What makes the division between these two houses resemble the English Wars of the Roses is not only the fact that Anglo-American philosophers have used the analytic/continental distinction to divide *themselves* into two separate factions; but the fact that the division has taken the form of an institutional struggle over who has the right to inherit the title of Philosopher.

In making their respective claims to the British crown, both the House of Lancaster and the House of York were able to affirm true lineal descent from King Edward III. In the analytic/continental version of this scenario, the role of Edward III would be played by the eighteenth-century German philosopher Immanuel Kant (1724–1804), the last common ancestor to whom each of the two factions proudly traces its genealogy. The fact that "it is not exactly the same Kant" to which the two houses appeal – as the non-partisan continental philosopher Paul Ricoeur has quipped (CC 50) – suggests that the analytic/continental division can be represented as a struggle over the Kantian legacy. Two non-partisan analytic philosophers, Richard Rorty and Michael Friedman, have separately tried to represent the division in just this way. They claim that the division has its roots in a distinction that Kant draws between two supposedly separable elements of human cognition, namely, "intuitions" and "concepts."

According to Kant, intuitions are immediate representations of individual objects that are somehow given to us through a faculty of receptivity, while concepts are spontaneously generated forms of thought in terms of which we cognize such objects (CPR A19/B33, A320/B376–7). This fundamental distinction organizes all of Kant's "critical" philosophy, eventually giving rise to a related distinction, namely that between "determining" and "reflective" judgments (CPJ 66–7). A determining judgment subsumes an object of intuition under a pre-given concept of the understanding (as in "This is a cat"), while a reflective judgment calls attention to our inability to subsume the form of an anomalous object under any concept that we possess (as in "Whatever this is, it is absolutely unique"). Kant associates the distinction between determining and reflective judgments with the difference between scientific cognition and aesthetics. The aim of science is to put forth determining judgments about that which is true or good, while the aim of aesthetic "taste" is to communicate to others our pleasurable encounters with objects that in some way resist conceptual determination.

In his 1981 essay, "Nineteenth-Century Idealism and Twentieth-Century Textualism," Rorty observes that this way of thinking about the relationship between science and art gave rise to a nineteenth-century polemic between "positivists" and "Romantics" as to which of the two should be accorded primacy in our sense of ourselves and the world (COP 142–3). Rorty goes on to suggest that the twentieth-century split between analytic and continental philosophers is just an extension of this debate, with the two sides functioning as "public relations agencies" of "scientific" and "literary culture" respectively (COP 149). In his view, this polemic is based upon a false dichotomy for which Kant's distinction between intuitions and concepts is to blame. By abandoning Kant's way of thinking about experience, late-nineteenth-century pragmatists such as William James (1842–1910) and John Dewey (1859–1952) – as well as Friedrich Nietzsche (1844–1900), whom Rorty classifies with the pragmatists – were able to reveal deep affinities between science and art (COP 150, 161). Rorty recommends that analytic and continental philosophers cultivate the neglected insights of these thinkers.

In *A Parting of the Ways: Carnap, Cassirer, and Heidegger* (2000), Friedman implicitly agrees with Rorty that the analytic/continental division concerns the relative importance of science and art, but instead of tracing the division between philosophy's "two cultures" (POTW ix, cf. COP 139) back to the split between positivists and Romantics, he locates it in the attempts made by rival schools of late-nineteenth and early-twentieth-century neo-Kantians to rid themselves of the intuition/concept dichotomy. In rejecting Kant's dualistic account of experience, his legatees found themselves torn between an account of human experience that gave primacy to the natural sciences (the view adopted by the Marburg School of neo-Kantianism) and one that privileged the *Geisteswissenschaften* or cultural sciences (the position of the Southwest School) (POTW 28, 155–6). Friedman goes on to show how an historically important debate between Rudolf Carnap (1891–1970) and Martin Heidegger (1889–1976) – two thinkers eventually regarded as standard-bearers of the analytic and continental traditions, respectively – arose out of this dilemma. In his 1932 essay, "The Elimination of Metaphysics Through Logical Analysis of Language" (*Überwindung der Metaphysik durch logische Analyse der Sprache*), Carnap criticized Heidegger's reflections on the sentence "Nothingness itself nothings [*Das Nichts selbst nichtet*]," maintaining that, since it violated the laws of logic, this sentence was utterly meaningless (POTW 11).[1] For his part, Heidegger dismissed the mathematical logic on which Carnap based his entire philosophy as "mere 'calculation'" (POTW 151n). Friedman regards both of these positions as one-sided, and he traces the philosophical roots of the debate to a public "disputation" that Heidegger had with the neo-Kantian philosopher Ernst Cassirer (1874–1945) in Davos, Switzerland in 1929 (with Carnap in attendance) (POTW x, 7). This encounter was significant not only for the role it would eventually play in defining the analytic/continental distinction, but because it led to the eclipse of Cassirer's "synthetic and conciliatory" alternative, his so-called "philosophy of symbolic forms," which attempted to do justice to both the natural and the cultural sciences (POTW 159). Thus Cassirer emerges on Friedman's account – much as the pragmatists do for Rorty – as a neglected thinker, the study of whose works could help analytic and continental philosophers resolve their philosophical differences.

Though Rorty and Friedman agree that the analytic/continental division has something to do with the Kantian dichotomy between intuitions and concepts, it is noteworthy that Rorty blames the division on Kant's *introduction* of his dualism, while Friedman traces it to various attempts made to *eliminate* it. These two views are not necessarily incompatible, because it is possible that the dilemma faced by the neo-Kantians – as to whether philosophy should have its point of departure in logic and science or in the *Geisteswissenschaften* – resulted from their inability to rid themselves of a pernicious distinction. But what if the neo-Kantians' failure reflected not the residual effects of a false dichotomy but the persistence of a genuinely irreducible one? Or, put differently, what if it were impossible to eliminate Kant's dualism without giving rise to philosophical controversy?

In the following section I will show that Kant's principal motive for introducing the intuition/concept dualism in the first place was to put an end to all hitherto existing philosophical controversies. By insisting on the ineliminability of his dualism, Kant hoped to bring about perpetual philosophical peace. Attending to this aspect of his project will show how exactly he came to play the role of the analytic/continental division's Edward III.

If Kant is our Edward III, then Rorty's characterization of the inaugural post-Kantian schism between Romanticism and positivism resembles Shakespeare's depiction – in *The Tragedy of King Richard the Second* – of the civil discord between the flamboyant Richard and the serious-minded Henry Bolingbroke, two of Edward's heirs. After the usurping Bolingbroke becomes King Henry IV, the conflict between the sobriety of determining judgment and the aesthetic license of reflective judgment is played out in the life of Henry's son, Prince Hal, who in *The First Part of Henry the Fourth* is torn between two ideals represented by the ambitious Hotspur and the life-loving Falstaff. The decisive moment of *The Second Part of Henry the Fourth* occurs when Hal, now King Henry V, banishes Falstaff. This event has its parallel in Rorty's account of the ascension of analytic philosophy to a position of institutional dominance in Anglo-American philosophy departments and the exiling of Romanticism to literary criticism. Henry V's subsequent efforts to unify his kingdom (portrayed in *The Life of Henry the Fifth*) can be likened to Rorty's attempts to overcome the analytic/continental division, but unlike Henry – who quelled civil dissension by conquering France – Rorty's approach has been to give up the Kantian pretension to constitute philosophy as a law-governed domain with borders that need to be defended or extended.

There is much to be said for this anarchic ambition, but in section three I will argue that Rorty does not so much resolve the analytic/continental division as suppress the underlying motives for it. In this respect his approach is too amicable, like that of the ineffectual Henry VI. In an effort to accentuate the stakes of the rivalry, in section four I will suggest that Nietzsche – a crucial figure in the genealogy of the House of Continental – was not a pragmatist, as Rorty claims, but a polemicist who, by challenging the Socratic conception of philosophical dialectics, radicalized the Romantic critique of positivism. In order to highlight Nietzsche's importance to the analytic/continental division, in section five I will show that in his confrontation with Cassirer, Heidegger essentially repeated the main argument of Nietzsche's *The Birth of Tragedy* (though probably without realizing it). This parallel will enable me to expand upon Friedman's analysis of the "parting of the ways" at Davos. Finally, in section six, I will suggest that the analytic/continental division can be represented as a series of divergent appropriations of the four questions that Kant took to be fundamental to philosophy. This model will guide my discussion throughout the rest of this book.

In performance, the three parts of Shakespeare's *Henry the Sixth* plays are sometimes broken down into two, the first presenting events pertaining to the reign of the House of Lancaster and the second to the period during which the House of York ruled – though it is important to remember that each of the two factions claimed legitimacy throughout the entire period. Analogously, the main chapters of this book can be regarded as telling only one half of the full story, for it does not chronicle the conceptual history of the House of Analytic. For that, the reader must turn to Roger Gibson's *Anglo-American Philosophy: A Contemporary Introduction*.[2] In the conclusion, I will offer a brief synopsis of how I would recount this other half of the story, and I will suggest that the analytic/continental division can be thought of as a controversy about the nature of philosophical controversies. The fact that this metaphilosophical conflict may be intrinsic to the philosophical enterprise (and not a mere by-product of the legacy of Kant) suggests that we have always been in the midst of the Wars of the Roses. In this spirit, my conclusion, though a mere epilogue, aspires to the philosophical equivalent of Shakespeare's *The Tragedy of Richard the Third*, that is, to a demonstration of the interminability of the winter of our discontent.

I.2   Kant's attempt to secure perpetual philosophical peace

> Civil dissension is a viperous worm
> That gnaws the bowels of the commonwealth.
> (*The First Part of Henry the Sixth*, III, i, 72–3)

In the preface to the first edition of the *Critique of Pure Reason* (*Kritik der reinen Vernunft*, 1781; second edition 1787), Kant characterizes metaphysics as a "battlefield of . . . endless controversies" (CPR Aviii). So interminable do these battles appear to be that metaphysics is no longer regarded (as it once was) as "the **queen** of all the sciences" (CPR Aviii). The aim of critique is to restore the queen to her rightful place of dignity by constituting "a court of justice" before which all metaphysical controversies can be lawfully resolved once and for all (CPR Axi).

The queen's claim to the throne had been called under suspicion by the seventeenth-century English empiricist John Locke (1632–1704). Locke impugned the honor of the queen by purporting to trace her genealogy back "to the rabble of common experience," that is, by claiming that the supposedly pure concepts of human understanding were actually derived from empirical intuitions (CPR Aix). Kant's metaphor of the falsely accused matron reappears in his 1783 book, *Prolegomena to Any Future Metaphysics that will be able to Come Forward as Science* (*Prolegomena zu einer jeden künftigen Metaphysik die als Wissenschaft wird auftreten können*), where he criticizes the Scottish empiricist David Hume (1711–1776) for having claimed that "reason was altogether deluded" in regarding the concept of causality "as one of her children" when it was actually just "a bastard of the imagination, . . . impregnated by experience" (PTAFM 55). Hume went even further than Locke in that he concluded from the queen's base origins that she was not fit to legislate over the rabble of sensibility. Against these slanderous claims, Kant promises to show that human understanding is equipped with genuinely "pure" concepts which arise from it alone, and that objects of experience are lawfully governed by them.

The empiricists are not the only ones to blame for the queen's misfortune. No less guilty are the "dogmatists," under whose influence the queen's rule had become "despotic" (CPR Aviii–ix). In order to ensure that this will no longer be the case, Kant seeks not only to legitimate the queen's rule over the rabble but to show that she oversteps her proper limits whenever she attempts to legislate beyond the field of sensible experience. In this regard he acts toward his queen like a minister who tells his monarch what she can and cannot do.[3] Just as he criticizes Locke and Hume for alleging that the pure concepts of the understanding were derived from sensible intuitions, so he criticizes the rationalist philosophers Gottfried Wilhelm Leibniz (1646–1716) and Christian Wolff (1679–1754) for thinking that through the use of concepts alone it was possible to have "intellectual" (i.e., nonsensible) intuitions of objects of the understanding.

In different ways, both the empiricists and the dogmatic rationalists failed to recognize the fact that intuitions and concepts are completely different kinds of representations. The mistake made by Locke and Hume was to think of concepts as abstractions or copies of sensible intuitions. In their view, concepts differed from intuitions only in having a lesser degree of liveliness or vividness. The symmetrical mistake made by Leibniz and Wolff was to think of intuitions as confused concepts. For them, intuitions differed from concepts only in having a lesser degree of clarity and distinctness. Kant contrasts these complementary errors by asserting that "Leibniz **intellectualized** the appearances, just as Locke totally **sensitivized** the concepts of understanding" (CPR A271/B327).

The intuition/concept dichotomy gives rise to a further distinction between "a priori" and "a posteriori" sources of cognition. In the introduction to the *Critique*, Kant says that while all human experience begins with a posteriori (i.e., empirical) sensations which provide the "matter" for our intuitions of empirical objects, we provide a priori (non-empirical) "forms" to which the matter of sensation must conform in order to be apprehended by us (CPR A1–2/B1–2). The discovery of pure forms of experience gives rise to the idea of a "transcendental philosophy" that will put forth a complete "system" of "*a priori* concepts of objects in general" (CPR A11–12). The narrower aim of critique is to prepare the way for such a system by identifying the a priori forms of cognition and distinguishing their legitimate contribution to experience from their illegitimate extension beyond the bounds of possible experience.

In order to carry out this project, Kant begins by drawing a distinction between analytic and synthetic judgments. A judgment of the form "A is B" is analytic if "the predicate B belongs to the subject A," while a judgment is synthetic if the predicate "B lies entirely outside the concept A" (CPR A6/B10). Analytic judgments can be known to be true a priori (i.e., independently of experience) because they do nothing more than make explicit something that has already been implicitly thought in the concept of the subject. According to Kant, I can know that all bodies are extended without having to appeal to sensible intuitions at all, because the concept of extension is contained within the concept of a body. By contrast, in order to know whether all bodies are heavy I have to appeal to my empirical intuitions of physical objects, because only these can teach me if heaviness is correctly predicated of bodies or not (CPR A7/B11). Thus, whereas the judgment that all bodies are extended is both analytic and (therefore) knowable a priori, the judgment that all bodies have weight is both synthetic and a posteriori. Because synthetic judgments can only be confirmed by appealing to an intuition of some sort, it is tempting to conclude that they are all a posteriori, i.e., that they can be known to be true only on the basis of empirical experience. But according to Kant, some synthetic judgments can be known to be true a priori. Such is the case with mathematics. Judgments like $7 + 5 = 12$ and *a straight line is the shortest distance between two points* are synthetic because their respective predicates (i.e., the concept of 12 and the concept of the shortest distance) are not contained in their subjects (the concept of the sum of 5 and 7, and the concept of a straight line) (CPR B16). Yet although they are synthetic, these judgments can somehow be known to be true a priori, that is, independently of the empirical content of experience.

Kant's discovery of the synthetic a priori character of arithmetic and geometry enables him to characterize critique as the project of surveying all of the different kinds of synthetic a priori judgments with an eye toward determining both their conditions of possibility and their scope of validity. In the case of mathematics, he argues in the section of the *Critique* entitled "Transcendental Aesthetic" that it is only because space and time are pure forms of human sensibility that we can know geometrical and arithmetical truths a priori. If space were something that we could have knowledge about only on the basis of empirical intuitions, then the judgments of geometry could only be known a posteriori (like the proposition that all bodies are heavy). But we know that geometrical truths are universally and necessarily valid for all possible objects in space, which is to say that we know them to be true a priori. Such knowledge cannot be arrived at analytically through the mere dissection of concepts, but only through an intuition of space. But since this intuition cannot be empirical, it follows that we must have an a priori intuition of space. Kant concludes that space itself is nothing more than a pure form of human sensibility, and that the actual objects which we intuit in space are only "appearances" and not "things in themselves." The same holds for time, the a priori intuition of which makes it possible for us to know arithmetical truths a priori. The difference between space and time is that space is the form of "outer" intuition, in which we represent objects (i.e., appearances) outside ourselves, while time is the form of "inner sense," by which each of us intuits our own representations (the appearance of oneself). To say that objects in space and time are just appearances is not to deny their "empirical reality," but it is to assert their "transcendental ideality" (CPR A28/B444, A35/B52). Because spatio-temporal properties pertain only to appearances and not to things in themselves, the validity of mathematics is restricted to the domain of objects of sensible intuition.

In the "Transcendental Analytic," Kant argues that just as our sensible intuitions of objects must conform to space and time as the a priori forms of human sensibility, so these same objects must conform to pure concepts which serve as the a priori forms of human understanding. These concepts are the "categories" which Locke and Hume (following Aristotle) had mistakenly tried to derive from empirical intuitions. By examining the logical structure of all acts of human judgment, Kant identifies twelve categories which he groups in threes under the four headings of "quantity," "quality," "relation," and "modality" (CPR A80/B106). To each category corresponds a particular synthetic a priori cognition by which something about experience can be known to be true, regardless of what the particular content of our empirical intuitions happens to be. Kant calls these a priori rules of experience "principles of pure understanding" (CPR A148/B187). To the headings of quantity, quality, relation, and modality, there correspond, respectively, "axioms of intuition," "anticipations of perception," "analogies of experience," and "postulates of empirical thinking in general" (CPR A161/B200). The axioms assert that every object of intuition must have an "extensive magnitude," that is, a spatial or temporal extent (CPR A161/B202). Likewise, the anticipations assert that every sensation must have an "intensive magnitude," that is, a degree of felt intensity that attests to a corresponding degree of reality (or force) in the sensed object itself (CPR A166/B207). The analogies tell us that objects of experience are necessarily governed by the relational categories of inherence (substance and accident), dependence (cause and effect), and concurrence (reciprocal causality between distinct substances) (CPR A182/B224, A189/B232, A211/B256). Finally, the postulates explain how the modal categories of possibility, existence, and necessity specify the different ways in which an object of experience can stand in relation to the thinking subject (CPR A218/B265–6).

The crucial argument of the Transcendental Analytic is the one that Kant presents as a "transcendental deduction" of the pure concepts of the understanding. In the first ("A") edition version of the deduction, Kant identifies "a threefold synthesis" involving the "apprehension" of a manifold of sensation in one intuition, the "reproduction" of this manifold in the imagination, and the conceptual "recognition" of the unitary object that is given to us thereby (CPR A97–103). The aim of this analysis – as well as of the second ("B") edition version of the deduction – is to show, first, that intuitable appearances in space and time are necessarily governed by the principles of pure understanding, and, second, that these principles are valid only in relation to appearances and not to things in themselves. Both of these conclusions are based on the idea that the categories derive their meaning solely through their reference to the spatio-temporal conditions of possible experience. To each of the pure concepts of the understanding there corresponds a "transcendental schema" by which the faculty of imagination relates that concept, through an act of synthesis, to a "time-determination" of a particular sort (CPR A138/B177). For example, to the category of substance there corresponds the schema of "the persistence of the real in time"; to the category of causality, "succession of the manifold insofar as it is subject to a rule"; and so on (CPR A144/B183). Apart from the schematism, the categories have a purely logical "function" but no sense.

Insofar as appearances are subject to categorial determination, Kant calls them "phenomena," the empirical study of which is reserved for the natural sciences. In order to mark the gap separating phenomena from things in themselves, he introduces the wholly negative concept of "noumena," a term that derives from the Greek word *nous*, which is often translated as "mind" or "understanding" (CPR A248–9/B306). Assuming we could know that such things exist (which we cannot), noumena would be the purely intelligible objects of thought that Leibniz and Wolff posited.

So long as the use of the categories is restricted to the "immanent" conditions of possible experience (and so barred from any "transcendent" employment), the understanding remains within its proper sphere of jurisdiction. But over and above the faculty of understanding we possess a faculty of reason which actively bids the understanding to transgress its limits (CPR A295–6/B352). In the "Transcendental Dialectic," Kant seeks to explain both why it is that reason does this, and why the synthetic a priori judgments to which it gives rise inevitably lead to "illusion" and not to truth (CPR A61–2/B86).

Kant characterizes reason as the capacity to draw inferences from premises. Accordingly, just as the categories of the understanding could be derived from the logical structure of judgments, so the pure "ideas" of reason can be deduced from the logical structure of syllogisms. Every syllogism has a major premise that is supplied by the understanding. Like all judgments, this premise must relate its concepts to one another categorically (S is P), hypothetically (if X then Y, where X and Y are themselves judgments), or disjunctively (either X or Y or Z). Depending on what this relation is, the syllogism itself will be categorical, hypothetical, or disjunctive in form.

In the Transcendental Analytic, Kant derived the categories of substance, causality, and community from the three types of relational judgments. To each of these categories there corresponded an analogy of experience by which the understanding bid itself to seek an empirical "condition" for something "conditioned." For example, the synthetic a priori principle that every event has a cause prompts the understanding to seek the actual cause of any particular event that happens to occur. This iterable procedure gives rise to a manifold of judgments. In order to bring unity to this manifold, reason posits the existence of an *unconditioned* condition for every series of conditions which the understanding posits. This is equivalent to demanding that rational demonstrations be grounded not merely in principles but in first principles. For each of the basic types of syllogism, reason generates a priori the idea of an object that could serve as the subject of such a (synthetic a priori) principle. Corresponding to the relational categories of substance, causality, and community are the ideas of the soul, the world (as totality), and God. The idea of the soul is the idea of the thinking subject as the absolutely unconditioned condition of all its representations; the idea of the world is the idea of the totality of appearances; and the idea of God is the idea of the unconditioned condition of all possibilities (CPR A334/B391).

Unlike the categories, whose employment is restricted to the conditions of possible experience, the ideas of reason refer the understanding to transcendent objects that can never be given in sensible intuitions. By appearing to extend human cognition in this way, reason seems to offer us the hope of purely rational – i.e., non-empirical – sciences of psychology (doctrine of the soul), cosmology (doctrine of the world-totality), and theology (doctrine of God) (CPR A334–5/B391–2). These hopes turn out to be in vain, because although the ideas are subjectively useful insofar as they direct the understanding to aspire to a standard of completeness which it can never actually attain, they have no objective employment whatsoever. The negative task of the Transcendental Dialectic is to prevent us from succumbing to the "transcendental illusions" of reason (CPR A295/B352). The supposed proofs in rational psychology of the substantiality, simplicity, and personal identity of the soul – as well as of the empirical ideality of objects in space – are only so many "paralogisms" (i.e., badly formed syllogisms). Likewise, rational cosmology can only generate "antinomies," apparent conflicts of reason with itself. Finally, the supposed proofs in rational theology for the existence of God can do no more than posit an "ideal" to which no actual object corresponds.

Of the three different types of fallacious dialectical inferences, the antinomies have a special status. Unlike the paralogisms and ideal – which give rise to "one-sided" illusions concerning the existence of the soul and God (CPR A406/B433) – the antinomies make it seem possible for reason both to prove *and* to disprove the existence of an unconditioned condition of appearances. In a 1798 letter to the German philosopher Christian Garve (1742–1798), Kant said that it was his discovery of the antinomies that first set him on the path of critique because he found it distressing to think that human reason might actually be in conflict with itself.[4] Were it impossible to discover the illusion that sustains the antinomies, it would be necessary to give up all hope of ever achieving perpetual philosophical peace. In the preface to the *Critique*, Kant blamed the dogmatists and empiricists for causing metaphysics to fall into disgrace, but in the chapter on the antinomies, he argues that the conflict between these two factions is rooted in human reason itself (CPR A466/B494). Each of the antinomies is presented as a conflict between a dogmatic metaphysical "thesis" and an empiricist "antithesis." For each of the instances in which the understanding posits a series of conditions of appearances, reason is able to complete the series in one of two ways. The dogmatic metaphysical strategy pursued in each of the theses is to posit a first term in the series that would serve as the unconditioned condition of all the other terms. By contrast, the empiricist strategy adopted by the antitheses is to deny the existence of such first terms by treating the entire series itself as the unconditioned (CPR A417/B445). What makes each of these conflicts so formidable is that reason appears to have perfectly sound arguments on both sides.

Kant identifies four antinomies of pure reason, one for each of the main headings of the principles of the understanding. The first antinomy concerns the existence or non-existence of a beginning of the world in time and an outer boundary of the world in space (CPR A426–7/B454–5). If such boundaries did not exist, an infinite number of events would already have occurred and an infinite number of things would co-exist simultaneously. But according to Kant both of these things would require the complete synthesis of an infinite number of terms, which is impossible. Thus it seems that the thesis of the first antinomy – "The world has a beginning in time, and in space it is also enclosed in boundaries" – must be true (CPR A426/B454). However, if we assume that the thesis is true, then there would have to exist an empty time and space in which the world was bounded. But this too is contradictory, for there would then be no sufficient reason why the world began *when* it did or existed *where* it did. Hence it appears that the antithesis must be true: "The world has no beginning and no bounds in space, but is infinite with regard to both time and space" (CPR A427/B455).

The second antinomy pertains to the existence or non-existence of simple parts of composite substances (CPR A434–5/B462–3). According to the thesis, such parts must exist because, otherwise, appearances would consist of nothing substantial at all. But according to the antithesis, such simple parts cannot exist, for if they did, they would have to be in space; but everything in space is divisible and so composite rather than simple.

The third antinomy involves a conflict about the concept of freedom. According to the thesis, there must be such a thing as freedom, for otherwise there would be no beginning to causal chains in nature (CPR A444–5/B472–3). According to the antithesis, there cannot be such a thing as freedom, for every event in time must be determined in accordance with a natural law from which it follows.

Finally, the fourth antinomy both affirms and denies the existence of "an absolutely necessary being." According to the thesis, there must be such a being in the world, for if there were not, the laws of nature would lack necessity – a conclusion that would contradict the results of the Transcendental Analytic. By contrast, the antithesis maintains that there cannot be an absolutely necessary being, for if there were, it would lack a cause of its existence – a conclusion that seems to contradict the principle that everything that exists in time depends upon the existence of something else (CPR A452–3/B480–1).

Kant characterizes the first two antinomies as "mathematical" in that – like the corresponding principles of the understanding with which they are associated – they pertain exclusively to the spatio-temporal character of phenomena. By contrast, the third and fourth antinomies are "dynamical" in that (again like their corresponding principles) they pertain to the existence of objects in nature.

Kant resolves all four of the antinomies by appealing to his distinction between appearances and things in themselves. The mathematical antinomies arise when space and time are mistakenly treated as transcendentally real. Once it is recognized that they are transcendentally ideal – though empirically real – it turns out that there neither is nor is not a beginning of the world in time or an outer boundary of space. Likewise, there are no indivisible parts of substances, but neither is anything composed of infinitely many parts. Kant resolves the dynamical antinomies in a different way, namely, by arguing that, while their antitheses are demonstrably true insofar as they deny the existence of freedom or a necessary being in (phenomenal) nature, their theses may also be true insofar as they posit the existence of these objects in the noumenal order of things in themselves. Without in any way extending human cognition, the theses vouchsafe for reason a "problematic" use of two of its cosmological ideas. Kant draws a similar conclusion with regard to the psychological idea of the soul and the theological idea of God (which he arrives at by connecting the idea of a necessary being with the idea of a "highest being"). Though the three ideas of soul, freedom, and God have only a "regulative" role to play in experience, they take on transcendent significance once they are considered from the moral point of view of "practical" (as opposed to "speculative") reason – an argument that Kant develops in his second *Critique*, the *Critique of Practical Reason* (*Kritik der praktischen Vernunft*, 1788).

Because the antinomies can only be resolved if objects in space and time are appearances and not things in themselves, Kant regards them as providing corroborating support for the argument presented in the Transcendental Aesthetic: "one can . . . draw from this antinomy a true utility, not dogmatic but critical and doctrinal utility, namely that of thereby proving indirectly the transcendental ideality of appearances, if perhaps someone did not have enough in the direct proof in the Transcendental Aesthetic" (CPR A506/B534). Kant reiterates this point in a marginal comment inserted in

Kant not only for failing to bring about perpetual philosophical peace but for fomenting the analytic/continental division. In his 1979 book, *Philosophy and the Mirror of Nature*, Rorty suggests that Kant's characterization of the history of philosophy as a struggle between those who would reduce concepts to intuitions and those who would reduce intuitions to concepts only makes sense if one is already convinced that human cognition consists of a synthesis of two different kinds of representations. But since Kant acknowledges that we have no direct awareness of pre-schematized intuitions, the very distinction between intuitions and concepts is merely theoretical and thus optional (PMN 154–5). Rather than characterizing human cognition as a synthesis of hypothetically separable components, Kant could simply have noted that to make a judgment is to hold a particular proposition to be true. He could then have cast the empiricism/rationalism dispute not as a conflict between rival reductionist strategies but as a disagreement about whether judgments about "secondary qualities" (i.e., empirical judgments) could be reduced to judgments about "primary qualities" (i.e., judgments that seem to depend upon reason alone):

> Had Kant instead said that the rationalists wanted to find a way of replacing propositions about secondary qualities with propositions which somehow did the same job but were known with certainty, and that the empiricists opposed this project, the next two centuries of philosophical thought might have been very different.
>
> (PMN 148)

Rorty concludes that, if Kant had said that the empiricist/rationalist debate was not about "putative *components* of propositions" but about "the degree of certainty attaching to them," the analytic/continental rift might never have opened up (PMN 149). Instead of distinguishing between determining and reflective judgments – i.e., between two different ways in which intuitions and concepts can be related to each other – a more pragmatically-minded Kant would have contrasted the act of describing things in a conventional vocabulary with the creative effort to articulate a new vocabulary. Rorty characterizes this as the difference between "systematic" and "edifying" philosophy. Systematic philosophers are those who provide useful descriptions of the world, while edifying philosophers are those who challenge our current ways of describing ourselves. Far from being in conflict with each other, these two activities are complementary (PMN 365ff.).

In *Contingency, Irony, and Solidarity* (1989), Rorty highlights the role that irony plays within edifying discourses. An ironist is someone who refuses to accept any "final vocabulary" as absolute. We are all forced to speak a particular idiom that commits us to a particular view of ourselves and the world, but ironists are always prepared to challenge the idiom that they presently use (CIS 73). Just as the Romantics wanted to make their lives works of art, so ironists seek to recreate themselves by inventing new vocabularies. Rorty goes on to suggest that continental philosophers such as Nietzsche, Heidegger, Foucault, and Derrida are ironists who aim not at truth – as do their analytic or systematic counterparts – but at self-transformation. This is an exemplary activity provided that it remains within its proper bounds. Invoking a classical liberal distinction between what one does in private and what one does in public, Rorty argues that an individual's efforts at self-creation should be carried out in such a way that they do not interfere with anyone else. Thus irony has its proper place in private, not in public (CIS 100). In public, what we need is a sense of solidarity which reflects our shared commitment to a particular way of describing ourselves and the world around us. For this, systematic philosophers are more helpful than ironists.

Edifying philosophers have nothing to contribute – as edifying philosophers – to the public domain because they are "useless": "Nietzsche, Derrida, and Foucault seem to me invaluable in our attempt to form a private self-image, but pretty much useless when it comes to politics" (CIS 83). Rorty also expresses concern about the "antiliberalism" of Nietzsche, who "often speaks as though he had a social mission, as if he had views relevant to public action" (CIS 99). But although Nietzsche's antiliberalism should be rejected, it is separable from his aesthetic conception of "self-knowledge as self-creation" (CIS 27). "Self-overcoming" is a merely private affair that has nothing to do with participation in the public domain: "For Proust and Nietzsche . . . there is *nothing* more powerful or important than self-redescription" (CIS 29, 99; Rorty's italics). Accordingly, Rorty distinguishes "Nietzsche the perspectivalist" (who wants to give himself a unique perspective on the world) from "Nietzsche the theorist of the will to power" (CIS 106).

In suggesting that systematic and edifying philosophers have complementary roles to play in a liberal society, Rorty purports to resolve the analytic/continental division. But his solution assumes that edifying – i.e., continental – philosophers should be happy about being relegated to the private domain. It is in this respect that he resembles King Henry VI. Henry thought that he could put an end to the Wars of the Roses by asking his rival Richard Plantagent to settle for a mere dukedom – or perhaps for the right to call himself a king in private. This solution proved to be ineffectual because the House of York would not settle for anything less than the English throne. Analogously, the very thinkers whom Rorty regards as edifying philosophers have not thought of themselves as merely seeking private grandeur at all; on the contrary, their principal claim has been on the public realm itself.

We might also wonder whether Rorty's redescription of the analytic/continental division is as far removed from Kant as he suggests that it is. Translated back into a Kantian vocabulary, ironists are thinkers who do not regard their determining judgments as definitive; they maintain a distance between themselves and the things they say by persisting in an attitude of reflective judging. Conversely, systematic philosophers are those who aim at making definitive determining judgments; for them, reflection is merely a means to an end. Thus the idea that ironists and systematic philosophers need one another is a way of asserting the complementarity of determining and reflective judgment. While it is true that the intuition/concept dichotomy disappears in Rorty's redescription, it is in a sense replaced by his reification of the public/private dichotomy. Kant also drew a sharp distinction between the public and the private realms, one that determined his conception of the proper role of philosophers within the body politic. The fact that Rorty can "overcome" the analytic/continental divide only by reverting to *this* Kantian dichotomy suggests that he has not resolved it but simply displaced it. This suspicion finds confirmation in the fact that, for both Nietzsche and the other continental philosophers whom Rorty regards as ironists, self-creation is an *essentially* public activity.

I.4   Nietzsche's clue to the persistence of the analytic/continental division

War, war, no peace! Peace is to me a war.
(*The Life and Death of King John,*
III, i, 113)

In one of his earliest essays, "Homer on Competition" (*Homers Wettkampf,* written in 1872), Nietzsche claims that for the ancient Greeks, the process of self-creation was inseparable from struggle with others and so could only be carried out in public. Without a good type of *Eris,* or discord, neither the individual nor the state could have flourished (HOC 190). Hence instead of consigning "selfishness" to the private domain, the Greeks regarded it as the principal virtue to be displayed in public: "without envy, jealousy and competitive ambition, the Hellenic state, like Hellenic man, deteriorates" (HOC 194). This attitude is echoed in *Ecce Homo: How One Becomes What One Is* (*Ecce Homo: Wie man wird, was man ist,* 1889; first published in 1908), in which Nietzsche proclaims: "I am warlike by nature. Attacking is one of my instincts" (EH 231). The very style in which *Ecce Homo* is written – a "testimony" to "*who I am*" (EH 217) – suggests a competition in which Nietzsche boasts about "why I am so wise," "why I am so clever," "why I write such good books," and "why I am a destiny."

If Nietzsche was in competition with anyone, it was with Socrates, the first of the Greeks to forswear "envy, jealousy, and competitive ambition." In the midst of the flourishing Greeks, he was an enigma, for while they affirmed life, he condemned it as a sickness from which death alone could provide a cure (TOTI 12). In a section of his book, *Twilight of the Idols* (*Götzendämmerung,* 1889), entitled "The Problem of Socrates," Nietzsche suggests that Socrates suffered from the sickness of "decadence." Unable to compete in the Greek manner, he sought revenge, using the art of philosophical dialectics to get his fellow citizens to question the value of their lives. Irony was his weapon of choice (TOTI 15). Thus, far from embracing Socratic irony – as Rorty implies – Nietzsche repudiates it in order to revive the Greek spirit of competition. To attack the Socratic "will to truth," the unconditional impulse to value truth above life, is not to adopt an ironic stance toward one's own beliefs but, on the contrary, to affirm one's "own" truths. Contending that life requires unconditional dogmas, Nietzsche raises a genealogical question, namely, how did Socrates succeed in converting the Greeks to a life of critical reflection?

In *The Birth of Tragedy* (*Die Geburt der Tragödie aus dem Geiste der Musik*, 1872), Nietzsche suggests that pre-Socratic Greek art was governed by two competing "drives," the Apollonian and the Dionysian (BOT 14). The Apollonian impulse expressed itself in beautiful images, while the Dionysian manifested itself in imageless music and in the sublime experience of intoxication associated with it. Drawing on the work of the German philosopher Arthur Schopenhauer (1788–1860), Nietzsche characterizes Apollo as the god of the *"principium individuationis,"* the principle according to which sensible objects are distinguished from one another. Lurking beneath the calm of Apollonian appearance is the chaos of Dionysus in which nothing can be distinguished from anything else. To gaze into the Dionysian abyss is to be filled with both "blissful ecstasy" and "horror" (BOT 17). The Apollonian and Dionysian principles came together in Greek tragedy, in which the chorus presented "a self-mirroring of Dionysiac man" (BOT 42). Through its identification with the chorus, the Greek spectators were able to lift the Apollonian veil of illusion in a communal affirmation of the Dionysian essence of life.

But suddenly a new form of dramatic art appeared, one that Nietzsche finds exemplified in the work of Euripides. Unlike Sophocles and Aeschylus, who were able to maintain an essential tension between the Apollonian and the Dionysian, Euripides provided the basis for "a non-Dionysiac art, morality, and view of the world" (BOT 59). His didactic dramas were intended to please a spectator who claimed the audacity to *judge* the tragic spectacle. This spectator was Socrates, in whom a "logical drive" (BOT 67) first came to the fore. The shift from tragedy to dialectics coincided with the formation of a new alliance, namely, that between Apollo and Socrates: "Here art becomes overgrown with *philosophical thought* which forces it to cling tightly to the trunk of dialectics. The *Apolline* tendency has disguised itself as logical schematism" (BOT 69).

Nietzsche's use of the word "schematism" in this context recalls that of Kant, who characterized the schematism as a "hidden art in the depths of the human soul, whose true operations we can divine from nature and lay unveiled before our eyes only with difficulty" (CPR A141/B180–1). Insofar as it makes possible the subsumption of objects of intuition under concepts – that is, insofar as it makes determining judgments possible – Kant's productive imagination remains subordinate to the understanding, but it is freed from this constraint in the encounter with the beautiful or sublime.

Nietzsche's account of the transformation of Apollonian figuration into logical schematism inverts this model, showing how an originally free imagination came to be subordinated to the understanding. More precisely, he shows how an original alliance between sensibility and imagination (Dionysus and Apollo) gave way to one between imagination and understanding (Apollo and Socrates). Support for this reading can be found in Nietzsche's posthumously published "On Truth and Lying in a Non-Moral Sense" (*Über Wahrheit und Lüge im aussermoralischen Sinne*, written in 1873), in which he explicitly characterizes concepts as congealed images: "Everything which distinguishes human beings from animals depends on this ability to sublimate sensuous metaphors into a schema, in other words, to dissolve an image into a concept" (OTL 146). Instead of serving as a mere vehicle for the subsumption of objects under concepts, the productive imagination transforms intuited images into concepts.

In his 1886 "An Attempt at Self-Criticism," a preface to the reissue of *The Birth of Tragedy*, Nietzsche retracts his earlier construal of Dionysian intoxication as a form of metaphysical communion, but he congratulates himself for having "dared . . . *to look at science through the prism of the artist, but also to look at art through the prism of life*" (BOT 5). In a sense, Kant did the exact opposite. In the third *Critique*, he considers the "feeling of life" through the prism or lens of art, and art through the lens of science (CPJ 90). He subordinates art to science by making the **free lawfulness** of the imagination in reflective judgment secondary with respect to the serious labor that the imagination performs in the service of the determining judgments of both the understanding (in science) and reason (in morality) (CPJ 124). The fact that Kant thereby "makes room for taste" in his critical philosophy does not settle Nietzsche's dispute with Socrates any more than Rorty does in reserving a private enclave for reflective judging. On the contrary, the very concept of taste as Kant conceives it – the capacity to recognize certain forms as beautiful – reflects the fundamental change introduced by Euripides when he conceived of a non-Dionysian artform. The closest that Kant comes to Dionysus is in his description of the feeling of the sublime. This feeling is prompted by an encounter with the formlessness of raw nature – i.e., with that which does not conform to the *principium individuationis* (CPJ 128). But here Kant recoils, or rather he describes the feeling of sublimity precisely *as* a recoiling from the "horrible" aspect of nature to an inner satisfaction in our moral vocation as rational beings (CPJ 129). Nietzsche refused to recoil: "I am a disciple of the philosopher Dionysus; I should prefer to be even a satyr to being a saint" (EH 217).

I.5   Heidegger's confirmation of Nietzsche's clue

The truth appears so naked on my side
That any purblind eye may find it out.
(The First Part of Henry the Sixth,
II, iv, 20–1)

In his encounter with Cassirer at Davos, Heidegger criticized the dominant neo-Kantian interpretation of Kant as an epistemologist, maintaining that he should instead be read as a thinker of being who came remarkably close to articulating the ideas about human existence that Heidegger himself had put forth in his 1927 book, *Being and Time (Sein und Zeit)*. Heidegger pursues this line of thought further in *Kant and the Problem of Metaphysics (Kant und das Problem der Metaphysik,* 1929). Prior to Kant, rationalists such as Wolff and Alexander Gottlieb Baumgarten (1714–1762) drew a distinction between "special" metaphysics – i.e., rational psychology, cosmology, and theology – and "general" metaphysics, or ontology. In his critiques of the paralogisms, antinomies, and ideal of pure reason, Kant showed that each of the celebrated branches of special metaphysics was a mere pseudo-science that could never establish the validity of its claims on behalf of pure reason. As for ontology, Kant regarded the Transcendental Analytic as sup-planting it: "the proud name of an ontology, which presumes to offer syn-thetic *a priori* cognitions of things in general ... must give way to the modest one of a mere analytic of the pure understanding" (CPR A247/B303). The neo-Kantians interpreted this claim as Kant's way of turning away from metaphysics to epistemology. But according to Heideg-ger, Kant's whole motivation in writing the *Critique* was to "lay the ground of metaphysics." To inquire into the transcendental conditions of possible experience is to identify the "ontological" grounds to which all empirical or "ontic" truths must conform: "Ontic truth, then, must necessarily conform to ontological truth. This is the correct interpretation of the meaning of the 'Copernican revolution'" (KAPOM 22). Unfortunately, Kant retreated from his deepest insights in a way that allowed the neo-Kantians to misconstrue the true nature of transcendental philosophy. The aim of Heidegger's book is to show exactly where Kant reneged on his attempt to lay the ground of metaphysics and to explain why he did so.

Heidegger breaks with the epistemological construal of transcendental philosophy by claiming that the primary locus of knowledge for Kant lies not in judgment but in intuition: "to interpret knowledge as judg-ment (thought) does violence to the decisive sense of the Kantian problem.... Knowledge is primarily intuition" (KAPOM 28, 32). This is not to deny the role that Kant accords to the understanding in empirical cognition, but to emphasize the fact that in his account of the schematism – the primordial synthesis by which the imagination relates the pure concepts of the understanding to pure determinations of time – he subordinates the understanding to sensibility: "It is only insofar as the pure understanding as understanding is the servant of pure intuition that it can remain the master of empirical intuition" (KAPOM 80). In other words, the fact that truth *can* pertain to determining judgments presupposes a prior schematization by which the categories are first "sensibilized." Thus, for Heidegger, the significance of Kant's treatment of the schematism lies in the privilege that it grants to the receptive dimension of human cognition.

Much of Heidegger's argument rests on his assessment of the A Deduction account of the three-fold synthesis by which the sensory manifold is apprehended in a single intuition, reproduced in the imagination, and conceptually recognized by the understanding. According to Heidegger, Kant accords the faculty of imagination a "central position" in this analysis not because it mediates between two wholly distinct faculties – i.e., sensibility and understanding – but rather because it is the "common but to us unknown root" from which these two faculties originally stem (KAPOM 67, 41; CPR A15/B29). Insofar as the imagination is the original source of both the receptive and spontaneous dimensions of human experience, it manifests itself as both a "spontaneous receptivity" (in pure sensibility) and as a "receptive spontaneity" (in pure understanding) (KAPOM 160, 162).[6] These two stems are not on an equal footing, however, because – as the analysis of the schematism shows – the understanding remains subordinate to sensibility. For Heidegger this implies that the imagination is fundamentally a faculty of receptivity: "The imagination is also and above all a faculty of intuition, i.e., receptivity" (KAPOM 159). Thus the imagination is first and foremost a kind of spontaneous receptivity, and only secondarily – and on this basis – a kind of receptive spontaneity.

Heidegger notes that, in his lectures on metaphysics from the mid-1770s – i.e., from the period when he was working out the details of the first edition of the *Critique of Pure Reason* – Kant identifies three distinct capacities of the faculty of imagination, each with its own temporal modality: (1) the capacity to form images in the present, (2) to reproduce the past, and (3) to anticipate the future (LOM-K 53, KAPOM 180). Heidegger argues that this three-fold analysis undergirds the three-fold synthesis of the A Deduction, so that the syntheses of pure apprehension, reproduction and recognition turn out to be structurally unified moments of a single synthesis by which the imagination constitutes, respectively, a pure present, a pure past, and a pure future (KAPOM 183ff.). On this interpretation, the imagination represents the primordial temporality of human existence. Heidegger suggests that Kant implicitly acknowledges as much when he cryptically asserts, in his lectures on logic, that the three questions posed in the first *Critique* – "What can I know?," "What should I do?," and "What may I hope?" – all point toward the more fundamental question: "What is man?" (KAPOM 213). Unfortunately, Kant "recoiled" (or "shrank back") from his discovery. Not only did he fail to provide the kind of "existential analytic" of human existence that Heidegger himself develops in *Being and Time*, but in the second edition of the *Critique*, he subordinated the function of synthesis — previously ascribed to the transcendental imagination — to the understanding. According to Heidegger, Kant did this because he remained under the spell of the rationalist conception of the subject as responsible for its judgments and actions (KAPOM 174). By delivering the imagination over to a legislative understanding, Kant prepared the way for German idealism. Thus Hegel — in an early work entitled *Faith and Knowledge* (*Glauben und Wissen*, 1802) — characterizes the productive imagination as the common root of the two stems of human cognition, but by this he means a faculty of intellectual intuition (i.e., receptive spontaneity) rather than the primordial temporality of human existence (i.e., spontaneous receptivity) (KAPOM 202, 252–3; FAK 73).

By opposing the B Deduction alliance between the imagination and the understanding to the more primordial alliance between the imagination and sensibility, Heidegger implicitly recapitulates Nietzsche's account of the shift from Aeschylean tragedy to Euripidean drama. For Nietzsche, Apollo was originally allied with Dionysus but later became subordinate to the Socratic will to truth. Analogously, for Heidegger, the Kantian imagination was originally allied with sensibility but was later made subordinate to the understanding. In both cases, what is being described is the transition from a fundamentally "aesthetic" orientation toward the world to the advent of an epistemic subject for whom knowledge is a matter of passing judgment on appearances. Though Heidegger does not make the connection explicit, his account of the manner in which Kant recoiled from his discovery of the hidden root of the two stems of human cognition clearly parallels Nietzsche's characterization of Socrates as recoiling from the horrors of the Dionysian. For Nietzsche, Apollonian figuration in Greek tragedy brought about a kind of synthesis between Dionysus and the spectators, one that did not simply bring together separate terms but that reunited that which it had first divided by introducing the *principium individuationis* into experience. These two stems are not on equal footing, for the spectatorial capacity of the spectator is itself rooted in the Dionysian, with the consequence that in the tragic work of art the spectator rediscovers its essential nature. Replacing the spontaneous receptivity of the tragic spectacle with the sovereign point of view of a receptive spontaneity, Socrates enslaves Apollo, forcing him to obey the dictates of reason. Henceforth the Euripidean work of art takes on a morally didactic character (a criticism that Heidegger implicitly levels at Kant as well), Dionysus disappears (the equivalent of what Heidegger refers to as the forgetting of Being), and Apollo becomes the agent of the scientific (merely ontic) determination of beings.

In his 1935 lecture, "The Origin of the Work of Art" (*Der Ursprung des Kunstwerkes*) — a title that tacitly recalls that of *The Birth of Tragedy* — Heidegger develops his own conception of what it means to say that truth is something that happens in works of art. The following year he devoted the first of a series of lecture courses on Nietzsche to the topic, "The Will to Power as Art" (1936–1937). Instead of focusing on *The Birth of Tragedy*, he concentrates on Nietzsche's later works, especially the posthumously published fragments that supposedly were to have comprised a magnum opus with the title *The Will to Power*. Heidegger suggests that Nietzsche failed to "overturn Platonism" because instead of opening up the question of being in a new way, he contented himself with inverting the Platonic subordination of the sensible to the intelligible. In a 1943 lecture entitled, "The Word of Nietzsche: 'God is Dead'" (*Nietzsches Wort 'Gott ist tot'*), Heidegger suggests that Nietzsche completes metaphysics by installing the spontaneous will of the subject as the true ground of being – thereby unwittingly completing the Socratic turn. In an attempt to revive the other thought that he attributes to Nietzsche – that we must seek anew the god whom we have killed – Heidegger attempts to go back to a conception of man as a kind of spontaneous receptivity (i.e., as a being to whom the gift of being calls forth gratitude) rather than as a kind of receptive spontaneity (exemplified in the history that stretches from the Socratic will to truth to the Nietzschean "will to will"). By hearkening to those poets who speak of the flight of the gods, we open ourselves up to a new way in which being might disclose itself. Thus it is only by returning to the primal power of great works of art that we can begin to loosen the hold which the reign of "modern technology" – i.e., determining judgment – has on us.

In 1929, Heidegger had not yet formulated this rearticulation of the basic argument of *The Birth of Tragedy*. But he did see that to adhere to the neo-Kantian construal of the schematism – as Cassirer did – was to persist in the forgetting of the question of being. In *The First Part of Henry the Sixth*, Shakespeare traces the origin of the Wars of the Roses to a confrontation in a garden in which red and white roses were first plucked as the respective emblems of the House of Lancaster and the House of York. Historically speaking, there probably never was such a rose-plucking episode. Nor, perhaps, did one take place at Davos. But both make good dramatic sense.

I.6   Kant's questions as taken up in the House of Continental

> Come, let us four to dinner. I dare say
> This quarrel will drink blood another day.
> (*The First Part of Henry the Sixth*,
> II, iv, 132–3)

In a chapter of the first *Critique* entitled "The Canon of Pure Reason," Kant claims that "All interest of my reason . . . is united" in three fundamental questions, namely:

1   **What can I know?**
2   **What should I do?**
3   **What may I hope?**

(CPR A804–5/B832–3)

In his lectures on logic, Kant adds to this list a fourth question – "What is man?" – suggesting (as we have seen Heidegger note) that, in some sense, it subsumes the other three ("At bottom all this could be reckoned to be anthropology, because the first three questions are related to the last") (L 29). The first question is speculative; the second practical; the third both speculative and practical in that it asks what I am entitled to believe in light of my practical interests (CPR A805/B833). Just as Kant claimed in the first *Critique* to have surveyed all of the antinomies that could possibly arise in attempting to respond to the first question, so in the second *Critique* he purports to resolve the only antinomy that can arise with respect to the second question. Likewise, all conflicts concerning the third question are resolved in Kant's third *Critique* and in his writings on rational theology, while those pertaining to the fourth (though less explicitly articulated) are addressed in his writings on philosophical anthropology.

Because Kant believed that he had resolved all of the fundamental philosophical controversies that could arise with respect to all of the fundamental philosophical questions, he would have expected that the analytic/continental division could be quickly dispatched. But if the House of Continental and the House of Analytic were simply putting forth different answers to shared Kantian questions, they would be able to recognize themselves as engaged in a common – albeit antagonistic – pursuit. Instead what has prevailed is a widespread sense of "mutual unintelligibility,"[7] with each side failing to understand how the other could regard itself as responding to serious philosophical questions at all. This predicament suggests that rather than giving different answers to Kantian questions, the two houses have divided by modifying these questions. In fact, each of Kant's questions presupposes an underlying dualism that analytic and continental philosophers have tried to undercut in diametrically opposed ways. As a result, they have been led to prioritize completely different questions of their own. Such, at any rate, will be the conceit guiding the rest of this book.

1   So long as the receptivity of sensibility and the spontaneity of thought are kept apart, the question "What can I know?" signifies: "What can I, insofar as I am a spontaneous thinker, know about a world that can only be given to me as appearance in space and time?" This question has two parts: first, "Can I be certain that the pure concepts of my faculty of understanding necessarily determine objects of experience?"; and second, "Do these concepts have any applicability to things in themselves?" By abandoning the transcendental ideality thesis, Kant's successors made the second question superfluous. By undercutting the intuition/concept dichotomy, they modified the first. In tracing the two stems of human cognition back to

a primordial "spontaneous receptivity," Nietzsche and Heidegger reduced knowledge to the aesthetic encounter with phenomena conceived not as "mere" appearances of underlying things in themselves but as disclosive manifestations of being itself. Hence Kant's question, "What can I know?," became subordinated to the more fundamental question: "How is truth disclosed aesthetically?" Conversely, for those who characterized cognition as a kind of "receptive spontaneity," knowledge became identified with the logical demonstration of propositional truths. Thus in the analytic tradition, the question, "What can I know?," became less pressing than the question, "What can be known on the basis of logical analysis alone?" Because these two questions – "How is truth disclosed aesthetically?" and "What can be known on the basis of logical analysis alone?" – derived their sense of urgency from the diametrically opposed "ordered conflations" on which they rested, neither of the two post-Kantian factions could understand why the other party's questions seemed so important to it. For the phenomenologists, logic was just the pale distillation of the discourse in which phenomenal givenness was disclosed; while, for their analytic counterparts, givenness was at best another name for logically analyzed truth.

2 Just as Kant's account of human cognition presupposed the intuition/concept dualism, so his account of moral obligation rests upon a sharp dichotomy between incentives of the will and pure practical reason. According to Kant, as finite rational agents we are all aware of a pure moral law (the "categorical imperative") that obliges us to act "autonomously" rather than "heteronomously." To act heteronomously is to allow one's will to be determined by incentives of some sort, while to act autonomously is to subordinate these incentives to the dictates of pure practical reason alone. Insofar as moral autonomy involves the subsumption of objects of the will under practical rules, it is the correlate of the spontaneity of the understanding, which subsumes objects of intuition under speculative rules. Thus the distinction between autonomy and heteronomy can be thought of as the practical analogue of the speculative distinction between spontaneity and receptivity. Kant characterizes the categorical imperative as an objective practical principle to which there corresponds the *pure* (i.e., non-sensuous or "non-pathological") incentive of "respect." Without the feeling of respect, the categorical imperative would be inefficacious; while, without the guidance of the categorical imperative, the incentive of respect would be "blind." Thus the dichotomy between moral incentives and moral principles is crucial to Kant's account of the phenomenon of obligation. But just as analytic and continental philosophers have divided over whether to conceive of human cognition as spontaneous receptivity or as receptive spontaneity, so they have divided over whether to conceive of moral obligation as autonomous heteronomy or as heteronomous autonomy. By "autonomous heteronomy" I mean a conception of obligation that subordinates moral principles to moral incentives. This construal of obligation has prevailed among phenomenologists (for whom respect is the practical analogue of

givenness) and continental philosophers influenced by psychoanalysis. Instead of prioritizing the question, "What should I do?" (or "What ought I do?"), these philosophers have posed the genealogical question, "To what does the feeling of respect attest?" By contrast, analytic ethicists have conceived of obligation as "heteronomous autonomy," that is, as reducible to the responsibility to acknowledge moral principles. Hence instead of inquiring into the nature of moral incentives per se, they have been guided by the question, "What is the force of moral prescriptives?"

3 Kant's third question – "What may I hope? – presupposes the dichotomy between immanence and transcendence. By restricting speculative reason to its immanent employment within the bounds of possible experience, Kant accorded a merely regulative status to the ideas of soul, freedom, and God. But he also argues that, from a practical point of view, reason reveals the transcendent – though inexplicable – fact of human freedom. In order to meet our obligation to pursue "the highest good," it is rationally necessary to believe not only that we are free, but that there is a God and that we have immortal souls. Thus the practical interests of reason entitle us to hope that the highest good is attainable. In the third *Critique*, Kant attempts to reconcile reason's two different vantage-points by analyzing the structure of "aesthetic" and "teleological" judgments, each of which both sustains and bridges the gap separating the immanent realm of phenomena from the transcendent realm of noumenal agents.

By abandoning Kant's transcendental ideality thesis, all of his successors were forced to give up the dichotomy between immanence and transcendence in favor of a conception of either transcendent immanence or immanent transcendence – but depending on whether they conceived of cognition as spontaneous receptivity or receptive spontaneity, they did so from either an aesthetic or a teleological point of view.[8] Kant claims that an object judged to be beautiful serves as an immanent symbol of the transcendent, while an idea judged to be sublime serves as a reminder of the gap separating our transcendent vocation as moral agents from our immanent existence in nature. Accordingly, those for whom cognition had become spontaneous receptivity – i.e., the aesthetic disclosure of truth – were torn between a conception of immanent transcendence as beautiful sublimity and a conception of transcendent immanence as sublime beauty. In Chapter 3, I associate these alternatives with, respectively, "critical theory" and "hermeneutics."

As Kant formulates it, the question, "What may I hope?," is eschatological in the sense that it is oriented toward the attainability of the highest good in a future life. But in the second essay of *The Conflict of the Faculties* (*Der Streit der Fakultäten*, 1798), he articulates an historical variant of the hope question, namely, "Is the human race constantly progressing?" (COF 297). This question concerns not the personal destiny of individuals in a future life but the collective destiny of the human species in the future course of its history. By problematizing the dichotomy between beauty and sublimity, Kant's continental successors have not only made it difficult to separate the eschatological and historical dimensions of hope to which works of art bear witness; they have also made it necessary to face the problem of whether art permits us to hope at all. To capture these two aspects of their shared concern, I have ascribed a common question to both critical theorists and hermeneuticians, namely, "Must we despair, or may we still hope?"

Analytic philosophers, for whom not the disclosure of phenomena but logically demonstrable truth had become the proper object of receptive spontaneity, could largely ignore the aesthetic dimension of the problem of immanence and transcendence in favor of its teleological dimension. The point of Kant's critique of teleological judgment is to ask whether "objectively purposive" natural phenomena can be exhaustively understood from the standpoint of natural science alone. Analytic philosophers have followed Kant in raising this question, though in the wake of Darwin they have been less interested in the ontological status of "organized beings" in general than in that of human beings as purposive agents.[9] Having done away with the phenomena/noumena dichotomy, they too have the option of thinking in terms of transcendent immanence or immanent transcendence. In the analytic context, I take this to be the difference not between beauty and sublimity but between scientifically ascertainable facts and metaphysical problems. Thus Kant's question, "What may I hope?," gives way to the seemingly more pedestrian question, "Are metaphysical questions still meaningful?"

4   Last but not least, Kant's enigmatic fourth question presupposes the dichotomy between the empirical and transcendental dimensions of human experience. My contention here is that continental philosophers have rejected this dichotomy in favor of a conception of human existence as empirically transcendental, and that analytic philosophers have instead opted for a conception of human existence as transcendentally empirical. By the former I mean the view that there is an important sense in which the natural world depends upon us; by the latter, the view that there is no feature of human existence that cannot be reduced to a manifestation of a nature that would continue to exist whether we were in it or not. But at issue is more than just two competing answers to Kant's question, "What is man?" By undoing the transcendental/empirical dichotomy, both continental and analytic philosophers have abandoned Kant's conception of philosophy as a strictly transcendental enterprise in favor of some other conception of philosophical methodology. In the House of Continental, this other conception is philosophical humanism; in the House of Analytic, philosophical naturalism. Both traditions have found themselves enmeshed in debates about the exact nature of these methodological commitments. In the continental tradition, it has especially been the existentialists and their critics who have raised the question, "What is the meaning of philosophical humanism?," while on the analytic side it has been the philosophers of science who have asked, "What is the meaning of philosophical naturalism?"

Such, in highly schematic form, are the different questions that I take to divide the two houses. After focusing on the continental variants in Chapters 1–4, I will briefly return to their analytic counterparts in Chapter 5. This will give me an opportunity to take up a fifth question also touched on by Kant, namely, "What is philosophizing good for and what is its ultimate end?" (L 27). As Jacques Derrida has noted, Kant's influence on the self-conception of professional philosophers runs so deep that it is difficult to question our Kantian inheritance:

> For many of "us" ("us": the majority of my supposed readers and myself), the authority of Kantian discourse has inscribed its virtues of legitimation to such a depth in our philosophical training, culture, and constitution that we have difficulty performing the imaginary variation that would allow us to "figure" a different one.
>
> (WAOP 49)

By going back to Kant's conception of the cosmopolitan ideal of the philosopher, I hope to be able to disturb both analytic and continental appropriations of the Kantian legacy.

Each of the narratives that I present aims at perspicuousness rather than truth per se. By "perspicuousness" I mean something like what John McCumber calls "Nobility": "the excellence of narrative linkage" (TITD 146). A system of notation is said to be "perspicuous" when it visually captures the relations that it is intended to represent. Through the art of the segue, I hope to make perspicuous how four different continental trajectories are related to an originating Kantian provocation. As already indicated, I associate the four problematics I have identified – though not exclusively – with (1) phenomenology, (2) psychoanalysis, (3) critical theory and hermeneutics, and (4) existentialism. Unlike the monolithic term "continental philosophy," these rubrics are indigenous to the historical trajectories that I am attempting to reconstruct. By situating them with respect to Kant's four questions, I hope to be able to identify the various "points of heresy"[10] that continue to divide those who insist upon sporting either a white philosophical rose or a red. That task I leave for Chapter 5, where I will also attempt to "demarcate" the analytic/continental division in McCumber's sense of opening it up to an unforeseeable philosophical future.

Perhaps I should make explicit the fact that in no sense do I claim completeness for this project ("Can this cockpit hold/The vasty fields of France?" [*The Life of Henry the Fifth*, Prologue, 11–12]). Since my topic is in large part an Anglo-American disciplinary formation, I have focused on European thinkers whose work has figured prominently in English-speaking academic forums. Not only are there many "continental" philosophers who do not appear in these pages at all, but those who do make an appearance are portrayed rather perfunctorily. In associating a particular philosopher with one or another of the four questions I have identified, I do not mean to imply that he or she has nothing interesting to say about the others. Finally, I regret that for reasons of space, I have been unable to address any of the secondary literature, and that the narratives I present, though roughly chronological, are only thinly historical. Like Shakespeare's apologetic chorus, I can only entreat the reader to "sit and see,/Minding true things by what their mock'ries be" (IV, Chorus, 52–3).

Notes

1 Cf. BW 103, where Heidegger's statement is rendered "The nothing itself nihilates."

2 Cf. J. Alberto Coffa's *The Semantic Tradition from Kant to Carnap: To the Vienna Station* and Robert Hanna's *Kant and the Foundations of Analytic Philosophy*, two comparable books which offer contrasting assessments of early analytic reactions against Kant.

3 Kant characterizes the relationship between a husband (the de facto ruler in a marriage) and his wife (the nominal monarch) in precisely these terms (AFPPV 172–3).

4 Kant, *Philosophical Correspondence*, p. 252.

5 Armstrong, *The Mind/Body Problem*, p. 10.

6 It should be noted that Kant explicitly rejects the "common root" hypothesis: "Understanding and sensibility . . . join together spontaneously . . . as intimately as if one had its source in the other, or both originated from a common root. But this cannot be – at least we cannot conceive how heterogeneous things could sprout from one and the same root" (AFPPV 53).

7 Cf. Daniel Price's "Against the Mutual Intelligibility of Analytic and Continental Philosophy," in which Heidegger's conception of an event is contrasted with that of Davidson.

8 In the phenomenological tradition, the difference between transcendent immanence and immanent transcendence is exemplified, respectively, in Husserl's conception of the ego as a "transcendence *within* immanence" and Sartre's conception of the ego as constituted outside consciousness.

9 Strictly speaking, there is nothing in the Darwinian theory of evolution that contradicts Kant's *reflective* ascription of objective purposiveness to natural organisms, because, he argues, such a view is compatible with the fact that it is always possible to provide mechanistic explanations for any seemingly purposive natural phenomena.

10 I borrow this expression from Foucault, for whom points of heresy are symptomatic of deeper "epistemic" conditions (OT 182). Much of what I will have to say in Chapter 5 about the analytic/continental division is prefigured in Foucault's account of the struggle in modernity between "critique" and "commentary" (OT 81; cf. 207).

1 The problem of the relationship between receptivity and spontaneity: how is truth disclosed aesthetically?

In the Introduction I suggested that by tracing the intuition/concept dichotomy back to a more primordial spontaneous receptivity, phenomenologists made the question, "How is truth disclosed aesthetically?," more fundamental than the Kantian question, "What can I know?" To do justice to this claim it would be necessary to reconstruct the history of the concept of phenomenology from Kant's contemporary Johann Heinrich Lambert (1728–1777) – the first writer to use the German term *Phänomenologie* – to Husserl and the phenomenological movement which he founded. Lambert took phenomenology to be a science of appearances. Kant borrowed the expression to refer to the doctrine concerning the motion or rest of matter with respect to a perceiving subject (MFNS 191). Hegel went further, conceiving of his "phenomenology of spirit" as a reflection on the process whereby the Kantian doctrine of the transcendental ideality of appearances is first posited and then overcome by a subject who discovers that the concept of the thing in itself is untenable. Hegel criticizes Fichte and Schelling for thinking that Kantian dualisms can be overcome simply by taking the possibility of intellectual intuition for granted. Instead, he seeks to show how a sustained reflection on the difference between intuiting and thinking *culminates* in an identification of the two in absolute knowing. In contrast to Hegel, Husserl suggests that phenomenology neither ends in absolute knowing nor begins in intellectual intuition per se. By ignoring the contribution that *sensible* intuition makes to the awareness of particular facts, the practicing phenomenologist discloses an accompanying *categorial* intuition of the ontological structure of the world. By generalizing the methodological "reduction" by which factual contents are put out of play, Husserl is led to characterize phenomenology as the scientific study of ideal essences disclosed in *eidetic* intuition. Heidegger's conception of the aesthetic disclosure of truth is indebted to Husserl's conception of categorial intuition, but unlike Husserl he comes to emphasize the way in which truth is revealed in works of art. The question of how to reconcile artistic truth with scientific truth is taken up not only by Heidegger but by Bachelard, who objects to Bergson's overestimation of the epistemic worth of pre-scientific intuition. Like Bachelard, Sartre focuses on the role played by the imagination in human cognition, reaching a different conclusion than Heidegger did about its ontological import. Merleau-Ponty (like Bergson) defends the view that scientific truth must be interpreted phenomenologically through the lens of a more primordial perceptual truth. By contrast, Foucault, Derrida, and

Deleuze all reject the phenomenological conception of truth as givenness in favor of a conception of truth as difference.

1.1   Kant's vigilance against fanaticism

And such a deal of skimble-skamble stuff
As puts me from my faith.
(*The First Part of Henry the Fourth*,
III, i, 152–3)

An important motive for Kant's insistence that human beings are incapable of intellectual intuition was his worry about a particular kind of madness that he calls "fanaticism," or *Schwärmerei*. As long as thought remains tethered to the conditions of sensible intuition, it cannot claim any extraordinary insight into "things hid and barr'd . . . from common sense" (*Love's Labor's Lost*, I, i, 57). But once the possibility of intellectual intuition is conceded, the door is open to any sort of extravagant claims – such as those put forth in the mystical writings of Emanuel Swedenborg (1688–1772). In his eight-volume *Arcana Coelestia* (1749–1756) Swedenborg claimed to have met with the dead and hence to be able to say what the next life would be like. What gave the "precritical" Kant pause was the idea that his own attempts to prove the existence of an intelligible realm of spiritual beings – i.e., a realm inhabited by God and departed souls – was perfectly compatible with Swedenborg's visionary ravings. This realization prompted him to ask in his "Dreams of a Spirit-Seer Elucidated by Dreams of Metaphysics" (*Träume eines Geistersehers, erläutert durch Träume der Metaphysik*, 1766), first, how Swedenborg's fanaticism was to be explained, and, second, whether human reason itself might be susceptible to an analogous condition.

In the first part of the essay, Kant asks whether it is possible to establish the existence of immaterial "spirits" which, though "present in space," do not exhibit the property of "impenetrability" by which we know material substances to exist (DOSS 310–11). Though the hope for immortality has led many philosophers – such as Kant himself – to try to prove that such substances do in fact exist, a chastened Kant now argues that the question entirely transcends the limits of human knowledge, and that we must remain content with a "*moral faith*" in a future life (DOSS 337–8, 359). The proper task of the metaphysician is not to extend human cognition – as the young Kant, trained in the dogmatic Wolffian tradition, had thought – but to develop "a science of the *limits of human reason*" (DOSS 354). In the second half of the essay, Kant offers an explanation as to how Swedenborg's visions might "have arisen from *fanatical intuition*" (DOSS 347). He conjectures that in ordinary perception there is a certain "motion of the nerves" of the brain, and that "the lines indicating the direction of the motion" converge in a "*focus imaginarius*" outside the subject in space, "whereas in the case of the images of imagination, . . . the *focus imaginarius* is located within me." What happens in cases of visionary "madness" is that, for some pathological reason, imaginary objects appear to exist outside the subject because this is where the *focus imaginarius* comes to be located (DOSS 333).

In the first *Critique*, published fifteen years later, Kant suggests that human reason is susceptible to a similar malady. The transcendental illusions to which reason is naturally prone arise because reason extends the "lines of direction" of the rules of the understanding so as to make them converge in a *focus imaginarius* that lies beyond the bounds of possible experience (CPR A644/B672). The aim of Kant's transcendental dialectic is to show that the "objects" which we place at these imaginary foci only have subjective validity for regulating the use of the understanding and not an objective validity that would arise from a constitutive use of the ideas of reason. Thus the conclusion of the transcendental analytic – that any attempt to extend the categories of the understanding beyond the bounds of possible intuitions can only come up against the limiting concept of *nothing* – remains in full force (CPR A292/B348).

Had Swedenborg understood why it *seemed* as if he could perceive objects that were really just figments of his own imagination, he could have prevented himself from being deluded by them; instead, he fell into fanaticism, insisting on the veracity of his visions. Reason is subject to an analogous temptation, not only because transcendental illusions continue to persist even after they have been subjected to critique, but because of the practical interest that we have in the immortality of our souls and the reality of a God who unites happiness with virtue (CPR A811/B839). In order to avoid succumbing to fanaticism, it is necessary to distinguish "subjectively sufficient" practical grounds for moral faith from the "objectively insufficient" speculative grounds for *proving* the existence of God and the immortality of our souls (CPR A822/B850ff.).[1] As Kant puts it in the preface to the second edition of the *Critique*: "I had to deny **knowledge** in order to make room for **faith**" (CPR Bxxx). Corresponding to the cognitive distinction between faith and knowledge is the affective distinction between the sublime mental state of enthusiasm [*Enthusiasm*] for unpresentable ideas and the *excessive* enthusiasm of fanaticism. Thus it is the task of critique both to promote enthusiasm and to curb it so that it does not give way to the madness of fanaticism – "**a delusion of being able to** *see* **something beyond all bounds of sensibility,** i.e., to dream in accordance with principles (to rave with reason)" (CPJ 156, 154).[2]

1.2   Nietzsche's commemoration of Dionysian intoxication

> Anon he finds him
> Striking too short at Greeks.
> (*The Tragedy of Hamlet, Prince
> of Denmark*, II, ii, 468–9)

Far from worrying that the fervor of religious enthusiasm might give way to fanaticism, Nietzsche longed for an experience of Dionysian intoxication not yet tempered by the sobriety of the will to truth. The problem with Swedenborg is not that he suffered from delusions but that his madness was Christian in character. In *Daybreak: Thoughts on the Prejudices of Morality* (*Morgenröte: Gedanken über die Moralischen Vorurteile*, 1881), Nietzsche extols madness as a state of mind that has always been sought by the most exceptional individuals (D 13–15). But he characterizes Christianity as an inherently life-denying religion that seeks consolation for human suffering in a future life rather than in this life. In *The Gay Science* (*Die Fröhliche Wissenschaft*, 1882, 1887), Nietzsche credits Kant with seeing that every attempt to extend the use of the understanding beyond the bounds of possible experience leads, literally, to nothing. But instead of abolishing the Christian conception of a realm of spirits, Kant preserves it as an object of faith: "like a fox who loses his way and goes astray back into his cage. Yet it had been *his* strength and cleverness that had *broken open* the cage!" (GS 264). Thus Kant ends up making the exact same mistake as Swedenborg, allowing the lines of direction of human understanding – and more importantly of human willing – to converge outside the world, that is, in nothing. In order to overcome this will to nothingness – what Nietzsche calls "nihilism" – it is not enough to recognize that "God is dead," for this is simply a way of revealing the nihilistic character of the orientation toward transcendence (GS 167). To affirm new values, we must bend the lines of direction of the will back toward the will itself. This can be accomplished by affirming the "eternal recurrence" (or eternal return) of every single moment of time (GS 230).

In *Beyond Good and Evil: Prelude to a Philosophy of the Future* (*Jenseits von Gut und Böse: Vorspiel einer Philosophie der Zukunft*, 1886), Nietzsche subordinates the epistemological question, "What can I know?," to the diagnostic question, "*What* in us really wants 'truth'?" – thereby making psychology the proper ground of a genuinely critical philosophy: "psychology is now again the path to the fundamental problems" (BGE 9, 32). Nietzsche agrees with Kant that the possibility of experience presupposes synthetic a priori judgments, but he considers all such judgments – not only those that Kant relegated to the dialectical illusions of reason – to be fictions that serve a particular form of life: "it is high time to replace the Kantian question, 'How are synthetic judgments *a priori* possible?' by another question, 'Why is belief in such judgments *necessary*?' – and to comprehend that such judgments must be *believed* to be true, for the sake of the preservation of creatures like ourselves; though they might, of course, be *false* judgments for all that!" (BGE 19; cf. 12). Because life requires illusion, the advent of the will to truth – the unconditional will not to be deceived – represents a symptom of decline. Nietzsche traces the beginning of this decline back to Socrates, Plato, and Christianity ("Platonism for 'the people'") (BGE 2). The only way of overcoming European nihilism is to overturn Platonism through a fundamental "revaluation of values" (BGE 117).

In *Twilight of the Idols, Or, How to Philosophize with the Hammer* (*Götzen-Dämmerung, oder: Wie man mit dem Hammer philosophirt*, 1889), Nietzsche characterizes the entire history of European philosophy as a series of responses to Plato's metaphysical distinction between a sensible realm of appearances and an intelligible realm of forms. Kant's denial of intellectual intuition represents a turning point in this history because it transformed Plato's "true world" into something unknowable and thus – in Nietzsche's view – expendable. By repudiating the appearance/reality distinction, post-Kantian positivists were able to revive the Greek spirit of "cheerfulness" (TOTI 23). But even the positivists did not go far enough, because they continued to think of nature – the "apparent world" – as somehow retaining its ontological integrity even after the illusion of a true world had been unmasked. To overcome this last remnant of Platonism, it is necessary to recognize that "*Along with the true world, we have also done away with the apparent!*" (TOTI 24). That is, in doing away with dogmatic metaphysics, we simultaneously undermine the truth claims of empirical science: "physics, too, is only an interpretation and exegesis of the world (to suit us, if I may say so!) and *not* a world-explanation." To look at science through the lens of art and art through that of life is to trace the will to truth back to the "will to power," the surging forth of life's tendency to "*discharge* its strength" (BGE 21). In the end, all phenomena are expressions of the will to power. Hence to the question concerning the "intelligible character" of the world, Nietzsche gives what he regards as a genuinely critical response: "'will to power' and *nothing else*" (BGE 48; my italics).

1.3   Bergson's intuition of duration

> I summon up remembrance of things past
> (Sonnet 30)

According to the French philosopher Henri Bergson (1859–1941), when we use language to describe phenomena, we subject them to conceptual demarcations that are appropriate for distinguishing objects in space but that are inapplicable to the lived duration of consciousness (TFW ix, TCM 89–90). As a result of our habit of thinking spatially, we falsely ascribe to our own mental states properties that pertain exclusively to physical objects (TFW 70). In order to avoid this illusion of "subreption" (as Kant would have called it), we must return to the "immediate data of consciousness" as they are given in intuition. By doing so himself, Bergson claims to be able to determine the boundaries of science in a different way than Kant had, and to resolve metaphysical problems concerning free will, the relationship between mind and body, and the nature of life.

   In his first book, *Time and Free Will: An Essay on the Immediate Data of Consciousness* (*Essai sur les données immédiates de la conscience*, 1889), Bergson argues that it is a mistake to claim – as late-nineteenth-century psychophysicists had – that conscious sensations or "intensities" admit of quantitative measurement in the same way that spatial "extensities" do (TFW

1ff.). Kant paved the way for psychophysics by claiming that just as every appearance of outer sense must have an extensive magnitude, so every sensation that we intuit through inner sense must have a degree of intensity or intensive magnitude. But, according to Bergson, sensations are wholly qualitative in character, exhibiting differences in kind but not differences in degree. The fact that we do ascribe degrees of intensity to them – as when we say that the pain in a tooth is increasing – is a consequence of the inevitable fact that we associate our sensations with the quantifiable extensities which they represent. For example, when we say that a particular sensation of warmth is more intense than another, it is only because we have learned that the former can be correlated with a heat source whose temperature is measurably higher than that which causes the "lesser" sensation of warmth, and because measurably distinct heat sources bring about different kinds of physiological reactions in our bodies (TFW 46–7). Likewise, when we try to lift a heavy object we feel a different sensation from the one that we feel when we try to lift a light object, and it is our recognition of this fact that encourages us to say that one sensation of effort has a greater degree of intensity than another. From a purely physical point of view, lifting a heavier object does require a greater amount of muscular activity than lifting a lighter one. But being aware of a greater extent of muscular activity is not the same thing as feeling sensations of greater intensity: "the apparent consciousness of a greater intensity of effort at a given point of the organism is reducible ... to the perception of a larger surface of the body being affected" (TFW 24). "Examine whether this increase of sensation ought not rather to be called a sensation of increase" (TFW 48).

Not only is it impossible to assign a degree of intensity to our sensations, but it is equally impossible to isolate any individual sensation from the manifold to which it belongs.[3] To do so, it would be necessary to treat the manifold as a collection of discrete units, and thus to apply numerical concepts to it. But according to Bergson, the concept of number is no less restricted to the order of extensity than geometrical concepts are, for in order to count a collection of objects it is necessary to juxtapose them to one another in a homogeneous medium of some sort – and only space can provide such a medium: "every clear idea of number implies a visual image in space" (TFW 79).[4] Kant thought that time was a homogeneous medium distinct from space, and that just as the intuition of space made geometry possible, so the intuition of time made arithmetic possible. But Bergson claims that the very idea of time as a homogeneous medium – like the concept of intensive magnitude – is based on a confusion of the qualitative life of consciousness with the quantitative order of space. Kant repeatedly insists that we can only represent time by drawing a line in space. For Bergson, this limitation is due to the fact that the very concept of time is (to borrow Kant's metaphor) a bastard one, born of "the trespassing of the idea of space upon the field of pure consciousness" (TFW 98). Thus, while Bergson accepts Kant's account of space – "we have assumed the existence of a homogeneous Space and, with Kant, distinguished this space from the matter which fills it" – he rejects his conception of time: "Kant's great mistake was to take time as a homogeneous medium" (TFW 236, 232).

Once it is admitted that quantitative concepts are inapplicable to consciousness, the seemingly promising idea of psychophysics turns out to be a pseudoscience (TFW 70). Kant made a similar point about empirical psychology, claiming that it could not be a genuine science because, although the flow of time can be represented in terms of the mathematical properties of a line, inner sense does not reveal the existence of anything that persists *in* time. This is why Kant restricted the use of the category of substance – the schema of which is "persistence of the real in time" (CPR A143–4/B183) – to objects of outer sense, and why he claimed that we could only know ourselves as appearances and not as things in themselves (CPR A381; MFNS 186). Bergson agrees with Kant that the categories of the understanding are applicable only to objects in space, but he disagrees with his conclusion that self-knowledge is impossible. The fact that the representation "I" does not refer to something that persists over time – like a pebble that would be carried along by a wave – is a consequence of the fact that, metaphysically speaking, I am nothing other than the lived flux of my own duration. Thus it is a mistake to claim, with Kant, that in intuition I apprehend only the appearance of myself in time, and that I can never know whether I really am a simple substance; on the contrary, it is precisely through intuition that I become aware of what I am as a "thing in itself."

Because he locates the noumenal subject outside the realm of appearances, Kant could only resolve the third antinomy by problematically ascribing freedom to an atemporal self whose actions would not *begin* in time even though they had *effects* in time (CPR A552/B580; TFW 235). By contrast, Bergson is able to claim that through intuition we have an immediate apprehension of our lived freedom. The difficulty of explaining how freedom can be made compatible with determinism in nature only arises when we represent human actions as if they could be subdivided into separable instants like points on a line. Such a representation leads us to think of freedom as the ability to choose one rather than another of two forking paths, a conception that cannot but imply that there is no such thing as freedom, for once a particular path has been chosen it is impossible to go back in time to show that the other could have been chosen as well. But lived freedom cannot be adequately represented by the image of forking paths. It is an ineffable fact that can only be intuited and not defined (TFW 219ff.).

Bergson's solution to the problem of free will rests on his claim that there is a difference in kind between the qualitative order of duration and the quantitative order of extensity. However, he does not conclude that there is a difference in kind between freedom and necessity. On the contrary, he suggests that because the acting subject is somehow located at the crossroads where duration and extensity intersect, its actions are always *more or less* free:

"Freedom . . . is not *absolute*, as a radically libertarian philosophy would have it; it admits of degrees." Bergson explains that this is due to the fact that "growths" which appear on the plane of extensity can influence the subject's actions without being incorporated into its consciousness: "The self, in so far as it has to do with a homogeneous space, develops on a kind of surface, and on this surface independent growths may form and float" (TFW 166). As examples, Bergson refers to post-hypnotic suggestions and deep-seated passions, both of which influence a person's actions without ever rising to the level of consciousness.

The idea that the acting subject both is and is not free insofar as it belongs both to the order of duration and to the order of extensity suggests that some account is needed of how exactly the two orders are related to each other. In *Matter and Memory* (*Matière et mémoire*, 1896), Bergson identifies extensive matter with perceptual "images" that cannot be reduced either to "that which the idealist calls a *representation*" or to "that which the realist calls a *thing*" (MAM 9). Our bodies are privileged images because it is always in relation to them that we perceive all of the other images that comprise the world. To perceive something is not to encounter it from a merely theoretical point of view but to be solicited by it to act in a certain way. So long as perception remains unconscious, actions occur automatically as instinctual reactions. Freedom arises when a moment of delay separates perception from action. This moment of delay marks the intrusion of the mental into the physical and of the past into the present. Since the distinguishing feature of the mental is duration, it is not consciousness per se but memory that accounts for freedom. To be free is to be capable of living in memory – or rather to bring the past to bear on present situations. Bergson likens the mind to an ever-expanding memory cone whose base contains the entirety of the past and whose apex lies on a plane containing all of the images that comprise the world in its present state. Thus the mind and body "meet" where the apex of the cone touches the plane of the present (MAM 152ff.). Thus to live a purely mental life would be to occupy the base of the cone, while to live an unthinking life of reaction would be to occupy the apex. But as Bergson observes, each of these alternatives represents a limit, for we ordinarily live in some "intermediate" zone between the two (MAM 162–3). Thus it is possible to live nearer to the apex, as "a man of *impulse*," or nearer to the base, as "a *dreamer*" (MAM 153).

Bergson suggests that, since images always have some minimal duration, matter itself must be "in great part the work of memory" (MAM 182). Matter can be thought of as memory in its most "relaxed" state, while memory can be thought of as matter in its most "contracted" state. The same can be said for the distinction between quality and quantity: "the heterogeneity of sensible qualities is due to their being contracted in our memory and the relative homogeneity of objective changes to the slackness of their natural tension" (MAM 182–3). Hence, although Bergson characterizes his account of matter and memory as "dualistic," the difference between the two orders turns out to be not one of kind but one of degree of "tension" (MAM 9, 183). Since matter and memory both spring from a common root, the same can be said of intellect and intuition. In *Creative Evolution* (*L'évolution créatrice*, 1907), Bergson notes that just as the intellect is suited "to think matter," so intuition is needed for apprehending "the true nature of life" (CE ix, 176). However, since matter differs from life (or memory) only to the extent that one of the two "tendencies" – relaxation or contraction – happens to predominate, it is only by degrees that one passes from phenomena that require conceptualization to phenomena that can only be grasped through an immediate intuition of some sort. Bergson criticizes Kant not only for maintaining a sharp dichotomy between intuitions and concepts, but for refusing to acknowledge that as we move from the objective to the subjective poles of experience, we gradually shift from sensible intuition to intellectual intuition (CE 359–60; cf. TCM 140). Kant's great discovery was to realize that metaphysical insight could only be achieved through a "superior intuition." Unfortunately he failed to recognize that we ourselves are capable of having such intuitions. Bergson claims that Kant's only motive for denying us this capacity was that he could not otherwise resolve the mathematical antinomies (CM 139–41). But Kant failed to see that the paradoxes of space and time only arise when we consider "change and duration" from the point of view of the discursive intellect rather than "in their original mobility" as this is revealed in an immediate intellectual intuition (CM 142).

Bergson takes his conception of intellectual intuition to differ from that of the German idealists in that they thought of it as "a non-temporal intuition" rather than as an intuition of lived duration (CE 362). Once this error is corrected, it becomes possible to complete Kant's critique of speculative metaphysics by showing that the very idea of eternal being is based on a confusion concerning the omnipresence of becoming. What Kant identified as the limiting concept of *nothing* does not open up genuine metaphysical problems concerning the origin of the world. On the contrary, as Kant himself points out – though he failed to appreciate the radical significance of his insight – the use of the logical function of negation is strictly regulative, i.e., it is limited to its immanent employment within experience (CE 275, 287). Hence it is meaningless to ask the question, "Why is there something rather than nothing?" Thus, by restricting intellectual intuition to the immanent domain of matter and memory, Bergson, like Nietzsche, bends the lines of direction of the understanding back toward life itself. Just as Nietzsche wanted to look at science through the lens of art and art through the lens of life, so Bergson attempts in *Creative Evolution* to look at science through the lens of intuition and intuition through the lens of the *élan vital*, the fundamental life force that manifests itself in different ways throughout the course of evolution. In animals, the *élan vital* expresses itself primarily as instinct; in human beings, as intellect. Because the function of the human intellect is practical rather than theoretical in character, it is well-suited to help us survive, but not to inform us about the ultimate nature of reality (CE 21). Thus while science is useful, its metaphysical significance can only be gleaned through intuition, our version of what instinct is in animals.

In *Duration and Simultaneity* (*Durée et simultanéité*, 1922), Bergson appeals to intuition in order to correct a "confusion" concerning Einstein's theory of relativity – a confusion pertaining not to the theory's "physical meaning," but to its "philosophical meaning" (DS xxvii). The theory of relativity had been taken to show that because two events may be simultaneous in one reference frame but not another, there could not be a single encompassing world-time to which all events belong. Against this interpretation, Bergson makes reference to the "twin paradox" associated with the special theory of relativity. Because each of two twins, one of whom is travelling away from the other, will perceive itself to be at rest and the other to be in motion, it will seem to each that her twin is growing older more slowly than she. But if this were really so, it would seem to follow that upon returning home, the traveller would be both younger and older than her twin. According to Bergson, the only way to avoid such an absurd conclusion is to admit that the two twins live through a single duration (DS 56). Throughout the period of their separation, each has an immediate intuition of the "real" duration through which she herself lives. When she ascribes a slowed-up motion to her twin, she merely projects an "imaginary" time to which nothing real corresponds – as will be discovered when the pair are reunited (DS 46). This argument assumes – as Bergson had already argued in *Time and Free Will* – that science can tell us nothing about motion because it is restricted to measuring simultaneities (DS 40).

Bergson was criticized by several physicists (including Einstein) for failing to see that the apparent symmetry between the twins' two reference frames breaks down once acceleration is factored in (DS 175). He had assumed that it would be possible for the twins to reunite without this violating the symmetry between their perceptions of each other. But the perceived symmetry is broken when the traveling twin turns around. In the second edition of his book, Bergson refused to concede this point, insisting that questions concerning acceleration were irrelevant to his argument because they concerned the general theory of relativity rather than the special theory. In his view, only the special theory had something to say about time, while the general theory was really just about space (or four-dimensional space-time) (DS 24, 122).[5] Whether this is so or not, Bergson seems to have been mistaken about the special theory itself. But whether the theory of relativity entails, precludes, or is neutral with respect to the idea of a single encompassing world-time seems to be less important than Bergson's main thesis, namely, that the metaphysical significance of science can only be assessed through intuition. To grasp metaphysical truths, he claims, we cannot rely on the intellect alone but must instead cultivate our capacity to intuit life as an insect does (CE 175–6). To Bertrand Russell's quip that instinct "is seen at its best in ants, bees, and Bergson," Bergson should, in principle, have thanked him for the compliment.[6]

1.4   Husserl's intuition of ideal essences

'Sblood, there is something in this more than natural,
  if philosophy could find it out.
                (*The Tragedy of Hamlet, Prince of Denmark*,
                                              II, ii, 366–8)

Although he does not appeal to the example of either bees or ants, Edmund Husserl (1859–1938) implicitly agrees with Bergson that the philosophical significance of science can only be adequately grasped through the lens of a special kind of intuition. According to Husserl, all science is grounded in intuitive evidence of a certain sort, but over the course of its development it gives rise to bodies of knowledge whose "authentic" meaning becomes obscured. One of the primary tasks of the phenomenologist is to recover the lost meaning buried in modern mathematical science by shifting attention from the factually existing states of affairs that it investigates to the essential structures of the mental acts by which logical and scientific truths are apprehended in the first place.

Before arriving at this conception of phenomenology, Husserl thought that the foundations of science could be adequately grasped from the standpoint of empirical psychology. This approach had been advocated by Franz Brentano (1838–1917), with whom Husserl studied in Vienna from 1884 to 1886. In his *Philosophy of Arithmetic* (*Philosophie der Arithmetik: Psychologische und logische Untersuchungen*, Vol. 1, 1891), Husserl provides a "psychologistic" account of the foundations of arithmetic. In particular, he attempts to show how numbers, and thus all arithmetical truths, are constituted by the mental operations of mathematicians. In 1894, Husserl's book was reviewed by the logician Gottlob Frege (1848–1925), whose criticisms of psychologism Husserl had brushed aside. Frege had argued that a psychologistic treatment of the foundations of arithmetic confuses numbers, which are mind-independent, with the mental acts by which we grasp them. In his review, he accused Husserl of blurring the distinction between the sense of mathematical expressions and their referents (FR 224–5).

Whether because of Frege's criticisms or not, Husserl soon abandoned his project. In his *Logical Investigations* (*Logische Untersuchungen*, 1900–1901), he repudiates psychologism in favor of a "'formal' or 'pure' logic" of the sort that Kant first envisioned and which the logician Bernard Bolzano (1781–1848) developed under the heading of a "theory of science" or "science of science" (LI I 318 n6, 2, 45, 27). Just as Kant's transcendental logic required a theory of judgment, so Husserl seeks to explicate the logical form of mental acts. For this purpose, empirical psychology must give way to a "pure" psychology – phenomenology – that can identify the essential structures of the acts by which we apprehend the "ideal objects" with which pure logic is concerned (LI I 176). For Husserl, "pure" refers not to the "form" as opposed to the empirical "matter" of a representation – as it did for Kant – but to the essence rather than the factual existence of a mental act or its object (but cf. IPTPP 359, where Husserl argues that this use of the term "pure" coincides with that of Kant).

In the sixth of his logical investigations – "Elements of a Phenomenological Elucidation of Knowledge" – Husserl claims that when we intuit objects we simultaneously apprehend both their sensible content and their categorial form. For example, seeing a sheet of white paper is accompanied by the act of seeing *that* the paper is white (or seeing the being-white of the paper). Thus, in contrast to Kant, for whom our experience of a categorially structured world is dependent upon acts of judgment by which we subsume intuitions under concepts, Husserl characterizes our capacity to make judgments as secondary with respect to a more primordial ability to *intuit* categorial forms. Kant took truth to be a function of judgment, but for Husserl it is first and foremost a function of intuitions and only derivatively of judgments (CPR A293/B350; LI II 273). Husserl draws a sharp distinction between categorial intuition and intellectual intuition, on the grounds that, while the latter purports to leave sensibility behind altogether, categorial intuition is rooted or "founded" in sensible intuition: "It lies in the nature of the case that everything categorial ultimately rests upon sensuous intuition, that a 'categorial intuition,' an intellectual insight . . . without any foundation of sense, is a piece of nonsense" (LI II 306). In this sense, Husserl agrees with Kant that thoughts without content are empty – i.e., that "empty" signifying acts are only meaningful or "authentic" insofar as they can be "fulfilled." But he also suggests that intuitions without judgments are not as blind as Kant had thought, for the categorial structure of the world must be intuited before it can be made explicit in an act of judgment.

In "Philosophy as Rigorous Science" (*Philosophie als strenge Wissenschaft*, 1910–1911), Husserl characterizes phenomenology as a transcendental enterprise. In words that echo both prefaces to the *Critique of Pure Reason*, he bemoans the fact that philosophy "is not yet a science," and that it still wallows in its "pre-Galilean" phase (PARS 73, 71, 100). Attempts to overcome this problem by grounding philosophy in the natural sciences have failed, because "naturalistic philosophy" is unable to comprehend the true ontological status of either consciousness – which cannot be reduced to a mere natural phenomenon – or nature itself, which is in a certain respect dependent on the existence of consciousness. Just as Kant complained that the failure of dogmatism to do justice to metaphysics had given rise to skepticism, so Husserl laments the fact that the inadequacies of naturalism have led to the suspicion that philosophy is incapable of becoming a rigorous science. And just as Kant warned against the dangers of "indifferentism," so Husserl worries about "a turn toward mere *Weltanschauung* philosophy," the idea that philosophy is just an expression of a particular culture's

"world-view" (PARS 79). In order to combat this irrationalist trend, naturalistic philosophy must be subjected to "a radical critique" (PARS 78,
translation slightly modified). Such a critique can only be carried out from
the standpoint of a transcendental phenomenology. In contrast to a merely
empirical phenomenology, which starts from the naturalistic assumption
that consciousness is a natural phenomenon like any other, transcendental
phenomenology begins by suspending "the naturalistic attitude" altogether.
To suspend the naturalistic (or natural) attitude is to treat objects of consciousness not insofar as they factually exist in nature but insofar as they are
first given to a consciousness who must recognize them *as* natural objects.
Thus the first requirement of a phenomenological critique is to show that
the foundational concept of objectivity – a necessary presupposition of any
science – is rooted in "objectivity's mode of givenness" for consciousness
(PARS 90–1). By disclosing the existence of "pure phenomena," "the 'phenomenological' attitude" opens up "the field for the genuine critique of
reason" (PARS 101–2, 109–10). We usually overlook the realm of pure phenomena because we remain under "the spell of the naturalistic point of view"
(PARS 110). Philosophical naturalism reinforces this illusion: "To follow
the model of the natural sciences almost inevitably means to reify consciousness" (PARS 103).

If "Philosophy as Rigorous Science" is Husserl's preface to a new critique
of pure reason, the critique itself is spelled out in his *Ideas Pertaining to a Pure
Phenomenology and to a Phenomenological Philosophy: First Book: General Introduction to a Pure Phenomenology (Ideen zu einer reinen Phänomenologie und phänomenologischen Philosophie, I. Buch: Allgemeine Einführung in die reine Phänomenologie,
1913).* To establish "pure phenomenology" as "the science fundamental to
philosophy," we must shift from the natural attitude to the phenomenological attitude (IPTPP xvii). We accomplish this shift by putting all posited
objects of consciousness out of play – that is, by carrying out a series of
"reductions." The first of these is the "eidetic reduction," the act of
systematically ignoring all "matters of fact." This exclusion does not abolish
the objects of consciousness *as* objects of consciousness; on the contrary, it
enables us to examine what pertains to them as such. In the *Investigations*, the
eidetic reduction was the only act deemed necessary for a phenomenological
description of ideal essences. But in "Philosophy as Rigorous Science,"
Husserl observed that a merely eidetic phenomenology was not sufficient for
escaping the natural attitude. Only by performing a second reduction that is
specifically transcendental in character do we definitively break with the
natural attitude (as well as with the more encompassing "dogmatic attitude"
by which we posit the existence of any "intentional" object whatsoever,
whether it be natural, mathematical, imagined, willed, etc.) (IPTPP 143). To
perform the transcendental reduction is to ignore not only everything that is
matter of factual as opposed to essential but everything that is posited by
consciousness as "real." What remains is a transcendentally "purified" consciousness for which pure phenomena are given as "irreal" (IPTPP xx).

In performing the eidetic and transcendental reductions – which Husserl sometimes refers to collectively as "the" phenomenological reduction, or *epochē* – we "neutralize" all positing acts of consciousness by "parenthesizing" their objects. Husserl likens this procedure to the methodical doubt with which René Descartes (1596–1650) begins his first meditation. Just as the attempt to doubt everything leads Descartes to discover the indubitability of the "I think," so Husserl suggests that by suspending the "thesis" of the existence of the objects of consciousness, the phenomenologist gains a reflective awareness of his or her own consciousness as something "absolute" (IPTPP 58).

In carrying out the phenomenological reduction, we do not "lose" the objects of our awareness; on the contrary, they are "still there" precisely as pure phenomena: "the positing undergoes a modification: . . . *we, so to speak, 'put it out of action' we 'exclude it,' we 'parenthesize it'*. It is still there, like the parenthesized in the parentheses, like the excluded outside the context of inclusion" (IPTPP 59). Instead of lingering in the field of pure phenomena, Descartes hastened to find his way back to the factually existing objects of consciousness, because his attention was focused exclusively on the epistemological question, "What can I know?" By contrast, Husserl proposes to thematize the essential structures of the pure phenomena that are disclosed from the perspective of the reduction. Doing so will provide a phenomenologically grounded account of how objectivity itself is first constituted.

For Husserl, phenomenology presupposes the ability of transcendentally purified consciousness to apprehend, through reflection, the essential structures of both our own mental acts and their objects (IPTPP 78). These essential structures can only be accessed by way of eidetic intuition, that is, by our capacity to "see" essences (IPTPP 8). Thus, just as Bergson stressed the need to forgo the use of the intellect in order to apprehend the nature of life, so Husserl insists upon phenomenology's "*principle of all principles*," the idea that we must attend only to that which is disclosed through "pure" intuition (IPTPP 44). By invoking this methodological principle, Husserl claims to be able to provide something that Kant could not, namely, a secure means of access to the domain of the transcendental. The closest that Kant comes to clarifying the method of transcendental inquiry is in his brief discussion of "transcendental reflection," the operation by which one determines whether representations that are to be compared with each other belong to sensibility or understanding (CPR A261/B317). Kant thought that, to adopt a transcendental point of view, it was sufficient to inquire into the conditions for the possibility of synthetic a priori cognition. But for Husserl, the concept of the synthetic a priori is in need of phenomenological clarification (IPTPP 136). The axioms of pure logic are analytic in the sense that they pertain to all objects, regardless of the particular "region" to which they belong. "Formal ontology" is the science of "*any region whatsoever*." By contrast, each of the various "regional ontologies" (such as mathematics and the natural sciences) has "regional axioms" that are synthetic a priori in the sense that they pertain only to a particular kind of object (IPTPP 21, 31).

Husserl suggests that Kant was unable to clarify the manner in which transcendental structures are first "constituted" in consciousness because he was only concerned with the epistemological question about how we could know synthetic a priori judgments to be true. To respond to Hume's skepticism, all Kant had to do was identify already-constituted features of experience such as space, time, and the categories. The closest that Kant came to providing a more genetic analysis is in the A Deduction account of the three-fold synthesis of apprehension, reproduction, and recognition. But according to Husserl, Kant was unable to clarify the distinction between a properly eidetic (and transcendental) account of this synthesis and a merely factual, psychologistic description of it. As a result, he was forced to abandon the analysis in the B Deduction (IPTPP 142). In the second edition introduction, Kant claims that it is impossible to provide an account of the manner in which the forms of experience are constituted, suggesting that a reduction can go no further than the parenthesizing of the empirical (CPR B5–6). Hence he implicitly limited himself to providing "static" analyses of the transcendental structures of human cognition.

To recognize the need for genetic analyses is not to claim that static analyses are superfluous or even secondary. On the contrary, Husserl suggests that the first task of transcendental phenomenology is to describe the static structures of mental acts. Kant was unable to provide an adequate account of these structures because he was unaware of the methodological import of the phenomenological reduction. To carry out the reduction is to bring into view the intentional structure of consciousness, that is, the eidetic fact that every mental act has the form of a "noesis" directed toward an ideal "sense" or "noema" (IPTPP 205). Thus "intentionality" (a term Husserl borrows from Brentano) is the "principal theme of phenomenology" (IPTPP 199). Because every intentional act has a two-fold structure, the phenomenologist must describe both its "act-stratum" (i.e., the various features pertaining to the noesis) and its "sense-stratum" (the corresponding features pertaining to the noema). What belong to the noesis as its "really inherent moments" are (1) the *hyle* or "matter," which, in the case of an act of perception, coincides with the Kantian sensible manifold, and (2) the "sense-bestowing" activity that synthesizes this manifold so as to direct consciousness toward a unitary object of some sort. By contrast, the noema "belongs" to the noesis as a "non-inherent moment" (IPTPP 237). As such it represents a kind of "transcendence within immanence." Insofar as it embodies an ideal meaning, the noema contains a "core" and a still more specific "noematic sense" that refers the noesis to its object. In the case of an act of perception, the synthesis of an hyletic manifold enables consciousness to "seize on" the identical "X" that is the object of perception. This analysis is intended to clarify Kant's account of the manner in which the synthetic unity of apperception is related to the "transcendental object = X" (CPR A109). However, where Kant took the object = X to refer to the unknowable thing in itself, Husserl instead interprets it as marking the difference between the physical object itself and the particular way it happens to present itself in perception. More precisely, he argues that in contrast to consciousness – which can be given to itself in a perfectly "adequate" way – physical objects and events are such that they can only ever be presented inadequately through finite "adumbrations." Each adumbration is "surrounded" by a "halo" of indeterminacies which could themselves be "filled out" through successive adumbrations. Hence the idea of a physical object – i.e., the idea to which the "X" refers – is the limiting concept of the sum total of all the different ways in which an object of perception could present itself to consciousness. Thus, far from being an unknown thing in itself, the essence "physical object" is "an 'idea' in the Kantian sense," that is, the idea of the complete disclosure of an infinite number of adumbrations (IPTPP 358). According to Husserl, the very idea of a non-spatial, non-temporal thing in itself is an "absurdity." Just as Bergson observed that it was necessary to wait for sugar to dissolve in water, so he claims that it would be a "countersense" to think that even God could have an "adequate perception" of a physical object (CE 9; IPTPP 92).

Having done away with the phenomena/noumena dichotomy, Husserl goes on to propose phenomenological "solutions" to the metaphysical problems that Kant took up in the Transcendental Dialectic. Instead of having to rely on rational psychology, which as Kant observed could only give rise to paralogisms, the phenomenologist is able to appeal to an intuition of the "phenomenological" or "pure Ego" which remains as a "residuum" after the reduction. Although it is not immediately apprehended in any reflective act of consciousness, the ego is always there as "a transcendency of a peculiar kind – one which is not constituted – a *transcendency within immanency*" (IPTPP 133). Similarly, a phenomenology of acts of willing can establish the reality of freedom, while the existence of God is disclosed as "*something transcendent in a sense totally different* from that in which the world is something transcendent" (IPTPP 134). In resolving each of these problems of "special metaphysics," Husserl seeks to show that the so-called ideas of reason refer not to noumenal objects that are posited by empty signifying acts, but to *immanent* transcendencies.

Although he thereby does away with the distinction between appearances and things in themselves, Husserl continues to regard time and space as transcendentally ideal insofar as they are constituted by consciousness. The task of "transcendental aesthetics" is to provide a phenomenological analysis of the constitution of time and space by going back to what is "truly absolute," namely, the "time-constituting" "flow" or "stream" of consciousness (CM 146; IPTPP 193; cf. OPCIT 77). Toward this end, Husserl attempts, in lectures delivered at Göttingen in 1905, to rework Kant's A Deduction account of the three-fold synthesis of apprehension, reproduction, and recognition.[7] To the synthesis of apprehension of a sensible (hyletic) manifold in one consciousness there corresponds the self-unifying flux of "*absolute subjectivity*." Like Bergsonian duration, it can be intuited, but it remains fundamentally ineffable ("For all of this, we lack names") (OPCIT 78–9). To Kant's second synthesis – the "synthesis of reproduction in the imagination" – corresponds Husserl's account of the constitution of "immanent time," the awareness of the sequential structure of successive states of consciousness. Finally, to Kant's "synthesis of recognition in the concept" there corresponds the constitution of "objective time" in which a sequence of worldly events is distinguished from the sequence of mental acts. The transition from immanent to objective time – or from "phenomenological time" to "cosmic time" – coincides with the constitution of Kant's "analogies of experience," the static principles that make it possible to distinguish an objective order of public events in nature from the subjective succession of private perceptions (IPTPP 192).

By showing that cosmic time is ontologically grounded in phenomenological time, Husserl is able to endorse what he takes to be the key tenet of Kant's transcendental idealism, namely, that the being of nature depends upon the being of consciousness rather than the other way around: "Nature *is* only as being constituted in regular concatenations of consciousness" (IPTPP 116). However, because he derives the objective temporal order from an independently given subjective flow, he cannot claim – as Kant did in his "refutation of idealism" – that the ability to determine one's own existence in time presupposes the apprehension of an objective time-order. Thus Husserl is faced with the problem of "transcendental solipsism" in a way that Kant was not. In order to preserve the ontological – not merely epistemic – priority of phenomenological time over cosmic time he must affirm that the *"being of consciousness"* would not be extinguished, but only *"modified,"* by *"an annihilation of the world"* (IPTPP 110). Likewise he claims that the existence of other persons – i.e., other streams of consciousness – can only be established through "empathy" after a prior constitution of physical objects in nature (IPTPP 6). Husserl addresses these phenomenological problems in the second and third volumes of the *Ideas*, as well as in his *Cartesian Meditations: an Introduction to Phenomenology* (*Cartesianische Meditationen: Eine Einleitung in die Phänomenologie*, 1931), in which he tries to show how an "inter-monadic" community is constituted on the basis of the acts of isolated transcendental subjects.

In *The Crisis of European Sciences and Transcendental Phenomenology* (*Die Krisis der europäischen Wissenschaften und die transzendentale Phänomenologie*, 1936–1937) Husserl returns to the problem concerning the crisis of meaning to which the natural sciences have given rise. When Galileo introduced his project for a "mathematization of nature," he did not find it necessary to explicate the phenomenological foundations of the new geometry (CES 23, 29). But for us, Galilean science is an inherited tradition whose original meaning is no longer present in it in an immediate way. Every cultural tradition is the result of "sedimentation," the building up of successive strata of meaning over time. Sedimentation is necessary in order for a science to attain the status of an on-going communal mode of inquiry. Through the use of writing, a science is able to constitute a kind of public – and transcendental – memory of an eidetic region that initially existed only in the mind of a particular individual. The problem is that this constitution of a transcendental memory simultaneously makes possible a forgetting insofar as the sedimented tradition becomes reified. Practitioners of geometry or mathematical physics can continue to make fruitful discoveries in their respective regions without ever inquiring into the phenomenological meaning of their activity. The natural attitude – as well as the more general dogmatic attitude – results precisely from such forgetting. Not only does the risk of oblivion open the way to skepticism and historical relativism (historicism) – as Husserl had already argued in "Philosophy as Rigorous Science" – but it threatens to undermine humanity's understanding of the peculiar kind of community that it constitutes as a whole. At stake is nothing less than "a struggle for the meaning of man" – the struggle between a naive scientism and the phenomenological movement itself (CES 14).

Husserl argues that all sciences have their roots in a shared cultural "lifeworld" – "the forgotten meaning-fundament of natural science" (CES 48) – in which ideal objects are first constituted. To carry out a phenomenological clarification of the sciences is to undertake a certain kind of historical mode of inquiry into their origins. Phenomenology must thematize the primacy of the lifeworld in order to correct the ontological distortion of the human condition that is expressed in the natural attitude. Just as Bergson sought to trace the sense of the theory of relativity back to the lived experience of duration, so in his Vienna lecture of 1935, "Philosophy and the Crisis of European Humanity" (*Die Krisis des Europäischen Menschentums und die Philosophie*), Husserl argues that the sense of the mathematical formulae in Einstein's theory of relativity can only be grasped by attending to the manner in which they "receive meaning on the foundation of life" – something about which the theory of relativity itself tells us "nothing" (CES 295).

Husserl's attack on naturalistic construals of science is anticipated in Kant's critique of "transcendental realism," the view that objects in nature are things in themselves rather than phenomena (CPR A369). But according to Husserl, Kant himself remained within the natural attitude insofar as he followed a merely "regressive" method in the first *Critique*, presupposing the validity of Galilean and Newtonian science and so failing to take up "genuine problems of foundation" (CES 104).[8] Kant criticized Locke's "physiology of the soul" for falling short of a properly transcendental point of view. But Husserl argues that in attempting to distinguish the transcendental subject from the phenomenologically given soul, Kant himself lapsed into an obscure metaphysics: "as soon as we distinguish this transcendental subjectivity from the soul, we get involved in something incomprehensibly mythical" (CES 118).

In the *Ideas*, Husserl claimed that every mental act *could* be expressed in language. But in "The Origin of Geometry" (*Die Frage nach dem Ursprung der Geometrie als intentionalhistorisches Problem*), a posthumously published fragment intended for inclusion in the *Crisis*, he suggests that no cultural tradition can exist apart from *actual* linguistic – and more precisely "literary" – expression (OOG 357n). The reason for this is that ideal objectivities such as geometrical objects are essentially public in character and so require sedimentation. Husserl conjectures that there must have been a "proto-geometer" through whose private mental acts the first geometrical idealities were constituted. These could have been communicated to others in spoken language. But in order for genuinely public objectivities such as the Pythagorean theorem to exist, oral communication would have been insufficient. Only by being written do ideal objectivities acquire that "virtual" reality by which they can endure even when no one happens to be (re-)constituting them (OOG 361). Put otherwise, it is by being written that geometrical truths – which are first constituted at a particular moment of cosmic time – become transhistorical truths. The paradox is that sedimentation – i.e., the condition for the possibility of both remembering and forgetting – thereby emerges as a condition for the possibility of the very existence of certain intentional objects. Insofar as written documents remain dependent on the animating acts of actual writers and readers, they are essentially "expressive" in character. But to the extent that the meanings they embody can only exist *as sedimented*, they retain an irreducible "indicative" dimension that escapes the order of sheer givenness (LI I 183). Thus the literary dimension of texts would appear to be ineliminable.

1.5   Heidegger's openness to being

My care is loss of care
[. . .] And nothing can we call our own but death
(*The Tragedy of King Richard the Second*,
IV, i, 196; III, ii, 152)

In his retrospective essay, "My Way to Phenomenology" (*Mein Weg in die Phänomenologie*, 1963), Heidegger recalls first becoming interested in the work of Husserl in 1907, after reading Brentano's *On the Several Senses of Being in Aristotle* (*Von der mannigfachen Bedeutung des Seienden nach Aristoteles*, 1862) (MWTP 74). Brentano had tried to show that, of the many different ways in which "being" is said according to Aristotle – it is said of accidents, truth (predication), potentiality and actuality, and the categories – its primary sense is the one pertaining to the categories, "the various highest concepts which are designated by the common name being" (SSB 53). Knowing that Husserl had studied with Brentano, Heidegger went on to read the *Logical Investigations* and discovered that Husserl's analysis of categorial intuition closely resembled Aristotle's account of the way in which the categories are encountered in *aisthesis*. In effect, sensuous intuition is to categorial intuition what beings are to the being of beings. By implicitly going back from a Kantian conception of categories as subjective forms of thought which we ourselves impose upon the world – and which accordingly require a "deduction" to demonstrate their validity – to an Aristotelian account of the categories as ways in which being shows itself in phenomena, Husserl had opened the way to a radical rethinking of the question concerning the unity of the manifold senses of being. After becoming Husserl's assistant at Freiburg in 1916, Heidegger conducted seminars on the *Investigations* (MWTP 78–9), suggesting to his students that the significance of phenomenological research lay not in Husserl's attempt to transform philosophy into a rigorous science but in its ability to renew the questions of "fundamental ontology."

In *Being and Time*, Heidegger notes that *"the question of the meaning of Being"* was of paramount importance for the ancient Greeks, but that today it has lost its sense of urgency (BAT 19). Aristotle claimed that the concept of being transcended all species and genera, and that for this reason it was of all concepts the one most in need of clarification (BAT 23). But apart from the medieval characterization of being as "transcendental," the entire history of Western metaphysics since Aristotle has tended toward the opposite conclusion, namely, that the concept of being is completely transparent since it is empty and without meaning (BAT 62). In this view, only determinate beings – and not being itself – are worthy of interrogation. The forgetting of the "ontological difference" – the difference between being and beings – culminates in Hegel's definition of being as "the 'indeterminate immediate,'" a formulation which serves as the foundation "for all the further categorial explications of his 'logic'" (BAT 22). With the success of Hegel's construal of being as "the most universal concept" – and of the neo-Kantian conception of categories as mere "forms of thought" – the Aristotelian problematic concerning the "unity of Being" has become completely eclipsed (BAT 23).

In order to raise anew the question of the meaning of being, Heidegger claims that it is necessary to interrogate a particular being about the kind of being that it has. This being is *Dasein* (BAT 27). The term *Dasein* – an ordinary German word used to refer to the existence of anything whatsoever – is reserved by Heidegger to refer specifically to the kind of being that we ourselves have (or are) insofar as our being is an "issue" for us (BAT 32). The unique kind of being that Dasein has Heidegger calls "existence" (*Existenz*) (BAT 32). To inquire into the being of Dasein is to disclose the structurally unified "existentialia" that essentially pertain to any Dasein whatsoever (BAT 33).

Existentialia are different in kind from categories (BAT 70). In his Transcendental Analytic, Kant sought to identify those categories that pertain to the being of objects of experience. But according to Heidegger, Kant's analysis suffered from the fact that he did not carry out a prior inquiry into the ontological structure of the "subject" for whom such objects are given. It is this lacuna that Heidegger's "existential analytic" is intended to fill. Kant saw that the categories could not be meaningfully predicated of the unity of apperception (BAT 366). But instead of recognizing that this was because

the being of Dasein is different in kind from that of those entities to which
the categories do pertain, Kant kept to a fundamentally Cartesian conception of the subject as something to which the category of substance could be
applied problematically (BAT 497 nxix). By failing to bring the phenomenon of Dasein into view, Kant was unable to recognize the difference
between categories and existentialia, let alone to take up the question of how
these fundamentally different kinds of being are unified in being itself.[9] In a
second part of *Being and Time* that was never published, Heidegger had
planned to carry out a "destruction" of "the history of ontology" in which he
would show how the forgetting of being in Western metaphysics had
originated in Aristotle's construal of the relationship between being and
time (BAT 41). With his discovery of the schematism, Kant did glimpse
what Heidegger's existential analytic will show, namely, that the being of
Dasein is temporality. But because he adhered to a Cartesian conception of
the thinking subject, Kant failed to recognize the true import of the
schematism (BAT 45).

The first task of Heidegger's existential analytic is to determine the
proper means of access to Dasein's way of being. That such a problem arises
at all is a consequence of the fact that, although its own existence is an issue
for it, Dasein is constituted in such a way that it understands itself "*proxi-
mally and for the most part*" in terms of the being of entities other than itself,
that is, in terms of the categories (BAT 36–7). Heidegger calls this mode of
being "average *everydayness*" (BAT 38). Everydayness is not something that
Dasein occasionally lapses into but is one of its existential (i.e., essential) features. Closely related to the phenomenon of everydayness is that of belonging to a tradition that has already interpreted being for Dasein in a way that
is obfuscatory rather than genuinely illuminating. In order to avoid the two-
fold temptation posed by everydayness and tradition, the existential analytic
must approach Dasein phenomenologically, that is, by allowing Dasein to
show itself as it exists in average everydayness, allowing this mode of being
to disclose itself as one in which Dasein misinterprets its own being. The
discovery of this misinterpretation will then point the way to a more "primordial" investigation of the ontological grounds of everydayness itself.

In its average everydayness, Dasein has the character of "being-in-the-
world" (BAT 65). *In* claiming that Dasein is essentially *in* a world – in a
sense different from the way in which entities other than Dasein are "in" a
surrounding space (BAT 79) – Heidegger departs from Husserl, who, like
Descartes, thought that the intentionality of consciousness did not preclude
the annihilation of the world. Kant's attempt to provide a "refutation of idealism" fares no better than Husserl's problematic solipsism, for the very idea
of proving the reality of the so-called external world only makes sense if one
mistakenly treats phenomena as "mere" appearances that are "in us" for
which corresponding objects "outside of us" must be found (BAT 247ff.).
Against this interpretation, Heidegger insists that "phenomena are *never*
appearances," but, on the contrary, are *things themselves* – i.e., beings –

showing themselves for what they are (BAT 53). Phenomenology and ontology are, in this view, one and the same (BAT 60–1). Dasein is inherently "phenomenological" in that it is the site through which phenomena disclose themselves. Only because the being of phenomena has been covered up in everydayness and tradition is it necessary for Dasein to *go back*, methodically, to the things themselves and to its own manner of being.

As the "logos" of phenomena, phenomenology has the discursive aim of providing an "interpretation" or "hermeneutic" of the being of beings (BAT 61–2). For Heidegger, phenomenology is hermeneutical not in the sense that it imposes an arbitrary interpretation on things but in that it allows the self-disclosure of phenomena to be brought to discourse. In keeping with the priority that both Aristotle and Husserl had accorded to intuition in the disclosure of the categorial structure of the world, Heidegger suggests that truth is a function of *aisthesis* before it is a function of judgment, i.e., that Dasein's capacity for asserting what is true presupposes its character as disclosive (BAT 57, 201). In section 44 of the Sixth Investigation, Husserl subordinated the truth of predicative judgments to the truth of (fulfilling) intuitions. Along similar lines, Heidegger argues, in section 44 of *Being and Time*, that truth in the sense of a factual correspondence between a judgment and a state of affairs (truth as *adequatio*) presupposes truth in the sense of disclosure (truth as *aletheia*) (BAT 258). But Heidegger goes further than Husserl does in emphasizing the "aesthetic" dimension of world-disclosure, for where Husserl clings to the Cartesian conception of the knowing subject to whom truth is disclosed, Heidegger identifies Dasein with world-disclosure itself. Hence instead of conceiving of phenomenology as the science of science, as Husserl does in "Philosophy as Rigorous Science," Heidegger treats it as the disclosure of world-disclosure, that is, as the *aisthesis* of *aisthesis*.

As everyday being-in-the-world, Dasein is practically "concerned" with objects whose mode of being is that of readiness-to-hand (*Zuhandenheit*) (BAT 83, 98). In its engagement with the ready-to-hand, Dasein is teleologically oriented toward possibilities which it seeks to realize, it itself functioning as that "for the sake of which" a network of telic significations exists. Dasein is also such as to exist with other Dasein toward whom it shows "solicitude," a term that denotes for Heidegger not an ethical orientation per se but rather the condition for the possibility of ethics, namely, existing in relation to others whose being is also that of Dasein rather than of readiness-to-hand (BAT 157). Although it is always possible to treat another Dasein (or oneself) as if it were merely a piece of equipment, this possibility is derivative with respect to the more fundamental way in which Dasein is taken to be a distinctive kind of being. Likewise, it is possible to treat that which is ready-to-hand as if it were merely present-at-hand (*vorhanden*), but presence-at-hand is itself a derivative mode of being of that which is ready-to-hand (which is a way of saying that Dasein's theoretical comportment toward the world is secondary with respect to its practical engagements in it) (BAT 100). Whenever Dasein takes its entire world – including itself – as exhibiting presence-at-hand, it interprets being in general as "reality" (BAT 245). In the mode of everydayness, Dasein exists not as itself but as "the 'they'" (*das Man*), interpreting itself and its world in an "inauthentic" manner (BAT 150). Heidegger calls this mode of existence "fallenness," which he takes to be characterized by "idle talk" (the discourse of "the they"), "curiosity" (an inauthentic mode of understanding), and "ambiguity" (the inability to distinguish between phenomenologically adequate and inadequate significations) (BAT 220). For each of the existentialia that make up Dasein's being, there are authentic and inauthentic ways in which Dasein can have an "existentiell" understanding of itself (BAT 33).

Dasein exists as fallen simply because being-in-the-world has the onto-logical structure of "care," which Heidegger defines as *"Being-ahead-of-itself,"* or, more precisely, *"ahead-of-itself-in-already-being-in-a-world"* (BAT 236). To say that Dasein has the character of being ahead of itself is to say that it is its potentiality-for-being, i.e., that it *is* only insofar as it is "projected" toward possibilities (BAT 185). To say that it is "already" in the world is to say that it is "thrown" (BAT 174). Taking these two existentialia together, care has the unitary character of "thrown projection" (BAT 188). All of the existen-tialia that pertain to Dasein – concern, solicitude, understanding, disclosed-ness (BAT 171), mood or state-of-mind (BAT 172), discourse (BAT 203–4), etc. – are so many structural moments of care. In this respect, Heidegger implies that care can be thought of as the mode of being that Kant would have ascribed to the unity of apperception, had he undertaken an existential analytic of "the subject." But is care the most primordial feature of the being of Dasein? Or is it grounded in a feature of Dasein's being that only emerges into view once the inauthenticity of Dasein's self-understanding in every-dayness is forsaken for a more authentic understanding?

In response to these questions, Heidegger does two things. In the second division of the first part of *Being and Time*, he points to the fact that the "whole" of Dasein can only be disclosed if care is taken not merely in its limited significance as the condition of Dasein's being toward worldly possi-bilities but in its more radical existential character as Dasein's being-toward-death (BAT 273, 277). In being ahead of itself, Dasein is in relation not only to worldly possibilities but to its most proper ("ownmost") possibility of no longer having any possibilities (BAT 294). Death is the one possibility that Dasein has for which no other Dasein can take its place (BAT 284). The other thing that Heidegger does to reveal the ontological ground of care is to show that within everydayness, Dasein "calls" itself to recognize that it is "guilty," i.e., that insofar as it is lost in "the they," it is inauthentic (BAT 314). In hearing the call of conscience, Dasein shows that it *"wants to have a conscience"* (BAT 277). To want to have a conscience means not to acknowledge one's moral obligations but something more existentially primordial, namely, to take on one's being-toward-death in a "resolute" manner (BAT 314). Far from presupposing a determinate conception of the morally good, the existential phenomenon of being-guilty serves as the condition for the possibility of such a conception: "The primordial 'Being-guilty' cannot be defined by morality, since morality already presupposes it for itself" (BAT 332).

The call of conscience manifests itself as "anxiety," a fundamental mood that "discloses Dasein *as Being-possible*" (BAT 232). In contrast to fear, which anxiety makes possible and which is always oriented toward some worldly object or event, anxiety is literally motivated by nothing, that is, by the phenomenon of Dasein's own possible nothingness (BAT 230–1). Thus anxiety is the way in which Dasein announces its being-toward-death to itself: "Anxiety arises out of Being-in-the-world as thrown Being-towards-death" (BAT 395). Resoluteness represents "readiness for anxiety" and so readiness for death (BAT 343). Every Dasein is faced with the choice of fleeing into everydayness or resolutely choosing its condition of thrown projection. Though Heidegger does not couch this either/or in explicitly religious terms, his description of it echoes the choice between persisting in sin and making a leap of faith as this alternative is thematized in the writings of the Danish philosopher Søren Kierkegaard (1813–1855). Heidegger acknowledges the psychological acumen of Kierkegaard's analysis of anxiety, though he criticizes him for failing to approach the phenomenon from an ontological point of view (BAT 492 niv; cf. 497 niii).

Insofar as anxiety calls Dasein away from its fallenness in everydayness, it provides an existential motive for what Husserl characterized as the suspension of the natural attitude. In Heidegger's terminology, it allows the transition from the phenomenology of everydayness to the phenomenology of authentic Dasein to be motivated by "the things themselves" and not by the arbitrary whim of the phenomenologist. To be fallen in everydayness is to interpret the phenomenon of the world – as well as Dasein's being-in-the-world – in terms of the "reality" of nature. By contrast, to become resolute is to recover the primordial dependence of the very "worldhood" of the world on Dasein itself: "worldhood itself is an *existentiale*" (BAT 92; cf. 94, 100). Thus the spatiality of the world is ontologically rooted in Dasein's "de-severance" (i.e., its existential motility) and in its "directionality" (BAT 138), but in fallenness these become thematized in terms of "the homogeneous space of Nature," an interpretation that can only arise if "the worldly character of the ready-to-hand gets . . . *deprived of its worldhood*" (BAT 147). Even Kant, despite the fact that he took space to be the mere form of outer sense, conceived of spatiality only categorially and not existentially (BAT 144). Such ontological distortions are rooted in the very character of Dasein as care, whose structure is precisely that of being-in-the-world. But care itself has a deeper ontological structure, namely that of temporality.

As temporality, care has the character of "being-ahead-of-itself" (projection), "being-already-in-a-world" (thrownness), and "being-alongside" that which is ready-to-hand and present-at-hand. In everydayness, these take the form, respectively, of "existence," "facticity," and "falling" (BAT 293). To say that Dasein is ahead of itself is just to say that it has a future. To say that it is already in a world is to say that it has a past. Finally, to say that it is alongside worldly entities is to say that it has a present. These three temporal "ekstases" constitute the most primordial being of Dasein insofar as it has the form of thrown projection (BAT 329). It is important not to construe futurity, pastness, and having-a-present on the basis of a conception of time derived from entities other than Dasein, for it is only insofar as Dasein is temporal that there is a "world-time" to which things ready-to-hand and present-at-hand belong. This is not to say that objects other than Dasein are in time only because we represent them that way. On the contrary, Heidegger argues against both Kant and Bergson that "the time 'in which' what is present-at-hand arises and passes away, is a genuine phenomenon of time" (BAT 382; cf. 471, 500–1 nxxx). Even Dasein can be said to be "in time" insofar as it situates itself with respect to a common time to which other Dasein belong (BAT 429). This common time is measured by ready-to-hand chronometric devices such as clocks and calendars. But the fact that there can be things like clocks and calendars remains rooted in Dasein's temporality, specifically insofar as "datability" pertains to its everyday engagements (BAT 459). Thus it is necessary to recognize that Dasein's capacity to belong to something like world-history is a consequence of the fact that it is itself essentially historical, rather than to say that it is historical because it belongs to world-history. In Heidegger's view, the mistake made by Hegel was to reverse this point of view. Like all of the philosophers who belong to the metaphysical tradition inaugurated by Plato and Aristotle, Hegel conceives of time as a series of "nows." Such a conception of time has its point of departure in the measurable "public" time that pertains to Dasein insofar as it is fallen in everydayness (BAT 470).

Heidegger's critique of clock time implies that there is a more primordial kind of temporality than the time that is measured by the theory of relativity (BAT 499 niv). But unlike Bergson, Heidegger does not want to reduce the "within-time-ness" of worldly events to "an externalization of . . . 'qualitative time'" as Bergson does (BAT 382). Heidegger criticizes Bergson for continuing to think of *worldly* time as a series of nows, that is, for thinking "time as space" (BAT 501 nxxx). He does not elaborate on this criticism, promising to do so in the never-published second part of *Being and Time*. Heidegger's book breaks off with an unanswered question as to how exactly one gets from the primordial temporality of Dasein to being, whose "horizon" appears to be time itself (BAT 488). This question is an important one, because it touches on the theme that motivates all of Heidegger's subsequent writings, namely, the idea that Dasein or "man" is *claimed* by being in such a way that to think is to listen to a call that comes not from Dasein itself but from being. The fact that we live in the forgetting of being is a consequence of the way in which being comes to presence, namely, as an "unconcealing" that conceals itself. To be lost as "the they" in everydayness is "not to have ears" to hear the *silence* of the concealment in which being presences out of (and possibly into) nothing.

In his 1955 lecture, "The Question Concerning Technology" (*Die Frage nach der Technik*), Heidegger implicitly distinguishes between two different modes of everydayness, one coinciding with the Greek conception of productive comportment as *techne*, and the other with the reign of modern technology. For Aristotle, *techne* was a way of revealing that which comes into being through the assistance of the work of the craftsman (QCT 13). By contrast, the essence of modern technology lies in the oblivion to which being is cast in the "presencing" of what is. According to Heidegger, modern technology represents the ultimate "danger" in that it installs man as a subject who is no longer even aware of the destituteness that attends to his condition because he no longer hears the call of being (QCT 26). We think of technology as something that we ourselves accomplish when, in fact, it is the mode in which being "destines" itself today, namely, by "challenging" man to "set upon" nature (QCT 14–15). Thus technology is not the product of the sheer spontaneity of man's will but is rather something that we *receive* as the setting-up of the will.

Heidegger uses the word "Enframing" – *Ge-stell* – to name the peculiar manner in which being reveals itself as "standing-reserve" in modern technology (QCT 19). To think the "essence of technology" is to hearken to the silence out of which, perhaps, another destining of being might once again call man into its midst. Construed in this way – i.e., as a mode of disinterested attentiveness rather than as instrumental determination – thinking represents a kind of "piety" (QCT 35). In the questioning stance of genuine thinking, we await an event – *Ereignis* – through which the essence of "the monstrousness that reigns" will be disclosed, and with it the glimpse of a new epoch of being (QCT 16). Modern science is incapable of thinking because it operates within the fixed metaphysical horizon of Enframing. The task of thinkers is to reflect on the essence of modern science by situating the conception of being as standing-reserve with respect to the history of the various ways in which being has revealed itself. In "Science and Reflection" (*Wissenschaft und Besinnung*, 1954), Heidegger suggests that it is only with Descartes and Galileo that being comes to be thought of as "objectness" rather than as "presencing" (QCT 163). Likewise, it is only with the advent of twentieth-century physics that objectness gives way to "the constancy of standing-reserve," a fundamentally new manifestation of being in which the subject–object relation congeals into the mode of Enframing (QCT 173). Despite this difference between classical and contemporary physics, they are essentially alike in that both construe science as the "entrapping" of the real (QCT 172–3). Hence, by virtue of its very essence, modern science cannot awaken us to the occlusion of being. Only poets can do this. In revealing the danger of forgetfulness, they prepare the way for a new destining of being. This is what the German poet Friedrich Hölderlin (1770–1843) means when he writes in his poem "Patmos" that "where danger is, grows/The saving power also" (QCT 28; cf. DOE 38).

In the *Ideas*, Husserl noted that when we encounter works of art we spontaneously perform "the *neutrality modification*" by which a "positing" act is transformed into an act of "phantasy" (IPTPP 260). This suggests that works of art draw us into the atmosphere of a reduction that has already been performed. Heidegger picks up on this idea, but instead of ascribing the reduction to the artist, he ascribes it to the work itself, or rather to the work insofar as it is disclosive of the truth of being. In "The Turning" (*Die Kehre*, 1955), Heidegger associates Hölderlin's saving power with the possibility of a "turning" in the way in which being comes to presence. By attributing such a turning to being rather than to Dasein, he implies that it is only through "grace" rather than "works" that man can be "saved" from Enframing. Thus, in contrast to Husserl, who urged his readers to overcome the crisis of modernity by *performing* an act of reduction – the *epochē* – Heidegger ascribes the transformative power of the *epochē* to being insofar as it destines itself differently in the transition from one *epoch* to another.

As the ever-increasing oblivion of being, the history of metaphysics represents the gradual coming to presence of man's hubris, exemplified in the shift from the pre-Socratic conception of man as openness to the Cartesian (and ultimately Nietzschean) self-assertion of the will of man – that is, in the shift from the destining of man qua spontaneous receptivity to the destining of man qua receptive spontaneity. At the time he wrote *Kant and the Problem of Metaphysics*, Heidegger thought that Kant had interrupted this trajectory by discovering in the schematism the primordial temporality of Dasein. But, in his 1961 lecture, "Kant's Thesis about Being" (*Kants Thesis über das Sein*), he instead claims that Kant conceives of being as "positedness," a way of thinking that leads directly to Hegel's conception of "being as Absolute concept" (P 363). In his critique of the ontological argument for the existence of God, Kant claimed that "the little word 'is' is not a predicate," since the modal concept of existence is one that refers not to a property of objects (beings), but to the relationship between a posited object and the perceiving subject (CPR A598/B626; P 352–3). Heidegger suggests that insofar as Kant thinks being in general in terms of the modal categories of being-possible, being-actual, and being-necessary, his metaphysics can be captured by the title "Being and Thought."

This interpretation implies that Kant remains within the metaphysics of spontaneity that stretches from the Cartesian subject through the Nietzschean conception of the will to power to the Promethean construal of technology as the product of man's activity. But this characterization overlooks the ontological significance of Kant's distinction between phenomena and noumena. For Kant, to posit an object is not to determine its being – something that pertains to it qua thing in itself – but to subsume its appearance under a concept. Thus he thinks being not as positedness but as that which escapes all positing. Support for this reading can be found in Kant's account of "the principle of homogeneity" and "the principle of specification," according to which it is always possible to find, for any given concept, both a higher conceptual genus under which it falls, and further species that fall under it (CPR A658/B686). Together, these two principles imply that we cannot reach the thought of being either by ascending to a highest genus or by finding a concept that would be perfectly adequate to an object of intuition. Thus the being of beings cannot be posited; it can only be indicated, negatively, through the idea of God – that is, through the idea of a highest being that subsumes all other beings under it: "because everything else, as conditioned, stands under it, it is called the **being of all beings** (*ens entium*)" (CPR A578–9/B606–7).

Kant notes that the being of beings can only be thought as an abyss from which we must *shrink back*: "What causes it to be unavoidable to assume something among existing things to be in itself necessary, and yet at the same time to shrink back from the existence of such a being as an abyss?" (CPR A615/B643). The answer to this question is that human cognition – for which there is an insurmountable gulf separating possibility from actuality – is inexorably led to posit that which can never be given to it, namely, a being whose mere possibility entails its actual existence, i.e., a necessary being. To say that we are called to think the idea of God *and* that such an idea must remain unthinkable for us is to indicate that human cognition can only vacillate between staring into the abyss and shrinking back, the being of beings forever concealing and revealing itself. Thus Kant is himself a thinker of the event by which being withdraws in the disclosure of a world.

In his 1929 lecture, "What is Metaphysics?" (*Was ist Metaphysik?*), Heidegger claims that such an event can only be glimpsed through the encounter with the nothing: "Human existence can relate to beings only if it holds itself out into the nothing" (BW 109). This is the lecture in which he reflects on the meaning of the sentence, "The nothing itself nihilates." Carnap thought that Heidegger was making a metaphysical assertion, but in effect he was simply restating the transcendental point that Kant made when he noted that the relation between the givenness of phenomena and the being of beings could only be thought through the concept of nothing. Thus in his 1935 lecture course, *Introduction to Metaphysics* (*Einführung in die Metaphysik*, published in 1953), Heidegger takes the fundamental question of metaphysics to be (pace Bergson), "Why are there beings at all instead of nothing?" (IM 1). To the extent that Kant's metaphysics can be captured by the expression "Being and Thought," so Heidegger's reflections on metaphysics might be entitled not "Being and Time" but "Being and Givenness." Yet just as Kant thinks being not as positedness but as the unpositable ground by which the positable is positable, so Heidegger ultimately thinks of being not as givenness but as that by which the given is given. Thus in his 1962 lecture, "Time and Being" (*Zeit und Sein*) – the title of the never-published third division of the first part of *Being and Time* – he calls attention to the peculiar idiom by which German speakers say that "there is" something, namely, through the words *es gibt*, which literally translate as "it gives": "We do not say: Being is, time is, but rather: there is Being [*es gibt Sein*] and there is time [*es gibt Zeit*]. . . . Instead of saying 'it is,' we say 'there is,' 'It gives'" (OTAB 5). This reflection leads Heidegger to ask about the "it" that gives, a question which he says has eluded Western metaphysics (OTAB 8). Thus it is not givenness per se but the "event" (*Ereignis*) by *which* givenness is given that Heidegger tries to think (OTAB 19). To inquire into the *Ereignis* is not to seek a transcendent *ground* of being – as Kant tried to think the unpositable ground of the positable – but to attend to that which eludes all "transcendental-horizontal re-presenting" (DOT 63ff.).

1.6   Bachelard's poetics of science

> We are such stuff
> As dreams are made on; and our little life
> Is rounded with a sleep.
> > (*The Tempest*, IV, i, 156–8)

In contrast to Heidegger, for whom twentieth-century physics was essentially just an extension of the early modern scientific project, Gaston Bachelard (1884–1962) – a chemist by training – thought that a "new scientific spirit" had opened up an entirely new way of thinking about being. Throughout his writings, Bachelard moves freely back and forth between technical considerations about the ontological implications of the new physics and metaphysical reveries about the imagery of lyric poetry.

Just as Bachelard is more amenable than Heidegger to the reconcilability of the claims of science and poetry, so he denies that there is as great a gap between intuition and intellect as Bergson supposed there to be. Intuitions have to be educated by the intellect, that is, by the very scientific accomplishments whose philosophical significance Bergson thought had to be assessed from the perspective of a naive or "pure" intuition. For Bachelard, the very capacity to intuit has a history, one that is dialectically informed by developments in science – a thesis he develops in *The New Scientific Spirit* (*Le nouvel esprit scientifique*, 1934). Just as intuition is first formed by science, so science has its point of departure in intuitions that it must "struggle" to overcome (NSS 77).

The distinctive feature of the new science is that it is based almost exclusively on a form of mathematics that has forsaken all reliance on intuition (NSS 55). Both Euclidean geometry and the Newtonian physics that rested upon it presupposed an intuitive conception of space. This is why Kant could regard the judgments of both pure mathematics and pure natural science as synthetic a priori. By contrast, the algebraic theory of groups that lies at the foundation of the new physics presupposes nothing more than the abstract concept of a set, together with a (closed) operation defined on its members. Because it relies exclusively on such concepts, group theory is an entirely discursive branch of mathematics. In showing that Euclidean geometry and Newtonian physics are just special cases of the new mathematics and science, the new scientific spirit has effectively established the primacy of theory over intuition: "By incorporating the group as one of its fundamental ideas, mathematical physics has demonstrated the primacy of theory" (NSS 35).

According to Bachelard, the applicability of group theory to science has ontological implications, because the concept of a group implies that relations are more primary than their relata: "With group theory we reach the ultimate abstraction, the realm in which relation has priority over being" (NSS 69; cf. 29). Kant claimed that within the order of phenomena, relations had priority over being, but he denied that this could be the case with things in themselves (CPR A285/B341). By contrast, Bachelard suggests that the new science confirms the *noumenal* priority of relations (NSS 31; cf. 147). In order for science to reach the level of the noumenal, it is necessary to abandon the plane of "empirical intuition" in favor of that of "mathematical intuition" (NSS 163): "Henceforth, to study phenomena one must engage in purely noumenal activity; it is mathematics that opens new avenues to experience" (NSS 60; cf. 6). Scientific method consists not in deductively progressing from one clear and distinct idea to another, but rather in inductively progressing from one obscure idea to another with the aim of synthesizing a recalcitrant body of individual results. When it succeeds in producing a new synthesis, a scientific achievement "realizes" a form of objectivity that makes possible new forms of intuition.

Bachelard characterizes this conception of scientific method as a kind of "applied rationalism," one that requires a "non-Cartesian epistemology." Descartes thought that the way to acquire knowledge was to analyze complex phenomena into their simple elements. But according to Bachelard, the priority of relations in the new physics implies that "every phenomenon is a fabric of relations," which is to say that the simple is a function of the complex rather than vice versa (NSS 147). In his second meditation, Descartes claimed that even though a piece of wax loses all of its sensible qualities when it is heated by the fire, we recognize it to be the same object over time because we apprehend its essence – specifically, its extendedness – through an act of intellectual intuition. As an alternative to this thought experiment, Bachelard describes the way in which a modern scientist would go about conducting an experiment on a piece of wax. Instead of attempting to get at its simple nature through an act of intellectual intuition, a chemist or physicist would begin by purifying the wax and then subjecting it to a number of tests in order to identify its chemical composition (NSS 165ff.). In carrying out such an "'objective meditation' in the laboratory," the modern scientist is as much constructing a reality as describing it (NSS 171).

Bachelard suggests that it was his reliance on Cartesian epistemology that led Bergson to overestimate the epistemic weight of intuition. Bachelard and Bergson agree that in order to comprehend the theory of relativity, we must abandon philosophical assumptions that derive from a Newtonian world-view (DS 189; NSS 138–9). But whereas Bergson thought that the theory of relativity demonstrated the ontological precedence of lived duration over objective time – and so of qualities over quantities – Bachelard suggests that the real lesson of all of the new physics is that we must pass from the intuition of qualities to discrete analyses carried out in thought: "it is essential to move from intuitive geometrization to 'discursive' arithmetization" not only in modern mathematics but in all branches of physics and chemistry (NSS 125). It is a mistake to think that philosophy can clarify the significance of science; on the contrary, "Science in effect creates philosophy" (NSS 3; cf. TPON 122).

For Bachelard, the new physics stands in a dialectical relationship to reality because it is at once both entirely abstract and thoroughly experimental. The tension between these two tendencies finds expression in the fact that modern science sanctions a priori theory construction ("rationalism"), while at the same time requiring fidelity to facts ("realism") (NSS 1ff.). Thus the new science is in a "constant state of crisis" in that it is an ongoing dialectic between synthetic a priori theorizing and experimentation (NSS 160, 140). Experimentation is not so much the empirical testing of particular cases as it is the instantiation of one of an indefinite number of possible cases given by the theory itself. Bachelard argues that in this sense, modern science has weakened the distinction between possibility and reality: "The possible has in a sense drawn nearer to the real; it has recaptured a place and a role in the organization of experience" (NSS 59). Insofar as it describes not just isolated phenomena but entire systems of possible phenomena, there is a "transcendental" dimension to the new science (NS 114).

In *The Philosophy of No: a Philosophy of the New Scientific Mind* (*La philosophie du non: Essai d'une philosophie du nouvel esprit scientifique*, 1940), Bachelard attempts to develop a conception of transcendental philosophy that would avoid Kant's mistake of reifying fixed conditions for the possibility of experience (TPON 12, 6). Such a philosophy must be founded on the discursivity of pure mathematics, which Bachelard regards not as a consequence of our ability to reason but as the fount of reason itself: "Arithmetic is not founded upon reason. It is the doctrine of reason which is founded upon arithmetic. Before knowing how to count I could hardly know what reason was" (TPON 123). Kant claimed that time was the form of inner sense, and arithmetic the science of time. By contrast, Bergson argued that we encounter lived duration only insofar as we become capable of "suspending" the discursive arithmetical overlay that thought imposes upon it. Against both of these points of view, Bachelard claims that the intuition of duration is a *product* of counting, that there would be no lived time apart from the discursive activity of ordinal numbering which is reason itself in its most primordial form. Thus time has a kind of digital character, which is to say that there are "lacunae in duration" (DD 19).

In *Dialectic of Duration* (*La Dialectique de la durée*, 1950), Bachelard suggests that "It is impossible to know time without judging it," a statement that recalls Kant's statement that intuitions without concepts are blind (DD 53; cf. NSS 9). But Bachelard goes further than Kant in arguing that "thought time" is ontologically prior to "lived time" (DD 37, 92). Bergson claimed that conceptual distinctions pertain to the domain of space alone. To the extent that they appear to pertain to time it is only insofar as we have shifted our attention from lived duration to "spatialized" time. But for Bachelard, conceptual discrimination belongs to an originary "thought time" that lies at the heart of "lived time": "Far from language having its roots in the spatial aspect of things, its true mental function lies for us in the temporal, ordered aspect of our actions" (DD 37; but cf. NSS 126, where Bachelard writes that "spatial localization underlies all language" [NSS 126]). Lived experience would thus be rooted in something like a "time of reasons" that is anterior to the time of lived duration: "What fragments thought is not the handling of solids in space but the dispersion of decisions in time" (DD 38–9). From the fact that counting, or discursive ordering, lies at the foundation of lived time, Bachelard concludes – again contra Bergson – that there is not one single time to which all events belong, but multiple times each of which has its own rhythmic structure. Perhaps all physical and psychic phenomena can be understood as either "consolidated" or "superimposed" temporal rhythms.

Bachelard envisions a "philosophy of repose" capable of teaching "the joys of poetry" (DD 17, 22). Whereas science must be guided by the intellect, poetry gives the lead to the imagination. For this reason, each requires its own vocabulary: "Two vocabularies should be organized to study knowledge and poetry. But these vocabularies do not correspond. And it would be useless to compose dictionaries to translate from one language to the other" (POR 15). Just as Kant distinguishes determining judgment (in which the imagination remains subordinate to the understanding) with reflective judgment (in which the understanding allows itself to be guided by the "free play" of the imagination), so Bachelard contrasts the rationalism of scientific practice with "the freedom of imagination . . . to liberate the psyche through poetry" (FPF 5). Throughout his writings he introduces a number of different terms to characterize the analysis of poetic reverie, including "poeticoanalysis" (FPF 24), "rhythmanalysis" (DD 21), and "psychoanalysis." Each of these stands in a dialectical relationship to Bachelard's "rationalism" or "applied rationalism." Psychoanalysis is not only a way of fathoming the unconscious import of poetic images – as in *The Psychoanalysis of Fire* (*La psychanalyse du feu*, 1938) – but a way of liberating ourselves from prejudices, as when mathematicians needed "a kind of psychoanalysis" to free themselves from their Euclidean habits of thought (NSS 39). Freud operated with too restricted a conception of psychoanalysis because he was unable to liberate himself from a biologistic conception of human existence. For Bachelard, aesthetic sublimation cannot be reduced to the force of drives; it is a response to "a call" (DD 146; cf. FPF 22). Poetry attests to this call, "the Orpheus complex" being "the antithesis of the Oedipus complex" (DD 152–3).

In order to capture the higher plane of existence to which we are called in poetic reverie, Bachelard distinguishes between different orders of reflective consciousness. Beyond the first-order cogito of Descartes's "*I think, therefore I am*," it is possible to rise to a second-order, "*I think that I think, therefore I am*," and even to a third-order, "*I think that I think that I think*" (DD 108–9). By ascending to these higher levels of reflection, we achieve successively more rarefied conceptions of the being of both ourselves as subjects and the world. The first-order Cartesian cogito – $(cogito)^1$ – represents objects as manipulable in accordance with laws of efficient causality. To consider how these laws might be put in service of some end – i.e., to reflect on $(cogito)^1$ from the standpoint of $(cogito)^2$ – is to adopt a teleological point of view, and thus to subordinate efficient causes to final causes (DD 110). Going one step further, to reflect on this second-order cogito from the perspective of $(cogito)^3$ is to contemplate the purposiveness of teleological thinking from a purely formal point of view, and thus to pass from final causes to formal causes (DD 111). Insofar as it is no longer concerned with existing objects but only with their forms, this third level of thought is "disinterested" in the same way that aesthetic reflection is for Kant. Bachelard regards the "pure aesthetics" of $(cogito)^3$ as the most exalted of the three forms of "thought time": "Let us live temporally at the power of three, at the level of the cogito cubed" (DD 110–11). To live at the level of $(cogito)^3$ is to seek "links, agreements, even Baudelairian correspondences" between "pure thought and pure poetry" (DD 22).

The three levels of reflection are not mere abstractions but concrete phenomenological attitudes that must be achieved through a series of reductions. Husserl thought that such a series could be continued indefinitely, referring in the *Ideas* to "the ideal possibility for continuing ad libitum the encasement of one objectivation into another" (IPTPP 247). But Bachelard cautions that it is a mistake to assume that it is possible to keep rising to the indefinite level of a $(cogito)^n$ for this is something that cannot be confirmed phenomenologically. Only with great difficulty, he reports, has he himself been able to glimpse what a fourth level of reflective consciousness is like: "We ourselves have found it exceedingly difficult, psychologically speaking, to attain to $(cogito)^4$. We believe that the true region of formal repose in which we would gladly remain is that of $(cogito)^3$" (DD 110).

Since Bachelard sees a correspondence between the three attainable levels of reflective consciousness and three of the kinds of causality identified by Aristotle – efficient, final, and formal – it is tempting to ask what order of cogito would correspond to the fourth, namely, material causality. One response would be to say that we conceive of the world in terms of material causality when we exist at the level of a *prereflective* zero-order cogito – $(cogito)^0$. This is the level of experience that Husserl identified as the natural attitude. Only by carrying out a first-order reduction did Descartes leave behind a physics of material causality for a physics of efficient causality. By implication, the post-Cartesian new scientific spirit – which Bachelard associates with the aesthetic stance of (cogito)³ – has given rise to a physics of formal causality (such as is based on the algebraic theory of groups).

Descartes thought that by reflecting on his own existence as a thinking thing he could prove the existence of the soul. This would be the stance of the "dogmatic" rationalist, the thinker of (cogito).¹ Kant criticized Descartes from the standpoint of a higher-order reflection which revealed that the thought of oneself as a simple substance does not suffice to establish the existence of such a thing. The subject of apperception can only represent itself teleologically as a moral end in itself. Bachelard takes Kant's critique of Descartes one step further. In aesthetic reflection, thought finds itself confronting not "objects" that can be determined by a legislative subject but "forms" that in some sense resist determination. Although at the level of (cogito)³ we find ourselves unable to subsume objects under determinate concepts, we experience this failure not as a cognitive shortcoming because the objects in question present us not so much with the demand that they be determined as with the meta-level (or higher order) demand that our thinking confront the very demand *that* objects be determined.

Kant saw that in aesthetic reflection, the suspension of the legislative rule of the understanding freed the imagination to engage in a free play with the forms of objects. But he regarded this as a temporary suspension of the serious business of knowing, a mere diversion with no power to transform the basic categories of the understanding. Kant's mistake was to think that Euclidean geometry and Newtonian science were not subject to revision. Had he recognized the historicity of the scientific enterprise, he would have seen that there is a dialectical interplay between reflective and determining judgment, that is, between poetic reverie and science. Heidegger saw that the imagination was the common root of sensibility and understanding, but he tried to go beyond a dialectical conception of the relationship between poetry and science by thinking of the history of both as a succession of epochs in the dispensation of being. For him, the imagination was not the subject's capacity to engage in reverie but the primordial temporality of Dasein. Thus, whereas Bachelard suggests that "it is through reverie that one must learn phenomenology," Heidegger suggests that phenomenology can only be learned by abandoning oneself to the self-disclosure of being (POR 14). The question would be whether Heidegger thereby manages to escape the Cartesian tradition, as he professes, or whether he simply radicalizes it by attempting to glimpse what it would be like to inhabit the elusive perspective of (cogito)⁴. For is not the "step back," by which the thinker allows Enframing to show itself as such, ultimately just a reflection on (cogito)³ from the standpoint of the *Ereignis* itself? In urging us to remain at the level of (cogito),³ Bachelard would have us see the chemist manipulating the wax not as Enframed but as engaged in the dialectics of reverie.

1.7   Sartre's nihilating cogito

And as imagination bodies forth
The forms of things unknown, the poet's pen
Turns them to shapes, and gives to aery nothing
A local habitation and a name.
                (*A Midsummer Night's Dream*, V, i, 14–17)

The idea that human existence is rooted in the capacity to engage in reverie
is also central to the work of the French existentialist, Jean-Paul Sartre
(1905–1980). Like Bachelard, Sartre takes the ability of consciousness to
reflect on itself to be its distinctive feature. In his critique of the paralogisms, Kant argued, against Descartes, that I cannot derive the existence of
my soul from the mere fact that all my representations are united in a single
consciousness: "I confuse the possible **abstraction** from my empirically
determined existence with the supposed consciousness of a **separate** possible
existence of my thinking Self" (CPR B427). Husserl defended Descartes in
the *Ideas*, claiming that through self-reflection I become aware of the existence of a transcendental ego as the animating pole of all my mental acts. In
The Transcendence of the Ego: An Existentialist Theory of Consciousness, (*La Tran-
scendance de L'Ego*, 1936–1937), Sartre rejects this argument. Kant conceded
that "The **I think** must **be able** to accompany all my representations" (CPR
B131). But the fact that the representation "I think" *can* accompany all of
my intentional acts does not mean that it actually does (TOTE 34). In prereflective consciousness, no "I" is present at all; only through an act of reflection do I *constitute* an "I" as the supposedly self-identical subject that had
been there all along. Thus it is necessary to distinguish the merely implicit
awareness that prereflective consciousness has of itself from the explicit self-
consciousness that arises with the reflective representation of a transcendental ego. Sartre concludes that, like every other intentional object, the ego is
something wholly transcendent: "the ego is neither formally nor materially
in consciousness: it is outside, *in the world*. It is a being of the world, like the
ego of another."(TOTE 31)

     Unlike Kant, for whom the existence of the soul remained a logical possi-
bility even though it could not be proved through intellectual intuition,
Sartre argues that the very idea of a soul is a psychological fiction. Pure consciousness is nothing but transcendental spontaneity, relentlessly synthesizing a temporal manifold. Just as it thereby constitutes worldly objects in
objective time, so it constitutes psychic states in immanent time. The
ego is nothing but the transcendent unity of psychic states, just as the
"world" represents the transcendent unity of things (TOTE 75). When
consciousness reflects on its own synthetic activity, it encounters this
passively constituted unity that hovers before it as if it were itself the agent
of unification. The only difference between psychic phenomena and physical
phenomena is that the former appear exclusively through reflective

consciousness, while the latter are the original objects of prereflective perceptual awareness. But since every act of perceptual consciousness is accompanied by the possibility of its being reflected upon, the entire "region" of the psychic haunts the physical world as a kind of "shadow" cast upon it by reflective consciousness. Insofar as it studies the ego and its states and actions, psychology is concerned with this region. Since the ego is transcendent to it, consciousness has no privileged access to its own psychic states; these can be approached either through introspection or behavioral observation. By contrast, the "transcendental sphere" of pure consciousness can be investigated only from a phenomenological standpoint (TOTE 96). To attain this standpoint it suffices to perform a "pure" reduction by which consciousness distinguishes its anonymous spontaneity from the ego and its psychic states.

Just as Bachelard equated the capacity to reflect with the capacity to engage in reverie, so in *The Imaginary: A Phenomenological Psychology for the Imagination* (*L'Imaginaire: Psychologie Phénoménologique de l'Imagination*, 1940), Sartre argues that the capacity to imagine is an essential feature of consciousness. In an effort to answer the question, "What are the characteristics that can be attributed to consciousness on the basis of the fact that it is consciousness capable of imagining?," Sartre distinguishes between three different kinds of cognitive acts: perceiving, conceiving, and imagining (Imag 179). As in Husserl, perception is essentially adumbrative in character; in perceiving a cube, I am only ever presented with particular aspects of something whose properties are infinitely rich. By contrast, when I think of the cube in an act of conception, I grasp it precisely in its infinite richness, albeit only abstractly (Imag 8). Imagining the cube shares certain features with both of these acts. Like perception, an image represents only a particular aspect of its object. But because it is unreal, the imagined object does not contain within itself anything more than is revealed in the image: "the imaged cube is given immediately for what it is" (Imag 9). Thus imagining is like conceiving in that it presents its object all at once. But this is only because there is no object apart from the image itself. Another way to specify the nature of imagining would be to say that while conceiving can be thought of as an empty intending, and perceiving as the fulfilling of such an act, imagining neither intends emptily nor fulfills – rather, it is an intending of emptiness itself (Imag 59, 180). Put otherwise, the imagined object is "given as absent to intuition . . . the image has wrapped within it a certain nothingness" (Imag 14; cf. 129). Precisely because they do not exist, "the objects of the world of images could in no way exist in the world of perception" (Imag 10). Thus it would be a mistake to think of the difference between perceiving and imagining as one of degree of vivacity and liveliness; on the contrary, there is an essential difference in kind by virtue of which it is always possible to tell when we are perceiving something and when we are merely imagining something. Because of this essential difference, Descartes was wrong to suggest that it is possible to be uncertain as to whether a particular object of consciousness belongs to the world of perception or to the order of imagination (Imag 160ff.).

Just as he locates the ego outside consciousness, so Sartre denies that images exist within consciousness as if they were immanent objects of inner sense (Imag 5). Like all intentional objects, the objects of imagination are wholly transcendent. To characterize an act of imagination as the intending of an image is just to say that the act intends a non-existent object. Thus the salient difference between an act of perception and an act of imagination is that the former is directed toward something that is really present to consciousness while the latter is directed toward something that is absent. Assuming that every intentional act has only one object, this implies that perceiving and imagining preclude one another: "to say 'I have an image of Pierre' is equivalent to saying not only 'I do not see Pierre,' but also 'I do not see anything at all'" (Imag 13). More precisely, every act of imagination is founded on the negation of an object of perception. That is, in order for an act of imagination to take place there must be something real – some underlying matter that *could* be perceived – the non-perceiving of which makes imagining possible: "In the different cases that we have studied, it has always been a question of animating a certain matter to make a *representation* of an absent or nonexistent object" (Imag 50). Thus every real object can function as the basis either for a perception that affirms it, or an act of imagination that negates it (Imag 20).

Sartre goes on to ask whether the power of imagination is accidental or essential to consciousness: "can we conceive of a consciousness that would never imagine . . . or rather, as soon as we posit a consciousness, must it be posited as always able to imagine?" "What therefore must a consciousness be in order that it can successively posit *real* objects and *imaged* objects?" (Imag 179–80). In response to these questions, Sartre notes that perception is essentially interwoven with retentions and protentions of aspects of objects that are not presently given to consciousness. Insofar as it has this temporal structure, perception carries within it the possibility of being suspended so that whatever is not presently given may be given *as* not given. Thus the possibility of perception necessarily goes hand-in-hand with the possibility of imagination. Consciousness is the capacity either to constitute or de-constitute objects of perception. To de-constitute an object of perception is not to cease to be conscious but to constitute something whose *non-being* is constituted through the de-constitution of the object of perception. Thus to be a conscious being – or more precisely, to be consciousness – is to be free either to perceive or to imagine at whim: "it is because we are transcendentally free that we can imagine" (Imag 186).[10] Conversely, freedom is nothing more than the capacity to negate objects of perception. Bergson claimed that a negating consciousness was really just an affirming consciousness in disguise. Sartre agrees with Bergson that it is impossible either to intuit or conceive of sheer nothingness, but he also maintains that insofar as consciousness has the ability to imagine, it is fundamentally a way of negating the entire world (Imag 187).

The idea that consciousness is intentional only insofar as it is a "lack-of-being" or ontological nothingness is developed in Sartre's monumental *Being and Nothingness: An Essay on Phenomenological Ontology* (*L'être et le Néant: Essai d'ontologie phénoménologique*, 1943): "My consciousness ... must arise in the world as a *No*" (BN 87). Like Bachelard, who also claimed against Bergson that the ability to affirm presupposes the ability to negate, Sartre derives the idea of the negativity of consciousness from Hegel. Heidegger claimed that human existence could apprehend beings only insofar as it "holds itself out into the nothing." Sartre objects to this formulation, claiming that it confines nothingness to the "beyond" of human existence instead of acknowledging the fact that the world is inhabited by "little pools of non-being," or *negatités*, each of which is constituted by a negating consciousness (BN 53). When I perceive the absence of Pierre from the cafe, it is indeed the *absence* of Pierre that I conjure, and not merely the present objects which serve as the perceptual ground upon which Pierre's absence can manifest itself as such. Consciousness introduces these little pools of nothingness into being only insofar as it is itself a "hole in being."

To characterize consciousness as a hole in being is not to deny its existence. As the privative correlate of its intentional objects, consciousness is always a "determinate nothingness" that gives it an ontologically ambiguous character. On the one hand, consciousness *is not*; on the other, it *is* in the sense that it "has to not be" the object it negates. Thus the being of consciousness represents a flight from being toward non-being. But it is a flight not toward sheer nothingness but rather toward determinate possibilities which the negation of its object discloses to consciousness. Consciousness is free in the sense that it can imagine various ways of not being the particular being that it negates.

Sartre uses the Hegelian terms "for-itself" and "in-itself" to characterize the difference between consciousness and the intentional objects that it negates. Being-in-itself is sheer ontological plenitude which can appear as such only through the eruption within it of the lack that is the for-itself. The for-itself, or consciousness, perpetually "nihilates" itself in that it "has to be" what it is not in the mode of not-being it. Put otherwise, consciousness is constantly realizing possibilities which, once actualized, must also be negated since it is "not that" either. Thus the for-itself is always torn between actuality and possibility, facticity and transcendence, an ambiguous ontological condition that Sartre calls "bad faith."

Though bad faith is ineluctable, it can be lived in two different ways: either by disavowing or identifying with one's facticity. If I disavow my facticity, I am in bad faith to the extent that I *am* the in-itself that I inherit from my past; but if I identify with it, I am again in bad faith because insofar as I am free, I *am not* it. Sartre suggests that there is no way of evading this double bind. In writing this sentence, for example, I become the person who has written it in an unavoidable way. But insofar as it exists on the page (or computer screen), I am not the sentence that I have written.

Roquentin, the narrator of Sartre's novel, *Nausea* (*La Nausée*, 1938), gives voice to this predicament:

> I had thought out this sentence, at first it had been a small part of myself. Now it was inscribed on the paper, it took sides against me. I didn't recognize it any more. I couldn't conceive it again. It was there, in front of me; in vain for me to trace some sign of its origin. Anyone could have written it. But *I* . . . *I* wasn't sure I wrote it.
>
> (Nau 95; Sartre's ellipses)

Though bad faith represents a kind of insincerity, sincerity would only be possible for a being whose for-itself and in-itself could coincide, something that Sartre considers to be impossible in principle. The only way that the for-itself can exist is in the mode of "being what it is not and not being what it is."

The double bind of bad faith is exemplified in Shakespeare's *The Tragedy of King Richard the Second*. Only when he is about to be deposed by the usurping Henry Bolingbroke does Richard realize that although he "is" a king, being a king belongs to his facticity as something that he can neither repudiate nor embrace in an authentic way. He also discovers that the property of being a king is something that depends on the existence of other people. In his final soliloquy, Richard – alone in prison – goes back and forth between imagining that he is a king and imagining that he is not, thereby dramatizing the dialectic of bad faith. But he also hints at what for Sartre will be the only way out of bad faith, namely, the possibility of identifying with the nothingness that consciousness essentially is: "But what e'er I be,/Nor I, nor any man that but man is,/With nothing shall be pleas'd, till he be eas'd/With being nothing" (V, v, 38–41). To be nothing is not to be dead, but to be free. Thus for Sartre, anxiety – the encounter with the nothing – is prompted not by the possibility of no longer having possibilities, but by the fact that one is not yet dead and so still has possibilities: "There is something distressing for each of us, to catch in the act this tireless creation of existence of which *we* are not the creators" (TOTE 99). Consciousness is free not just in the sense that it "can" choose its manner of being but in the sense that it is always *ineluctably* choosing. In this respect, there is something paradoxically mechanical about the spontaneity of consciousness: "Consciousness is frightened by its own spontaneity because it senses this spontaneity as *beyond* freedom" (TOTE 100). We flee from anxiety not so much by immersing ourselves in everydayness as by identifying with our egos, "blaming" our actions on the psychological character that we acquire through our choices. Thus equating consciousness with the ego is a way of trying, in vain, to absolve ourselves of responsibility.

Thus it is not the certainty of death but the necessity of having to live that causes us to be anxious. Since even the act of suicide would be a choice, there is no escape from freedom. To be condemned to be free is, in a certain sense, to be unable to die, a theme that Sartre explores in his play, *No Exit* (*Huis Clos*, 1944). Thus we do not flee *into* everydayness but *from* it. By denying that being-in-the-world has the character of consciousness, Heidegger treats the nothingness that I have to be in the world as if it were merely a transcendent nothingness that I will be at the end of my life. But death is not nothingness. Rather, death represents the moment when the nothingness that I perpetually resurrect by negating my facticity will have given way to sheer ontological plenitude. In this sense, "my" death is not mine: "death can not be my peculiar possibility; it can not even be one of *my* possibilities" (BN 691).

According to Sartre, it is impossible to define the ekstatic character of Dasein's temporality without making reference to consciousness: "This ekstatic character of human reality will lapse into a thing-like, blind in-itself unless it arises from the consciousness of ekstasis" (BN 120). Of the three temporal ekstases, Heidegger accorded primacy to the future. By contrast, Sartre takes the present to be the defining mode of human temporality: "it is best to put the accent on the present ekstasis and not on the future ekstasis as Heidegger does" (BN 202). Each of us is condemned to live our temporality as an empirically engaged imagination – that is, as a transcendence from facticity toward determinate possibilities. There are many possible ways in which I can comport myself with respect to the fact that I will die. But these are precisely ways of living, not of dying: "My project toward a particular death is comprehensible (suicide, martyrdom, heroism) but not the project toward *my* death as the undetermined possibility of no longer realizing a presence in the world" (BN 691).

By defining the for-itself not just as negation but as a lack of what it negates, Sartre captures two conflicting aspects of the relationship between consciousness and its facticity, namely, refusal and desire. On the one hand, the for-itself is a kind of ontological denial of being-in-itself; yet it is also the desire to coincide with itself: these were the two possible ways of being in bad faith. This desire has a very specific sense: it is the desire to "return" to the in-itself without having to give up being-for-itself. Thus the object of desire is an unattainable possibility that might be characterized as the possibility of being dead without having to be dead, that is, the ideal of coinciding with one's past while miraculously retaining one's relationship to the future. The idea of an immortal soul speaks to this desire. For Sartre it is an inherently contradictory idea, since being-for-itself and being-in-itself are antithetical metaphysical conditions. Even if I could survive my own death I would not have been responsible for my birth; in this sense, my "initial" in-itself would perpetually escape me.

The ideal of a being whose being-in-itself would completely coincide with its being-for-itself is given to us as the idea of God, a necessarily existing being whose possibility (for-itself) would be the ground of its actuality (in-itself). Thus human desire can be characterized as the desire to be God. Like the idea of a being who could survive its own death, the idea of God is the idea of an impossible being. And yet this impossibility remains our highest aspiration, functioning as a kind of regulative ideal. Kant left room for faith by claiming that although the idea of God lacked "real" possibility, it retained its "logical" possibility. By contrast, Sartre, like Nietzsche, argues that we should cut the Gordian knot in favor of a thoroughgoing atheism, since *for us* the idea of God remains as meaningless as the possibility of not having to wait for sugar to dissolve in water.[11] Human existence is inherently absurd in the specific sense that we are forever attempting to become God, that is, to achieve a complete coincidence of our facticity – the "sedimented" past that we inherit – with our freedom. Sartre's principled atheism can be thought of as the correlate of his repudiation of Heidegger's conception of authentic being toward death, for God is impossible in exactly the same way that my death is: "even if God did exist, that would change nothing" (EHE 51). At the end of *Being and Nothingness*, Sartre offers his alternative to Heidegger's conception of authenticity: this would be for the for-itself to forsake the desire to be God altogether, to take itself rather than a transcendent ideal as its highest value. Whether it is possible to accomplish such a reorientation of one's "fundamental project" is a question that he leaves open, promising to take it up in a never-completed "future work" on existential ethics (BN 798).

By a "fundamental project," Sartre means the way in which a particular for-itself relates to being. So long as I remain within a particular fundamental project, it colors everything that I do. Though my fundamental project is something that I myself have freely chosen, I am not necessarily aware of it because living something at the level of one's prereflective consciousness does not guarantee reflective awareness of it: "if the fundamental project is fully experienced by the subject and hence wholly conscious, that certainly does not mean that it must by the same token be *known* by him; quite the contrary" (BN 729). The aim of what Sartre calls "existential psychoanalysis" is to disclose someone's fundamental project, that is, to provide a kind of "*moral description*" of a person's character. But there is also an ethical aim of existential psychoanalysis, namely, "to make us repudiate the *spirit of seriousness*" (BN 796). Like Nietzsche, Sartre equates the spirit of seriousness with the belief in transcendent values. Thus to overcome the spirit of seriousness is to reclaim one's freedom and so to be able to choose – consciously – a different fundamental project.

Just as a person's fundamental project colors her perception of the world's qualities, so the world's qualities have personalities of their own which color a person's fundamental project. Thus Sartre refers to "the metaphysical import of yellow, of red, of polished, or wrinkled," and he provides an existential analysis of the quality of sliminess: "The horror of the slimy is the horrible fear that time might become slimy, that facticity might progress continually and insensibly and absorb the For-itself which *exists it*. It is the fear not of death, not of the pure In-itself, not of nothingness, but of a particular type of being, which does not actually exist any more than the In-itself-For-itself and which is only *represented* by the slimy" (BN 770, 778). Unlike Bachelard, who relied on poetic images for his psychoanalysis of the elements, Sartre suggests that the analysis of the existential import of worldly qualities should be grounded in perception rather than imagination. To perceive a cloudy sky as gloomy is not to superimpose an imagined idea or even a feeling of gloominess onto an indifferent perception; it is to perceive *gloomy clouds*. Thus we do not view the clouds as gloomy because our perception of them is accompanied by poetic reverie; rather, if the perception spurs us to poetic reverie it is because we directly perceive the clouds' gloominess, a property that is no less real than that of being composed of microscopic droplets of water.

1.8   Merleau-Ponty's return to primordial perception

> I will say of it,
> It tutors nature. Artificial strife
> Lives in these touches, livelier than life.
> (*The Life of Timon of Athens*, I, i, 36–8)

Like Sartre – with whom he co-founded the journal *Les temps modernes* in 1944 – the French phenomenologist Maurice Merleau-Ponty (1908–1961) argues that much of what we treat as our subjective overlay of objectively given facts is actually inherent in things themselves. To see this, it is necessary to show how objectivity is phenomenologically grounded in perception. Husserl's great discovery was not intentionality – something already thematized not only by Brentano but by Descartes – but "a deeper intentionality," that "others have called existence" and which for Merleau-Ponty is the "actual experience" of primordial perception: "The first philosophical act would appear to be to return to the world of actual experience which is prior to the objective world" (POP 121 n57).

In *The Phenomenology of Perception* (*Phénoménologie de la perception*, 1945), Merleau-Ponty agrees with Husserl that it is possible to go further than Kant did in accounting for the genesis of "static" forms of experience. Kant conceived of "phenomenology" as a "doctrine of appearance" whose aim was to distinguish subjective representations of matter in motion from the objectively real movement of bodies in space (MFNS 265n). Such an analysis makes it possible to distinguish a mere "judgment of perception" about the relative motion of an object with respect to the perceiving subject from an objectively valid "judgment of experience" about the object's actual motion with respect to space (PTAFM 92). For Kant, judgments of experience go beyond judgments of perception by subsuming perceptual phenomena under pure concepts of the understanding, thereby making natural science possible. Thus phenomenology has a merely propaedeutic role to play in distinguishing mere perception from experience proper. For Merleau-Ponty, by contrast, the task of phenomenology is to correct the error of subreption that arises when we treat perception as a privative form of experience. Like Husserl, he accuses Kant of remaining within the natural attitude by presuming the existence of already constituted objects of experience and then regressively inquiring into their possibility. Despite his effective critique of the abstract intellectualism of rationalist metaphysics, Kant succumbs to the same intellectualist temptation in his account of the conditions for the possibility of experience (POP 304).

Just as Heidegger criticized Kant for subordinating the activity of the productive imagination to the determining power of the understanding, so Merleau-Ponty characterizes the productive imagination as a more primordial form of intentionality than that which is manifest in intellectual cognition: "We found beneath the intentionality of acts, or thetic intentionality, another kind which is the condition of the former's possibility: . . . an 'art hidden in the depths of the human soul'" (POP 429). It is at the level of this deeper intentionality that one must seek the phenomenon of perception, not in order to describe it in its pristine purity but to show how it gives rise to the sense of experience that informs the natural attitude itself. This deeper level of our intentional contact with the world is not a mere abstraction, something that we posit on the basis of theoretical considerations. That is the mistake made by an empiricist epistemology which imagines that experience is built up out of a multiplicity of sensory data. Like Sartre, Merleau-Ponty appeals to the Gestalt psychologists who showed that perception is always already the grasping of forms, not the piecemeal synthesis of discrete sensations. Just as Sartre rejected Husserl's conception of the transcendental ego, so Merleau-Ponty argues that Husserl's conception of a pre-thetic stratum of *hyle* (akin to the Kantian sensible manifold) is a fiction. The primordial perception of forms can be captured in terms of Kant's conception of a "synopsis of the manifold" to which no synthesis proper need correspond: "we prefer, to the notion of synthesis, that of synopsis, which does not yet point to an explicit positing of diversity" (POP 276n; cf. CPR A94). Thus for Merleau-Ponty there is a primordial level of perception that can be disclosed through the phenomenological reduction. To the extent that we have lost sight of this originary "lived experience" of ourselves and the world, it is because we typically view it through the lens of science: "In the natural attitude, I do not have *perceptions*" (POP 281).

In contrast to Kant, for whom perception was merely a privative form of experience, Merleau-Ponty treats science as an alienated form of perception: "We shall no longer hold that perception is incipient science, but conversely that classical science is a form of perception which has lost sight of its origins" (POP 57). Thus it is a question of disclosing the transcendental illusions to which the understanding is prone in natural science, just as Kant revealed the transcendental illusions to which reason was prone in pure metaphysics. Kant carried out his critique of reason by tracing the origin of the ideas back to the categories from which they were derived. Analogously, Merleau-Ponty will show how the categories are themselves derived from a more primordial perception that Kant did not detect. Whereas Kant was content to describe static conditions for the *possibility* of experience, the phenomenology of perception will disclose the generative "operations" by which "conditions of reality" come into being (POP 38, 439).

The first task of the phenomenology of perception is to correct Kant's conception of the forms of sensibility by showing how space and time are rooted in the perception of bodily motility. Kant was aware of the body's role in spatial orientation,[12] and he acknowledges that "we cannot think of a line without **drawing** it in thought" (CPR B154). But according to Merleau-Ponty, he failed to recognize that the very idea of an objective space in which the subject can get its bearings – or in which lines may be drawn – has *its* roots in bodily motility. Thus it is not enough to say that the geometer must construct his or her objects, or even to acknowledge the role played by bodily motility in geometrical construction; one must go further and recognize that there would be no "form of outer intuition" at all without such motility: "The subject of geometry is a motor subject ... motion is productive of space" (POP 387). An analogous point can be made about time. Like Heidegger, Merleau-Ponty argues that the idea of worldly time as the objective medium in which events in nature succeed one another is derived from the more primordial temporality of human existence. In *Being and Time*, Heidegger subordinated Dasein's spatiality to the supposedly more fundamental condition of temporality – a view he later characterized as "untenable" (BAT 418ff.; OTAB 23). Merleau-Ponty regards both temporality and spatiality as equiprimordial structures of being-in-the-world, whose ultimate ontological significance lies in the phenomenon of embodiment.

In order to arrive at a phenomenologically adequate conception of the human body, it is once again necessary to turn to perception rather than to science. My perceived body is a body that I live in the first person, whereas the body as it is represented by science is the impersonal seat of third-person processes. For Merleau-Ponty, the latter is ultimately just a privative abstraction of the first: "the body, as a chemical structure or an agglomeration of tissues, is formed, by a process of impoverishment, from a primordial phenomenon of the body-for-us" (POP 351). The central aim of Merleau-Ponty's first book, *The Structure of Behavior* (*La Structure du comportement*, 1942), was to demonstrate the inadequacy of any third-person description of any aspect of our bodily comportment. As he explains in *The Phenomenology of Perception*, "If it is once conceded that it may be the seat of third person processes, nothing in behaviour can be reserved for consciousness" (POP 123). So long as we remain within the snares of objectivist thinking, we are forced to choose between two false alternatives. One is "idealism" (or else some version of mind/body dualism), according to which the subject is a constituting consciousness distinct from all objects. This model preserves the subject's first-person perspective but at the expense of its estrangement not only from its own body but from the world itself. The other is that of "naturalism" (or any reductive materialism) that eliminates the first-person point of view altogether. Only by restoring to perception its preobjective grasp of our body's motility can we clarify what it means to be a corporeal subject: "It is because it is a preobjective view that being-in-the-world can be distinguished from every third person process, from every modality of the *res extensa*, as from every *cogitatio*" (POP 80).

My body is an original motility without which there would be neither space nor time. Yet because it situates me within space and time, it is always possible for me to regard my body as if it were an objectively existing thing in space. This explains the genesis of the natural attitude. In claiming to have discovered that space and time are forms of intuition and not things in themselves, Kant challenged a key tenet of the natural attitude, but he continued to regard the embodied subject as an empirically real object in relation to which other bodies can be in motion. Thus it was Kant's empirical realism that led him to misconstrue the relationship between phenomenology and science. For Kant, to attend to the manner in which bodies subjectively "appear" to be moving is to take a partial view that is ultimately determined by the objective position of one's own body in physical space. It is therefore necessary to "correct" the appearances, and to accept the "true" account of motion that science teaches us. Although it may appear that the sun rises, we "know" that it is in fact the earth that moves and not the sun. For Merleau-Ponty, by contrast, the very idea of an empirically real space is ontologically dependent upon bodily motility, which implies that it is the scientific account of motion that needs to be corrected in light of what perception reveals (POP xvi). Husserl claimed that to return to the lifeworld was to provide a secure foundation for Kant's Copernican Revolution (CES 199). But to return to the lifeworld is to show that the very sense of the Copernican discovery – that the earth orbits the sun – is grounded in the lifeworld experience of the sun orbiting the earth. In this sense, Husserl's Copernican turn represents a Keplerian Restoration.

Merleau-Ponty's restoration of the ontological dignity of the lifeworld enables him to defend Bergson's construal of the theory of relativity. The physicists had accused Bergson of unnecessarily introducing an "observer" into a theory that depends exclusively on the presence of "measuring instruments." But according to Merleau-Ponty, Bergson was right to insist that the idea of simultaneity is meaningless apart from the perspective of a perceiver for whom two events are simultaneous: "what Bergson wants to show is precisely that there is no simultaneity between things in themselves, which no matter how closely they border on one another exist each one in itself. Perceived things alone can participate in the same line of present" (S 185). In effect, the physicists treated the question of the presence or absence of an observer as a question pertaining to a physical object like any other. But Bergson was calling attention to the fact that every conception of the physical world has its ontological roots in perception itself. Thus his insistence that there is a single over-arching cosmic time to which all events belong was not a bit of speculative metaphysics but a phenomenologically rigorous restitution of what perception teaches us about the world:

> A profound idea: rationality and the universal are founded anew, and not upon the divine right of a dogmatic science, but upon the prescientific evidence that there is one single world, upon that reason prior to reason which is implicated in our existence, in our commerce with the perceived world and with others.
>
> (S 196)

Although Merleau-Ponty criticizes Bergson for relying on a conception of intuition that remains introspective and abstract (POP 57–8), he credits him with recognizing that "The absolute knowledge of the philosopher is perception" (IPOP 16).

Bachelard criticized Bergson for basing his interpretation of the theory of relativity on an uneducated intuition. By contrast, Merleau-Ponty suggests that it was the physicists who refused to allow the new physics to inform their intuitions. For it is precisely classical physics, and not the theory of relativity, that encourages us to think of perceivers merely as empirical bodies embedded in a spatio-temporal field. In recognizing that the special theory of relativity undermined this intuition, "Bergson made an advance on Einstein's classicism" (S 196). From a strictly phenomenological point of view, it is not surprising that the assumptions of classical physics should ultimately undermine themselves. Thus it is not intuition that needs to be educated by science but science that needs to be informed by the sense of reality that is revealed in "primordial perception": "The scientist too must learn to criticize the idea of an external world in itself" (POP 10). "Scientific thinking ... must return to the 'there is' which underlies it" (PrOP 160).

Just as Heidegger thought that poetry could disclose the truth about being in a way that science could not, so Merleau-Ponty suggests that painting has the ability to reveal the primordial world of perception. In contrast to music – which for Nietzsche invoked the Dionysian excess *behind* phenomena but which for precisely this reason remains "too far beyond the world and the designatable to depict anything but certain outlines of Being" (PrOP 161) – or poetry – which for both Heidegger and Bachelard was a way of thinking that *transcended* phenomena – painting is for Merleau-Ponty the one form of art that is capable of presenting the phenomena of perception: "Only the painter is entitled to look at everything without being obliged to appraise what he sees" (PrOP 161). In order to achieve this perspective, the painter must avoid two temptations: one, the "impressionist" (or quasi-empiricist) attempt to reconstruct phenomena on the basis of discrete sensations; the other, the "academic" (or intellectualist) mistake of attempting to reconstruct phenomena on the basis of the categories of objective thought. For Merleau-Ponty, the greatness of the French painter Paul Cézanne (1839–1906) was that he tried to steer a course between these two nineteenth-century approaches to painting. Instead of attempting to reconstruct nature as it is for the scientist – whether through sense impressions or the delineation of well-defined forms – Cézanne relentlessly strove to paint that more primordial phenomenal nature upon which scientific constructions are built: "Cézanne wanted to paint this primordial world.... He wished, as he said, to confront the sciences with the nature 'from which they came'" (SAN 13–14).

Cézanne's work calls attention to two features of perceived nature that typically elude scientific understanding. One is the phenomenon of indeterminacy; the other is that of kinaesthesis. An example of indeterminacy in perception is given in the "Müller-Lyer illusion," in which one of two lines that have the same "objective" length appears to be longer than the other. From the standpoint of the natural attitude, we are inclined to say that the two perceived lines must "really" be identical in length and that accordingly they only "appear" to be non-identical. But this analysis is based on the presumption that everything we perceive must be fully determinate. What we actually confront are two lines that are neither equal nor unequal in length: "In Müller-Lyer's illusion, one of the lines ceases to be equal to the other without becoming 'unequal': it becomes 'different'" (POP 11). Cézanne captures the indeterminacy of primordial perception by representing colors, edges, and perspectives as they actually appear rather than as they "should" appear. Likewise, his paintings aspire to express the kinaesthesis of everyday experience, the fact that "we *see* the depth, the smoothness, the softness, the hardness of objects; Cézanne even claimed that we see their odor" (SAN 15). We never encounter an isolated quality of red but something like the "woolly red" of the carpet, as Sartre – who also cites Cézanne in this context (BN 257–8) – puts it (POP 5; cf. POI 248). It is only by way of a retroactive illusion generated by the habits of objective thought that we learn to draw sharp distinctions among the separable qualia contributed to perception by the various senses: "These distinctions between touch and sight are unknown in primordial perception. It is only as a result of a science of the human body that we finally learn to distinguish between our senses" (SAN 15; cf. POP 229). It would therefore be a mistake to content ourselves with recognizing a mere "evocation" of tactile qualities in painting in general, and in Cézanne's paintings in particular (PrOP 166). In attempting to capture the kinaesthesis of primordial perception, Cézanne was in effect creating a *Gesamtkunstwerk* – a total art work – without having to *add* music or poetry to his painting (in contrast to Wagner, whose musical dramas are mixed works of art). Given the kinaesthetic nature of perception in general, any type of aesthetic experience should be able to accomplish what painting can, but Merleau-Ponty suggests that vision has a privileged status with respect to the other senses.

For Merleau-Ponty, Cézanne's paintings do not just illustrate phenomenological truths; they are placeholders for a philosophy that is still to come: "this philosophy still to be done is that which animates the painter ...

when, in Cézanne's words, he 'thinks in painting'" (PrOP 178). Such a philosophy must be able to do justice both to physics and phenomenology: "If we ever again find a balance between science and philosophy, between our models and the obscurity of the 'there is,' it must be of a new kind" (PrOP 177). We do not yet possess such a balance because our science and philosophy are under the sway of a kind of hyper-Cartesianism (PrOP 177). Descartes separated the mind from the body, but at least he was still able to recognize their mysterious unity in lived experience. For us, this unity has been torn asunder – as in the radical division that Sartre recognizes between the for-itself and the in-itself. Merleau-Ponty criticizes Sartre's ontology for being

> too exclusively antithetic: the antithesis of my view of myself and another's view of me and the antithesis of the *for itself* and the *in itself* often seem to be alternatives instead of being described as the living bond and communication between one term and the other.
>
> (SAN 72)

To overcome this dichotomy, Merleau-Ponty defines the embodied subject as a "fold" or "hollow" in being rather than as a "hole" or sheer nothingness inhabiting it: "I am not, . . . in Hegel's phrase, 'a hole in being,' but a hollow, a fold, which has been made and which can be unmade" (POP 215; cf. 431). Sartre is right to point out that my eye cannot see itself; but reflexivity is the very essence of embodiment – which is to say that the subject *is* its body.

Thus whereas Sartre considered the subject's body to be what it is "for others," Merleau-Ponty claims that it is necessary to overcome this residual Cartesianism by rediscovering within ourselves "the junction of the *for itself* and the *in itself*" (POP 373). I am not irrevocably cut off from the world and other people; or rather, if I can be so cut off it is only on the basis of a deeper ontological commonality. Merleau-Ponty regards the Hegelian struggle for recognition, which figures so prominently in *Being and Nothingness*, as rooted in the "peaceful co-existence in the world of childhood" (POP 355). In order to recapture Husserl's sense of the living body as *Leib* rather than as mere *Körper*, he introduces the concept of "flesh," a term that cuts across the for-itself/in-itself dichotomy. My flesh is of a piece with that of both things and other persons: "That is why we say that in perception the thing is given to us 'in person,' or 'in the flesh'" (POP 320; cf. PrOP 163). In his unfinished *The Visible and the Invisible, Followed by Working Notes* (*Le Visible et l'invisible; suivi de notes de travail*, 1964), Merleau-Ponty develops the idea that "the presence of the world is precisely the presence of its flesh to my flesh" (VAI 127).

Unlike Leonardo da Vinci (1452–1519), for whom painting posed cognitive problems, Cézanne's problems were corporeal in nature (SAN 22). Or, rather, since every painter "takes his body with him" – as the writer Paul

Valéry (1871–1945) observed – the difference between Leonardo and Cézanne is that between someone who lived his embodiment the way that a separable Cartesian mind would, and someone who struggled to express Merleau-Ponty's own vision of the world as flesh (PrOP 162). Descartes admired engraved line drawings because their well-defined contours and lack of color enabled them to represent the essentially geometrical properties of physical objects. We grasp the essence of the wax not through the perception of its sensible qualities, but by an "inspection of the mind." Leonardo's anatomical drawings could be said to represent the zero point at which perception first gives way to science. By contrast, Cézanne's paintings consist of nothing but sensible qualities which are presented as the primordial reality out of which the so-called "primary" qualities are abstracted. As such they represent not the birth of science but the reverse moment when science rediscovers its phenomenological origins. To know what the wax is it is not enough either to inspect it with the mind or to subject it to Bachelard's calibrated experiments: we must look at it with the eyes of Cézanne, whose paintings – with their multiple outlines of objects, "modulated" colors, and "distorted" perspectives – provide us with an apprenticeship in phenomenological intuition (SAN 14–15).

Merleau-Ponty's suggestion that Cézanne's task was an endless one – that the philosophy to which his work attests is one "still to be done" – is of a piece with Husserl's characterization of himself as a perpetual beginner. In the work of Cézanne, Merleau-Ponty finds not merely an expression of a philosophical point of view but an effort to express the phenomenon of expressiveness itself, an endlessly reflective task that in *The Phenomenology of Perception* he seemed to think only the philosopher is burdened with: "it is possible to speak about speech whereas it is impossible to paint about painting . . . every philosopher has dreamed of a form of discourse which would supersede all others, whereas the painter or the musician does not hope to exhaust all possible painting or music" (POP 190). Cézanne does in fact dream of painting about painting, and it is precisely therein that the eloquence of his work lies: "Cézanne's difficulties are those of the first word" (SAN 19).

If the work of art enjoys a privileged status for Merleau-Ponty it is because our bodies themselves are in a sense works of art. This is the fundamental insight that science has lost sight of: "The body is to be compared, not to a physical object, but rather to a work of art" (POP 150). The work of art that I am is not a self-contained monad but a "communion" (POP 213) with the world and with others: "That is why we said with Herder that man *is a sensorium commune*" (POP 238). The task of the painter is to effect this experience of communion, to reawaken us to our shared perception of the world we hold in common (PrOP 166).

By appealing to the notion of a common world, Merleau-Ponty implicitly offers his own version of Kant's analogies of experience, the principles by which we distinguish between our own subjective perceptions and our experience of an objective world. Kant claimed that in order to rise from mere judgments of perception to judgments of experience, it was necessary to subject appearances to the categories of relation. By contrast, Merleau-Ponty suggests that perception itself is capable of apprehending a shared phenomenal world. Thus instead of establishing the world's objectivity at the level of thetic intentionality, he seeks to identify the world's proto-objectivity at the level of pre-thetic intentionality. It is this shared perceptual world that Cézanne captures, for instead of painting his own private sensations, he paints *things themselves* as they reveal themselves to perception: "It is the mountain itself which from out there makes itself seen by the painter; it is the mountain that he interrogates with his gaze" (PrOP 166).

Thus to say that the wax is the wax of Cézanne is not to reduce it to a collection of merely "subjective" qualities. On the contrary, the wax of Cézanne *is* the wax itself, that unitary piece of the world's flesh which we encounter through perception and about which we can make judgments of experience. What we must not say, for Merleau-Ponty, is that Cézanne's wax is a mere appearance in contrast to the "real" wax of the physicist, nor must we "explain" Cézanne's wax as a consequence of the ontological properties of the physicist's wax. But we can envision a scientific analysis of the wax which, instead of "replacing" the wax of perception by its intelligible essence (as Cartesian science does) would perpetually hearken back to it as its proper object. Thus, even though Bachelard's chemist might purify the wax to detect otherwise undetectable properties, the properties disclosed thereby remain properties of the perceived wax. Put otherwise, cinnabar is not red *because* it is mercuric sulphide; rather, it is mercuric sulphide *because* it is a certain kind of red (i.e., "cinnabar-red" in contrast to "woolly-red"). To say this is not just to restore perception to its proper epistemic status; it is to accord ontological dignity to perceptual phenomena that are indeterminate. Hence instead of assuming that the objective world has a fully determinate character, the "new kind" of science that Merleau-Ponty envisions will abandon "the prejudice of determinate being" (POP 51n).

There is a sense in which Kant abandoned "the prejudice of determinate being" in his solution to the first antinomy, namely, insofar as he argued that the world was neither finite nor infinite because it lacked *any* determinate magnitude (CPR A519/B547). But Merleau-Ponty goes much further than Kant by suggesting that things themselves might be indeterminate. In taking this view, he comes close to the position that Kant refers to as "naturalism." In the concluding chapter of the first *Critique*, "The History of Pure Reason," Kant first distinguishes between "sensualist" and "intellectualist" conceptions of the object of cognition, and between empiricist and "noologist" (or rationalist) conceptions of the origin of cognitions. Like Kant, Merleau-Ponty repeatedly argues against all four of these positions. Kant then goes on to distinguish two different conceptions of philosophical method: "naturalism" and "science." In contrast to the scientist, whose approach to the problems of pure reason is systematic, the naturalist assumes that "common understanding without science" is a more reliable guide than "speculation." Dismissing such a point of view as misologistic, Kant goes on to suggest that the real battle is between two alternative ways of pursuing a scientific method in philosophy, namely, dogmatism and skepticism. Against both of these alternatives, he recommends, of course, the path of critique.

Keeping in mind that naturalism in the Kantian sense is entirely different from the sort of naturalism that Husserl and Merleau-Ponty reject – the latter being akin to what Kant calls transcendental realism – it is tempting to say that it is the path of the naturalist of pure reason that Merleau-Ponty seeks to rehabilitate, for although he appeals to perception rather than "common understanding," he is trying to show that the method of phenomenology cannot be scientific. Just as within the order of science, there is a conflict between dogmatism and skepticism, so within "naturalism" there is a dispute between the defenders of "common understanding" and the defenders of phenomena as they are perceived. But the real dispute is ultimately that between the critical method as Kant conceives it and the phenomenological method as Husserl first practiced it. For although it might seem as if phenomenology, as a species of "naturalism" – again in Kant's sense of the term – is prereflective, it is precisely in its return to the prereflective stratum of experience that phenomenology is most rigorously reflective: "The task of a radical reflection . . . consists, paradoxically enough, in recovering the unreflective experience of the world" (POP 241). According to Kant, the naturalist is someone who "asserts . . . that one can determine the magnitude and breadth of the moon more securely by eye than by mathematical rigmarole" (CPR A855/B883). In *The Phenomenology of Perception*, Merleau-Ponty claims not that we can better determine the actual size of the moon with the eye than with "mathematical rigmarole," but that the moon as seen with the eye has *no* determinate magnitude:

> When I look quite freely and naturally, the various parts of the field interact and *motivate* this enormous moon on the horizon, this measureless size which nevertheless is a size. Consciousness must be faced with its own unreflective life in things and awakened to its own history which it was forgetting: such is the true part that philosophical reflection has to play.
>
> (POP 31)

1.9   Foucault's archaeology of imagination

> Mad call I it, for to define true madness,
> What is't but to be nothing else but mad?
> (*The Tragedy of Hamlet, Prince of Denmark*,
> II, ii, 93–4)

In contrast to Merleau-Ponty, for whom phenomenology was a way of remaining faithful to the lifeworld, Michel Foucault (1926–1984) dreamed of an "archaeology" that would be able to plumb the depths of what it is tempting to call the "deathworld," the night out of which the imagination shapes the human relation to nothingness. In his early writings, Foucault conceives of such an archaeology as a history of "unreason," or rather as an historical reconstruction of the different ways in which unreason has been confronted in European history from the Middle Ages up until the present. Insofar as it is akin to intellectual history, archaeology remains oriented toward a linear past whose successive strata it seeks to unearth. But insofar as it tries to disclose the permanence of the night that perpetually threatens the daylight of reason, archaeology aspires to undo everything that is reassuring in the linear representation of time – thereby remaining faithful to unreason itself, and resisting the forces that would reduce it to the object of a clinical gaze (MC 212). Foucault is critical of psychoanalysis because although it recognizes "this heterogeneity of two temporal structures," it ultimately reduces "the experience of Unreason" to "the knowledge of madness, and to the science it authorizes" (MC 297 n9).

In his first publication, "Dream, Imagination, and Existence: an introduction to Ludwig Binswanger's 'Dream and Existence'" (*Introduction* in *Le Rêve et l'Existence*, 1954), Foucault suggests that a "phenomenological analysis" of dreaming "must be completed and grounded" in an existential analysis (DIAE 63). Binswanger (1881–1966) had argued that, though we flee the anxiety of being-toward-death while we are awake, when we sleep we are "awakened" to death by our dreams: "In the depth of his dream, what man encounters is his death ... death is the absolute meaning of the dream" (DIAE 54–5). Foucault concludes from this insight that far from representing a mere respite from existence, dreaming is the primordial way in which existence first blossoms forth as being-in-the-world. This implies that the dream is not rooted in archaic images; rather, it is "the first condition of ... possibility" of the imagination itself (DIAE 67). In contrast to Sartre, for whom the power of imagination was anchored in the perception of the real, Foucault agrees with Bachelard that the perception of the real is grounded in the imagination (DIAE 67, 70). But since the imagination is itself rooted in the dream's relationship to death, it is necessary to carry out a "transcendental reduction of the imaginary" by which a "passage" is made "from anthropology to ontology" (DIAE 73). This step was taken by Binswanger (following Heidegger) but not by Bachelard. Binswanger's analysis of the dream makes it possible to thematize the relationship between two very different paths that the imagination can take, namely, madness and the constitution of the world: "What he brought to light regarding dreams is the fundamental moment where the movement of existence discovers the decisive point of bifurcation between those images in which it becomes alienated in a pathological subjectivity, and expressions in which it fulfills itself in an objective history" (DIAE 74–5).

In *Folie et déraison: Histoire de la folie à l'âge classique*, 1961) – translated (in abridged form) as *Madness and Civilization: a History of Insanity in the Age of*

Reason – Foucault seeks to return to this "point of bifurcation," thematizing it as the moment when reason and madness first diverged: "We must try to return, in history, to that zero point in the course of madness at which madness is an undifferentiated experience, a not yet divided experience of division itself" (MC ix). Just as Nietzsche suggested that in the pre-Socratic experience of tragedy no firm distinction existed between the frenzy of the chorus and the rationality of the spectators, so Foucault suggests that, although the Greeks distinguished between "hubris" and "logos," they did not oppose these in any absolute way (MC xi). In the Middle Ages, madness was still in dialogue with reason, manifesting itself as a sign of divine transcendence from the world.[13] The first glimmers of a division only appear when the "ship of fools" enters "the imaginary landscape of the Renaissance" (MC 7). Not yet the sign of a rigorous division, the ships upon which madmen were exiled from European cities – both in literature and in reality – had the "symbolic" value of sending those who had lost their reason on a "pilgrimage" to recover it (MC 9). Like mediators between the world of men and the beyond, the mad were set apart without being entirely excluded, "put in the interior of the exterior, and inversely" (MC 11). A more decisive break occurs in the middle of the seventeenth century, at the dawn of the period that the French refer to as "the classical age," when the mad were suddenly locked up along with anyone else perceived as posing a threat to social order, such as the poor, the unemployed, and criminals. It is with this "great confinement" of all the representatives of unreason that Foucault locates the definitive divergence between reason and madness, the moment when rational men – by virtue of an "other form of madness" – assured themselves of their own rationality by locking up those who had lost theirs (MC ix).

At the beginning of the Renaissance there lurked in the paintings of Hieronymus Bosch (*c.*1450–1516) the anxiety that reason could succumb to madness at any moment. Just before this period, it had been death rather than madness that haunted the imagination of Europeans (MC 15). The substitution of madness for death as the primary object of anxiety represents for Foucault the symbolic replacement of death's *imminence* by its *immanence* (MC 16–17). Over the course of the Renaissance, the threat of madness was gradually dissipated by a humanistic discourse that spoke ironically of men's folly (MC 26–7). Thus it was precisely when madness ceased to be perceived as dangerous that it was subjected to confinement (MC 38). Foucault explains this paradox by showing that the true motive for confinement was to subject the representatives of unreason to the partly economic, partly moral requirement to labor (MC 55). Though confined with all the others, the mad were singled out and put on display, treated by the spectators who came to observe them as circus creatures who had reverted to a condition of sheer animality (MC 70).

In the classical period, madness was taken to originate in the passions, the undifferentiated intermediaries between body and soul (MC 88). During the

Renaissance, madness was equated with a visionary imagination, but in the classical period, an unruly imagination was seen as only a necessary, but not sufficient, condition for madness. To be mad was not just to suffer from hallucinations but to "affirm" them to be true (MC 93). This was how Kant assessed the case of Swedenborg, whom he diagnosed as a fanatic not because the objects of his imagination appeared to exist outside him as objects of perception but because he judged them to be so. According to Foucault, madness was construed throughout the eighteenth century as "delirium," that is, as the subjection of an otherwise healthy reason to the fascination of unreal images: "Whereas tradition compared the delirium of the madman to the vivacity of the dream images, the classical period identified delirium only with the complex of the image and the night of the mind" (MC 103). The difference between reason and delirium corresponds to the distinction that Kant draws between a discourse that subordinates sensible images to the schematism of the understanding and a discourse that subordinates the laws of the understanding to the allure of the image. According to Foucault, Descartes thought he could free himself from the very possibility of madness by severing the link between a sovereign rational discourse and the sensible images that might be deceptive products of the imagination (MC 108). So long as madness was conceived as delirious discourse, it was treated by insinuating the force of an "exterior Cogito" – that of the physician – into the discourse of the patient (MC 185). This imposition was accomplished either by appealing directly to the patient's own reason or by conjuring images designed to restore the patient to the truth.

At the beginning of the nineteenth century, attitudes toward the mad changed in significant ways. No longer treated as inhuman animals, those deemed mad were supposedly "liberated" from their places of confinement by reformers who recognized the inadequacy of earlier forms of therapy (MC 240). But although the nineteenth century freed those labeled as mad from their physical chains, it did so by subjecting them to moral chains that were in a sense even more confining (MC 247). To build a house of confinement was to erect a barrier between the Same and the Other within the very heart of the Same; neither assimilated nor simply excluded, the confined Other was included *as* excluded from the order of the Same. What the nineteenth-century asylum did was to replicate this structure within the psyche of the individual by subjecting the otherwise unconstrained patient to the constant pedagogical supervision of the doctor, who according to Foucault functioned less as a "medical personage" than as "Father" and "Judge" – i.e., as a representative of social order (MC 272–3). This paternal relationship between doctor and patient was inherited by Freud, who did renew the "dialogue with unreason" that the classical age had interrupted, but only by tightening the moral constraints that his predecessors introduced (MC 198). Insofar as psychoanalysis surrounds the patient in a "milieu" of responsibility and guilt for unconscious transgressions, it is but a new type of confinement.

Just as Freud claimed that he wrote *The Interpretation of Dreams* to disturb the sleep of his readers, so Foucault could be said to have written *Folie et déraison* to rouse his readers from their psychoanalytic slumber. To the extent that psychoanalysis represents an attempt on the part of reason to acknowledge its own rootedness in the irrational, Foucault is sympathetic with it. But psychoanalysis does not disturb so much as reassure, for in explaining madness it fails to engage with unreason: "psychoanalysis can unravel some of the forms of madness; it remains a stranger to the sovereign enterprise of unreason" (MC 278). The twentieth century recognizes itself as haunted by this other kind of madness, which so frequently appears – or rather disappears – at the moment when a work of art bursts forth into the world (MC 286ff.). Unlike Kant, who felt that it was incumbent upon him to explain away the madness of Swedenborg, Foucault feels obliged to attest to the mysterious depths of "Nietzsche's madness," before which modernity itself must be judged.[14]

In *The Order of Things: an Archaeology of the Human Sciences* (*Les mots et les choses: Une Archéologie des sciences humaines*, 1966), Foucault characterizes the entire "history of madness" as "the history of the Other – of that which, for a given culture, is at once interior and foreign, therefore to be excluded (so as to exorcize the interior danger) but by being shut away (in order to reduce its otherness)." He now proposes to relate the flip side of this history: "the history of the order imposed on things would be the history of the Same – of that which, for a given culture, is both dispersed and related, therefore to be distinguished by kinds and to be collected together into identities" (OT xxiv). During the Renaissance, knowledge was governed by the play of resemblances among visible forms, so much so that language itself appeared merely as a "fold" within visible being" (OT 17). As the embodiment of divine intentions, the natural world appeared as the obscure expression of "an original Text" (OT 41) that had to be deciphered. Because knowledge could only slide from one appearance to another, every interpretation of the world called forth a duplicating commentary which called forth another and so on ad infinitum.

Instead of equating knowledge with the interpretation of resemblances, the classical episteme defined knowledge in terms of ordered representations of identities and differences. For this transition to take place, language had to be separated from the world: "that uniform layer, in which the *seen* and the *read*, the visible and the expressible, were endlessly interwoven, vanished. . . . Things and words were to be separated from one another" (OT 43). From Descartes through Port-Royal Logic, language serves as a medium in which the world can be represented. Knowledge must still take its initial cue from sensible resemblances, but these must be ordered in and by a language that analyzes its representations of the world. This denigration of resemblance in favor of representation is exemplified in Descartes's subordination of imagination to the intellect. Before Descartes, the color or smell of the wax might very well be a sign of its hidden essence, but for Descartes it is merely an incitement to an ordering activity that will grasp the essence of the wax on the basis of the intellect alone. Foucault shows how the fields of general grammar, natural history, and the analysis of wealth all function as sciences of order during the early modern period. Crucial to each of these discourses is the assumption that it is possible to say what we see, for with the separation of articulable speech from the visible world, it becomes both necessary and sufficient for science to bring these two orders into coincidence through the construction of a table of names: "to speak or to write ... is to make one's way towards the sovereign act of nomination, to move, through language, towards the place where things and words are conjoined in their common essence, and which makes it possible to give them a name" (OT 130, 117).

The shift from the Renaissance to the classical episteme coincides with the reduction of madness to reason's "other." So long as knowledge is understood in terms of an open-ended play of resemblances, the madman cannot be rigorously distinguished from the scientist. On the contrary, the madman is the visionary to whom the secrets of nature are revealed in a privileged way. The rise of representation puts an end to this view and sets up for the first time a sharp distinction between the madman and the man of knowledge. According to Foucault, Don Quixote is a comic figure precisely because he is guided by the *mere* play of resemblances; like the madman, he "is Different only in so far as he is unaware of Difference" (OT 49).

The classical episteme begins to fall apart at the end of the eighteenth century, when the gap between language and being is first felt as a profound ontological gap. Kant problematizes the limits of representation by inquiring into the synthetic activity of a subject who represents things not as they are in themselves but as they appear to a certain kind of being: "whereas before it was a question of establishing relations of identity or difference against the continuous background of similitudes, Kant brings into prominence the inverse problem of the synthesis of the diverse" (OT 162). In the early nineteenth century, new sciences appear whose aim is no longer to classify objects of representation but to fathom the quasi-transcendent objects that supposedly ground our representations of them. These quasi-transcend*ent* objects – notably, life, labor, and language – function as quasi-transcendent*al* conditions for the possibility of experience: "the conditions of possibility of experience are being sought in the conditions of possibility of the object and its existence, whereas in transcendental reflection the conditions of possibility of the objects of experience are identified with the conditions of possibility of experience itself" (OT 244). It is in Kant that the problem concerning the relationship between the empirical and the transcendental first manifests itself (OT 318ff.). This problem persists in the post-Kantian split between the impulse toward formalization characteristic of the natural sciences and logic, and the impulse toward interpretation that informs the hermeneutic sciences. The demise of representation as the medium in which the order of language and the order of being would one day coincide brings with it the constitution of a new object of inquiry: man.

So long as it held sway, the classical episteme was predicated upon the homology between the order of being and the order of thought. Within this framework, discourse functioned as the representative medium in which being and thought could be united. In one way, Kant's first *Critique* belongs to the classical episteme, namely, insofar as the schematism ensures that the sensible manifold can be classified in accordance with the table of categories. But Kant's Copernican turn also opens up the distinction between phenomena and noumena, with the consequence that the order which we encounter in nature pertains not to things in themselves but only to appearances. Man is situated at the suturing-point of these two orders as both the inaccessible transcendental ground of experience and an empirical object in nature. In taking up the question, "What is man?," Kant tried to keep transcendental philosophy separate from empirical anthropology. By contrast, the post-Kantian human sciences that first arose in the nineteenth century came to treat man as an "empirico-transcendental doublet," that is, as a natural being whose quasi-transcendental grounds were to be found in life, labor, and language (OT 248). So conceived, man – "an invention of recent date" – is an inherently unstable object on the verge of disappearing "like a face drawn in sand at the edge of the sea" (OT 387; cf. xxiii). Whereas Heidegger criticized Kant for failing to distinguish between an anthropology of man and an existential analytic of Dasein, Foucault suggests that Heidegger's own attempt to pursue "the retreat and return of the origin" – that is, the unfathomable event of the *Ereignis* – remains squarely within the problematic of "man and his doubles" (OT 334).

Foucault suggests that it is in some sense impossible to think outside the horizons determined by a prevailing episteme: "In any given culture and at any given moment, there is always only one *episteme* that defines the conditions of possibility of all knowledge, whether expressed in a theory or silently invested in a practice" (OT 168). This is not to say that everyone living in the same time and place will share the same opinions, but rather that the *range* of possible opinions is structurally determined. Thus every episteme has its "points of heresy," controversies that attest less to intellectual freedom than to the hold that the dominant episteme has over thought. For example, in classical natural history there was a raging debate as to whether plants and animals should be classified on the model of "the system" of Linnaeus – Carl von Linné (1707–1778) – or "the method" of Michel Adanson (1727–1806). But as "ways of defining identities by means of the general grid of differences," both were essentially equivalent, the only difference being in how they went about constructing such a table (OT 145).

Foucault's account of the relationship between an episteme and its points of heresy can be likened to Kant's account of the relationship between a distributive judgment and its parts. As Kant observes, a distributive judgment carves up a field of mutually exclusive but exhaustive possible positions on a particular question; as an example he gives the judgment, "The world exists either through blind chance, or through inner necessity, or through an external cause" (CPR A74/B99). Since one of these possibilities must be true (but no more than one), the distributive judgment itself must be true. Insofar as a distributive judgment appears to exhaust all conceivable alternative solutions to a particular problem, it determines the range of what it is possible to think. Thus the only way to transform an episteme is to challenge its distributive judgments. This is precisely what Kant did in resolving the antinomies. He showed that the seemingly exhaustive points of heresy of classical metaphysics did not in fact cover the entire field of what it was possible to think. For instance, instead of being forced to think that the world is either finite or infinite in magnitude, Kant showed that it was possible to think that it has no determinate magnitude whatsoever. In a precisely analogous way, Foucault's survey of the limits of the post-Kantian episteme represents an attempt to find unsuspected ways of thinking that would break out of the dominant distributive judgments. Thus although he claims that thought is constrained by whatever the dominant episteme happens to be, he does not draw the fatalistic conclusion that it is impossible to escape it. Unlike phenomenology, which in his view remains caught within the distributive alternatives of the problematic concerning man and his doubles, archaeology purports to be a genuinely liberating exercise.

In *The Archaeology of Knowledge* (*L'Archéologie du savoir*, 1969), Foucault contrasts the archaeological investigation of epistemic breaks with the phenomenological search for archaic meanings. In contrast to Husserl, who used the expression "historical a priori" to refer to the sedimented traces of past intentions, Foucault characterizes the "historical a priori" as having nothing to do with conscious intentions (OOG 372; OT 157–8; AOK 127ff.). Whereas for Husserl the task of the genetic phenomenologist was to reconstruct the process by which successive strata of the historical a priori were laid down by a living consciousness, for Foucault the task of the archaeologist is to treat textual marks as indicative "monuments" rather than as expressive "documents" (AOK 7). Just as Bachelard (from whom Foucault borrows the notion of an epistemic break or "threshold") criticized Bergson for relying on the authority of intuition, so Foucault criticizes phenomenology for its "transcendental narcissism," that is, for its reliance on the point of view of the self-reflective subject (AOK 4, 203; cf. OT xiv). Like Husserl's conception of genetic phenomenology, both Sartre's account of the for-itself/in-itself doublet and Merleau-Ponty's conception of the flesh are so many ways of attempting to think man from the point of view of man himself. Merleau-Ponty was drawn to Cézanne's paintings because they tried to represent a lived experience of nature that was anterior to the birth of language. By contrast, in *This is Not a Pipe: With Illustrations and Letters by René Magritte* (*Ceci n'est pas une pipe: Deux lettres et quatre dessins de René Magritte*, 1973), Foucault calls attention to works of art – such as those of Magritte

(1898–1967) – in which language and image clash like "the fragments of an unraveled calligram" (TINAP 22; cf. OT 129) – ironically attesting to the impossibility of a superimposition of articulable words and visible things.

In calling attention to the unbridgeable rift between the orders of the visible and the articulable, Foucault implicitly hearkens back to Kant's distinction between the receptive and spontaneous dimensions of human cognition. Like Heidegger, Foucault finds the "common root" of this division in the imagination. Just as Heidegger's reflections on the imagination led him to think "The nothing nothings," so Foucault's reflections on madness led him, in effect, to think "Unreason unreasons." But whereas Heidegger tried to overcome the tyranny of reason ("the most stiff-necked adversary of thought") by returning to the piety of questioning, Foucault attempts to recover that experience of *hubris* which the Greeks did not yet distinguish from the logos (QCT 112; MC xi). Thus, whereas Heidegger took Nietzsche's pronouncement of the death of God to mean that we must seek God, Foucault suggests that it is "Nietzsche's pride" – not his piety – that challenges the sovereignty of modern reason (MC 288). Thus there is a fundamental difference between Heidegger and Foucault – not just over how to read Nietzsche, but over the question of whether we suffer from too much hubris or too little. Just as psychoanalysis remains complicitous with nineteenth-century techniques of "liberation," so Heidegger's critique of man's hubris is perfectly in keeping with nineteenth-century attitudes toward madness: "For the nineteenth century, the initial model of madness would be to believe oneself to be God, while for the preceding centuries it had been to deny God" (MC 264).

1.10   Derrida's deconstruction of the metaphysics of presence

Now am I dead
(*A Midsummer Night's Dream*,
V, i, 301)

For the Algerian-born French philosopher Jacques Derrida (1930–2004), "deconstruction" is what phenomenology becomes, when, attempting to carry out the eidetic reduction, we discover that what makes the reduction possible also makes it impossible. This is not to say that we are entitled – or even able – to lapse back into the natural or dogmatic attitude. Against the "irresponsibility" of a simply anti-phenomenological "empiricism," Derrida emphasizes the obligation to think that which eludes phenomenology in principle (IOG 120). In his view, phenomenology represents the self-critical vigilance of Western metaphysics, which has always taken the form of a "metaphysics of presence." The ultimate aim of both the eidetic and transcendental reductions is to purify what Husserl calls "the living present" so that it can apprehend itself in an intuition of pristine immanence (SAP 6).

But for reasons that Husserl himself brings out without realizing their implications, the phenomenological reductions cannot take place without a paradoxical detour through language in general and writing in particular. The necessity of this detour is not merely a methodological limitation affecting phenomenological reflection; more radically, it is constitutive of "self-presence" itself, which therefore can no longer be conceived as *pure* presence. Thus deconstruction is a way of thinking about writing as that which reveals "the closure of metaphysics" (SAP 52).

In his 1962 essay, *Edmund Husserl's Origin of Geometry: an Introduction* (*Introduction à "L'Origine de la géométrie" de Husserl*), Derrida argues that Husserl's critique of the foundations of mathematics is more radical than that of Kant because it recognizes the need to address the problem of constitution. Kant does call attention to the role that must have been played by a first geometer – "a single man ... whether he was called 'Thales' or had some other name" (CPR Bxi; cf. IOG 39) – but he does not conceive of the act of this first geometer as *constituting* geometry in Husserl's sense of this term. Thus Kant's first geometer merely discovered that "in order to know something securely *a priori*," it was necessary to "produce" figures "according to *a priori* concepts" (CPR Bxii). But because these a priori concepts – as well as the a priori form of space – are "already constituted," there is nothing genuinely creative or constituting in what Kant calls the "construction" of a geometrical concept (IOG 40; cf. CPR Bxii; A713/B741). For Kant the origin of geometry can be situated only in an "ideal history" that would be "the history of an operation, and not of a founding.... And if there is a birth of geometry for Kant, it seems to be only the extrinsic *circumstance* for the emergence of a truth (which is itself always already constituted for any factual consciousness)" (IOG 41). By separating ideal history from factual history, Kant forecloses the problem of constitution altogether – at least after the A Deduction, which Derrida does not discuss: "to avoid empiricism from the start and at any price, Kant had to confine his transcendental discourse to a world of ideal constituted objects, whose correlate was therefore itself a constituted subject" (IOG 42). By contrast, Husserl recognized that, in order to account for the "protohistory" (IOG 42) of geometry it was necessary to avoid both the Scylla of "historicism" and the Charybdis of "objectivism" (IOG 26).

As Derrida observes, Husserl's attempt to account for the protohistory of geometry requires an entirely new kind of reduction that is different in kind from both the eidetic and the transcendental. The eidetic reduction is a way of suspending all reference to matters of fact so that static analyses of *already* constituted idealities can be carried out. By contrast, the genetic problem of constitution requires an "historical reduction" (IOG 47) by which the phenomenologist purports to "reactivate" a factual act of a singular kind, namely, one by which a particular class of iterable idealities (such as those that belong to geometry) were first constituted as such.

In returning to the realm of factuality it might seem as if the historical reduction requires that the eidetic reduction be suspended. But Derrida argues that in one sense the historical reduction presupposes the eidetic, for it is only by first identifying an iterable ideality that one is able to inquire into its genesis: "the reactivating reduction supposes the iterative reduction of the static and structural analysis, which teaches us once and for all what the geometrical 'phenomenon' is" (IOG 50). "I must already have a naïve knowledge of geometry and must not *begin* at its origin" (IOG 38; cf. 49). But the relationship between the two reductions is more complicated than this suggests, for it is only by going back to the sense of the inaugural act that the sense of what was thereby constituted can be apprehended. This point is underscored by one of Husserl's principal motives for carrying out genetic analyses in the first place, namely, the fact that through historical sedimentation the very sense of Galilean geometry has become eclipsed. Derrida concludes that "there is no simple response to the question of the priority of one reduction over another" (IOG 48).

In attempting to carry out the reactivating historical reduction, Husserl is led to discover the paradoxical role that writing plays in the constitution of idealities that are "free" as opposed to "bound," that is, independent of (rather than dependent upon) the factual languages in which they are expressed (IOG 71–2). In order for geometrical idealities to exist independently of the mind of the protogeometer they had to be expressed in language. But in order to exist independently of the actual animating acts of every particular geometer – as geometrical idealities must – they had to be expressed not just in language but specifically in writing, that is, in a "virtual" form of communication that would continue to exist even when no one was reanimating its sense (OOG 360–1; IOG 87). Derrida concludes that every written text functions as "a kind of autonomous transcendental field from which every present subject can be absent. . . . Thus a subjectless transcendental field is one of the 'conditions' of transcendental subjectivity" (IOG 88). To write is to produce an iterable ideality that exists for any possible subject whatsoever. As such, the act of writing functions as a kind of transcendental reduction by which the one who writes adopts the point of view of a transcendental "we": "The authentic act of writing is a transcendental reduction performed by and toward the *we*" (IOG 92). Moreover, since according to Husserl writing plays an irreducible role in the constitution of *every* cultural tradition (OOG 356–7) – that is, every ideal objectivity that essentially exists for a collective "we" – it is only through writing that such a transcendental reduction can be carried out.

The historical reduction has led to a kind of transcendental reduction that would serve as the basis for the constitution of iterable ideal essences. From this it follows that the eidetic reduction – which in the *Ideas* served as the necessary foundation for the more radicalizing transcendental reduction – is grounded in a more originary transcendental reduction. But this "more originary" reduction can only take place in writing and not in the interiority of consciousness. The paradox is that this "transcendental" reduction is essentially dependent upon an "empirical" medium which serves as the condition for the possibility of the "freeing" of the transcendental from the empirical: "Historical incarnation frees the transcendental, instead of binding it. This last notion, the transcendental, must then be rethought" (IOG 77; cf. 89n). The empirical dimension of writing cannot be altogether reduced, since it enables free idealities to continue to exist when no actual subject happens to be attending to them. Conversely, writing cannot be reduced *to* a merely empirical phenomenon, for then the idealities it constitutes would not be freed from their dependence upon a particular sensible manifestation. Thus writing would be transcendental only insofar as it is empirical and empirical only insofar as it is transcendental. It is precisely here that Husserl is at his most radical, for not only does he refuse to reduce the historical to the transcendental – as Kant did in foreclosing the entire problematic of the proto-geometer – he simultaneously resists the temptation to reduce the transcendental to the historical: "If we consider this question to be *at once* historical and transcendental, we see to what irresponsible empiricism all the 'phenomenologies' of prescientific perception are condemned, phenomenologies which would not let themselves be beset by that question" (IOG 120). Derrida intimates that this is the mistake made by Merleau-Ponty (IOG 116).

If the concept of the transcendental can no longer be opposed to that of the empirical in a simple way, the same holds for the related "oppositions" between the factual and the ideal, the sensible and the intelligible, the real and the irreal, etc. And yet it was these very distinctions upon which the eidetic and transcendental reductions of the *Ideas* depended. This problem could be forestalled only if it were possible to carry out static analyses of already constituted idealities without having to return to their founding acts. But according to Derrida, the role played by writing in the constitution of such idealities makes this impossible in principle. Writing is an inherently double-edged phenomenon in that it performs its work of transcendental memory only by subjecting the idealities it constitutes to that peculiar form of transcendental forgetting which Husserl designates by the term "crisis": "That *virtuality* . . . is an ambiguous value: it simultaneously makes passivity, forgetfulness, and all the phenomena of *crisis* possible" (IOG 87). As the virtual embodiment of sedimented meanings, writing functions simultaneously as both a living body (*Leib*) and an inanimate corpse (*Körper*), that is, as both a living memory and an entombed forgetting (IOG 97). It is as if written texts were zombies, living-dead repositories of "lost intentions and guarded secrets" (IOG 88).

Faced with the task of reanimating a sedimented text, there are always two competing interpretative choices. On the one hand, it is possible to aim at reactivating the "univocal" intention that was originally sedimented in a body of writing. Husserl does this in responding to the crisis of European humanity. But it is also possible to aim instead at multiplying the number of different readings to which any text can in principle lend itself. Derrida associates this latter ideal – that of maximizing "equivocity" – with James Joyce's (1882–1941) *Finnegans Wake* (IOG 102–3). To maximize equivocity would be to exacerbate the forgetting that writing makes possible and thus to worsen the condition of crisis. Husserl concedes that, as a matter of fact, it is impossible for any text to escape the threat of equivocity altogether, but he nonetheless maintains that every text can be treated as univocal insofar as it expresses an original animating intention. But here Derrida argues that the very sense of such an original act of constitution must itself remain equivocal as long as the constituted idealities themselves are subject to equivocity. Only if it were possible to identify a univocal meaning from the point of view of the eidetic reduction would it be possible to identify a univocal sense for the original constituting act. But this is not possible if the idealities in question have been constituted in writing.

The only way Husserl can resolve this tension is by regarding the univocity of sense as a telos to be aimed at. It is here that he relies on the concept of an "Idea in the Kantian sense," that is, on the supposition that although univocity is never given in fact it is proleptically promised in advance. But what exactly is meant by this appeal to an "Idea in the Kantian sense"? Derrida points out that Husserl has recourse to this notion whenever the value of presence, or givenness, needs to be guaranteed by something that is not present: "Every time this value of presence becomes threatened, Husserl will awaken it, recall it, and bring it back to itself in the form of a telos – that is, an Idea in the Kantian sense" (SAP 9, translation slightly modified; cf. IOG 106, 137). What is paradoxical about Husserl's appeal to ideas in the Kantian sense is that it is a way of anticipating a form of evidence that can never be given as such, since Kantian ideas can only play a regulative, limiting role in experience. For Derrida, such appeals contradict the "principle of principles" that Husserl articulated in the *Ideas*, namely, the stricture that phenomenology attend only to that which is presently given in intuition. Somehow an idea in the Kantian sense must be presently given despite the fact that it is given as ungivable.

But the problem goes still further, for the threat of equivocity suggests that it is only through the ungivable telos of an idea in the Kantian sense that it is possible to identify the sense even of those idealities that are supposed to be immediately given to eidetic intuition. For, in suggesting that the univocity of constituted idealities is something only promised and never given as such, Husserl implicitly concedes that it would be possible to identify the sense of an original constituting act only by anticipating the completion of an incompletable tradition: "The *primordial* sense of every intentional act is *only* its *final* sense, i.e., the constitution of an object. . . . That is why only a teleology can open up a passage, a way back toward the beginnings" (IOG 64). In the case of geometry, for instance, the founding act of the protogeometer will have acquired its sense only at an unattainable end of geometrical inquiry. But this is just to say that the founding act is itself given only as an idea in the Kantian sense, that geometry rests as much upon an infinitely receding arche as it does on an infinitely deferred telos: "Must we not say that geometry is on the way toward its origin, instead of proceeding from it?" (IOG 131).

All this could be avoided if it were possible for the protogeometer to have constituted geometry while remaining within the interiority of his or her own stream of consciousness. For then it would have been possible for the protogeometer to have intuited idealities whose iterability would not depend upon their being written. Husserl attempts to vouchsafe this possibility by making the public iterability of geometrical idealities secondary with respect to their private iterability for the protogeometer (IOG 86). But this position proves untenable since there can be no "private" iterability of free idealities apart from their public iterability. Derrida concludes that there is an unresolvable tension between the "living present," in which the individual subject is supposed to be able to intuit essences, and the irreducible relation to alterity through which the immediate intuition of essences is perpetually deferred. But this tension turns out to be nothing more nor less than "the movement of primordial temporalization" which Husserl attempts to describe in his account of the constitution of time (IOG 143). There Husserl was forced to acknowledge the role played by retentions and protentions in the constitution of the present. For Derrida, retentions and protentions are not apprehensions of something that was or will be present. On the contrary, to think of the present as an effect of retentions and protentions is to acknowledge a primordial non-presence at the heart of "presence" itself. But this is just to say that there is no such thing as presence, or rather that presence "is" itself only an idea in the Kantian sense, something promised as indefinitely deferred: "Here delay is the philosophical absolute" (IOG 152). More precisely, temporalization would be "the dialectic between the dialectical (the indefinite mutual and irreducible implication of protentions and retentions) and the nondialectical (the absolute and concrete identity of the Living Present, the universal form of consciousness)" (IOG 143). The fact that free idealities must be constituted in writing is just a consequence of the more radical fact that presence *in general* can be "constituted" only through "writing," here identified with the network of retentions and protentions.

Thus Husserl's principle of principles – the claim that phenomenology must rely exclusively on senses that are revealed in pure intuition – would be compromised by the role that writing plays in the constitution of presence: "Phenomenology would thus be *stretched* between the *finitizing* consciousness of its *principle* and the *infinitizing* consciousness of its final *institution*" (IOG 138). In fact, the very possibility of phenomenology is called into question once it is admitted that it too has its condition of possibility in language (IOG 69–70n). Husserl attempts to contain this threat by maintaining that recourse to language in static phenomenology is not necessary, or that it is necessary only in order to *express* idealities which do not themselves depend upon language in the way that geometrical idealities do.

Derrida challenges this assumption in *Speech and Phenomena: Introduction to the Problem of Signs in Husserl's Phenomenology* (*La Voix et le Phénomène*, 1967). Once again his argument will consist in drawing out the implications of Husserl's analyses of "the movement of temporalization and of the constitution of intersubjectivity," which reveal "an irreducible nonpresence" and "an ineradicable nonprimordiality" at the very foundation of the so-called "living present" (SAP 6–7; cf. 64). Derrida observes that after putting forth certain "essential distinctions" concerning the nature of signs in the *Logical Investigations* (LI I 183–205), Husserl repeatedly deferred any direct engagement with the problems posed by the phenomenology of language – at least until "The Origin of Geometry." From the *Logical Investigations* on, he assumes that there is a pre-expressive stratum of mental life whose sense can be apprehended in a form of reflection which is itself not yet expressive in character. Only in a secondary (and supposedly contingent) manner is this sense brought to a form of expression that is not yet subject to the threat of equivocity because it represents a perfectly transparent and therefore univocal means of signification.

As Derrida points out, Husserl bases this analysis on the supposition that a rigorous distinction can be drawn between "expressive" and non-expressive or "indicative" signs (LI I 183). For Husserl, all signs contain an indicative stratum as a matter of fact, but it is possible to isolate a stratum of language that is purely expressive in character (LI I 189). Such a stratum can be found in the solitary monologue in which a subject gives expression to the sense of its own mental acts: "In a monologue words can perform no function of indicating the existence of mental acts, since such indication would there be quite purposeless. For the acts in question are themselves experienced by us at that very moment" (LI I 191). In other words, the signs used in an inner monologue are purely expressive because they do nothing more than bring to linguistic signification what is immediately intuited as a pre-expressive sense. To carry out the eidetic reduction would be to bring this pre-expressive stratum of experience into view. Thus it is possible to carry out static analyses of noematic senses and their noetic correlates without addressing the problems posed by indication. That topic need only be broached when one passes from a phenomenological description of that which can be intuited by an individual consciousness in the living present to a phenomenology of intersubjectivity.

Against this point of view, Derrida argues that it is impossible to reduce the indicative dimension of signs from expressive language, and, more radically, that it is impossible to identify a pre-expressive stratum of experience at all. Husserl claims that by performing the eidetic reduction, the conscious subject is able to apprehend the living present as the ideal form in which pre-expressive senses in general manifest themselves. To bring these senses to expression it suffices for the subject to "point" them out to itself through an imaginary linguistic signification. Because such signification is merely imagined and not real, it is not supposed to be subject to the problem of equivocity that inevitably adheres to indicative signs. But Derrida points out that, in order for any sign to function as a sign – whether it is imagined in the purported interiority of consciousness or put forth in communication – it must be essentially repeatable or iterable. The ideality of the sign consists of nothing other than its repeatability: "When in fact I *effectively* use words, and whether or not I do it for communicative ends..., I must from the outset operate (within) a structure of repetition whose basic element can only be representative" (SAP 50). Moreover, ideality in general would have its essence in its repeatability; that is, to apprehend an ideality as an ideality would be to recognize the difference between the given fact in which that ideality happens to manifest itself and the possibility of an indefinite proliferation of other such facts. This is to say that all idealities would function as signs. But if this is so, then even the ideality of the living present must be given as a sign, that is, as a structure of iterability which, as such, is distinct from any particular living present in which it happens to manifest itself. Put otherwise, one apprehends an actual living present – a concrete particular "now" – only on the basis of recognizing the contingency of *this* now in the apprehension of a now-in-general: "The presence-of-the-present is derived from repetition and not the reverse" (SAP 52).

Derrida asks what it means to say "I am" or "At this very moment I am alive." From the structure of iterability it follows that such statements are meaningful only insofar as one's actual existence at the moment of their utterance is contingent. In other words, it is a condition for the possibility of the very meaningfulness of "I am alive" that it be possible that I *not* be alive: "The *I am*, being experienced only as an *I am present*, itself presupposes the relationship with presence in general, with being as presence. The appearing of the *I* to itself in the *I am* is thus originally a relation with its own possible disappearance." Put otherwise, "The relationship with *my death* (my disappearance in general) thus lurks in this determination of being as presence" (SAP 54). Here, the possibility of being dead would function as a condition for the possibility of being able to say that one is alive. But Derrida goes on to argue that to recognize the dependence of expression on iterability is tantamount to acknowledging the irreducibility of indication in signification in general. Husserl claimed that there could be no indication in the subject's silent monologue with itself, because an immediate intuition of an object would preclude the possibility of its being indicated. If this is so, and if it is impossible to purge expression of its indicative dimension, it follows that signification is not merely compatible with the non-givenness of what is signified; on the contrary, signification only takes place on the assumption that what is signified is not given in intuition. This enables Derrida to draw the paradoxical conclusion that the statement "I am" can effectively take place only on the condition of my actual death: "My nonperception, my nonintuition, my *hic et nunc* absence are expressed by that very thing that I say and *because* I say it" (SAP 93). "The statement 'I am alive' is accompanied by my being dead, and its possibility requires the possibility that I be dead; and conversely" (SAP 96–7).

In the *Introduction*, Derrida characterized writing as a living-dead repository of "lost intentions and guarded secrets." Here he concludes that the so-called living present, insofar as it is constituted through writing, is in the same predicament. Husserl attempts to avoid this conclusion by appealing to the concept of a phenomenological "voice" that would be able to hear itself speak without having to pass through the medium of indication. Speech plays a privileged role here because it appears to be a purely temporal medium of expression that would not be contaminated by the irreducibly indicative dimension of spatial (i.e., written) signs: "What constitutes the originality of speech . . . is that its substance seems to be purely temporal" (SAP 83). But Derrida once again observes that Husserl's own analyses of the constitution of temporality and intersubjectivity undermine the account that he wants to give of this experience of pure "auto-affection": "Is not the concept of pure solitude . . . *undermined* by its own origin, by the very condition of its self-presence, that is, by 'time,' to be conceived anew on the basis now of difference within auto-affection. . .?" (SAP 68). Derrida's entire argument thus amounts to a hearkening back to Husserl's attempt to rework the three syntheses of Kant's A Deduction, and he introduces the term *différance* to refer to that "primordial" play of difference and deferral by which both "time" and "space" would first be constituted as such. In the *Introduction*, Derrida suggested that in the movement of temporalization, "Difference would be transcendental" (IOG 153). This is to affirm something like the ontological primacy of difference, but Derrida resists characterizing *différance* as a first principle since it is rather that which indicates that there are no first principles.

In his critique of the paralogisms of the soul, Kant himself argued that there is no such thing as an experience of self-presence because the thought "I am" is never accompanied by an intellectual intuition of myself as the one who thinks. The Kantian subject does have an empirical intuition of itself, but only in time. Like Husserl, Derrida attempts to account for something like the genesis or constitution of time, so that the impossibility of self-presence would be a consequence not of an a priori form of time but of *différance*. For Derrida, *différance* is that by which both "temporalizing" and "spacing" take place. In the "Refutation of Idealism," Kant argues that the possibility of intuiting oneself in time is rooted in a prior apprehension of objects of outer sense. Analogously, Derrida suggests that there is no time-constitution apart from the primordial relation to alterity by which something like space is first constituted as such. Here he introduces the concept of a "trace," that is, of that whose essential non-appearance serves as the basis for appearance in general. Insofar as the subject is the effect of a play of traces, it is itself a trace. Therefore to preserve, with Kant, the idea of the soul as a regulative idea would be to dream of an impossibility, namely, the appearance "in person" of that which is only in not appearing: "the self of the living present is primordially a trace" (SAP 85).

Sartre claimed that the subject is always torn between its for-itself and its in-itself, so that the subject who writes would be in an unavoidable relationship of bad faith to his or her writing. Derrida suggests that the very split between the for-itself and the in-itself is a function of writing itself, of that which constitutes the subject as a play of traces. In a footnote in the *Introduction*, Derrida characterizes Sartre's phenomenology of imagination as a "breakthrough" that "has so profoundly unbalanced – and then overthrown – the landscape of Husserl's phenomenology" (IOG 125n). But rather than take the for-itself/in-itself dichotomy for granted, Derrida thematizes *différance* as that which both generates and problematizes all metaphysical oppositions: "We could thus take up all the coupled oppositions on which philosophy is constructed, and from which our language lives, not in order to see opposition vanish but to see the emergence of a necessity such that one of the terms appears as the differance of the other" (SAP 148). This would apply to all of Kant's dichotomies, such as

> the sensible and the intelligible, phenomenon and noumenon, internal and external phenomenon, the pure sensible and the empirical sensible, the transcendental and the empirical, the pure and the impure, the *a priori* and the *a posteriori*, the objective and the subjective, sensibility, imagination, understanding, and reason.
>
> (WAOP 52–3)

Insofar as writing both founds and ruins all philosophical oppositions – perhaps first and foremost that between the empirical and the transcendental (IOG 90–1) – it can be thought of as a kind of "empirico-transcendental doublet." But unlike Foucault, for whom the empirico-transcendental doublet "man" was "an invention of recent date" whose condition of possibility had to be sought in an archaeological inquiry for which phenomenology was only one of a series of modern forms of thought, Derrida maintains that it is impossible to date the advent of writing and that phenomenology represents the most rigorous philosophical attempt to account for it. Moreover, if writing is that which makes something like historicity itself possible, its aporetic status as an empirico-transcendental doublet is no less presupposed by Foucault than it is by Husserl. In his 1963 lecture, "Cogito and the History of Madness" (*Cogito et l'histoire de la folie*, first published in 1964), Derrida questions Foucault's attempt to locate the zero point at which reason would separate itself from madness at a determinate point in history, since any such break would have to be thought of both as occurring within history and as the ground of historicity itself. Framing this concern around a question of where exactly in the *Meditations* Descartes attempts to preclude the possibility of his being mad, Derrida argues that thought is always inescapably engaged in something like "the great confinement": "the reign of finite thought can be established only on the basis of the more or less disguised internment . . . of the madman within us" (WAD 61).

Just as it would be impossible to return to a time before reason's exclusion of madness, so it is impossible to regard the forgetting of being as an event that would have occurred in time. In *"Ousia* and *Grammē*: Note on a Note from *Being and Time"* (*Ousia et Gramme*: Note sur une note de *Sein und Zeit*, 1968) Derrida argues that it is impossible to draw a sharp distinction between authentic and inauthentic conceptions of time as Heidegger tries to do in *Being and Time*, since all such distinctions are already inscribed within the metaphysical tradition that Heidegger wants to challenge: "we can only conclude that the entire system of metaphysical concepts, throughout its history, develops the so-called 'vulgarity' of the concept of time . . . but also that an *other* concept of time cannot be opposed to it, since time in general belongs to metaphysical conceptuality" (MOP 63). It is in part for this reason that Derrida speaks of *différance* rather than time per se. The idea of a "deconstruction of metaphysics" is in some sense a modification of Heidegger's project for a "destruction of the history of ontology." But Derrida thinks that Heidegger himself remains within the metaphysics of presence to the extent that he seeks a "first word of Being," that is, a word that would give a proper name to the event of *Ereignis* (SAP 160). To the extent that *différance* precludes the possibility of such a word, it can be thought of as "older" than the "ontological difference" between being and beings (SAP 154). The "Heideggerian *hope*" that Derrida rejects can be likened to what Sartre called the desire to be God insofar as both bespeak the dream of pure presence (SAP 159). In "The Transcendence of the Ego," Sartre characterized "the transcendental *I*" as "the death of consciousness," suggesting that "All the results of phenomenology begin to crumble if the *I* is not . . . an object *for* consciousness" (TOTE 40, 42). In effect, Derrida can be said to take seriously the idea that the "transcendental I" *is* the death of consciousness and to show in precisely what sense the results of phenomenology do in fact begin to crumble. For Derrida, death is no longer that which is merely *imminent*, as it was for Heidegger, but *immanent* in the sense that it has always already overtaken us, precluding the possibility of presence to self. Or, in the words of Macbeth: "Life's but a walking shadow"[15] (*The Tragedy of Macbeth*, V, v, 24).

1.11   Deleuze's transcendental empiricism

> The time is out of joint
> (*The Tragedy of Hamlet, Prince of Denmark*,
> I, v, 188)

Just as deconstruction affirms the primacy of *différance* over the living present, so the "transcendental empiricism" of the French philosopher Gilles Deleuze (1925–1995) affirms the ontological primacy of difference over identity. Hence just as Derrida tries to break with the metaphysics of presence, so Deleuze rejects the metaphysical interpretation of difference as "external" difference – that is, as the difference that exists between self-identical terms that are themselves ontologically primary – in favor of an "internal" difference through which the diversity of relata is first given. Thus internal difference – or difference as such – is not the diversity of the given but "that by which the given is given" (DR 222). Just as Derrida connected *différance* to the phenomenon of iterability, so Deleuze argues that difference manifests itself in the phenomenon of repetition.

Before developing these ideas in his own name, Deleuze attributes them to Bergson. In contrast to Bachelard, who criticized Bergson for relying on a naive faith in the epistemic power of intuition, Deleuze argues – in "Bergson's Conception of Difference" (*La Conception de la différence chez Bergson*, 1956) and *Bergsonism* (*Le Bergsonisme*, 1966) – that Bergsonian intuition is actually a rigorous method for going beyond the order of sheer givenness. To appeal to intuition is to carry out a "transcendental analysis" of the given, dividing its "bad mixtures" into their separable tendencies: "intuition presents itself as a method of difference or division: that of dividing the mixture into two tendencies" (BCD 46; cf. B 13). These two tendencies – duration and extensity – correspond to two different kinds of difference: difference in kind and difference in degree. At first, Bergson thinks of the difference between these two kinds of difference as external, but he goes on to show that it is, in fact, internal. He does so by conceiving of duration as that which *"differs from itself"* (BCD 48), thereby giving rise to its other: "the mixture decomposes itself into two tendencies, one of which is the indivisible, but the indivisible differentiates itself into two tendencies, the other of which is the principle of the divisible" (BCD 49). Thus the difference between duration and extensity is not a merely external difference but the result of the primordial self-differentiation of duration itself.

Deleuze distinguishes Bergson's conception of difference from that of Hegel, for whom a thing differs from itself only insofar as it differs from something else that it is not: "According to Hegel, the thing differs from itself because it differs in the first place from all that it is not, such that difference goes to the point of contradiction" (BCD 53). Though contradiction might seem to represent an extreme of difference, it is only the extreme of external difference. Insofar as identity serves as both its arche and its telos, "the dialectic of contradiction lacks difference itself" (BCD 53). But Bergson shows that all of the categories that govern the Hegelian dialectic – the so-called "determinations of reflection," namely, identity, external difference, opposition, and contradiction – are so many dialectical illusions arising from the tendency to project back to the point of origin what is in fact merely an effect (what Nietzsche calls the *"error of confusing cause and effect"*) (TOTI 30). What is truly primary is not identity but difference – i.e., duration – which, in its movement of self-differentiation, gives rise to that which manifests itself *as* the identical. In *Time and Free Will*, Bergson still treated the difference between duration and extensity as external, so that his position seemed to be fundamentally dualistic. But in *Matter and Memory* he shows that both duration (i.e., difference in kind) and extensity (i.e., difference in degree) are *"degrees of difference itself"* (BCD 61). Thus Bergson is a monist for whom difference is all that there is (BCD 47).

Deleuze develops his own conception of difference in *Difference and Repetition* (*Différence et Répétition*, 1968). Just as Husserl read Kant as opening up – but not exploring – the realm of transcendental phenomenology, so Deleuze reads Kant as "the analogue of a great explorer – not of another world, but of the upper or lower reaches of this one" (DR 135). Just as Husserl criticized Kant for succumbing to psychologism in the A Deduction, so Deleuze argues that all of Kant's arguments are psychologistic:

> Kant traces the so-called transcendental structures from the empirical acts of a psychological consciousness. . . . In order to hide this all too obvious procedure, Kant suppressed this text in the second edition. Although it is better hidden, the tracing method, with all its "psychologism," nevertheless subsists.
>
> (DR 135; cf. 143)

Kant's true point of departure is "the Image of thought," a precritical – and therefore dogmatic – idea of what thought itself is supposed to be like. In principle, nothing could be better "equipped to overturn the Image of thought" than Kant's critique of pure reason, but in its execution, nothing turns out to do a better job of buttressing it (DR 136). The reason for this is that Kant conceives of critique as the process by which one validates synthetic a priori judgments whose legitimacy is taken for granted from the very beginning. For example, instead of asking *whether or not* we are entitled to think that $5 + 7 = 12$, Kant asks how it is that we *know* it. Such a procedure amounts to a forsaking of the very project of critique: *"Critique has done nothing insofar as it has not been brought to bear on truth itself"* (NAP 90). Kant presumes precisely what should be questioned, masking the questionability of the image of thought behind a tacit dogma of the form "'Everybody knows...'" (DR 129–30). If philosophy has any true task it is to challenge all claims of the "Everybody knows" form. Socrates exhibits an exemplary pugnaciousness when he questions the things that every Greek "knows" – i.e., the opinions whose universalization constitutes the image of thought as such (DR 134). Such pugnaciousness or "ill will" (DR 130) is needed in order to challenge the dogmatism of appeals to so-called "good sense." In the *Discourse on Method*, Descartes claims that "Good sense is of all things in the world the most equally distributed" (cited in DR 131). This implies that every person with the capacity to think has a natural affinity for the truth. But in Deleuze's view, thought has an inherent inertia or sluggishness; it must be prodded by force. Appeals to good sense only serve to reinforce thought's laziness.

Closely related to the principle of good sense, which imposes a "norm of distribution" determining the proper use of each faculty, is that of common sense, which represents an overarching "norm of identity" for thought (DR

133–4). This norm functions as the highest principle of the image of thought, positing "the unity of a thinking subject" whose manifold acts converge on self-identical objects: "For Kant as for Descartes, it is the identity of the Self in the 'I think' which grounds the harmony of all the faculties and their agreement on the form of a supposed Same object" (DR 133). Kant comes close to challenging the image of thought insofar as he discovers the heterogeneity of the faculties of imagination, understanding, and reason. But rather than using this insight to critique the principle of common sense he instead multiplies it by granting to each of the three faculties a domain in which it determines the form of the unification of thought. Thus each of the three *Critiques* has its own common sense: a "logical common sense" determined by a legislative understanding, a "moral common sense" determined by a legislative reason, and an "aesthetic common sense" determined by the free play of the imagination (DR 137; cf. KCP 68). *Critique* then amounts to nothing more than ensuring that the diverse faculties function in a harmonious rather than disharmonious manner in each of thought's three domains. In each of its avatars, common sense has its telos in the recognition of a self-identical object by a self-identical subject. Thus common sense in general is the principle by which thought has its destiny in recognition. Not only does recognition as re-cognition tend to confirm pre-existing prejudices, but by its very form it subordinates difference to identity. For this reason, Deleuze characterizes the Kantian image of thought – as Nietzsche did – as inherently "moral" in character. Despite its genuinely revolutionary potential, the Kantian critique overturns nothing: "*Critique* has everything – a tribunal of justices of the peace, a registration room, a register – except the power of a new politics which would overturn the image of thought" (DR 137).

To abandon the principles of common sense and good sense would be to open the way for a very different doctrine of faculties, one that was anarchic and conflictual in character rather than legislative and harmonizing. Kant came close to discovering such a condition of the faculties in his account of the violence that reason does to the imagination in the judgment of the sublime. But even here he shrinks back, allowing a "dissension" between the faculties to become an "accord" (KCP 51). A genuine suspension of the dogma of common sense would reveal the inherently anarchic relation among the faculties. Again Deleuze suggests that Kant's mistake was to derive the transcendental from the empirical rather than identifying its "superior" form: "The transcendental form of a faculty is indistinguishable from its disjointed, superior or transcendent exercise. . . . The transcendent exercise must not be traced from the empirical exercise precisely because it apprehends that which cannot be grasped from the point of view of common sense" (DR 143). Thus it is necessary to pursue a "superior empiricism" or "transcendental empiricism," that is, an empiricism that has as its object not the sensible per se but rather the *being* of the sensible, not that which can be imagined but the *being* of the imaginable, etc.: "What is it that can only be sensed, yet is imperceptible at the same time? We must pose this question not only for memory and thought, but also for the imagination ... transcendental empiricism is the only way to avoid tracing the transcendental from the outlines of the empirical" (B 30; DR 143–4; cf. 55–6).

According to Deleuze, Kant's philosophy is not a philosophy of difference but of representation. Thus it is governed by four concepts whose function is to tame difference: identity, opposition, analogy, and resemblance, the "four branches of the Cogito" on which "difference is crucified" (DR 138). Deleuze suggests that these concepts are merely derivatives (predicables) of difference itself: "*Opposition, resemblance, identity and even analogy are only effects produced by these presentations of difference*, rather than being conditions which subordinate difference and make it something represented" (DR 145). Deleuze associates these "four iron collars of representation: identity in the concept, opposition in the predicate, analogy in judgement, and resemblance in perception" with the four-fold distinction that Foucault detected in the classical episteme, namely, "articulation," "attribution," "designation," and "derivation" (DR 262, OT 201). But whereas Foucault read Kant as calling attention to the limits of the classical conception of representation, Deleuze reads Kant as adhering to the philosophy of representation. In a section of the first *Critique* entitled "On the Amphiboly of the Concepts of Reflection," Kant identifies four pairs of concepts in terms of which representations can be reflectively compared with each other: identity/difference, agreement/opposition, inner/outer, and determinable/determination (CPR A261/B317). These are the very concepts that Deleuze associates with the philosophy of representation. Kant criticizes Leibniz for failing to ask whether the representations we compare belong to sensibility or understanding. By neglecting this question, Leibniz was led to think that he could establish the reality of an intelligible world of simple substances – his so-called "monadology." In showing that his arguments rested on a confusion of intuitions with concepts, Kant purports to show that a genuine transcendental philosophy must limit itself to accounting for conditions for the possibility of experience, not to providing an account of things in themselves. But if the Kantian conception of possible experience is illicitly derived from the dogmatic image of thought, as Deleuze argues it is, then it becomes necessary to reassess Leibniz's metaphysics.

For Deleuze, the problem with Kant's A Deduction is not that it attempts to go back to an absolutely primordial time-constituting consciousness; on the contrary, the problem is that it has its true point of departure in its telos, namely, the synthesis of recognition. Moreover, it is the very form of recognition, rather than a reliance on empirical examples, that makes the deduction psychologistic: "The form of recognition has never sanctioned anything but the recognisable and the recognised; form will never inspire anything but conformities" (DR 134). Here one would have to ask whether Husserl escapes this difficulty. In the static analyses of the *Ideas*, the form of common sense does seem to be predominant insofar as Husserl emphasizes the identity of objects apprehended through different modes of presentation (perception, memory, judgment, etc.). In order to carry out a genuine critique, phenomenology would have to suspend the norm of common sense, thereby bringing into view the disparity of different mental acts. Whether Husserl goes this far or not would depend on how he takes up the genetic problems of phenomenology, and in particular on whether these analyses are governed by the telos of recognition or not. In *Difference and Repetition*, Deleuze notes that Husserl, like Bergson, was able to go back to the idea of consciousness as a genuine "multiplicity" (DR 182). But in *The Logic of Sense* (*Logique du sens*, 1969), he suggests that "the Husserlian genesis" remains under the sway of "an originary faculty of *common sense*" insofar as it is guided by the telos of "the Kantian object $= x$" (LOS 97). Thus Husserl's version of the A Deduction ends up being no less psychologistic than that of Kant: "What is evident in Kant, when he directly deduces the three transcendental syntheses from corresponding psychological syntheses, is no less evident in Husserl when he deduces an originary and transcendental 'Seeing' from perceptual 'vision'" (LOS 98).

In carrying out his own reworking of the A Deduction, Deleuze follows Heidegger in regarding the three syntheses of apprehension, reproduction, and recognition as the constitution of the present, past, and future. But instead of grounding this account in a rereading or reworking of the Kantian schematism, he looks to the role played by repetition in the sensible manifold itself. At the most primordial level of experience is a "passive synthesis" by which repetition in the pure flow of sensations (or hyle) constitutes a kind of transcendental "habitus," the capacity for acquiring habits (DR 72). Thus the "living present" would have its origin in habitus itself, the principle governing the synthesis of apprehension. The question as to why it is that the present passes (a question that Sartre addresses in *Being and Nothingness*) is equivalent to the question of why a second synthesis takes place. To answer this question, Husserl appealed to the retentional structure of consciousness, i.e., to the fact that past presents are retained in consciousness *as* past. By contrast, Deleuze suggests that there is a "pure past" which does not have to wait upon the present. It is constituted by the second synthesis, which Deleuze takes to be governed by the transcendental principle of "Mnemosyne" (DR 80–1). Like Bergsonian memory, the pure past co-exists with the present. Likewise, there is a "pure" future that also co-exists with the present and which is constituted by "a third synthesis" that is ruled by the principle of the Eternal Return (DR 85).

According to Deleuze, Kant's mistake was to construe this third synthesis as a synthesis of recognition, as if having a future coincided with the ability to apprehend past presents. Yet despite this fundamental shortcoming, it was Kant who opened the way to a completely new conception of the future, insofar as he "introduced time into thought as such" (DR 87). For Descartes, the subject who exists *in* time is not fractured *by* time. More precisely, if the "undetermined" Cartesian subject can be "determined" in accordance with

the concept of the "I think," this is because there is no essential difference
between the two. What Kant does is to show that thought can only be
determined in accordance with the "determinable" form of time, and that for
this reason the subject is irreducibly split: "time moves into the subject, in
order to distinguish the Ego from the I in it" (KCP ix).

> The consequences of this are extreme: my undetermined existence can be
> determined only *within time* as the existence of a phenomenon, of a
> passive, receptive phenomenal subject *appearing within time*. As a result,
> the spontaneity of which I am conscious in the "I think" cannot be under-
> stood as the attribute of a substantial and spontaneous being, but only as
> the affection of a passive self which experiences its own thought . . . being
> exercised in it and upon it but not by it.
>
> (DR 86)

Thus, like Hamlet, Kant discovers a time that is "out of joint" (DR 88;
KCP vii).

Deleuze claims that Kant's discovery of the out-of-jointness of time
should have led him to dismiss the claims of rational psychology and rational theology altogether (DR 87). Instead, and despite his critique of dogmatic metaphysics, Kant salvaged a problematic use for the ideas of the soul
and God. According to Deleuze, Kant shrinks back at the precise moment
when he retroactively projects the "I think" – a result of passive synthesis –
back to the beginning, as if the synthesis of apprehension were active and
sensibility were merely a medium of receptivity. Deleuze regards this as a
last-ditch effort to rescue the philosophy of representation:

> It is impossible to maintain the Kantian distribution, which amounts to a
> supreme effort to save the world of representation: here, synthesis is
> understood as active and as giving rise to a new form of identity in the I,
> while passivity is understood as simple receptivity without synthesis.
>
> (DR 87)

Henceforth Kant conceives of synthesis as the process by which a spontaneous understanding determines an indifferent object of receptivity. This is
the same mistake that Sartre accused Husserl of making.

In order to avoid this error of "subreption," Heidegger tried to return to
Kant's account of the schematism, identifying the imagination as the hidden
root of the two stems of human cognition. Deleuze pursues a different strategy, turning to a suggestion made by Kant's contemporary, Salomon
Maimon (1754?–1800). Maimon saw that the intuition/concept dualism
leaves us with a merely "extrinsic" relation between the determinable object
(of intuition) and its determination (by a concept of the understanding).
Returning to this most primordial level of experience, Deleuze suggests
that, following Maimon, the sensible manifold should be regarded not as an

indifferent diversity of qualities awaiting synthesis by the understanding but as a reciprocal determination of intensive magnitudes each of which is to be regarded as a "differential" (DR 173). On this account, space, time, and the categories – as well as the "given" sensible manifold – would be generated within and by a *differential* manifold. Kant thought it was impossible to provide a genetic account of this sort; the sensible manifold is an empirical given, the indifferent "matter" of cognition whose source must remain an inexplicable mystery, while the "forms" of experience are pure givens. But Maimon suggests that the concept of an intensive magnitude already points to the idea of a differential genesis; it suffices to regard intensive magnitudes as differentials whose reciprocal determination gives rise to the diversity of apparently self-identical qualities that appear as the "matter" of sensation.

Kant introduced the concept of an intensive magnitude in the section of the first *Critique* entitled "Anticipations of Perception": "The **principle**, which anticipates all perceptions, as such, runs thus: In all appearances the sensation, and the **real**, which corresponds to it in the object (*realitas phaenomenon*), has an **intensive magnitude**, i.e., a degree" (CPR A166; cf. B207). Husserl implicitly appealed to this concept in suggesting that there were degrees of fulfillment or givenness that range from "zero" (in the case of an empty intention) to "one" (IPTPP 154). But Bergson rejected the very idea of an intensive magnitude, regarding it as a "bad mixture" of qualities and extensities. This left him with an analogue of the Kantian distinction between intuitions and concepts, which is to say with a merely external conception of difference. Deleuze concludes that "the Bergsonian critique of intensity seems unconvincing. It assumes qualities ready-made and extensities already constituted" (DR 239). In effect Bergson had provided a merely "static" analysis of experience in *Time and Free Will*, the equivalent of Kant's "transcendental doctrine of elements." Only in *Matter and Memory* did he find a way to treat duration and extensity as different degrees of difference itself. But what are these degrees of difference if not intensive magnitudes?

> Difference is a matter of degree only within the extensity in which it is explicated; it is a matter of kind only with regard to the quality which covers it within that extensity. Between the two are all the degrees of difference – beneath the two lies the entire nature of difference – in other words, the intensive.
>
> (DR 239)

Thus intensities or intensive magnitudes are not "badly formed composites" which must be separated according to the principles of a dualism; on the contrary, they are differentials that give rise to the difference between qualities and extensities. Bachelard claimed that "a discontinuous Bergsonism" would have to accept intensities as the quantifiable units of which qualities are composed, thereby taking account of Bernhard Riemann's

(1826–1866) arithmetization of the continuum (DD 133). Deleuze suggests that Bergson had already reached this conclusion and that Bergsonian memory is a "multiplicity" (or "manifold") in the Riemannian sense (DR 182). He also suggests that Bergson went further than Bachelard in overcoming artificial dualisms, for though Bachelard "denounces the recognition model of philosophy," he is unable to overcome "the duality of science and poetry" (DR 320 n9; F 20).

The difference between Heidegger's attempt to trace the intuition/concept division back to the schematism and Maimon's attempt to derive it from the reciprocal determination of intensive magnitudes has to do with the Kantian distinction between concepts of the understanding and ideas of reason. According to Deleuze, Maimon showed that "there is a step-by-step, internal, dynamic construction of space which must precede the 'representation' of the whole as a form of exteriority."(DR 26) That is, he showed that the representation of space is rooted in a differential field of intensive magnitudes. Following Maimon, Deleuze equates ideas with the differentials whose reciprocal determination constitutes reality (DR 174). Thus ideas are not problematic extensions of categories, as they were for Kant, but problematic objects of thought, that is, "virtual" problems that have their "solutions" in the trajectory taken by a given course of events (DR 168). This view is captured in Bergson's representation of memory as a virtual cone whose solutions are found on the plane of the present that cuts through it. To explore the realm of the virtual is equivalent to carrying out a differential analysis of ideas: "If Ideas are the differentials of thought, there is a differential calculus corresponding to each Idea, an alphabet of what it means to think" (DR 181).

Thus to trace the intuition/concept dualism back to intensive magnitudes is to show that the true vocation of thought is to think difference. By appealing instead to the transcendental schematism, Heidegger is unable to do this. Despite his "more and more pronounced orientation towards a philosophy of ontological Difference" – indicated in his claim that "Difference cannot . . . be subordinated to the Identical" – he nonetheless invokes a conception of being as the Same which fails to escape the philosophy of representation (DR xix, 65–6). Deleuze agrees with Heidegger that being is "univocal" but he maintains that the univocity of being must be said of difference itself (DR 35). That Heidegger fails to do this is revealed by his critique of Nietzsche's conception of the eternal return of the same: "Does he conceive of *being* in such a manner that it will be truly disengaged from any subordination in relation to the identity of representation? It would seem not, given his critique of the Nietzschean eternal return" (DR 66).

In his 1953 lecture, "Who is Nietzsche's Zarathustra?" (*Wer ist Nietzsches Zarathustra?*), Heidegger argues that "Nietzsche's thought of eternal recurrence" remains within the horizon of metaphysics since it fails to think adequately the Same that returns in the eternal return (N II 233). By contrast, Deleuze claims that, for Nietzsche, the thought of the eternal return is the thought not of the return of the Same but rather of the return of difference (DR 242, 298–9). As such, the eternal return pertains neither to the past nor to the present but solely to the future: "Eternal return, in its esoteric truth, concerns – and can concern – only the third time of the series. Only there is it determined. That is why it is properly called a belief of the future, a belief in the future" (DR 90). This is what Nietzsche meant when he envisioned his "philosophers of the future" (BGE 52) – not philosophers who would one day be present but philosophers for whom the future itself is the highest object of affirmation. To think the eternal return as the return of the future is to think the future itself as that which is constituted in and through the return. Whereas Habitus and Mnemosyne represent the transcendental principles governing, respectively, the syntheses of the present and the past, Dionysus is the god of the synthesis of the pure future. All three syntheses concern repetition as the being of difference, but only the future is repeated as such: "The present is the repeater, the past is repetition itself, but the future is that which is repeated" (DR 94). As the antithesis of Mnemosyne, the eternal return involves not the insomnia of incessant memory but "active forgetting" (DR 55).

In *Nietzsche and Philosophy* (*Nietzsche et la philosophie*, 1962), Deleuze reads Nietzsche as carrying out a more rigorous critique than that of Kant, one that manages to put forth "a new image of thought" based on "sense and value" rather than "truth" (NAP 104). Like Maimon and Bergson, Nietzsche offers a genetic account of the so-called conditions for the possibility of experience, tracing these to a differential play of forces: "All sensibility is only a becoming of forces" (NAP 63). "We require a genesis of reason itself, and also a genesis of the understanding and its categories: what are the forces of reason and the understanding?" (NAP 91). Heidegger resists this genetic analysis, preferring "the metaphors of gift" to "those of violence" (DR 321 n11), the schema of the future remaining guided by the horizon of the ever-renewed giving of the *Ereignis*. Once again, his decision to ground the intuition/concept dualism in the schematism rather than in the differential play of intensive magnitudes attests to a failure to follow through on his attempt to think the ontological primacy of difference. Despite these shortcomings, Deleuze praises "Heidegger's profound texts showing that as long as thought continues to presuppose its own good nature and good will, in the form of a common sense, a *ratio*, a *Cogitatio natura universalis*, it will think nothing at all but remain a prisoner to opinion" (DR 144). Heidegger challenged the image of thought by calling attention to the primacy of finitude over the image of a divine intellectual intuition. Likewise, it was Heidegger who emphasized that the third synthesis of time should not be construed in terms of a philosophy of recognition: "if the function of this pure synthesis is recognition, this does not mean that its prospecting is concerned with an essent which it can pro-pose to itself as identical but that it prospects the horizon of pro-position in general" (KAPOM 191). Nonetheless, Heidegger does not escape the image of thought, as is evident in his allowing the existential analytic of Dasein to be guided by Dasein's "pre-ontological understanding of Being" (DR 129; cf. 321 n11).

Far from being the true root of the intuition/concept dualism, schematism represents a kind of "bad mixture" that transcendental empiricism must divide into its separable tendencies (without remaining at the level of a mere dualism). In *Foucault* (*Foucault*, 1986), Deleuze reads the Foucauldian problematic of the visible and the articulable as a way of undoing an analogous bad mixture. At issue are no longer intuitions and judgments but "bodies" and "statements." Just as the Kantian schematism mediated between intuitions and concepts, so "power-knowledge" sutures articulable discourses to visible bodies. In separating out the visible and articulable tendencies that make up power-knowledge formations, Foucault unmasks the moral image of thought. In the classical episteme, all the forms of unreason were reduced to the single figure of error, which Deleuze characterizes as the negative image of recognition (DR 149). In place of this conception, he provides a "transcendental" description of "stupidity" as something that belongs to thought by right (DR 151). Kant defined stupidity as "the lack of the power of judgment" (CPR A133/B172). But this is to conceive of stupidity merely as the possibility of error. For Deleuze, stupidity represents thought's confrontation with "the indeterminate, but the indeterminate in so far as it continues to embrace determination" (DR 152).

In "Theatrum Philosophicum," an essay on *Difference and Repetition* and *Logic of Sense*, Foucault claims that the conceptual determination of objects of intuition marks the moment when thought excludes the possibility of its own stupidity (LCMP 188). Something analogous occurs in Descartes when he rules out the very possibility of his being mad. But just as the exclusion of madness represented another kind of madness, so the exclusion of stupidity represents another kind of stupidity. Foucault concludes that there is something profoundly stupid about determination itself: "Underneath the ovine species, we are reduced to counting sheep. This stands as the first form of subjection" (LCMP 182). Deleuze's transcendental empiricism provides a way of going back to a kind of "zero point" at which stupidity still appears as such and not yet merely as the error of unintelligence. To return to this zero point is to encounter "the terrible revelation of a thought without image" (DR 147). Sartre referred to the anxiety that consciousness undergoes in discovering that it is a pure spontaneity wholly distinct from the recognizable psychic objects with which it ordinarily identifies. Sartre's description of consciousness as a kind of subjectless transcendental field is taken up in Deleuze's conception of a "plane of immanence," the locus of the primordial syntheses of time. Sartre characterized consciousness as a hole or "pool" of nothingness within the immanence of sheer being. Deleuze, like Bergson, rejects the being of negativity in favor of the being of difference (DR 170). Thus instead of characterizing subjectivity as a hole in being, he describes it – following Heidegger and Merleau-Ponty – as a "fold" (F 110). Like Bergson, Merleau-Ponty also sought to go beyond static conditions of possibility to genetic conditions of actuality, invoking the "vertical" fold through which thought becomes flesh, thereby opening up the "horizontal" difference between the visible and the articulable (F 110).[16] Foucault also spoke of a "fold in being," but according to Deleuze he rejected the concept of intentionality as "too pacifying," conceiving of the horizontal relation between the visible and the articulable as an "interlacing" of competing forces, "a battle between two implacable foes" (OT 20; F 112–13). The question is whether thought has its proper destination in the fidelity to givenness or in the affirmation of difference. Insofar as the latter requires a critique of the image of thought, Nietzsche saw that it must disturb and not reassure: "Philosophy does not serve the State or the Church, who have other concerns. It serves no established power. The use of philosophy is to *sadden*. A philosophy that saddens no one, that annoys no one, is not a philosophy. It is useful for harming stupidity, for turning stupidity into something shameful" (NAP 106).

Notes

1 Cf. CPR B128, where Guyer and Wood translate *Schwärmerei* not as "fanaticism" but as "enthusiasm."
2 Cf. RRT 17, where "enthusiasm" again translates *Schwärmerei*.
3 In this view, the fact that it is impossible to say whether two "qualia" are identical or different would not count as an objection to their existence. Likewise, for Bergson it is not consciousness per se but memory that is the salient feature of the mental.
4 Against Mill's claim that we derive our concept of number from the sensible perception of aggregates of objects in space, Frege observes that not every collection of objects is a spatial aggregate. If Mill were right, it should follow that "it is really incorrect to speak of three strokes when the clock strikes three, or to call sweet, sour and bitter three sensations of taste" (FR 9–10). In defense of Mill, Bergson could have said that when we think of the strokes of the clock as three, or of several sensations as three, it is only because we have projected them into space. Moments of duration are not external to one another like distinct parts of a spatial aggregate; rather, they interpenetrate one another in a way that eludes all spatial representation. Likewise, only insofar as we subject our lived experience to a spatial analysis does it seem possible to separate out isolated sensations of sweet, sour, and bitter. Perhaps the concepts of sweet, sour, and bitter are three, but the qualities they name are not.
5 In *Time and Free Will*, Bergson characterized the "homogeneous time" of the physicist as "a fourth dimension of space," an imaginary representation that is useful from the point of view of the intellect but which falsifies lived duration (TFW 109).
6 Russell, *A History of Western Philosophy*, pp. 803, 793. Cf. OKEW 31ff.
7 I am indebted to Jean Tan for calling my attention to the relevance of these lectures in the present context.
8 Thus for Husserl there is no significant difference between the "synthetic" and "analytic" approaches that Kant says he followed in, respectively, the first *Critique* and the *Prolegomena* (PTAFM 60).
9 In the second *Critique*, Kant does put forth a "table of the categories of freedom," but these pertain to the *object* of practical freedom – just as the

categories of the understanding pertain to objects of experience – rather than to the existential structure of Dasein as care (CPrR 193–4).

10 Likewise, for Husserl, it is only through the eidetic variations of "free phantasy" that the phenomenologist is able to identify invariable features of experience.

11 For Kant, God is precisely that being who – since his intuitions are intellectual rather than sensible in character – does *not* have to wait for sugar to dissolve in water. According to his biographers, the elderly Kant had an aversion to having to wait for coffee, expressing the hope that in the next life – for which, however, one could only wait – having to wait for coffee would no longer be necessary.

12 Cf. both the precritical "Concerning the Ultimate Ground of the Differentiation of Directions in Space" (*Von dem ersten Grunde des Unterschiedes der Gegenden im Raume*, 1768) and the postcritical "What is Orientation in Thinking?" (*Was heißt: Sich im Denken orientiren?*, 1786).

13 Cf. Nietzsche's reference to "the madman as the mask and speaking-trumpet of a divinity" (D 14).

14 No wonder Foucault called Pierre Klossowski's *Nietzsche and the Vicious Circle* (*Nietzsche et le Cercle Vicieux*, 1969) – an attempt to connect Nietzsche's madness to the thought of the eternal return – "the greatest book of philosophy" (NAVC vii).

15 Cf. DIAE 54, where Foucault attributes to Macbeth the insight that "the dream . . . murders sleep." The distinction between the "I will die" and the "I am dead" is prefigured in Foucault's description of the difference between the *memento mori* of the Middle Ages and the Renaissance characterization of madness as the "*déjà-là* of death" (MC 16). According to Foucault, in the classical period, one was not considered to be mad if one merely *imagined* that one were dead, but only if one *believed* it (MC 93).

16 Deleuze expresses sympathy with Merleau-Ponty's characterization of Cézanne as "the painter par excellence," but he interprets Cézanne, like Francis Bacon (1909–1992), as a painter of "sensations" rather than of the flesh of the world (FBLOS 156 n1, 32–3).

2 The problem of the relationship between heteronomy and autonomy: to what does the feeling of respect attest?

According to Kant, the answer to the question, "What should I do?," is provided by the categorical imperative, the universal moral law that has its origin in pure practical reason. To follow the categorical imperative is to subordinate one's desire for happiness – i.e., the totality of one's inclinations – to the duty to follow subjective rules, or maxims, that have the form of law. Insofar as one gives these rules to oneself, to act from duty is to act autonomously. By contrast, to allow independently given incentives to determinate the rules one follows is to act heteronomously. As members of the phenomenal realm of nature, our wills are unavoidably subject to such pathological incentives, but when we act we must think of ourselves as autonomous members of an intelligible kingdom of ends. The first thinker to highlight the difficulties that arise from such a divided conception of the will was the German philosopher Arthur Schopenhauer (1788–1860). In contrast to Kant, who, despite his moral argument against hedonism, tries to reconcile reason's demand that we obey the moral law with the inclinations' demand for sensuous gratification, Schopenhauer offers a pessimistic argument against hedonism, maintaining that true contentment can be found only in the complete renunciation of desire, the source of all human suffering. In this view, virtue consists not in willing autonomously, but in not willing anything at all. Nietzsche responds to this nihilistic conclusion by renouncing the Kantian opposition between appearances and things in themselves. If will to power is all that there is, then the supposed opposition between reason and pathological incentives of the will is illusory. Every action is autonomous insofar as it arises from the spontaneity of the will, but fundamentally heteronomous in that it is impossible for the will to will otherwise than it does. By providing a genealogy of the feeling of respect, the affective correlate of the categorical imperative, Nietzsche reveals the "pathological" roots of morality itself. Freud complicates this account by calling attention to the role played by the death drive in the genesis of the superego. Lévi-Strauss offers a different explanation than Freud of the normative force of the prohibition of incest, but like Freud he emphasizes the ineluctability of submission to the law. Going back to Nietzsche, Bataille affirms the sovereignty of transgression, an experience that Blanchot characterizes as essentially literary in character. Like Bataille and Blanchot, Levinas attests to an experience of alterity that undercuts the ego's false pretension to autonomy, but unlike them he seeks to preserve a distinction between the immanent violence of the will to power and ethical transcendence toward the good. Lacan problematizes this distinction by noting a secret complicity between transgression and fidelity to the moral law, while his critics – Althusser, Deleuze and Guattari, and Kristeva – sustain the desire to subvert a law that they perceive less as normative than as normalizing. For Derrida, finally, the obligation of hospitality bears witness to the interminability of the condition of autonomous heteronomy.

2.1   Kant's fact of reason

> Virtue and that part of philosophy
> Will I apply that treats of happiness
> By virtue specially to be achiev'd.
> (*The Taming of the Shrew*,
> I, i, 18–20)

In the *Critique of Pure Reason*, Kant criticized Locke for sensualizing concepts and Leibniz for intellectualizing appearances. Likewise, in the *Groundwork of the Metaphysics of Morals* (*Grundlegung zur Metaphysik der Sitten*, 1785), he criticizes empiricist moral doctrines for sensualizing the will and rationalist moral doctrines for intellectualizing the inclinations. The common mistake made by both is to subordinate the intrinsic dignity of a pure will to the value of an object outside it. To correct this error, Kant insists that the only thing that is good absolutely or "without limitation" is a "good will," by which he means a will that acts "from duty" (G 49, 53). To act from duty it is not sufficient to comply with what the moral law commands, for actions that *merely* accord with duty are motivated by inclinations rather than by "respect" for the law (G 55). A will not subject to the "pathological" influence of the inclinations would always necessarily act in conformity with duty, and as such would be "holy" (G 67). No human being can be called holy because, as finite beings with needs, our wills are unavoidably subject to the influence of inclinations. For us, holiness is the ideal that the moral law – the categorical imperative – commands us to strive for.

Imperatives that are merely "hypothetical" (rather than categorical) direct the will to act in order to attain an object posited by an inclination (G 67). As such, they make gratification the "determining ground" of the will. Some hypothetical imperatives are "assertoric" in the sense that they can be ascribed to everyone as "counsels of prudence." Their universality derives from the fact that all sensuously embodied rational beings desire happiness. Others are "problematic" in that they bear on possible objects of desire; the precepts that they prescribe to the will are "rules of skill." In contrast to both of these pathologically (i.e., sensuously) grounded imperatives, the categorical imperative is a "command" that holds irrespective of whatever claims the inclinations make upon us (G 68–9).

Kant claims that all rational beings are aware of what specific duties the categorical imperative commands. He distinguishes between "perfect" and "imperfect" duties – i.e., between those that are unconditionally binding and those whose applicability to specific cases depends on circumstances – and between "duties to oneself" and "duties to others." These two distinctions cut across each other, so altogether there are four different kinds of duties: perfect duties toward ourselves (such as the duty not to commit suicide); perfect duties toward others (such as the duty never to make a false promise); imperfect duties toward ourselves (such as the duty to cultivate our talents); and imperfect duties toward others (such as the duty to be benevolent) (G 73–5).

Kant gives several different formulations of the categorical imperative. The first tells us which "maxims" or subjective practical principles it is permissible for the will to act upon: *"act only in accordance with that maxim through which you can at the same time will that it become a universal law"* (G 73). We know that it is wrong to kill ourselves or to make false promises because it is impossible to will it to be a universal law that everyone did these things (since such an order would undermine itself). Likewise, we know that we have a duty to cultivate our talents and to be benevolent toward others, for although a world in which no one did these things is conceivable, a will that posited such a world "would conflict with itself" (G 32). Thus the first version of the categorical imperative specifies the "form" of a morally permissible maxim but not its "material" object. In order to make explicit the requirement that no such object be the determining ground of the will, the second version states that it is our duty to treat all rational wills as ends in themselves rather than as means to ends set by the inclinations: *"So act that you use humanity, whether in your own person or in the person of any other, always at the same time as an end, never merely as a means"* (G 80). Put together, these two expressions of the categorical imperative give rise to a third that is based on the idea of a "kingdom of ends" in which all co-existing rational wills would be autonomous (i.e., self-legislating) members: "act only *so that the will could regard itself as at the same time giving universal law through its maxim"* (G 84).

Thus the categorical imperative is based on a principle of autonomy. By contrast, imperatives that are hypothetical are based on a principle of "heteronomy" in that they bind the will to something other than itself – i.e., the inclinations (G 83). This is the problem with empiricist and rationalist moral doctrines. Empiricist moral doctrines base the worth of an action on "physical or moral feeling" (G 90). In the *Critique of Practical Reason*, Kant characterizes both physical and moral feeling as "internal" subjective determining grounds of the will (CPrR 172). The idea that our actions should be motivated by the desire for *physical* happiness was advocated by the ancient Hellenistic philosopher Epicurus (*ca.*341–270 BCE). Kant admires Epicurus for restricting his conception of happiness to that which accords with virtue, but he faults him for subordinating the latter to the former (CPrR 173). In principle, Epicureanism is the most dangerous of all the heteronomous moral doctrines because it subordinates the will to selfish hedonistic ends

(G 90). Somewhat less objectionable is the view of the Scottish philosopher Francis Hutcheson (1694–1746), that actions should be motivated by moral sentiment, for it takes into account the welfare of others. But Hutcheson's doctrine, like that of Epicurus, would still make moral principles subordinate to the desire for happiness. Rationalist moral doctrines have the merit of recognizing the priority that virtue ought to have over happiness. They locate the *objective* determining ground of the will either in the internal idea of a perfect will – the view of Wolff and the ancient Stoics – or in the external idea of "the will of God" – a thesis advocated by Christian August Crusius (1715–1775) (CPrR 172). Of the two, Kant regards Crusius's as the more objectionable doctrine because it makes the idea of the moral law subordinate to an independently given theological conception of the divine will (G 91). Without the guidance of the moral law, any such conception is subject to caprice.

Kant's criticism of Crusius's "theological morality" echoes Socrates's argument in Plato's *Euthyphro* that holiness or piety cannot be defined as what is pleasing to all of the gods. Just as Socrates suggests that we should say that the gods love the pious because it is pious – rather than that the pious is pious because the gods love it – so Kant argues that our conception of God as a holy will from whom the categorical imperative issues must be derived from our prior acquaintance with the moral law itself: "So far as practical reason has the right to lead us, we will not hold actions to be obligatory because they are God's commands, but will rather regard them as divine commands because we are internally obligated to them" (CPR A819/B847). Provided that we fashion our idea of God on the basis of our prior acquaintance with the moral law, it is permissible and even necessary to think of our obligations as divine decrees. We then represent God as the sovereign in the kingdom of ends, that is, as a supreme moral being who gives laws without being subject to any. But we must not conceive of God as capable of commanding anything that conflicts with the categorical imperative. According to Kant, when Abraham heard a voice commanding him to sacrifice his son, he should have concluded that the voice could not be that of God (RRT 283n; cf. 124, 204).

The Stoics avoided the problems of theological morality by basing their conception of virtue on an *internal* idea of a perfect will. Kant regards this as the least unacceptable of the heteronomous moral doctrines. But apart from our independent awareness of the moral law – from which all conceptions of the good must be derived – the concept of perfection is "empty" (CPrR 190; G 91). Lacking the capacity for an intellectual intuition of the good itself, the only content that we can provide for the concept of perfection – apart from our prior grasp of the categorical imperative – is empirical (CPrR 173). Thus the Stoic doctrine can become efficacious only by intellectualizing some pathological object of the inclinations, treating it as the determining ground of the will. The mistake made by both rationalist moral doctrines is more difficult to expose than that made by the empiricist doctrines, because the latter explicitly make happiness the determining ground of the will, while the former do so only implicitly. But even if it were possible to have a direct intellectual intuition of the good, the idea of perfection could only motivate the will heteronomously by appealing to the incentive of either desire (for the good) or fear (of a just God) (G 91; CPrR 173).

Just as in the first *Critique* Kant identified the pure concepts of the understanding (categories) in terms of which we could know objects of experience, so in the second *Critique* he identifies pure practical "categories of freedom" in terms of which we think "the concepts of the good and evil" (CPrR 193). And just as the categories could be applied to the sensible manifold only through the intermediary of the schematism, so the categories of freedom can be applied to a "manifold of *desires*" only through the intermediary of the "typic of pure practical judgment" (CPrR 192, 194). Unlike the schematism, which was supplied by the imagination, whose pure time-determinations were homogeneous with both sensibility and the understanding, the typic must rely on the intermediary of the understanding, whose concept of a law of nature (considered only with respect to its form) is homogeneous with both the idea of the moral law and the idea of an autonomous will (CPrR 195). In representing ourselves as subject to "laws of freedom," we treat nature as subject to our will rather than the other way around (CPrR 175). In the first *Critique*, pure speculative reason synthesized not the sensible manifold – the task of the understanding – but a manifold of laws of the understanding. Analogously, pure practical reason is incapable of directly determining a material object for the will but must determine which maxims of the understanding can be used to determine such a material object. Just as thoughts without content are empty and intuitions without concepts blind, so a moral law without determinate maxims would be empty, while maxims without the guidance of the categorical imperative would be morally blind.

For the categories of the understanding, it was necessary to supply a "deduction" – i.e., a demonstration of both their purity and their applicability to appearances. But according to Kant, a deduction of the categories of freedom is both unnecessary – insofar as our awareness of the purity of the moral law is an unimpeachable "fact of reason" that guarantees that it is possible for us to do what duty commands – and impossible, because we cannot trace the origin of the moral law back to a higher ground (CPrR 164, 198). However, we can deduce *from* the moral law the existence of a unique, non-pathological feeling that serves as an incentive to morality, namely, the feeling of respect.

Insofar as we are subject to the influence of the inclinations, we are guided by a principle of "self-love," which, when made into an overriding principle of action, is "self-conceit." Consciousness of the moral law "restricts" self-love by allowing us to seek our own happiness only to the degree that this is consistent with obedience to the moral law. But it "*strikes down* self-conceit altogether," for it demands of us nothing less than a practical revolution by which we abandon our selfish motive for happiness in favor of the moral incentive to act from duty. Considered negatively, the pure feeling that corresponds to this awareness is one of "humiliation"; but considered positively as the subjective acknowledgment of the authority of the moral law, it is respect (CPrR 199). Kant emphasizes that "respect for the law is not the incentive to morality; instead it is morality itself subjectively considered as an incentive" (CPrR 201). Just as the typic tells us how to determine whether a particular action *accords* with the moral law, so an action done out of respect for the moral law enables us to say that it was performed *from* duty. It is impossible to know whether anyone has ever genuinely acted out of respect for the law because every action that accords with duty might be performed because of some hidden pathological motivation. Indeed, we know that every phenomenal appearance – including human actions – can be explained in terms of heteronomous laws of nature. But since heteronomy in the order of appearances is compatible with autonomy in the noumenal kingdom of ends, to strengthen our resolve to live virtuously it is good to look for examples of individuals who have withstood the incentive of happiness for the sake of virtue (CPrR 263). While it is true that we cannot know whether anyone has ever acted from duty, respect for the moral law is omnipresent even in evil-doers since it is nothing but subjective awareness of the fact of moral obligation.

Kant resolved the third antinomy by arguing that, although every action we perform necessarily follows from our "empirical character" in nature, this fact did not contradict the possibility that, as things in themselves, we were responsible for our "intelligible character" (CPR A538/B566ff.). From a merely speculative point of view, this was all that reason could accomplish. But from a practical point of view, our consciousness of the moral law shows that we are in fact free. We cannot extend our speculative insight into the nature of our freedom because mere consciousness of the moral law does not provide us with an intellectual intuition of ourselves as noumenal agents. But for practical purposes alone, reason is able to extend its cognition beyond the bounds of possible experience. Kant characterizes the concept of freedom as "the *keystone* of the whole structure of a system of pure reason," because it unites the speculative and practical interests of reason by pointing the way to solutions to the other two outstanding problems of the first *Critique*, namely, the immortality of the soul and the existence of God (CPrR 139).

Just as speculative reason encountered an antinomy when it demanded an unconditioned condition for every series of conditions in the order of appearances, so an antinomy arises when practical reason seeks an unconditioned object of the will, namely, "the *highest good*" (CPrR 227). As pathologically motivated beings with practical reason, we have an interest both in virtue and in happiness. The ancient Hellenistic philosophers believed that there was an "analytic" connection between the concept of virtue and the concept of happiness, but they disagreed about which of the two was primary (whence the antinomy). For Epicurus, the pursuit of happiness logically entailed the pursuit of virtue; for the Stoics, the pursuit of virtue was sufficient for happiness. To resolve this disagreement, Kant argues, first, that the connection between the concepts of virtue and happiness is synthetic rather than analytic. Second, he claims that while the Epicurean doctrine is *"absolutely false"* (for reasons indicated above), the Stoic doctrine is "only *conditionally false*" (CPrR 232). It is false to think that virtue is sufficient for happiness *in nature*, because the most we can expect from acting virtuously is a merely negative "intellectual contentment" that is not the same as gratification of our morally permissible desires (CPrR 234). But because nature is only the realm of appearances, it is conceivable that in the intelligible kingdom of ends, happiness is apportioned in accordance with moral worth. Kant concludes that insofar as we have a practical interest in promoting the highest good for human beings, it is necessary to posit the existence of "a *highest original good*" – i.e., God – who guarantees "the possibility of the *highest derived good* (the best world)" (CPrR 241). In other words, the only way of resolving the antinomy of practical reason is to posit the existence of God, as well as the immortality of our souls – both to support our hope for happiness commensurate with virtue and because we can only expect to achieve holiness of will through "endless progress" (CPrR 238, 240). Thus what for speculative reason were mere "hypotheses" turn out for practical reason to be necessary "postulates" (CPrR 254). The interests of reason in its speculative vocation remain distinct from those that pertain to its practical employment, but the latter must take precedence over the former (CPrR 238). Hence speculative reason is prompted – but not coerced – to a "moral faith" in the reality of God and the immortality of the soul (CPrR 255–6). In contrast to the theological morality of the rationalists, such a "moral theology" is practically necessary for "it is only with religion that the *hope* of happiness first arises" (CPrR 245). Kant regards Christianity as superior to the Hellenistic doctrines in that it grounds the possibility of the highest good in the idea of God rather than on the basis of the human will alone (CPrR 242–3n).

In *Religion within the Boundaries of Mere Reason* (*Die Religion innerhalb der Grenzen der bloßen Vernunft*, 1793), Kant argues that, from a speculative point of view, we cannot understand how imperfect moral creatures such as ourselves could attain holiness of will without divine assistance. However, from a practical point of view, we cannot expect divine assistance to compensate for our own evil dispositions. Thus it is necessary to hope for grace while at the same time believing that our salvation depends upon works alone. In order to sustain this double point of view, the idea of divine benevolence must be subordinated to the idea of divine justice. Just as in his political philosophy Kant characterizes a "right of pardon" as "the most equivocal of all the rights exercised by the sovereign," so he acknowledges God's capacity to forgive while emphasizing the inexorable justice of a God who punishes or rewards solely on the basis of moral desert (PW 160). The

Christian idea of hell is salutary because it would be wrong to think that God forgives all wickedness (EOAT 224).

The paradox of believing in a sovereign who is both unforgiving and merciful is explored in Shakespeare's *Measure for Measure*. At the beginning of the play, the Duke of Vienna laments that he has forgiven so many crimes that the citizens no longer obey the law. To remedy this situation, he pretends to leave the city, putting the strict and seemingly virtuous Angelo in his place. True to expectations, Angelo condemns to death a man named Claudio for impregnating his fiancée. When Claudio's sister Isabella asks Angelo to pardon her brother for his misdeed, Angelo refuses on the grounds that "Mine were the very cipher of a function,/To fine the faults whose fine stands in record,/And let go by the actor." To this, Isabella responds: "O just but severe law!" (II, ii, 39–41). She goes on to argue that there is no human being who is not in need of *undeserved* mercy. Angelo refuses to yield, but soon finds himself tempted by his desire for Isabella, to whom he promises to pardon Claudio if she will sleep with him. When the Duke finally reappears, it is Angelo who stands in need of forgiveness, and true to her principle, Isabella now pleads on *his* behalf. Just as Angelo refused to pardon Claudio, so the Duke at first refuses to pardon him – thereby reinstating the necessary gap between justice and mercy – relenting only when it is discovered that Claudio is still alive and that Angelo has slept not with Isabella but with *his* (ex-)fiancée, Mariana. He is forgiven not so much for having succumbed to temptation as for having held to too strict a moral standard. During his brief reign, the population of the local prison swells to such a size that one wonders if anyone in Vienna is still at large. Were God like Angelo, everyone would end up in hell "for the rebellion of a codpiece" (III, ii, 115).

Kant repudiates the "moral asceticism" of the Stoics, not only because it expects too much of us (we are not God and so cannot be perfect) but because it denigrates the inclinations which *"considered in themselves* . . . are *good"*: "to want to extirpate them would not only be futile but harmful and blameworthy as well; we must rather only curb them, so that they will not wear each other out but will instead be harmonized into a whole called happiness" (MOM 597; RRT 102; cf. G 104). We have an indirect duty to promote our own happiness as well as that of others to the extent that this is consistent with duty. Though we know a priori that performing our duty will be painful, we should not lacerate ourselves in an effort to live up to an unattainable ideal. It is enough to strive for ever-increasing moral improvement over time, knowing that it would take an infinite duration (in a non-temporal afterlife) to achieve holiness of will. So long as we do so strive, worldly happiness within the bounds of morality remains a legitimate aspiration. No one is "diabolically" evil in the sense of being capable of making evil itself into the principle of his or her actions, for even evil-doers have respect for the moral law. But all human beings are "radically evil" insofar as our wills are subject to the pathological influence of the inclinations (RRT

80, 82). Just as the forgiving Duke must disappear behind the strict Angelo before reappearing, so for Kant the God of mercy must remain hidden behind the God of justice. This principle holds not only for the way we judge ourselves, but for the way that we judge others – i.e., a rational being striving to act from duty is entitled not just to hope that good people will be happy but also to expect that wicked people will be punished. Forgiveness is a duty, but it should not be confused with *"meek toleration* of wrongs" (MOM 578).

2.2   Nietzsche's genealogy of the ascetic ideal

'Tis torture, and not mercy.
(*The Tragedy of Romeo and Juliet*,
III, iii, 29)

Instead of treating the categorical imperative as an unimpeachable and a priori "fact of reason," Nietzsche suggests that it is a highly questionable product of a complex history. In *Beyond Good and Evil* and *On the Genealogy of Morality: A Polemic* (*Zur Genealogie der Moral: Eine Streitschrift*, 1887), Nietzsche argues that Kant failed to carry out a genuine *"critique* of moral values" because, like all other moral philosophers, he dogmatically accepted "morality itself" as "given" rather than as "problematic" (OGOM 8; BGE 97–8). A genuine critique of practical reason requires a careful psychological study of the motives of moral philosophers, for "Even apart from the value of such claims as 'there is a categorical imperative in us,' one can still always ask: what does such a claim tell us about the man who makes it?" (BGE 99). In insisting that all human beings necessarily feel respect for the moral law, Kant simply purports universality for a personal idiosyncracy: " 'What deserves respect in me is that I can obey – and you *ought* not to be different from me' " (BGE 100). But if moral principles are ultimately derived from felt incentives of the will, it follows that each should have "*his own* categorical imperative" (AC 132).

Just as he replaced the question, "What can I know?," with the psychological question, "What in us demands truth?," so instead of raising the normative question, "What should I do?," Nietzsche poses a diagnostic one: "Under what conditions did man invent the value judgments good and evil? *and what value do they themselves have?*" (OGOM 5). Drawing on his background in philology, Nietzsche argues that, in all languages, the word for "good" was originally used by an aristocratic nobility to characterize everything that they affirmed. By contrast, the antithetical label "bad" referred to those "base" individuals who were incapable of affirming themselves. Only with *"the slaves' revolt"* inaugurated by the Jews did "slave morality" come to prevail over "master morality" (OGOM 19; cf. BGE 108, 204). Nietzsche characterizes the ancient Jews as a "priestly people" who were filled with *ressentiment* (resentment) toward others (OGOM 18). They were able to exact an "imaginary revenge" on their enemies by inverting the values that had prevailed in master morality (OGOM 21). Whatever their enemies called good, they called "evil," thereby enabling themselves to affirm as good what their enemies called bad. It is crucial to the psychology of slave morality that self-affirmation presupposes such a reactive denigration of the values of others. While the masters' characterization of others as bad was a mere "afterthought" to their primary act of affirmation, the slaves' designation of others as evil was their creative "deed" par excellence (OGOM 24). The contrast here is not so much between autonomy and heteronomy, for according to Nietzsche there is no such thing as free will (TOTI 35). Rather, master morality has its origin in the spontaneity of a will that cannot will otherwise than it does – i.e., in an experience of heteronomous *autonomy*, while slave morality arises "when **ressentiment** itself turns creative and gives birth to new values" – i.e., in an experience of autonomous *heteronomy* (OGOM 21). The latter is exemplified in "the philosophy of Kant," which Nietzsche pithily characterizes as "the civil servant as thing in itself established as a judge over the civil servant as appearance" (TOTI 67).

For Nietzsche, Christianity not only inherits a morality that is based on hate; it disguises it as a religion of love. This duplicity is manifest in the teachings of Paul – "the genius of hatred" – whose proclamation of the good news of eternal salvation is betrayed by his fervid promise that unbelievers will suffer eternal damnation (AC 164). Far from being a mere corollary of the hope that good people will be rewarded for their good deeds, the expectation that others will suffer eternal torment motivates the belief that "good" people will go to heaven. Traces of this idea survive in Kant's insistence that we must not think that evil people are forgiven for their sins. In Christian morality, the instinct for cruelty that in antiquity found expression in festivals is redirected inward in the form of "bad conscience" (OGOM 60–1). This is why "the categorical imperative smells of cruelty" (OGOM 45).

The ancient festival of cruelty has a close affinity with the Greek experience of tragedy. In tragedy, a spectacle is staged on behalf of a spectator who takes great satisfaction in witnessing suffering. In the festival, passive beholding gives way to active participation: "To see somebody suffer is nice, to make somebody suffer even nicer" (OGOM 46). Just as the Apollonian tragic image can be thought of as an original schema or symbol for concepts of the understanding, so the festival provided a primordial figure for Kant's "typic" of morality. And just as the decline of Greek tragedy eclipsed the aesthetic origin of reason itself, so the slave revolt masks the true origin of the "moral law." By encouraging the Greeks to reflect on their own instincts – i.e., to ask themselves, "What should I do?" – Socrates himself contributed to the slave revolt (BGE 103–4). Nietzsche also traces the capacity for reflection to the period in man's "pre-history" when he inflicted suffering on himself not just to burn something in his memory but to create the very faculty of memory, which ran counter to his natural instinct of "active forgetfulness" (OGOM 38, 41).

Nietzsche detects a certain "voluptuousness" in Kant's description of the feeling of respect (OGOM 92). Not only is the sense of suffering that Kant associates with this feeling rooted in the reversal whereby spontaneous cruelty toward others is turned around on the subject itself; the very idea of the subject with an "interior" psychic life has its origin in "this uncanny, terrible but joyous labour of a soul voluntarily split within itself, which makes itself suffer out of the pleasure of making suffer" (OGOM 64). At the heart of this phenomenon is what Nietzsche calls "the ascetic ideal," the paradoxical appearance of life turned against itself (OGOM 93). Since even the ascetic ideal must be a manifestation of the will to power, Nietzsche seeks to identify its value for life. But the ascetic ideal represents different things for different people; in artists and philosophers, for example, it is pressed into the service of some higher end. What especially interests Nietzsche is its value for the "ascetic priest," the type of individual for whom the ascetic ideal appears to be an end in itself. According to Nietzsche, it is the ascetic priest in whom *ressentiment* becomes creative for the first time: "an ascetic life is a self-contradiction: here an unparalleled *ressentiment* rules, that of an unfulfilled instinct and power-will which wants to be master, not over something in life, but over life itself" (OGOM 91). So understood, the ascetic priest is a kind of perverse double of the noble aristocrat, for although he is unable to affirm anything in a genuinely autonomous way – "'autonomous' and 'ethical' are mutually exclusive" – he seeks to impose his will on others (OGOM 40). Toward this end, he exploits "the *herd instinct*": "wherever there are herds, it is the instinct of weakness that has willed the herd and the cleverness of the priests that has organized it" (OGOM 13, 106).

Nietzsche condemns the hateful ascetic priest for hypocritically espousing the love of one's neighbor. Only the noble aristocrat is capable of such love: "here and here alone is it possible, assuming that this is possible at all on earth – truly to '*love* your neighbour'" (OGOM 24; cf. 107). In the name of such a higher love, Nietzsche opposes to the Christian ethic of mercy a *merciless* ethic of "severity and hardness" (OGOM 52; BGE 205). Thus it is not the smell of cruelty per se that he finds repellent in the categorical imperative, but its hypocrisy: "This workshop where *ideals are fabricated* – it seems to me just to stink of lies" (OGOM 31). In contrast to the false friendship that is rooted in the commonality of the herd, Nietzsche imagines a true friendship based on the "*pathos of distance*": "In a friend one should have one's best enemy. You should be closest to him with your heart when you resist him" (BGE 201; Z 56).

2.3   Freud's diagnosis of superegoic cruelty and his speculative anthropology

We band of brothers
(*The Life of Henry the Fifth*,
IV, iii, 60)

Following Nietzsche's lead, Sigmund Freud (1856–1939), the founder of psychoanalysis, also tried to peer into the workshop where values are made, that is, into the unconscious. According to Freud, some mental representations are unconscious in the merely "descriptive" sense that the subject is presently unaware of them. But others are actively repressed and so unconscious in the "dynamic" sense (GPT 49–50; EATI 4–6). The aim of psychoanalysis is to help individuals negotiate the psychic difficulties – such as neuroses and psychoses – that arise from the dynamical conflicts between the instinctual forces that animate repressed mental representations and the instinctual forces that repress them. In his 1895 "A Project for a Scientific Psychology" (*Entwurf einer Psychologie*, first published in 1950), Freud proposed a neurological model that was intended to explain how repression worked. But he soon abandoned this model in favor of a "metapsychological" explanation that was neutral with respect to questions concerning its physical instantiation. Freud's metapsychology has three tasks: first, to provide a "topographical" picture of the division of the "psychical apparatus"; second, to explain the psychic "dynamics" that give rise not only to repression but to the topographical divisions themselves; and third, to describe the "economic" processes whose aim is to "discharge" painful excitations (GPT 130).

In *The Interpretation of Dreams* (*Die Traumdeutung*, 1900), Freud suggests that every dream represents the fulfillment of an unconscious wish or desire. To explain the mechanism of dream formation he supposes that the mental apparatus is divided into systems that function like the several parts of a "compound microscope or a photographic apparatus" (IOD 574). The images of such an instrument are located at "ideal points, regions in which no tangible component of the apparatus is situated" (IOD 575). The same may be supposed for the location of mental representations. Just as a camera takes in light and then produces a photograph, so the mental apparatus begins by taking in stimuli and ends in "motor activity" (IOD 576). However, it does not merely take snapshots of the present; it also stores them in memory. Freud speculates that conscious perception and memory take place in two different parts of the mental apparatus and that representations which appear in one of the two regions do not appear in the other. Thus there would be a division separating the "permanent traces" of memory – located in the interior of the apparatus – from the fleeting appearances of conscious perception (IOD 577). While we are awake, there is a normal progressive path by which conscious stimuli give rise to muscular innervations. But when we sleep – and so are not engaged in practical activities – a "regressive" route can be followed by unconscious memory traces that conjure appearances which seem to be caused by external objects impinging on our senses. This is what it means to dream. What enables dreaming to take place is the fact that, between the region of the unconscious and the perceptual consciousness that accompanies motor activity stands an intermediate region which Freud calls the "preconscious" (IOD 580). To it belong thoughts that are not strictly unconscious but which are ordinarily kept apart from consciousness by a "censoring" agency of some sort (IOD 581). When we sleep this censorship is relaxed, allowing the thoughts into consciousness. As they travel a regressive route to give rise to the dream images that will represent them, these thoughts become distorted by genuinely unconscious representations that have been actively repressed before they were allowed to enter consciousness. The crucial aspect of what Freud calls the "dream-work" concerns not the preconscious thoughts that find expression in the "manifest content" of the dream, but the way in which these thoughts are distorted so as to be given "plastic" form (IOD 311). Through the semantic overloading of "condensation" and the "displacement" of an affective charge from a repressed representation to an associated representation, the dream-work enables repressed material to work its way into a dream's representation of a preconscious thought (IOD 312ff., 340ff.). To interpret a dream is to unravel the dream-work. Insofar as psychoanalysis seeks to undo the work of repression, it helps to bring unconscious ideas into – or under the control of – the preconscious so that they can then become conscious (IOD 617). Dreams are not the only examples of compromises between the repressive and repressed aspects of the psychic apparatus. Jokes, "inadvertent" slips of the tongue or pen and other "parapraxes" also lend themselves to psychoanalytic interpretation.

Freud conjectures that, prior to the advent of repression, the undifferentiated mental apparatus is governed by an "unpleasure principle" or, equivalently, a "pleasure principle," that is, by an a priori tendency to discharge excitations by the shortest possible – i.e., "most economic" – route (IOD 639). Some of these excitations arise from the external world, but others arise from instinctual pressures from within the psychic apparatus. Since it is impossible to eliminate the latter altogether, the pleasure principle must follow a "principle of constancy" by which the apparatus strives to keep the level of excitations at as low a level as possible (as opposed to eliminating them altogether) (IOD 604). Repression arises only when the most economic route to discharging excitations can no longer be taken, or rather when something within the psychic apparatus seeks to prevent an excitation from being discharged. The dynamical tensions that result from such conflicts divide the psyche into an unmodified part that is still governed by the pleasure principle and a part that has come under the sway of the "reality principle" (GPT 24). To the extent that it is governed by the reality principle, the modified part of the psyche becomes engaged in "reality-testing," the sampling of perceptual excitations from the external world for the sake of negotiating the obstacles that it places in the way of the functioning of the pleasure principle.

So long as the psyche is governed by the pleasure principle alone, mental representations take the form of "primacy process" hallucinations. Only when the solipsistic pleasure principle fails to be adequate to its task of discharging excitations is a part of the apparatus prompted to take an interest in reality so that suffering may be avoided. This corresponds to a shift from "primary process" imagining to "secondary process" reasoning (IOD 640). To the extent that the reality principle also aims at a reduction of suffering, it functions as an extension of the pleasure principle. But insofar as it provides the apparatus with motives for deferring gratification, it stands in opposition to it. Thus the transition from the pleasure principle to the reality principle marks the beginning of repression and the division of the apparatus into separable regions. Henceforth barriers separating the unconscious part of the apparatus from the preconscious and the preconscious from consciousness function as censors, preventing repressed mental representations from discharging their associated charges. These representations attempt to circumvent the censorship by facilitating new pathways toward discharge. It is this dynamic struggle between repressing and repressed forces that gives rise to the various psychic disturbances that psychoanalysis tries to cure. Prior to developing his theory of the unconscious, Freud treated a significant number of patients, mostly women, who were diagnosed as "hysterics." At first he thought that each of them had been the victim of an early childhood seduction, but later he came to believe that all of the various "transference neuroses" – notably hysteria (which he subdivides into various types such as "anxiety hysteria" and "conversion hysteria") and obsessional neurosis (which, in his case study of the Rat Man, he characterizes as a "dialect" of hysteria) – result from a conflict between distinct psychic instincts.

Without reducing the psychic instincts (or "drives") to biological instincts, Freud vaguely characterizes the former as "representatives" of the latter (GPT 87). In his first attempt to put forth a theory of the drives, Freud supposes that corresponding to the biological distinction between an organism's instinct to survive and its instinct to procreate – tendencies that can impel it in two different directions – are "ego instincts" and "sexual instincts." In the course of early childhood development, the various external pressures that comprise the "Oedipus complex" lead to the repression of sexual instincts that, until then, had freely manifested themselves since infancy. In this way the ego instincts gain the upper hand, giving rise to a "latency period" that stretches from the end of the Oedipus complex (around the age of six) to the onset of puberty, when the sexual instincts begin to manifest themselves again.

In its rudimentary form, the Oedipus complex represents a conflict between the sexual and ego instincts that is played out as a relationship between the subject and its parents. From the standpoint of what he later calls the "complete" Oedipus complex (EATI 28), a child of either sex will treat one of its parents as a sexual object and the other as a rival. To work through the Oedipus complex is to accede to the external demand that one renounce whatever "object choice" has been made and replace it with an "identification" of some sort – i.e., the choice of a sexual object must be replaced by an ego identification. Thereafter, until puberty, the ego instincts predominate over the sexual instincts. Freud's generalized version of the complete Oedipus complex allows for all possible permutations of this scenario. That is, given Freud's assumption of "constitutional bisexuality," it is possible for a boy (or girl) to choose either his (or her) mother or father as a sexual object and then to replace this object choice with an identification with either parent (EATI 26). In those cases where a child ends up identifying with the parent of the same sex, the revival of the sexual instincts in puberty will manifest itself in heterosexual object choices, and, when the child identifies with the opposite-sex parent, in homosexual object choices. Though Freud's description of the complete Oedipus complex seems to allow for exactly eight distinguishable trajectories, it is further complicated by a distinction between primary identifications that are formed prior to the Oedipus complex and secondary ones that set in with its dissolution. Some of these secondary identifications are characterized as regressions to primary identifications. Complicating matters still further is Freud's suggestion that in the earliest "oral" stage of infancy, there is no difference between object choice and identification (EATI 23). Only later does this difference emerge as that between the desire to "*have*" and the desire to "*be*" an object (GPAE 47).

The distinction between having and being plays an important role in Freud's account of the different ways in which girls and boys work through the Oedipus complex. As a subject with a penis, a boy who has chosen his mother as a sexual object "has" something that he does not want to lose. Fear of being castrated by his father prompts him to abandon this object choice. Thus the boy's Oedipus complex is dissolved when his ego instincts repress his sexual instincts in order to ward off the threatening consequences that might arise from giving them free rein. Since the girl "lacks" a penis, she has no fear of being castrated, but according to Freud, she too suffers from a "castration complex," one that is based on "envy for the penis" (NILOP 155). Thus her motive for abandoning an Oedipal object choice is not fear of being castrated but the desire to acquire a penis by bearing a child. For both sexes, the Oedipus complex is resolved when the child internalizes the prohibition of incest through secondary identification with the father, thereby acquiring the rudiments of a moral conscience. According to Freud, men tend to have a stricter sense of morality than women because their identification with the father tends to be stronger and because their traversal of the Oedipus complex is typically filled with greater anxiety.

An adult's character is largely determined by how the Oedipus complex was traversed in childhood and how the sexual instincts reappear during puberty. Neurotics accept reality and then attempt to flee it, psychotics deny reality and then attempt to reconstruct it, and so-called normal people work at transforming a reality they neither flee nor deny (GPT 204). Because of the different ways in which they resolve the Oedipus complex, men are more prone to obsessional neurosis and women to hysteria. Each of these neuroses results from an ineffectual repression, specifically when a repressed representation threatens to manifest itself in consciousness in an insufficiently disguised form. In such cases the "return of the repressed" leads to fresh efforts at repression that are only partially successful. The resultant neurosis represents an unstable "compromise formation" that differs from a dream or parapraxis in that it requires a great psychic effort for the ego to keep the repressed content at bay. The main difference between obsessional neurosis and hysteria is that, while the latter concerns the return of a repressed sexual instinct, the former involves a regression to the "sadistic" stage that succeeds the oral stage of early childhood development. Thus in obsessional neurosis it is not a sexual instinct but a hostile ego instinct that has undergone repression and which now threatens to return. Whereas hysteria tends to manifest itself either in phobic reactions to external objects (anxiety hysteria) or in bodily symptoms (conversion hysteria), obsessional neurosis expresses itself through the development of an especially strict moral conscience and a felt need to perform ritual actions that unconsciously aim at both gratification of the repressed instinct and expiation for such gratification. Freud's case studies of little Hans, Dora, and the Rat Man illustrate his assessment of the basic structures, respectively, of anxiety hysteria (phobia), conversion hysteria, and obsessional neurosis.

Differing from hysteria and obsessional neurosis, both of which result from a failed effort to repress socially prohibited instinctual urges, are the various psychoses that arise from an opposite reaction to the conflict between the demands of the instincts and the demands of external reality. In these cases an effort is made to repress or "flee" from external reality itself. Just as neurotic symptoms emerge not through primary repression but through the return of the repressed and the subject's efforts at a secondary repression, so psychotic symptoms in illnesses such as paranoia and schizophrenia (or "paraphrenia") emerge not in the initial fleeing from reality but when a "return of reality" threatens and the subject meets this threat through desperate efforts to create his or her own version of reality (GPT 41; cf. 204). In his "Psycho-Analytic Notes on an Autobiographical Account of a Case of Paranoia (Dementia Paranoides)" (*Psychoanalytische Bemerkungen über einen autobiographisch beschriebenen Fall von Paranoia (Dementia Paranoides)*, 1911) – an analysis of the memoirs of Daniel Paul Schreber (1842–1911) – Freud identifies "projection" as the crucial mechanism by which something intrapsychic is treated as if it came from an object in the external world. Schreber's delusions of persecution are explained in terms of a series of unconscious mental operations by which an unconscious homosexual desire – represented linguistically as "I love him" – is transformed first by reversal into "I hate him" and then by projection into "He hates me" (GPT 33). In an analogous manner, the schizophrenic recreates external reality through sensory hallucination (GPT 46).

In "On Narcissism: an Introduction" (*Zur Einführung des Narzissmus*, 1914), Freud suggests that the distinction between sexual instincts and ego instincts might be artificial, since it is possible for the former to be directed either toward an external object or (as in narcissism) toward the subject's own ego (GPT 57–8; cf. TAT 111). Thus the only crucial distinction to be drawn is that between "ego libido" and "object libido": "only where there is object-cathexis is it possible to discriminate a sexual energy – the libido – from an energy pertaining to the ego-instincts" (GPT 59). The libido is to be understood as a single sexual energy whose "reservoir" is the ego and which can be directed outward or withdrawn inward like the "pseudopodia" of a "protoplasmic animalcule" (GPT 58). This account implies that the subject can react to the forsaking of an external object choice either through identification or by substituting its own ego for the lost object. To accommodate this second possibility, Freud modifies his original topographical picture of the mind. Identification still represents the way in which the subject models its ego on that of another person, but substitution for an abandoned object divides the ego into an "ego ideal" (or "ideal ego") and the unmodified ego proper (GPT 74). The ego ideal proposes itself to the libido as an object of love, while the ego both aspires to its ideal and reproaches itself for failing to live up to it. Freud conjectures that this is the origin of the sense of conscience, and that the functions of repression and reality-testing should be credited to the ego ideal rather than to the ego (later reversing himself on this point) (GPT 74; EATI 22n).

The idea that the phenomenon of moral awareness is rooted in the division of the ego is developed further in Freud's essay, "Mourning and Melancholia" (*Trauer und Melancholie*, 1917). Under "normal" circumstances, the ego reacts to the loss of an object by carrying out a "work of mourning," the slow and painful process of undoing each of the many cathexes or "investments" that had linked it to the lost object (GPT 165–6). After a period of time, the grieving subject is able to enjoy life again. By contrast, melancholia manifests itself as a seemingly interminable process of mourning for the loss of something unconscious: "he knows whom he has lost but not *what* it is he has lost in them" (GPT 166). Freud suggests that instead of withdrawing its cathexes from the lost object, the melancholic "incorporates" it into itself in a way that seems to involve both identification and object choice, or rather to blur the distinction between the two. As such, incorporation represents a regression to the oral stage of early childhood development when the external world was taken to consist only of things to be eaten or not eaten. As in the case of narcissism, melancholic incorporation leads to the setting up of an ego ideal that the ego is reproached for failing to live up to. Freud hears this reproach in Hamlet's "use every man after his desert, and who shall scape whipping?" (though perhaps it is more explicitly conveyed in his subsequent words: "O, what a rogue and peasant slave am I!") (GPT 168; II, ii, 529–30, 550). Freud suggests that the melancholic's self-accusations are actually directed at the lost object, for whom the subject had experienced ambivalent feelings of both love and hate (GPT 169; cf. TAT 77). By identifying itself with this object, the ego is able to deflect – and so make manifest – an aggression that would otherwise remain unconscious. Crucial to this dialectic is the paradoxical fact that the suffering melancholic enjoys his or her suffering because it represents an opportunity for gratifying an unconscious sadistic impulse (GPT 172). In those cases where melancholia is succeeded by mania, Freud supposes that after the subject's aggression has been spent, its libido (which has now been detached from the lost object) turns back toward the ego, so that mania would in effect represent a kind of narcissism (GPT 179).

Insofar as narcissism and melancholia illustrate the genesis and functioning of an ego ideal, they are especially stark instances of the typical process by which individuals acquire a sense of moral conscience. But there is one feature of melancholia that still needs to be explained, namely, the extreme severity with which the ego ideal chastises the ego. In his original theory of the psychic instincts Freud had been able to suppose that just as love is rooted in the sexual instincts, so hate, its affective opposite, is rooted in the ego instincts. It was then possible to distinguish between a "pure" sadistic impulse that would have its source in the ego and a "sexual" sadistic impulse that would arise from a commingling of ego instincts and sexual instincts. But by reducing the ego instincts to a manifestation of narcissistic libido, Freud is no longer able to explain aggression in quite the same way. In *Beyond the Pleasure Principle* (*Jenseits des Lustprinzips*, 1920), he offers a solution to this problem by returning to a dualistic theory of the instincts. But instead of reintroducing the distinction between ego instincts and sexual instincts – these are still identified with the libido or "Eros" as two manifestations of "life instincts" – he opposes both of these to a wholly unheard-of "death instinct."

As the title of his book suggests, Freud's conception of the death instinct arises from a reflection on the limits of the pleasure principle. Because the reality principle is ultimately just a modification of the pleasure principle – one that is prompted by the needs of life – it would seem as if all psychic phenomena are governed by the tendency to discharge painful excitations. Why then in certain situations do painful excitations appear to be actively sought? Originally Freud thought that any masochistic tendencies, whether conscious or unconscious, had to be explained in terms of the "turning around" of a more primordial sadistic impulse that could readily be traced to the ego instincts (GPT 91–2). But since the libido theory makes sadism just as difficult to explain as masochism there is no longer a reason to assume that sadistic trends are more primordial than masochistic trends. After reflecting on instances of an apparent "repetition compulsion" both in "war neuroses" (BPP 10) – in which patients repeatedly relive traumatic experiences in their dreams – and in play (BPP 13–15), Freud is led to make the supposition that over and above the pleasure principle that governs the life instincts there is a "Nirvana principle" (BPP 67) that governs a largely "silent" and "elusive" (EATI 41) death instinct. Here Freud is not just putting forth a new theory of the psychic instincts. More radically, he is advancing a speculative cosmology whose two opposing forces – Eros and Thanatos – are tendencies toward combination and division. By appealing to the dialectical interplay of these two forces, he is able to speculate on how life itself first developed, why all individual organisms eventually die, how multicellular organisms and sexual reproduction evolved, and why the individual members of some species tend to form societies. Since Eros and Thanatos are constantly struggling against each other, the latter seeking to destroy whatever the former creates, every achievement of life depends upon a "fusion" of forces whereby Eros somehow binds Thanatos to its own ends. In psychic life this is reflected in the subordination of the Nirvana principle to the pleasure principle, which explains why the pleasure principle seems to enjoy hegemony over all mental operations. But in fact the death instinct is always operative, even when its ends are brought into compliance with the ends of the life instincts. Only in those cases where a "defusion" of instincts occurs do we find the death instinct manifesting itself in a pure (or relatively pure) form, namely, as a tendency toward destruction.

Just as Freud characterized the ego as a reservoir of libido that could be directed either externally toward objects or internally toward the ego itself, so he imagines the death instinct as a mobile force that can be turned either toward external objects (in the form of aggression) or toward the ego (in the form of masochism).[1] Freud's new theory of the instincts enables him to complete the topographical revisions that he had begun to introduce with the distinction between the ego and the ego ideal. In *The Ego and the Id* (*Das Ich und das Es*, 1923) he introduces the term "id" (*Es*) to refer to the pre-differentiated psyche that serves as a reservoir of both Eros and the death instinct, continuing to think of the ego as that portion of the mind which, under the influence of external reality, comes to be governed by the reality principle. Though the ego is still conceived as an agency of repression, Freud now suggests that a portion of it is itself unconscious – thereby indicating that something that is not itself repressed (and so not unconscious in the dynamic sense) can remain inaccessible to consciousness (EATI 8–9). He bases this claim on the fact of "resistance," namely, the ego's apparent ignorance of its unwillingness to undo a repression. By focusing on the ways in which the ego plays a mediating role between the demands of the id and the demands of external reality, Freud provides a general account of the process by which a portion of the ego is transformed into an ego ideal or "superego." The resultant defusion of the death instinct from Eros explains not only why the melancholic's self-reproaches are so severe but why in general moral conscience manifests itself through feelings of (conscious or unconscious) guilt.

Freud assumes that every time the demands of external reality prompt the ego to force the id to give up an object choice, the ego attempts to mitigate the loss by incorporating the lost object within itself. The ego ideal or superego can then be conceived as the "precipitate" of a series of such modifications (EATI 30). This implies that the superego is essentially a compromise formation in that it represents both the demands of the id (both those of Eros and the death instinct) and the demands of external reality (notably in the form of internalized prohibitions inherited through the dissolution of the Oedipus complex). But insofar as instinctual defusion results from this process – not so much from the repression of the sexual instincts as from the "sublimation" by which they become "aim-inhibited" and so directed toward "higher" social ends that are consonant with the ends of civilization – the superego inherits a purified death drive that achieves satisfaction through treating the ego cruelly: "it may be said of the id that it is totally non-moral, of the ego that it strives to be moral, and of the super-ego that it can be super-moral and then become as cruel as only the id can be" (EATI 56). Ostensibly the ego is criticized for failing to live up to its ego ideal, but from an economic point of view this criticism is a mere pretext for the gratification of a sadistic impulse that the superego directs toward the ego on behalf of the id. Thus it is not that we feel guilty because we fail to live up to an ego ideal; rather, we reproach ourselves for failing to live up to an ego ideal *in order to* feel guilty (as if the gods were to punish unholy actions not because they were intrinsically unholy but just for the sheer pleasure of punishing mortals). This explains why "the categorical imperative smells of cruelty." As "a direct inheritance from the Oedipus-complex," it is wielded by a sadistic superego to punish the ego (GPT 198; cf. EATI 31, 49; TAT xxviii, 29). In support of this interpretation, Freud observes that it is precisely those individuals who come closest to living up to their ego ideals who feel the guiltiest. In "The Economic Problem in Masochism" (*Das ökonomische Problem des Masochismus*, 1924), he distinguishes between the relatively mild sadism associated with a superego that has been desexualized through instinctual defusion and the abnormal condition of "moral masochism" that results from a resexualization of morality: "Conscience and morality arose through overcoming, desexualizing, the Oedipus-complex; in moral masochism morality becomes sexualized afresh" (GPT 199). In order to distinguish between the contributions made by Eros and the death drive to the phenomenon of moral masochism, Freud clarifies the difference between the pleasure principle and the Nirvana principle. Originally, the pleasure principle had been characterized as a tendency toward discharging excitations. But Eros is defined by its striving for excitations. In order to preserve the idea that Eros is governed by the pleasure principle (and not by the Nirvana principle), Freud supposes that pleasure must involve some qualitative and not merely quantitative factor (GPT 191).

In *Civilization and its Discontents* (*Das Unbehagen in der Kultur*, 1930), Freud likens the superego to a "garrison in a conquered city" (CAID 84). Because it is the result of identifications and incorporations, it functions like a "foreign body" inhabiting and persecuting the ego. As such, its injunctions are fundamentally heteronomous in character. Freud regards the ego as having to struggle for autonomy; it is "a poor creature owing service to three masters," psychoanalysis being "an instrument to enable the ego to achieve a progressive conquest of the id" (EATI 58). The metaphor of the garrison in a conquered city illustrates the peculiar logic of a foreign body as something that is both included and excluded from the psyche, or rather as something that is included *as* excluded. The very concept of incorporation suggests an ingestion that does not result in digestion, the ego ideal remaining inassimilable to the ego. Kant attributed the inclinations to a "foreign impulse" that a rational subject must protect itself against: "he does not . . . ascribe them to his proper self, that is, to his will" (G 92, 104). Hence the inclinations must be confined by a will that listens only to an autonomous voice within, subjecting them to constant surveillance. But according to Freud, it is this very voice that represents a foreign body for it is nothing but an incorporation of the voice of the father.[2] To obey the moral law is not to act autonomously but to act heteronomously. Or rather, by way of marking the difference between a merely external authority and an internalized representation of an external authority, to act from duty is to act in an *autonomously heteronomous* manner. Kant would have denied that the concept of autonomy could have any pertinence in Freud's model, since the opposition between determination of the will by external coercion and determination of the will by one's own inclinations is merely a contrast between two different forms of heteronomy. But Freud is trying to show that there is no such thing as autonomy in the strict Kantian sense, that the only meaningful sense of autonomy is self-determination of the drives – thereby echoing Nietzsche's claim that the terms "'autonomous' and 'ethical' are mutually exclusive" (OGOM 40).

Thus the only meaningful way to define the opposition between heteronomy and autonomy would be in terms of the conflict between the moral demands of civilization and the individual's demand for gratification – and here Freud draws the pessimistic conclusion that the well-being of the community is necessarily paid for by the increased suffering inflicted on the individual by the superego. Only sublimation offers a way of harmonizing the instinctual aims of the individual with the moral aims of civilization. But in effect sublimation is just the process by which heteronomous demands are taken on as if they coincided with the "autonomous" demands of the drives, precisely what happens when one learns to identify with the superegoic garrison, taking its voice to be one's own. This is what Kant called the task of learning to love the law: "The highest goal of the moral perfection of finite creatures, never completely attainable by human beings, is . . . the love of the Law" (RWBMR 170). For Kant this kind of love is "practical" rather than "pathological." But Freud remains suspicious of this solution, regarding the commandment to "love one's neighbor as oneself" as an almost unbearable injunction that "is impossible to fulfill" (CAID 109). Denying that the idea of a morally good will is a priori, he supposes that the original sense of "good" and "bad" is derived from the oral stage when a child distinguishes between "good" and "bad" things to eat. The subsequent genesis of the superego marks a reversal by which what had been viewed as "bad" comes to count as "good" and vice versa. This account of a kind of "slave revolt in morality" differs from Nietzsche's only in that it appeals to a dynamic interplay between the life and death instincts, whereas Nietzsche accounts for the phenomenon of life turned against itself (ascetic values) in terms of a single drive, the will to power (CAID 83ff.).

Freud had already presented a fuller analogue to Nietzsche's *Genealogy* in *Totem and Taboo: Some Points of Agreement between the Mental Lives of Savages and Neurotics* (*Totem und Tabu*, 1913), where he attempts to demonstrate his thesis that man is not a "herd animal" but "a horde animal, an individual creature in a horde led by a chief' (GPAE 68). Drawing on both ethnographical reports of other cultures and speculative accounts of the origins of civilization put forth by J.G. Frazer (1854–1941), Wilhelm Wundt (1832–1920), William Robertson Smith (1846–1894), Charles Darwin (1809–1882), and others, Freud draws a comparison between taboo restrictions in primitive cultures and the rituals of obsessional neurotics, both of which he explains as attempts both to gratify and to expiate a prohibited desire. This suggests that obsessional neurosis represents an atavistic regression to an earlier stage of civilization, an idea that leads to the supposition that the process by which a child works through the Oedipus complex is itself an atavistic repetition of an actual stage of human history (cf. Nietzsche's reference to "a pre-history which . . . exists at all times or could possibly re-occur" [OGOM 50]). Freud conjectures that at the dawn of civilization the exiled sons of a tyrannical "primal father" banded together in order to murder him and devour his corpse, thereby authorizing themselves to engage in previously prohibited sexual intercourse with the women of his "primal horde"; thus at the dawn of human history we would have an *actual* murder, *literal* incorporation, and *consummated* incest, acts which eventually get symbolically re-enacted in the Oedipus complex. Freud supposes that the murderous brothers would have felt guilty for their crimes, particularly since their attitude toward the primal father would have been ambivalent, based not only on fear but also on love. Simultaneously liberated and guilt-stricken, they henceforth attempt both to commemorate and expiate their crimes by ritually partaking of a "totem meal" in which they slaughter and consume a totem animal that stands in for the dead father (and with which they themselves are identified), prohibiting any individual from performing these acts on their own. The resultant institutions associated with totemism, based upon the founding taboos against murdering the totem animal and committing incest, would represent both the first form of a social contract and the first form of organized religion. All that would distinguish the totemic band of brothers from the modern nation-state and modern religion would be a series of modifications involving the establishment of matriarchy, the subsequent return of patriarchy coinciding with the elevation of the dead father to the level of a divine abstraction or ideal – Nietzsche had also suggested that "inevitably the ancestor himself is finally transfigured into a *god*" (OGOM 65–6) – and the separation of social and religious functions. Freud is well aware of the conjectural nature of all this (TAT 177n), insisting that his account of the primal horde is "only a hypothesis" (GPAE 69) – much as Kant characterized his own "Conjectures on the Beginning of Human History" (*Mutmaßlicher Anfang der Menschengeschichte*, 1786), as "a pleasure trip" (PW 221). Despite these caveats, all of Freud's subsequent reflections on the nature of moral obligation are based upon this account of early human history. The superegoic guilt that we experience today is explained not in terms of the Oedipus complex alone but in terms of the originary scene of crime and expiation whose traces have somehow survived in the collective unconscious.

One reason for the implacability of the superego's cruelty is that it holds up to the ego not merely an ideal that it ought to aspire to but an ideal that it simultaneously may not aspire to – the idea being that brotherly equality is predicated on a prohibition against any individual assuming the authoritative position of the primal father.[3] Freud concludes that the Nietzschean overman represents this forgotten primal father: "He, at the very beginning of the history of mankind, was the 'superman' whom Nietzsche only expected from the future" (GPAE 71). Nietzsche had already found an equivalent of Freud's primal father in his conception of the self-affirming master. Where Nietzsche detects the transition from master morality to slave morality, Freud sees a transition from the morality of the primal father to the morality of the repentant brothers. In the last chapter of *Totem and Taboo*, Freud provides his own genealogy of Christianity – a "son-religion" that has changed the nature of the totem meal by structuring communion around the body of the expiating son rather than that of the dead father (TAT 191) – and he attempts to offer his own explanation for the "birth of tragedy": "the Hero of tragedy . . . had to suffer because he was the primal father . . . and the tragic guilt was the guilt which he had to take on himself in order to relieve the Chorus from theirs" (TAT 193). The significance of Dionysus lies in the fact that he is the divine animal totem who must be dismembered for the sake of the members of a goat-clan (the Chorus, and by extension the spectators) (TAT 194). Freud characterizes the totem meal in all its avatars as a "festival" in the specific sense of a communal transgression of social laws, a ritual in which both the mourning for the slaughtered totem animal and the subsequent feelings of "festive rejoicing" become *obligatory*: "A festival is a permitted, or rather an obligatory, excess, a solemn breach of a prohibition . . . excess is of the essence" (TAT 174). This points to an important aspect of the superego, namely, the fact that it commands not just obedience to the law but ritual disobedience as well.

In *Group Psychology and the Analysis of the Ego* (*Massenpsychologie und Ich-Analyse*, 1921) Freud suggests that the tendency of modern individuals to form anti-social groups – that is, groups that enable individuals to throw off

the ordinary social constraints which they have internalized in their ego
ideals – is an instance of an atavistic tendency *both* to return to the primal
horde *and* to repeat the festive excesses of the totem meal. The essential
feature of such a group is that it is structured around a leader who comes to
occupy the ordinarily proscribed place of the primal father; each member is
able to identify with the others (at the level of their egos) only insofar as
each puts the leader in the place of its own ego ideal. A powerful motivation
for so abandoning the moral strictures of the ego ideal is once again the fact
that it makes possible "a magnificent festival for the ego" (GPAE 81). Nietzsche had already anticipated the manner in which a leader can provide individuals with such a motivation: "the appearance of one who commands
unconditionally strikes these herd-animal Europeans as an immense comfort
and salvation from a gradually intolerable pressure" (BGE 111). Freud
regards group formation as akin to hypnotic suggestion whereby each individual acquires a set of beliefs that is immune to the critical examination of
the ego ideal, suggestion being "a conviction which is not based upon perception and reasoning but upon an erotic tie" (GPAE 76–7). Often credited
for anticipating here the social logic of fascism, Freud regards it as an ethical
imperative for the practicing psychoanalyst to resist putting himself or
herself in the position of the patient's ego ideal. Referring to this as a
"temptation for the analyst to play the part of a prophet, saviour and
redeemer to the patient," he insists that "the rules of analysis are diametrically opposed to the physician's making use of his personality in any such
manner." The aim of analysis is not "to make pathological reactions impossible, but to give the patient's ego *freedom* to decide one way or the other"
(EATI 51n). Thus the moral obligation of the analyst is not to cure an
analysand of sufferings that are themselves traceable in one way or another to
the experience of obligation but to enable the subject to respond to that
experience in an autonomous manner. But since obligation is itself something inherited from others, the true aim of psychoanalysis is to make possible an experience of autonomous heteronomy.

2.4   Lévi-Strauss's structural anthropology

Good Lord, for alliance!
(*Much Ado About Nothing*, I, i, 318)

Throughout his writings, the French anthropologist Claude Lévi-Strauss
(1908–) repeatedly likens Freud's *Totem and Taboo* to a myth that, like any
other, reveals something important about the culture to which it belongs
but without explaining anything about it. Instead of resorting to speculations about the pre-history of human culture, Lévi-Strauss relies on ethnographic reports of actual cultures whose symbolic practices he submits to
"structural analysis." While acknowledging the potential significance of "the
bringing together of ethnology and psychoanalysis," he also notes "the dis-

tressing trend which, for several years, has tended to transform the psychoanalytic system from a body of scientific hypotheses that are experimentally verifiable in certain specific and limited cases into a kind of diffuse mythology" (IWMM 5; SA 181). In his 1949 essay, "The Sorcerer and His Magic" (*Le sorcier et sa magie*), Lévi-Strauss compares the practicing psychoanalyst to a shaman who is capable of giving individuals a "sense of security," but without bringing about "real cures" (SA 183).[4] In 1962, he claims that his attitude toward *Totem and Taboo* has only "hardened" in the intervening years (T 70n), while in 1985 – in *The Jealous Potter* (*La potière jalouse*) – he attempts to situate Freud's book within the larger field of myths to which it belongs.

Like Freud, Lévi-Strauss takes the prohibition of incest to be the defining feature of human culture, observing that if a biological instinct to avoid consanguineous sex existed, no such cultural institution would be needed (TAT 153–4; ESK 24; T 94). But instead of conjecturing about the historical origins of the incest prohibition, Lévi-Strauss seeks to account for the way in which it functions in different cultures. In *The Elementary Structures of Kinship* (*Les Structures élémentaires de la Parenté*, 1949) he notes that despite its universality – which would seem to suggest that it is rooted in human biology – the incest prohibition functions not as an instinct but as a rule: "The prohibition of incest has the universality of bent and instinct, and the coercive character of law and institution" (ESK 10). He characterizes this as an "antinomic" fact, because it would appear to sanction both the thesis that it is nature that is responsible for the rule (since all other rules vary from culture to culture), and the antithesis that not nature but culture is responsible for it. Lévi-Strauss resolves this antinomy in the same way that Kant resolved the dynamical antinomies of the first *Critique*, namely, by suggesting that the truth of the antithesis is compatible with the truth of the thesis. No longer a fact of reason but a fact of culture – or rather *the* fact of culture – the prohibition of incest is that natural phenomenon by which human beings acquire sovereignty over nature: "It is the fundamental step because of which, by which, but above all in which, the transition from nature to culture is accomplished. . . . Before it, culture is still non-existent; with it, nature's sovereignty over man is ended. The prohibition of incest is where nature transcends itself" (ESK 24–5).

Thus the prohibition of incest, like the categorical imperative, attests to the fact of human autonomy, but autonomy is something that we are heteronomously determined to have by virtue of "the structure and functioning" of our brains (SA II 14). Kant could resolve the antinomy between freedom and natural causality only by distinguishing between two distinct orders of causality, one natural and one transcendent. By contrast, Lévi-Strauss tries to reconcile autonomy and heteronomy within the framework of a strictly naturalistic ontology – so much so that he later softens the distinction between nature and culture, claiming in *The Savage Mind* (*La Pensée sauvage*, 1962) that it "now seems to be of primarily methodological importance" (SM 247n). Insofar as the prohibition of incest is unconscious, it functions merely as a natural cause, determining human actions in a heteronomous manner; but insofar as it is a rule that human beings consciously invoke, it legislates actions that are genuinely autonomous. Thus the biological capacity for rule-governed behavior and our actual rule-governed practices require different kinds of explanation:

> although it may be legitimate or even inevitable to fall back upon a naturalistic interpretation in order to understand the emergence of symbolic thinking, once the latter is given, the nature of the explanation must change as radically as the newly appeared phenomenon differs from those which have preceded and prepared it.
>
> (SA 51)

Insofar as the human sciences are concerned with laws of culture, they cannot be "smoothly" reduced to biology.[5]

The prohibition of incest does not simply forbid consanguineous marriages; it manifests itself as the positive obligation of the members of a culture to exchange women in accordance with determinate rules whose logical structure is in some sense unconscious even though everyone knows how to follow them: "The prohibition of incest is less a rule prohibiting marriage with the mother, sister or daughter, than a rule obliging the mother, sister or daughter to be given to others" (ESK 481). Particular rules pertaining to the exchange of women vary from culture to culture in precisely the same way that linguistic rules do. Lévi-Strauss suggests that this is because all rules are inherently linguistic in character, the transition from nature to culture coinciding with the acquisition of language. Because language – like the incest prohibition itself – is an inherently social phenomenon, the individual's capacity to signify (the Kantian "I think") must be rooted in a cultural "we signify." Analogously, the prohibition of incest pertains to individuals only insofar as they are members of a group whose relationship to one another is defined by a "kinship system." Thus the primary subject of both cognition and duty is a collective one such as a tribe whose individual members count as cognitive and moral subjects only insofar as they occupy specific positions within it. Since kinship systems are structured in the same way that languages are, Lévi-Strauss concludes that anthropology – as well as the other "human sciences" – must be modeled on structural linguistics.

For N.S. Troubetzkoy (1890–1938) and Roman Jakobson (1896–1982), the founders of structural linguistics, all manifest linguistic phenomena are governed by unconscious rules that specify the various ways in which "phonemes" – the distinguishable sounds that serve as the building blocks of language – can and cannot be combined so as to produce meaningful speech. These rules pertain not to individual phonemes per se but to their relations with one another (SA 33–5). Lévi-Strauss's science of kinship systems is based on exactly the same principle, except that in place of individual phonemes he puts elementary kinship terms such as mother, father, son, daughter, mother's brother, father's sister, etc.: "Like phonemes, kinship terms are elements of meaning; like phonemes, they acquire meaning only if they are integrated into systems. 'Kinship systems,' like 'phonemic systems,' are built by the mind on the level of unconscious thought" (SA 34). The basic function of a kinship system is to impose the obligation of an exchange of women so that incest will be avoided. But how it accomplishes this task is just as variable as are the rules that different languages impose on phonemes. Kinship rules resemble linguistic rules in that they govern relations among a set of individuals each of which occupies a specific position in an overall structure. By isolating a small number of "elementary structures," Lévi-Strauss seeks to show how both "simple" kinship systems and more lax "complex" systems are constructed.

The method of structural analysis can be applied to any cultural phenomenon whatsoever. The first thing to do is to characterize a particular cultural product as "a relation between two or more terms, real or supposed." For example, a particular food, such as honey, can be characterized as sweet rather than bitter, and as liquid rather than solid. These "infrastructural" elements are the equivalent of phonemes or kinship terms. We then draw up "a table of possible permutations between these terms," the original phenomenon representing only one of the conceivable outcomes. Finally, we treat this table – not the phenomenon in question – as "the general object of analysis" (T 16). This procedure has a certain affinity with the process by which Kant derived his table of categories from the manifest structure of empirical judgments. Just as for Kant the categories were conditions for the possibility of actual experience, so, for Lévi-Strauss, structures account for an array of possibilities, only some of which might be selected in actual experience. It is possible to confirm or disconfirm a particular structural analysis by checking its "transcendental deductions" against empirical reports provided by ethnographers. Conversely, it is also possible to work from "empirical deductions" based on both ethnographic reports and naturalistic observations to systemic analyses.

Lévi-Strauss follows this method in his *Introduction to a Science of Mythology* (*Mythologiques*, 1964–1971), a four-volume study of North and South American myths. Instead of trying to interpret individual myths, he breaks them down into their elementary "mythemes" and then allows the relations among their various permutations to guide his analysis of great families of myths. Because the mythemes themselves are meaningless, it would be a mistake to try to explain what a particular mytheme might mean apart from its systemic position in a structure. Psychoanalysts make this mistake when they try to set up a one-to-one correspondence between particular dream symbols and their hidden meanings.

It would also be a mistake to remain at the level of "a purely phenomenological given, on which scientific analysis has no hold" (IWMM 41). In his

Introduction to the Work of Marcel Mauss (*Introduction à l'oeuvre de Marcel Mauss*, 1950) Lévi-Strauss credits Mauss (1872–1950) with being the first ethnologist to appreciate the need for going beyond empirical givens to underlying structures. In *The Gift: The Form and Reason for Exchange in Archaic Society* (*Essai sur le don: Forme et raison de l'échange dans les sociétés archaïques*, 1923–1924), Mauss had argued that individual cultural phenomena had to be understood in terms of the "*total social fact*" to which they belonged (Gift 5–6, 3). Lévi-Strauss interprets this idea as an anticipation of his own conception of unconscious infrastructures (IWMM 25). In the *Elementary Structures*, he had credited Mauss with showing that the giving away of wives in both primitive and modern cultures is determined in accordance with rules of reciprocity – but he also emphasized the necessity of going beyond the observable phenomena of giving, receiving, and returning to the underlying structure governing such practices of reciprocal gift-giving (ESK 52). Mauss argued that gift-giving was fundamentally different from exchange, even when the former obliged the recipient to give something back in return. Though he acknowledges that there is something paradoxical in the idea of a gift retaining its gratuitous character while simultaneously obliging its recipient to make a counter-gift – since this would seem precisely to reduce the gift to the term of an exchange – he tries to account for this paradox by ascribing a mysterious property to gifts, a property by virtue of which they ensure their economic circulation. The members of a New Zealand tribe call this property *hau*.

Lévi-Strauss objects that Mauss treats giving, receiving, and returning as if they were separate actions that somehow need to be synthesized, thereby reneging on his own insight into the total social fact. In appealing to *hau* as that which performs this synthesis, Mauss succumbs to the "danger of confusing the natives' theories about their social organization (and the superficial form given to these institutions to make them consistent with theory) with the actual functioning of the society" (SA 130). This is to allow ethnology to degenerate into "a verbose phenomenology" (IWMM 58) at the very moment when it should be pushing toward a genuinely structural analysis. Against Mauss, Lévi-Strauss claims that what makes the return of a gift obligatory is precisely the fact that reciprocal gift-giving *is* at bottom a form of exchange: "the primary, fundamental phenomenon is exchange itself, which gets split up into discrete operations in social life; the mistake was to take the discrete operations for the basic phenomenon" (IWMM 47).

Freud makes the same kind of mistake. Like structural analysis, psychoanalysis is supposed to disclose "the permanent structure of the human mind" (ESK 491). Insofar as Freud tries to fathom "the structure of the conflicts to which a sick man is prone," he keeps to this task. But in *Totem and Taboo* he forsakes the path of genuine explanation in favor of myth-making – his version of *hau*: "In the one case, the progression is from experience to myths, and from myths to structure. In the other, a myth is invented to explain the facts, in other words, one behaves like the sick man instead of diagnosing him" (ESK 492). In *The Jealous Potter*, Lévi-Strauss writes approvingly of Freud's account of the various techniques by which primary significations are transformed in dreams and other psychic phenomena. But instead of advancing to a properly structural analysis of the underlying grammar of the mind, Freud characterizes unconscious thought as pregrammatical and prelogical. The other mistake that Freud makes is to think that all symbols express a single code – specifically, a "psycho-organic code" pertaining to bodily orifices (JP 186) – when in fact every symbol is an attempt to establish a semantic relationship across two or more different codes (JP 205). As a result of these two shortcomings, Freud ends up constructing myths that are essentially just variations on the very myths he is trying to elucidate. This is equally the case for the Oedipus complex and the story of the primal father. Instead of uncovering the transformational grammar of the human mind he merely *exhibits* it in his own thinking: "The variants elaborated by Freud obey the laws of mythic thought; they respect the same constraints and apply the same transformational rules.... These rules are precisely those of a grammar he considered from the start to be nonexistent" (JP 191).

Lévi-Strauss draws a sharp distinction between the two typical characteristics of so-called primitive cultures that had been thought to comprise the totemic phenomenon: one is the principle of exogamy, the obligation for a member of one moiety or section of a tribe to take a wife from a different moiety or section (or from another tribe); the other is the supposed tendency of primitive people to identify themselves with animal totems in some way. Having already explicated the logic behind exogamy in his classification of kinship systems, Lévi-Strauss attempts in his book *Totemism* (*Le Totémisme aujourd'hui*, 1962) to explain what exactly is involved in the various practices by which members of primitive cultures classify their relationships both with one another and with the natural world in categories borrowed from nature. Claiming that the very concept of totemism is a European invention whose main function was to deny any affinity between Christian cultures and non-Christian cultures (T 3), Lévi-Strauss argues that what so-called totemism really represents is not a tendency among primitive tribes to associate particular animal or plant species with particular individuals or clans in a one-to-one manner, but rather an ability to use the relations among distinct natural kinds (of any sort, i.e., not just animal or plant species) to represent human relations. Thus it is not the resemblance between particular animal species and particular persons that is of interest to primitive thought, but the way in which the *differences* among various animal species resemble the *differences* among human beings (T 77). This distinction is crucial for it shows that totemic thinking is just as "logical" as modern scientific thinking. The only difference is that one is guided by a system of abstractions, the other by a system of natural kinds. Earlier ethnologists thought that totemism was to be explained in terms of the fact that animals are "good to eat," but Lévi-Strauss counters that animals are rather "good to think" (T 89).

In distinguishing between "totemic," "primitive," or "mythic" thought on the one hand and "abstract" or "scientific" thought on the other, Lévi-Strauss implicitly returns to the Kantian problem concerning the relationship between receptivity and spontaneity, a theme he develops at length in *The Savage Mind*. Scientific thought, exemplified in modern European cultures, can be characterized in terms of determining judgments by which objects of intuition are grouped in accordance with abstract categories of the understanding. By contrast, primitive thought, instead of using abstract categories to determine natural objects, uses natural objects to determine concrete conceptual rubrics that are then used to classify other kinds of objects. This is precisely what is accomplished in using an opposition between two species of animals to represent an opposition between two clans; in such a case the species are selected precisely because of some particular traits in terms of which they can be opposed. Thus totemic thought contains a moment of aesthetic reflection in the Kantian sense, proceeding from a mere play of cognitive faculties to the determination of natural kinds as symbols. Kant claimed that the difference between a schema and a symbol is that whereas the former enables an object of intuition to be determined in an immediate way, the latter makes possible the indirect determination of an entirely different object of reason. Thus symbolism involves a double operation, "first applying the concept to the object of a sensible intuition, and then, second, applying the mere rule of reflection on that intuition to an entirely different object, of which the first is only the symbol." For example, "between a despotic state and a handmill there is, of course, no similarity, but there is one between the rule for reflecting on both and their causality" (CPJ 226). This is precisely what Lévi-Strauss has in mind when he suggests that totemic thought is based on a reflection upon the relations holding among the elements of two series of objects. Moreover, just as Kant suggests that we make use of symbols precisely where it is impossible to have scientific cognitions, so Lévi-Strauss regards totemic or mythic thought as something that all cultures have recourse to when they come upon the limits of experience – conceived now as the limits of signification: "mythic thought . . . is inherent in the workings of the mind every time it tries to delve into meaning . . . mythic thought should not thereby be opposed to analytical reason" (JP 206). The principles of totemic classification were misunderstood because European anthropologists thought that they were attempts to explain nature when in fact they were attempts to use relations among natural kinds as logical operators: "The mistake of Mannhardt and the Naturalist School was to think that natural phenomena are *what* myths seek to explain, when they are rather the *medium through which* myths try to explain facts which are themselves not of a natural but a logical order" (SM 95).

Lévi-Strauss concludes that primitive thought is essentially "metaphorical," confirming the view of Jean-Jacques Rousseau (1712–1778) that "the first language must have been figurative" (T 102). But this is not to say – as both Rousseau and Giambattista Vico (1668–1744) had concluded

(JP 194–5) – that primitive thought is pre-logical; on the contrary, logical thought can manifest itself in either of two complementary ways, "totemic" (symbolic) or "scientific" (schematic). In those cases where individual animal species fulfill a symbolic function, they can be thought of as "zoemes," the analogues of phonemes, whose meaning is also a function of their relations to one another (JP 97). Kant himself seems to be aware of this relational criterion, for when he invokes the idea of the handmill as a symbol for a despotic state, he does so by contrasting the handmill with a living organism that can serve as the symbol for a monarchical state: thus it is the *difference* between a totemic animal and a (no less) totemic machine that stands in for the difference between monarchical and despotic European tribes.

Once a particular set of phonemes, mythemes, zoemes, or any other x-emes has been selected and put to work (Lévi-Strauss isolates elementary "gustemes" such as savory/bland to illustrate how a structural analysis of the differences between English cooking and French cooking might be pursued [SA 86]), the elements lose the character of arbitrariness that they had before being pressed into semantic service: "the linguistic sign is arbitrary a priori, but ceases to be arbitrary a posteriori" (SA 91). This explains why particular terms may come to be associated with relatively stable meanings, despite the fact that their meaning is always a function of their structural relations with other terms (for example, why a handmill can serve as a common vehicle for symbolizing a despotic state) (JP 148–9). Lévi-Strauss goes so far as to suggest that "there is no position that we more urgently need to put behind us" than the belief of Ferdinand de Saussure (1857–1913) in "the arbitrary nature of the linguistic sign" (IWMM 72 n17). Instead what is needed is "a reintegration of content with form" that "opens the way to a genuine structural analysis, equally far removed from formalism [of the Saussurean variety] and from functionalism [that is, of attempts to explain totemism in terms of either circular or vacuous speculations about its usefulness]" (T 86).

Primitive and scientific forms of thought thus represent two complementary ways of solving a problem concerning the relationship between signifiers and the objects that they signify: "a fundamental situation perseveres which arises out of the human condition: namely, that man has from the start had at his disposition a signifier-totality which he is at a loss to know how to allocate to a signified, given as such, but no less unknown for being given" (IWMM 62). Lévi-Strauss notes that there is always an "inadequation" between these two orders, "a non-fit and overspill which divine understanding alone can soak up; this generates a signifier-surfeit relative to the signifieds to which it can be fitted. So, in man's effort to understand the world, he always disposes of a surplus of signification" (IWMM 62). This is a remarkable passage because it transposes into the vocabulary of structural analysis the very problem that Kant poses in terms of the gap separating intuitions from concepts, and because, like Kant, Lévi-Strauss suggests that this gap could be adequately overcome only by a divine knower capable of intellectual intuition. Just as Kant can appeal to both schematism and symbolism as two different ways of bridging the gap, so Lévi-Strauss regards scientific thought as only one of two structurally distinct ways of negotiating the inadequation between signifier and signified, language and world. Moreover, just as Kant regards fanaticism as an illicit attempt on the part of reason to determine objects without having to go through the mediating realm of intuitive symbols, so this has its parallel in Lévi-Strauss's critique of what we might call "hypermythical" thought, the effort on the part of thinkers such as Freud to try to use mythological thinking to explain mythological thinking. The reason that Lévi-Strauss is able to liken the psychoanalyst to the shaman is that both individuals occupy social positions that are charged with negotiating the inadequation of language and world. Since every culture is faced with a problem of inadequation not just between signifier and signified but between its various "symbolic systems" or codes, it compensates for a certain inability to negotiate the transitions from one code to another by isolating specific individuals who "figuratively represent certain forms of compromise which are not realisable on the collective plane" (IWMM 16–18). These "abnormal" individuals function as "docile witnesses" who are "sensitive to the contradictions and gaps in the social structure." By virtue of their very abnormality they confirm the "normality" of the rest of the population. Without their presence on the margins of society, "the total system would be in danger of disintegrating into its local systems" (IWMM 18–19).[6]

2.5   Bataille's heterology and his transvaluation of sovereignty

"Who chooseth me must give and hazard all he hath."
[. . .] And here choose I. Joy be the consequence!
(*The Merchant of Venice*, II, ix, 21; III, ii, 107)

The idea that homogeneous social systems maintain themselves through the production and exclusion of excessive heterogeneous elements is a central theme in the early writings of the French writer Georges Bataille (1897–1962). Unlike Lévi-Strauss, for whom structuralism offered a ready-made scientific approach to this phenomenon, Bataille suggests that all conventional science reduces heterogeneity to homogeneity by specifying laws to which the heterogeneous must conform. Nietzsche objected to the very concept of laws of nature on the grounds that it represented a false interpretation of the will to power (BGE 30). Following Nietzsche, Bataille characterizes all existing science as the expression of a "servile" attitude (VOE 97; cf. 224–5). In "The Use Value of D.A.F. de Sade (An Open Letter to my Current Comrades)" (*La valeur d'usage de D.A.F de Sade (lettre ouverte à mes camarades actuels*, ca. 1929–1930), he envisions under the name of "heterology" an entirely different kind of science, one that would be, precisely, a science *of* the entirely different or "completely other" (VOE 102 n2). Instead of trying to make the heterogeneous conform to laws, heterology must be an essentially subversive science that "serves excretion" (VOE 97).

For Bataille, the homogeneous part of society is governed by a principle of production; it renders things useful for its own growth and maintenance. By contrast, the heterogeneous part is the site of expenditure and waste, containing everything that homogeneous society excludes. To liberate the heterogeneous part of society from the domination of the forces of homogeneity, a new "economic and political organization of society" must implement an "asocial organization having as its goal orgiastic participation in different forms of destruction. . . . Such an organization can have no other conception of morality than the one scandalously affirmed for the first time by the Marquis de Sade" (VOE 101). In *Philosophy in the Bedroom* (*La Philosophie dans le boudoir*, 1795), Sade (1740–1814) had admonished his contemporaries with the words, "Frenchmen, One More Effort if You Want to be Republicans!" Bataille gives this formula a Marxist twist, exhorting his readers to make one more effort if they want to be proletarians. The class struggle that Marx revealed is less a struggle for control of the means of production than it is a struggle between forces of useful consumption and forces of useless consumption – i.e., between the "tendency toward homogeneity" and the "tendency toward heterogeneity." Bourgeois subjects are no less enslaved to the forces of production than are proletarians, for although the latter are unable to enjoy the surplus value that their labor produces, the former fail to exercise their capacity for sovereign enjoyment; their consumption is never excessive, as it remains within the service of production: "the bourgeois cannot *violate the sense of proportion*" (AS III 347).[7] Against such a measured consumption, Bataille opposes a useless expenditure that would not just violate all sense of measure but would celebrate everything heterogeneous that civilization abhors: feces, cadavers, violence, madness, and so on.

Freud traced the advent of civilization to the evolutionary moment when human beings first assumed an upright posture, thereby making it possible for us to avoid having to smell our own excretory organs (CAID 54n). In his posthumously published, "The Jesuve" (*Le Jésuve*, written in 1930), Bataille puts forth an analogous suggestion, speculating on how "the reduction of the projection of the anal orifice" in human beings has its corollary in the role that laughter and tears have come to play as privileged modes of human expression (VOE 76–7). Lévi-Strauss would have no trouble locating "The Jesuve" – or "The Solar Anus" (*L'Anus Solaire*, 1931; written in 1927) – among the myths about bodily orifices that he analyzes in *The Jealous Potter*. But unlike Freud, for whom the story of the primal horde purported to be scientific rather than literary, Bataille is aware of the literary character of his myths. Freud drew a sharp distinction between art – which, like religion, presents illusions, but which, unlike religion, represents its illusions *as* illusions – and science, which claims to represent a non-illusory truth. But for Bataille the very opposition between art and science succumbs to the servility of what Nietzsche called the "will to truth."

Freud equated the unremitting furtherance of the aims of Eros with an increase in the general malaise of individuals. Likewise, Bataille regards any society based on perpetual accumulation – such as capitalism – as one in which all subjects are reduced to a condition of base servility. Like Freud, Bataille argues that every increase in social conformity leads to the increased risk of an explosion of forces of social disruption. For Freud, the tension between social constraint and instinct could only be resolved through sublimation, that is, through the subordination of desire to the demands of civilization. For Bataille, the aim of heterology is not sublimation but subversion, the deliberate transgression of moral laws. Thus to the image of an "Icarian revolt," which equates human aspiration with the soaring of an eagle, he opposes that of the "subterranean" digging of a mole who "begins in the bowels of the earth, as in the materialist bowels of proletarians" (VOE 35).[8]

Just as for Freud the superegoic repression of the instincts drew its strength from the instincts themselves – specifically from the death drive – so for Bataille the bourgeois exclusion of heterogeneity draws upon an "imperative" heterogeneous element from which it derives its force. Thus there comes about a distinction between a "high" (quasi-superegoic) heterogeneity, which functions in bourgeois society as its "sovereign" element, and the "low" (id-like) heterogeneity that this sadistic agency degrades and subjugates. Insofar as it serves the productive forces of homogeneity, bourgeois sovereignty is not genuinely sovereign in the sense of serving no end whatsoever. To achieve true sovereignty, the degraded forces of low heterogeneity must reclaim the very sadistic impulses which the forces of high sovereignty turn against them. Put otherwise, the only way to combat sadism is to adopt a Sadean ethic. In Freudian terms, it is a question of acting directly on the death instinct instead of suffering the effects of superegoic cruelty. The choice is not between cruelty toward others and cruelty toward oneself. For Bataille, there is no sharp distinction between inflicting violence and suffering violence, for the tendency toward heterogeneity manifests itself in "limit experiences" in which the boundaries between self and other disappear. Thus the distinction between Eros and the death drive becomes problematic: "it is difficult to know to what extent the community is but the favorable occasion for a festival and a sacrifice, or to what extent the festival and the sacrifice bear witness to the love individuals give to the community." Like Nietzsche, Bataille regards the festival as the privileged occasion for communal "laceration" (VOE 251).

In "The Psychological Structure of Fascism" (*La structure psychologique de fascisme*, 1933), Bataille notes that, as long as the modern bourgeois state excludes the heterogeneous part of society, it exists in "a precarious form" as "threatened homogeneity" (VOE 139). The fascist state resolves this problem by incorporating the heterogeneous part of society – i.e., the proletariat – into the fascist army, thereby transforming an element that is neither assimilable nor simply eliminable into an agency of state oppression:

"In the midst of the population, the army retains the distinction of being *wholly other*, but with a sovereignty linked to domination" (VOE 151). Like the superego, which Freud characterized as "a garrison in a conquered city," the fascist army functions as a foreign body that is included as excluded in the manner of what Foucault, inspired by Bataille, will call "the great confinement." Bataille had complained that the Surrealists reduced Sade to a mere *"foreign body,"* treating him as "an object of transports of exaltation" only "to the extent that these transports facilitate his excretion" (VOE 92). Analogously, the sadistic fascist army is used merely to inoculate the homogeneous part of society from a true Sadean ethic.

During the German occupation of France, Bataille wrote three books – *Inner Experience* (*L'Experience intérieure*, 1943), *Guilty* (*Le Coupable*, 1944), and *On Nietzsche* (*Sur Nietzsche*, 1945) – which he later planned to include in a six-volume *Summa Atheologica*. In these works, he suggests that authentic sovereignty – in contrast to its distorted manifestation in bourgeois or fascist subjectivity – can only be achieved in lacerating experiences when the subject verges on the brink of immolation, attaining the sacred at the very moment when consciousness lapses into a condition of "unknowing."

In the first volume of *The Accursed Share* (*La Part Maudite*, 3 vols, 1949, 1976), Bataille develops an economic theory based upon the idea that human history is guided not by processes of production but by processes of expenditure. Toward this end he distinguishes between "restrictive economy" and "general economy." A restrictive economy is a relatively closed system whose relations to extraneous factors are of minimal importance. The concept of a restrictive economy is a useful fiction that makes it possible to ignore the larger "general economy" to which a relatively "isolable system" belongs (AS I 19). But it is a legitimate fiction only when the extraneous factors in question are truly negligible. Bataille argues that both Marxist and bourgeois economic theories have failed to recognize the importance of taking the more general point of view. This requires taking into account the entire circulation of energy in the "biosphere," a perspective which shows that everything that happens on the surface of the earth is ultimately part of the entropic process by which the biosphere expends the excess energy that it stores up from the sun's rays. Such is the basis of Bataille's "Copernican transformation" of economic theory (AS I 25). Viewed from the narrow perspective of restrictive economy, the primary aim of a society is to increase its wealth. But viewed from the perspective of general economy, its real aim is to decrease it – just as the aim of the pleasure principle is to decrease excitations. Bataille also suggests that it is only the *excess* wealth that a society produces which must be shed, his analogue of Freud's constancy principle.

Throughout history, different strategies have been used to deal with the problem of excess wealth. Of particular interest to Bataille are those cultures that employ the practice of "potlatch," the ritual destruction of wealth that takes place in ceremonies of reciprocal gift-giving. From a restricted point of view, the aim of the potlatch is to increase wealth. This is how Mauss characterized the logic of gift-giving in general; insofar as the gift calls forth a counter-gift, it functions like a wise investment. Indeed, according to a quasi-Hegelian "cunning of reason," gift-givers always receive more than they give: "we must remain something other than pure financial experts, even in so far as we wish to increase our own wealth" (Gift 77). Acknowledging that it is paradoxical to offer a utilitarian defense of altruism, Mauss suggests that it is a question of finding the mean between extremes: "The life of the monk, and the life of a Shylock are both equally to be shunned" (Gift 69). In the specific case of the potlatch, the group that destroys the most gains the most prestige – so that even if they lose material goods, they are compensated with a symbolic good.

Bataille claims that it was his reading of Mauss's description of the potlatch that led him to formulate his conception of general economy. The fact that the potlatch aims at prestige shows how difficult it is to identify a form of useless expenditure that cannot be capitalized upon. Unlike Mauss, who exhorts his readers to be more generous on the grounds that "we run no risk of disappointment," Bataille envisions a potlatch that would truly squander everything (Gift 71). Under the present conditions of the Cold War, squandering everything represents the only way of forestalling another world war. Thus we must choose between "an acceptable loss, preferable to another that is regarded as unacceptable: a question of *acceptability*, not utility" (AS I 31). By distinguishing between acceptability and utility, Bataille attempts to avoid the paradox of the potlatch, that is, the paradox of finding a use for uselessness. However, in the preface to the second volume of *The Accursed Share*, he suggests that he did not entirely succeed in this regard: "I could not then prevent consumption from being seen as something useful" (AS II 16).

In a new attempt to locate sovereignty in the phenomenon of eroticism, Bataille proposes a number of revisions to Lévi-Strauss's account of the transition from animal nature to human culture. First, like Freud, he suggests that the prohibition of murder is just as crucial to this transition as is the prohibition of incest, the former being only one particular manifestation of a more general abhorrence of death that is also expressed in prohibitions against contact with corpses.[9] Second, he observes that not just incest but animal sexuality in general is subject to prohibition. This implies that even permitted marriages must originally have represented transgressions of a certain sort (AS II 58). Bataille concludes that all human institutions are intended to distinguish humanity from animality. Accordingly, it would be impossible for human beings to avoid violating their prohibitions without altogether ceasing to obey their animal needs. Not all transgressions involve a lapsing back into animality. On the contrary, what is most distinctively human is revealed not in obedience to human prohibitions but in their deliberate violation. Through the use of ritual transgression, festivals divide the profane world from the sacred domain of the erotic. Eroticism differs from mere animal sexuality as a dialectical "negation of the negation" differs from the originally negated state. The allure of the erotic consists not in the attractiveness of animal sexuality per se but in the appeal of transgression. By *deliberately* violating a prohibition that thereby retains its status *as* a prohibition, transgression confirms humanity's break with animality at the very moment when it appears to rescind it. The main shortcoming of Lévi-Strauss's *Elementary Structures* is that it recognizes only the first step through which humanity distinguished itself from animality (namely, prohibition) and not the second (transgression) (AS II 43).

Thus transgression is less the opposite of prohibition than its extension, at least insofar as the aim of prohibition is to break with the givenness of our natural condition as animals. Once we have made the break from nature to culture, it is the human world – i.e., our second nature – that functions as what is "naturally" given: "*the negation of nature* . . . is the negation of the given," but "as soon as nature, which a spirit of revolt had rejected as the *given*, ceased to appear as such, the very spirit that had rejected it no longer considered it as the given . . .; it then regarded nature's antithesis, prohibition, as the given" (AS II 76–7). Thus the dialectical progression from prohibition to transgression constitutes a single movement, "a constant pursuit of autonomy (or of sovereignty)" – though Bataille warns against taking "an abstract view" according to which autonomy or sovereignty would be the motive for prohibition and transgression (AS II 84). Bataille elaborates on the dialectic of givenness and transgression in the third volume of *The Accursed Share*, suggesting that "we find the *human quality* not in some definite state but in the necessarily undecided battle of the one who refuses *the given* – whatever this may be, provided it is *the given*" (AS III 343).

Insofar as he affirms "an end that would not be subordinate to any other, a *sovereign* end," Bataille seems to echo Aristotle, who in his *Nicomachean Ethics* claims that there must be some ultimately "useless" end for the sake of which everything else is useful (AS III 226). But for Bataille sovereign experience is an end that has no relationship whatsoever to subordinate ends; as pure expenditure, it occurs precisely when we renounce all utilitarian "counsels of prudence." This is why we cannot aim at having sovereign experiences, though they are the only ones in which humanity has genuine dignity. The fact that it is human dignity that Bataille takes to be at stake suggests that his conception of sovereignty is closer to Kant's conception of man as an end in itself. But, like Nietzsche, Bataille thinks that Kant does not truly regard man as an end in itself but instead treats him as a mere instrument of the moral law. In order to overcome the new type of heteronomy expressed in the categorical imperative, he asks: "how can we imagine, in spite of Kant, an ethics that does not *commit itself*, that does not place us in the service of some means?" (AS III 380). Kant characterized man as a "member" of the kingdom of ends and not as its "sovereign," reserving this latter status for God alone. But if man's dignity can be attained only in genuinely sovereign moments, then it is "practically necessary" either that there be no God or, if there is, that man rebel against him. Following a suggestion of the French writer André Gide (1869–1951), Bataille concludes that Nietzsche had to proclaim the death of God because he was "jealous" of him (AS III 375).

Thus Bataille's account of the relationship between servile and sovereign forms of experience can be regarded as a dialecticization of Kant's distinction between "heteronomous" and "autonomous" forms of the will. While prohibition issues in an initial distinction between heteronomous (animal) and autonomous (human) forms of life, it immediately transfigures the latter into a second-order kind of heteronomous existence. This explains why "an autonomous decision may have no sovereign quality at all; it may even be servile" (AS III 311). Transgression marks not the return to the heteronomy of nature but a second-order autonomy by which we transcend the heteronomous autonomy of culture. But since we can transcend the latter only by deliberately plunging ourselves back into an animality that remains, from the standpoint of culture, an object of horror, there is a sense in which eroticism represents a kind of autonomous heteronomy that would be opposed to the heteronomous autonomy ("subjugated sovereignty" [AS III 380]) of culture. The only way of attaining an experience of pure sovereignty would be for transgression to be pushed to the point at which absolutely everything, including the subject itself, were to be destroyed. Bataille thinks of this as the moment of the miraculous, where something "impossible" suddenly appears (AS II 206). We thereby enter a region that is truly "beyond good and evil": "the region where the autonomy of the subject breaks away from all restraints, where the categories of good and evil, of pleasure and pain, are infinitely surpassed" (AS II 183–4).

At times Bataille suggests that such an experience can only be represented in literature (AS III 177). Drawing on Blanchot's *Lautréamont et Sade* (1949), he locates the sovereignty of Sade's literary characters in their "utter solitude," their unconditional refusal to recognize themselves as having something in common with anyone or anything else (AS II 175; cf. LAE 125). Juliette and Clairwill isolate themselves by cultivating a fundamental apathy that leaves them indifferent not only to other persons and things but to their own pleasures and pains as well (AS II 180). This is done not in the name of the ascetic ideal but for the sake of a sovereignty whose point of departure lies in crime. Sade's characters aspire to carrying out crimes so total that nothing short of total destruction could satisfy them, and they regard as justified any imaginable cruelty that might bring them the least bit of satisfaction. In this way a second conception of pleasure arises, one that is sovereign as opposed to utilitarian (AS III 408).

Despite his admiration for this "unparalleled" literary representation of sovereignty, Bataille criticizes Sade for failing to extend his vision of sovereign experience to humanity as a whole: "The world is not, as Sade tended to represent it, made up of myself and things. But the idea he formed of rebellion is nevertheless at the limit of the possible" (AS III 253). "Nothing is more evident in reading Sade than the absurdity of a continual denial of the value of men for one another: this denial militates against the truth value of Sade's thought, involving it in the most banal contradictions" (AS II 176). Thus Bataille criticizes Sade for failing to articulate a conception of sovereign solidarity, just as he criticizes Nietzsche for confusing sovereignty with power: "Nietzsche's main shortcoming is in having misinterpreted the opposition of sovereignty and power" (AS III 453 n1). The error of both thinkers lies in a misconception about the relationship between sovereignty and subjectivity. What enables the Hegelian master to attain sovereignty is a willingness to look death in the face, to "tarry with the negative," to sacrifice everything – in contrast to the slave who becomes a slave by pulling back from the abyss, by prudentially keeping himself from going "too far." Unfortunately Hegel himself makes the mistake of equating sovereignty with mastery. True sovereignty represents that "deep subjectivity" (AS III 237) which has nothing to do with the order of objectivity because its essence is "NOTHING": "Sovereignty is NOTHING" (AS III 256). "'I am NOTHING': this parody of affirmation is the last word of sovereign subjectivity, freed from the dominion it wanted – or had – to give itself over things" (AS III 421).

By linking sovereignty to an experience of solidarity, Bataille's idea of the sovereign subject as NOTHING differs from Sartre's nihilating cogito in that the latter remains perpetually enslaved to an "in itself" over which it seeks mastery (the desire to be God). For Bataille, any construal of sovereignty as mastery is based upon the point of view of the slave. This was the mistake made by the fascists, who homogenized Nietzsche's doctrine of the will to power just as they reduced Sadism to the servile end of the domination of humanity. In the early 1930s, Bataille had advocated excessive violence as a way of combating fascism, a stance that the Surrealists denounced as "surfascist" (VOE xviii). The vicariousness of this distinction is implicitly acknowledged in Bataille's novel, *L'Abbé C* (1950), when the narrator shrinks back from the recollection of the familiarity between his brother, the Sadean priest Robert, and the sadistic butcher Henri: "all the associations that I had, up to this point, refused to make . . . are finally forcing themselves upon me – and scaring me out of my wits" (LC 130).

By linking sovereignty to an experience of solidarity, Bataille is led to contrast both Sade and Nietzsche, who sacrificed solidarity in the name of sovereignty, with Stalin, who sacrificed sovereignty in the name of solidarity. According to Bataille, Joseph Stalin (1879–1953) mistakenly equated sovereignty with the debased version of it that bourgeois society inherited from feudalism. But just as Nietzsche's ascetic priest achieved mastery through the denunciation of all claims to mastery, so Stalin renounced sovereignty in a paradoxically sovereign way (AS III 323). Hence Stalinism represents a highly ambiguous phenomenon. On the one hand, it has made possible "that return to sovereignty which is represented by all the forms of the sovereignty of others" (AS III 301). But, on the other, it "is still obsessed with primitive accumulation" in the manner of nascent capitalism (AS III

360). Insofar as true communism seeks to destroy "the bourgeois debasement of sovereign subjectivity," Bataille concludes that "nothing counts more" than "the *cause*" of communism, which he characterizes as "an obligation that falls on all men" (AS III 360, 366). This obligation is absolutely unique for it is the only one that is not servile. It cannot be expressed in the form of a categorical imperative for the very reason that, according to Kant himself, a sovereign is a being who is not subject to imperatives of any sort. Thus if there is a kind of obligation that communism imposes, it must be coincident with the exigency of sovereignty itself.

Bataille invokes the figure of "the man of sovereign art" who "occupies the most common position, that of destitution." Precisely because sovereignty is the antithesis of dominion, the man of sovereign art does not lead but rather "remains on the side of the *led*," in what it is again tempting to recognize as a condition of autonomous heteronomy (AS III 422). The distinctive feature of the man of sovereign art lies in his refusal to regard himself as superior to anyone else – except to those who imagine that *they* are superior to others (AS III 423). Thus what gives him his sovereignty is nothing else than a sense of solidarity. This attitude is less moral than aesthetic, having its privileged form of expression in literature, a kind of domain-without-dominion that epitomizes sovereignty in its purest form.

Neither servile nor claiming mastery, the man of sovereign art is drawn to a form of communism that is "literary" not in the sense that it has nothing to do with the real world but in the sense that it approaches the real world from the point of view of sovereign experience. Literature is not solitary; on the contrary, it is the domain in which sovereignty can be communicated. Bataille sought such an experience of loyalty and friendship in a series of collectives to which he belonged from 1935 to 1939: *Contre-Attaque*, *Acéphale*, and the *Collège de Sociologie*. In each of these groups – especially *Acéphale* – he envisioned the possibility of a community that would be founded on the sacrifice of one of its members. But with the outbreak of the Second World War he turns to his quasi-mystical "inner experience" and to literature as the royal road to community. For Bataille – who wrote such "transgressive" literary works as *The Story of the Eye* (*Histoire de l'oeil*, 1928) and *Madame Edwarda* (*Madama Edwarda*, 1941) – literature represents not the route to sublimation but an approach toward evil: "Literature is *communication*. Communication requires loyalty. A rigorous morality results from complicity in the knowledge of Evil, which is the basis of intense communication" (LAE ix).

2.6   Blanchot's art of discretion

> Horatio, I am dead,
> Thou livest. Report me and my cause aright
> To the unsatisfied.
> (*The Tragedy of Hamlet, Prince of Denmark*,
> V, ii, 338–40)

No one better exemplified Bataille's man of sovereign art than his friend, the French writer Maurice Blanchot (1907–2003). Following Bataille and the writer André Malraux (1901–1976), Blanchot suggests that modern art became the object of an "absolute passion" when it freed itself from external forms of sovereignty found in religion and the state (Fr 17). Art has the power "of putting an end to the world, of standing before or after the world . . . the condition of being outside the world" (Fr 33–4). For Blanchot, "the outside" represents a radical form of exteriority to which works of art – particularly works of literature – call us. To respond to this call is to inhabit the work's space as an unremitting condition of exile from the world, a condition in which we endure the "anonymous" existence of a "neuter" subjectivity: "the 'I' that we are recognizes itself by sinking into the neutrality of a featureless third person" (SOL 30). Literature plays an exemplary role in this regard because it is not just a particular form of art but the ubiquitous condition of a certain being-in-language by virtue of which we always already belong to the outside: "Where I am alone, I am not there; no one is there, but the impersonal is: the outside, as that which prevents, precedes, and dissolves the possibility of any personal relation" (SOL 31). What distinguishes the artist or writer – Bataille's man of sovereign art – is a commitment to the interminability of this experience: "the artist . . . is he for whom there exists . . . only the outside" (SOL 83). To persist in the experience of the outside – whether as reader or writer – is to participate in the communication of an incommunicable thought, the sharing of an unsharable secret. This requires a sense of discretion, the art of respecting the "secret without secret" (Fr 131; cf. 173) which is the animating passion of a particular literary work or body of works. For Blanchot, discretion is not merely one particular virtue that a writer or reader ought to exhibit; it is a fundamental "guardian power" (Fr 169) which preserves "the place of literature" (Fr 171) as the place of shared experience.

In his book, *The Space of Literature* (*L'Espace Littéraire*, 1955), Blanchot calls attention to the close relationship that literature has with death, not just because writing presupposes the absence of the one who writes but because writing is itself a way of dying – and dying a way of writing: "The writer . . . is one who writes in order to be able to die, and he is one whose power to write comes from an anticipated relation with death" (SOL 93). Thus there is a kind of "circular demand" between writing and death: "*Write to be able to die – Die to be able to write*" (SOL 94). Heidegger claimed that there was a difference between the inauthentic way in which "everyone" (*das Man*) dies a worldly death and the authentic manner in which an individual relates to death as the very limit of his or her possibility. Rather than treating this as an either/or distinction, Blanchot suggests that there is an essential "doubleness" to death, "the *doubleness* within which such an event withdraws as if to preserve the void of its secret. . . . It is death as the extreme of power, as my most proper possibility, but also the death which never comes to me, to which I can never say yes, with which there is no authentic relation possible" (SOL 155). To write so as to be able to die is to strive for an authentic death, while to die so as to able to write is to accept the anonymity of an inauthentic death as the condition for the possibility of access to literature. Writing thus retains a double relationship to death, a death that is both hidden and exposed, secret and disclosed. Whence the absolute risk that pertains to it: "each of us . . . is menaced by his Golem, that crude clay image, our mistaken double, the derisory idol that renders us visible and against which, living, we protest by the discretion of our life, but once we are dead perpetuates us" (IC 203).

Discretion is the art of protecting what remains secret in a secret that is completely divulged. As such it is a way of respecting what is authentic in a work of literature despite the fact that – or rather precisely because – it is impossible to maintain Heidegger's strict dichotomy between authentic discourse (*Rede*) and inauthentic idle talk (*Gerede*): "to give speech to this neuter movement which is, as it were, all of speech: Is this to make a work of chatter, is this to make a work of literature?" (Fr 126). To try to decipher a text's secret – as opposed to calling attention to its irremediably secretive character – would be to reduce it to idle talk despite one's best intentions. Still worse would be deliberately to characterize another's words as idle talk: "The person who calls the other a chatterbox causes himself to be suspected of a chattering that is worse still, pretentious and authoritarian" (Fr 125). Discretion protects literary works from the "homogeneous space" of culture, from an imperative to "say everything," to make everything public (Fr 71). But the secret to which discretion bears witness is not secret in the sense that it masks something radically hidden or private; on the contrary Blanchot calls it a "secret without secret" to indicate the fact that it lacks any such depth, its secrecy being a function of its very publicity: "the secret *as* secret, . . . secret in that it discloses itself" (Fr 151). Discretion's virtue therefore lies not so much in the holding back of facts as in its affirmation of a certain distance; of *The Book of Questions* (*Le livre des Questions*, 1963), by Edmond Jabès (1912–1991), Blanchot writes: "It is a book of discretion, not because he refrains from saying all that must be said, but because he holds himself back in the space or the time of pause" (Fr 226). This distance or pause separates the one who writes from himself or herself, imposing a condition of exile which writing is the attempt to share. Only in this sense is literature an effort to communicate, the aim of which is not to convey information but to affirm "a speech that is altogether *other*" (Fr 56).

Discretion makes possible a shared experience of exile, an experience that can be characterized, with Bataille, as one of community or communism – or of friendship: "He once called it *friendship*, the most tender of names. Because his entire work expresses friendship, friendship for the impossible that is man" (IC 211; cf. Fr 95–6). Blanchot's 1971 collection of essays, *Friendship* (*L'Amitié*), practices a certain art of discretion with respect to the works of Bataille, from whom he borrows two epigraphs concerning the nature of friendship and whose work he evokes in the book's opening and closing sections. In the first essay, "The Birth of Art" (*Naissance de l'art*), Blanchot discusses Bataille's *La Peinture préhistorique: Lascaux ou la naissance de l'art* (1955), which equates the advent of both transgression and art (Fr 6). Bataille's book exemplifies discretion in that "it does not do violence to the figures it nonetheless tears from the earth" (Fr 2). In the concluding essay of *Friendship* – also entitled "Friendship" and printed in a different typeface from the rest of the text – Blanchot responds to the question, "*How could one agree to speak of this friend?*," by emphasizing his own responsibility not to betray the person whom he, in a sense, has torn from the earth: "*Here discretion lies not in the simple refusal to put forward confidences (how vulgar this would be, even to think of it), but it is the interval, the pure interval that, from me to this other who is a friend, measures all that is between us*" (Fr 289, 291; cf. IC 202). In this passage, Blanchot implicitly distinguishes his own silence concerning Bataille with the indiscretion of Max Brod (1884–1968) toward the writings of Franz Kafka (1883–1924). Blanchot implies that Brod failed to attest to the "enigma" of his friend's work; with any author, the critic has a responsibility to resist "the pleasure of deciphering" and "*the worst of histories, literary history*" (Fr 244, 142, 290). In contrast to Heidegger's distinction between authenticity and inauthenticity, which concerned an individual Dasein's relationship to its own death, Blanchot's distinction between discretion and indiscretion pertains to a shared relationship to death, a relationship that the survivor is obliged to respect. This is why the obligation of discretion only increases with the other's death.

Like Bataille, Blanchot regards the demand of sovereign art as equivalent to "the communist exigency," communism being "the incommensurable communication where everything that is public ... ties us to the other (others) through what is closest to us" (Fr 64, 97, 149). In "Marx's Three Voices" (*Les Trois Paroles de Marx*), he suggests that Marx's texts are written in at least three distinct registers – philosophical, political, and scientific – each of which must be taken into account. Against Althusser's insistence on an exclusively scientific reading, Blanchot denies that there is any simple opposition between science and literature: "let us remember that no writer, even Marxist, could return to writing as to a knowledge, for literature ... becomes science only by the same movement that leads science to become in its turn literature" (Fr 100). In *The Unavowable Community* (*Communauté inavouable*, 1983) Blanchot develops his conception of a "literary communism." In *The Inoperative Community* (*La communauté désoeuvrée*, 1986), Jean-Luc

Nancy (1940–) had expressed sympathy with Bataille's conception of communism as the sharing of what is unsharable, but he also voiced concern that, by invoking an experience of sacrificial communion, the *Acéphale* group came too close to fascism. Blanchot was not a member of *Acéphale*, nor did he express any sympathy with Marxism in the 1930s; on the contrary, he was a regular contributor to the far right journal *Combat*, apparently being drawn to communism only after meeting Bataille in late 1940.

In response to Nancy, Blanchot concedes that "Death is indeed present in Acéphale," but he emphasizes the "literary" dimension of Bataille's conception of sacrifice – literary not merely in the sense that it was never meant to be put into practice but in that it was a way of representing something that could not be put into practice, namely, a certain experience of the impossible. In contrast to "Freud's reverie" of the murder of the primal father – something all too possible, even if fanciful – Bataille envisioned "a completely different kind of sacrifice, a sacrifice that would no longer be the murder of one person or of all persons, but gift and abandonment, the infinite of abandonment" (UC 58 n7; cf. F 113): "the person who could destroy in a pure movement of loving, would not wound, would not destroy, would only give"). Blanchot thinks that Bataille would agree with Nancy that community can be realized only in its own "unworking" (UC 33), that it can exist only as "a solitude lived in common and bound to an unknown responsibility" (UC 21). This is precisely what Bataille had in mind in speaking of "the community of those who do not have a community" (UC 1), namely, a certain "absence of community" (UC 15) to which *Acéphale* aspired. For both Bataille and Blanchot, community exists precisely when "community dissolves itself, giving the impression of never having been able to exist, even when it did exist" (UC 53). This happened during the student protests in Paris in May 1968, when "it was not even a question of overthrowing an old world; what mattered was . . . a *being-together*" (UC 30).

If death remains at the basis of community, this is to be understood not in the sense of sacrificial communion but rather as what Blanchot calls "mortal substitution," an impossible sharing of death (UC 11). For both Bataille and Blanchot every death is in a sense prohibited insofar as it is the object of horror, so that dying would be the exemplary instance of transgression or what Blanchot calls "the step beyond." The impossibility of sacrifice – or of any transgression – would thus be a function of the impossibility of dying authentically, while to become capable of dying authentically would be to become capable of an impossible transgression that is "radically out of reach" (IC 453 n3). Transgression is impossible not only because it purports to violate a law that is essentially inviolable, but because it always obeys a higher law governing it (SNB 24). But it is also not merely a secondary act by which an already existing prohibition would be both violated and confirmed; on the contrary, it is the primary act by which the prohibition itself would first be constituted, "producing the Law only by infraction" (Fr 166).

The step beyond can never be taken, and yet we live the perpetual immi-nence of it, eternally dying an impossible death – a condition that Blanchot likens to Nietzsche's vision of the eternal recurrence of the same (Fr 33, 35).

In *The Step Not Beyond* (*Le Pas au-delà*, 1973) Blanchot characterizes the eternal recurrence not as the permanent renewal of the present but, on the contrary, as an immediate consequence of the fact that the present as such is fractured. To say that everything that has ever happened has happened an infinite number of times and that it will again happen an infinite number of times is to specify a relationship to the past and the future, but without thereby indicating that either the "what has happened" or the "what will happen" ever *happens* in an immediate present. On the contrary, the eternal recurrence spells the ruin of presence, since nothing ever takes place except as a "re-" or "pre-" taking place:

> the event that we thought we had lived was itself never in a relation of presence to us nor to anything whatsoever . . . in the future will return infinitely what could in no form and never be present, in the same way that in the past that which, in the past, never belonged in any form to the present, has returned.
>
> (SNB 15, 22)

To think the eternal recurrence in this sense is to think a form of tempo-rality that is entirely different from either a linear conception of time as a series of nows or an existential conception of temporal ekstases that would situate the thinker within a world. The recurrence has the character of a being-outside-time-inside-time, and as such it is the temporal analogue of the outside, or simply another name for it.

To write under the exigency of the thought of the eternal recurrence is thus again to take up the position of a neuter subject forever bereft of any proper experience of "mineness." In *The Step Not Beyond*, Blanchot adopts the standpoint of a "he" or "it" (*il*) as opposed to an "I" as if by way of a strange literalization of Kant's reference to "this I, or He, or It (the thing), which thinks" (CPR A346/B404). To write from the position of the neuter subject is not so much to divest oneself of an already existing personal identity as to reveal a certain anonymity that would be constitutive of the one who writes. Writing thereby becomes less a technique of memory than one of forgetting, the aim of written traces – as opposed to determinate marks – being to erase rather than record a life. The narrator of Bataille's *L'Abbé C* writes:

> The only way to atone for the sin of writing is to annihilate what is written . . . I can, however, tie negation so closely to affirmation that my pen gradually effaces what it has written . . . I believe that the secret of literature is there, and that a book is not a thing of beauty unless it is skillfully adorned with the indifference of the ruins.
>
> (LC 128)

Likewise in *Death Sentence* (*L'Arrêt de Mort*, 1948) Blanchot's narrator says of the text he writes: "Once I am dead, it will represent only the shell of an enigma, and I hope those who love me will have the courage to destroy it, without trying to learn what it means" (DSe 30).

In keeping with his construal of the eternal recurrence, Blanchot suggests that the movement of erasure paradoxically comes before that which it erases: "Effaced before being written. If the word trace can be admitted, it is as the mark that would indicate as erased what was, however, never traced" (SNB 17). Conceived in this way, writing does not have the telos of the presence of a book; on the contrary it attests to a certain "absence of book" (Fr 281; IC 422–35), the book that it erases. Just as the aim of being-together is not the presence of community but a certain absence of community, so writing aspires not to the condition of the book – emblem of culture – but to the condition of its absence. This suggests another way of practicing the art of discretion, namely, by thinking of a written "corpus" not as the presentation or representation of the one who writes but as the trace of the disappearance of the one who, in a sense, does not write: "*The absence of the book* revokes all continuity of presence just as it eludes the questioning borne by the book" (IC 423). "One can say that writing, dying are what are most discreet, although always made known by the public Last Act, the great tomblike rock of the Book" (SNB 104).

Though the neuter subject is singular rather than plural, it especially comes to the fore in what Blanchot calls "plural speech," a style of writing in which the confessional idiom of the first-person narrator is replaced by a multi-voiced conversation. In *The Infinite Conversation* (*L'Entretien infini*, 1969), Blanchot characterizes plural speech as speech that passes by way of the other:

> Plural speech would be this unique speech where what is said one time by "me" is repeated another time by "*Autrui*" and thus given back to its essential Difference. What therefore characterizes this kind of dialogue is that it is not simply an exchange of words between two Selves, two beings in the first person, but that the Other speaks there in the presence of speech, which is his sole presence; a neutral speech.
>
> (IC 215–16)

Throughout *The Step Not Beyond*, Blanchot's fragmentary reflections on the eternal recurrence are interrupted by the plural speech of two friends. One of the two eventually dies, leading the survivor or narrator or Blanchot (the *il*) to beseech: "Free me from the too long speech" (SNB 137; cf. 50). When death finally makes its appearance it is as an impossible limit that cannot be crossed, yet in relation to which friendship remains as ineliminable as fear and dread. The possibility that friendship might mitigate anxiety is hinted at in *The Infinite Conversation* where Blanchot defines the philosopher – "borrowing words from Georges Bataille – as someone who is afraid" (IC 49).

In a brief narrative *récit* entitled, "The Instant of My Death" (*L'instant de ma mort*, 1994), Blanchot recounts how a "young man" managed to escape execution by a firing squad in 1944, an experience of which he writes, "In his place, I will not try to analyze. He was perhaps suddenly invincible. Dead – immortal. Perhaps ecstasy. Rather the feeling of compassion for suffering humanity, the happiness of not being immortal or eternal. Henceforth, he was bound to death by a surreptitious friendship" (IOMD 5). The idea of being bound to death by friendship – and of being bound to friendship by death – is a constant theme in Blanchot's writing: "I know, I imagine that this unanalyzable feeling changed what there remained for him of existence. As if the death outside of him could only henceforth collide with the death in him. 'I am alive. No, you are dead'" (IOMD 9). "The Instance of My Death" can be characterized as an autobiographical narrative, but everything that Blanchot has to say about writing, discretion, and the neuter subject cautions us against hastily invoking the categories of biography and autobiography. The obligation of discretion – not the obligation to remain silent but the obligation to speak or write discreetly – imposes the problem of how to "tell a story" in such a way as to produce not a book but that absence of book which alone could do justice to the life it would recount. To the extent that the obligation of discretion arises from an "exigency," as Blanchot likes to say, it is the exigency of bearing witness to the wholly other, of that which links death to friendship. This obligation is fundamentally heteronomous in that it remains bound to death and friendship, about which one is never authorized either to speak or to remain silent. Perhaps it is the obligation to sustain a certain silence through speaking or writing; as such, discretion would be the experience of autonomous heteronomy.

Blanchot's conception of the relationship between friendship and discretion is exemplified in Hamlet's words to Horatio: "Give me that man/That is not passion's slave, and I will wear him/In my heart's core, ay, in my heart of heart,/As I do thee" (III, ii, 71–4). Horatio is a man of discretion because he is "not a pipe for Fortune's finger/To sound what stop she please" (III, ii, 70–1), and because unlike Rosencrantz and Guildenstern, he does not treat Hamlet as a pipe to "pluck out the heart of my mystery" (III, ii, 365–6). Diametrically opposed to Horatio is the constantly spying Polonius, who explicitly advocates a policy of indiscretion: "By indirections find directions out" (II, i, 63). When Hamlet hears of the players' arrival, his first thought is of the sovereignty of art: "He that plays the king shall be welcome" (II, ii, 319). Polonius – in the service of a false king – has no sense whatsoever of the sovereignty of art, impatiently interrupting the player-king with a peremptory, "This is too long" (II, ii, 498). When he praises Hamlet's acting with the words, "'Fore God, my lord, well spoken, with good accent and good discretion" (II, ii, 466–7), he is evidently thinking of discretion as a skill or technique – an "art" in the sense that the queen has in mind when she admonishes him with the words, "More matter with less art" (to which

Polonius protests, "Madam, I swear I use no art at all") (II, ii, 95–6). By contrast, when Hamlet advises the players to "let your own discretion be your tutor" so as "to hold as 'twere the mirror up to nature" (III, ii, 16–17, 21–2), he advocates an "artless" art, a certain "absence of art." Horatio exemplifies this art of discretion. At the end of the play, he is the survivor who would have preferred to die with his friend: "I am more an antique Roman than a Dane./Here's yet some liquor left" (V, ii, 341–2). Prevented from dying, and lacking in art, Horatio must bear witness to Hamlet's story not by relating an ostentatious chronicle of events, but by erasing the trace of that which is always in some sense "to come." In accepting this obligation, he testifies to attestation itself as the undisclosable secret of friendship.

2.7   Levinas's ethics of alterity

No more evasion.
(*Measure for Measure*, I, i, 50)

Just as Blanchot conceived of friendship as discretion, so his friend Emmanuel Levinas (1906–1995) takes discretion to be the proper response to any encounter with the "face of the other." In contrast to Bataille, who located the "wholly other" in sheer heterogeneity, Levinas finds it exclusively in the alterity of another human being, that is, in a personal other (*autrui*) rather than in an impersonal other (*autre*): "it is only man who could be absolutely foreign to me" (TAI 73). "The absolutely other [*Autre*] is the Other [*Autrui*]" (TAI 39; cf. 71). To think the other as *wholly* other requires that the other be in no way reducible to the order of sameness or homogeneity, and thus that the other entirely escape the horizon of phenomenological givenness. To encounter another person is to encounter someone who is in the most fundamental of senses unencounterable. Levinas characterizes such an encounter in terms of the "epiphany of the face" (TAI 51) of the other, the face being not a phenomenological given but that within the order of givenness which marks its own non-givenness, its character as a trace of that which never appears as such: "The way in which the other presents himself, exceeding *the idea of the other in me*, we here name face" (TAI 50; cf. OTB 91: "A face is a trace of itself"). Insofar as it exceeds the order of givenness, the face or trace of the other completely eludes phenomenological description. This is not to say that phenomenology can be simply by-passed, however. On the contrary, Levinas suggests that it is only by working through phenomenology that what is beyond it – "metaphysical exteriority" (TAI 29) – can be reached. In the *Cartesian Meditations* Husserl tried to found intersubjectivity in the subject's relationship to an "alter ego." Levinas thinks that this does not go far enough, for even if the subject has no immediate intuition of an alter ego – since for Husserl, like Leibniz, every subject is a windowless "monad" – it is still represented as another "me" rather than as that which escapes the order of egoity in general (TAI 67). Despite an initial sympathy with Heidegger's conception of care as the fundamental mode of Dasein's being-in-the-world (TIHP 119), Levinas also finds Heidegger's conception of *Mitsein* ("being-with") to be woefully inadequate, because it characterizes the relation to the other as always already belonging to the order of being rather than as that which in some sense founds ontology itself. Following Plato, Levinas characterizes the good as "beyond being and non-being." Insofar as Heidegger remains within the horizon of the question of being, he reduces the ethical relation to "a coexistence, a *we* prior to the I and the other, a neutral intersubjectivity" (TAI 68). Though Blanchot also invoked a conception of "impersonal neutrality," Levinas reads him as criticizing Heidegger's "philosophy of the neuter" (TAI 298). Instead of lamenting the metaphysical forgetting of being, Levinas reproaches Heidegger for forgetting the – metaphysical – question of the good. Ethics, not ontology, is "first philosophy."

In *The Theory of Intuition in Husserl's Phenomenology* (*Théorie de l'intuition dans la phénoménologie de Husserl*, 1930), Levinas expresses sympathy for the "intuitionism" of Husserl's *Ideas*, noting that the phenomenological principle of principles – the strict reliance on givenness – is grounded in the suspension of the natural attitude (TIHP liv, lviii). For Levinas, the principal error of naturalism is to equate "the existence and the conditions of existence of the physical world with existence and the conditions of existence in general" (TIHP 9). Husserl showed that *"to exist does not mean the same thing in every region,"* but he failed to recognize that this entailed that some intentional objects are not subject to objectifying acts of consciousness ("doxic theses") (TIHP 4, 134). By maintaining that every act is subject to doxic modification, Husserl privileges a particular kind of intentionality, namely, that of judging and knowing. Levinas agrees with Heidegger that practical and axiological attitudes such as caring and valuing have a unique structure that Husserl did not manage to elucidate (TIHP 158).

In *Existence and Existents* (*De l'existence à l'existant*, 1947), Levinas characterizes the ethical relation not as an intentional relation to a unique region of being but rather as a relation to that which is beyond being: "the movement which leads an existent toward the Good is not a transcendence by which that existent raises itself up to a higher existence, but a departure from Being . . . an *ex-cedence*" (EAE xxvii). Heidegger is criticized for construing anxiety as the encounter with the nothing rather than with the unremitting condition of being itself, the sheer *il y a* ("there is"): "It is because the *there is* has such a complete hold on us that we cannot take nothingness and death lightly, and we tremble before them" (EAE 5). What horrifies is not nothingness but "the haunting spectre, the phantom," as when Macbeth encounters the ghost of Banquo (EAE 56).[10] The "horror" of the *il y a* concerns the threat of an "anonymous existence": "what cannot disappear, the sheer fact of being in which *one* participates" (EAE 55, 44, 53). For Blanchot, the anonymity of the outside took place both "before" and "after" the existence of the world in the manner of the eternal recurrence. But, for

Levinas, the *il y a* – "the absence of the world, the elemental" – pertains to a condition that terminates in "hypostasis," the event by which the subject is constituted as a subject, thereby putting an end to its impersonality (EAE 44). To give an account of hypostasis it is necessary to go beyond mere phenomenological description, for phenomena only appear as such after hypostasis, that is, after the ego has already taken a "position" within the world: "A method is called for such that thought is invited to go beyond intuition" (EAE 63). Likewise, the relation to the other escapes phenomenological thematization: "Neither the category of quantity nor even that of quality describes the alterity of the other, who does not simply have another quality than me, but as it were bears alterity as a quality" (EAE 97).

According to Levinas, Heidegger conceived of intersubjectivity as a kind of "communion" in which the other was reduced to the order of "the solitary subject" who had to face death alone (EAE 98; cf. TAI 68). Against this point of view, Levinas argues in *Time and the Other* (*Le temps et l'autre*, 1947) that death represents the limit of possibility not in the ontological sense of a possible impossibility but rather in the ethical sense of an impossible possibility. Though "apparently Byzantine" (TAO 70), this distinction is crucial, for death is not something that the subject can appropriate as its own; on the contrary, death always comes to us as the most passive of events: "Death is thus never assumed, it comes. Suicide is a contradictory concept.... *Hamlet* is precisely a lengthy testimony to this impossibility of assuming death" (TAO 73; cf. SOL 102ff.). As the announcement of alterity, death does not individuate Dasein but rather breaks apart its solitude: "My solitude is thus not confirmed by death but broken by it" (TAO 74). Analogously, there is no relation to the future apart from the relation to the other. Heidegger's conception of the temporality of Dasein remains within a monotonous present, just as his conception of the call of conscience remains within the order of the same. As a result of his obliviousness to ethics, Heidegger can only think of obligation as "obedience to Being" (TAI 45). For Levinas, by contrast, obligation originates in the call of the other and exceeds the subject's pretension to mastery.

In *Totality and Infinity* (*Totalité et Infini: Essai sur l'extériorité*, 1961) Levinas distinguishes between ontology and metaphysics, being and the Good, politics and ethics, philosophy and prophecy (TAI 21). Once again it is a question not of sidestepping phenomenology but of carrying it to its limit, to the point where transcendence erupts within the order of phenomenality. Transcendence bespeaks a kind of "metaphysical desire," a desire for the infinite, where infinity would represent the "beyond" of a closed ontological totality. The idea of the infinite exceeds the subject's capacity to think it, arising in the welcoming encounter with another person who, irreducible to the thematic object of a noesis, first constitutes the intentionality of the subject: "This book will present subjectivity as welcoming the Other, as hospitality; in it the idea of infinity is consummated.... All knowing qua intentionality already presupposes the idea of infinity, which is preeminently *non-adequation*" (TAI 27). Insofar as it represents the "beyond" of totality, alterity cannot be reduced to a mere worldly obstacle against which the freedom of consciousness would measure itself. Thus we do not think alterity so long as we think it, with Hegel, merely as the presence to consciousness of that which is distinct from it (TAI 36). Only the other can bracket the hegemony of phenomenological givenness: "It is not I who resist the system, as Kierkegaard thought; it is the other" (TAI 40).

Levinas's conception of the "overflowing" character of the idea of the infinite is indebted to Descartes's attempt to derive the existence of God from the idea of an infinite being. According to Levinas, the Cartesian God is neither *a* being nor *being* itself but the transcendence that takes place in the encounter with another person. Here transcendence is to be conceived not as the traversal of a space already co-inhabited by separate beings but as the inaugural constitution of a shared world. Insofar as the other exists at an infinite "height" above me, this shared world exhibits "the primary curvature of being" (TAI 86; cf. EAE 100). The strange "curvature" of ethical space is exemplified in "proximity" to the other, which Levinas characterizes as both an infinite closeness and an infinite distance. Only with the appearance of a third party, an "other other," is this asymmetrical space supplemented by the advent of a shared public space in which each subject has rights. But even in this triangulated public realm, the dyadic relation to the other retains its fundamentally asymmetrical character. In this respect it is irreducible to Kant's kingdom of ends, which Levinas regards as an ontological totality of multiple rational wills (TAI 217; cf. OTB 129).

Kant claimed that, although the moral law has no heteronomous foundation, we inevitably treat it as if it did: "*conscience* is peculiar in that, although its business is a business of a human being with himself, one constrained by his reason sees himself constrained to carry it on as at the bidding *of another person*" (MOM 560). Levinas takes this idea one step further, suggesting that the feeling of respect attests not to the autonomy of the will but to the heteronomous encounter with the face of the other. Insofar as it represents the true ground of the categorical imperative, the face is not a phenomenal appearance but an interpellating discourse of the form "Thou shalt not kill." Thus autonomy is grounded in heteronomy: "The presence of the Other, a privileged heteronomy, does not clash with freedom but invests it" (TAI 88; cf. OTB 148). Whereas for Kant, only an intellectual intuition of the divine could justify the otherwise fanatical attempt to ground obligation on an encounter with the Other, for Levinas, it is not through intellectual intuition that the subject encounters the divine but through the face – or discourse – of another person: "The dimension of the divine opens forth from the human face" (TAI 78; cf. 196).

For the epiphany of the face to be truly radical, the subject must first be in a not-yet-worldly condition of "separation," entirely immersed in the "enjoyment" of sensibility. Thus hypostasis – the advent of enjoyment – stands half-way between the *il y a* and transcendence (TAI 191). The anteriority of enjoyment grounds the "absolute difference" (TAI 195) that separates one person from another, thereby making transcendence something more than a relation between beings already constituting a totality. When the epiphany of the face interrupts the subject's condition of "being-at-home-with-oneself," it calls the subject to respond to a welcoming speech that invites it to respond (TAI 52, 88). Only through this inviting/obliging speech of the other does the subject find itself in a world. Thus care in the Heideggerian sense is a consequence – not the foundation – of the ethical relation, while the face is not a thematizable object but an intelligible speech anterior to the subject's initiation into a world.

Whereas *Totality and Infinity* emphasizes the role played by the interpellating face of the other, Levinas's *Otherwise Than Being or Beyond Essence* (*Autrement qu'être ou au-delà de l'essence*, 1974) calls attention to the condition of the interpellated subject who, always appearing "too late" in relation to the call, nonetheless is obliged to attest to its having taken place. This retroactive character of interpellation manifests itself as "obsession." Just as hypostasis riveted the subject to its own being in such a way as to make sleep and death impossible, so responsibility precludes any "evasion" of ethical responsibility (OTB 195). Thus it is (ethically) impossible to "slip away" from the call of the other (OTB 53). The impossibility of ethical evasion is not mitigated by the fact that it is possible to evade the order of being, a theme that Levinas pursues in his 1935 essay, "On Escape" (*De l'évasion*). Ethical evasion is impossible because the subject has always already responded to this call through a primordial "here I am," thereby committing itself to the good: "before the bipolarity of good and evil presented to choice, the subject finds himself committed to the Good" (OTB 122). This does not mean that it is impossible to act "contrary to duty" in the Kantian sense, but it does imply that we are incapable of "diabolical evil." Conversely, the fact that the subject always responds too late to the call of the other (or has never done enough for the other) would be a mark of the subject's "radical evil."

Obsession is not only a confession of radical evil; it is an impossible attempt to forestall one's guilt by returning to the scene of a crime that never took place. In this respect, there is an important affinity between Levinas's conception of obsession and Freud's construal of obsessional neurosis. Not only does Freud associate obsessional neurosis with an exaggerated sense of moral conscience, but he observes that the more the obsessional sacrifices to the superego, the greater its guilt becomes. Analogously, Levinas describes the "approach" to the other as a kind of inverse Zeno's Paradox: no matter how "close" one gets, one always has infinitely far to go – not because every step only gets one half-way there but, on the contrary, because every step closer paradoxically *doubles* the distance: "The more I answer the more I am responsible; the more I approach the neighbor . . . the further away I am" (OTB 93). However, whereas Freud regards obsession as a symptom of superegoic cruelty, Levinas characterizes it as a mark of the "glory" of the infinite, specifically of the "infinition" involved in the approach to the other

(OTB 193 n35). Obsession is not "pathological" in either a Kantian or Freudian sense, for it is without any libidinal basis whatsoever: "Beneath the erotic alterity there is the alterity of the-one-for-the-other, responsibility before eros" (OTB 192 n27). Levinas refers in passing to the unconscious in *Existence and Existents*, but he does not accord any fundamental significance to a psychoanalytic conception of alterity (EAE 28). Whereas Freud characterized the retroactive attempt to bind cathexes that had overwhelmed the subject as an effort at mastery, he characterizes the obsessional attempt to attest to the ethical relation as an effort to divest oneself of mastery. Thus, far from representing a striving for mastery, ethical obsession is a (non-erotic) passion for passivity: "This response answers, but with no eroticism, to an absolutely heteronomous call" (OTB 53; cf. 123).

To "say" that the relation to the other involves a passivity more passive than any passivity is to bear witness to something that precedes the subject's very capacity for capacity; in this sense the encounter with the other is "older" even than the faculty of receptivity. To attest to this passivity is to "say" something that cannot be mastered as something "said." All meaningful assertions, considered either as sentences or propositions, belong to the order of the said (*le dit*). By contrast, every "saying" (*le dire*) – though it issues in the production of something said – attests to that which does not belong to the order of being, to the non-ontological "fact" of the ethical relation. This is why Levinas's own discourse is structured by a kind of repetition compulsion. Attestation always fails, not because speech is unable to master the ethical relation but, on the contrary, because it can *only* master it, reducing it to something thematized, to something merely said. Hence the work of attestation must be perpetually – obsessively – renewed.

Levinas characterizes the ethical relation as one of "substitution." In substitution, I put myself in the place of the other, or more precisely I find myself always already obliged to assume responsibility for the other – even to the point of being responsible for the other's responsibility: "I have to answer for his very responsibility" (OTB 84, cf. 117). Levinas characterizes substitution as the state of being "held hostage" by the other, of being wounded with a "good violence" that is different in kind from all ontological forms of violence (OTB 43; cf. TAI 47). As the taking on of the other's responsibility, substitution involves not only the subject's persecution, but the subject's responsibility for its own persecution by the other: "It is as though persecution by another were at the bottom of solidarity with another" (OTB 102).

Since it was Levinas who first suggested to us that the entire history of philosophy can be found in Shakespeare, perhaps his account of substitution can be illustrated by considering the ethical predicament of Desdemona in *Othello* (TAO 72). Othello has been deceived by the nefarious Iago into thinking that Desdemona has been having an affair with Othello's lieutenant, Michael Cassio. When Othello accuses her of being a whore, the innocent Desdemona does not express outrage for her persecution, but instead assumes responsibility for it: "'Tis meet I should be us'd so, very meet" (*The Tragedy of Othello, the Moor of Venice*, IV, ii, 106). Likewise, when Iago's wife Emilia asks the dying Desdemona who killed her, she responds: "Nobody. I myself. Farewell!/Commend me to my kind lord" (V, ii, 123–4). Desdemona does not blame herself for any transgression ("A guiltless death I die"); nor is her substitution for Othello based on her "pathological" affection for him (V, ii, 121). On the contrary, her act attests to the experience of ethical obsession. Iago is well aware of Desdemona's excessive goodness, and he uses it to deceive Othello. Thus, after Othello has stripped Cassio of his lieutenantship, Iago advises him to plead to Desdemona for assistance, because "She is of so free, so kind, so apt, so blessed a disposition, that she holds it a vice in her goodness not to do more than she is requested" (II, iii, 20–3). As Iago anticipates, so earnestly does Desdemona intercede on Cassio's behalf that her husband cannot but grow suspicious. It is tempting to say that just as Iago might be described as diabolically evil – though this is contestable, since his antipathy toward Othello appears to be motivated by pathological jealousy rather than by principled rebellion against the moral law – so Desdemona verges on being *diabolically good*. In the second *Critique*, Kant criticizes moral teachers who extol not the simple actions that duty prescribes but "supermeritorious" deeds that fill us with "empty wishes and longings for inaccessible perfection" (CPrR 263–4). The same criticism might be applied to Desdemona. Instead of doing what she could for Cassio and leaving it at that, she adopts the morally fanatical stance of the Levinasian subject for whom the experience of "too much" of the good is always experienced as "not enough."

Shakespeare hints that the true ethical subject of the play is not Desdemona but Emilia, who in the final scene confesses to having given Iago the fateful handkerchief that appeared to confirm Desdemona's infidelity. Emilia is situated between two extremes – one represented by Cassio's mistress Bianca, whom she calls a "strumpet"; the other by Desdemona, whom she insists is not a "whore" (V, i, 121; IV, ii, 137). The overly good Desdemona refuses to believe that any woman would cuckold her husband – not even "for all the world." But Emilia argues to the contrary that, under the right circumstances, an act of infidelity would be ethically justified: "Say they slack their duties ... or say they strike us" (IV, iii, 88–91). Desdemona resists Emilia's reasoning, ending the conversation with the words, "God me such usage send,/Not to pick bad from bad, but by bad mend!" (IV, iii, 105–6). In other words, even in the face of persecution one must persist in the ethical act of fidelity to the other. When Othello finally smothers her, Desdemona literally enacts what Levinas describes as the "breathlessness" of ethical "inspiration" (OTB 5). At the moment when Emilia knocks on the door, she represents the entry of the "third party," which Levinas associates with the advent of justice. But she does not merely triangulate the scene; she confesses her own inadvertent complicity with Iago's crime. According to Levinas, substitution takes place prior to the subject's very capacity for having capacities. But Emilia's confession derives its moral worth from the fact that she makes it *despite* being a subject with capacities. Earlier she had suggested to Desdemona that ontology trumps ethics: "Why, the wrong is but a wrong i' the world; and having the world for your labor, 'tis a wrong in your own world, and you might quickly make it right" (IV, iii, 81–3). But now she does the exact opposite, gratuitously assuming responsibility even if it will *cost her* the entire world: "Let heaven and men and devils, let them all,/All, all, cry shame against me, yet I'll speak" (V, ii, 220–1).

Despite Desdemona's seemingly inevitable fate, Levinas does not believe that substitution involves sacrifice. On the contrary, there is a way in which it preserves, and even constitutes, the integrity of the subject: "it is through this substitution that I am not 'another,' but me" (OTB 127). Yet the subject only acquires "breathing space" with the appearance of the third party, *another* other to whom the subject is also obliged. Instead of merely multiplying the subject's responsibilities, the third person mitigates the smothering condition of proximity to a sole other: "The relationship with the third party is an incessant correction of the assymetry [sic] of proximity . . . there is also justice for me" (OTB 159). In *Measure for Measure*, when the third party (the Duke) reappears at the end of the play, Isabella immediately demands of him "justice, justice, justice, justice!" (V, i, 25). However, when Emilia appears at the door just after Othello has strangled her, the dying Desdemona does not ask for justice; instead, she persists in substitution by taking Othello's guilt on herself.[11] It is precisely here that the excessiveness of her goodness manifests itself. It is Emilia who, against her own interest, demands justice for Desdemona. Analogously, Isabella's ultimate ethical act occurs not when she intercedes on behalf of her brother, but at the end of the play, when – *after* receiving justice from the Duke – she performs the "unthinkable" and wholly gratuitous act of asking him to pardon her persecutor, Angelo (V, i, 443–54).

Since the position of Desdemona is not altogether different from that of Sade's virtuous Justine, it is tempting to compare Levinas's account of ethical substitution with Bataille's Sadean ethic. There is a moment in Bataille's novel, *L'Abbé C*, when Robert (or "Chianine") sees a light shining under his door and becomes convinced that when he opens it he is "going to find Immanuel Kant waiting for me" (LC 134). But he imagines that it will be a transformed Kant: "He didn't have the diaphanous face that distinguished him during his lifetime: he had the hirsute mien of a bushy-haired man wearing a three-cornered hat" (LC 135). This uncanny, hirsute Kant can be thought of as Kant's – or Bataille's – disavowed alter ego. According to Deleuze, a good philosophical commentary ought to reveal such figures: "In the history of philosophy, a commentary should act as a veritable double and bear the maximal modification appropriate to a double. (One imagines a *philosophically* bearded Hegel, a *philosophically* clean-shaven Marx, in the same way as a moustached Mona Lisa.)" (DR xxi). The question to be asked here is what it would mean to imagine a hirsute Levinas. For Bataille, as for Levinas, transcendence "exceeds 'being's limits'" (ON 149). But unlike Bataille, the clean-shaven Levinas finds the wholly other not in orgiastic works of literature but in sober "prose" (TAI 203). To be interpellated by the other is to be called *away from* the obscene anonymous heterogeneity of the *il y a*, rather than *toward* it; in this sense there is something analogous to sublimation in Levinas's ethics. But what if it were only by keeping the good at a certain distance – precisely "beyond being" – that one could be sure to avoid "the very worst"? To keep one's distance from the other – to recoil from something in the commandment to love thy neighbor – would be to seek an excluded middle between smotheredness and evasion of responsibility, an "otherwise" that would escape the either/or of both ontology and ethics.

Levinas suggests that all speech is rooted in a primordial "Here I am" (*me voici*) by which the subject answers "for everything and for everyone" (OTB 114). In attesting to this "Here I am," Levinas is not making a personal confession but putting forth a prophetic discourse, one that purports universality. Just as in Descartes, the reader is obliged to adopt the standpoint of the nominative subject (the "I" of the "I think"), so in reading Levinas one is called upon to adopt the standpoint of the accused or accusative subject (the "me" of the *me voici*). This implies that only a subject *like* Levinas – a subject whose relation to alterity is the *same* as his – will be able to read him properly. It is impossible to disagree with Levinas because as soon as one articulates one's disagreement one has already said, "Here I am."

Levinas likens the "saying" of obligation to skepticism. When the (dogmatic) skeptic says, "There is no truth," a logician can always point out that this claim is self-refuting because either it is false or else, if it is true, it is again false. But Levinas likes to point out that it is always possible for the skeptic to respond by once again challenging the presumption that there is truth. This is possible because the "saying" of skepticism stands in a diachronic relation to the conditions of the content that is "said" in the skeptic's utterance: "skepticism has the gall to return ... because in the contradiction which logic sees in it the 'at the same time' of the contradictories is missing" (OTB 7). Thus there is a kind of delay between the significance expressed in the skeptic's utterance and the realization that the utterance is self-refuting. This lag time is also present in the paradox of the Cretan liar – the subject who says "I am lying" – which Lacan resolves by distinguishing between the "subject of the enunciation" and the "subject of the enunciated statement" (S XI 139). In distinguishing between the saying and the said, Levinas suggests that while logic or ontology can always refute skepticism, it cannot do so in any final way. The ever-renewed saying of the skeptic attests to a certain otherwise-than-truth or otherwise-than-being. Levinas regards his own attempt to attest to the otherwise-than-being as akin to skepticism in that it can always be refuted by ontology, but never definitively.

But this argument seems to stop half-way, since it addresses only skepticism about truth and not moral skepticism. Moral skepticism can be expressed in a statement of the form, "I am not obliged." But since for

Levinas all speech is first and foremost a saying-to-the-other, it always represents an acceptance of obligation. Hence the statement "I am not obliged" refutes itself in the same way that "There is no truth" refutes itself – with one crucial difference, namely, that whereas truth-skepticism is refuted by ontology, moral skepticism is refuted by (Levinasian) ethics. But here it would seem possible to resist the Levinasian refutation of moral skepticism by making precisely the same move that he makes with respect to truth-skepticism. Is there not a diachronic separation between the saying of *moral* skepticism and its "said" content? The subject who says "I am not obliged" can always be refuted, but not once and for all – or at least not without recourse to the same kind of violence to which ontology resorts in refuting ethics. But if moral skepticism is just as irrepressible as skepticism about truth, then does not saying "I am not obliged" attest to something other than Levinasian obligation – i.e., to something other than the otherwise-than-being? And would not this represent the evasion of the order of the ethical?

To attest to the otherwise-than-obliged would be to claim that the relation to the other might take a different form than Levinas suggests. Levinas's "Here I am" bespeaks a primordial fidelity to the other, an attitude akin to what Freud describes as the neurotic's primordial acceptance of reality. But Freud also allows for a psychotic refusal of reality. If the "Here I am" is to cover this possibility as well, it must be able to signify not merely an acceptance of responsibility but its refusal as well. So understood, "Here I am" would express a relation to the other that is "ethical" not insofar as it precludes the possibility of diabolical evil but precisely insofar as it includes it within its purview. Levinas sees psychoanalysis as an extension of ontology, objecting to the violence with which the analyst purports to attest on behalf of the other to the other's relation to alterity. But is it possible to conceive psychoanalysis otherwise, not as the transferential identification of the subject with the analyst but as "a dialogue in which, perhaps – perhaps – something would come to light that would enlighten us about ourselves when we speak by way of the other" (IC 233)? For Blanchot – if not Levinas – this is a possibility opened up in the work of Lacan.

2.8   Lacan's detection of a secret alliance between Kant and Sade

> I am the dog – no, the dog is himself, and I am the dog –
>   O! the dog is me, and I am myself; ay, so, so.
> > (*The Two Gentlemen of Verona*, II, ii, 21–3)

> For, sir,
> It is as sure as you are Roderigo,
> Were I the Moor, I would not be Iago.
> > (*The Tragedy of Othello,*
> > *the Moor of Venice*, I, i, 55–7)

Originally trained as a psychiatrist, the French psychoanalyst Jacques Lacan (1901–1981) re-articulated Freudian metapsychology in terms borrowed from structural linguistics. Under the banner of a "return to Freud" he developed his ideas in a seminar that he gave from 1953 until 1980, first to analysts in training and later to a broader audience (E 114). Among the themes that are central in the published transcriptions of this seminar, as well as in his collected *Écrits* (1966), are the relationship between psychoanalysis and modern science and the nature of moral experience. His ethics, like that of Levinas, has its point of departure in an attempt to think the subject's relation to "the other." But, for Lacan, there are two different kinds of others that need to be distinguished, the little other (*autre*) and the big Other (*Autre*). The little other – or *objet petit a* – emerges in an early phase of childhood development which he calls "the mirror stage," when an infant between the ages of six to eighteen months identifies itself with an image in its visual field. Identification is to be understood not as the equating of an already constituted ego with an empirical object but as the primordial experience by virtue of which a sense of self is first acquired. Because it is founded on an "imaginary" object in the subject's visual field, the ego arises from a fundamental "misrecognition" or alienation: "the initial synthesis of the *ego* is essentially an *alter ego*, it is alienated" (S III 39).[12] Lacan suggests that misrecognition is a consequence of the infant's lack of motor coordination, so that the image with which it identifies would anticipate a bodily integrity it has not yet acquired. But he often makes the Hegelian point – recognized by Sartre and Bataille – that in itself the subject is nothing, so that it could only identify itself as something by identifying itself with something that it is not; Kant makes a similar point in claiming that it is only through objects of outer sense that the subject becomes capable of inner sense. The primordial object with which the subject identifies its ego is the *objet petit a*, or rather it is the first of a series of empirical objects to play its role of "filling in" for the subject by purporting to fill in its primordial lack.

So long as the subject remains exclusively within this relation of imaginary identification it stands in a relation of potential aggressive rivalry to all those empirical others who can play the part of the *objet petit a*. In his early seminars, Lacan often likens this rivalry to the "struggle for recognition" that Hegel describes in the *Phenomenology of Spirit* (S I 170; S III 40). This condition is only interrupted by the intervention of another agency, namely, that of the big Other. In developmental terms, the big Other is the symbolic function that a child's father represents – what Lacan calls the *nom-de-père*, the name-of-the-father (with a pun on *non-de-père*: the no-of-the-father). Through a secondary identification that takes place by way of the big Other, the subject acquires a "symbolic" identity that is different in kind from the "imaginary" identity acquired at the level of the ego. Symbolic identification consists in being recognized by the big Other, thereby obviating the need for struggle at the imaginary level. Unlike the little other, which constantly reappears in the order of intuitable objects, the big Other transcends the order of phenomenal appearance. In this sense the relation to the big Other has the character of transcendence in Levinas's sense of the term: "when the Other with a big O speaks it is not purely and simply the reality in front of you, namely the individual who is holding forth. The Other is beyond that reality" (S III 50–1). Like the Levinasian face, the big Other manifests itself as interpellating discourse, constituting the subject as a speaking subject. But whereas for Levinas discourse appears in the subject's initial relation to the other, so that "peace" would precede the aggressivity of war, for Lacan discourse emerges only with that "other other" or "third party" whose intervention makes peace possible (S III 39). Since any of an indefinite number of persons or institutions can stand in for it, the big Other's recognition of the subject ultimately depends upon the subject's recognition of someone or something *as* the big Other: "It has to be recognized for you to be able to make yourself recognized" (S III 51). Symbolic identification is just as unstable as imaginary identification in that it is always possible for the subject to revert to mere aggressive rivalry in its relations with others. The imaginary dimension of the dialectic of subjectivity does not disappear with the advent of the symbolic function.

Lacan's distinction between imaginary and symbolic identification corresponds to Freud's distinction between the primary identifications that take place prior to the onset of the Oedipus complex and the secondary identifications that result from its traversal. The only difference is that where Freud speaks indifferently of the "ideal ego" of narcissism and the "ego ideal" that forms the kernel of the superego, Lacan distinguishes between the imaginary ego and the symbolically recognized subject. The latter – which is to be distinguished from the ego – is the subject of the unconscious. According to Lacan, "the unconscious is structured like a language" because symbolic identification passes through language in precisely the same way that imaginary identification takes place through objects in the subject's visual field. To be recognized by the big Other is to be identified with a particular signifier which "represents" the subject for all those other signifiers which collectively comprise the ellipse of language whose other focal point is the big Other. Put otherwise, symbolic identification takes place when the subject accedes to a language that already represents it. To this extent symbolic identification is no less "alienating" than imaginary identification, since the language that the subject henceforth speaks is always already speaking it. Thus there is a fundamental split within the speaking subject, namely, between the subject who produces conscious discourse and the subject who is spoken by an unconscious language that its conscious discourse itself expresses. For Lacan this is the only way of making sense of Freud's conception of the unconscious: that it represents the division which language introduces into human subjectivity. Freud claimed that the unconscious represents things rather than words, and that the representation of words should be located at the level of the preconscious (GPT 147). But the very split between these two levels is a function of the difference between the signifier and the signified. Put otherwise, the fact that word-presentations do not appear in the unconscious is a consequence of the fact that the unconscious consists of nothing but the very signifiers which first make word-presentations possible.

This structuralist interpretation of Freud is indebted to the work of both Jakobson and Lévi-Strauss. In his essay, "Two Aspects of Language and Two Types of Aphasic Disturbances," Jakobson had suggested a way of reading Freud's account of the dreamwork in linguistic terms; dream symbolism would be akin to the use of metaphor in language (the substitution of one signifier for another), while condensation and displacement would exhibit the trope of metonymy (the linking of signifiers in combinatorial relations with one another). Lacan modifies this suggestion by equating condensation with metaphor and displacement with metonymy (S III 221); the work of dream interpretation then consists in the attempt to track down the linguistic chain by which the signifying elements of a dream are linked to the primordial signifier with which the subject is identified. From Lévi-Strauss, Lacan borrows the idea that kinship systems are structured in the same way as languages, reading his explanation of the dynamics of the exchange of women back into Freud's account of the origins of the Oedipus complex:

> If Freud insisted on the Oedipus complex to the extent of constructing a sociology of totems and taboos, it is obviously because for him the Law is there *ab origine*. It is therefore out of the question to ask oneself the question of origins. . . . This fundamental law is simply a law of symbolization. This is what the Oedipus complex means.
>
> (S III 83)

Whereas Lévi-Strauss emphasizes the differences between structural anthropology and psychoanalysis, Lacan posits a fundamental identity:

> Lévi-Strauss demonstrates that there is a correct classification of what the elementary structures of kinship make available to us. This presupposes that the symbolic agencies function in the society from the start, from the moment it takes on a human appearance. But this is nothing more nor less than what is presupposed by the unconscious such as we discover and manipulate it in analysis.
>
> (S II 30)

Non-human animals experience something akin to imaginary identification; indeed, for Lacan, they remain exclusively at the level of images which captivate their attention. What is distinctive about human experience is that it is structured by language, which retroactively affects the way in which we relate to the imaginary dimension itself – thus while "the ego is an imaginary function" (S II 36), it "intervenes in psychic life only as symbol" (S II

38). Lacan accordingly associates the symbolic dimension of human experience with the order of the signifier and the imaginary dimension with the order of signified meanings, while to discourse as it unfolds in time he assigns a third dimension, that of "the real" (S III 52, 54). The idea that imaginary formations are retroactively affected by symbolic interventions indicates the inadequacy of taking a simple genetic or sequential point of view on human development: "do not allow yourselves to be fascinated by this genetic moment . . . the symbol is already there" (S III 81). From the standpoint of the individual, the transition from nature to culture has always already taken place by way of the kinship rules which enable human relations to be governed not by imaginary aggression but by symbolically structured exchange (S II 52). These rules, which Lévi-Strauss recognized to be unconscious, lend a strictly mechanical aspect to human behavior which animals do not exhibit; indeed it is the very automatism of the signifier in human affairs that frees us from our environment: "It is in as much as, compared to the animal, we are machines, that is to say something decomposed, that we possess greater freedom" (S II 31).

In his 1959–1960 seminar, *The Ethics of Psychoanalysis* (*L'Éthique de la Psychanalyse*), Lacan suggests that there is a gap in Lévi-Strauss's conception of the elementary structures of kinship, for while it is perfectly capable of explaining why fathers do not marry their daughters, it cannot account for the real enigma concerning human sexuality, namely, the fact that sons do not marry their mothers. But this is precisely what Freud's account of the Oedipus complex tries to explain: "the result of the law is always to exclude incest in its fundamental form, son/mother incest, which is the kind Freud emphasizes" (S VII 67). The law that prohibits incest has a positive side other than the obligation to exchange wives. It also has the function of constituting the very desire that it proscribes, namely, desire for the mother. Here the mother is to be understood as a primordially lost object from whom the subject has been separated. In keeping with the logic of retroactive constitution, this lost maternal object never really existed as such; or rather it exists in the first place only *as* lost. This is why Freud sees the advent of the reality principle not in the appearance of a real object but in the subject's attempt to "refind" in reality something that it has already lost (GPT 216). This search for "the first outside" is necessarily futile: "It is in its nature that the object as such is lost. It will never be found again" (S VII 52). Like the Kantian "transcendental object = x," the lost object – *das Ding*, or the Thing – is different in kind from any empirical object that might appear within phenomenal – i.e., imaginary – reality. As such it belongs to the order of the real, which is to be understood not as a transcendent noumenal realm from which we are barred by our lack of intellectual intuition, but as that primordially lost maternal object to which the law prevents us from returning. Access to the real would require a transgression that is strictly impossible because the Thing exists only as a function of the law that prohibits access to it.

Thus the desire for the mother (like the allure of the erotic for Bataille) only originates with the prohibition of incest. Insofar as it is directed toward the lost object qua lost, this desire – or rather desire as such – can never be satisfied. In effect, to desire is to desire the past qua past, so that even if the past were to be miraculously reconstituted in the present, it would not satisfy the subject because it would not be present *as past*.[13] Paradoxically, it is by "searching for lost time" that a relation to the future is opened up. The idea that it is necessary for the subject to keep its distance from the lost object of desire is developed by Lacan in his 1958–1959 seminar, *Le Désir et son Interprétation*. There he suggests that "desire is always the desire of the other," i.e., that desire is primordially "misrecognized" in the same way that the ego is. In support of this thesis he argues that, far from wanting to sleep with his mother (as a conventional psychoanalytic interpretation would have it), Hamlet is horrified at his mother's desire, which represents for him an unfathomable abyss from which he must separate himself. Thus the lost object is something that must be strictly avoided. Lacan concludes that the maternal Thing is the ultimate traumatic object, a too intimate alterity or "extimacy" from which the subject must keep a certain distance in order to sustain its own relation to reality as a desiring being (S VII 139). For Lacan, desire is to be distinguished not only from biological "need" but also from the narcissistic "demand" that the ego addresses to various imaginary substitutes for the lost object. To maintain the purity of desire would be to refuse all such surrogates as so many "graven images" of the sublime Thing (S VII 175). Conversely, sublimation can be understood as the process by which the subject raises some particular empirical object "to the dignity of the Thing" (S VII 112). Courtly love as depicted in medieval poetry exemplifies the logic of sublimation (S VII 128). The Lady to whom the poet pledged his absolute devotion was able to function as an object of desire only insofar as she was put in the position of the unattainable Thing; in this way she could be simultaneously pursued and kept at a distance.

Lacan suggests that Freud's great contribution to ethics lies in his recognition that the ultimate object of desire – the good – is unattainable:

> the step taken by Freud at the level of the pleasure principle is to show us that there is no Sovereign Good – that the Sovereign Good, which is *das Ding*, which is the mother, is also the object of incest, is a forbidden good, and that there is no other good. Such is the foundation of the moral law as turned on its head by Freud.
>
> (S VII 70)

Freud turns the moral law on its head by dissociating it from the concept of the good, or more precisely by interpreting it as a radical foreclosure of the good (S VII 96). Lacan notes that it was Kant who first conceived of a gap separating the moral law from the idea of the good. Kant does this, first, by distinguishing between all pathological goods – objects of inclination –

and the moral Good; and second by relegating the latter to the status of the sublime Thing in relation to which the moral law situates us. For Lacan, this marks "the great revolutionary crisis of morality" (S VII 70) that separates Kantian ethics from the ethical systems of antiquity in a profound way. Aristotle's *Nicomachean Ethics* exemplifies the traditional conception of the good as pleasurable (S VII 36). Only with Kant is a difference in kind between pathological goods and the Good introduced, the moral law requiring us to sacrifice all pleasure in the name of something that is "beyond the pleasure principle." What Kant failed to see, however, is that this sacrifice – carried out in the name of fidelity to the sublime object that the law represents as unrepresentable – gives rise to another kind of gratification, one that is different in kind from pathological pleasure because it pertains to the satisfaction of the death drive. Lacan calls this other kind of gratification *jouissance*.

Kant's failure to recognize the dimension of *jouissance* in moral experience – something Freud had already alluded to in his conception of moral masochism – is evidenced in a thought experiment that appears in the *Critique of Practical Reason*. Kant contrasts two hypothetical situations – one in which a man is given the opportunity to gratify his lust with a woman, knowing that on his way out the door he will be hanged; the other in which a man is asked by his prince to bear false witness against his friend, knowing that if he does not he will be killed. Kant thinks that no one would give up his life just for a night of great sex, but that everyone would at least hesitate before bearing false witness against a friend, even if they knew that the alternative was death (CPrR 163–4). Lacan suggests that this argument rests on an empirical appeal to human behavior: "The striking point is that the power of proof is here left to reality – to the real behavior of the individual" (S VII 108). In effect, Kant simply purports universality for a "normal" response to the scenario that he depicts. But Lacan notes two "abnormal" cases in which someone might act differently. The first involves "overestimation," where the subject raises the object to the dignity of the Thing; the other is perversion, in which the subject maintains a certain fidelity to the Thing precisely by transgressing the law: "All of which leads to the conclusion that it is not impossible for a man to sleep with a woman knowing full well that he is to be bumped off on his way out" (S VII 109).

The case of perversion is exemplified by Sade. Following Blanchot, Bataille noted the crucial moment of apathy in Sade's representation of cruelty: "In the first stage of her career, Juliette hears herself reproached constantly by Clairwill about this: she commits crime only when inflamed by the passions; she places lust, the effervescence of pleasure above all else. Dangerous indulgences. Crime is more important than lust" (AS II 180). The idea that crime is more important than lust suggests that Sade's evil is not merely "radical" but "diabolical." Shakespeare gives expression to the principled character of diabolical evil in *The Tragedy of Titus Andronicus*, when the unrepentant Aaron (a character far more evil than Iago) proclaims as his final words: "If one good deed in all my life I did,/I do repent it from my very soul" (V, iii, 189–90). Because of its principled character, diabolical evil is formally indistinguishable from holiness of the will (or at least from deep-seated virtue). This can be seen by substituting the word "duty" for "crime" in Bataille's characterization of Sade's ethic: "*Duty* is more important than lust." Conversely, Lacan observes that, from a merely formal point of view, Sade's maxim – "'Let us take as the universal maxim of our conduct the right to enjoy any other person whatsoever as the instrument of our pleasure'" – fully accords with the categorical imperative. This maxim is universalizable because it affirms a universal right: "everyone is invited to pursue to the limit the demands of his lust and to realize them." Lacan concludes that "the Sadian world is conceivable – even if it is its inversion, its caricature – as one of the possible forms of the world governed by a radical ethics, by the Kantian ethics" (S VII 79).

Kant claims that no one could choose to live in a world without mutual benevolence, for although such a world is not inherently contradictory – as is the idea of a world in which everyone always lied – a rational will could not affirm such a world without entering into "conflict with itself" (G 75). A fortiori, it is impossible to will the universalizability of Sade's maxim because no one could choose to live in a Sadean "kingdom of means." But Lacan chides Kant for being naive on just this point. Not only is it possible for Sade to universalize his maxim, but the enjoyment that serves as the determining ground of his will is not pathological in character. Moreover, by overlooking the distinction between the pathological incentive of pleasure and the non-pathological incentive of *jouissance*, Kant fails to detect the *jouissance* that surreptitiously motivates his own feeling of respect for the moral law: "Anyone can see that if the moral law is, in effect, capable of playing some role here, it is precisely as a support for the *jouissance* involved.... That's what Kant on this occasion simply ignores" (S VII 189).

According to Lacan, both Kant and Sade were responding to a crisis that began with the advent of modern science. The idea of the real as that which always returns to the same place was problematized by Copernicus and Galileo, who liberated the notion of "the same place" from its phenomenological (imaginary) moorings in the lifeworld (S II 297; S VII 70). This transformation is evidenced in the separation of astronomy from astrology (S XI 152). Paradoxically, the real disappeared at the very moment when humanity attained technical mastery over nature by representing it algebraically – i.e., through a combinatory of signifiers (S II 299–300). For Freud, the Copernican revolution was the first of three blows to man's narcissism, the other two coming from Darwin and Freud himself (whom Lacan regards as the founder of a new science) (S XI 8). Lacan argues that the Copernican blow led directly to Kant's conception of the Good as an unattainable Thing beyond all imaginary goods. But the moral law does not merely orient us toward the Good; it also protects us from it, so that, conversely, transgression in the form of diabolical evil represents an approach to the Good. Thus, just as Freud revealed the sadism of the categorical imperative, so Lacan detects a moral – i.e., Kantian – element in Sade. Freud discerned the uncanny proximity between Kant and Sade not only in his account of the sado-masochistic structure of the superego–ego relationship, but in his reflections on the Christian commandment to "love thy neighbor as thyself." Lacan suggests that Freud recoiled from this commandment in "horror" because he saw that the approach to the other coincided with the approach to "the evil in which he doesn't hesitate to locate man's deepest heart" (S VII 194). Just as imaginary identification gave rise to the dialectic of aggressivity, so love of one's neighbor leads to an intolerable festive cruelty in which all boundaries disappear: "to love him as myself, is necessarily to move toward some cruelty. His or mine? . . . nothing indicates they are distinct" (S VII 198).

The three-fold distinction between the *objet petit a*, the big Other, and the Thing – which correspond, respectively, to the imaginary, the symbolic, and the real – results from a "spectral analysis" of the object, to which there corresponds a comparable spectral analysis of the subject (S VII 274). Thus there are not three different kinds of others, but three different ways in which the subject can relate itself to alterity. Lacan suggests that the distinction that Freud drew between hysteria, obsessional neurosis, and psychosis reflects three alternative ways in which a speaking subject can be constituted in relation to some primordially encountered object. An hysteric is someone for whom the other "failed to give satisfaction," while the obsessional neurotic is someone who received "too much pleasure" from it. Both of these forms of neurosis – in which, according to Freud, the subject accepts reality rather than turning away from it – are to be distinguished from psychosis, which reflects a primordial disavowal of the alterity of the other: "The paranoid doesn't believe in that first stranger in relation to whom the subject is obliged to take his bearings" (S VII 54). In effect, the paranoiac is someone whose relation to the other does not take the form of Levinas's "Here I am," since the other – or at least the big Other, the other with whom the subject is engaged in discourse – has been radically "foreclosed" (this is the way in which Lacan represents Schreber's psychosis). Lacan distinguishes between "empty speech" and "full speech," that is, between an alienated discourse in which the unconscious remains hidden and an authentic discourse that attests to the subject's primordial desire. Full speech is characterized by the fact that "the subject receives his message from the other in an inverted form" (S III 36). An example of this might be Levinas's "Here I am," in which, say, a neurotic subject attests to his or her fidelity to the primordially lost object. But according to Lacan, psychotic speech works otherwise. Cut off from a relation to the big Other, the psychotic's discourse takes place at the imaginary level of the mirror relation, so that here the subject receives her own message back from the other – but precisely not in an inverted form (S III 51). To the extent that the psychotic's speech takes the form of the attestation "Here I am," it will represent not fidelity to the other but, on the contrary, the attitude of the radical moral skeptic.

Blanchot suggested that Lacanian analysis was a way of enabling a subject to attest to its unique relation to alterity. For Lacan, it is also a way of responding to the untenability of eudaimonistic ethics – that is, an ethics that aims at happiness – in modernity. According to Lacan, Freud discovered that happiness is simply impossible to achieve. Thus the first imperative for the analyst is not to promise to make analysands happy: "That's something to remember whenever the analyst finds himself in the position of responding to anyone who asks him for happiness. . . . Not only doesn't he have that Sovereign Good that is asked for him, but he also knows there isn't any" (S VII 300). The aim of analysis is not (as it is in ego psychology) to enable individuals to "adapt" themselves better to a reality that is always structured by an imaginary fantasy of some sort, but on the contrary to "traverse" that fantasy so as to be able to confront desire in its pure form: "a form of ethical judgment is possible, of a kind that gives this question the force of a Last Judgment: Have you acted in conformity with the desire that is in you?" (S VII 314). In accepting the Kantian/Sadean renunciation of all pathological objects of demand – "the service of goods" – Lacan acknowledges the "tragic" dimension of the human condition (S VII 313).

Lacan suggests that it is not Oedipus but Antigone who embodies the essence of tragedy. In rejecting the service of goods, she puts herself in direct relation to the Thing as the ultimate object of desire. On Lacan's reading of Sophocles' play, Antigone is motivated neither by love of her brother nor (as Hegel thought) by a divine law; on the contrary, her will is entirely without "material incentives" of any sort. On the contrary, her actions are governed exclusively by the death instinct: "from Antigone's point of view life can only be approached, can only be lived or thought about, from the place of that limit where her life is already lost, where she is already on the other side" (S VII 280). What makes Antigone so fascinating is that by violating Creon's decree that her brother be refused proper burial rites, she performs an ethical act of transgression, the extreme point where Kant and Sade meet. "Antigone in her unbearable splendour" is not so much the Lady of courtly love raised to the dignity of the Thing, as the Thing itself lowered to the level of an empirical object (S VII 247). But through our fascination with the image of Antigone, we undergo catharsis: "we are purged, purified of everything of . . . the order of the imaginary. And we are purged of it through the intervention of one image among others" (S VII 248). The analyst attempts to bring about an analogous effect by isolating the privileged signifier around which a subject's "fundamental fantasy" has been constructed.

Unlike tragedy, which represents the "triumph of being-for-death," comedy exhibits the triumph of life, or, "not so much the triumph of life as its flight." Though psychoanalytic categories owe more to classical tragedy than to comedy, "the experience of human action" has the character of "tragi-comedy," which is to say that it is lived as the conflict between Thanatos and Eros (S VII 313–14). Just as the Thing belongs to the order of tragedy, so there is a comic dimension to the dialectic of identification, as is illustrated in Shakespeare's *The Two Gentlemen of Verona*. At the beginning of the play, the young Valentine and his friend Proteus have not yet made the transition from the imaginary realm of the home to the symbolic realm of the world abroad. Valentine is about to make this transition by leaving Verona for Milan, but Proteus prefers to remain at home so that he can be with Julia, with whom he is in love. In the opening lines of the play, Valentine responds to an unspoken request by Proteus that he stay in Verona: "Cease to persuade, my loving Proteus:/Home-keeping youth have ever homely wits" (I, i, 1–2). Valentine chides his friend with being obsessed with love, intimating that Proteus is in love less with Julia than with love itself. Valentine spurns love, preferring to seek "honor" abroad. Before departing, the two friends agree to correspond by letter.

Much to his displeasure, Proteus is forced by his father to join his friend in Milan, where Valentine has fallen in love with a young woman named Silvia. Immediately upon seeing her, Proteus becomes enamored as well, determining to thwart Valentine's plan to elope with her. The fact that Proteus's love is subject to the metonymy of demand shows that his former affection for Julia was still at the imaginary stage – as was his identification with Valentine, with whom he now enters into the dialectic of aggressivity. Through Proteus's machinations, Valentine is banished by Silvia's father. Once again Valentine must leave his friend, but this time Proteus encourages him to do so by inverting Valentine's opening words of the play: "Cease to lament for that thou canst not help,/And study help for that which thou lament'st" (III, i, 243–4). Again an exchange of letters is promised, with Proteus (falsely) claiming that he will deliver Valentine's letters to Silvia.

The action of the play culminates in the woods outside Milan, where Silvia has fled to seek Valentine. Proteus is about to force himself upon her when suddenly the hidden Valentine steps forward, preventing the rape and denouncing Proteus as a false friend. Proteus pleads for forgiveness – not from Silvia but from Valentine, who agrees to forgive his friend in a highly significant way, namely, by offering to *give Silvia to him*: "And that my love may appear plain and free,/All that was mine in Silvia I give thee" (V, iv, 82–3). At the moment that this gift is proposed, Julia (disguised as Sebastian), swoons. When she comes to, she gives Proteus a ring to give to Silvia, but it is the ring that he had first given to Julia herself. Proteus recognizes it, and when Julia reveals her true identity, he *gives Silvia back to Valentine* and takes up Julia once again. Only now is Proteus able to undergo symbolic identification by accepting his position in the kinship structure: "What is in Silvia's face, but I may spy/More fresh in Julia's with a constant eye?" (V, iv, 114–15). With the symbolic pact between the two men sealed, they can return to a shared home – "One feast, one house, one mutual happiness" (V, iv, 173) – that is no longer the imaginary space in which the action of the play began but the paternal order governed by kinship rules (for Silvia's father has now agreed to "give" his daughter to Valentine).[14]

Lacan claims that Freud's account of the Oedipus complex explains something that Lévi-Strauss could not, namely, why it is that only daughters – not sons – are exchanged. To traverse the Oedipus complex is to undergo "symbolic castration," the subordination of the subject to the signifier that represents it in the big Other. The difference between being "not yet" and "always already" castrated reflects two different ways of being situated with respect to the "name-of-the-father," the signifier of the Other. Men "have" the phallus but only insofar as they lack it, while women "are" the phallus but at the expense of not having it. Just as for Sartre the desire of the for-itself to coincide with the in-itself – i.e., the desire to be God – was futile, so for Lacan the desire to be a full subject for whom having and being would coincide – i.e., the desire to take the place of the mythical father of the primal horde – is foreclosed to all subjects in the symbolic order. But insofar as women lack the phallus, they are treated not as subjects but as objects of exchange.

While still in Milan, Proteus begged Silvia to give him a portrait of herself, which she agreed to do only because she knew that her image was a mere trifle. This insight is expressed in Lacan's claim that "Woman does not exist" (*La femme n'éxiste pas*, with a slash through the *La*). But "Woman does not exist" in a second sense as well, namely, insofar as actually existing women are included within a patriarchal kinship system *as* excluded from it (in the manner of "the great confinement") (S XX 72–3). It is significant that from the moment that Silvia becomes the object of an exchange between the two men, she does not speak.[15] The social order that has been (re-)constituted at the end of Shakespeare's play truly is a "society of brothers." Lacan's claim that "there is no sexual relationship" reflects the tragic rather than the comic side of the human condition. In *Two Gentlemen* there is every indication that the two couples will live happily ever after. But in tragedies – such as *Othello* – the possibility of a reconciliation between the sexes comes too late.

2.9   Althusser's attempt to forge an alliance between Marx and Freud

> *1. Witch* Hail!
> *2. Witch* Hail!
> *3. Witch* Hail!
> (*The Tragedy of*
> *Macbeth*, I, iii,
>   62–4)

In 1963, when Lacan was dismissed from the International Psychoanalytical Association and so forced to abandon his seminar at the Hôpital Sainte-Anne, the Algerian-born French philosopher Louis Althusser (1918–1990) enabled him to resume his seminar at the École normale supérieure, encouraging his own students – including Jacques-Alain Miller, Lacan's future son-in-law and heir apparent – to attend. The structuralist reading of Marx that Althusser was developing at the time was intended to parallel, and ultimately encompass, Lacan's structuralist reading of Freud, for the economic class struggle that "in the last instance" determines manifest social phenomena does so in exactly the same way that the unconscious determines manifest psychic phenomena (FM 112). Though Lacan took little note of his work, Althusser regarded their intellectual alliance as important for both theoretical and political reasons. Marx and Freud had not merely discovered comparable objects; they had both developed inherently "conflictual" sciences that took aim at bourgeois ideology (WOP 108). Because the Marxist and Freudian movements were opposed by reactionary forces, they both had to struggle against "revisionist" tendencies (WOP 109–10). By defending the properly scientific character of Marx and Freud's respective discoveries, Althusser and Lacan were furthering the proletarian struggle against capitalist relations of production. Although Althusser eventually became disillusioned with Lacan – calling him a "pitiful Harlequin" in 1980 – he never abandoned his own effort to situate psychoanalysis within a Marxist framework (WOP 126).

In the essays collected in *For Marx* (*Pour Marx*, 1965), Althusser tries to explain the exact nature of Marxist philosophy (FM 31). To do this, it is necessary to distinguish between the early Marx's account of the alienation of man and the mature Marx's scientific understanding of the social relations of production in capitalism – because *"the young Marx is not Marx"* (FM 53). According to Althusser, the crucial breakthrough in Marx's thinking occurred in 1845, but it was only in the first volume of *Capital*, published in 1867, that Marx was able to articulate his discovery of the structural character of the capitalist mode of production (FM 227). In his early writings, Marx was still under the influence of Hegel, from whom he had learned to think of history as the dialectical process by which an alienated humanity overcomes its alienation. But he eventually formulated a completely different conception of the dialectic, one that is concerned with the manner in which a dominant mode of production determines social relations of production and vice versa. "Humanistic" interpretations of Marx – such as those of Sartre and Merleau-Ponty – fail to appreciate just how different the Marxist dialectic is from that of Hegel.

Althusser characterizes Marx's discovery as an "epistemological break," a term he borrows from Bachelard to refer to the moment when a new science suddenly emerges out of its own ideological pre-history (FM 32, 168, 185, 257). Epistemological breaks occur whenever a new form of "knowledge" appears, whether it is a genuine science or a mere pseudo-science. Overemphasizing the continuity between a new science and its pre-history is a mistake because it makes it seem as if the new "object of knowledge" had already been there before. By freeing the history of science from its prejudice in favor of genetic continuities, both Bachelard and Foucault – as well as

Jean Cavaillès (1903–1944) and Georges Canguilhem (1904–1995) – were able to develop a scientific history that has as its object those very ruptures by which something radically new emerges (RC 44). This new approach is exemplified in Foucault's accounts of the birth of "madness" and "the 'gaze' of clinical medicine" (RC 45). Marx prepared the way for the new history by emphasizing the radical difference between feudal and capitalist economies, while Freud emphasized the radical break that occurs when an infant becomes a human subject with an unconscious. Both rejected evolutionary explanations of manifest phenomena in favor of analyses of how such phenomena are determined by underlying structures that are in a certain sense "atemporal" (WOP 62). Althusser suggests that just as he had to rescue Marx from the humanists, so Lacan had to rescue Freud from supposedly orthodox analysts (WOP 53). In a pair of letters to his own analyst, René Diatkine, Althusser defends Lacan's claim that "the child is caught up in language from the time of his birth," thereby emphasizing the fact that symbolic identification is not to be understood in genetic or developmental terms (WOP 66). Althusser gives this idea a Marxist twist by further claiming that the child is caught up in *ideology* from the time of its birth.

In *Reading Capital* (*Lire le Capital*, 1968) – a collection of papers written by members of a seminar that he gave in 1965 – Althusser likens Marx's "reading" of the discourse of political economy to Freud's way of listening to the speech of a subject undergoing analysis. In both cases it is a question of attending not to a manifest discourse but to something that escapes the order of immediacy. Althusser credits Benedict de Spinoza (1632–1677) with being the first philosopher to thematize the question, "*What is it to read?*" (RC 15). Spinoza's "theory of the difference between the imaginary and the true" was obscured by the triumph of Lockean empiricism, a philosophical ideology that continues to hold sway not only in the work of later classical empiricists such as Berkeley and Hume but even in the work of Leibniz, Kant, and Hegel (RC 17, 35). For Althusser, empiricism is the presumption that there is an equivalence between "the true" and "the given." Knowledge is then conceived on the model of a "mirror" relation between the knower and the known; to read a phenomenon is to attend to it in the manner in which it is given (RC 19). But givenness is an imaginary lure, as Lacan shows in his account of the mirror stage (RC 53). Such a lure is ideological in the sense that it is produced by something that disappears behind it: "there can never be a given on the fore-stage of obviousness, except by means of a giving ideology which stays behind. . . . If we do not go and look behind the curtain we shall not see its act of 'giving': it disappears into the given as all workmanship does into its works" (RC 163). Thus empiricism is an *essentially* ideological doctrine because it bars the way to a structural analysis of that by which the given is given.

Marx's critique of the discourse of the political economists was based on this very insight. Adam Smith (1723–1790) and David Ricardo (1772–1823) failed to discover the role played by surplus value in capitalist relations of production because they attended merely to manifest economic phenomena such as the exchange of a laborer's services for a wage. The problem is not that they failed to see something that was equally manifest but that they limited themselves to the order of visible phenomena:

> Political Economy gives itself as an object the domain of "economic facts" which it regards as having the obviousness of *facts*: absolute givens which it takes as they "give" themselves. . . . Marx's revocation of the pretensions of Political Economy is identical with his revocation of the obviousness of this "given," which in fact it *"gives itself"* arbitrarily as an object, pretending that this object *was given it.*
>
> (RC 158–9).

Just as Freud discovered that the overt speech of his patients was conditioned by something that remained silent within it – "Only since Freud have we begun to suspect what listening, and hence what speaking (and keeping silent), *means*" – so "only since Marx have we had to begin to suspect what, in theory at least, *reading* and hence writing *means*" (RC 16). In his early conception of *homo oeconomicus*, Marx thought it was possible to read the immediate presence of "abstract" essences in "concrete" phenomena (FM 109; RC 162, 16). What enabled him to go beyond this Hegelian point of view was his discovery of something "symptomatic" about the discourse of the political economists, namely, its systematic confusion of the concept of labor with that of labor power (RC 28). Marx treats this confusion in the same way that Freud treats a slip of the tongue – i.e., as attesting to something that remains repressed while nonetheless massively governing the discourse as a whole: "Marx makes us . . . see what the classical text itself says while not saying it, does not say while saying it . . . *it is the classical text itself which tells us that it is silent*" (RC 22). A critical reading of the discourse of political economy becomes possible only when "an *informed* gaze" – as opposed to a merely "acute or attentive gaze" – discovers that there are "blanks" within it (RC 27).

In contrast to an empiricist reliance on the given, a structural analysis must "construct" its object: "there is no *immediate* grasp of the economic, there is no raw economic 'given,' . . . the identification of the economic is achieved by *the construction of its concept*" (RC 178). In the preface to the second volume of Marx's *Capital*, Engels likened Marx's discovery of surplus value to Antoine Laurent Lavoisier's (1743–1794) discovery of oxygen, observing that both Marx and Lavoisier had to subject their respective fields (political economy and chemistry) to a thorough-going critique. Althusser agrees with Engels that Marx's relationship to Smith and Ricardo is akin to that of Lavoisier's relationship to Joseph Priestley (1733–1804) and Carl Wilhelm Scheele (1742–1786). Just as the latter could not see the very thing that they produced – namely, oxygen – because they were still caught in " *'phlogistic' categories*," so the political economists could not see what they produced – surplus value – because they were thinking in ideological categories (RC 152). To revolutionize the old discourses, Lavoisier and Marx had to construct new theoretical objects.

Kant defined the construction of a concept as the process whereby "a **non-empirical** intuition" of "an **individual** object" is used to represent any of the indefinite number of objects that fall under that concept (CPR A713/B741). This is what geometers do when they draw a triangle and then reason about it as if it were any triangle whatsoever. According to Kant, Thales (or whoever the first geometer was) discovered a new science that could not have been founded either on the basis of concepts alone or on the basis of intuitions alone (since the geometer does not simply "read off" the properties of a given object in an empiricist manner, but must "ascribe to the thing nothing except what followed necessarily from what he himself had put into it in accordance with its concept"). Analogously, when Galileo "rolled balls of a weight chosen by himself down an inclined plane," he did not rely on mere observation of natural phenomena but rather used reason to "compel nature to answer its questions, rather than letting nature guide its movements" (CPR Bxii–xiii).

Althusser also credits Thales and Galileo with "opening up" the "great 'continents'" of mathematics and physics (LAP 15; cf. 39). But his conception of construction differs from that of Kant. For Kant, to construct a concept is to exhibit in intuition an object that is subsumed under an *already given* concept. For Althusser, by contrast, construction is required for concept formation itself: no concept is ever "immediately 'given,' . . . *legible* in visible reality," but "must be . . . *constructed*" (RC 101). Kant acknowledges that geometers and natural scientists have to invent new concepts, but the conditions for the possibility of their respective sciences are a priori and so are themselves insusceptible to revolutionary transformation. Althusser suggests that Kant remains within a fundamentally empiricist point of view for precisely this reason. By merely inquiring into the possibility of synthetic a priori judgments, Kant – like the political economists – surreptitiously *gives himself* what he takes to be given: "this problem has been formulated on the basis of its 'answer,' as the exact *reflection* of that answer, i.e., not as a real problem but as the problem that had to be posed if the desired *ideological* solution was to be the solution to this problem" (RC 52).[16] Likewise, Kant's characterization of the subject as a synthetic unity of apperception reflects the bourgeois demand that "*the conflictual rift of the class struggle . . . be lived by agents as a superior and 'spiritual' form of unity*" (WOP 116). Though Kant made a significant contribution to the critique of ideology by characterizing rational psychology, cosmology, and theology as "'*sciences' without objects*," he himself succumbed to "*an ideology of 'man'*" (as do all those who persist in reading Marx as a theorist of alienation) (RC 115n; cf. WOP 91).

Instead of continuing to plow the pseudo-scientific field that had been sown by the political economists, Marx constructed an entirely new theoretical object, namely, the totality of the relations of production. Unlike an isolated act of exchange, a "manifest" phenomenon whose deeper significance lies concealed, the relations of production comprise a structural whole which – like the Freudian unconscious – "overdetermines" manifest economic phenomena (FM 206n; RC 188). In *The Interpretation of Dreams*, Freud suggested that the meaning of an element of a dream could be overdetermined through the mechanisms of condensation and displacement. For Althusser, "overdetermination" refers to the fact that every element of a structure is determined by its position with respect to the structure as a whole, and that within a particular structure, each level or substructure both determines and is determined by the others. Whereas Hegel, like Leibniz, treated manifest phenomena as the direct "expression" of a unified totality, Marx anticipated the structuralists by recognizing the priority that relations have over their terms (RC 180). For Hegel, the dialectic proceeded by way of contradiction and its sublation. As such, it involves not the mutual determination of disparate structures, but the integrity and identity of a unitary subject who assimilates what is external to it through "cumulative *internalization*" (FM 101). Thus for Hegel, every contradiction remains "simple," involving a single subject capable of sustaining multiple determinations. For Marx, by contrast, dialectical contradiction is overdetermined in the sense that it involves a genuine manifold of structures that determine one another through a kind of conflictual reciprocity. Although he singles out a dominant structure – the economic mode of production – it does not function as a central element in a unified totality: "this dominance of a structure ... cannot be reduced to the primacy of a *centre*" (RC 98). The priority that Marx accords to structures over their elements requires that every contradiction involve a complex interaction among elements and levels that are inextricably bound up with one another. "In the last instance" it is the dominant mode of production that determines the character of social relations, but only insofar as a relation of mutual determination holds among various structures within society as a whole. Thus it is possible to preserve the classic Marxist priority given to the economic "infrastructure" over the ideological "superstructure" while providing a more nuanced account of the various ways in which each can influence the other.

The concept of overdetermination enables Althusser to make sense of the peculiar kind of temporality pertaining to structures that are in some sense atemporal. Once again he identifies Marx's position by distinguishing it from that of Hegel. Just as Hegel thinks contradiction only in terms of a central unifying subject, so he conceives of events as occurring in a single, unified, homogeneous time that is grounded in the subject's perpetual presence to itself: "Two essential characteristics of Hegelian historical time can be isolated: its homogeneous continuity and its contemporaneity" (RC 94). In this account, *"nothing can run ahead of its time. The present constitutes the absolute horizon* of all knowing" (RC 95). Against this point of view Althusser suggests that each of the different levels of a structure is governed by a different temporality so that "it is no longer possible to think the process of the development of the different levels of the whole *in the same historical time*" (RC 99). As Marx conceives it, "the time of economic production ... is a complex and non-linear time – a time of times ... that cannot be *read* in the continuity of the time of life or clocks" (RC 101). This suggests that Lévi-Strauss's way of thinking the relation between the "synchronic" and "diachronic" dimensions of structural causality is inadequate. Like Hegel, Lévi-Strauss conceives of the synchronic in terms of "contemporaneity" and the diachronic as the sequence of events that occur in a linear homogeneous time (RC 96). As a result he is unable to account for the manner in which structures adapt themselves to events: "by what miracle could an empty time and momentary events induce de- and re-structurations of the synchronic?" (RC 108). By contrast, Althusser's own conception of multiple temporalities allows him to think the synchronic as "rhythm and punctuation" (RC 100), whereby "events" have to be located at the specific level of the system at which they occur: "it is no longer possible to think the process of the development of the different levels of the whole *in the same historical time*" (RC 99). Once again he finds a model for this in Foucault's account of the different temporal rhythms exhibited in the history of madness and the clinical gaze; he also appeals to Freud's account of the complex relationship between "the time of the unconscious" and "the time of biography" (RC 103).

Thus, despite the fact that Lévi-Strauss is no less critical of humanism than Althusser, and that he also explicitly appeals to Marx as the founder of structural analysis – Mauss's "total social fact" being essentially equivalent to the social relations of production – Althusser thinks that his account of kinship structures falls short of a genuinely Marxist point of view for a number of reasons. For one thing, Lévi-Strauss is unable to explain why a particular kinship structure takes the form that it does; instead of demonstrating how it is the necessary consequence of a particular mode of production, he contents himself with indicating that it is a combinatorial possibility (HCOW 26). This is connected with the fact that he has no real conception of a mode of production, with the consequence that his account of social relations of production is "left hanging in the air" (HCOW 25). Lacking such an account he can only resort to biologistic or functionalist explanations of kinship systems. Finally, he is unable to account for the specifically ideological dimension in which particular kinship roles are "concretely lived" (WOP 71; cf. 29, 177 n4; HCOW 27). The ultimate task of a unified structural theory would require bringing Marxist, Freudian, and Lévi-Straussian doctrines together: "how is one to think rigorously the relation between first, the formal structure of language, ... second, the concrete structures of kinship, and finally, the concrete ideological formations in which the specific functions (paternity, maternity, childhood) implied in the structures of kinship are experienced?" (WOP 30).

But here it is necessary to proceed cautiously. In one of the letters written to Diatkine in 1966, Althusser speculates that the unconscious "needs 'something' to function," and that "this 'something' is, it seems to me, in the last analysis, *the stuff of ideology*" (WOP 75). This suggests "that the unconscious is structured like that 'language [*langage*]' ... which is *ideological*" (WOP 76). But in an essay composed in 1976, "On Marx and Freud," he emphasizes the fact that Marx and Freud did not have the same object; the mistake made by Wilhelm Reich's (1897–1957) attempt to bring Marx and Freud together was to assume that they did (WOP 107). In "The Discovery of Dr. Freud," also written in 1976, he suggests that it is necessary to avoid two different extremes, one represented in Lacan's avoidance of the connection between Marx and Freud; the other in Reich's haste to make such a connection (WOP 98–9). Here Althusser offers a revised assessment of the significance of Lacan's achievement, suggesting that Lacan failed to "*constitute a scientific theory of the unconscious*," providing instead "*a philosophy of psychoanalysis*" (WOP 90–1). Freud's achievement is now said to rest on his hesitancy to pronounce as final any results that could not yet lay claim to genuine scientificity. Precisely by exercising such caution Freud demonstrated the truly scientific character of his enterprise (WOP 93–4). When asked by a correspondent in the late 1970s to explain the connection between ideology and the unconscious, Althusser demurred, appealing to the rigor of Freud's scientific caution. Just as Freud could not specify the connection between biology and the unconscious even though he knew that some such connection must exist, so Althusser says that he too is unable to see the connection that he presumes to exist between ideology and the unconscious (WOP 5).

In "Ideology and Ideological State Apparatuses (Notes Towards an Investigation" (*Idéologie et appareils idéologiques d'état (Notes pour une recherche)*, 1970), Althusser attempts to explain the manner in which existing social relations of production are themselves reproduced. Here he suggests that it is necessary to isolate the specific role played by "ideological state apparatuses" such as schools, churches, and armies whose function is to "educate" subjects to accept "*the ruling ideology*" (LAP 133). All along Althusser had been arguing that the focal point of the ideology of capitalism was the bourgeois subject, conceived equivalently either as *homo oeconomicus* or *homo psychologicus* (WOP 149). What he now does is to ascribe to ideology the function of constituting this subject as such:

> I say: the category of the subject is constitutive of all ideology, but at the same time and immediately I add that *the category of the subject is only constitutive of all ideology insofar as all ideology has the function (which defines it) of "constituting" concrete individuals as subjects.*
>
> (LAP 171)

The mechanism by which this is accomplished is "interpellation": "ideology 'acts' or 'functions' in such a way that it 'recruits' subjects among the individuals (it recruits them all), or 'transforms' the individuals into subjects (it transforms them all) by that very precise operation which I have called *interpellation* or hailing, and which can be imagined along the lines of the most commonplace everyday police (or other) hailing: 'Hey, you there!'" (LAP 174).

Interpellation is equivalent to what Lacan called "symbolic identification," except that its ideological dimension is underscored. Thus the police officer who hails the subject represents the big Other, but this function must be understood in terms of the class struggle. To be "successfully" interpellated in ideology is to traverse the Oedipus complex in such a way as to acquire a superego whose demands are specifically tied to the dominant mode of production. Lacking a materialist conception of the relationship between a dominant mode of production and the social relations of production, Freud could posit only a generic superego that would befit every social formation. Conversely, Marxism, lacking an account of the formation of the superego, was unable to explain the process by which a dominant mode of production reproduces itself. Althusser solves both of these problems simultaneously by putting forth a kind of "second topography" for Marxism. According to Marxism's first topography, there is an economic infrastructure at the base of society, and two superstructural levels supported by it. At the top is the "politico-legal" structure of the state. Between this level and the infrastructure are "the different ideologies" that mediate between them (LAP 134). This relatively static model is akin to Freud's first topographical division between the unconscious, consciousness, and the mediating preconscious. In *Civilization and its Discontents*, Freud used his dynamic model of the id, ego, and superego to show that it is through the mechanisms of identification and incorporation that subjects assimilate the norms of their culture, thereby enabling social structures to reproduce themselves. By conceiving of identification as interpellation, Althusser manages to apply this solution to Marxism while at the same time situating Freud's account within a Marxist framework.

So understood, interpellation is the process by which individuals come to accept the "obviousness" of all those normative "truths" that pertain to existing relations of production, thereby enabling these relations to reproduce themselves.[17] Thus once again ideology "imposes ... obviousness as obviousness, which we cannot *fail to recognize*" (LAP 172). This explains why "those who are in ideology believe themselves by definition outside ideology ... It is necessary to be outside ideology, i.e. in scientific knowledge, to be able to say: I am in ideology (a quite exceptional case) or (the general case): I was in ideology" (LAP 175). To recognize that one is in ideology one must be outside it – or rather, one must be outside it insofar as one is inside it, as if by way of a structure of transcendence within immanence or autonomous heteronomy. Levinas also conceived of interpellation – the discourse of the other – as the mechanism by which a subject is called to assume its status as a subject. But for him this was an ethical relation "older" than war (TAI 21).

By contrast, Althusser claims that interpellation takes place in an inherently antagonistic social space that can only be theorized from the standpoint of a "conflictual science," that is, a science which *takes sides*. This explains why Marxism, not ethics, is first philosophy. Althusser credits the idea of a conflictual science to Niccolò Machiavelli (1469–1527), who discovered that contrary to what a positivistic empiricism teaches, there is no *"null* position, *outside of conflict"* that one could adopt (WOP 111).

The idea that society is inherently antagonistic suggests that there are subjects who successfully resist interpellation. But ideology infects bourgeois and proletarian subjects alike. This is because interpellation is not merely a secondary operation by which already constituted subjects are exposed to ideology, but the primary operation by which subjects become subjects in the first place. Put otherwise, interpellation is the same thing as Oedipalization, which is something that every subject must undergo: "the Oedipus complex is the dramatic structure, the 'theatrical machine,' imposed by the Law of Culture on every involuntary and constrained candidate to humanity" (WOP 29). Psychoanalysis can take the form of yet another interpellating mechanism (helping subjects to become "successfully" Oedipalized) or it can function as a site of resistance to the dominant ideology. In 1963, Althusser regarded Lacan's attack on ego psychology as pointing in the second direction: "Outside. You are henceforth outside . . . it is enough to begin working with those who are working within that outside" (WOP 158). But in 1980, when Lacan was orchestrating the breakup of his École Freudienne de Paris, Althusser accused him and his cohorts of not considering the consequences of their actions from the point of view of the analysands: "it won't come crashing down on your heads, since you are well protected and know how to lie low . . . it will come crashing down on the unfortunates who come to stretch out on your couch and on all their intimates and the intimates of their intimates and on to infinity" (WOP 133).

Unlike Lacan, who theorized from the standpoint of a practicing analyst, Althusser wrote exclusively as an analysand, having undergone various forms of treatment for severe depression since the 1940s. Eight months after his speech to the Lacanians, he was hospitalized for strangling his wife, Hélène Légotien (1910–1980). In his posthumously published, *The Future Lasts Forever: A Memoir* (L'avenir dure longtemps, suivi de Les Faits, 1992), Althusser claims to have been massaging his wife's neck and then suddenly to have realized that she was dead. Though he says that he is writing to give "the response" that he would like to have given in court had he not been "declared unfit to plead," Althusser's memoir reads less like the legal defense of a subject accused of a crime than the testimony of a suffering human being: "I hope my readers will forgive me. I am writing this book principally for my friends, and for myself if that is possible" (FLF 13, 18).

2.10 Deleuze and Guattari's schizoanalysis

> I am but mad north-north-west. When the wind is southerly I know a
> hawk from a hand-saw.
>
> (*The Tragedy of Hamlet, Prince of Denmark*, II, ii, 378–9)

In his 1967 essay, "How do we Recognize Structuralism?" (*A quoi reconnaît-on le structuralisme?*, first published in 1973), Deleuze characterizes structuralism as "a new transcendental philosophy" (HDWRS 263). For Lévi-Strauss, Lacan, and Althusser (as well as Foucault), the relationship between structures and events is that between a virtual differential manifold and the various combinations of elements which actualize themselves in time (HDWRS 268). On this interpretation, structuralism is nothing less than a philosophy of difference. In *Difference and Repetition*, Deleuze characterized thought as a kind of "differential calculus" that has ideas as its objects (DR 181–2). In the essay on structuralism he suggests that this differential calculus pertains to the "symbolic" order discovered by Lévi-Strauss and Lacan (HDWRS 265). Lacan's tripartite distinction between the real, the imaginary, and the symbolic can be understood in terms of the difference, respectively, between a unitary ideal, the dual mirror relation, and a tertiary play of terms, one of which is always absent (HDWRS 260–1). Lacan shows that it is this third dimension – or dimension of the third – that governs formations of subjectivity and intersubjectivity (HDWRS 263). Likewise, Lévi-Strauss discerns the "differential relations" governing kinship systems (HDWRS 266), while Althusser discovers beneath manifest economic phenomena the "structural space defined by relations of production" (HDWRS 262). In each case, the structures in question are both unconscious and linguistic, giving rise to a distribution of "singularities" that "shift from place to place" (HDWRS 280). Hence the subject revealed by structuralism is essentially "nomadic," different in kind from the unified and unifying Kantian subject in that it is an effect of the passive syntheses of "a differential unconsciousness" (HDWRS 270).

This conception of a differential unconscious that produces a nomadic subject is developed in *Anti-Oedipus: Capitalism and Schizophrenia* (*L'Anti-Oedipe*, vol. 1 of *Capitalisme et schizophrénie*, 1972), the first of a series of books that Deleuze wrote with the Lacanian-trained psychoanalyst, Félix Guattari (1930–1992). Deleuze and Guattari criticize structuralism for locating structures at the level of the symbolic order rather than at that of the real, the locus of "desiring-production" (AO 97, 1ff.). They also suggest that the unconscious is better thought of in "machinic" rather than "structural" terms, because desire manifests itself not through a "logical combinatory" of signifiers but in a network of binary "desiring-machines" each of which is coupled to another (AO 53, 109). Althusser saw that there was a connection between Oedipalization and capitalism, but he was unable to specify its exact nature. This is because he failed to take his own eminently machinic account of social production to its logical conclusion, lapsing into a philosophy of representation (as opposed to a philosophy of difference) (AO 306). Explaining Oedipalization in terms of interpellation is insufficient because it "is not an ideological problem, a problem of failing to recognize, or of being subject to, an illusion. It is a problem of desire, *and desire is part of the infrastructure*" (AO 104). Thus it is necessary "to show how, in the subject who desires, desire can be made to desire its own repression" (AO 105). Lacan resisted the normalizing tendencies of psychoanalysis by calling attention to the differential character of the unconscious: "he does not enclose the unconscious in an Oedipal structure. He shows on the contrary that Oedipus is imaginary, nothing but an image, a myth" (AO 310). But the fact that Lacan's followers continue to regard successful Oedipalization as the aim of analysis suggests that his efforts did not fully succeed (AO 73).

In *Difference and Repetition*, Deleuze criticized Kant for subordinating the passive syntheses of the manifold to the transcendent forms of the "I think" and the object = x. In *Anti-Oedipus*, Deleuze and Guattari suggest that psychoanalysts make an analogous mistake when they impose a "transcendent" use on the syntheses of the unconscious (AO 109). Instead of seeing desire as "the set of *passive syntheses* that engineer partial objects, flows, and bodies, and that function as units of production" (AO 26) – an entirely immanent operation – they represent it as lacking something beyond itself. In order to complete Lacan's Copernican turn, it is necessary to carry out a truly transcendental analysis of the unconscious, one that will critique the various "paralogisms of the unconscious" to which psychoanalysis has succumbed and account for the mechanisms by which psychic and social repression are produced by desiring-production itself (AO 177). Such is the task of Deleuze and Guattari's "schizoanalysis" (AO 75, 109). Its therapeutic aim is to bring about a "de-oedipalizing" reversal of the subjection of the passive syntheses of desire to transcendent uses, thereby "restoring the syntheses of the unconscious to their immanent use" (AO 112).

In *Difference and Repetition*, Deleuze distinguished the three time-constituting syntheses of Habitus, Mnemosyne, and the Eternal Return. In *Anti-Oedipus* this becomes the three-fold division between (1) a "connective synthesis of production" by which a linear sequence of the form "and then" is constituted, (2) a "disjunctive synthesis of recording" of the form "either ... or ... or," and (3) a "conjunctive synthesis of consumption–consummation [*consommation*]" that has the concluding form of a "so it's ..." (AO 12, 16). These syntheses once again belong to the field of a differential manifold but they are now considered with respect to their "practical" employment. Thus they are syntheses of desire. *Anti-Oedipus* can therefore be described as an attempt to carry out a genuine critique of practical reason, just as *Difference and Repetition* represented a truly transcendental critique of pure reason.[18] Deleuze and Guattari credit Kant with the discovery that desire is essentially productive (AO 25; cf. CPrR 144n: "The **faculty of desire** is a being's *faculty to be by means of its representations the cause of the reality of the objects of* *these representations."*). Unfortunately, Kant once again shrinks back from one of his insights, relegating the object produced by desire to the status of a mere "psychic reality." In doing so he continues to adhere to the long metaphysical tradition for which desire is conceived as a lack of something that transcends it. Against this point of view, Deleuze and Guattari maintain that desire is productive not of mere psychic representations of something missing but of the real itself: "If desire produces, its product is real" (AO 26).

Since desire is not a faculty of a unified and unifying subject but a differential manifold, it can be characterized as a field of "desiring machines." Each desiring-machine produces a "flow" that is siphoned off by another which produces a flow that is in turn siphoned off by another, and so on (AO 1ff.). These are the connective syntheses of the unconscious. Collectively they give rise to a non-productive "body without organs," a kind of virtual object that is less the totality of the series of connective syntheses than an additional entity existing "alongside" it: "The body without organs is in fact produced as a whole, but a whole alongside the parts – a whole that does not unify or totalize them, but that is added to them like a new, really distinct part" (AO 326). At the first level of synthesis, the body without organs distinguishes itself from its desiring-machines, repelling them in the manner of a "paranoiac machine" (AO 9). In effect, this is the practical equivalent of what, in *Difference and Repetition*, Deleuze called the pure present, immediately freeing itself from whatever appears on its surface so that something new can appear. Corresponding to the constitution of a pure *past* would then be the disjunctive syntheses by which whatever is produced by the connective syntheses is recorded on the surface of the body without organs. This time the body without organs functions as a gigantic memory or "miraculating machine," attracting rather than repelling the desiring-machines that constitute it (AO 11). Finally, the conjunctive synthesis corresponds to the pure future – the eternal return – as the object of a practical affirmation. Here Deleuze and Guattari refer to the production of a "celibate machine," in which the repulsive tendency of the paranoiac machine and the attractive tendency of the miraculating machine are brought together. The celibate machine is the site of enjoyment or *jouissance*, and as such it can be thought of as producing and consuming intensive magnitudes (AO 18, 84). In *Difference and Repetition*, intensive magnitudes were characterized as differentials whose reciprocal determination gave rise to manifest qualities. In *Anti-Oedipus*, Deleuze and Guattari suggest that the entire process of desiring-production can be understood as the production of differential intensities, with the body without organs functioning as their "degree zero" place of inscription (AO 20).

It is at the level of the third synthesis that the subject proper appears, but only as "a mere residuum alongside the desiring-machines," a residuum that "confuses" itself with the celibate machine (AO 17). This confusion is akin to that described by Lacan in his account of the mirror stage. The jubilant cry "So it's *me*!" (AO 20) is the expression not of a unified and unifying subject but of a subject that is a mere surface effect of desiring-production. The point of Lacan's account of imaginary identification – like that of Sartre's account of the transcendence of the ego – was to show that the subject is a result of fundamentally passive syntheses, not the agent of a series of active syntheses governed by a principle of common sense. The problem was to show how this originary experience of misrecognition serves as the basis for a symbolic identification by which the subject takes itself to be unified and unifying. Lacan, following Freud, characterized this as the process of Oedipalization. In effect, it is Oedipus that imposes on desire what in *Difference and Repetition* Deleuze called a "norm of identity" (the principle of common sense) and a "norm of distribution" (the principle of good sense). The first manifests itself in the subject's filiative position within a kinship system; the second in the rules of alliance that distinguish permissible from prohibited sexual partners.

Oedipalization is the process by which the three syntheses take on a transcendent as opposed to an immanent use. The connective synthesis of desiring-production, originally geared to "partial" and "non-specific" objects, is now oriented by parental figures and a system of conjugal rules. Desire is repressed, but in such a way as to give rise to the illusion that what had been desired all along is what is now explicitly prohibited by the conjugal rules themselves: "Incest is only the retroactive effect of the repressing representation *on* the repressed representative: . . . it projects onto the representative, categories, rendered discernible, that it has itself established" (AO 165). It is precisely through this "paralogism of extrapolation" that desire comes to appear as lack (AO 73, 110). In a similar way, the disjunctive synthesis, which had been inclusive ("either . . . or . . . or") now becomes exclusive ("either/or") as it is forced to think of differences in terms of rigid oppositions (AO 76). Here desire can only choose between subjecting itself to a transcendent law that directs it toward the symbolic order and retreating to an undifferentiated imaginary space – the choice between "normality" and "neurosis." In either case, its "real" nature as desiring-production is dissimulated. Deleuze and Guattari call this the "paralogism of the double bind" (AO 80). Finally, the conjunctive synthesis, whose immanent use had been "nomadic and polyvocal," becomes "segregative and biunivocal" (AO 110–11). This occurs when the third synthesis is subjected to a transcendent signifier which, as Lacan put it, "represents" the subject in the symbolic order. Segregation involves the demarcation of a previously mobile field of intensities into series of determinable objects or persons. Biunivocalization occurs when the mobile and immanent conjunctive synthesis "so it's . . ." gives rise to the determinate and transcendent "so *that* is what *this* meant" (AO 101). This corresponds to what *Difference and Repetition* called "the form of recognition." Deleuze and Guattari call it "the paralogism of application" (AO 111).

The problem with psychoanalysis is that instead of helping to unravel these paralogisms it actively encourages them. Nowhere is this more evident than in the way that psychoanalysis treats schizophrenics. Freud regarded schizophrenics as subjects who had "failed" to undergo successful Oedipalization. But the real question is whether clinically diagnosed schizophrenics suffer from "too much" or "too little" Oedipalization. It is to Lacan's credit that he repudiated the idea that the aim of analysis should be to strengthen the ego. This implies that Oedipalization is something to be resisted. But "certain disciples of Lacan" have put forth "oedipalizing interpretations of Lacanism" which suggest that the way to treat schizophrenics is to make them more like neurotics, subjects who remain trapped within the triangular Oedipal paradigm (AO 53, 73). Against this tendency, Deleuze and Guattari argue that the aim of analysis should be not Oedipalization but schizophrenization: "Wouldn't it be better to schizophrenize – to schizophrenize the domain of the unconscious as well as the sociohistorical domain, so as to shatter the iron collar of Oedipus and rediscover everywhere the force of desiring-production...?" (AO 53). This is not to valorize the psychic condition of clinically diagnosed schizophrenics but to recognize in schizophrenia a process of desiring-production that has been thwarted:

> Before being a mental state of the schizophrenic who has made himself into an artificial person through autism, schizophrenia is the process of the production of desire and desiring-machines. How does one get from one to the other, and is this transition inevitable? This remains the crucial question.
>
> (AO 24)

In order to understand what exactly Oedipalization is, and why it should be resisted rather than encouraged, it is necessary to specify its precise relationship to capitalism. Lévi-Strauss showed that the Oedipus myth is not universal. But he too remained short of a properly machinic point of view. A kinship system is not "a logical combinative arrangement" but a "physical system where intensities are distributed" (AO 187; cf. 147: "A kinship system is not a structure but a practice, a praxis, a method, and even a strategy."). Deleuze and Guattari suggest that Mauss was right to emphasize the priority of the gift over exchange, for while it is true that gifts necessarily call forth counter-gifts, it is only through a secondary operation that gift-giving comes to be stamped with the symbolic form of exchange (AO 185–6). By conceiving of kinship systems as structures rather than machines, Lévi-Strauss assumes that this secondary operation is already there at the beginning, and that the only crucial distinction to be made is that between elementary and complex kinship systems. Against this point of view, Deleuze and Guattari identify three basic kinds of social machines – territorial, despotic, and capitalist (AO 33) – the first of which has nothing to do with symbolic exchange: "Society is not first of all a milieu for exchange where the essential would be to circulate or to cause to circulate, but rather a *socius* of inscription where the essential thing is to mark and to be marked" (AO 142).

Mauss was the first to put forth a comprehensive theory of the gift, but "the great book of modern ethnology" (AO 190) is Nietzsche's *Genealogy*, whose second essay calls attention to the role played by mnemotechniques in "man's pre-history" (OGOM 41; AO 145). Nietzsche shows how the "primitive" territorial machine operates, namely, by "coding" the flows of desiring-production so that they will be channeled toward specific ends. It is here that desiring-production is converted into social production, which rebounds upon desire itself. Inscription serves not merely as a production of marks but as a production of painful intensities, and of visible *signs* of pain that will be recognized as such. Thus the territorial machine functions as what the schizophrenic writer Antonin Artaud (1895–1948) called a *"theater of cruelty"* (AO 189). Deleuze and Guattari emphasize that the signs or codes inscribed by the territorial machine are not yet symbolic in character. This is because there is as yet no transcendent signifier that would govern the process of inscription. Everything is subject to rigid codes, but these are not grounded in any transcendent point of unification. The possibility of such a thing "haunts" the primitive territorial machine as a threat lurking on the horizon. Indeed, it is the threat of the horizon itself in the form of what Kant called a *focus imaginarius*, a transcendent object = x to which all the codes would ultimately refer.

The arrival from the horizon of such an object = x corresponds to the overthrow of the territorial machine and the advent of a "despotic" or "barbarian" machine. Here the "immanent unity of the earth ... gives way to a transcendent unity of an altogether different nature – the unity of the State" (AO 146). Once again it is Nietzsche who provides an exemplary description of how the ancient system of "festive" cruelty gives way to the "terror" and "vengeance" of the state apparatus (AO 212). The primordial state or *Urstaat* represents "a terror without precedent, in comparison with which the ancient system of cruelty, the forms of primitive regimentation and punishment, are nothing" (AO 192). The principal function of the despotic machine is to "overcode" all of the codes that appeared at the level of the primitive machine, thereby subjecting the order of signs to that of a despotic signifier, whether this be God, the king, or the State itself (AO 199, 206). Thus it is here that the symbolic order first appears. It is also here that the prohibition against incest manifests itself as such, again as a retroactive overcoding of desire. But the figure of Oedipus has not yet arrived, for the system of terror does not require it. All desiring-production is directed toward the body of the despot – a figure equivalent to the father of Freud's primal horde – who is the only subject exempt from the incest prohibition.

Only in the transition from the barbarian machine to the capitalist machine does Oedipus finally appear. The function of the capitalist machine is to "decode" all of the overcoded codes, thereby allowing desiring-production to circulate freely. However, in carrying out this general "deterritorialization" of flows – thereby representing nothing less than the schizophrenization of desire – capitalism simultaneously reterritorializes them by subjecting them to the body of capital itself. As such capitalism represents "the *relative* limit of every society," whereas schizophrenia represents "the *absolute* limit that causes the flows to travel in a free state on a desocialized body without organs" (AO 246).

Capitalism represents the process by which desiring-production is freed from the despotic signifier, thereby undoing all of the overcoded codes of the barbarian machine. As Marx and Engels put it in the *Manifesto of the Communist Party*: "All the settled, age-old relations with their train of time-honoured preconceptions and viewpoints are dissolved; all newly formed ones become outmoded before they can ossify" (LPW 4). In effect this corresponds to "the death of God," the elimination of the despotic signifier. And yet under capitalism it is not the case that "everything is permitted." For it is as if capitalism has sped up the dialectic of prohibition and transgression to the point where both occur simultaneously in a festival that is perpetually renewed and canceled. This reflects the fact that the capitalist machine maintains a relationship to both the form of the despotic state and the territorial body of the earth. These manifest themselves as internal limits of social production, checks which prevent the deterritorialization of desire from going too far. In other words, to ensure that all social production remains directed toward the body of capital, the capitalist machine introduces mechanisms that keep desiring-production from becoming revolutionary. In particular, the family comes to function as a private domain in which desiring-production is kept from manifesting its real nature as social production. Foucault traced this mechanism back to the asylum structure of the nineteenth century: "the asylum would keep the insane in the imperative fiction of the family" (MC 254). It is here that Oedipus enters the scene. Oedipalization is the process by which an essentially "schizo" subject is made to think of itself as a unified ego who wants to sleep with its mother (the representative of the territorial earth) but is prevented from doing so by its father (the inheritor of the despotic signifier) (AO 265). Psychoanalysis then accentuates the predicament of the subject by insisting that all its genuinely revolutionary manifestations of desire are really just expressions of a private Oedipal triangle (AO 92).

Deleuze and Guattari suggest that the three kinds of social machines can be understood as manifestations of the three basic forms of passive synthesis: "the savage territorial machine operated on the basis of connections of production, . . . the barbarian despotic machine was based on disjunctions of inscription derived from the eminent unity. But the capitalist machine, the civilized machine, will first establish itself on the conjunction" (AO 224). Corresponding to each of the three social machines, therefore, is a representation of the transcendent use of one of the three syntheses:

the system of connotation-connection in the savage territorial machine, corresponding to the coding of the flows; the system of subordination-disjunction in the barbarian despotic machine, corresponding to overcoding; the system of co-ordination-conjunction in the civilized machine, corresponding to the decoding of the flows.

(AO 262)

Thus Oedipalization corresponds to the paralogism of application. At the two poles of biunivocalization are an imaginary Oedipus and a symbolic Oedipus, between whose two poles desire is constrained to oscillate: "Oedipus says to us: either you will ... 'resolve' Oedipus, or you will fall into the neurotic night of imaginary identifications" (AO 79). This is why "The true difference in nature is not between the Symbolic and the Imaginary, but between the real machinic ... element, which constitutes desiring-production, and the structural whole of the imaginary and the Symbolic." It is also why the aim of schizoanalysis should be not to "oedipalize the schizo" but to follow through on the work of Lacan, who "schizophrenized even neurosis" (AO 83; cf. 175).

Deleuze and Guattari suggest that Bataille's conception of "sumptuary, nonproductive expenditure" exemplifies an immanent use of the third synthesis of consumption (AO 4n; cf. 190). In reterritorializing all the flows that it decodes, the capitalist machine transforms expenditure into investment (productive consumption), thereby producing servile (Oedipal) subjects rather than sovereign subjects (schizos). Just as Bataille characterized Sade as a genuine sovereign subject, so in *Coldness and Cruelty* (*Le Froid et le Cruel*, 1967) Deleuze reads both Sade and Leopold von Sacher-Masoch (1836–1905) as revolutionary subjects. Bataille is credited with bringing out "Sade's hatred of tyranny," and with distinguishing genuine Sadism from the sadism of the Nazis (CAC 87, 17). Contrary to Freud's view of masochism as a simple inversion of sadism, Deleuze argues that the two express completely different forms of revolutionary desire (CAC 39–40). They both subvert the law of Oedipus, but Sade does so through irony; Masoch through humor (CAC 86–8). Following Blanchot, Deleuze reads Sade as forging an alliance between the father and the daughter against the mother, and Masoch as uniting the son and a disavowed mother against the father (CAC 60ff.). Each of these strategies exploits the "structural split" between the ego and the superego, finding in perversion a "third alternative" to "the functional disturbance of neurosis and the spiritual outlet of sublimation" (CAC 117). Thus the pervert, like the schizo, represents for Deleuze a solution to the double bind of Oedipalization.

2.11 Kristeva's semanalysis

And such a want-wit sadness makes of me,
That I have much ado to know myself.
(*The Merchant of Venice*, I, i, 6–7)

When the Bulgarian-born theorist Julia Kristeva (1941–) came to France in 1966, she immediately became involved in a number of different fields associated with the structuralist movement: linguistics, Marxism, and Lacanian psychoanalysis (JKI 13). Bringing these together, she developed a unique way of reading literary texts, an approach that she calls "semanalysis." Like psychoanalysis, semanalysis is concerned with the unconscious, whose formations it regards as signifying operations. It is also akin to schizoanalysis in that it is geared toward a critique of capitalism. In her 1974 book, *Revolution in Poetic Language* (*La révolution du langage poétique: L'avant-garde à la fin du XIXe siècle: Lautréamont et Mallarmé*), Kristeva poses the same basic question as Deleuze and Guattari, namely, how can analytic practice be made to stimulate rather than stifle the revolutionary potential of subjects? She suggests that this question can be answered by attending to a particular kind of discourse – "text-practice" (RPL 88) – which is exemplified in avant-garde works of literature that disrupt the very language in which they are written: "The text is a practice that could be compared to political revolution: the one brings about in the subject what the other introduces into society" (RPL 17). Agreeing with Deleuze and Guattari that there is something "liberating" about the "de-structuring and a-signifying machine of the unconscious," Kristeva notes that "their examples of 'schizophrenic flow' are usually drawn from modern literature" (RPL 17).[19]

In order to highlight the role played by signification in the constitution of subjectivity, Kristeva characterizes the primordial play of psychic drives not in terms of desiring-production – "*desire* cannot completely account for the mechanisms of the signifying process" (RPL 145–6) – but in terms of what she calls "signifiance" (RPL 22). Freud's distinction between primary and secondary processes is said to correspond to the difference between the "semiotic" and "symbolic" levels of discourse (RPL 24). Prior to the subject's acquisition of the linguistic competence to make judgments – an ability that coincides with access to the symbolic order – the pre-thetic subject is immersed in a semiotic "chora" or primal place in which the drives manifest themselves in a relatively free state (RPL 25). The chora is characterized by the proto-syntactic processes of displacement (metonymy) and condensation (metaphor); and with the advent of symbolic discourse it also manifests itself through a third process which Kristeva calls "*transposition*," that is, the "*passage from one sign system to another*" (RPL 59–60). To make the transition from the semiotic to the symbolic requires that the subject cross the "threshold" of the "thetic phase" (RPL 48). This involves two distinct stages that correspond to what Lacan called "imaginary" and "symbolic" identification, namely, "the mirror stage and the 'discovery' of castration" (RPL 46). For Kristeva, to traverse the Oedipus complex is to enter the thetic phase as an articulate subject with the capacity to signify desires that would otherwise remain inchoate.

Kristeva's account of the path from the semiotic chora to the advent of the thetic subject has a certain affinity with Nietzsche's representation of the passage from the Dionysian to the Socratic. Like the Greek chorus, the chora represents a kind of pulsating "spirit of music" that is more primordial than Apollonian figuration: "the *chora* precedes and underlies figuration and thus specularization, and is analogous only to vocal or kinetic rhythm" (RPL 26; cf. 24, where music is described as one of the few "nonverbal signifying systems that are constructed exclusively on the basis of the semiotic"). Just as the Dionysian manifested itself through Apollonian figuration, so the semiotic remains present in the mirror stage. Like the Greek spectator who identifies with the tragic chorus, the child is still identified with the maternal body. In order for the thetic phase to be completed, the subject must separate itself from its mother, thereby acquiring the ability to make judgments about objects from which it distinguishes itself (RPL 47). This is like the moment when Socrates made his appearance in the Greek theater. According to Nietzsche, Socrates's arrival coincided with the disappearance of the Dionysian from the Greek stage. Likewise, for Kristeva, separation from the maternal requires a repression of the semiotic as the subject now finds itself situated within a symbolic milieu.

Just as Nietzsche mourned the loss of Greek tragedy, so Kristeva suggests that we are all in mourning for the primordial maternal body from which we have had to separate ourselves. There are various ways of compensating for this loss, many of which represent a refusal or denial of separation. Fetishism, perversion, and psychosis – the results, respectively, of negation, disavowal, and foreclosure of the discovery of castration – are three different consequences of a failure to complete the thetic phase (RPL 63–4). Like Deleuze and Guattari, Kristeva suggests that these failures bespeak a certain resistance to the demands of the symbolic order. But just as they distinguished between suffering schizophrenics and revolutionary schizos, so she contrasts the inability of fetishists, perverts, and psychotics to respond to loss in a satisfactory way with a genuinely transformative solution. Instead of refusing to cross the threshold separating the semiotic from the symbolic, avant-garde writers like Stéphane Mallarmé (1842–1898) and Comte de Lautréamont (1846–1870) achieved symbolic mastery while allowing for semiotic disruption of their discourses. In this way they remained what Kristeva calls subjects "in process" (RPL 22). To remain in process is to make the transition from the semiotic to the symbolic without succumbing to the pretensions of an exclusively symbolic subject – a position that Kristeva associates with the Cartesian and Husserlian conceptions of the ego, but which can also be likened to Nietzsche's depiction of Socrates. In contrast to the metalinguistic discourse that Kristeva associates with such a claim to total mastery, the subject in process is like a "text" whose grammatical rules are "disturbed" by the return of the semiotic (RPL 37). Like the fetishist, the subject in-process refuses to forsake the semiotic dimension altogether, but unlike the fetishist she is able to signify this refusal in symbolic language: "The text is completely different from a fetish because it *signifies*" (RPL 65).

In order for the subject-in-process or the text to avoid the two extremes of either disavowal of castration or complete repression of the semiotic, a delicate balance between competing forces is required. This can be likened to the interplay that Nietzsche detected between the Dionysian and the Apollonian. Kristeva associates an excess of the semiotic with Dionysian intoxication: "The Dionysian festivals in Greece are the most striking example of this deluge of the signifier, which so inundates the symbolic order that it portends the latter's dissolution in a dancing, singing, and poetic animality" (RPL 79). Like Bataille, she characterizes the ecstacy to which art can give rise as an experience of "excess" and "heterogeneity" (RPL 204, 191, 212).

Corresponding to the distinction between the semiotic and symbolic registers is the semanalytic distinction between "genotext" and "phenotext" (RPL 86–7). According to Kristeva, the genotext represents the process by which choral drives and rhythms manifest themselves in a signifying discourse, while the phenotext represents the manifest level at which that discourse makes thetic – i.e., propositional – claims of a certain sort. She then goes on to offer a "provisional and schematic" typology of four different types of discourse. In his 1969–1970 seminar, *L'Envers de la psychanalyse*, Lacan distinguished between the discourses of the master, the university, the hysteric, and the analyst. Kristeva proposes "a different classification, which, in certain respects, intersects these four Lacanian categories." Her contrast is between "narrative, metalanguage, contemplation, and text-practice" (RPL 88).

Each of these forms of discourse represents a unique type of signifying practice which Kristeva associates with both a particular kind of social formation and a corresponding modality of the subject who enunciates the discourse in question. For example, narrative is associated with situations in which kinship relations dominate either social life as a whole or the psychic life of individuals who identify themselves in terms of familial coordinates. Kristeva credits psychoanalysis with uncovering the role played by narrative in neurosis. But just as Deleuze and Guattari criticized those psychoanalysts who reinforced the reign of Oedipus by forcing subjects to identify themselves in terms of a Mommy–Daddy–me triangle, so she suggests that psychoanalysts tend to reduce all signifiance to narrative (RPL 90–3). The second form of discourse, metalanguage, represents a hierarchical social or psychic position in which the thetic subject becomes dominant. Kristeva suggests that metaphysics and science are governed by this type of discourse, and that insofar as it represents the apotheosis of the subject it can also manifest itself in paranoia (RPL 94–5, 89). Contemplation, the third type of discourse, is typical of certain relatively isolated communities that exist as enclaves within hierarchical societies. Though endlessly critical of the existing order, contemplation is ineffective, being the discourse of an obsessional or quasi-obsessional subject who problematizes all pretension to mastery. According to Kristeva, both philosophy and deconstruction exemplify this mode of discourse (RPL 95–7).

Finally, the text is characterized as the form of signification proper to "a *hierarchically fluctuating* social system" in which subjects remain essentially in-process (RPL 99). In the text symbolization takes place in such a way as to allow for a perpetual reconfiguration of its coordinates. Like Deleuze and Guattari, Kristeva locates both schizophrenia and revolutionary subjectivity at this level, characterizing each as a form of transgression which only *"revolutionary practice"* succeeds in making meaningful (RPL 102–5). To read a text as a text is to attend not only to what it signifies at the manifest level of symbolic discourse but also to the way in which semiotic flows manifest themselves in its rhythms, alliterations, and other poetic devices. This is the task of semanalysis:

> To understand this practice we must ... break through the sign, dissolve it, and analyze it in a semanalysis, tearing the veil of representation to find the material signifying process. ... In the case of texts by Lautréamont, Mallarmé, Joyce, and Artaud, *reading* means giving up the lexical, syntactic, and semantic operation of deciphering, and instead retracing the path of their production.
>
> (RPL 103)

Because it is both musical and signifying – Dionysian and Apollonian – poetry is an exemplary form of textual practice.

Unique to textual practice is "negativity," a term that Kristeva borrows from Hegel to refer to the restless movement that "prevents the immobilization of the thetic" (RPL 99, 113). Negativity hearkens back to the originary "event" by which the semiotic chora first gives rise to symbolization (RPL 146). In "Negation" (*Die Verneinung*, 1925), Freud had interpreted the logical function of negation – a manifestation of the death drive – as an "intellectual" substitute for repression, locating the origin of repression itself in the infant's impulse to expel, or reject, objects that cause it pain (GPT 214–16). For Kristeva, the negativity that manifests itself in texts refers not to the intellectual (symbolic) concept of negation but to this more primordial (semiotic) experience of rejection (RPL 150). In his account of the relationship between art and sublimation, Freud hinted that "aesthetic productions" exhibit the non-intellectual expression of rejection that Kristeva associates with texts (RPL 161). Rejection is "normalized" when instead of finding an outlet in text practices it is subjected to Oedipalizing narratives which constitute the thetic subject as an ego with the capacity to make affirmative and negative judgments (RPL 161). Like Deleuze and Guattari, Kristeva regards Oedipalization as both psychically deadening and complicitous with capitalism. Just as they claimed that capitalism produces damaged schizos, so she sees it as producing both neurotics and paranoid subjects (RPL 139). To cope with the subversive threat of text practices, capitalism also tends to produce avant-garde texts as isolable enclaves of heterogeneity – a form of inoculation not unlike the production of fascist armies (Bataille) or asylums (Foucault).

Instead of redirecting negation toward familial identifications, the production of texts unleashes negativity as a form of "expenditure and implementation" (RPL 162). Like Bataille, Kristeva conceives of expenditure as an expression of heterogeneity. By channeling rejection into "identificatory, intersubjective, and sexual stases," "the heterogeneity of drives" is subordinated to the "homological economy" of the symbolic order (RPL 167, 175–6; cf. 190). Just as for Bataille heterology was not only a science but a practice, so for Kristeva a text is not just an "experience of heterogeneous contradiction" but a "practice" (RPL 195). It was Bataille who discovered in literature "the discreet, yet so profound and upsetting, means for struggle against oppressive unity and against its reverse side, exuberant or macabre nihilism" (BEP 262). In "The Use Value of D.A.F. de Sade," Bataille had criticized the Surrealists for considering the work of Sade from a merely aesthetic point of view rather than as a model for proletarian revolutionary activity. Likewise, Kristeva suggests that textual practices should serve the revolutionary end "of bringing about new social relations, and thus joining in the process of capitalism's subversion" (RPL 105).

Kristeva agrees with Marx that Hegel conceived of negativity only from the standpoint of a contemplative philosophical discourse, extending this criticism to deconstruction ("grammatology") as well (RPL 140–5). Among those said to have appreciated the necessity for poets to become revolutionaries and for revolutionaries to become poets are Vladimir Ilyich Lenin (1870–1924) and Mao Zedong (1893–1976) (RPL 199–201; cf. BEP 258–60). In 1973, Kristeva and other members of the Tel Quel group of literary critics with which she was associated visited Maoist China. In a 1988 interview, she claims that this trip left her disillusioned with "leftist movements" and "leftist ideology" (JKI 7). Though still critical of capitalism, her subsequent work no longer couches the transformative potential of texts and analytic practice in the vocabulary of revolution.

In *Black Sun: Depression and Melancholia* (*Soleil noir: dépression et mélancolie*, 1987), Kristeva develops the psychoanalytic idea that melancholia is rooted in the primordial loss of the maternal Thing. Artists come to terms with this loss through sublimation (BS 13–14). The "work of the imagination" – an inherently melancholy faculty – has its origin in the attempt to compensate for loss by producing a work that masks the fact of castration (BS 6, 9). In order for this process to be successful, the work of art must serve as a means of entry into the symbolic order rather than as a mere substitute for the lost object (BS 23). Just as it was necessary for text practice to cross the threshold separating the semiotic from the symbolic, so coming to terms with loss requires an acknowledgment of the inevitability of "matricide" (BS 27–8).

Kristeva goes on to analyze various types of "feminine depression," each of which arises from the difficulty that women have in separating from their mothers: "the melancholy woman is the dead one that has always been abandoned within herself and can never kill outside herself" (BS 30; cf. 69ff.).

For Kristeva, sublimation represents the only way around this double bind between psychic murder and suicide: "Sublimation alone withstands death" (BS 100). But instead of attending exclusively to the text's capacity for perpetual negativity, she highlights the role played by beauty in the process by which the "artist and the connoisseur" acquire "a sublimatory hold over the lost Thing" (BS 97). A product of the imagination, beauty would be that which "is not affected by the universality of death" (BS 98). Drawing on Benjamin's *The Origin of German Tragic Drama*, Kristeva suggests that the work of the aesthetic imagination is inherently allegorical in that it is capable of representing the universal experience of mourning that lies at the basis of melancholia (BS 101).

Kristeva's account of sublimation echoes a number of themes in Kant's critique of aesthetic judgment. For Kant, genius – like the subject-in-process – is capable of producing a work that both does and does not make sense: it strikes us as purposive (i.e., as signifying) without indicating exactly what its purpose (meaning) is. If the imagination of the genius is given too much freedom, then the work becomes meaningless; while if the understanding is given too much control, the work becomes merely didactic (precisely what Nietzsche complained about in Euripidean drama). Kristeva's chora can be thought of as representing an originary free play of the imagination prior to the advent of a schematism that will subject it to (symbolic) laws of the understanding. As for the sublime, Kant suggests that a potentially traumatic encounter with something formless (akin to the threat of castration) gives rise to a conflict between the imagination and reason whose outcome is a triumphal feeling of enthusiasm on the part of the subject. Although Kristeva does not explicitly engage with Kantian aesthetic categories, her distinction between the subject who remains in process and the subject who refuses to come to terms with castration is akin to the difference between the genius and the sublime enthusiast who always risks succumbing to fanaticism.

An example of such fanaticism is analyzed in Kristeva's *Powers of Horror: An Essay on Abjection* (*Pouvoirs de l'horreur: essai sur l'abjection*, 1980), a semanalytic study of the writings of the anti-Semitic French novelist Louis-Ferdinand Céline (1894–1961). For Kristeva, the "abject" – that which provokes horror and repulsion – represents the pre-objective maternal Thing from which every subject must separate itself. Bataille recognized the crucial role played by abjection in the transition from animality to humanity and in the advent of the subject/object relationship (POH 64). Insofar as it precedes the distinction between subject and object, the relation to the abject eludes the opposition between introjection and rejection. Heterogeneity – alterity – does not exist "outside" the subject in any simple way since the very split between inside and outside only arises through a forgetting of the undifferentiated condition of the semiotic chora. Phobia represents an attempt on the part of the subject to localize the abject through projection or rejection. But the danger of abjection is always present, requiring perpetual vigilance – particularly since the abject is not only horrifying; as Bataille saw, it also exerts a powerful attraction. Just as perversion represents the choice of transgression rather than sublimation, so paranoia results from the phobic subject's identification with the superegoic demand to repudiate the abject. Whereas the normal or neurotic ego suffers from the superegoic accusation of its abjectness (treating oneself as a piece of shit), the paranoid subject tries to project abjectness outside of itself onto others, thereby endlessly repeating the abjection of the mother's body. In the writings of Céline, abjectness is projected onto Jews who are represented as "staining" the body politic. In contrast to paranoia, textual practice represents a nonphobic way of inscribing the heterogenous within the symbolic order.

Closely akin to anti-Semitism is xenophobia. In *Strangers to Ourselves* (*Étrangers à nous-mêmes*, 1988), Kristeva traces the hatred of foreigners to an inability on the part of individuals to come to terms with their own constitutive relationship to alterity. Reflecting on the history of religious and political responses to the threat of foreignness, she notes the frequency of a compromise formation between banishment and assimilation, namely, the tactic of including "the other" within the body politic *as* excluded from it (i.e., the tactic of "the great confinement"). Whether geographically isolated or merely politically disenfranchised, the incorporated but unassimilated foreigner is merely "tolerated." In the name of cosmopolitanism, a number of attempts have been made throughout European history to acknowledge foreigners as members of a universal human community. Not only did the French Revolution invoke universal "rights of man"; it spoke of extending "rights of citizens" to foreigners living in France. Following Kant, Kristeva envisions a cosmopolitan "right to hospitality" that would grant foreigners rights *as* foreigners. But to overcome the paranoia of xenophobia and the neurotic compromise formation of tolerance, we must come to terms with the "foreignness in ourselves," for "That is perhaps the only way not to hound it outside of us" (STO 191). Insofar as it "dissolves . . . narcissistic fixations," psychoanalysis represents "a journey into the strangeness of the other and of oneself, toward an ethics of respect for the irreconcilable" (RPL 233; STO 182).

2.12   Derrida's hauntology

I'll bury thee in a triumphant grave.
(*The Tragedy of Romeo and Juliet*,
V, iii, 83)

Nay, come, let's go together.
(*The Tragedy of Hamlet,
Prince of Denmark*, I, v, 190)

In *Speech and Phenomena*, Derrida argued that in his account of the genesis of internal time consciousness, Husserl discovered that there could be no "living present" without a constitutive relationship to alterity and death. Though Husserl persisted in thinking that the subject could nonetheless have an immediate apprehension of itself in the living present, Derrida concluded that it could not, and that life, rather than simply being the opposite of death, was death in its *différance* from itself (SAP 148). To indicate this fact, Derrida introduces the expression "life death," connecting it with a passage from *The Gay Science* in which Nietzsche cautions: "Let us beware of saying that death is opposed to life. The living is merely a type of what is dead, and a very rare type" (GS 168; TPC 269). Freud develops a similar idea in *Beyond the Pleasure Principle*, suggesting that life is simply a round-about way in which something that was originally dead seeks to return to its original state. In "Freud and the Scene of Writing" (*Freud et la scène de l'écriture*, 1966), Derrida notes that, as early as his "Project for a Scientific Psychology," Freud took life to be an effect of difference and repetition:

> there is no life present *at first* which would *then* come to protect, postpone, or reserve itself in *différance*. The latter constitutes the essence of life. . . . Life must be thought of as trace before Being may be determined as presence. This is the only condition on which we can say that life *is* death.
>
> (WAD 203)

Just as Husserl showed that consciousness of the present presupposed a synthesis of retentions of the past, so Freud argues that consciousness only arises in the wake of memory. But Freud goes further than Husserl in noting that memory eludes all phenomenological description in principle (WAD 202). Yet despite Freud's denial that the subject can be fully present to itself in consciousness, Derrida suggests that he too ultimately reverts to the metaphysical view that the living present is uncontaminated by its relation to death and alterity.

In "A Note on the 'Mystic Writing-Pad'" (*Notiz über den Wunderblock*, 1925), Freud suggests that the entire psychic apparatus – both its topographical divisions and its dynamic relays – can be represented on the model of a writing machine of a peculiar sort. Derrida claims that this model cannot be regarded as merely metaphorical for it solves a theoretical problem for which Freud could find no other solution (WAD 199). From 1895 on, Freud had tried to explain how one and the same system could function both as an unconscious recording machine (i.e., as a repository of "memories" registered in the system before becoming conscious) and as a perpetually blank slate that was ever-ready for new conscious perceptions. How could one and the same system be permanently modified and yet completely unaffected by that which enervates it? (WAD 200). What made this problem seem intractable was Freud's beliefs that consciousness must be secondary with respect to memory, and that memory is the recording of *differences* between forces that have "breached" the system by overcoming its resistances. Together these ideas implied that consciousness was merely an effect of a play of differential traces, that is, an effect of a kind of writing. Older than the empirical writing that can be located in space and time – but without leaving the empirical/transcendental distinction intact – such a "proto-" or "arche-writing" would be constitutive of space and time themselves (WAD 212, 227, 209). Derrida notes that whenever Freud attempts to explain the functioning of the unconscious – for example, in his account of the dreamwork as a "rebus" and in his conception of the psychic censorship – he is forced to appeal to the "metaphor" of writing. But all of "the classical writing surfaces" prove to be inadequate because they involve a merely external relation between the recording agency and the surface of inscription. In effect, Freud's problem was that he kept looking for a spatiotemporal image of that through which an originary "spacing" and "temporalizing" would take place. Only with his discovery of the mystic writing pad does he find a model that can capture the scene of writing as an activity of auto-affection (WAD 222).

The mystic writing pad (also known as a "magic slate") is a toy for children. It has three layers: a wax slab, a waxed sheet of paper that is attached to the slab at one end, and a celluloid covering that protects the paper from being ripped. By pressing an object hard enough against the celluloid covering, one leaves marks in the slab that "appear" on the sheet of paper where the paper has been pressed into the slab's grooves. By lifting the sheet of paper away from the slab, the marks disappear from view but remain etched on the slab. Thus, as Freud points out, the waxed sheet of paper can be likened to consciousness – which remains ever-ready for new inscriptions – while the slab functions as a kind of memory. Significantly, it is only by being etched in "memory" that the marks appear in "consciousness." As for the celluloid covering, Freud likens this to the psychic apparatus's resistance to excitations. To complete the analogy, Freud imagines that the wax slab representing the unconscious periodically sends out "feelers" to sample excitations from the external world. To this back-and-forth movement he traces "the origin of the concept of time" (GPT 212; WAD 225). All this suggests that the so-called psychic apparatus *is* a kind of writing machine. But according to Derrida, precisely here Freud shrinks back, for if the psychic apparatus really were an autonomic writing machine it would have to be something that is only alive insofar as, *dead*, it writes itself (WAD 227). Just as Freud refuses to think the relationship between life and death (or Eros and Thanatos) as one of *différance*, so he fails to recognize that all of the oppositions governing his metapsychology – notably the distinction between the pleasure principle and the reality principle – are relations of *différance* (SAP 150).

In "Mourning and Melancholia," Freud contrasted the so-called "normal" work of mourning, in which the subject manages to complete the arduous process of coming to terms with loss, and the pathological failure or refusal to mourn that is characteristic of melancholia. Melancholia was said to result from an identification with a lost object against which the subject directs reproaches that are ostensibly aimed at itself. This account served as the basis not only for Freud's distinction between the ego and the ego ideal, but for his analysis of the moral phenomena of conscience and guilt. An originary melancholia would lie at the basis of the sense of obligation. But if this is so, then perhaps there is an "ethical" moment in the melancholic's refusal or inability to mourn, a refusal to commit "matricide," as Kristeva called it. Derrida observes that the very idea of a completed work of mourning is equivalent to the ideal of a living present that would be purified of all relationship to alterity and death. But if this relationship is constitutive of subjectivity – as Freud's account of the ego as a precipitate of identifications implies – then instead of characterizing melancholia as a pathological case of mourning, mourning – or at least the triumphalist fantasy of a completed work of mourning – should be regarded as a pathological case of a "constitutive" melancholia. In effect, we are always in what Derrida calls "mid-mourning," the perpetual – because perpetually deferred – work of "originary" or "impossible" mourning.

Derrida develops this idea in "Fors," his foreword to *The Wolf Man's Magic Word: A Cryptonymy* (*Cryptonymie: Le verbier de L'Homme aux loups*, 1976) by the Hungarian-born psychoanalysts Nicolas Abraham (1919–1975) and Maria Torok (1925–1998). To account for the difference between mourning and melancholia, Abraham and Torok contrast "introjection" – an "authentic" process of mourning by which the ego responds to a loss that it learns to accept – with "incorporation," a fantasmatic process by which the melancholic ego, refusing to mourn, "encrypts" the lost object within itself. Thus, in melancholia, the incorporated other is, as it were, buried alive: "I pretend to keep the dead alive, intact, *safe (save) inside me*, but it is only in order to refuse, in a necessarily equivocal way, to love the dead as a living part of me" (Fors xvi). Though sympathetic with Abraham and Torok's account of incorporation, Derrida asks whether it is possible to draw a rigorous distinction between incorporation and introjection:

> The question could of course be raised as to whether or not "normal" mourning preserves the object *as other* (a living person dead) inside me. This question – of the general appropriation and safekeeping of the other *as other* – can always be raised as the deciding factor, but does it not at the same time blur the very line it draws between introjection and incorporation, through an essential and irreducible ambiguity?
>
> (Fors xvii)

Derrida goes on to suggest that it is both necessary and impossible to distinguish between incorporation as the process by which the ego attempts to inoculate itself against alterity – thereby making it akin to the triumphalist claim to have completed a work of mourning – and another way of being haunted by someone who both "must" and "must not" be mourned.

Besides the metapsychological concept of a crypt, Abraham and Torok also introduce the term "phantom" to refer to something that haunts the subject "from within" but which has come to it from the unconscious of another person. Like the crypt, the phantom is something inaccessible to consciousness – in this case, not because the subject represses it, but because the subject has inherited it from the other's unconscious.[20] Freud implicitly thematized the problematic of the phantom in his account of the inheritance of the repressed murder of the father of the primal horde.

As early as his introduction to Husserl's "Origin of Geometry," Derrida had explicitly characterized writing as a problem of inheritance. To belong to a culture – a condition for the possibility of being a subject at all – is to inherit a sedimented tradition in which buried intentions are entombed (IOG 88). To inherit is to be obliged to watch over these intentions, an obligation that is inherently conflictual since it amounts to the simultaneous demand to keep something that is dead *alive* – and to keep something that is alive *dead*. The responsibility of the inheritor is ineluctable insofar as one cannot *not* inherit. Likewise it is impossible not to *bequeath* an inheritance to others.[21] Thus ethics – the relation to the other – is first and foremost a relation of bequeathal and inheritance.

In *The Post Card: From Socrates to Freud and Beyond* (*La carte postale: De Socrate à Freud et au-delà*, 1980), Derrida contrasts two different construals of the aim of psychoanalysis, one corresponding to triumphalism, the other to perpetual mourning – the two tendential limits of the responsibility for an inheritance. In "To Speculate – on 'Freud'" (*Spéculer – Sur «Freud»*), he reads *Beyond the Pleasure Principle* as an expression of Freud's anxiety over his own legacy. Then, in "*Le Facteur de la vérité*" ("The Deliverer of Truth") – "a contribution to a decrypting still to come of the French analytic movement" – he reads Lacan's "Seminar on *The Purloined Letter*" as attesting to Lacan's jealous struggle with other French psychoanalysts – such as Marie Bonaparte (1882–1962) – for control over the Freudian legacy (TPC 335). Without renouncing the Freudian inheritance, Derrida tries to articulate another way of responding to it. Toward this end, he effectively puts his own problematic of inheritance on display in the lengthy "Envois" – "sendings" – with which the book begins. The *envois* are said to be fragments of a series of postcards whose addressee(s) are apparently never named. Lacan claimed that a letter which circulates in the course of Poe's short story – a letter that is initially in possession of the queen before being stolen by the minister, from whom it is stolen in turn by Dupin, who gives it back to the queen – represents the phallus. By returning to the queen – i.e., to a woman who, as such, "lacks" it – the letter would thereby attest to the role played by castration in the constitution of the symbolic order. Lacan concludes with the confident assurance "that a letter always arrives at its destination" (SPL 53).

Derrida challenges this reading by maintaining that "a letter can always not arrive at its destination" (TPC 441). The possibility of not arriving pertains to all writing by its very nature. According to Derrida, Lacan effectively ignores the problematic of writing, attending only to the signified content that Poe's text purports to represent (the "story" that its narrator recounts) (TPC 428). Ostensibly, Lacan takes the signifier (as opposed to the signified) to be the proper object of psychoanalytic interpretation, and Derrida regards this as "an indispensable phase in the elaboration of a theory of the text" (TPC 424). But in order to carry out this program it would be necessary to examine the textual character of the signifier itself. Instead of doing this, Lacan relies on a classical conception of the signifier whose materiality would be that of an iterable ideality. In particular, his account of castration requires that the signifier — i.e., the letter or phallus — remain intact: "the signifier must never risk being lost, destroyed, divided, or fragmented without return" (TPC 438). According to Derrida, Lacan preserves the integrity of the signifier by identifying the proper place of its lack — that is, on the body of a castrated woman. To say that the letter always arrives at its destination would be to affirm the circulation of the phallus as the perpetual return of the same to the same. But in fact the iterability of the signifier — that which supposedly guarantees its ideality and integrity — also subjects it to an originary bifurcation which threatens to ruin its circular return to its point of origin. Far from having a unique destiny, the letter would be subject to what Derrida calls "destinerrance":

> The divisibility of the letter ... is what chances and sets off course, without guarantee of return, the remaining [*restance*] of anything whatsoever: a letter does *not always* arrive at its destination, and from the moment that this possibility belongs to its structure one can say that it never truly arrives, that when it does arrive its capacity not to arrive torments it with an internal drifting.
>
> (TPC 489)

This condition of destinerrance is highlighted in the fragments of the epistolary "Envois." Like Blanchot — whose "Death Sentence" he characterizes as "perhaps a truly cryptic story" (Fors xxxix) — Derrida characterizes writing as the sharing of an unsharable secret, the attestation to something unavowable (GT 94). Every text contains a secret not insofar as it keeps something from view — like a sealed letter — but precisely insofar as it discloses it for all to see: like a postcard. To read is always to inherit public secrets, and thus to be haunted by what Abraham and Torok characterize as phantoms.

Derrida elaborates on the concept of the phantom in *Specters of Marx: the State of the Debt, the Work of Mourning, and the New International* (*Spectres de Marx: L'État de la dette, le travail du deuil et la nouvelle Internationale*, 1993), introducing the term "hauntology" (*hantologie*) (SOM 10, 51) to refer to the "logic of the ghost" (SOM 63). Hauntology is to psychoanalysis what deconstruction is to phenomenology — a radicalization of the problematic of the relationship between life and death. In *Speech and Phenomena*, Derrida had derived the sense of the expression "I am" from that of "I am dead" (SAP 97). In *Specters of Marx* he connects the "I am" to an originary "I am haunted" (SOM 133). Or, as he puts it in a memorial to Althusser: "we are . . . only *ourselves* from that point within us where the other, the mortal other, resonates" (TRLAF 244).

The title, *Specters of Marx*, refers both to the ghosts that belong to Marx's legacy and to the ghosts with which he himself was haunted. The theme of spectrality appears frequently in Marx's writings, notably in the opening sentence of the *Communist Manifesto* ("A specter is haunting Europe – the specter of communism"); in the *Eighteenth Brumaire of Louis Bonaparte*, where Marx writes that "The tradition of all the dead generations weighs like a nightmare on the brain of the living"; in *The German Ideology*, where Max Stirner (1806–1856) is relentlessly chided for appearing to believe in ghosts; and in the first chapter of *Capital*, where Marx characterizes commodity fetishism as a kind of "phantomalization" of things (SOM 4, 108, 126ff., 159). Derrida suggests that Marx was obsessed with the figure of the ghost, and that he sought to exorcize it by ontologizing it, that is, by reducing that which haunts to the exclusive alternatives of being or non-being. In effect, he sought to complete a work of mourning that would eliminate spectrality by reducing alterity to the order of ontology (SOM 29). Against this triumphalist gesture, Derrida seeks to articulate another way of taking up the Marxist inheritance, a way of affirming an ethical communism that would be based on the irreducibility of alterity to the order of the same. Appealing to Blanchot's conception of a communism whose condition of possibility would be a certain "unworking," Derrida characterizes this as a communism "to come" (SOM xix). The expression "to come" (*à-venir*) suggests a future (*avenir*) that can only take place *as* irreducibly futural. In stressing the "to-come" of communism (as well as of democracy), Derrida intends not to postpone the coming of an event but to insist on an irreducible diachrony in every such coming.

Derrida reads Hamlet's "The time is out of joint – O cursed spite,/That ever I was born to set it right!" (I, v, 188–9) as an expression of the ineluctable obligation of inheritance.[22] Uttered as a response to the apparition of a ghost, Hamlet's words attest to an irreducible problem concerning the relationship between time and the spectral. On the one hand, "setting right the time" can mean adjusting the disadjusted so that everything would belong together to the order of the same. This is how Heidegger understood Anaximander's use of the Greek word for justice, *dikē* (SOM 28). On the other hand, it can also mean preserving that disadjustment of time which, for Levinas, was a condition for the possibility of justice. Derrida suggests that Hamlet's lament takes place in "the space opened up by this question" (SOM 23). To preserve the sense of this question is to keep open the relation to the "to-come" as a relation to that which resists ontologization, namely, alterity. But this requires that one be prepared to welcome rather than banish ghosts. Freud characterized Hamlet as a melancholic (GPT 168). For

Derrida, Hamlet represents the exemplary figure of someone who does not allow himself the luxury – or alibi – of not being haunted. In his remarkable "The Phantom of Hamlet or The Sixth Act preceded by The Intermission of 'Truth'" (*Le fantôme d'Hamlet ou le VIᵉ Acte, précédé par l'Entre'Acte de la Vérité*, 1975), Abraham tries to provide Shakespeare's play with some sort of closure, so that the reader or spectator would no longer be haunted by the buried secret with which Hamlet himself is haunted.[23] Although Derrida does not refer to Abraham's sixth act in *Specters of Marx*, he suggests that "Hamlet could never know the peace of a 'good ending'" – thereby emphasizing the incompletability of every work of mourning (SOM 29).

In the "Exordium" that opens up *Specters of Marx*, Derrida discusses the phrase, "*I would like to learn to live finally*" (*je voudrais apprendre à vivre enfin*) (SOM xvii). Hauntology is, in effect, a way of learning to live with ghosts – just as psychoanalysis, for Kristeva, is about learning to live with foreigners ("Foreigners must confront a ghost from the past that remains hidden in a secret part of themselves." [JKI 4]). Both Kristeva and Derrida invoke an ethic of hospitality, of a welcoming of the wholly other. For Levinas, to welcome the other was to escape the order of violence or war. In "Violence and Metaphysics: an Essay on the Thought of Emmanuel Levinas" (*Violence et métaphysique: Essai sur la pensée d'Emmanuel Levinas*, 1964), Derrida suggests that it is impossible to escape the order of violence altogether – "One never escapes the *economy of war*" – and that there could be no violence apart from an encounter with the other (WAD 148). This does not mean that Levinas's ethics is vitiated, but that the relationship between ontology and ethics is more complicated than he suggests, that the problematic of hospitality is in a certain way inseparable from the question of being. This theme reappears in *Aporias: Dying – Awaiting (One Another at) the 'Limits of Truth'* (*Apories: Mourir – s'attendre aux limites de la vérité*, 1993) where Derrida addresses the question, "My death – is it possible?" Taking up Levinas's polemic with Heidegger as to whether death represents the possibility of impossibility or the impossibility of possibility, he suggests that the relationship to death can only manifest itself as an aporia since at issue is a relationship to the impossible itself.

In *Given Time: 1. Counterfeit Money* (*Donner le temps: 1. Fausse monnaie*, 1992), Derrida characterizes the gift as the impossible: "Not impossible but *the* impossible" (GT 7). In order for a gift to function as a gift it must in no way oblige its recipient to offer something in return. But as soon as a gift exists *as such*, some form of circular restitution has already taken place. Hence the "conditions of possibility of the gift (that some 'one' gives some 'thing' to some 'one other') designate simultaneously the conditions of the impossibility of the gift" (GT 12). This does not mean that there is no such thing as a gift but that *if* there is, it cannot exist "*in* time" in a simple way: "There would be a gift only at the instant when the *paradoxical* instant . . . tears time apart" (GT 3, 9). Heidegger referred to the *Ereignis* as the giving of time itself, but in doing so he remained within a thought of the proper [*eigen*] (GT 21–2). Without dismissing this Heideggerian problematic, Derrida proposes another way of thinking about the giving of time, one that leads him to engage with Lévi-Strauss's debate with Mauss as to whether all apparent examples of gift-giving can be reduced *without remainder* to economic exchange. Derrida agrees with Lévi-Strauss that Mauss fails to isolate a single phenomenon that would not reduce to the moment of an economic circuit. But this is because the gift, insofar as it "is" nothing but sheer excess, necessarily exceeds the order of phenomenality. Likewise, the desire to give can only manifest itself as a passion for excess – i.e., as an excessive passion – which is to say, as a kind of "madness" or fanaticism (GT 37). Indeed, at the very moment when Mauss writes of the potlatch, his very language "goes mad," "the process of the gift *gets carried away with itself*" (GT 46).

Insofar as it opens up the ethical relation to the other, the potlatch also makes possible the worst violence. Kant tried to negotiate this problem by distinguishing between two different kinds of madness – enthusiasm and fanaticism. Derrida suggests that it is both necessary and impossible to make such a distinction by somehow maintaining a kind of measure between measure itself and the immeasurable. Like Bataille, he dreams of an expenditure that would be "without reserve": "a kind of potlatch of signs that burns, consumes, and wastes words in the gay affirmation of death." But there is always recuperation: "this transgression of discourse . . . must, in some fashion, and like every transgression, conserve or confirm that which it exceeds" (WAD 274). There is no writing without calculation, but it is writing that opens up "the question of the gift" (GT 101).

In an "Epigraph" to the first chapter of *Given Time*, Derrida quotes a letter from Madame de Maintenon (1635–1719), the "secret wife" of Louis XIV (1638–1715): "The King takes all my time; I give the rest to Saint-Cyr, to whom I would like to give all" (GT 1). In *The Space of Literature*, Blanchot had written: "Even if one gives 'all one's time' to the work's demands, 'all' still is not enough, for it is not a matter of devoting time . . . but of passing into another time where there is no longer any task" (SOL 60). Like Blanchot, Derrida attempts to think this "other time" not eschatologically (as in Kant's future life) but in terms of the out-of-jointness of time. Madame de Maintenon has no time to give and yet she gives a certain "remainder" of it, wishing she *had* more of it to *give* (GT 3). In *Specters of Marx*, Derrida characterizes the relation to the future to-come as a "desert-like messianism," a messianic hope oriented not toward the fulfillment of a promise but toward the coming of the unforeseeable (SOM 28). Blanchot spoke of "a kind of messianism announcing nothing but its autonomy and its *unworking*" (UC 33). If the condition of this unworking is the irreducible disadjustment of time, the obligation to set the time right is the responsibility to maintain this disadjustment, that is, to allow unknown guests to be welcomed.

Notes

1 Cf. Nietzsche: "All instincts which are not discharged outwardly *turn inwards –* this is what I call the *internalization* of man: with it there now evolves in man what will later be called his 'soul' " (OGOM 61).

2 The cruelty that the superego directs against the ego has an ambiguous representational dimension, for, on the one hand, it expresses the child's hostility toward the father and, on the other, the father's revenge against the child. Given the dialectical complexity of the relationship between the ego and the superego, as well as between the id and the superego, it is difficult to say what exactly counts as host and what as foreign body, where the "city" ends and the "garrison" begins.

3 Cf. Kant: "Even the dead are not always safe from this critical examination, especially if their example appears inimitable" (CPrR 202).

4 This assessment echoes Nietzsche's diagnosis of the ascetic priest: "It is only suffering itself, the discomfort of the sufferer, that he combats, *not* its cause, *not* the actual state of being ill" (OGOM 101). Foucault suggests that Freud inherited the "thaumaturgical virtues" of the nineteenth-century doctor whose alleged power to heal rested more on the force of moral example than on any medical competence (MC 277).

5 Expressed in the language of the analytic philosopher John McDowell, this is to reject "bald naturalism" in favor of an account of human beings as somehow having the ability to acquire a "second nature" (McDowell, *Mind and World*, pp. 84–5). For Lévi-Strauss, the transition from first nature to second nature is made possible by the unconscious rule-following behavior that serves as the foundation for deliberate rule-following behavior.

6 Kristeva makes a similar point: "Society protects itself from negativity precisely by producing such social groups – the 'specialists of the negative,' the contemplatives, 'theoretical' and 'intellectual' types – which represent negativity as sublimated and set apart. Through them, society purges itself of negativity and endlessly calls itself into question so as to avoid breaking apart" (RPL 97).

7 Cf. Marx: "To be sure, the industrial capitalist also takes *his* pleasures . . . but his pleasure is only a side-issue – recreation – something subordinated to production; at the same time it is a *calculated* and, therefore, itself an *economical* pleasure" (EAPM 157).

8 Cf. Kant's characterization of man as a being "designed to stand upright and to scan the heavens," not to fix a "mole-like gaze . . . on experience" (PW 63).

9 Cf. Bataille's novel, *Blue of Noon* (*Le Bleu du ciel*, 1957), where transgression takes the form of sexual contact with a maternal corpse.

10 Cf. Hamlet's "dread of something after death" (III, i, 77), and the words of his father's ghost: "O horrible, O horrible, most horrible!" (I, v, 80). Levinas notes that "this impossibility of escaping from an anonymous and uncorruptible existence constitutes the final depths of Shakespearean tragedy" (EAE 56).

11 For Othello, by contrast, the sound of Emilia knocking at the door awakens in him a sense of remorse. The same thing happens to Macbeth, who when he hears someone knocking cries out: "Wake Duncan with thy knocking! I would thou couldst!" (*The Tragedy of Macbeth*, II, ii, 71).

12 As Žižek (SOI 24) points out, Marx anticipates Lacan's account of imaginary identification (C 144 n19).

13 In *Gravity and Grace* (*La Pesanteur et la grâce*, 1947), Simone Weil (1909–1943) makes the inverse point, suggesting that fulfilled desires are generally disappointing because what we really yearn for is the future qua future: "When we are disappointed by a pleasure which we have been expecting and which comes, the disappointment is because we were expecting the future, and as soon as it is

there it is present. We want the future to be there without ceasing to be future" (1947: 20). According to Weil, the true object of desire is eternity, which suggests that there is no real difference between desiring an inaccessible past and desiring an inaccessible future. In a slightly different vein, Bergson suggests that fulfillment is disappointing because desire aims at an indefinite manifold of possible futures only one of which can be actualized in the present (TFW 10).

14 In a reading of "The Purloined Letter" by Edgar Allan Poe (1809–1849), Lacan suggests that "a letter always arrives at its destination" (SPL 53). Proteus's letters to the two women never arrive at their destination since Julia and Silvia both tear them up. Only at the end of the play does Proteus become capable of full speech – with Valentine. As for Valentine – who was already capable of full speech with Proteus – he receives his message to Silvia back in an inverted form, writing at her request a love letter that she delivers to him.

15 Another Sylvia, née Maklès, was married first to Bataille and then to Lacan.

16 Cf. Deleuze's critique of Kant's reliance on the "image of thought."

17 In effect, to be interpellated is to be introduced into what Sellars characterizes as "the space of reasons." For Althusser, this space is inherently ideological, so that the Sellarsian distinction between the "manifest" and "scientific" images of the world would have to be developed from a Marxist point of view.

18 Deleuze reads Nietzsche's *Genealogy* as a reworking not of Kant's second *Critique* – as one might expect – but of the first, since prior to the question, "What can I know?," one must ask the *ad hominem* question, "Who or what wants to know?": "According to Nietzsche the question 'which one?' (*qui*) means this: what are the forces which take hold of a given thing, what is the will that possesses it?" (NAP 88, 76–7). Thus Nietzsche, like Levinas, takes ethics to be first philosophy.

19 Among others, Deleuze and Guattari refer to works by Samuel Beckett (1906–1989), Antonin Artaud (1896–1948), and D.H. Lawrence (1885–1930).

20 See the essays collected in Abraham and Torok, *The Shell and the Kernel*, especially Abraham, "Notes on the Phantom: a Complement to Freud's Metapsychology," p. 175, and Torok, "Story of Fear: the Symptoms of Phobia – the Return of the Repressed or the Return of the Phantom?" p. 181; also cf. Fors 118–19 n21.

21 I thank Jean Tan for reminding me of this corollary.

22 Cf. Arendt: "Hamlet's words, 'The time is out of joint. O cursed spite that ever I was born to set it right,' are more or less true for every new generation, although since the beginning of our century they have perhaps acquired a more persuasive validity than before" (BPAF 192).

23 Nicolas Abraham, "The Phantom of Hamlet *or* The Sixth Act *preceded by* The Intermission of 'Truth,'" in Abraham and Torok, *The Shell and the Kernel*, p. 188.

3 The problem of the relationship between immanence and transcendence: must we despair or may we still hope?

In Chapters 1 and 2, my narratives skipped directly from Kant to Nietzsche, neglecting all other nineteenth-century thinkers. In this chapter, the key transitional figure will be Marx, whose critique of philosophical quietism prompted continental philosophers to reformulate Kant's hope question. Ideally, a separate section would also be devoted to the work of the German poet Friedrich Schiller (1759–1805), whose *On the Aesthetic Education of Man in a Series of Letters* (*Über die Ästhetische Erziehung des Menschen in einer Reihe von Briefen*, 1795; rev. 1801) opened up the aestheticist approach to what I am calling the problem of the relationship between immanence and transcendence. Kant's distinction between the immanent realm of phenomena (to which reason in its speculative employment is restricted) and the transcendent kingdom of ends (to which reason in its practical vocation transports us) underlies his formulation of the eschatological question, "What may I hope?" To ask what I may hope is to ask what I am entitled to believe in order for the highest good to be attainable. According to Kant, this question can only be answered by religion, which promises divine assistance not only for the eventual apportionment of happiness in accordance with moral worth but also for the individual's striving for perfect virtue (or holiness of will). But Schiller, taking his cue from the conceptions of beauty and sublimity that Kant presents in the first part of the *Critique of the Power of Judgment*, suggests that not religion but art promises the attainment of the highest good, conceived as the harmonization of inclination and reason. Instead of projecting the object of human aspiration onto a transcendent future life, as religion does, art anticipates an immanent reconciliation in the course of human history. Kant claimed that through divine assistance in nature (i.e., providence) the highest good in human history would eventually be achieved. Picking up on this idea, the German idealists characterized history as the dialectical overcoming of the dichotomy between the immanence of the human and the transcendence of the divine. But after the death of Hegel – who rejected Schiller's valorization of art in favor of a valorization of philosophy as the self-comprehension of the truth of religion – his successors split into two rival camps. For the so-called "Old Hegelians," the task of philosophy was to articulate already established religious truths. But for Ludwig Feuerbach (1804–1872), the most celebrated of the "Young Hegelians," the task of a genuinely critical philosophy was to free an alienated humanity from the religious dichotomy between the immanent and the transcendent. Marx agrees with Feuerbach that all of the great Kantian dualisms are so many symptoms of alienation, but he argues that religion is not the cause but merely the effect of underlying social conditions, and that the highest good can only be achieved in communist society. Marx characterizes communist society on the model of Schiller's aesthetic utopia, that is, as a world in which the human capacity for aesthetic play will have finally been achieved. In bourgeois society, art can only exist in a stunted form. This aesthetic dimension of Marx's thought became the salient point of reference for critical theorists such as Lukács, Benjamin, Adorno, and Marcuse. For each of these thinkers, art inherits the burden of reconciliation that religion once fulfilled. Hence the problem of the relationship between transcendence and immanence becomes the problem of the relationship between the sublime and the beautiful. Insofar as this Kantian dualism admits of two complementary ordered conflations, it opens up one of the points of heresy within the House of Continental. For critical theorists such as Benjamin and Adorno, art exhibits a beautiful sublimity that serves as a placeholder for a religion that is in some sense still to come. By contrast, for hermeneuticians such as Heidegger, Gadamer, and Ricoeur, art exhibits a sublime beauty that symbolizes religious truth. A comparable point of contention separates Arendt from Lyotard, the one modeling political discourse on aesthetic quarrels about the beautiful; the other on attestations to the sublime. Habermas attempts to overcome these dilemmas by preserving Kant's three-fold distinction between cognitive, moral, and aesthetic claims, while Žižek seeks to revive the aspirations of critical theory by radicalizing – rather than undermining – this very distinction.

3.1   Kant's prophetic response to the French Revolution

> In God's name cheerly on, courageous friends,
> To reap the harvest of perpetual peace
> By this one bloody trial of sharp war.
> (*The Tragedy of Richard the Third*,
> V, ii, 14–16)

Because Kant thinks that we are entitled to hope for happiness only to the degree that we are worthy of it, the proper form of the question, "What may I hope?," is conditional: "If I do what I should, what may I then hope?" (CPR A805/B833). In his solution to the antinomy of practical reason, Kant answered this question by arguing that, although virtue is neither a means to the end of happiness nor itself sufficient for happiness, we are entitled to posit the synthetic unity of virtue and happiness in the idea of the highest good. Because the subjective highest good for man is conceivable only in "a future life," it is necessary to posit both the existence of the objective highest good – i.e., a morally benevolent God – and the immortality of our souls (CPR A811/B839). In *Religion Within the Boundaries of Mere Reason*, Kant attempts to reconcile the requirements of a purely rational moral faith with the doctrines of an "ecclesiastical" or historical religion such as Christianity. He acknowledges that ecclesiastic traditions have authority as possible sources of revelation, but only if their teachings do not contradict those of reason. This restriction of ecclesiastical authority was not taken kindly by the Prussian king, Friedrich Wilhelm II (1744–1797), who in 1794 forbade Kant from "disparaging" the Church in like manner again. Kant agreed, "*as Your Majesty's most loyal subject,*" not to publish anything more on the subject of religion, but he eventually took this pledge to expire upon the king's death in 1797 (COF 242).

Although Kant claims that the highest good for individuals can only be achieved in a future life, he also posits a highest good for the species as a whole that should be the object of all our striving. Thus the question, "What may I hope?," has an analogue that concerns the destiny of the human race: "What may *we* hope?" In his "Idea for a Universal History with a Cosmopolitan Purpose" (*Idee zu einer allgemeinen Geschichte in weltbürgerlicher Absicht*, 1784) – as well as in "Perpetual Peace: A Philosophical Sketch" (*Zum ewigen Frieden: Ein philosophischer Entwurf*, 1795) and the second essay of *The Conflict of the Faculties* (*Der Streit der Fakultäten*, 1798) – Kant attempts to prove that human history is guided by providential laws of nature toward "*a perfect civil union of mankind*" (PW 51). But the proofs that he offers are less speculative than practical in character, as if he were trying to provide grounds for an unshakable faith in human progress. Without such faith, the "spectacle" of human history "would force us to turn away in revulsion, and, by making us despair of ever finding any completed rational aim behind it, would reduce us to hoping for it *only* in some other world" (PW 53; my italics).

It is important for Kant that the goal of human history can only be attained through man's "own efforts." Had nature intended for us to live peacefully with one another, it would have made us docile like sheep – but then peace would not be something that we ourselves had achieved (PW 45). This is in keeping with the claim in the *Groundwork* that nature intends not for men to be happy but for men to make themselves worthy of being happy. The fact that we are naturally aggressive toward one another – "the *unsocial sociability* of men" (PW 44) – spurs us to find a solution to "*the greatest problem for the human species,*" namely, "*that of attaining a civil society which can administer justice universally*" (PW 45).

The path to perpetual peace involves several stages. First, it is necessary for human beings to leave behind the state of nature by founding a civil society on principles of right (laws) whose aim is to secure – not curtail – the freedom of all. Kant regards the requirement to live in civil society as a duty that takes precedence over all others – so that the worst of crimes would be to revolt against the prevailing government and so regress to the state of nature. Second, it is necessary that over the course of human history civil constitutions be perfected so that genuinely "republican" rather than "despotic" governments prevail. A republican government is one in which the legislative and executive functions are kept separate. Kant regards democracies as despotic because they identify those who legislate with those who execute the legislation (PW 101). A genuinely republican government requires a sharp distinction between the power of the sovereign – whether embodied in a single autocrat or a group of aristocrats – and the subjects who are governed by this power. As the law-maker, the sovereign must be "above" the laws. Thus whereas the civil duties that subjects have toward one another are "coercive" in the sense that they can be legitimately enforced, those that the sovereign has toward the subjects are not.

Kant also distinguishes between "passive" and "active" members of a republic, that is, between those who are mere subjects (in the sense of being "subject" to the laws) and those who in addition to being subjects are "citizens" with the right to vote on the laws (PW 77). Except in the case of women and children – both of whom Kant regards as naturally unfit for citizenship – the right of citizenship should be based neither on natural nor hereditary factors but on a subject's economic independence: "The only qualification required by a citizen (apart, of course, from being an adult male) is that he must be his *own master* (*sui iuris*), and must have some *property* (which can include any skill, trade, fine art or science) to support himself" (PW 78; cf. 139–40). For example, a wig-maker is deserving of citizenship whereas a barber is not, for the latter depends upon others for his livelihood in a way that the former – despite the fact that he may require the hair of others to make his wigs – does not.[1]

A third requirement for perpetual peace is that an international analogue of civil society be founded. So long as separate nations exist in a state of nature with respect to one another, they will remain in a condition of perpetual war, for even when they are not actually at war they are constantly preparing for it, whether for aggressive, defensive, or pre-emptive purposes. Kant thinks that this problem cannot be resolved through the founding of a world government, in part because existing nations would not (and in some sense ought not) forsake their sovereignty and in part because the sheer size of such a super-nation would lead to inevitable civil divisions. It can only be resolved if individual nations voluntarily establish a joint "federation" whose sole aim would be the securing of a genuine peace (as opposed to a mere truce) with one another (PW 90, 102). Eventually this federation can be expected to include all nations, at which point a meaningful "international right" will have been established. But this can come about only if each nation has a republican constitution under which its people get to decide whether they will go to war or not. Once a federation of republics is formed, perpetual peace will enable all human beings to enjoy a further "cosmopolitan" right of world-citizenship, that is, a right to sojourn anywhere on the face of the earth and receive the "right of hospitality" (though not the "*right of a guest* to be entertained") (PW 106).

According to Kant, the possibility of perpetual peace rests only on the gradual enactment of coercive laws, and not on the virtue of individuals.

Ideally, both sovereigns and citizens ought always to obey the categorical imperative. What distinguishes the "moral politician" from a Machiavellian "political moralist" is that the former adheres to the "transcendental and affirmative principle of public right" according to which "All maxims which *require* publicity if they are not to fail in their purpose can be reconciled both with right and with politics" (PW 118, 130). This principle applies at both the national and international levels. But the problem of perfecting civil constitutions – a sufficient condition for perpetual peace – is one that "can be solved even by a nation of devils" (PW 52, 112). The aim of a "universal history with a cosmopolitan purpose" is to study the defects of earlier constitutions so as to make future constitutional reforms possible. Citizens can recommend such reforms but only sovereigns can enact them. Because obedience to existing law overrides all other duties, revolutionary acts are never justified. So sacrosanct is this principle that after a hitherto illegitimate revolution has established a new government, citizens owe their allegiance to it and should not attempt to restore the ousted regime. The justification for this paradoxical requirement is not that "might makes right" – a principle that subordinates morality to politics – but on the contrary that sovereignty should be regarded not as originating in contingent events in history but as issuing from a divine will: "A law which is so sacred (i.e. inviolable) that it is practically a crime even to cast doubt upon it and thus to suspend its effectiveness for even an instant, cannot be thought of as coming from human beings, but from some infallible supreme legislator" (PW 143). Thus Kant endorses the doctrine of the divine rights of kings on the grounds that an existing sovereign must be regarded as an embodiment of an idea of reason (the idea of right) (PW 83n).

Kant's attitude toward sovereignty is akin to that taken by the Duke of York in Shakespeare's *The Tragedy of King Richard the Second*. Although he believes that Richard is a bad king, York refuses to take part in Henry Bolingbroke's rebellion against him. However, once the rebellion is successful, York acknowledges Henry's legitimacy, going so far as to disclose his son Aumerle's plot to restore Richard to the throne. In support of such an action, Kant writes: "For instance, it might be necessary for someone to betray someone else, even if their relationship were that of father and son, in order to preserve the state from catastrophe" (PW 81n). The problem faced by York is what to do during a time of transition, that is, while an on-going revolutionary situation is taking place. Kant forestalls this problem by suggesting that there is a precise moment of reversal at which we move from a state in which revolutionary actions are unconditionally wrong to a new state in which they are no longer revolutionary. In Shakespeare's play, York only acknowledges Henry as king at the precise instant when Richard hands the crown and scepter to him. Earlier, when the banished Henry first returned to England while King Richard was abroad, York conceded that he had no power to suppress the rebellion, but persisted in recognizing Richard as England's anointed king.

Although Kant argues against revolutionary actions, he expresses great sympathy for both the American and, especially, the French Revolution. To reconcile his enthusiasm with his principles, Kant suggests in *The Metaphysics of Morals* (*Die Metaphysik der Sitten*, 1797) that the French Revolution was not a true revolution, for by convening the Estates-General in 1789, the French king had implicitly abdicated the throne (PW 164).[2] This claim invites us to interpret Kant's prohibition against revolution less as a defense of blind obedience to authority than as an argument against regarding justifiable resistance against a purported authority *as* revolutionary. However, because he does not think that a government loses its legitimacy merely by obliging its subjects to perform otherwise immoral acts, there is no fixed criterion by which one could determine when exactly a government has forfeited its right to govern.

Kant also refers to the French Revolution in the second essay of *The Conflict of the Faculties*, where he attempts to answer the "old" question, "Is the human race constantly progressing?" Kant's aim in this essay is to justify hope on behalf of the future course of human history. While simply denouncing as "terroristic" the hypothesis that humanity becomes more and more depraved over time, he worries that if we only look at the historical record of past human actions, there is no way of proving that humanity is improving over time either (COF 298–9). But he notes that just as the pre-Copernican theory of the heavens only made it *seem* as if the planets wandered back and forth, so it is possible that this way of looking at history leaves us with a false impression (COF 300). Although there is no Copernican vantage point from which we can predict the future course of human history – only God could know in advance the actions of beings who are free – perhaps instead of trying to extrapolate future actions based on past actions we can instead find a clue to the future destiny of humanity by attending to the feelings that are aroused in spectators who *bear witness* to great efforts to achieve moral progress. The French Revolution provides an occasion for such observations. Whether the attempt made by the revolutionaries to found a republic succeeds or not, it is significant that those who witnessed their efforts from afar felt a sense of solidarity – "a wishful *participation* that borders closely on enthusiasm" – on their behalf (COF 302). However, this sense of solidarity for the *cause* of the revolutionaries was not necessarily accompanied by any predisposition to assist them. On the contrary, the reaction of the spectators was completely "disinterested," a sine qua non for an aesthetic, rather than a moral, judgment. Yet, according to Kant, such a reaction could not have arisen if there were not "a moral predisposition in the human race" (COF 302). Kant concludes from the existence of this disposition that it is only a matter of time before the human race achieves its goal of perpetual peace among federated republican states. Though it is impossible to predict when exactly this will occur, we can be certain that it will, for an event such as the French Revolution "*will not be forgotten*" (COF 304). Thus Kant bases his prophecy on the expectation that a past event will be remembered – and redeemed.

The idea that the success or failure of the French Revolution is irrelevant to the question concerning human progress is in keeping with the anti-consequentialist thrust of Kant's moral philosophy; what matters in assessing the worth of a will is its goodness, not its efficacy. But it is not the will of the revolutionaries that justifies Kant's expectation of the moral progress of the species. On the contrary, those who took part in the French Revolution – assuming it was a revolution – could not have been acting from duty. In contrast to the disinterested spectators, who felt *enthusiasm* on behalf of an idea of pure reason, they succumbed to a kind of moral – or political – *fanaticism*.

In his earlier essays on the philosophy of history, Kant based his optimism about the future on the idea that there are purposes in nature. In the second part of the *Critique of the Power of Judgment*, he attempts to justify this view by showing that although teleological judgments do not provide us with objective knowledge about the world, they are subjectively necessary for our faculty of judgment. Crucial to Kant's argument is the distinction that he introduces between "determining" and "reflective" judgments – a distinction anticipated in the first *Critique* contrast between the "apodictic" and "hypothetical" uses of reason (CPR A646–7/B674–5). Determining judgments subsume particular objects under already given universal concepts. By contrast, reflective judgments begin with particulars and seek universal concepts under which to subsume them. Kant distinguishes two different kinds of reflective judging: one in which we compare a multiplicity of particulars with an eye toward identifying their common marks; and one in which we attend solely to a single object. The former serves as a propaedeutic to determining judgment; the latter has no end outside itself. In any act of reflection, the power of judgment is not constrained by the rules of the understanding but rather operates under a rule of its own. The "transcendental principle" which the faculty of judgment gives itself as a "law" states that "since universal laws of nature have their ground in our understanding, which prescribes them to nature . . ., the particular empirical laws . . . must be considered in terms of the sort of unity they would have if an understanding (even if not ours) had likewise given them for the sake of our faculty of cognition" (CPJ 66). In other words, reflective judgment is governed by the indemonstrable but subjectively necessary assumption that natural objects have been created by an intelligent designer. This principle does not guarantee that there are purposes in nature, but it prompts us to look for such purposes. Kant distinguishes two different applications of this principle: aesthetic judgment and teleological judgment.

The "analytic" of Kant's critique of aesthetic judgment is divided into two parts, one pertaining to judgments about the beautiful and the other to judgments about the sublime. We call an object beautiful when its form strikes us as "subjectively purposive" – i.e., when it seems to have been designed for the purpose of giving us pleasure, even though we cannot ascribe a definite intention to its author (CPJ 75). By contrast, we judge an idea to be sublime when the apparent *contrapurposiveness* of nature turns out to bespeak a higher purpose.

In the case of an aesthetically reflective "judgment of taste" – i.e., the judgment that something is beautiful – we attend to an object whose very singularity makes us unable to compare it to others. Finding no particular concept of the understanding to be adequate to it, we nonetheless find our imaginative representation of its form to agree with the faculty of understanding "in general" (CPJ 102). It is as if the object's form *promised* its determinability under a concept that is not immediately forthcoming. This sense of promised but unfulfilled determinability corresponds to a harmonizing of the free (but lawlike) imagination with the lawful (but idle) understanding. Pleasure in the judgment of taste can thus be characterized as a pleasure that we take in a reflective judgment that promises an indefinitely deferred determinate judgment. In other words, to say that an object is beautiful is to report that the encounter with its form brings about a pleasurable harmony between the faculties of imagination and understanding. In contrast to both the merely sensuous delight that one takes in something merely "agreeable," and the intellectual pleasure that one takes in recognizing something to be "good," the pleasure that accompanies the encounter with a beautiful object is completely disinterested (CPJ 91).

Because the judgment of taste is not a judgment about the determinable properties of an object but about the subjective response that we have to its form, it is impossible to "prove" that an object is beautiful. Yet unlike judgments about the agreeable, a considered judgment of taste does not merely reflect our personal idiosyncrasies, because it rests solely on cognitive capacities that all human beings share. Thus although no one can expect others to share his or her particular likes and dislikes in matters concerning the agreeable – some people enjoy the taste of broccoli, while others do not – we do expect, and even "demand," that others share our judgments of taste. The fact that judgments of taste purport universality – despite the fact that they are not objective and so cannot be proven to be true – gives rise to what Kant calls "the antinomy of taste" (CPJ 214). The thesis states that "The judgment of taste is not based on concepts, for otherwise it would be possible to dispute about it (decide by means of proofs)." By contrast, the antithesis states, "The judgment of taste is based on concepts, for otherwise, despite its variety, it would not even be possible to argue about it (to lay claim to the necessary assent of others to this judgment)" (CPJ 215). Kant resolves this conflict by arguing that, while the judgment of taste is not based on a "determinate" concept, it is based on one that is "indeterminate," that is, on a "rational concept of the supersensible, which grounds the object (and also the judging subject) as an object of sense" (CPJ 126). That is, the judgment of taste is prompted by an indeterminate concept of the intelligible ground of the object whose form gives us pleasure. Thus the judgment of taste is "based on a concept" but because this concept is indeterminable we can never settle any "arguments" or "quarrels" in support of it.[3]

Aesthetic quarrels are unique in that they aim at consensus without our being able to guarantee that consensus can actually be attained. By contrast, arguments about what things are good always admit of consensus because they are based upon determinate concepts, while arguments about what things are agreeable are pointless. To quarrel on behalf of a judgment of taste is to purport "subjective" as opposed to "objective" universality without being able to prove that we are right (CPJ 100). Thus taste gives rise to a dialogue whose telos is agreement but whose outcome is uncertain. Kant suggests that our capacity to make judgments of taste presupposes the existence of a *sensus communis* – a shared common sense – and that the aim of aesthetic quarreling is to cultivate such a faculty (CPJ 173). Whether the *sensus communis* should be thought of as "a constitutive principle of the possibility of experience, or whether a yet higher principle of reason only makes it into a regulative principle for us first to produce a common sense in ourselves for higher ends" is a question that Kant leaves unanswered (CPJ 124). The ideal of a fully achieved *sensus communis* can be thought of as the subjective analogue of the political ideal of a "general will."

In his analytic of the sublime, Kant distinguishes the "mathematically" sublime from the "dynamically" sublime (CPJ 131). An experience of the mathematically sublime – the "absolutely great" – occurs when we attempt to grasp in a single intuition the full magnitude of an object that exceeds our power of aesthetic comprehension. This failure on the part of the imagination is experienced by us as painful, particularly insofar as it bespeaks our inability to provide reason with a sensible image that would be adequate to its idea of the infinite. But this failure on the part of the imagination then gives rise to a "higher" pleasure as we are reminded of our vocation as moral agents, a vocation that makes us greater than nature itself. Thus the very failure of the imagination is purposive for the faculty of reason which thereby recognizes itself as what is absolutely great, a fact attested to by the circumstance that it is not nature in its hugeness but reason in its infinite demand that does violence to the imagination.

In the case of the dynamically sublime, it is an encounter not so much with the large as with the terrifying that prompts the subject to try to imagine the full force of nature's power. Though this attempt again causes pain, it gives way to the pleasurable feeling of our vocation as rational wills whose ability to resist all natural incentives transcends the power of nature. Thus in the feeling of both the mathematical and the dynamical sublime – which may simply be two aspects of one and the same experience – it is not nature itself but only the moral disposition of the human mind that we experiences as sublime: "Hence it is the disposition of the mind resulting from a certain representation occupying the reflective judgment, but not the object, which is to be called sublime" (CPJ 134).

In contrast to the pleasure felt in the judgment of the beautiful – which attests to a harmonizing of the imagination and the understanding – in the experience of the sublime we feel pleasure because the *discord* between imagination and reason reminds us of our dignity as rational agents. More precisely, the feeling of the sublime represents an aesthetic response to our moral vocation, our responsibility to realize the highest good. For this reason, Kant characterizes the feeling of enthusiasm as sublime: "This state of mind seems to be sublime, so much so that it is commonly maintained that without it nothing great can be accomplished" (CPJ 154). Thus enthusiasm is associated not only with the experience of bearing witness – as in the case of the spectators of the French Revolution – but with the standpoint of moral agency.

Kant characterizes the beautiful as a "symbol of morality," thereby indicating how taste can play an edifying role in human experience (CPJ 225). But he resists the rationalist view of Alexander Gottlieb Baumgarten (1714–1762) that the beautiful is the sensible expression of the idea of perfection, for this would be to blur the distinction between sensible forms and intelligible concepts. Because he treats the beautiful and the good as different in kind, Kant also forestalls both a moral aesthetics and an aesthetic morality.

In the first *Critique*, Kant characterized ideas as concepts of reason to which no intuition could be adequate. In the third *Critique*, he supplements this account by acknowledging the existence of "aesthetic ideas," sensible images that cryptically express indeterminate concepts. "Genius" – or more precisely "spirit" – is the faculty for presenting aesthetic ideas (CPJ 192). To say that a work of art is a product of genius is to say that the artist, without really knowing what he or she was doing, somehow managed to exhibit an indeterminate concept in a sensible image. The encounter with such a work stimulates our cognitive faculties as we seek words or concepts that would be adequate to the aesthetic idea. Ultimately, this task is futile, but we experience this futility not as a failure – not as a disharmony between the faculties of imagination and understanding – but as revelatory of precisely that which is inexpressible in the work. The beautiful is a symbol of the good in the precise sense that aesthetic ideas express the inexpressible, perhaps, as such, necessarily making reference to the sublime.

In his "critique of the teleological power of judgment" Kant argues that living organisms, or "organized beings," exhibit a peculiar kind of reciprocal causation that cannot be explained on the basis of the mechanical conception of causality employed by the understanding (CPJ 244–5). Such objects must be regarded as "objectively purposive" – though only for reflective judgment (CPJ 233ff.). This stipulation preserves for teleological judgments the same sort of promissory character that was exhibited in aesthetic judgments about the subjective purposiveness of beautiful forms in nature. In both cases, nature provides us with "hints" that it has been designed by an intelligent creator but not with guarantees. Once again, Kant preserves the boundary separating enthusiasm from fanaticism. To succumb to fanaticism would be to believe that it is possible to identify divine purposes in nature from the standpoint of a determining judgment. Such a claim would overstep the bounds of possible experience. Although we can only make sense of natural organisms by taking them to be designed in accordance with divine intentions, we do this from the standpoint of reflective judgment alone. Thus the hints that nature provides us with retain their merely promissory character.

To have faith is, in effect, to believe that there are promises in nature. To have faith that the human race is morally improving is to believe that the "final end of nature" – the highest good for humanity – will be attained. But because a promise is not an epistemic guarantee, to have faith is to recognize the promise of the highest *as* promised rather than as given:

> It is a matter of trusting the promise of the moral law; not a promise that is contained in the moral law, but one that I put into it, and indeed on a morally adequate basis. For a final end cannot be commanded by any law of reason without reason simultaneously promising its attainability, even if uncertainly.
>
> (CPJ 335)

If enthusiasm is the necessary affective complement to faith, fanaticism arises when we believe that a promise either has already been fulfilled or will be fulfilled at a definite point in time. Put otherwise, whereas enthusiasm can be correlated with the right to hope, fanaticism can be characterized as a sense of entitlement. As a defender of the Enlightenment separation of the claims of science from the claims of faith, Kant resists the Romantics' tendency toward fanaticism. This comes through not only in his satirical critique of Swedenborg but in his reviews of Johann Gottfried Herder's (1744–1803) *Ideas for a Philosophy of the History of Mankind* (*Ideen zur Philosophie der Geschichte der Menschheit*, 1784, 1785), in which his former student ascribes divine purposes to nature in a determinate rather than a merely reflective way.

Kant worries not only about "theological" fanaticism but about "political" fanaticism as well – which is why his argument against revolution plays such a foundational role in his political philosophy. In "An Answer to the Question: 'What is Enlightenment?'" (*Beantwortung der Frage: Was ist Aufklärung?*, 1784) he draws a sharp distinction between our "private" duty to obey the law and our "public" right to protest against unjust laws. According to Kant, we are fully justified – and even obliged – to make public pleas for reforms that will eventually lead to a republican form of government, but we are never justified in striving to instantiate the idea of right through revolutionary means. Enthusiasm gives way to fanaticism at the precise moment when reformists become revolutionaries – that is, at the moment when enthusiasm on behalf of a promise becomes a fanatical attempt to realize that promise. This explains why Kant condemns not only revolution but even acts of civil disobedience, while nonetheless defending – passionately – the right of individuals to protest against any and every perceived injustice. From this point of view, Kant's attack on political fanaticism is as much an attack on "state" fanaticism as it is against "revolutionary" fanaticism. A government becomes fanatical – and not merely despotic – when it legislates how its subjects ought to think, censoring all dissenting voices. In claiming to express the voice of a fully determinate general will, a fanatical government stifles the public quarrels that are necessary for preserving the promissory character of the idea of a general will. By contrast, a merely enthusiastic government – such as Kant attributes to the rule of Frederick the Great (1712–1786) – favors public dissent in the hope that political quarreling will further its own ends (PW 55). Only in a perfect civil society – exemplified for Kant in Plato's ideal Republic – would rulers be entitled to act "fanatically," for then they would have genuine insight into the good (CPR A316–17/B372–4). But since such an ideal can never be achieved by men, Kant assigns philosophers not the role of kings but of citizens with the right to dissent (PW 115). Just as he thinks it would require an infinite (non-temporal) duration for a finite being to realize the ideal of moral perfection or holiness – this is why it is necessary to posit the immortality of our souls – so the attainment of both an ideal republic and perpetual peace can only be approached asymptotically (CPrR 238; PW 171).

Kant's insistence on the merely promissory character of ideals bears on his distinction between beauty and sublimity. Both the beautiful and the sublime attest to the division between intuitions and concepts, the one presenting an object of intuition to which no concept is adequate, the other a concept to which no intuition is adequate. Only a being for whom intuitions and concepts are distinct – i.e., a being incapable of intellectual intuition – can experience beauty and sublimity. Conversely, the experiences of beauty and sublimity represent, in different ways, the closest we can come to an intellectual intuition of the divine. Thus, an object strikes us as beautiful when the mere sensible intuition of its form *seems* to reveal its intelligible character, while an idea counts as sublime when it *demands* – while simultaneously precluding – intuitive fulfillment. That neither experience can succeed in overcoming the gap separating our cognitive faculties is a consequence of the fact that each lacks what the other alone could provide. In this sense, the beautiful and the sublime beckon to each other as if longing for a union that is strictly impossible – which is to say that there is no such thing as either sublime beauty or beautiful sublimity. Even if a natural object could qualify as something sublime, it would be difficult – if not impossible – for a single object to exhibit *both* the form requisite for natural or artifactual beauty *and* that "formlessness" of "raw nature" the encounter with which prompts an experience of sublimity (CPJ 136).

In the *Anthropology*, Kant does refer to the possibility of representing the sublime in a beautiful manner: "the *representation* of the sublime can and should be beautiful in itself; otherwise it is coarse, barbaric, and in bad taste" (AFPPV 109). Likewise, in the third *Critique* he suggests that "the presentation of the sublime, so far as it belongs to beautiful art, can be united with beauty in a **verse tragedy**, a **didactic poem**, and **oratorio**"

(CPJ 203). Kant's examples – all of which involve "the arts of speech" – suggest that beauty and sublimity can only be united in representations of the actions of human beings (CPJ 198). If this is so, what counts as sublime in such a representation is not raw nature but that which is itself truly sublime, namely, humanity itself. Because human actions have a moral character, the beauty that they exhibit must be "adherent" rather than "free" – in other words, it must be the beauty of something that can also be judged to be good because, despite the fact that the object's form resists conceptual determination, it is *also* something that we have a determinate concept of (CPJ 114). In suggesting that representations of the sublime not only can but ought to be beautiful, Kant implies that the "ideal" of beauty – human beauty – is itself an example of beautiful sublimity or sublime beauty (CPJ 117). He does not say that the sublime itself can be beautiful but only that the sublime ought to be *represented* in a beautiful way. In light of Nietzsche's suggestion that Wagner managed to unite beauty and sublimity in his operas, which were conceived as "total works of art" (*Gesamtkunstwerke*), it is noteworthy that Kant also implies that beauty and sublimity can only be united in mixed artforms. The fact that he expresses doubt about the success of "the combination of the beautiful arts in one and the same product" – "in these combinations beautiful art is all the more artistic, although whether it is also more beautiful (since so many different kinds of satisfaction are criss-crossed with each other) can be doubted in some of these cases" – suggests that the *Gesamtkunstwerk* represents an unattainable ideal, one that, like a perfect constitution, could only be achieved at the end of an infinite (aesthetic) progression over time (CPJ 203).

3.2 Marx's prophecy of a proletarian revolution

What is here?
Gold? Yellow, glittering, precious gold?
No, gods, I am no idle votarist;
Roots, you clear heavens! Thus much of this will make
Black white, foul fair, wrong right,
Base noble, old young, coward valiant.
(*The Life of Timon of Athens*, IV, iii, 25–30)

Karl Marx (1818–1883) also thought that history was inexorably progressing toward the fulfillment of the highest ends of humanity, but he conceived of this telos not as a perpetual peace among federated states each of which would be governed by a republican constitution, but as the realization of communist society in which the abolition of private property would put an end to the class struggle. Marx also rejected any appeal to the providence of nature. The highest good for humanity could only be achieved by humanity itself.

Like other post-Hegelian German philosophers, the young Marx sought a more radical conception of the critical project, one that would show that the philosophy of Kant was the expression of a fundamentally bourgeois point of view. Feuerbach had taken an important step in this direction by denouncing the privilege that the German idealists accorded to the abstract life of the "spirit" over the actual existence of living human beings. After studying in Bonn and Berlin, Marx moved to Paris in 1843, where he wrote his posthumously published *Economic and Philosophic Manuscripts of 1844* (*Ökonomisch-philosophische Manuskripte aus dem Jahre 1844*), noting in the preface that "It is only with *Feuerbach* that positive, humanistic and naturalistic criticism begins" (EAPM 64). Marx was drawn to Feuerbach's idea that what distinguishes human beings from other animals is our "species-being," the fact that we are conscious of ourselves as individuals only insofar as we are conscious of the species as a whole (EAPM 113). Like Hegel, Feuerbach also thought that history is the movement by which humanity becomes alienated from itself and then overcomes its self-alienation. But Hegel had been unable to make this idea concrete because, like Kant, his thought was determined by the bourgeois society to which he belonged (EAPM 177).

As Marx conceives it, alienation is a function of private property, or rather, of any economic system in which the products of human labor are appropriated by a subset, or class, of society as a whole. In such a world, humanity becomes "estranged" from itself in several interrelated ways. The worker is estranged from the product that his or her labor produces, since this comes to exist as an "alien power" standing over against it: "the object which labor produces . . . confronts it as *something alien*, as a *power independent* of the producer" (EAPM 108). As a consequence of estrangement from the thing, the worker also suffers from "*self-estrangement*." Finally, through the division of humanity into laborers and owners, the species as a whole becomes estranged from itself: "In estranging from man (1) nature, and (2) himself, . . . estranged labor estranges the *species* from man. It changes for him the *life of the species* into a means of individual life" (EAPM 112; cf. 114).

In leaving behind the mercantile system of the feudal period, modern bourgeois society had brought humanity to its most extreme point of self-alienation by dividing all human beings into two opposed classes (EAPM 100; LPW 2). Only by overcoming this division would it be possible to achieve a reconciliation of alienated humanity with itself. Feuerbach was right to criticize Hegel for his belief that such a reconciliation could take place at the level of mere thinking, but Marx thinks that Feuerbach's materialist alternative to idealism remains too abstract insofar as it offers only a critique of religion rather than a revolutionary transformation of the economic conditions of civil society. The division between the classes will be overcome only when the development of bourgeois society reaches a crisis that will allow workers to abolish the institution of private property: "In order to abolish the *idea* of private property, the *idea* of communism is completely sufficient. It takes *actual* communist action to abolish actual private property" (EAPM 154). Until this is accomplished, the two classes will remain locked in an antagonistic struggle with each other. So long as the owners of capital control the means of production they will continue to appropriate all of the profit produced by the labor of the workers. Marx is contemptuous of the greed of the capitalists, but he especially despises the "political economists" – besides Smith and Ricardo, Jean-Baptiste Say (1767–1832), and James Mill (1773–1836) – who defend the interests of the capitalists by hypocritically pretending that the alleged "laws" of political economy benefit society as a whole. In making the "critique of political economy" his starting-point, Marx purports to carry out a more radical Copernican turn than that of Kant, one that is capable of revealing the complicity between German idealism and the interests of the bourgeoisie.

Marx suggests that the discourse of the political economists is dogmatic in that it fails to develop a genuine critique of the concept of private property: "Political economy starts with the fact of private property, but it does not explain it to us" (EAPM 106). Instead of providing a deduction of the entire system of private property, the political economists invoke speculative myths about "a fictitious primordial condition" in which primitive human beings are supposed to have naturally stumbled upon modern bourgeois practices such as trade, the division of labor, and wage-labor (EAPM 107).[4] Against this mystifying point of view, Marx proposes to analyze the actual structure of bourgeois economic practice so as to expose the contradictions of political economy. Toward this end he focuses on the phenomenon of wage-labor, that is, on the form that labor has in any system that is based upon private property: "*wages* and *private property* are identical: since the product, as the object of labor pays for labor itself, therefore the wage is but a necessary consequence of labor's estrangement" (EAPM 117). Wage-labor is inherently dehumanizing because it reduces the worker who must sell his or her labor on the marketplace to the status of a commodity, "indeed the most wretched of commodities" (EAPM 106; cf. 65). Like all commodities, the value of wage-labor is a function of supply and demand. As long as there are hungry workers, the value of their labor will tend to be reduced to the bare minimum: "the only necessary wage rate is that providing for the subsistence of the worker for the duration of his work . . . and for the race of laborers not to die out" (EAPM 65). Political economy reveals its cynical character when instead of distinguishing wage-labor from labor per se, it treats them as equivalent (EAPM 72).

In being reduced to the level of a commodity, the worker has no choice but to sell himself or herself in the marketplace, thereby acquiring a price. In the *Groundwork*, Kant claimed that human beings had "dignity" precisely insofar as no "price" could be put on their value (G 84). The political economists pay lip service to this idea, but Marx suggests that they dissemble when they argue that it would be morally wrong for a woman to prostitute herself or for another to sell his friend into slavery, for ethical considerations have no proper place within the discourse of political economy (EAPM 152).

In bourgeois society, "the nobility of man" is forsaken as money alone comes to function as "an *end in itself*" (EAPM 155). The degradation of man and the idolatry of money are thus two sides of the same coin: "Man becomes ever poorer as man, his need for *money* becomes ever greater if he wants to over-power hostile being.... The need for money is therefore the true need pro-duced by the modern economic system" (EAPM 147).

"The power of money in bourgeois society" is insidious not only because of the systematic way in which workers are deprived of acquiring more than the bare minimum – though this would be indictment enough – but because all of humanity comes to be enslaved by it (EAPM 165). As money alone is elevated to the status of an end in itself, it ceases to function merely as a means of reckoning the exchange value of goods and comes to be equated with value in general. For this reason, everyone – even wealthy capi-talists – become misers:

> The less you eat, drink and buy books; the less you go to the theater, the dance hall, the public house; the less you think, love, theorize, sing, paint, fence, etc., the more you *save* – the *greater* becomes your treasure which neither moths nor dust will devour – your *capital*.

Despite the fact that political economy remains premised on greed, it is "the science of *asceticism*, and its true ideal is the *ascetic* but *extortionate* miser and the *ascetic* but *productive* slave." Thus Marx sees the capitalist in the same light that Nietzsche saw the ascetic priest. Though money retains its poten-tial to enable us to do various things, in bourgeois society its natural tend-ency is to do nothing but grow: "and all the things which you cannot do, your money can do" (EAPM 150). This tendency is reinforced by competi-tion among the capitalists, who can only avoid falling into the ranks of the workers by reinvesting their profits. The end result is that the capitalists do not control capital but are instead controlled by it – as of course are the workers, since they must sell themselves to the capitalists in order to survive.

The autonomization of capital – closely connected with its accumulation in the hands of ever fewer capitalists – manifests itself as a restless drive for ever-increasing profits. In order to satisfy this constant need for growth, capital breaks down all local and national boundaries, thereby bestowing upon it a certain "cosmopolitan" character: "This political economy, con-sequently, displays a *cosmopolitan*, universal energy which overthrows every restriction and bond so as to establish itself instead as the *sole* politics, the sole universality, the sole limit and sole bond" (EAPM 129; cf. LPW 4). Thus, unlike Kant, who saw the trend toward cosmopolitanism as a con-sequence of the costs of war, Marx interprets it as the inevitable consequence of the laws governing the capitalist mode of production. This process will eventually divide the entire world into a vast class of dispossessed workers and a tiny class of capitalists – at which point the workers will seize collective control over private property, the first stage of communism: "*communism is the positive* expression of annulled private property – at first as *universal* private property" (EAPM 132). With the abolition of the system of private property, the history of the class struggle and self-estrangement of humanity will have come to an end. In this sense, communism represents "the riddle of history solved" (EAPM 135). But communism is not so much the end of human history as it is the beginning of the history of non-alienated humanity (EAPM 146). Hence it is necessary to distinguish between communism conceived as the immediate abolition of private property – a still negative, mediated definition – and communism as it will exist in and for itself (EAPM 187).

Human beings are unique in that we alone have the capacity to "form things in accordance with the laws of beauty," but although great works of art have been created under conditions of alienation, this capacity has never been fully developed (EAPM 114). Just as Schiller envisioned an "aesthetic state" in which the constraint of labor would be transformed into the freedom of play, so Marx characterizes communist society as a world in which a reconciled humanity will become capable of play: "A man cannot become a child again unless he becomes childish. But does he not enjoy the artless ways of the child, and must he not strive to reproduce its truth on a higher plane?" (KMAR 20). Under capitalism, the human senses have degenerated to such an extent that the capacity for aesthetic pleasure has been reduced to the bare need for animal sustenance: "The care-burdened man in need has no sense for the finest play." But in communist society, truly human senses – i.e., senses attuned to beauty: "a musical ear, an eye for beauty of form" – will develop (EAPM 141). The inability to intuit the world in a properly human way is connected for Marx, as it was for Schiller, with the separation of sensing and thinking into two distinct activities. Kant's supposed discovery of a transcendental division between the receptivity of sensibility and the spontaneity of thought was merely the obscure coming-to-consciousness of an historically conditioned, alienated form of human experience. Hegel tried to overcome Kant's various dualisms by showing that they were the product of alienation. But, although Hegel saw history as the dialectical process by which human labor produced – and transcended – its own self-estrangement, he reduced sensuously embodied labor to the abstract labor of mere thinking, which is to say that he did not reconcile thinking and intuiting so much as *think* their reconciliation (EAPM 177). Even when Hegel attempts to make the transition from the abstractions of logical thought to the concrete intuition of nature, he manages only to represent a contentless mode of intuition: "the abstract thinker who has committed himself to intuiting, intuits nature abstractly" (EAPM 191).

Instead of conceiving of the dialectic idealistically as the labor of the concept, it needs to be understood materialistically as the activity by which naturally existing human beings transform both nature itself and themselves. But Marx emphasizes the importance of not allowing the critique of idealism to fall into another theoretical abstraction, one that would represent the material world merely as an object of intuition rather than as an object of practice. This was Feuerbach's mistake. Accordingly, in the first of his posthumously published "Theses on Feuerbach" (*Thesen über Feuerbach*) from 1845, Marx writes: "The chief defect of all hitherto existing materialism (that of Feuerbach included) is that the thing, reality, sensuousness, is conceived only in the form of the object or of intuition, but not as *sensuous human activity, practice*, not subjectively" (KMAR 21, translation slightly modified). Abstract materialism and abstract idealism are ultimately just two different expressions of the same alienated reality – the one privileging intuition, the other thought: "Feuerbach, not satisfied with *abstract thinking*, wants *intuition*; but he does not conceive sensuousness as *practical*, human-sensuous activity" (KMAR 22, translation slightly modified). Whence Marx's famous eleventh thesis: "The philosophers have only interpreted the world, in various ways; the point is to change it" (KMAR 23).

The history of the various ways in which human beings have changed the world is the history of the class struggle. In the *Manifesto of the Communist Party* (*Manifest der Kommunistischen Partei*, 1848), written on behalf of the international Communist League, Marx and his collaborator Friedrich Engels (1821–1895) provide an overview of the manner in which the class of capitalists – the bourgeoisie – has changed the world. They also call upon the class of workers – the proletariat – to change the world again by overthrowing the bourgeois system of private property so as to bring the entire class struggle to an end once and for all. In order to accomplish this goal, it is necessary for proletarians to recognize their common interests and thus to adopt a genuinely cosmopolitan point of view: "*Proletarians of all countries unite!*" (LPW 30; cf. 13). In contrast to the merely cynical cosmopolitanism of the bourgeoisie, that of the proletariat is genuine because it represents the interest of humanity as a whole: "All previous movements were movements of minorities or in the interest of minorities. The proletarian movement is the independent movement of the vast majority in the interests of that vast majority" (LPW 11).

In 1848, the year that the *Manifesto* was published, the second French Republic nourished the hope that the bourgeois French Revolution had paved the way for a communist, or at least socialist, revolution. This optimism was undermined with the reactionary *coup d'état* of Louis Bonaparte (1808–1873), who dissolved the republican National Legislative Assembly in December 1851. In *The Eighteenth Brumaire of Louis Bonaparte* (*Der achtzehnte Brumaire des Louis Bonaparte*, 1852), Marx attempts to account for this setback by contrasting the revolutions of the past with the coming proletarian revolution. Eighteenth-century bourgeois revolutions were able to occur swiftly and decisively because the class struggle had reached a point where it remained only for the bourgeoisie to seize control of the government. In 1848, by contrast, economic conditions were not yet ripe for a proletarian revolution because bourgeois society had not yet reached the point of an exclusively bipolar class antagonism between the bourgeoisie and the proletariat. Diverse classes with their own interests, including the large French peasantry, enabled the bourgeoisie to form alliances in their struggle against the proletariat. Eventually, however, it would become impossible for the peasantry to resist the process by which it too would be absorbed by the proletariat. One important lesson of the history of the second Republic is "that in Europe the question of today is something other than 'republic or monarchy'" (LPW 39). Another reason for the comparative difficulty of the proletarian revolution is its novelty. Previous revolutions were essentially alike in that they pitted one class against another. But the proletarian revolution is unique in that it signals the end of the class struggle itself. Thus, whereas the bourgeois French revolutionaries were able to dress themselves up in Roman costumes, the communists require an entirely new wardrobe: "The social revolution of the nineteenth century cannot create its poetry from the past but only from the future" (LPW 34).

In 1849 Marx moved to England, where he wrote a number of extensive studies of bourgeois society, including *Capital: A Critique of Political Economy* (*Das Kapital: Kritik der politischen Ökonomie*), the first volume of which was published in 1867 (revised edition 1872). Marx begins with the supposition that what is distinctive about "the capitalist mode of production" is the commodity form (C 125). In order for a product of human labor to become a commodity, several conditions have to be met. First, it must have a "use-value," which is a function of the specific qualities that it has. Second, it must stand in a quantitative relation to other objects with different use-values. In order for such a relation to exist, there must be a common measure of the "value" of each thing, a value that is independent of use value (C 127). Marx claims that a thing's value is determined by the amount of human labor required to produce it – or, more precisely, by the quantity of "socially necessary labour-time" that is necessary for its production (C 129). This implies that value can fluctuate in accordance with changes in the means of production. The third criterion for a thing's becoming a commodity is that its value be expressed as "exchange-value." For this to happen, qualitatively distinct forms of labor – to which there correspond qualitatively distinct use-values – must be "performed in isolation" (C 132). In other words, there must be "a social division of labour" that has the form of "a complex system" (C 133). In such a system, the exchange of things of equal value can take place only when a particular use-value comes to serve as the common unit for measuring all values: "the magnitudes of different things only become comparable in quantitative terms when they have been reduced to the same unit" (C 140–1). The commodity that "acquires the form of universal equivalent" – for example, gold – thereby comes to function as money. Thus a thing becomes a commodity when it acquires a price (C 160).

Under the feudal economy that prevailed in Europe in the Middle Ages, exchange was governed by social relations of dependence rather than by money per se. Hence value was reckoned not in terms of exchange-value but in terms of labor-time. A serf was expected to work for a certain amount of time for his lord in exchange for the right to work the land (C 170). But once the commodity comes into existence, value seems to inhere in it as a "mysterious" property that it possesses over and above its physical qualities: "The mysterious character of the commodity-form consists therefore simply in the fact that the commodity reflects the social characteristics of men's own labour as objective characteristics of the products of labour themselves, as the socio-natural properties of these things" (C 164–5). As a result of this illusion, exchange ceases to take place as a relation between human beings and instead assumes "the fantastic form of a relation between things." Marx refers to this as the "fetishism of commodities" (C 165).

Thus the advent of the commodity marks the true beginning of what Marx referred to in the 1844 Manuscripts as the phenomenon of estranged labor. Whereas Feuerbach thought that alienation found its primary expression in religion, Marx locates it more precisely in the religion of commodities, which is based on the distinction between use-value and exchange-value. Insofar as a commodity is a use-value, it is a sensible object with physical properties. But insofar as it is an exchange-value it functions as if it were a *supersensible* object with spiritual properties: "as soon as it emerges as a commodity, it changes into a thing which transcends sensuousness" (C 163; cf. 149). Thus the fetishism of commodities occurs at the precise moment when the relationship between a thing and its value becomes inverted: instead of serving as a mere measure of the socially necessary labor-time that is needed to produce a thing, abstract value appears as a transcendent entity that manifests itself in the thing. Marx characterizes this as the revelation of the commodity's "sublime objectivity" (C 144).

Insofar as it treats a merely regulative principle as if it were constitutive of a transcendent object, the fetishism of commodities can be thought of as a transcendental illusion. Kant claimed that it was a peculiarity of such illusions that even after seeing through them, they continued to persist, seducing reason with their allure (CPR A297/B353). Marx makes a similar point about the fetishism of commodities:

> The belated scientific discovery that the products of labour, in so far as they are values, are merely the material expressions of the human labour expended to produce them, marks an epoch in the history of mankind's development, but by no means banishes the semblance of objectivity possessed by the social characteristics of labour.
>
> (C 167)

Here Marx implicitly reiterates his critique of Hegel and Feuerbach, both of whom thought that alienation could be overcome by understanding it. In fact, the fetishism of commodities can be effectively overcome only when the institution of private property is abolished: "The veil is not removed from the countenance of the social life-process, i.e. the process of material production, until it becomes production by freely associated men, and stands under their conscious and planned control" (C 173).

The fact that the fetishism of commodities *can* be overcome shows that it is not so much a *transcendental* illusion as one that is historically generated. Indeed, the illusion consists in thinking that the commodity-form is itself a transcendental condition of the possibility of experience in general rather than being a condition for the possibility of bourgeois experience – i.e., that there is no other way of organizing economic production and exchange apart from commodity-production. In contrast to Hegel and Feuerbach – who tried to overcome man's self-estrangement by acknowledging its historicity – Kant implicitly treats alienation as if it were an essential feature of human existence as such. Not only does he consider the separation of the receptivity of sensibility from the spontaneity of thought to be an a priori condition for the possibility of experience, but he locates man's value in a supersensible kingdom of ends. For precisely this reason, Kant accords a higher value to the sublime than to the beautiful. Insofar as it harmonizes the imagination and understanding, a beautiful object promises a reconciliation of humanity with itself – though in order to actualize such a reconciliation it would be necessary to pass from the merely contemplative stance of disinterested taste to the active stance of engaged practice. By contrast, the feeling of the sublime reinforces the division between the imagination and reason, giving rise to the subject's conviction that its "true" life lies in a supersensible beyond.

By tracing the feeling of the sublime to the commodity-form, Marx suggests that the Kantian conception of *man* as an end in itself is really just a disguised form of the view that *money* is an end in itself. Or rather, though Kant makes a valiant effort to retain the pre-capitalist idea that man is an end in itself who cannot be assigned a price, he espouses an alienated moral theory that is simultaneously divorced from – and therefore complicitous with – bourgeois political economy. As Marx and Engels put it in their posthumously published *The German Ideology* (*Die deutsche Ideologie*, written in 1845–1846): "Kant was satisfied with 'good will' alone, even if it remained entirely without result, and he transferred the *realisation* of this good will, the harmony between it and the needs and impulses of individuals, to *the world beyond*" (GI 193). This characterization of Kant's moral philosophy might be said to overlook the importance that Kant attaches in his philosophy of history to the promise of perpetual peace, but Marx and Engels regard Kant's reaction to the French Revolution as reactionary rather than progressive. In effect, he based his conception of the will on that of the bourgeoisie and then "recoiled in horror from the practice of this energetic bourgeois liberalism as soon as this practice showed itself, both in the Reign of Terror and in shameless bourgeois profit-making" (GI 195).

Marx's critique of the commodity-form enables him to explain how the capitalists make their profit, namely, by the extraction of the "surplus-value" that labor produces (C 251). But his critique of capitalism ultimately rests not on the claim that the wages that workers receive for their labor have *less* value than the commodities that they produce. On the contrary, it is the very form of wage labor – inextricably bound up with the production of commodities – that is inherently de-humanizing. One way to characterize the condition of de-humanization would be to say that it occurs whenever the collective human vocation for creating a beautiful world gives way to the isolation of individuals who have become transfixed by the sublimity of abstract value. What makes political economy so insidious is that it justifies the separation of beauty from value by making money the sole object of desire. To say that political economy is the science of asceticism is to say that it orients human desire away from the immanence of the beautiful and toward the transcendence of the sublime. An effective – i.e., practical – critique of political economy requires that the artificial separation of labor from value be abolished. In communist society, human beings will at last become capable of creating a truly beautiful world. Thus in contrast to Schiller, who thought that alienation would be overcome *through* the aesthetic education of man, Marx suggests that it is only when alienation has been overcome that the aesthetic education of humanity will truly begin.

3.3 Lukács's conception of reification and his development of a Marxist aesthetics

> When that this body did contain a spirit,
> A kingdom for it was too small a bound,
> But now two paces of the vilest earth
> Is room enough.
> [. . .] What, old acquaintance! could not all this flesh
> Keep in a little life?
> *(The First Part of Henry the Fourth,*
> V, iv, 89–92, 102–3)

In his early writings, the Hungarian philosopher Georg (György) Lukács (1885–1971) laments the fact that in bourgeois society humanity appears to be irremediably estranged from itself. Taking his cue from Kant and Hegel rather than from Marx, he expresses a kind of despairing nostalgia for the unattainable Romantic ideal of a reconciled humanity. At first, not even the Russian Revolution of October 1917 could cure Lukács of his unremitting pessimism. But in 1918, he converts to a Marxist point of view, from which he derives the confident expectation that the world-wide proletarian revolution will succeed in redeeming an alienated humanity. In retrospect, he now regards his pre-Marxist sense of hopelessness as a product of the very bourgeois subjectivity that he had sought, in vain, to critique.

In "The Bourgeois Way of Life and Art for Art's Sake," one of the essays in *Soul and Form* (*A lékék és a formák*, 1910; *Die Seele und die Formen*, 1911), the young Lukács reflects "with impotent nostalgia" on a lost experience of perfection that the German Romantics associated with the "bourgeois way of life" (SAF 55). The Romantics regarded the asceticism of the bourgeois way of life as aspiring to a kind of perfection akin to that enjoyed by works of art. But, according to Lukács, it is no longer possible to regard the self-absorption of bourgeois asceticism as having anything in common with artistic perfection; on the contrary, it is entirely cut off from that which alone could give it a kind of dignity and grace: "The bourgeois way of life is merely a mask that hides the bitter, useless pain of a failed and ruined life, the life-pain of the Romantic born too late" (SAF 56). In terms that suggest Nietzsche's (as well as Marx's) critique of the ascetic ideal, Lukács accuses bourgeois culture of something like *ressentiment*: "it is only the opposite of something, it acquires meaning solely through the energy with which it says 'No' to something" (SAF 56). Thus despite their purported affinity, there is an unbridgeable gulf separating "the bourgeois way of life" from "art for art's sake." This gulf poses a problem for the modern artist, whose crafts-manship represents an attempt to put bourgeois professionalism in the service of the perfection to which art aspires. At issue in the artist's sense of craft is not merely the creation of art but the redemption of life itself, or at least of life as it has been deformed by bourgeois society.

Whether such an effort at redemption can succeed or not is the guiding question of Lukács's *The Theory of the Novel: a Historico-Philosophical Essay on the Forms of Great Epic Literature* (*Die Theorie des Romans*, 1916). In his 1962 preface to its reissue, Lukács says that this work, composed during the First World War, "was written in a mood of permanent despair over the state of the world" (TOTN 12). In the book itself he had referred to his age, in terms borrowed from Fichte, as "the epoch of absolute sinfulness" (TOTN 152). Absolute sinfulness is the extreme manifestation of a more pervasive condition of "transcendental homelessness" (TOTN 41) that has plagued Europe throughout the modern period. Man becomes transcendentally homeless whenever "life" is cut off from "essence," that is, whenever the individual subject experiences itself as alienated from the world. In this historical constellation, the novel has a unique role to play, for unlike other forms of literature, it has the alienated subject seeking reconciliation with the world as its protagonist. Unfortunately, so great is the rift within human experience in the age of absolute sinfulness that even the novel proves unable to heal it. Lukács concludes with a wistful hope for a new form of art that might succeed where the novel fails, acknowledging that such a hope may be futile (TOTN 153).

In order to indicate the specificity of the novel form, Lukács situates it with respect to earlier forms of literature from which it is distinct. Lying at the basis of his typology is a fundamental distinction between "integrated" and "problematic" civilizations. An integrated civilization, such as he imag-ines ancient Greece to have been, is one in which life and essence are not dis-tinct, that is, in which human beings live their lives within a world which they regard as inherently meaningful. Since no sharp division between the interior life of a subject and the external world yet exists, nature represents a transcendental home for human action. Corresponding to such "happy ages" (TOTN 29) is the epic, which Lukács represents as that form of literature which provides an answer to the question "how can life become essence?" (TOTN 30).[5] Here the answer precedes the question, for it is only when a civilization becomes problematic that it is forced to pose the problem of reconciliation. This occurs not in the epic but in tragedy, whose appearance in ancient Greece is symptomatic of a crisis. Tragedy registers the loss of a sense of unity but finds reconciliation in the destiny of the tragic hero (TOTN 35). The advent of philosophy represents the self-consciousness of tragedy, or rather a taking-stock of the arbitrariness of tragic destiny and the tenuousness of its reconciliation of life and essence. Thus unlike Nietzsche, for whom Socrates disturbed a perfect balance between Apollo and Dionysus, Lukács conceives of Socratic questioning as making explicit a problem that tragedy itself implicitly poses. Plato's vision of the soul's contemplation of the forms represents the last great Greek answer to the question concerning life and essence. The subsequent history of European philosophy inherits from Plato not his solution to the problem of the lost transcendental home but the problem itself, which in Kant manifests itself in the seemingly unbridgeable gulf separating the exigency of a pure moral "ought" from the contingency of the empirical world (TOTN 36).

Lukács regards the history of European culture since antiquity as a series of responses to this crisis, with some ages (like the medieval) succeeding in reconstituting a relatively integrated civilization and others failing to do so. The distinctive feature of modernity, coinciding with the rise of bourgeois society and finding expression in the philosophy of Kant, is that its crisis has been accentuated to the point where reconciliation of life and essence appears to be impossible. Lukács characterizes this condition as "the abandonment of the world by God" (TOTN 97). In a world devoid of metaphysics, only art preserves a slender possibility of redemption (TOTN 37). But so long as it stands opposed to reality, art cannot take the place of metaphysics; only by remaking the world in its own image could it do that – but for this art is too weak. In effect the task faced by modern art – and by the novel in particular – is to recreate the epic, but in order to accomplish this goal it would also have to recreate the social conditions for the possibility of the epic. For Lukács, Miguel de Cervantes' (1547–1616) *Don Quixote* is the first, and to some extent the most successful, attempt to respond to the enormity of this challenge. Cervantes's hero aspires to nothing less than a transfiguration of the world so as to make it a transcendental home for chivalrous acts. The fact that such an effort is patently absurd is one of the key themes of the novel. Yet despite the ridiculousness (as opposed to sublimity) of his adventures, Don Quixote's high-minded sense of purpose endows him with an undeniable dignity. According to Lukács, the hero of every subsequent modern novel has had the task of struggling to recapture the conditions for the possibility of an epic experience of the world. But because this task must be accomplished under the condition of absolute homelessness or sinfulness, it is impossible to fulfill. Thus the history of the novel is a history of failure.

Over the course of this failed history, the novel has been torn between two extremes: in aspiring to the status of an epic hero, the soul of the hero of the novel is always either "'too narrow' or 'too broad' in relation to reality" (TOTN 13; cf. 97). The first of these extremes manifests itself in "abstract idealism," epitomized in *Don Quixote*: "*Don Quixote* is the first great battle of interiority against the prosaic vulgarity of outward life" (TOTN 104). Don Quixote's struggles to invest prosaic life with poetic meaning would be of truly epic proportion were it not for the fact that they are completely at variance with the world in which he actually lives; in this sense his soul is "too narrow." The novel of abstract idealism represents this failure as comic rather than as tragic, revealing how the most "sublime" of aspirations for the ideal can only lead to "monomania" (TOTN 100). At the other extreme is what Lukács calls the novel of "romantic disillusionment," exemplified in the figure of Oblomov, the title character of a novel by the nineteenth-century Russian writer, Ivan Alexandrovich Goncharov (1812–1891) (TOTN 120). In this genre, it is as if a sobered Don Quixote had retreated from the field of battle without giving up his lofty aspirations. In a gesture analogous to what Kierkegaard calls "infinite resignation," the heroic subject of this type of novel forsakes action altogether, taking refuge in a soul that has become decidedly "too broad" for the world around it. This is just another extreme, as both types of novel are faced with – and unable to resolve – the problem of utopia. Genuine reconciliation would require a return to the "happy age" of the epic, but in the age of absolute sinfulness the most that can be accomplished is a choice between privileging one of the two sides of the schism between life and essence, inner soul and outer world.

Thus the main problem faced by Lukács is whether it is possible for the novel to straddle these two extremes, to reconcile the opposition between abstract idealism and the romanticism of disillusionment. This leads him to consider *Wilhelm Meister's Years of Apprenticeship*, a work by the German poet Johann Wolfgang von Goethe (1749–1832), which represents a "humanist" attempt to solve this problem: "Humanism, the fundamental attitude of this type of work, demands a balance between activity and contemplation, between wanting to mould the world and being purely receptive towards it" (TOTN 135). In effect this is the problem of the relationship between receptivity and spontaneity, carried over into the domain of action. It can also be characterized in aesthetic terms as the problem of the relationship between the beautiful and the sublime, where abstract idealism aims, in vain, at the construction of a beautiful world and the romanticism of disillusionment settles for the worldless sublimity of the merely ideal. Goethe's *Bildungsroman* represents an attempt to bring these two extremes together, which it does by situating its heroic subject in a social milieu in which everyone seeks the same reconciliation between life and essence. Lukács characterizes this artistic solution as a potential breakthrough, but he claims that it ultimately fails because art by itself can only do so much; the *Bildungsroman* can at best reveal the utter impossibility of carrying out its reconciliation in bourgeois society as it actually exists. In contrast to ancient tragedy, whose hero was redeemed through fate or destiny, the *Bildungsroman* glimpses an impossible redemption by projecting its characters into an unreal and therefore merely utopian setting. In so doing it shows that "no artist's skill is great and masterly enough to bridge the abyss" (TOTN 143). In the final pages of *The Theory of the Novel*, Lukács looks for a successor to the *Bildungsroman* in the work of Leo Tolstoy (1828–1910), whose promise is due, in part, to the supposed fact that Russian civilization is less alienated than Western European culture (TOTN 145). But here he finds only "restless *ennui*" and so confirmation for his thesis that "Literary development has not yet gone beyond the novel of disillusionment" (TOTN 149, 151). More precisely, the novel is still torn between the extremes of abstract idealism and the romanticism of disillusionment, attesting to the impossibility of redemption from the age of absolute sinfulness. A glimmer of hope might be found in Fyodor Dostoyevsky (1821–1881), whose works – insofar as they escape the dilemma between abstract idealism and romantic disillusionment – transcend the novel form (TOTN 152; cf. 20). But whether Dostoyevsky "is merely a beginning or a completion" remains an open question (TOTN 153).

Given his critique of bourgeois culture and his interest in Russian literature, it is not surprising that the Russian Revolution had a major impact on Lukács's thinking, but at first he expressed moral reservations about the Bolshevik seizure of power. In "Bolshevism as an Ethical Problem" (*A bolsevizmus mint erkölcsi probléma*, 1918) he argues in favor of social democracy as the only ethically viable route to socialism:

> one must decide whether socialism indeed personifies the will and power to redeem this world – or whether socialism is really just an ideological cover for class interest. . . . Bolshevism rests on the metaphysical assumption that good can issue from evil. . . . This writer cannot share this faith and therefore sees at the root of Bolshevism an insoluble ethical dilemma.
> (TLR 218, 220)

By the time this essay appeared in print, however, Lukács had joined the communist party, serving as commissar of education in the short-lived Hungarian Workers' Republic in 1919.[6]

After the despairing tone on which *The Theory of the Novel* ends, nothing could be more striking than the sense of sheer optimism that pervades the essays collected in *History and Class Consciousness* (*Geschichte und Klassenbewusstsein: Studien über Marxistische Dialektik*, 1923). In 1967, looking back at this transition, Lukács himself observes that "*The Theory of the Novel* was written at a time when I was still in a general state of despair . . . any hopes of a way out seemed to be a utopian mirage. Only the Russian Revolution really opened a window to the future" (HACC xi). What had been recognized before from a merely bourgeois point of view as the problem of transcendental homelessness is now seen – correctly – through the proletarian lens of the contradictions of capitalism. Far from being inescapable, these contradictions can be overcome provided that the proletariat recognizes itself as the subject whose collective actions as a class will at last make possible a genuine reconciliation of soul and world, subject and object. Only the proletariat can accomplish this reconciliation because it alone is in a position to recognize that what appears to the bourgeois sensibility to be a timeless rift between life and essence is in fact an historical consequence of "the reification of all human relations," the alienation of humanity from the second nature that it has created for itself (HACC 6). In seeing through the quasi-transcendental character of reification, the proletariat is capable not merely of *hoping* for a reconciled humanity but of *acting* in such a way as to jumpstart the stalled historical dialectic. Thus the proletarian revolution represents the great epic adventure of our day.

In "Reification and the Consciousness of the Proletariat," Lukács reconstructs the philosophical trajectory that leads from Kant's critical project to Marx's account of the proletariat as revolutionary subject. Prior to the advent of capitalism it would have been impossible for any individual or collective subject to adopt the point of view of society as a whole. This possibility manifests itself only under capitalism, in which the commodification of social relations has become so pervasive that the difference from previous societies is one of quality rather than quantity (HACC 84). Every subject in bourgeois society – whether proletarian, bourgeois, petty bourgeois, or peasant – is alienated. But only the proletariat as a class – due to its collective commodification as a source of labor power – can become conscious of reification as the truth of capitalism. Such consciousness cannot be achieved by isolated individual workers because it represents the point of view of the totality itself. Thus, in order for the proletariat to assume its position as the collective subject of human history, individual workers must acquire the ability to represent the point of view of their class – and ultimately society – as a whole. Otherwise capitalism might continue indefinitely, for the contradictions of capitalism have created only the conditions for the possibility of its defeat. The epic struggle of the proletariat ultimately rests on the successful cultivation of class consciousness.

In "Bolshevism as an Ethical Problem," Lukács insisted that only the ability to "redeem" the world as a whole could justify proletarian revolutions. In *History and Class Consciousness*, he explicitly ascribes such a "messianic" power to the proletariat, a point of view he would later repudiate as too idealistic (HACC xiii). Lukács's messianism enables him to suspend his earlier reservations concerning the Bolsheviks' use of violence and disdain for existing democratic institutions. Whereas previously he had claimed that good could not come from evil, he now sees revolutionary violence as a means to ending all recourse to violence (HACC 252). Hence it would be a mistake to refuse to have recourse to illegal actions in fighting for an end to the class struggle, though it would be just as much of a mistake to fetishize illegal actions in a spirit of "romantic" revolutionary fervor (HACC 263). In all such questions *"the legitimacy of the Revolution"* (HACC 269) should not be lost sight of.

Thus Lukács fully accepts Marx's claim that the aim of philosophy should be to change, rather than merely interpret, the world: "for the dialectical method the central problem is *to change reality*" (HACC 3). Bourgeois subjectivity is unable to change reality, for even when it acts it merely modifies surface phenomena, leaving unchanged the fundamentally reified character of the "second nature" in which it has enslaved all of humanity (including itself) (HACC 128). More precisely, bourgeois subjectivity was capable of changing reality only in its properly revolutionary moment, when it was overthrowing feudalism. This explains why it had been possible for the Romantics to glorify the bourgeois way of life just before and after the French Revolution. But once it has succeeded in commodifying social relations, bourgeois subjectivity can henceforth only adapt itself to its own environment by cleverly anticipating the likely outcomes of economic processes that appear to be governed by fixed eternal laws; such action is more akin to contemplation than it is to genuine praxis:

> this "action" consists in predicting, in calculating as far as possible the probable effects of those laws and the subject of the "action" takes up a position in which these effects can be exploited to the best advantage of his own purpose. . . . The attitude of the subject then becomes purely contemplative in the philosophical sense.
>
> (HACC 130)

Despite the fact that it is itself the author of the social relations it has established, the bourgeoisie remains fascinated by the fetishism of commodities. Only the proletariat can see through this mirage by realizing that what appear under capitalism as fixed essences have their origin in fluid historical processes: "when the dialectical method destroys the fiction of the immortality of the categories it also destroys their reified character and clears the way to a knowledge of reality" (HACC 14). Lukács concludes that Marx's *Capital* has no other aim than "the retranslation of economic objects from things back into processes" (HACC 183), and that "the chapter dealing with the fetish character of the commodity contains within itself the whole of historical materialism" (HACC 170). Class consciousness of the proletariat on behalf of society as a whole will only be achieved when "we shall have raised ourselves in fact to the position from which reality can be understood as our 'action'" (HACC 145). Here class consciousness must not be understood merely as an abstract awareness on the part of a still contemplative subject. This was the shortcoming of the German idealist tradition, which perfectly understood what was necessary to overcome reification but only on the level of abstract thought: "classical philosophy is able to think the deepest and most fundamental problems of the development of bourgeois society through to the very end – on the plane of philosophy" (HACC 121).

For Lukács, the entire German idealist tradition from Kant through Hegel can be understood as a rigorous response to the inherent "antinomies of bourgeois thought," but without its being understood that these antinomies had their origin in historically contingent social contradictions that could be resolved only through the revolutionary activity of the proletariat (HACC 156). Kant inaugurated the critical tradition by challenging the rationalist pretension to provide a complete systematic comprehension of the world. He does this in two ways: first, by indicating that it is impossible to complete such a system (since this can only be thought as a regulative idea); second, by emphasizing the irreducibility of the "irrational" kernel of that which is given in intuition. In Kant's third *Critique*, these two limits turn out to coincide in the problem concerning the objective purposiveness of nature (HACC 116). In recognizing the insolubility of this problem – the principle of purposiveness is valid only for reflective, not determining, judgment – Kant indicates that it is impossible to regard the world as fully rational. But rather than recognize this as a feature of the particular character of bourgeois society he instead treats it as an unchanging transcendental condition of possible human experience in general. Thus, far from resolving the antinomies of bourgeois thought, Kant succumbs to them, as can be seen in the sharp dichotomy that separates the first *Critique* from the second, that is, the account of nature as a law-governed realm in which all human actions are heteronomous from the ideal of a kingdom of ends (HACC 41). Despite the fact that the categorical imperative bids us to change the world by regarding ourselves as legislators in nature, it remains a merely abstract and utopian principle, paradoxically affirming the very world it would supposedly have us transform. This can be seen in the fact that Kant regards the categories of experience as fixed transcendental limits rather than as the expression of bourgeois social relations (HACC 119).

Hegel makes a decisive advance beyond Kant by recognizing the historical and dialectical character of both the Kantian forms of thought and the Kantian conception of the moral law, thereby passing from the point of mere "conditions of possibility" to (genetic) conditions of actuality (HACC 110). But Hegel fails to take the next step, which is to recognize that the antinomies of bourgeois thought can be resolved not by the thought of philosophers but only through the revolutionary actions of the proletariat:

Hence classical philosophy had nothing but these unresolved antinomies to bequeath to succeeding (bourgeois) generations. The continuation of that course which at least in method started to point the way beyond these limits, namely the dialectical method as the true historical method was reserved for the class which was able to discover within itself on the basis of its life-experience the identical subject-object, the subject of action; the "we" of the genesis: namely the proletariat.

(HACC 148–9)

At present "man" does not yet exist; or rather he exists only as not yet existing, as the telos toward which proletarian consciousness (i.e., activity) points (HACC 69, 190). Thus the coming – or rather on-going – proletarian revolution is the process of restoring to humanity its very humanity. As such it represents not a mere utopian possibility but the realization of a "tendency" inherent in the existing contradictions of capitalism.

This account enables Lukács to reconceive the role of art in human experience. Schiller claimed that man is fully human "only when he plays" (HACC 139). However, as long as this principle is conceived from the standpoint of bourgeois subjectivity, it poses an insoluble dilemma:

either the world must be aestheticised, which is an evasion of the real problem and is just another way to annihilate "action." Or else, the aesthetic principle must be elevated into the principle by which objective reality is shaped: but that would be to mythologize the discovery of intuitive understanding.

(HACC 140)

This is the opposition that Lukács had earlier detected between abstract idealism and the romanticism of disillusionment – the former mythologizing or mystifying reality; the latter retreating to the contemplative standpoint of the disengaged observer. This opposition, which had earlier seemed to Lukács to be insurmountable, now appears as just another one of the antinomies of bourgeois thought: "The truly critical, metaphysically non-hypostatised, artistic view of the world leads to an even greater fragmentation of the unity of the subject and thus to an increase in the symptoms of alienation" (HACC 215 n53). In other words, the very impotence to which bourgeois works of art attest confirms that they are themselves products of reification. Under these conditions, bourgeois society threatens to reduce art to a mere commodity:

Under capitalism the scope of art is much more narrowly confined; it can exercise no determining influence upon the production of consumer goods and indeed the question of its own existence is decided by purely economic factors and the problems of technical production governed by them.

(HACC 236)

Shortly after its publication, *History and Class Consciousness* was condemned by Soviet officials as contradicting the reigning scientific interpretation of Marxism, and Lukács found it expedient to repudiate his work.[7] When Hitler came to power in 1933, he left Berlin for the Soviet Union, having already studied at the Marx–Engels Institute in Moscow, where he was one of the first to read Marx's still-unpublished 1844 Manuscripts. In subsequent publications, Lukács defends – though not uncritically – the aesthetics of Soviet realism against what he regards as the decadence of Western European modernism. In *The Historical Novel* (*Der historische Roman*, 1955; originally published in Russian in 1937), he distinguishes the historical novel from the historical drama, and attempts to explain why the former emerged around the time of the French Revolution. Since works of literature not only reflect material social conditions but have the capacity of raising class consciousness, Lukács argues that certain forms of literature should be promoted over others. In the realistic historical novel, he detects a "new humanism" of the same sort that he had earlier praised in Goethe's *Wilhelm Meister* (THN 301–4).

In a 1909 lecture, "Shakespeare and Modern Drama" (*Shakespeare és a modern dráma*, 1911), Lukács distinguished Shakespearean drama from modern drama by claiming, with the nineteenth-century Austrian dramatist Friedrich Hebbel (1813–1863), that whereas modern dramatists represent conflicts between abstract ideas, Shakespeare presents conflicts between concrete individual characters (TLR 74–6). Hegel criticized Shakespeare for having failed to show that Macbeth was acting not merely out of a personal motive but on the basis of an abstract principle concerning hereditary rights (TLR 75). Against this reading, Lukács argues that Shakespeare is uninterested in abstract principles, and that he treats everything other than character as a mere backdrop for the dramatic action of his plays. It is modern drama that subordinates character to the representation of the clash of ideas. These two types of drama constitute a kind of dialectical unity, since "every literary work, especially drama, is the result of the mixture of concrete and abstract elements, and . . . neither the one nor the other can ever dominate the whole" (TLR 78). As in *The Theory of the Novel*, two literary forms are contrasted, each of which strives to achieve something that the other cannot. Works of art are situated historically, but they are subject to an over-arching condition governing literary forms in general. In *The Historical Novel*, Lukács reiterates his earlier rejoinder to Hegel's criticism of *Macbeth*, but he now emphasizes Shakespeare's ability to represent the specific historical condition to which his characters belong: "Shakespeare shows the human qualities which inevitably arise in just this social-historical context. . . . And he is quite right to portray this human essence (socially and historically conditioned) and not to clutter up the clear outlines of his work with trivial motifs" (THN 138). Throughout his plays, Shakespeare reveals "a whole set of the inner contradictions of feudalism," such as in *King Lear*, where he "creates the greatest and most moving tragedy of the break-up of the family *qua* human community" (THN 153, 93).

Perhaps most revelatory with respect to Lukács's own historical situation are the two parts of Shakespeare's *Henry the Fourth*. In the first part, which corresponds to Lukács's pre-Marxist period, the idle Prince Hal is not yet capable of "redeeming time" (I, ii, 216). His two principal foils, Falstaff and Hotspur, represent the complementary misfits that Lukács had detected in *The Theory of the Novel* – the one, with a body vaster than his spirit, falling short of world-redemption; the other, with a spirit too large for his small stature, overshooting it. At the end of the play, as Hal eulogizes the two men (only one of whom is actually dead, since the cowardly Falstaff has carefully avoided the life of action), Shakespeare invites us to expect great things from him in the second part of the play. However, this second part – the complement of Lukács's Soviet period – is permeated with an atmosphere of general debauchery and a sense of futility. Significantly, Hal assumes his father's crown twice – first, precipitously, when he falsely believes that his father is dead (the analogue of the ill-fated Hungarian Soviet); and second, when he really does become king, but then heartlessly repudiates Falstaff (as if beginning the Great Purge). At this moment, the English do not know what the reign of King Henry the Fifth will be like, whether he really will redeem time or not. This is the same predicament that Lukács found himself in when Stalin came to power.

3.4   Heidegger's dialogue with Nietzsche about great art

Let it be so.
(*The Merchant of Venice*, V, i, 300)

In the final pages of *Being and Time*, Heidegger alludes to *History and Class Consciousness*, suggesting that the phenomenon of reification has not yet been ontologically clarified: "It has long been known that ancient ontology works with 'Thing-concepts' and that there is a danger of 'reifying consciousness.' But what does this 'reifying' signify? Where does it arise? . . . *Why* does this reifying always keep coming back to exercise its dominion?" (BAT 487; cf. 72, 472).[8] Unlike Lukács, Heidegger saw no difference between capitalism and Bolshevism, as is indicated by his 1935 remark that "Russia and America, seen metaphysically, are both the same: the same hopeless frenzy of unchained technology and of the rootless organization of the average man" (IM 40).[9] In a post-war letter to Marcuse, Heidegger contends that it was his antipathy toward Bolshevism that led him to join the Nazi Party in 1933, a decision that he says he later regretted. Though still convinced that Bolshevism is no less caught up in the age of technology than capitalism or fascism, Heidegger tentatively indicates the possibility of "a productive dialogue with Marxism" in his "Letter on Humanism" (*Brief über den Humanismus*, 1947), in which he credits Marx with recognizing that human estrangement is the fundamental plight of modern existence (BW 243). Human estrangement from being is characterized in "Building Dwelling Thinking" (*Bauen Wohnen Denken*, first presented in 1951) as "homelessness," the key concept of Lukács's *The Theory of the Novel*. According to Heidegger, true homelessness has nothing to do with a shortage of houses but with the fact "that mortals ever search anew for the nature of dwelling, that they *must ever learn to dwell*" (PLT 161). In *Being and Time*, Heidegger had criticized Hegel for characterizing reification as the falling-into-time of spirit (BAT 486). This point is clarified in "The Question Concerning Technology," where he suggests that reification must be understood not as the self-externalization of either spirit or labor, but as the unfolding of the history of being, from the Greeks' relationship to things to the Enframing of man in modern technology.

In his 1935 lecture, "The Origin of the Work of Art" (*Der Ursprung des Kunstwerkes*, first published in 1950), Heidegger argues that works of art play a unique role in alerting us to the fact of reification by revealing both the "equipmental" character of equipment and the "thingly" character of things. A painting by Van Gogh of a pair of peasant's shoes evokes the earth to which they belong and the world in which they have their everyday function: "This equipment belongs to the *earth*, and it is protected in the *world* of the peasant woman" (PLT 34). Instead of conceiving of art in terms of the metaphysical categories of form and matter – which pertain only to equipment – Heidegger characterizes the work of art as the site of a conflict between earth and world (PLT 28). Earth, the concealing ground of what is, is revealed as such in the world opened up by the work, just as this world can be revealed only in the earthly element in which the work is cast. As the intimate conflict of earth and world, the work of art allows the "happening of truth" to take place. Truth can be "established" in science, but only art can "open up" a world: "science is not an original happening of truth, but always the cultivation of a domain of truth already opened" (PLT 62). This leads Heidegger to ask: "What is truth, that it can happen as, or even must happen as, art?" (PLT 57).

In his 1936–1937 lecture course on Nietzsche's conception of the will to power as art, Heidegger suggests that Nietzsche's eventual break with Wagner – whose music he had initially taken to exemplify the tension between Apollo and Dionysus but later derided as insipid – was inevitable, because "Wagner sought sheer upsurgence of the Dionysian upon which one might ride, while Nietzsche sought to leash its force and give it form" (N I 88). To "give form" to the formless without violating the rights of the formless is to create art in "the grand style" (N I 124). Nietzsche associates "intoxication" or "rapture" (*Rausch*) with the experience of the Dionysian, but Heidegger suggests that rapture – the "fundamental mood" of Nietzsche's aesthetics – should be associated with works that unite the Dionysian and Apollonian. Nietzsche failed to see how close his own conception of the beautiful was to that of Kant because he was led astray by Schopenhauer, who equated Kant's conception of disinterestedness with a nihilistic quiescence of the will. But not only does Kant observe that we can and do take a moral interest in that which we experience in an aesthetically disinterested manner, he also notes that in the judgment of taste we "favor" the beautiful, recognizing it as worthy of "honor." Insofar as "comportment toward the beautiful" involves "*unconstrained favoring*," the will plays an active role in Kant's account of taste (N I 109). Just as an effort of the will is required to resist all natural inclinations, so it takes an effort of the will to resist all sensuous and cognitive enticements that would interfere with the object's disclosure of its mere form. Heidegger concludes that "Kant alone grasped the essence of what Nietzsche in his own way wanted to comprehend concerning the decisive aspects of the beautiful" (N I 111).

In a note inserted in his own copy of *Kant and the Problem of Metaphysics*, Heidegger claims to have found confirmation for his interpretation of the first *Critique* in the conception of "beauty as a symbol of morality" that Kant develops in section 59 of the third *Critique*: "Only considered far enough to be able to see that it is not contradicted. But now the highest corroboration of the interpretation; see § 59, p. 258...!!, likewise p. 238...; the intelligible! whererupon [sic] taste (reflection–imagination) looks out (into itself)" (KAPOM-T 175–6). Though cryptic, this passage suggests that although Heidegger rejects the view that a work of art is both a thing and a symbol, his critique pertains to post-Kantian aesthetics and not to Kant's own conception of the beautiful. Indeed, "The Origin of the Work of Art" can be characterized as an attempt to rework the idea that the beautiful is a symbol of morality – by tacitly exploiting Kant's conception of an aesthetic idea. Aesthetic ideas prompt us to think:

> Now if we add to a concept a representation of the imagination that belongs to its presentation, but which by itself stimulates so much thinking that it can never be grasped in a determinate concept, hence which aesthetically enlarges the concept itself in an unbounded way, then in this case the imagination is creative.
>
> (CPJ 193)

This statement could be read as a description of Heidegger's own hermeneutic procedure. In his account of the Van Gogh painting, the "mere" image of a pair of shoes prompted an inconclusive discourse whose end was not to determine what the shoes were but to "enlarge" our concept of equipment in general. Elsewhere, Heidegger inquires into what is implied by the concept of a thing. Since mere conceptual analysis appears to get us nowhere, he turns to a particular presentation of a thing in the imagination: an ordinary jug. By inviting us to reflect on the jug – rather than merely subsuming it under its concept – Heidegger is able to "enlarge" our concept of what a thing is. We are led to think that which is inexpressible or "concealed" in it, that which necessarily eludes the determining judgments of science: "Science always encounters only what *its* kind of representation has admitted beforehand as an object possible for science. . . . The thingness of the thing remains concealed, forgotten" (PLT 170). The fact that works of art can disclose the thingly character of things attests to the "aesthetic" character of *aisthesis*, or sensible intuition. But a great work of art is not merely beautiful – that is, not merely world-disclosive – but also sublime in the sense that it discloses the undisclosable concealment of the earth. Thus a work that exhibits such sublime beauty is able to disclose both itself and that which is undisclosable in it, the "secret" that gives rise to a reflective judging or "thinking."

Heidegger's conception of the relationship between the task of the poet and the task of the thinker is akin to that between genius and taste in Kant. Kant ranked poetry highest among the various forms of art because "it is really the art of poetry in which the faculty of aesthetic ideas can reveal itself in its full measure" (CPJ 193). In "What are Poets For?" (*Wozu Dichter?*, 1946), Heidegger implicitly responds to this Kantian provocation by taking up Hölderlin's question, "And what are poets for in a destitute time?" Our time is "absolutely" destitute because not only have the gods disappeared, but so have the traces of what could lead us to them (PLT 93). It is the task of poets to preserve the memory of their flight: "Poets are the mortals who, singing earnestly of the wine-god [Dionysus], sense the trace of the fugitive gods" (PLT 94). Thus the task of the poet is one of remembrance. If human time is defined by the flight of the gods – i.e., by the withdrawal of being – then the gods have never been present. In sensing the traces of the fugitive gods, poetry commemorates not the past but that which forever disappears in the arrival of time itself. That which disappears in giving time cannot be conceived as a first cause acting at the beginning of the world. On the contrary, the flight of the gods to which the poets bear witness is an "event" (*Ereignis*) whose traces come from the future as much as the past: "we experience what-has-been, returning in the *remembrance*, swinging out beyond our present, and coming to us as something futural" (EOHP 123). Hölderlin's poem, "*Andenken*," bears witness to the flight of the gods by recalling the "well-spring" from which being itself comes forth. Hölderlin's distinction between the "holy pathos" of the Greeks and their "Occidental *Junonian sobriety* of representational skill" not only anticipates Nietzsche's distinction between the Dionysian and the Apollonian, but it represents it "in an even more profound and lofty manner" (N I 103–4).

In "Who is Nietzsche's Zarathustra?," Heidegger says that Zarathustra is, above all, someone who experiences a certain kind of "terror" (*Schrecken*): "Whoever has failed and continues to fail to apprehend from the start the terror that haunts all of Zarathustra's speeches – which often sound presumptuous, often seem little more than frenzied extravaganzas – will never be able to discover who Zarathustra is" (N II 215, translation slightly modified). For Heidegger, Zarathustra is the teacher of the thought of the being of beings, that is, the thought of the eternal return. Contending that the angel whom the poet Rainer Maria Rilke (1875–1926) conjures in his *Duino Elegies* (*Duineser Elegien*, 1923) is "*metaphysically the same* as the figure of Nietzsche's Zarathustra," Heidegger implicitly identifies Nietzsche's experience of "holy dread" at the "raging discord" between truth and art with Rilke's characterization of the beautiful as "the beginning of the terrifying, a beginning we but barely endure" (PLT 134; N I 116). If truth represents the "unconcealment" of beings as they are entrapped within Enframing, art represents the poetic turning that calls us to recognize the unholiness of what is. Thus Rilke's angel would be located at the horizon of the world's "absolute" destitution, not on the side of the gods but on the side of the poets who witness their flight, preserving the condition for the possibility of their return: "Poets . . . are under way on the track of the holy because they experience the unholy as such" (PLT 141). To deliver the "balance" of the world's being from the hand of "the merchant" to the angel, from "the calculating will" to the poet's song, is the task of the thinker who takes seriously what Hölderlin and Rilke tell us poets are for in a destitute time.

3.5   Benjamin's angel of history

> Did heaven look on,
> And would not take their part?
> (*The Tragedy of Macbeth*,
>   IV, iii, 223–4)

The poetry of Hölderlin was also important to the philosophical reflections of Walter Benjamin (1892–1940), who as a German Jew had a different perspective than Heidegger on what it meant to live in a destitute time. Hannah Arendt, who knew them both, thought that Benjamin resembled Heidegger in that he "thought poetically, but he was neither a poet nor a philosopher" (I 4). Like Heidegger, Benjamin studied in Freiburg with the Neo-Kantian philosopher Heinrich Rickert (1863–1936). In an early essay, "On the Program of the Coming Philosophy" (*Über das Programm der kommenden Philosophie*, 1918), he suggests that the task of "the coming philosophy" is to transform "the Kantian system" to provide "religious experience" with the same sort of justification that Kant provided for "mechanical" experience (SW I 102, 105). As is, Kant's philosophy is "oriented so one-sidedly along mathematical–mechanical lines" that it fails to recognize a non-scientific conception of knowledge upon which the possibility of religious experience rests (SW I 108). Along with Johann Georg Hamann (1730–1788), who criticized Kant for underestimating the spiritual depth of words, Benjamin looks to language for a clue as to the nature of such knowledge. In "On Language as Such and on the Language of Man" (*Über Sprache überhaupt und über die Sprache des Menschen*, 1916), he argues that language is not merely an instrument to facilitate human communication; it is the "medium of creation" (SW I 68). To say that human beings have the capacity to use language is to say that we are endowed with the ability to respond to the hidden language of things. Thus to name something is to try to give voice to its own silent murmuring: "There is no event or thing in either animate or inanimate nature that does not in some way partake of language" (SW I 62).

The fact that human beings speak a multiplicity of languages is a consequence of the infinite distance separating the divine speech hidden in things from human discourse. Together, the diverse human languages aspire to the condition of a divine or "pure" language. In "The Task of the Translator" (*Die Aufgabe des Übersetzers*, 1923), Benjamin suggests that this is the ideal toward which every authentic translation strives: "It is the task of the translator to release in his own language that pure language which is exiled among alien tongues, to liberate the language imprisoned in a work in his re-creation of that work" (SW I 261). The dimension of human speech that refers to divine or pure language is occluded by a view of language as a mere tool used to convey information. Benjamin distinguishes the signified content of language from the manner in which it is signified. This contrast between "what is meant" and the "way of meaning" (SW I 257) resembles Frege's distinction between that which an expression refers to (its *Bedeutung*) and the way in which it refers (its *Sinn*). But whereas Frege dreamed of a purely formal language in which information would be conveyed without any logical or semantic ambiguity, and which could thereby serve as a medium for univocal translations from one language to another, Benjamin thinks of pure language as an unattainable ideal toward which all empirical languages collectively strive in vain.[10] Translation can only evoke this ideal by refusing to recognize univocity of content as the standard of faithfulness. Thus a good translation must aim not at repeating what is meant but at recreating how what is meant is said, thereby bringing about a resonance between different languages.

Benjamin agrees with Hamann that Kant did not appreciate the hermeneutical depths of language. While Kant acknowledged the capacity of genius to represent aesthetic ideas, he did not recognize that "there is a philosophical genius that is characterized by a yearning for that language which manifests itself in translations" (SW I 259). In "The Concept of Criticism in German Romanticism" (*Der Begriff der Kunstkritik in der deutschen Romantik*, 1920), Benjamin looks for such a conception in the works of Schlegel and Novalis, for whom the essence of the linguistic was to be found in works of literature. Schlegel and Novalis saw themselves as carrying out a new form of philosophical critique, one that had its point of departure in Hamann's insight into the divine nature of language. In contrast to Fichte, who invoked an intellectual intuition by which the subject would overcome its separation from the objects that it itself posits, the Romantics took as their point of departure a conception of the work of literature, one that presupposes a certain distance separating subject and object. In direct contrast to Kant, for whom aesthetic reflection was an activity performed by the judging subject, the Romantics ascribed the work of reflection to literary works themselves. On this view, the task of the (literary) critic is to respond to the work's own reflection, in effect serving as a kind of witness whose critical discretion or askesis allows the object to relate itself in reflection to the absolute. According to Benjamin the work of the critic is not incidental to the work's movement; on the contrary, the Romantics tended to exalt the role of the critic to such an extent that it eclipses that played by the work itself: "in the theory of Romantic art one cannot avoid the paradox that criticism is valued more highly than works of art" (SW I 185). By transforming the role of the philosophical critic into that of the literary critic, the Romantics conceived of aesthetics as first philosophy. Or rather, they thought that works of art and philosophical reflection call each other forth in such a way that a genuine critical theory must attend to both:

> What critique basically seeks to prove about a work of art is the virtual possibility of the formulation of its contents as a philosophical problem. . . . Critique makes the ideal of the philosophical problem manifest itself in a work of art . . . such a manifestation may be assigned to every philosophical problem as its aura [*Strahlenkreis*], so to speak.
>
> (SW I 218; cf. 333–4)

In the "Epistemo-Critical Prologue" to his book, *The Origin of German Tragic Drama* (*Ursprung des deutschen Trauerspiels*, 1928), Benjamin criticizes the Romantics for relying on the concept of "reflective consciousness" instead of on the "linguistic character" of works of art (OGTD 38). The task of the critic is not to lend wings to the work so that it can immediately ascend to heaven but to describe, in "sober prose," the constellation to which the work belongs (OGTD 29). By "constellation," Benjamin envisions an ideal relationship that is strictly intelligible in character. In order to be redeemed, phenomena must be described not as they manifest themselves empirically but as they appear in the intelligible constellation: "Phenomena do not, however, enter into the realm of ideas whole, in the crude empirical state, adulterated by appearances, but only in their basic elements, redeemed" (OGTD 33). "Ideas are to objects as constellations are to stars. . . . Ideas are timeless constellations, and by virtue of the elements' being seen as points in such constellations, phenomena are subdivided and at the same time redeemed" (OGTD 34).

This description hearkens back to Kant's distinction between empirical phenomena and intelligible noumena. Benjamin also invokes Kant's distinction between concepts of the understanding and ideas of reason, but instead of treating the ideas as products of reason, he treats them as if they were aesthetic ideas: "Whereas the concept is a spontaneous product of the intellect, ideas are simply given to be reflected upon" (OGTD 30). Such ideas are "given" not as objects of "intellectual intuition," but in the Kantian sense as problems (OGTD 35). Likewise, ideas are given only through those visible phenomena whose constellation they comprise. For this reason, "philosophy may not presume to speak in the tones of revelation" but must instead recall "the primordial form of perception" (OGTD 36). In seeking the idea within the work of art, the philosopher strives for something like beautiful sublimity, an effort that stands between that of the artist (who aims at mere beauty) and the scientist (who aims at mere truth): "If it is the task of the philosopher to practise the kind of description of the world of ideas which automatically includes and absorbs the empirical world, then he occupies an elevated position between that of the scientist and the artist" (OGTD 32).

Thus despite the fact that "On the Program of the Coming Philosophy" characterizes "the distinction between intuition and intellect" as "a metaphysical rudiment" that the Neo-Kantians were right to "eliminate" (SW I 105), Benjamin seeks not an intellectual intuition of the divine but a conception of redemption that remains within the bounds of "sober" experience. For Kant this possibility was preserved through teleological judgment, by which the temporality of mechanical causality was made compatible with a non-temporal form of teleological causality. But Benjamin resists any teleological conception of nature as intrinsically purposive. Redemption can take place only through an overturning of natural time. To hope for the messiah is not just to hope on behalf of a future that the preceding history of nature has prepared but to hope for a redemption that would be capable of acting on this very temporal order itself – and thus on the past as much as on the future. Newton – whose laws of nature presuppose the existence of an empty uniform time in which all events take place – thought that God could perform miracles by acting, so to speak, *in* time. By contrast, Benjamin envisions a messiah capable of acting *on* time: "No one says that the distortions which it will be the Messiah's mission to set right someday affect only our space; surely they are distortions of our time as well" (SW II 812). Thus the messianic promise of redemption is to be understood not in terms of a linear model of time according to which a future reconciliation of humanity would be the goal toward which history is progressing. Benjamin regards the linear march of time as an unremitting disaster from which a messiah alone could redeem us. To regard either the present or the past from the point of view of mere historiography would be to find only occasions for despair, so that it would be impossible to answer Kant's question, "Is the human race constantly progressing?," in the affirmative. But historical materialism offers another way of thinking about time, not as a linear sequence of nows but as a constellation of moments any one of which is capable of being "blasted" out of its historical context and charged with the task of redemption. So conceived, historical materialism is not only a way of thinking about the course of history; it is a way of salvaging the past so as to interrupt and overturn the linear progression of homogeneous time.

As early as 1916, Benjamin distinguished the "mechanical time" of nature from the "historical time" or "messianic time" of religious experience (SW I 55–6). In contrast to "mythical" experience, which seeks an empirical determination of the divine, religious experience respects the indeterminability of the ideal by protesting against "graven images" (SW II 808). Kant claimed that "there is no more sublime passage in the Jewish Book of the Law than the commandment: Thou shalt not make unto thyself any graven image" (CPJ 156). Benjamin's critique of myth can be likened to Kant's critique of theological fanaticism, just as his attempt to prevent the messianic from disappearing into the night of "homogeneous" or mechanical time is a way of keeping alive the flame of Kantian enthusiasm. In the third *Critique*, Kant claimed that the analogy with human creation entitles us to attribute intelligence to a divine author of the world, but only from the standpoint of reflective judgment; our analogical reasoning must, in effect, remain sober. Benjamin makes a similar point in a posthumously published 1919 fragment with the title "Analogy and Relationship" (*Analogie und Verwandtschaft*): "Analogy ... cannot be examined too soberly.... Feeling should not allow itself to be guided by analogy" (SW I 208).

In "Two Poems by Friedrich Hölderlin" (*Zwei Gedichte von Friedrich Hölderlin*, 1914–1915), Benjamin contrasts sobriety with sublimity: "Only now shall Hölderlin's phrase 'sacredly sober' be uttered ... sobriety now is allowed, is called for, because this life is in itself sacred, standing beyond all exaltation [*Erhebung*] in the sublime" (SW I 35). Analogously, in the essay on romanticism, he contrasts sobriety with ecstasy: "the core of the work remains indestructible, because this core consists not in ecstasy ... but in the unassailable, sober prosaic form" (SW I 176). However, in a 1919–1920 fragment, "On Semblance" (*Über «Schein»*) and in his essay "Goethe's Elective Affinities" (*Goethes Wahlverwandtschaften*, 1924–1925), Benjamin refers to "the sublime violence of the true" (SW I 224, 340) as a moral force which "shatters whatever still survives as the legacy of chaos in all beautiful semblance" (SW I 340). Insofar as it attests to "a being beyond all beauty," the sublime represents an inexpressible divine violence which interrupts the natural order of the world (SW I 351). In his "Critique of Violence" (*Zur Kritik der Gewalt*, 1921), Benjamin suggests that all human legal institutions are founded on a mythical "lawmaking" violence that is countered by "law-destroying" divine violence (SW I 249). Thus, whereas Kant adhered to the early modern conception of the divine rights of kings, Benjamin explicitly separates, and even opposes, the orders of human and divine law. Kant went so far as to argue that we must not try to fathom the human origins of a sovereign power – thereby recommending that we systematically ignore the dimension of lawmaking violence. By emphasizing precisely this dimension and opposing it to divine retribution, Benjamin undercuts Kant's distinction between obedience to the law and revolutionary fanaticism. The point is not that revolutionary violence can be justified as an expression of divine violence – on the contrary, divine violence remains inscrutable and inaccessible to human intervention – but rather that obedience to human law is itself always founded on another kind of violence (SW I 252). Against a state that serves the exclusive interest of the bourgeoisie, a revolutionary "general strike" represents not an act of violence but its very opposite: "Against this deep, moral, and genuinely revolutionary conception, no objection can stand that seeks, on grounds of its possibly catastrophic consequences, to brand such a general strike as violence" (SW I, 246). Thus, rather than sanctioning the use of violence, Benjamin's historical materialist takes on the role of a kind of biblical prophet, ascribing a divine mission to the revolutionary proletariat. By contrast, fascism represents not the overthrow of human law but its extreme manifestation in the form of a police state. Here mythical violence reaches an extreme, tending to collapse the distinction between the state's "lawmaking" and "law-preserving" functions (SW I 242–3).

In "The Work of Art in the Age of its Technological Reproducibility" (*Kunstwerk im Zeitalter seiner technischen Reproduzierbarkeit*) – the first version of which was published in a French translation in 1936 – Benjamin suggests that as art loses its religious "aura" it gains a potentially revolutionary significance. The aura of an object is a kind of halo or mystique by virtue of which it appears as unapproachable. In the case of natural objects, a thing's aura is "the unique apparition of a distance, however near it may be" (SW IV 255). Likewise, the aura of historical objects, particularly works of art, is a function of their unapproachability by "the masses." Here the quasi-magical effect of aura is seen to play a social role, lending itself to the "cult value" which works of art take on.

Benjamin claims that with the advent of modern techniques of reproduction, works of art tend to lose their aura. The invention of lithography and photography in the nineteenth century accelerated this process in two ways: first, by making relatively cheap reproductions of works of art available to the masses; second, by giving rise to new forms of art – such as film – whose products are essentially lacking in aura. Earlier techniques of reproduction (e.g. reproduction "by hand") could not duplicate "the here and now of the work of art," the spatio-temporal singularity that gave an original an "authenticity" that no copy could possess (SW IV 253). But modern techniques of reproduction have tended to undermine the primacy of the original in a number of ways, for example by making it possible to "place the copy of the original in situations which the original itself cannot attain" (SW IV 254). In losing their quality of authenticity or aura, works of art – especially those that depend upon new technological media such as the camera – become accessible to the masses. This in turn makes possible an important change in artistic production itself: "*as soon as the criterion of authenticity ceases to be applied to artistic production, the whole social function of art is revolutionized. Instead of being founded on ritual, it is based on a different practice: politics*" (SW IV 256–7). The decline of the aura of traditional forms of art, along with the ascendancy of photography and film, together mark the birth of a proletarian art, one that will herald the coming revolution by breaking down reified oppositions between artists and spectators. In his posthumously published "The Author as Producer" (*Der Autor als Produzent*, written in 1934), Benjamin singles out the "epic theater" of Bertolt Brecht (1898–1956) as an exemplary instance of such a political art: "Brecht . . . succeeded in changing the functional connection between stage and public, text and performance, director and actor" (SW II 778). In contrast to fascism, which seeks to appropriate the phenomenon of aura by aestheticizing politics, proletarian art aims at a politicization of art. This distinction recalls Benjamin's earlier distinction between mythical violence and revolutionary violence (SW IV 270). Both of these distinctions reflect the "sobriety" of Benjamin's messianism, and can be thought of as his analogue of Kant's distinction between political enthusiasm and political fanaticism.

Like Kant, Benjamin distinguishes between a properly religious sense of hope and "that heathen concern which, instead of keeping immortality as a hope, demands it as a pledge" (SW I 317). But he goes further than Kant in suggesting that hope "must never be kindled from one's own existence" (SW I 355). In its most authentic form, hope exists for the sake of others, specifically for those for whom hope itself is no longer possible. Thus at the end of his study of Goethe's *Elective Affinities*, he asks: "What does it matter if they never gathered strength for battle? Only for the sake of the hopeless ones have we been given hope" (SW I 356). The same idea is expressed even more forcefully in "On the Concept of History" (*Über den Begriff der Geschichte*, 1940), where the messianic promise of redemption is oriented not so much toward the future as toward a *past* future that has already been foreclosed. To say that hope is only given to us for the sake of "the oppressed past" – for those who have already experienced, without necessarily knowing it, their "last hope" – is to say that we ourselves are charged with "a *weak* messianic power, a power on which the past has a claim" (SW IV 396; SW I 355; SW IV 390). For Benjamin, historical materialism is nothing less than the consciousness of this weak messianic power, doing best when the theology that pulls its strings makes sure to "keep out of sight" (SW IV 389).

In order to fulfill its messianic mission, historical materialism opposes "homogeneous, empty time" (SW IV 395). Subjected to the rhythms of mechanized production, the lived duration of the proletariat is distorted and cannot be redeemed merely by appealing to a dialectical model of history according to which history is inevitably tending toward the resolution of the class struggle. Insofar as the concept of progress is an unending disaster essentially connected to the idea of linear time, the question, "Is the human race constantly progressing?," is the wrong one to ask. If hope nonetheless remains permissible – for the sake of others – it is because it is possible to give an affirmative answer to the question, "Is history redeemable?" Like Bergson and Heidegger, Benjamin rejects the linear conception of time as a spatial sequence of nows, but he ascribes to calendars a memorial function that clocks lack: "calendars do not measure time the way clocks do; they are monuments of a historical consciousness of which not the slightest trace has been apparent in Europe, it would seem, for the past hundred years" (SW IV 395).

Kant mentions the desire to alter the course of time as an example of a desire for the "absolutely impossible":

a person may desire something in the most lively and persistent way even though he is convinced that he cannot accomplish it or even that it is absolutely impossible: e.g., to wish that which has been done to be undone, to yearn for the more rapid passage of a burdensome time, etc.

(CPJ 32; cf. 65)

Benjamin's messianism involves precisely this kind of hope for the impossible. The fate to which the tragic hero is condemned – and against which he rebels in vain – differs in kind from the temporal condition of the moral agent who retains the capacity to hope for redemption, however impossible it may be (SW I 201–6). Benjamin finds such hope not in classical tragedy – in which fate precludes its very possibility – but in the German "mourning play" or *Trauerspiel*, which he describes as "mathematically comparable to one branch of a hyperbola whose other branch lies in infinity" (SW I 57).[11]

Kant suggests that the experience of the sublime does violence to the ordinary flow of linear time. The experience of the mathematical sublime is occasioned by a failure on the part of imagination to present a successively apprehended sequence as a simultaneously apprehended image. In straining to accomplish this unattainable task, the imagination "does violence to the inner sense," that is, to time as a form of inner intuition (CPJ 142). There is a regressive movement in this experience that can be likened to an attempt to halt the flow of time and recapture the past. Benjamin envisions precisely such a cessation of the flow of time, a freezing of the present, "a present . . . in which time takes a stand [*einsteht*] and has come to a standstill" (SW IV 396). For Kant, the attempt to freeze the present necessarily fails, giving rise to the pain of having to endure our subjection to linear time. But the enthusiastic feeling of pleasure that we subsequently take in our vocation as moral beings can be likened to a feeling for the messianic redemption of time.[12]

In an unpublished fragment on the poet Charles Baudelaire (1821–1867) written in 1921–1922, Benjamin follows Kant in suggesting that the significance of an historical event such as the French Revolution cannot be determined on the basis of mere events in time: "no one can deduce from the negative, on which time records the objects, the true essence of things as they really are" (SW I 361). Likewise in the very early essay, "The Life of Students" (*Das Leben der Studenten*, 1915) he writes, "This condition cannot be captured in terms of the pragmatic description of details (the history of institutions, customs, and so on); in fact, it eludes them. Rather, the task is to grasp its metaphysical structure, as with the messianic domain or the idea of the French Revolution" (SW I 37). Marx claimed that the philosophers had merely interpreted the world and not changed it. But in order to be redemptive, change cannot be oriented exclusively toward the future, as it appears to be in *The Eighteenth Brumaire*, where Marx writes: "The revolution of the nineteenth century must let the dead bury the dead" (LPW 34). Without giving up on the imperative to change the world, Benjamin charges the proletariat with nothing less than the responsibility *not* to let the dead bury the dead:[13]

> We know that the Jews were prohibited from inquiring into the future: the Torah and the prayers instructed them in remembrance. This disenchanted the future, which holds sway over all those who turn to soothsayers for enlightenment. This does not imply, however, that for the Jews the future became homogeneous, empty time. For every second was the small gateway in time through which the Messiah might enter.
>
> (SW IV 397)

In the ninth "thesis" of "On the Concept of History," Benjamin invokes an extraordinary image, from a drawing by Paul Klee (1879–1940), of an "angel of history" who, facing the past, "sees one single catastrophe, which keeps piling wreckage upon wreckage and hurls it at his feet." Driven "irresistibly into the future," the angel stares in horror at "what we call progress" (SW IV 392). It is tempting to say of this image what Benjamin says about the interpretation of Kafka's parables: "his parables are never exhausted by what is explainable; on the contrary, he took all conceivable precautions against the interpretation of his writings. One has to find one's way in them circumspectly, cautiously, and warily" (SW II 804). So intertwined is Benjamin's messianism with his conception of historical materialism that one could also say of his vision of historical redemption what he says of the work of the Russian writer Nikolai Leskov (1831–1895):

> Both the chronicler, with his orientation toward salvation, and the storyteller, with his profane outlook, are so represented in his works that . . . one can hardly determine whether the web in which they appear is the golden fabric of a religious view of the course of things, or the multicolored fabric of a worldly view.
>
> (SW III 153)

From 1927 until his death, Benjamin worked on a massive socio-cultural history of nineteenth-century Paris whose materials were eventually published in 1982 as *The Arcades Project* (*Passagenwerk*). Originally entitled "Paris Arcades: a Dialectical Fairyland" (*Pariser Passagen: Eine dialektische Feerie*), its name and scope changed as he worked sporadically on it throughout the 1930s. In a 1935 exposé, "Paris, the Capital of the Nineteenth Century" (*Paris, die Hauptstadt des XIX. Jahrhunderts*), the project is represented as a compendium of "dialectical images" that will illuminate "the collective unconscious" of the nineteenth century, a period of European history in which "the old and the new interpenetrate" (AP 4). At the center of the enterprise are the Parisian arcades. Long, corridor-like iron structures with glass ceilings that were built "in the decade and a half after 1822" (AP 3), the arcades were half-interior, half-exterior public spaces in which not-yet-fully-commodified objects stood on public display. Part dream-world and part marketplace, the arcades represent a kind of half-way point between the past and the present, the archaic and the modern, the pre-commodified thing and the fetishized commodity. They also stand half-way between two other inventions of the nineteenth century: world exhibitions – "places of pilgrimage to the commodity fetish" (AP 7; cf. 8) – and the private collection, a kind of anti-exhibition which seeks, in vain, to rescue the thing from its commodification: "The interior is the asylum of art. The collector is the true resident of the interior. He makes his concern the transfiguration of things . . . the Sisyphean task of divesting things of their commodity character by taking possession of them. But he bestows on them only connoisseur value" (AP 9). The space of the arcade was also to have been situated by Benjamin with respect to the on-going social struggle over public space that took place throughout Paris in the 1800s. Thus he sees the major renovations of Paris, carried out by Georges-Eugène Haussmann (1809–1891) during the reign of Napoleon III (1808–1873), as part of a counter-revolutionary effort against the barricades that French revolutionaries had periodically erected ever since 1789: "The true goal of Haussmann's projects was to secure the city against civil war" (AP 12). The disastrous Paris Commune of 1871 can be regarded as the last great effort on the part of the nineteenth-century proletariat to redeem a world that commodification had almost completely disenchanted. Benjamin's work would attest to the hopes of the past by bearing witness to their betrayal.

The images to be assembled around the arcades purport to exhibit a peculiar kind of "ambiguity" which Benjamin characterizes as that of "dialectics at a standstill": "This standstill is utopia and the dialectical image, therefore, dream image. Such an image is afforded by the commodity per se: as fetish. Such an image is presented by the arcades" (AP 10). In one of the many fragments for the project, he writes: "Dialectics at a standstill – this is the quintessence of the method" (AP 865). Here it is tempting to recall Kant's account of the impossible effort to stop the flow of time; the historical materialist has the task not of jump-starting a stalled dialectic but of rescuing the dialectical image from the dialectics of the commodity-form. Two figures of the nineteenth century anticipate the historical materialist in this respect: the collector and the Baudelairean *flâneur*. In "Eduard Fuchs, Collector and Historian" (*Eduard Fuchs, der Sammler und der Historiker*, 1937), Benjamin attributes to the historical materialist something which the passion of the collector does not quite manage to attain, namely, "a consciousness of the present which explodes the continuum of history": "The historical materialist blasts the epoch out of its reified 'historical continuity,' and thereby the life out of the epoch, and the work out of the lifework" (SW III 262). Likewise, in "The Paris of the Second Empire in Baudelaire" (written in 1938) he regards the *flâneur* as exhibiting a kind of "empathy" both for and with the commodity, which never entirely loses its own ability to redeem those who alone could redeem it:

> If there were such a thing as a commodity-soul (a notion that Marx occasionally mentions in jest), it would be the most empathetic ever encountered in the realm of souls, for it would be bound to see every individual as a buyer in whose hand and house it wants to nestle.
>
> (SW IV 31)

This suggests, as Benjamin puts it in a 1938 letter to Adorno, that "empathy with the commodity is probably empathy with exchange-value itself" (TCC 295). Besides the collector and the *flâneur*, Benjamin finds other expressions of this experience of empathy with exchange value in the nineteenth-century figures of the gambler, the stock market speculator, and the masses who attended world exhibitions (TCC 296).

The surviving *Arcades Project* is largely a pastiche of quotations whose juxtapositions Benjamin conceived as *correspondances*, Proustian evocations of a "lost time."[14] In "On the Image of Proust" (*Zum Bilde Prousts*, 1929, 1934), Benjamin expresses admiration for Marcel Proust's (1871–1922) "involuntary recollection" (*mémoire involontaire*), a literary technique that he regards as much as a work of forgetting as one of recollecting (SW II 238). Proust interweaves images which appear not "singly" but as a "net" that he "casts . . . into the sea of the *temps perdu*" (SW II 247). Benjamin suggests that "It took Proust to make the nineteenth century ripe for memoirs" (SW II 240). The *Arcades Project* is itself a vast Proustian memoir of the nineteenth century. After the Nazis invaded France in 1940, Benjamin left the manuscript with Bataille and fled Paris, hoping to join Adorno and other members of the exiled Institute for Social Research (*Institut für Sozialforschung*) in New York. Forbidden to cross into Spain, he decided to take his life.

At several places in his early writings, Benjamin invokes Hölderlin's poem "Timidity," in which the poet asks, "Does not your foot stride upon what is true, as upon carpets?" Benjamin suggests that this image became a figure of despair for Goethe: "In his old age, Goethe had penetrated profoundly enough into the essence of poetry to feel with horror the absence of every occasion for poetry in the world that surrounded him, yet want to stride solely and forever upon that carpet of truth" (SW I 329). This construal of what it means to be aware of poetry in a destitute time is echoed in a 1938 letter that Benjamin sent to his friend Gershom Scholem (1897–1982): "So, as Kafka says, there is an infinite amount of hope – only not for us." But then Benjamin immediately adds, "This statement truly contains Kafka's hope. It is the source of his radiant serenity" (SW III 327).

3.6   Adorno's ambivalence about the possibility of poetry after Auschwitz

More, I prithee more. I can suck melancholy out of a song,
  as a weasel sucks eggs.

(As You Like It, II, v, 12–13)

Beshrew thee, cousin, which didst lead me forth
Of that sweet way I was in to despair!

(The Tragedy of King Richard the Second,
III, ii, 204–5)[15]

The idea that redemption is promised only in works of art that mourn the unfulfillability of this very promise is central to the thought of Benjamin's friend, the critical theorist Theodor Wiesengrund Adorno (1903–1969). From 1928 until 1940, Adorno maintained an active correspondence with Benjamin, who refers to their "shared work" and "the mutual confirmation we found in one another's thoughts" (TCC 21, 155). Like Benjamin, Adorno seeks to unite a dialectical understanding of history with a clandestine messianism, referring in a 1934 letter to "the secret coded character of our theology" (TCC 67). But whereas Benjamin believed that the loss of the work of art's aura represented the possibility of a revolutionary mass art, Adorno considers this loss to be nothing more than the flip side of the hegemony of "the culture industry." He repeatedly urges Benjamin to complete the Arcades Project ("the Holy of Holies"), occasionally criticizing him – as a defender of "Arcades orthodoxy" – for sacrificing its theological dimension to a crassly conceived historical materialism (TCC 284–5). Unlike Benjamin, Adorno did not share Lukács's faith in the redemptive power of the proletariat, eventually claiming in his *Negative Dialectics* (*Negativ Dialektik*, 1966) that the moment when philosophy might have changed the world "was missed" (ND 3). Whereas Lukács never abandoned his view that the dialectical contradictions of the class struggle would eventually lead to the emancipation of humanity, Adorno – who in 1937 emigrated not to the Soviet Union but to the United States – characterizes the "dialectic of Enlightenment" as inexorable. In the preface to *Dialectic of Enlightenment: Philosophical Fragments* (*Dialektik der Aufklärung, Philosophische Fragmente*, 1944, 1947), Adorno and Max Horkheimer (1895–1973) – the director of the Institute for Social Research that had originally been based in Frankfurt – echo Benjamin in suggesting that the task of a critical theory of society "is not conservation of the past but the fulfillment of past hopes" (DOE xvii). But in the wake of fascism and the triumph of "instrumental reason" in both the capitalist and communist worlds, Horkheimer and Adorno suggest that the weak messianic power which Benjamin ascribed to the present has been all but extinguished.

For Horkheimer and Adorno, "enlightenment" is the process by which civilization becomes increasingly rational. Insofar as reason enables humanity to free itself from the dominion of blind nature, it is intrinsically emancipatory. But insofar as it subjugates both the nature outside it and the nature within it, the very reason that promises to liberate humanity ends up enslaving it to increasingly *irrational* instrumental ends. Marx saw – as did the sociologist Max Weber (1864–1920) – that capitalism represented a fundamentally ascetic world-view, with both proletarians (because of deprivation) and bourgeois subjects (because of the imperative to accumulate wealth) being unable to gratify their inclinations. But whereas Marx (unlike Weber) had enough confidence in the dialectic of enlightenment to expect that capitalism would be replaced by an economic system that would achieve the highest good for humanity – i.e., universal happiness no longer subordinated to virtue – Horkheimer and Adorno observe that all that has come out of the proletarian movement is fascism and the "total administration" of post-fascist societies. To explain this outcome, they seek to show that from its very inception the process of enlightenment has run counter to the goal of achieving the highest good.

According to Horkheimer and Adorno, the entire dialectic of Enlightenment is encapsulated in the *Odyssey*, "the basic text of European civilization" (DOE 37).[16] Homer's epic represents the process by which a proto-bourgeois rational subject establishes its dominion over nature. Throughout his adventures, Odysseus must constantly reassert the separability of humanity from animality – as when he rescues his men from Circe, who had turned them into pigs, and drags them away by force from the land of the Lotus-eaters. These episodes mark the transition from mythical thinking, which Freud associated with the reign of the pleasure principle, to scientific rationality, the cognitive correlate of the reality principle. Like Freud, Horkheimer and Adorno suggest that civilization's repression of instinctual urges is not merely temporary but perpetual, and perpetually increasing. Homer captures the sense of loss with which Odysseus must constantly reassert the egoic principle of self-preservation against the claims of the inclinations to gratification. As they leave the hedonistic land of the Lotus-eaters, Odysseus and his men are "sick at heart" (DOE 50). Especially significant is the moment when Odysseus has himself bound to the mast as they sail by the Sirens. Knowing in advance that the sensuous power of their song will cause him to rebel against his own reason, Odysseus "has taken the precaution not to succumb to them even while he succumbs" (DOE 46). When Odysseus calls to his men, they can hear neither him nor the song, for their ears are stopped with wax. As they keep the ship on its steady course away from danger, Odysseus is unable to free either himself or them from subjugation.

In the song of the Sirens, Horkheimer and Adorno detect the contradiction to which all subsequent works of art have been condemned, namely, to awaken in spectators a futile hope for redemption: "The fettered man listens to a concert, as immobilized as audiences later, and his enthusiastic call for liberation goes unheard as applause" (DOE 27). Art preserves the memory of the costs of enlightenment, but only insofar as aesthetic contemplation remains disinterested – just as, according to Freud, dreams require the motor paralysis of sleep to enable otherwise repressed desires to express themselves (IOD 607). Bourgeois works of art use the pretext of their uselessness to protest against domination. As such, they are both subversive and guilty of complicity at the same time. In the confines of the theater, the dream of utopia does not change the world. Outside, order reasserts itself.

The triumph of epic rationality over myth is dialectically complicated, in part because myth is already a kind of enlightenment. At a first, "preanimistic" stage of civilization, humanity adapts itself to nature through "mimesis." Later, as humanity begins to separate itself from nature, "mimetic behavior" is replaced by "the organized manipulation of mimesis" in the "magical phase" of civilization (DOE 148). At this level, mythical thinking represents the "enlightened" banishment of preanimistic ways of thinking. Finally, the transition from myth to rationality – exemplified in Homer's epic – represents the rise of scientific rationality, which has prevailed in Western civilization ever since. Or rather, ever since Homer, enlightenment has stood in a dialectical relationship to myth, continually unmasking its own accomplishments as insufficiently rational. This process culminates in the ruthlessly formal conception of instrumental rationality that prevails in modernity – i.e., in "the age of Enlightenment" and its aftermath.

Kant believed that the path of enlightenment led directly to the achievement of the highest good on earth – an optimistic faith still shared by Marx and Lukács. But Horkheimer and Adorno suggest that Kant's division between theoretical and practical reason was unable to forestall the totalitarian turn that instrumental reason was later to take (DOE 65). On their reading, pure speculative reason is already equivalent to formal instrumental reason, while pure practical reason represents an ineffectual bulwark against its hegemony. Fifteen years before Lacan, Horkheimer and Adorno suggest that Sade (as well as Nietzsche) carries out a more "intransigent critique of practical reason" by repudiating all traces of moral sentiment which surreptitiously motivate Kant's conception of respect for the moral law (DOE 74). Sade does not merely oppose Kant; rather, he transfers on to the plane of practical reason what Kant himself had already accomplished on the theoretical: "Sade demonstrated empirically what Kant grounded transcendentally: the affinity between knowledge and planning" (DOE 69). At the other end of the history of civilization, the works of Sade represent "the Homeric epic after it has discarded its last mythological veil: the story of thought as an instrument of power" (DOE 92).[17]

Although they regard Kant as unwittingly complicitous with the dialectic of enlightenment, Horkheimer and Adorno acknowledge that the Kantian conception of critique remains faithful to the true task of philosophy, namely, "to resist suggestion" (DOE 202). But like Marx and Lukács, they regard all of Kant's dualisms as symptoms of divisions that he is unable to resolve. Chief among these is the rift between sensuous nature and human rationality – i.e., between intuitions and concepts. Indeed, Horkheimer and Adorno go so far as to suggest that the fundamental task of philosophy is to "close" the "chasm" between the two. Unfortunately, philosophy has been unable to succeed in this regard, and in fact it has "usually . . . sided with the tendency to which it owes its name" (DOE 13). In other words, philosophers have typically "resolved" the opposition by subordinating sensibility to the hegemony of the concept. Because they regard rationality itself as equivalent to domination, Horkheimer and Adorno characterize the Kantian schematism (and presumably the typic of pure practical judgment as well) as a mechanism of control. As social control over individuals has increased, the function of schematization has been taken away from individuals and put in the hands of industry: "The active contribution which Kantian schematism still expected of subjects . . . is denied to the subject by industry" (DOE 98). "The true nature of the schematism which externally coordinates the universal and the particular, the concept and the individual case, finally turns out, in current science, to be the interest of industrial society" (DOE 65). By relieving individuals of the responsibility to make judgments, industry replaces the "act of synthesis" with "blind subsumption . . . blind intuition and empty concepts are brought together rigidly and without mediation" (DOE 166–7).

If determining judgments function as instruments of domination, reflective judgments sustain the possibility of critique. Just as aesthetic reflection *resists* schematization, so the culture industry *imposes* it by substituting mere commodities for genuine works of art (DOE 65). The subordination of sensuous intuitions to concepts is the flip side of the deferral of sensual pleasure for the sake of self-preservation. Through sublimation, works of art attest to the "mutilated" character of cultural pleasures by representing "fulfillment in its brokenness" (DOE 111). In other words, precisely by sustaining the gap between mere sensuous gratification and aesthetic satisfaction – i.e., the gap that Kant detects in the difference between the agreeable and the beautiful – works of art protest against reason's repression of the inclinations – i.e., against the gap that should *not* exist between the agreeable and the (instrumental) good.

The requirement that art be more than "culinary" or "pornographic" – i.e., more than merely agreeable – is at the heart of Adorno's essays on music, which he studied with the composer Alban Berg (1885–1935) in 1925. Adorno's need to distinguish genuine works of art from mere cultural commodities leads him, in "On Jazz" (*Über Jazz*, 1936), to insist that jazz is "beyond redemption" (EOM 492). But not even "autonomous" works of art are immune to the vicissitudes of the commodity form. In "On the Fetish-Character in Music and the Regression in Listening" (*Über den Fetishcharakter in der Musik und die Regression des Hörens*, 1938), Adorno argues that the performance of classical music on the radio has made it increasingly difficult for listeners to hear it as music: "Where they react at all, it no longer makes any difference whether it is to Beethoven's Seventh Symphony or to a bikini" (EOM 295). The "regression of listening" pervades all aspects of culture, leading to a general distraction whereby all music becomes mere "background music," a fitting testament to a culture in which it has become impossible to speak as well (EOM 289). To Benjamin's suggestion that the distraction of the viewer of silent films could serve a revolutionary purpose, Adorno responds that "However it may be with films, today's mass music shows little of such progress in disenchantment" (EOM 312).[18] In a letter from 1936, Adorno criticizes Benjamin for underestimating the subversive potential of "autonomous" works of art and for exaggerating that of the supposedly non-auratic new media (TCC 128).[19] Benjamin is right to emphasize the decline of aura, but he fails to recognize that this is brought about by the autonomous work itself: "I agree with you that the auratic element of the work of art is in decline, and that not merely on account of its technical reproducibility, incidentally, but also through the fulfillment of its own 'autonomous' formal laws" (TCC 129). Art responds to its degradation by resisting commodification, and it does this by refusing to be either agreeable or beautiful.

In his posthumously published *Aesthetic Theory* (*Ästhetische Theorie*, 1971), Adorno argues that art needs to preserve its aura precisely so as to avoid commodification: "Aura is not only – as Benjamin claimed – the here and now of the artwork, it is whatever goes beyond its factual givenness, its content; one cannot abolish it and still want art" (AT 45). Art can no more dispense with aura than aesthetics can the concept of beauty: "putting the concept of beauty on the Index . . . would amount to resignation on the part of aesthetics" (AT 50). This suggests that it is in some sense for the sake of beauty that modern art becomes willfully dissonant, even ugly. Dissonance occasions that feeling of pain which Kant associated with the judgment of the sublime. However, whereas Kant associated the feeling of the sublime with the subject's mastery over nature, Adorno suggests that the contrapurposiveness of dissonant art places the *work* above both the subject and subjugated nature in the name of de-subjugated nature. In the encounter with art's sublimity, the subject is reminded of its lost affinity with nature: Odysseus now strains at the terrible cries of Arnold Schoenberg's (1874–1951) *Erwartung*, which remembers on his behalf the forgotten song of the Sirens. In effect, art's sublimity serves as a memorial to beauty. What Kant characterized as beauty's "purposiveness without purpose" was co-opted by the culture industry as "purposelessness for purposes dictated by the market" (DOE 127–8). Hence modern art can no longer be beautiful. Despite Kant's intentions to the contrary, his aesthetic theory became complicitous with the bourgeois reduction of taste to culinary appetite. After Kant, art had to refuse to give pleasure to bourgeois subjects who would otherwise enjoy them without taking cognizance of their critique of existing social conditions. Though the third *Critique* seeks to articulate the conditions under which humanity can feel "at home" in nature, it is ultimately predicated on the very division between nature and reason that is the central teaching of Kant's moral philosophy. The feeling of the sublime goes hand-in-hand with the domination of both nature and humanity. Hegel tried to complete Kant's critique of pure reason by reducing nature to spirit. But in Adorno's view, this was just another expression of the will to domination. In place of Hegelian reconciliation, Adorno adheres to a dialectical construal of the dualism that sustains Kantian aesthetics. Not only do works of art bear witness to the true nature of social alienation; they alone hold out the promise of an authentic reconciliation of nature and reason.

Thus Kantian aesthetics remains a crucial point of departure for Adorno precisely because it takes seriously the division between nature and reason. As such, it not only remains faithful to the experience of alienation, but it simultaneously preserves the capacity for hope – a capacity evidenced negatively in the awareness of failure rather than positively in utopian representations. For Kant, the difference between the respective objects of sensibility and reason corresponded to the distinction between the actual and the possible: nature is the actual realm of human cruelty, while the kingdom of ends is the possible (though practically necessary) realm of human goodness. To heed the categorical imperative is to respond to the demand to make the possible actual ("ought" implies "can"). In contrast to Kant, Hegel identified the real with the rational and the rational with the real. Adorno is nowhere more faithful to Kant than when he insists that the real is the irrational, for he thereby remains true to the *demand* for a reconciliation that has not yet taken place. But Adorno relocates the origin of this demand. Instead of situating the categorical imperative on the side of a reason whose ultimate destiny is distinct from that of nature, he places it squarely within sensible experience itself – specifically, in the work of art. It is in the song of the Sirens – not in the bourgeois subject's guilty voice of reason – that something like the categorical imperative originates. Thus the work of art is that in sensible nature which, by conjuring the *semblance* of a reconciliation between nature and reason (whether positively or negatively), attests to the condition of their mutual alienation, thereby calling for their *actual* reconciliation. That call is a demand whose ultimate telos lies not in the repression of the inclinations but in their free, uncoerced sublimation. In a sense, the work of art always says one and the same thing: so act that you use the *nature in humanity* as an end in itself, not merely as a means. But works of art are not merely sensible representations of intelligible speech. If they were, they would remain objects to be subsumed under concepts rather than objects to be responded to mimetically. This is one reason why Adorno objects to didactic works of art whose protest against domination takes place exclusively at the level of content. The fact that intuitions without concepts are dumb – a point that underlies the critique of Husserl's conception of categorial intuition that Adorno presents in *Against Epistemology: a Metacritique: Studies in Husserl and the Phenomenological Antinomies (Zur Metacritik der Erken-*

ntnistheorie: Studien über Husserl und die phänomenologischen Antinomien, 1956) – poses a problem for art, whose task is to give expression to the inarticulable, to speak on behalf of that in sensible nature which is incapable of speech. Unlike Kant, Adorno does not claim that the beautiful is a "symbol" of the good, a solution that he considers to be too facile. If the split between sensibility and intelligibility is a consequence of social alienation, art cannot have recourse to a symbolism that would effectively smooth over social antagonisms. Instead of appealing to art's symbolism, Adorno invokes its "enigmaticalness." Every genuine work of art is an enigma in that it harbors a meaning which cannot be fully disclosed. It is precisely art's enigmaticalness that enables it to fulfill the task of expressing the inexpressible – but at the price of simultaneously failing to fulfill this task.

Adorno rejects Hegel's idea that the beautiful is the expression of a rational idea; the idea of art's enigmaticalness is intended to counter Hegelian rationalization with an account of art's properly sensible eloquence. Though Adorno does not make the connection explicit, his sense of art's enigmaticalness resembles Kant's conception of aesthetic ideas, for to say that a work is an enigma is to say that it prompts us to try to articulate what the work "says" without saying it. For Adorno, as for Kant, it is the work's form that carries the burden of art's eloquence. Adorno likens artworks to dreams. According to Freud, what is distinctive about a dream is neither its manifest content nor its latent meaning (what the dream "says") but the manner in which the dream-work expresses its meaning. What is unconscious is to be located not at the level of the latent content but at that of the dream's "form." The psychoanalyst might succeed in making a determining judgment about the latent thought, but the dream's enigma – its "kernel" – is like an aesthetic idea in that it bespeaks a truth that the dream precisely does not speak.

Because its expression is thoroughly enigmatical, the work of art cannot say what it wants to say; it cannot express its aesthetic categorical imperative in as bald a form as suggested above. Moreover, the aesthetic imperative requires ever-changing forms of expression. Kant himself gave several different versions of the categorical imperative, claiming that they were essentially equivalent. Works of art provide different versions as well, not only because their enigmaticalness prompts them to try out alternative forms of expression (a remnant of the Kantian doctrine of genius), but because changing historical circumstances require different ways of articulating art's demand. Art becomes sublime when it can no longer express the inexpressible as beautiful form. As the *form* of the formless – that is, as sublime form – modern art presents its unfitness for consumption, its contrapurposiveness for subjective consciousness. Were it possible to translate it into speech, sublime art's version of the categorical imperative would be something like, "Resist commodity fetishism." But works of art neither judge nor communicate. They themselves resist, and therein lies their autonomy (though this too must be compromised by art's heteronomous response to social conditions) (AT 226).

For Kant the beautiful was a symbol of morality. Likewise, for Adorno, sublime art represents an enigma of reconciliation. Like Marx and Lukács, Adorno regards the Kantian distinction between intuitions and concepts as a symptom of an historical condition that originated in antiquity, namely, the condition of unreconciled humanity. Ever since Plato, philosophy has taken cognizance of this condition, but it has done so by siding with the interests of domination (DOE 13). Every philosophy that engages in the task of covering up this social wound is ideological. Thus the intuition/concept dualism is a symptom of a profound social antagonism, one that cannot be eliminated through vague attempts at mediation. What remains false in Hegelian dialectics is its presumption to resolve antinomies which at present must be endured: "Ever since Plato, bourgeois consciousness has deceived itself that objective antinomies could be mastered by steering a middle course between them, whereas the sought-out mean always conceals the antinomy and is torn apart by it" (AT 298). Against the "negation of the negation" by which Hegelian dialectic purports to attain positive reconciliation of opposites, Adorno insists upon a purely "negative dialectics" that refuses all false appeasement.

The challenge of art is to do justice to the antinomical character of social antinomies without compromising its own integrity and autonomy. Only through mimesis, construed not as imitation at the level of content but as sympathetic response at the level of form, can art hope to carry out this double task. But the effort to do so is almost too much: for internal reasons, art carries within it the seeds of its own destruction. Art's sublimity is a last-ditch effort at self-preservation and, after Auschwitz, even sublime art may no longer be possible. Any art that fails to register its own impossibility today is a priori condemned to being a mere commodity, an obscene sacrifice to barbaric "taste," a term that acquires an exclusively pejorative connotation in Adorno's later work since he associates it with bourgeois aesthetics. To the extent that art can still exist, it is the site of the world's hope; but to the extent that it is no longer entitled to exist, it registers the world's despair. In his account of the sublime, Kant called attention to a certain kind of "double bind" affecting the imagination.[20] On the one hand, the imagination is obliged to provide a sensible image of an idea of reason; yet at the same time it must not provide such an image, thereby respecting the unpresentability of such ideas.[21] In effect, this is equivalent to the double requirement of providing an "incarnation" of the divine while respecting the prohibition against graven images, which Horkheimer and Adorno characterize as a way of bearing witness to despair: "The Jewish religion brooks no word which might bring solace to the despair of all mortality" (DOE 23). Thus, the work of art is summoned both to appear (as a sign of hope) and *not* to appear (as a sign of despair). Lukács anticipated this predicament in *The Theory of the Novel*, referring to works that "show polemically the impossibility of achieving their necessary object and the inner nullity of their own means" (TOTN 38–9; cf. 72).

This double bind finds expression in Adorno's assessment of the possibility of art "after Auschwitz." In *Prisms* (*Prismen*, 1955), he claims that "To write poetry after Auschwitz is barbaric" (Prisms 34). But in *Negative Dialectics* he modifies this view to account for both the obscenity and the necessity of seeking consolation: "it may have been wrong to say that after Auschwitz you could no longer write poems" since "perennial suffering has as much right to expression as a tortured man has to scream" (ND 362). These two statements can be thought of as two sides of an antinomy that cannot be resolved but only endured. Unlike Lukács, Adorno does not think that the proletariat can resolve such antinomies any more than the bourgeoisie could. In 1962, Lukács accused Adorno of having "taken up residence in the 'Grand Hotel Abyss,'" where "the daily contemplation of the abyss between excellent meals or artistic entertainments, can only heighten the enjoyment of the subtle comforts offered" (TOTN 22).[22] In response, Adorno criticized Lukács for sacrificing the critical rigor of his earlier works – in which he had correctly identified the problem of reconciliation – to the "lie" that the proletariat had succeeded in fulfilling its destiny as the subject–object of history in Eastern European countries (NTL I 240).

In "Parataxis: on Hölderlin's Late Poetry" (*Parataxis. Zur späten Lyrik Hölderlins*, 1964), Adorno criticizes Heidegger for distorting Hölderlin's poetry by highlighting its allusions to German mythology and ignoring or distorting its references to foreignness (NTL II 117). In contrast to Heidegger, who failed to recognize the dialectical relationship between the form and content of Hölderlin's late fragments, Benjamin reveals their "paratactic" character. Adorno defines parataxes as "artificial disturbances that evade the logical hierarchy of a subordinating syntax" (NTL II 131). Through the paratactic juxtaposition of dialectical images, Hölderlin brings about "aconceptual syntheses" that have "escaped from the spell of the domination of nature" (NTL II 130). This technique resembles the use of dissonance in "Beethoven's late style" (NTL II 133; cf. EOM 564–8). Like Beethoven, Hölderlin knew that all "great music is aconceptual synthesis," an insight that informs his conception of song (NTL II 130). Though the sublimity of parataxis and dissonance remains merely aesthetic – as Lukács implied in his critique of the Grand Hotel Abyss – the mixed feeling of pain and pleasure to which it gives rise attests both to suffering nature and to the hope, however fragile, for redemption.[23] The paradox of paratactic art is that it can only prevent its aestheticization or commodification by becoming ever more fractured, thereby undermining its status as art. It is possible that this dialectic will lead to the complete disappearance of art, thereby belatedly fulfilling Hegel's premature characterization of art as a thing of the past. In paratactic works, Adorno discerns a kind of apotropaic work of mourning by which art grieves over its own imminent disappearance.[24] Poetry written after Auschwitz bears witness not to the flight or promised return of the gods, but to that which has been reduced to silence. As such we could say that its vocation lies not in sublime beauty (i.e., the fractured symbolism that Heidegger detected in Hölderlin), but in beautiful sublimity (i.e., the hermeticism of ruins).

3.7   Marcuse's Great Refusal

> I' th' commonwealth I would, by contraries,
> Execute all things
> *(The Tempest*, II, i, 148–9)

After studying with Heidegger in Freiburg from 1928 until 1933, Herbert Marcuse (1898–1979) moved to Frankfurt, where he became a member of the Institute for Social Research. Having read *Being and Time* through the lens of Lukács's *History and Class Consciousness*, he was shocked when Heidegger joined the Nazi Party. In 1934, Marcuse emigrated to the United States, where he eventually became the most prominent representative of the Frankfurt School's ideal of the socially engaged critic.

Marcuse reflects on the complicity of German existentialism with National Socialist ideology in "The Struggle Against Liberalism in the Totalitarian View of the State" (*Der Kampf gegen den Liberalismus in der totalitären Staatsauffassung*, 1934). Despite his claim to be concerned in this essay "not with the philosophical form of existentialism but with its political form," Marcuse implicitly criticizes Heidegger's conception of historicity for being abstract, irrational, and uncritical (Negations 31, 34). The seeds of irrationalism had been sown by bourgeois liberalism, which Marcuse blames for the "functionalization of reason" (Negations 15). Reason becomes functional when it bows before "irrational pregivens," sacrificing its autonomy to heteronomous economic and administrative forces: "such functionalization of reason . . . leads to a reinterpretation of the irrational pregivens as *normative* ones, which place reason under the heteronomy of the irrational" (Negations 15). Instead of responding to the functionalization of reason by advocating a genuine critique of historically situated reason – such as Marx and Lukács had done – the existentialists accentuated the tendency toward irrationalism by replacing the liberal ideal of the self-determining rational subject with an ideological affirmation of the individual whose identity was supposedly rooted in "existential" conditions in an irremediable way. Such conditions, typically said to be biological and racial in character, could only be acknowledged and accepted, not subjected to critical appraisal. By thereby closing off the very possibility of critique, German existentialism – despite its professed opposition to bourgeois liberalism – represented a conservative reaction against the Marxist critique of capitalism. All of the appeals to the German *Volk*, to "blood and soil," and to Nietzsche's "blond beast" were so many ways of encouraging workers to forsake their critical rationality in favor of an ideological identification that ran contrary to their own interests (Negations 15).

Just as Heidegger accused Kant of "shrinking back" from his discovery of the imagination as the primordial temporality of Dasein, so Marcuse implicitly accuses the new rector of the University of Freiburg of shrinking back from the Marxist implications of his own account of historicity. In *Being and Time*, Heidegger characterized Dasein as a concretely existing historical subject engaged in praxis. By undermining the traditional philosophical distinction between human beings qua laboring animals and human beings qua thinking subjects – which ever since the Greeks had served as an ideological justification of the division of humanity into two separate classes – this analysis should have lent itself to a genuinely critical social theory. But instead of providing a concrete analysis of Dasein's historicity, Heidegger succumbed to the same irrationalist temptation as did the "political" existentialists, appealing not to the spontaneity of critical reason but to the "authentic" embracing of Dasein's "destiny." Though Heidegger denies that Dasein is defined by biological and racial pre-givens, the abstractness of his analysis of historicity makes it suitable to any and all political purposes: "the place of abstract reason was taken by an equally abstract 'historicity,' which amounted at best to a relativism addressed indifferently to all social groups and structures" (Negations 78).

Heidegger explicitly capitulated to the dominant Nazi ideology in his 1933 Rectoral Address, "The Self-Assertion of the German University" (*Die Selbstbehauptung der deutschen Universität*), in which he asserts that not the individual Dasein but the German nation has an historical destiny that needs to be authentically seized. Marcuse regards this claim as a betrayal of philosophy itself:

> At this point concretion stopped, and philosophy remained content to talk of the nation's "links with destiny," of the "heritage" that each individual has to adopt, and of the community of the "generation," while the other dimensions of facticity were treated under such categories as "they" (*das Man*), or "idle talk" (*das Gerede*), and relegated to "inauthentic" existence.
>
> (Negations 32)

In allowing for a racist construal of existential categories, "existentialism accompanies its debacle with a self-abasement unique in the history of ideas" (Negations 40).

Marcuse argues that even from the standpoint of *Being and Time*, there is no demonstrable criterion by which one could determine which aspects of human existence are genuinely "ontological" and which merely "ontic" (Negations 31). The same holds for the related distinctions that Heidegger draws between the "existential" and the "existentiell," and between authenticity and inauthenticity. The fact that Heidegger does not justify his analyses with arguments reflects the "irrationalist" credo of the existentialists according to which a demand for justification could arise only from the standpoint of those unwilling or unable to acknowledge the self-evidential force that existential conditions supposedly carry with them. But on what non-ideological basis could one determine that identification with the "destiny" of the *Volk* is one of Dasein's authentic possibilities, while calling attention to the exploitation of labor is only so much inauthentic "idle talk"?

Marcuse sees himself as defending the Kantian critical tradition against the "quietistic indifference" of a merely descriptive phenomenology (Negations 60). But he also suggests that Kant's critical project inherits ideological tendencies that have plagued philosophy from its inception. In particular, he follows his fellow critical theorists in characterizing all Kantian dualisms – notably that between theoretical and practical reason – as symptoms of alienation. Instead of characterizing "the spontaneity of the concept" as the possession of an autonomous subject standing over and against an object to be determined, Marcuse ascribes it to the dialectical interplay between subject and object, thought and being. On this dialectical view, reason is not a mere cognitive instrument that utilitarian subjects use in order to get a purchase on a "one-dimensional" world of facts; rather, it is the *logos* that manifests itself in human history (Negations 65; ODM 97). In *One-Dimensional Man* (1964), Marcuse characterizes this dialectical conception of reason as "two-dimensional" in that it sees humanity as charged with the task of *becoming* rational over time, that is, of attaining an "essential" rationality that remains merely "potential" within it. Traditional philosophical distinctions between essence and appearance, possibility and actuality, freedom and necessity, all carry with them a normative demand: humanity *ought* to attain its essence, its highest possibility, its capacity for freedom (ODM 133). Anything that stands in the way of these goals ought to be subjected to critique.

In order for humanity to achieve its essence, it is necessary to transform the social conditions that currently prevent it from being actualized. Marcuse concludes that a genuinely dialectical philosophy must be confrontational, challenging the existing social order for its shortcomings. Thus philosophy capitulates whenever it abandons its political orientation, preferring to valorize itself at the expense of those it leaves behind. Aristotle, who abandoned the political realm "lest Athens sin against philosophy twice,"[25] took this fateful step when he rejected Plato's dialectical construal of the rules governing philosophical reflection in favor of a conception of abstract "laws of thought." So long as philosophy remained dialectical, not only did statements of fact carry with them a normative force, but "logic" itself was conceived in terms of the world's inherent, if unfulfilled, rationality. With Aristotle, a sharp division is introduced between the formal laws of logic and the concrete content on which these laws are brought to bear. As a result, logical thought acquires a highly abstract character; the forms of syllogistic reasoning strip dialectical logic of its politically subversive potential. Distinctions such as that between essence and appearance lose their normative force and are reduced to mere contrasts between a term and its contrary.

This "flattening out" of dialectic's two-dimensional universe has contributed to the reification of dialectical distinctions, their hypostatization as dualisms. Chief among these are Kant's distinctions between theoretical and practical reason, categorial judgments and categorical imperatives (ODM 133). In accepting these dichotomies, the Kantian project itself remains grounded in "irrational pre-givens" (ODM 15). As Lukács had already pointed out, the most that Kant can accomplish in his practical philosophy is a merely abstract comparison of an actual state of affairs with an abstract or formal possibility. For Marcuse, this is the epitome of one-dimensional thought. In order for philosophy to become truly critical it must transcend itself, reclaiming its status as a two-dimensional critical theory of society. Instead of positing abstract utopian possibilities, such a theory must seek *real* – not merely abstract – possibilities for social transformation. In some sense the distinction between abstract and real possibilities is still present in Aristotle, for whom an acorn contains within it the real potentiality of becoming an oak (as opposed to the merely "utopian" possibility of becoming, say, an elm). In a similar vein, Marcuse suggests that the conflict between existing forces and relations of production contains the seeds of real tendencies and not merely abstract possibilities. The liberation of humanity from its subservience to economic needs stands in relation to actuality as humanity's essence does to its mere appearance. To identify this inherent possibility is equivalent to making a normative demand for its realization. The fact that there are countervailing forces working against this tendency attests both to the antagonistic character of society and to the need for critical theorists to side with the liberating tendency.

Marcuse suggests that in advanced industrial societies the distinctions between classes have become blurred as the benefits of industrial production have come to be enjoyed by workers as well as those who own and control the means of production. This is a consequence not of an inherent tendency within capitalism to heal social antagonisms but, rather, of its need to accelerate the rate of consumption of the goods it produces. Thus the "need" for workers to enjoy commodities is of a piece with planned obsolescence in that both enable the capitalist mode of production to perpetuate itself. But, although the lives of workers have thereby improved since the time of Marx, such improvement is merely "quantitative" rather than "qualitative." Exploitation still exists; the transformation of workers into consumers does not alleviate the social contradictions that Marx originally discerned. Marcuse concludes that both in capitalist societies and in the Soviet Union traditional class antagonisms have largely given way to universal subservience to a system of "total administration." In some sense no one controls the reified means of production; the economic system exists as an objective set of relations governed by fixed economic "laws." This is not to say that class divisions have disappeared, for both Western and Soviet economic systems serve the interests of only a portion of humanity. By masking class antagonisms, they are able to represent themselves as completely rational. In Marcuse's view, modern industrial society has become completely one-dimensional because no one – not even those exploited – any longer recognizes the gap separating the existing society from its proper, "real" possibility. Thus it is necessary to distinguish between "true" and "false" consciousness, "true" and "false" needs, etc. Those who believe that they can find contentment from the consumption of commodities are deceived. Their "happy consciousness" is even more miserable than the alienated "unhappy consciousness" that Hegel and Marx identified because it fails to recognize the poverty of the administered diversions it settles for.

Like Horkheimer and Adorno, Marcuse distinguishes between art, whose images "recall and preserve in memory [what] pertains to the future," and cultural commodities whose essence is to neutralize the two-dimensional promise of art: "The absorbent power of society depletes the artistic dimension by assimilating its antagonistic contents" (ODM 60–1). Aesthetic experience is a sublimated awareness of that which has been lost through repression; as such it is simultaneously an experience of alienation, unhappy consciousness, and potential revolutionary fervor. Society neutralizes art by *desublimating* aesthetic experience, transforming it into an *apparently* non-alienated contentment with innocuous forms of libidinal satisfaction: "What happens is surely wild and obscene, virile and tasty, quite immoral – and, precisely because of that, perfectly harmless" (ODM 77). The culture industry is thus construed as simultaneously "diminishing erotic and intensifying sexual energy," its products exhibiting a paradoxically repressive liberation of desublimated desire (ODM 73).

Marcuse's account of repressive desublimation complicates the opposition between sublimation and subversion. Like Adorno, he believes that the subversion of one-dimensional society depends not upon refusing sublimation on the grounds that it is repressive but on refusing repression by *completing* the interrupted process of aesthetic sublimation. The legitimate claims of the pleasure principle can be honored only by accepting the reality principle – without, however, having to accept social domination. Marcuse criticizes the sociologist Norman O. Brown (1913–2002) for calling for the abolition of the reality principle, a position he regards as no less fanatical than the irrationalism of German existentialism: "What is to be abolished is not the reality principle; not everything, but such particular things as business, politics, exploitation, poverty" (Negations 235–6). Marcuse's reference to the political "harmlessness" of cultural products that are "wild and obscene" attests to his view that desublimation is merely reactionary.

In *Eros and Civilization* (1955), Marcuse had already distinguished between the minimal instinctual repression necessary for society to exist at all and the "surplus-repression" characteristic of social domination. Freud drew the pessimistic conclusion that civilization requires an ever-increasing level of instinctual renunciation, thereby making happiness incompatible with social morality. But if Freud's analysis is situated within a Marxist framework, a different picture emerges. The modern tendency toward increased repression – an expression of what Marcuse calls the "performance principle" – is a consequence of the structure of industrial society (EC 44). In effect, surplus repression is the psychic correlate of the extraction of surplus value. At the same time that modern industrial society has increased repression, it has simultaneously obviated the need for it. Thus surplus repression reflects the contradiction between relations of production (which depend upon excess repression) and mode of production (which contains the real possibility of an end of social domination).

In *Civilization and its Discontents*, Freud claimed that only aesthetic sublimation could enable individuals to find happiness within civilization. But sublimation as he conceived it had nothing revolutionary about it; on the contrary, it was a way of conforming to existing social demands. In order to revolutionize Freud's conception of sublimation, Marcuse goes back to Schiller's *On the Aesthetic Education of Man*. Just as Kant discerned a free play between imagination and understanding in the judgment of taste, so Schiller claims that in aesthetic play our "sensuous" and "form" drives are harmonized. But Schiller goes further than Kant in characterizing the division between the sensuous and intellectual dimensions of human existence as something to be overcome through the cultivation of a "play" drive. For Kant, aesthetic play was merely a diversion from, or an incitement to, the serious business of understanding and reason. But for Schiller, the ability to play is itself the true telos of human education.

Marcuse suggests that what Schiller identifies as the "tyranny of reason" corresponds to the domination of the reality principle over the pleasure principle (EC 187). To cultivate the play drive is to liberate the repressed demands of the pleasure principle. Once freed from the fetters of the form-giving understanding, the sensuous drive would be able to sublimate itself, thereby bringing the pleasure principle into harmonious accord with the reality principle. This harmony, made possible through aesthetic sublimation, is different from the pseudo-harmony – "the obscene merger of aesthetics and reality" – that Marcuse associates with repressive desublimation (ODM 248). So long as we fail to distinguish between play as the expression of aesthetic sublimation and play as the expression of repressive desublimation, the concept of play remains ambiguous. Adorno criticized Schiller's conception of play as "the opposite of freedom" on the grounds that it supposedly represented a proto-fascist sacrifice of the autonomous subject's ability to engage in serious critical reflection (AT 317). Perhaps with Marcuse in mind, Adorno claims that, in an alienated world, seriousness in art is more important than aesthetic play. But Marcuse's distinction between sublimated play and desublimated play seems to speak to this concern, and could be said to correspond to Benjamin's distinction between the politicization of aesthetics and the aestheticization of politics.

Insofar as art represents "the Great Refusal," it does not merely offer an escapist fantasy (desublimated play); it shows that it is possible to *realize* what we can imagine (sublimated play) (ODM 63). According to Marcuse, imagination remains "merely" utopian in the former case, but it becomes a genuine power in the latter:

> If phantasy were set free to answer . . . the fundamental philosophical questions asked by Kant, all of sociology would be terrified at the utopian character of its answers. . . . In replying to the question 'What may I hope?,' it would point less to eternal bliss and inner freedom than to the already possible unfolding and fulfillment of needs and wants.
>
> (Negations 155)

Art's refusal of one-dimensional society manifests itself as a force of negativity, a rejection of what is in the name of what might be. As such it reminds conceptual thinking – that is, philosophy – of its own critical responsibility, a vocation it has largely forsaken. Just as Marcuse criticized German existentialism for its irrationalist tendencies, so he criticizes the dominant schools of analytic philosophy for leveling down the critical potential of two-dimensional thinking. Marcuse concedes that, compared with German existentialism, logical positivism "retains a certain critical tendency." Both Carnap and Otto Neurath (1882–1945) were both avowed Marxists who saw their "debunking" of metaphysics as socially progressive. But Marcuse argues that by insisting on the absolute character of positive "facts," logical positivism remains no less beholden than German idealism to irrational pre-givens (Negations 66). This reactionary tendency was exacerbated in the ordinary language philosophy of J.L. Austin (1911–1960) and the philosophical behaviorism of Gilbert Ryle (1900–1976), both of which Marcuse regards as attempts to dissolve all two-dimensional problems by adhering to the status quo.[26] Such a program amounts to the self-abasement of philosophy, an "almost masochistic" submission to "the established reality" (ODM 177, 173). By indiscriminately attacking all metaphysical concepts, analytic philosophy has had the effect of purging everyday reality of its inherent capacity for critical transformation. Though it prides itself on exorcizing metaphysical "ghosts," it gives rise to a false picture of the world, "a ghost much more ghostly than those which the analysis combats" (ODM 194).[27]

In contrast to the complacency of analytic philosophy, critical theory promotes the virtue of obstinacy: "Critical theory preserves obstinacy as a genuine quality of philosophical thought" (Negations 143). Just as Socrates claimed that his obstinacy benefited the Athenians, so Marcuse suggests that the obstinacy of the critical theorist benefits those who – knowingly or unknowingly – suffer from the oppression of total administration. Invoking Benjamin's claim that hope is only given to us for the sake of those without hope, he characterizes the critical theorist as someone who "wants to remain loyal to those who, without hope, have given and give their life to the Great Refusal" (ODM 257).

3.8 Arendt's articulation of the democratic principles of the American revolution

What need we any spur but our own cause
To prick us to redress?
(*The Tragedy of Julius Caesar*, II, i, 123–4)

Hannah Arendt (1906–1975), who also studied with Heidegger in Freiburg, left her native Germany when the Nazis came to power in 1933, going first to Prague and then to Paris, where she met Benjamin and helped fellow Jewish refugees emigrate to Palestine. In 1941 she settled in the United States, eventually becoming an American citizen in 1951. In contrast to the members of the Frankfurt School, who saw little difference between the fascist state which they had fled and the rest of the "administered" West, Arendt sought to emphasize the differences. In her view, the "totalitarian" regimes that came to power in both Nazi Germany and the Soviet Union under Stalin represented an entirely new form of government whose genealogy had to be understood in order to preserve, and nurture, the democratic principles that the ancient Greeks and Romans had recognized as the hallmarks of a true republic. These principles were invoked by all of the great modern revolutions – especially the American – but they were quickly forgotten, due to a failure of self-understanding for which Arendt seeks to provide both an explanation and a new political vocabulary.

In *The Origins of Totalitarianism* (1951), Arendt suggests that, unlike mere tyranny or authoritarianism – two oppressive types of government that go back to antiquity – totalitarianism is unique in that it seeks to control not only the public realm where political action takes place but the private lives of individuals (OOT 475). She traces the roots of totalitarianism to nineteenth-century antisemitism – from which the Nazis derived an ideology – and to the period of imperialist expansionism that stretched from the mid-1880s until the outbreak of the First World War – from which all totalitarian movements derived their quest for global domination. But she also suggests that, in some sense, both antisemitism and the quest for expansion were mere pretexts used by totalitarian movements to establish "total domination," that is, "to organize the infinite plurality and differentiation of human beings as if all of humanity were just one individual" (OOT 438). The project of total domination could only arise after modern social movements had produced significant numbers of "stateless people" without public places of their own (OOT 292). Such was the condition of the Jews in Nazi Germany. After being deprived of their public rights as citizens, they were reduced to the merely animal condition of living human beings without any rights whatsoever. In the Declaration of the Rights of Man, the French Revolutionaries had affirmed the inalienability and universality of rights that human beings possess not by virtue of being members of a state, but simply by virtue of being human. But no sooner had these "rights of man" been recognized than they were quickly equated throughout Europe with the eminently "unenforceable" "rights of peoples" (OOT 293, 291). The lesson to be learned from the subsequent fate of stateless peoples under totalitarian rule is that, far from possessing inalienable rights simply by virtue of being born, we *acquire* rights when, as members of a group, we collectively attribute them to one another: "We are not born equal; we become equal as members of a group on the strength of our decision to guarantee ourselves mutually equal rights" (OOT 301). Thus instead of reaffirming the universality of innate human rights, Arendt emphasizes the universal capacity of human beings to give ourselves rights by founding democratic republics. This capacity, first discovered by the ancient Greeks and Romans, was rediscovered by the French and American Revolutionaries. But instead of building on their new-found political experience, the eighteenth-century revolutionaries blurred the distinction, crucial in antiquity, between two aspects of human existence. One is our need to labor, something that we share with all animals. The other is our capacity to constitute a polis by mutually recognizing one another. The former corresponds to the rights of man; the latter to the rights of citizens.

In *The Human Condition* (1958), Arendt credits the ancient Greeks with being the first people to demarcate a sharp boundary separating the "public realm" of the polis from the "private realm" of the home (HC 22). In the polis, Greek citizens – i.e., adult, male heads of households – freely conducted the properly "political" affairs of state, while in the private realm of the household, or *oikos*, they separately ruled over the women, children, and slaves who tended to their "economic" necessities (HC 28). Though based upon a system of oppression that consigned women and slaves to the less than fully human condition of *animal laborans*, this separation of realms enabled the Greeks to protect the polis, in which they created a common world, from the incursion of private interests. By consigning the ruler/ruled relation to the household, they were able to preserve the democratic polis as a space of freedom. In antiquity, to be free meant not to be *from* politics but to be free *for* it. Only in late antiquity, when the economic relation between ruler and ruled came to dominate the public realm as the art of "government," did freedom come to be construed in the negative sense as mere "liberty" (i.e., as freedom from political oppression). At first, the decline of democracy reflected not a sudden preference for economic matters over political affairs but the Christian emphasis on the contemplative life over the practical life in general. This preference is already found in Plato, for whom the life of the philosopher is superior to that of the statesman. Lumping together both labor and action under the heading of the *vita activa*, or life of worldly activity, early Christian thinkers treated all practical matters as mere necessities for the sake of the *vita contemplativa*, or a life spent in contemplation of the divine. Arendt suggests that it was this denigration of politics that eventually allowed the economic model of government to overrun the polis. From the Holy Roman Empire to the rise of the modern nation-state, the properly political dimension of human experience was eclipsed. In the modern nation-state, politicians are more economic "administrators" than true political statesmen. This is a consequence not only of the Christian denigration of the *vita activa* but of the increased importance that "social" – i.e., economic – concerns have come to play in modernity. To explain how this came about, Arendt finds it necessary to accentuate a distinction that the Greeks never made fully explicit, namely, the distinction between labor and work.

All animals, including humans, must labor in order to survive. To labor is to produce for the sake of consumption, but since consumption itself takes place for the sake of future production, a life condemned to mere laboring is caught in a monotonous natural cycle interrupted only by an equally meaningless death. Though laboring is a purposive activity, it has no purpose outside itself. By contrast, to work is to make something in accordance with a plan, something that is intended to be used repeatedly rather than consumed. Work is teleologically oriented toward a preconceived goal at which we aim; its linear means–end structure interrupts the natural cycle of production and consumption, literally giving direction to our lives. Unlike the products of labor, which are intended to be consumed and thus destroyed, the products of work are intended to endure. Mere animal labor takes place within nature, but human work transforms nature into a "world."

Whereas the Greek slave was condemned to remain merely an *animal laborans*, work elevated the economically autonomous craftsman to the properly human status of *homo faber*. If the ancient Greek philosophers nonetheless failed to clarify the distinction between labor and work, it was because they viewed both as subordinate to the higher vocation of human action. For Arendt, this failure to distinguish carefully between labor and work, coupled with the later Christian subordination of the entirety of the *vita activa* to the *vita contemplativa*, is reflected in the modern subordination of political action proper to social movements. Whereas the great revolutions of the eighteenth century were directed against existing forms of government, the revolutions of the nineteenth and twentieth – notably those carried out in the name of Marx – were primarily "directed against society" (BPAF 200). Arendt agrees with Marx that the modern state is controlled by economic interests, but rather than seeking to liberate human beings from economic necessities – an impossibility in any event – she seeks to liberate the political domain of action from its colonization by society. What misled Marx to view politics as an extension of economics was his correct assessment of the French Revolution as having culminated in the political hegemony of *homo faber* – i.e., the modern bourgeoisie – which had been vying with the nobility for control of the government since the beginning of modernity. What makes the reign of *homo faber* morally as well as politically objectionable is its tendency to reduce everything in nature, including human beings, to "mere means" (HC 155–6). A spiritual child of the French revolutionary, Maximilien Robespierre (1758–1794), Marx saw the triumph of *homo faber* as a defeat of *animal laborans*, for whose sake the proletarian revolution would eventually have to take place. The fact that Kant granted citizenship to wig-makers but not to barbers – i.e., to those who work but not to those who labor – confirms the degree to which he remained a philosopher of the bour-geoisie. But, from Arendt's perspective, Kant's distinction – though no less problematic than the ancient Greek distinction between citizens and slaves – was an attempt to prevent economic inequalities from undermining the political equality needed in the public realm. In that sense, Kant remained truer to the "revolutionary élan" (BPAF 200).

In *On Revolution* (1963), Arendt distinguishes the properly political con-cerns of those who took part in the American Revolution from the social agenda that became the principal catalyst and legacy of the French Revolu-tion. Though the American intention to found a republican form of govern-ment ultimately failed to provide an adequate mechanism by which all citizens could play an active part in political decision-making, the ideal of such a republic remains the proper model to which true revolutionaries ought to look. What kept the American Revolution from achieving its full potential was the inability of the framers of the Constitution to explain to themselves what they had discovered during the course of the Revolution, namely, that the preservation of political freedom – not mere freedom from tyranny – is essential for human flourishing. Only when they rebelled – ini-tially with the sole intention of reclaiming private freedoms that had been curtailed – did the eighteenth-century revolutionaries stumble upon an awareness of the centrality of public freedom to human dignity (OR 34). Although the revolutionaries themselves failed to articulate this insight, Arendt claims that "the central idea of revolution . . . is the foundation of freedom, that is, the foundation of a body politic which guarantees the space where freedom can appear" (OR 125; cf. 35). Thus genuine revolutions are nothing but attempts to reclaim the Greek experience of political life.

In *Between Past and Future: Eight Exercises in Political Thought* (1968), Arendt argues that the modern conception of freedom as the capacity of an isolated individual to act on his or her "will" could only arise once govern-ments had divested citizens of their "worldly" capacity to act together as equals in the public realm (BPAF 147). True freedom lies not in the sover-eignty of the individual but in the manifest political actions that mutually recognizing citizens perform in concert with one another. Arendt finds this conception of freedom exemplified in the words and deeds of Brutus in Shakespeare's *The Tragedy of Julius Caesar* (BPAF 151). What Brutus keenly recognizes is that, if Caesar becomes emperor, the Romans will be deprived of their dignity *as Romans* – i.e., as citizens. When Cassius suggests that the conspirators swear to their resolution to kill Caesar, Brutus vehemently protests, noting – as does Arendt – that there can be no transcendent ground for the actions that human beings initiate with one another. Arendt suggests that whereas in ancient Greece "the foundation of a new body politic" was a "commonplace" occurrence, the Romans regarded themselves as bound to the originary act by which Rome had been founded by their ancestors (BPAF 121). Thus, whereas the Greeks lacked a conception of political authority, the Romans invested the authority of their "founding fathers" in the Senate, while granting to the people as a whole the power to act. Brutus recognizes that by usurping both the authority of the Senate and the power of the people, Caesar will become a tyrant – whether he acts benevolently toward the Roman citizens or not (for example, by bequeathing his fortune to them in his will). Valuing his citizenship more than his life, Brutus assumes that the only "spur" that he and the others need "to prick us to redress" is the fact that they are Romans. Arendt notes that the signal feature of political action is that it depends upon a willingness to continue deeds that have already been begun by others, knowing that what one begins anew is likely to be undone or redone by others. Significantly, when his fellow conspirators ask if Cicero should be included in the plot, Brutus says no, "For he will never follow any thing/That other men begin" – in other words, he is not a true Roman (II, i, 151–2). At the end of the play, Antony memorializes Brutus as "the noblest Roman of them all" because of all the conspirators, only he killed Caesar for the "common good" (V, v, 68, 72). In the *Eighteenth Brumaire*, Marx noted that the French Revolutionaries decked themselves out in Roman dress. Arendt suggests that this was true of all modern revolutionaries, who like Brutus understood that it was better to prefer liberty to death (BPAF 139).

In Arendt's view, the crucial mistake made by the French Revolutionaries was to substitute for the American concern with forms of government the doctrine of the rights of man (OOT 290–302; OR 56). Instead of founding a political space in which citizens could freely debate their different points of view, the revolutionaries appealed to the Rousseauian fiction of a monolithic general will embodied in those who represented the French nation as a whole. The "Reign of Terror" was but a forerunner of the totalitarian regimes in which Rousseau's general will was equated with the will of the Leader, with which the regime's right-less "citizens" were obliged to identify. Unfortunately, it was not the American Revolution but the French which captivated the imagination of Hegel and Marx, and of all those "professional revolutionists" inspired by their ideas. Arendt suggests that Hegel and Marx were wrong not only to emphasize the social dimension of the French Revolution at the expense of the political character of the American Revolution but to view the French Revolution itself through the eyes of the historian, the spectator, rather than those of the agents who took part in it. By construing the course of the French Revolution as if it were governed by inexorable historical laws, Hegel and Marx encouraged their revolutionary successors to think of themselves and those whom they would liberate from poverty as instruments of history rather than as autonomous agents (OR 52–3). It is because they followed Hegel and Marx that those who took part in the Russian Revolution – at its inception, the most hopeful political event of its day, as the French Revolution had been for Kant – were eventually willing to sacrifice the political freedom of Soviet subjects to the historical mission of the Bolshevik Party. Had Lenin and his fellow revolutionaries been schooled in the writings of Jefferson rather than Marx – and been aware of Jefferson's belated realization that the American Constitution had failed to subdivide the government into local wards, "elementary republics" that would collectively comprise the American republic as a whole – they would have given genuine political power to the "soviets" rather than impose a dictatorial form of government from above (OR 255). Lenin's failure in this regard led directly to the rise of Stalinism. What had started out, like the French Revolution, "crystallizing the best of men's hopes," ended up, like the Terror, "realizing the full measure of their despair" (OR 57).

Marx accepted Hegel's belief that individual human agents are inexorably swept up by forces of "historical necessity" because he was impressed with the way in which "biological necessity" – manifest in the "misery" and "abject poverty" of the Sans-Culottes – "burst on to the scene of the French Revolution" (OR 59–60). It was this sudden eruption of the "social question" that led the revolutionaries to appeal to the rights of man, that is, to the rights of *animal laborans* (OR 61). The abolition of poverty and the alleviation of suffering were noble causes inspired by genuine compassion, but compassion, for Arendt, is not a political virtue (OR 86). Though she shares Marx's concern with the liberation of the masses from poverty, she rejects his belief that such liberation can be accomplished through the establishment of a "dictatorship of the proletariat" to be followed by a "withering away of the state." Wresting political control from the administrative elite who rule the modern nation-state is desirable, but its goal should be to liberate politics from economics, that is, to abolish government for the sake of a genuine social compact, rather than to complete the reduction of politics to economics.

By defining the goal of revolution as the elimination of the need to labor – a chimerical goal – Marx implicitly identified the highest good with the human capacity to engage in hobbies, that is, with the capacity to play (HC 128n). But according to Arendt, we become fully human not by playing – as Schiller and Marcuse suggested – but, on the contrary, by working and acting. The difference between Marcuse and Arendt is nowhere more vivid than in their differing assessments of the "crisis in education" in the 1960s. Whereas Marcuse championed the students' right to rebel against authority, Arendt suggests that education is the one domain in which authority must be defended (BPAF 195). The aim of education is to "prepare the child for the world of adults," and this takes place, precisely, through "the gradually acquired habit of work and of not-playing" (BPAF 183). Arendt's point is not that the freedom of children must be broken in order to prepare them to enter a world whose values must be conserved at all costs, but on the contrary that it is precisely for the sake of the revolutionary freedom of the future adult that the child must forsake the realm of play: "Exactly for the sake of what is new and revolutionary in every child, education must be conservative" (BPAF 192–3). By mistakenly construing freedom as liberation from all facets of the *vita activa*, Marx unwittingly equated happiness with the happiness of the consumer rather than with the "public happiness" that human beings can only acquire through joint political action (HC 133; OR 127; BPAF 5). Ironically, Marx's vision of the reign of the *animal laborans* has been realized in advanced industrial capitalism, which has succeeded in putting man qua consumer in a position of hegemony. In contrast to both Adorno and Marcuse, for whom happiness is to be found in the liberation of the sensuous dimension of human existence, Arendt maintains that the legitimate demands of *animal laborans* remain outside the scope of the public realm and should be satisfied through technological and administrative means, rather than through politics (OR 112–14).

The failure of past revolutions "to solve the social question" is not a mere accident of history but turns on the difference between work and action. To work is to create something in accordance with a preconceived plan; one of Arendt's favorite examples is Plato's account of the bed-maker who makes beds in accordance with his or her access to a form. Because it treats the material on which it works as a mere means to its end, work is inherently violent; it *imposes* a form on its material. Work, moreover, is a solitary activity. Though some sort of apprenticeship is generally needed to acquire mastery of a craft, the craftsman works in isolation, knowing exactly what the outcome of his or her activity should be.

For Arendt, action differs from work in all these respects. Drawing on Augustine's conception of "natality," of the fact that human beings are essentially "beginners," she suggests that to act is to begin something without knowing in advance what the outcome will – or even should – be (HC 9; OR 211; BPAF 167; LOM II 109–10). To act is to "make an appearance" of some sort in public. As such, action requires the existence of other persons who serve not only as witnesses but as fellow actors. When individuals act in concert, they do not merely perform purposive bodily movements together as in the case of shared manual labor or work; as in the case of the Greek polis, they constitute the very public space within which their actions take place. Cooperative constituting acts of this sort generate power, namely, the power of a plurality of individuals to act in a mutually regarding way. Unlike the violence which the craftsman exercises over his or her material, power accrues equally to all parties who participate in constituting acts.

The real reason why the social question will never be solved by political means is not that economic problems are insoluble; on the contrary, it is precisely their solubility through technical means that makes them "work problems" rather than "action problems"; as such they could theoretically be entrusted to competent administrators. By contrast, the task of political constitution is one that administrators can only bungle, since their forte is not action but work. At the heart of Arendt's vision of political life is not blithe indifference toward economic matters, as it can appear at times, but an insistence on the difference in kind, even incompatibility, between work and action. Unlike Plato, who insisted on conflating the roles of philosophers and kings, Arendt maintains that what we need is for statesmen to stop being administrators and administrators to stop being statesmen, "for the qualities of the statesman or the political man and the qualities of the manager or administrator are not only not the same, they very seldom are to be found in the same individual" (OR 274).

While the Greek polis exemplifies Arendt's vision of a public space constituted by and for acting subjects, Plato's conception of the ideal republic represents a perversion of the Greek model because it conceives of the task of constituting a republic as a matter of work rather than action. Plato's philosopher-king is essentially a craftsman, no different in kind from the bedmaker; knowing in advance what his or her republic should look like, the philosopher-king is entitled to treat other persons as means to its realization. It is only with Plato that the oxymoronic idea of political government creeps into Greek thought, a model which eventually became dominant in European history. When the eighteenth-century revolutionaries rediscovered the Greek experience of political action, they did so when the problem of political constitution came to the fore, that is, the problem of inaugurating a new political space. But at precisely this crucial point the revolutionaries – both American and French – faltered. Instead of making sure that all citizens would be able to exercise political power, the framers of the American Constitution concentrated on protecting them from the violence of a tyrannical government. In the case of the French Revolution, the result was even more insidious. When Maximilien Robespierre (1758–1794) and the Jacobins seized control of the government, they did so precisely in the manner of Plato's philosopher-king, pretending to know what was in the interest of the French people. This entitled them to treat everyone – ultimately even one another – as means to preconceived ends. In both the American attempt to protect the people *from* tyranny as well as the French (and later Soviet) attempt to help the people *through* tyranny, Arendt discerns the same failure to appreciate the difference between action and work, that is, between the power generated from genuine constituting acts and the violence that will always be associated with the imposition of a form on recalcitrant material.

Benjamin called attention to the violence said to lie at the basis of all human legal institutions. Once a legal framework is in place, all attempts to preserve the law can be defended by appealing to it. But what legitimates the framework itself? One response to this problem is to appeal to a divine mandate; human law justifies itself as sanctioned by divine law. But Benjamin suggests that any legal appeal to a purported divine authority is a form of idolatry. Divine violence is law-destroying precisely insofar as it refuses to sanction any lawmaking violence. Arendt shares Benjamin's suspicion of lawmaking violence, but her distinction between violence and power enables her to suggest another solution to the problem of how to justify the constitution of a legal framework. Simply by virtue of our natality, of our being beginners, human beings have the capacity to constitute a body of laws that is without divine authorization. Thus instead of grounding action in law, Arendt grounds the law itself in action: "The way the beginner starts whatever he intends to do lays down the law of action for those who have joined him in order to partake in the enterprise and to bring about its accomplishment" (OR 211).

For Arendt, to act is to begin something whose end is unforeseeable because it is always done in concert with others whose actions are just as free. Thus there is a purposiveness to action but not a guiding purpose. In this sense, actions are like beautiful works of art. Just as Kant thought that no one living on a desert island would decorate his or her home since there would be no one else to see it, so Arendt suggests that no one would perform an action if no one were there to witness it (LKPP 61–2). To set out the boundaries of the polis is akin to demarcating a theatrical space on which a play can be staged. Those who act do so for their own sake, but also for the sake of those witnesses who will remember their deeds. For the Greeks, the aim of action was not to be "worthy of happiness" (as it was for Kant) but to be "worthy of an immortality which surrounds men but which mortals do not possess" (HC 232). In *On Revolution*, Arendt emphasized the difference between the standpoints of the actor and the spectator, faulting Marx and his revolutionary successors for attempting to act from an historical, rather than a political, point of view. But although it is impossible to inhabit simultaneously the interested standpoint of the actor and the disinterested standpoint of the spectator, both points of view are essential to human existence, as Arendt tries to show in her posthumously published *Lectures on Kant's Political Philosophy* (1982). In contrast to Hegel, who sacrificed the standpoint of the individual actor to the universal standpoint of the historian or (worse) philosopher of history, Kant tried to reconcile the human need to pass judgment on past actions with the "dignity" of the standpoint of the individual agent. Although "Kant nowhere takes action into account" – on the contrary, his response to the question, "What ought I to do?." treats human deeds as if they could be deduced from fixed rules – this lacuna in his moral philosophy is compensated for in the political philosophy that Arendt teases out of his Analytic of the Beautiful (LKPP 19).

Because they are reflective rather than determining, judgments of taste treat particulars as particulars rather than as instances of universal rules. Unlike knowledge claims, judgments of taste are recognized to be mere opinions; but because they purport subjective universality we feel compelled to reach consensus about them. Aesthetic quarrels – different in kind from cognitive disputes – are oriented toward the realization of a *sensus communis*, a shared point of view that is perpetually subject to revision as newcomers (both artistic geniuses and new aesthetic judges) arrive. Arendt regards this representation of aesthetic quarreling as a perfect description of the process of political deliberation. Kant failed to recognize the political significance of his account of taste for two reasons: first, because he subordinated politics to morality; and second, because he remained committed to a "workmanlike" model of moral theory according to which judgments of the form "This is good" are not reflective but determining. By contrast, Arendt suggests that all judgments about particulars qua particulars – including moral judgments – are akin to judgments of taste.

To say, "This rose is beautiful" is not to deduce a consequence of the universal judgment, "All roses are beautiful," but to call attention to a singular fact (LKPP 13). But what about a judgment like, "This is a rose" or "This action is good"? Kant would have regarded these as determining judgments because they subsume particulars under universals – the concepts *rose* and *good* being different in kind from the concept *beautiful* in this respect. But Arendt argues that all singular judgments are reflective because, as Kant himself acknowledges, there is no rule that can tell us whether or not an object falls under a given concept. Thus, rather than distinguishing between reflective and determining judgments, Arendt characterizes judgment in general as reflective. Just as judgments of taste seek to reach consensus about the beautiful, so political judgments seek to reach consensus about the rightness or wrongness of actions. To participate in a political deliberation is to put forth an opinion (rather than a knowledge claim) which needs public approval. This construal of judgment also enables Arendt to address the problem of how to reconcile our double standpoint as actors and spectators, political animals and historical judges. As actors, we are occasionally presented with "unprecedented" situations that require us to judge how we should act (EIJ 295; cf. LKPP 98). Failure to exercise the faculty of judgment can lead to the sort of culpable complicity that Arendt refers to as the "banality of evil," that is, the unthinking participation in truly diabolical crimes. Conversely, it is possible to make historical judgments without reducing past actors to pawns in the great game of History (a mistake she attributes to Hegel and Marx): "If judgment is our faculty for dealing with the past, . . . we may reclaim our human dignity, win it back, as it were, from the pseudo-divinity named History of the modern age, without denying history's importance but denying its right to be the ultimate judge" (LKPP 5).

3.9   Gadamer's fusion of horizons

Laud we the gods
(*Cymbeline*, V, v, 476)

Like Marcuse and Arendt, Hans-Georg Gadamer also studied with Heidegger in the 1920s, but since he was not Jewish, he did not have to leave Germany when Hitler came to power in 1933. Neither did he join the Nazi Party, as Heidegger did. Instead of turning his philosophical attention to on-going social and political issues, Gadamer became interested in Heidegger's reflections on the way in which truth takes place in works of art. This led him to emphasize the hermeneutical – i.e., interpretative – dimension of human understanding, something that Heidegger had thematized in *Being and Time*. Over the years, Gadamer developed an original conception of philosophical hermeneutics, to which he first gave systematic expression in his 1960 book, *Truth and Method* (*Wahrheit und Methode*).

The main aim of *Truth and Method* is to critique the narrowly scientistic construal of truth which has come to prevail in modernity. Toward this end, Gadamer takes as his clue the distinctive kind of truth that art expresses: "through a work of art a truth is experienced that we cannot attain in any other way" (TM xxii–xxiii). In order to clarify the nature of artistic truth, it is necessary to combat the "aestheticist" construal of art to which the work of Kant inadvertently gave rise. Prior to Kant, "taste" was conceived not simply as an "aesthetic" assessment of the pleasure afforded by an object of intuition, but as a cognitive reflection on the content of a work of art. So long as art was embedded in a shared religious context, it was recognized as an inherently meaningful object to be encountered on its own terms. Only as art became independent of such contexts did it come to be treated in a *merely* aesthetic way: "Whereas a definite taste differentiates – i.e., selects and rejects – on the basis of some content, aesthetic differentiation is an abstraction that selects only on the basis of aesthetic quality as such" (TM 85). Kant contributed to this process of aesthetic differentiation by stripping taste of determinate conceptual content: "the price that he pays for this legitimation of critique in the area of taste is that he denies taste any *significance for knowledge*" (TM 43).

Only with the rise of modern science and the philosophical demand that all truth claims be submitted to the methodical scrutiny of reason did the distinction between truths of taste and truths of reason begin to disappear. Giambattista Vico (1668–1744) defended the idea that there was a sense of truth proper to the humanities, but according to Gadamer, he failed to recognize the full scope of the problem, contenting himself with the claim that humanistic inquiry is capable of attaining the sort of truth demanded by the new science instead of making the case that a different kind of truth is at stake in judgments of taste. In the Kantian judgment of taste, the understanding is present, but only as a faculty of concepts "in general." In its free play with the imagination, the understanding is, as it were, on holiday. Its employment is only "serious" – i.e., geared toward truth – when it is called upon to make determining judgments. Against this point of view, Gadamer argues that works of art – and ultimately natural beauties as well, which, he claims, we learn to appreciate with eyes trained by works of art (TM 59; RBOE 31) – do in fact make truth claims. To recognize the force of such claims is to acknowledge that there is a form of knowing proper to taste. But instead of simply defending reflective judgment as just as epistemically valid as determining judgment, Gadamer suggests, following Hegel, that all judgments involve an element of both reflection and determination (TM 39n). Kant acknowledged that the ability to make a determining judgment – i.e., to subsume a particular object under a universal concept – presupposes an act of reflection by which we compare the object to others of its kind. But Gadamer claims that even reflection on a singular particular qua singular particular counts as knowledge. To bring this out, he compares Kant's distinction between reflective and determining judgment to Aristotle's distinction (developed in the *Posterior Analytics*) between experience and science.

According to Aristotle, experience arises from a manifold of perceptions and it culminates in science when we acquire universal concepts that can be applied to particulars. But Aristotle also regards experience itself – i.e., reflection – as a kind of knowledge on its own. This is the point of his distinction between *theoria* (theoretical knowledge) and *phronesis* (practical wisdom). Whereas *theoria* reaches truth through logical demonstrations – thereby subsuming particulars under universals – *phronesis* attends to particulars as particulars. Against Plato, whom he regarded as reducing all truths to demonstrable truths, Aristotle claims that the truths apprehended through *phronesis* cannot be taught like a doctrine but can only be acquired and put to work by way of experience itself. According to Gadamer, this Aristotelian sense of *phronesis* was still present in pre-Kantian conceptions of taste. Kant's mistake was to restrict the concept of truth to the kind of truth that is revealed in natural science. This conception of truth retains its force for Kant even in his metaphysics. Thus, despite his insistence that there is a difference in kind between theoretical and practical cognition, his moral philosophy retains the form of *theoria*, the specificity of *phronesis* having been relegated to an entirely marginal status. This can be seen in Kant's quasi-Platonic (and un-Arendtian) rejoinder to Aristotle: though ethical decision-making depends upon a capacity of reflective discernment – this is why examples of morally good actions can play a useful pedagogical role – what is decisive is the deductive movement from the universal moral law to the particular cases that fall under it. Kant recognizes that skill in judgment must be acquired through practice, calling judgment "the kind of understanding that comes only with years" (AFPPV 71). But judgment in this sense still remains subordinate to the understanding.

Gadamer's distinction between aesthetic and hermeneutic approaches to art can be likened to Marcuse's distinction between desublimated play and sublimated play. Kant treated aesthetic play as something merely subjective, the beautiful object occasioning a free play of the subject's faculties. Gadamer suggests that from here it is but a short step to Schiller's conception of aesthetic consciousness, a state of mind in which the subject is capable of experiencing anything and everything in a playful way. Like Adorno, Gadamer is uneasy with Schiller's conception of merely aesthetic play, but like Marcuse, he develops a more authentic conception. Genuine play is to be located not on the side of the subject but in the way in which the subject is drawn into the play of the work itself. Not only is play an inherently purposive activity (we try, for example, to get a ball through a hoop), but insofar as it involves role-playing, it is representational as well, calling forth an audience. As such, it lies at the basis of all art. Advancing by steps from an analysis of games that we play to dramatic plays that we stage and ultimately to the plastic arts and literature, Gadamer ascribes to the experience of art a unique kind of seriousness. Like Arendt, Gadamer considers theater to be the most political of artforms because it literally stages the actions of human beings (TM 147; HC 188). Arendt repeatedly likens human agents to actors taking part in a play, but she resists equating action with play, criticizing Marx for his vision of a "leisure society" in which people would find fulfillment in mere "hobbies" (HC 127–8). But like Marcuse, Gadamer suggests that the opposition between mere play and serious work is artificial: "Seriousness is not merely something that calls us away from play; rather, seriousness in playing is necessary to make the play wholly play" (TM 102; cf. RBOE 130).

To experience the play of art in a serious way is not to have a merely subjective "lived experience" (*Erlebnis*) but to have an "experience" (*Erfahrung*) in the sense of an encounter with truth (TM 98). In order to recapture this possibility, Gadamer invokes the ideal of "aesthetic *non*-differentiation," that is, an experience of art that does not divorce aesthetics from the encounter with something meaningful that calls for interpretation. Once again, Gadamer suggests that Kant did not entirely succumb to the subjectivism of aesthetic differentiation. This can be seen from the fact that he distinguishes the pleasure that accompanies the judgment of taste from the mere feeling of agreeableness. In this respect, taste remains a kind of *Erfahrung* rather than a mere *Erlebnis*. We do not dispute about judgments of taste precisely because they do not belong to *scientific* experience, but we quarrel on their behalf because they do not pertain merely to *lived* experience either. But instead of simply praising Kant for acknowledging the unique status of judgments of taste, Gadamer regrets that insofar as Kant draws a sharp distinction between the cognitive character of judgments about the good and the quasi-cognitive character of judgments about the beautiful and sublime, he opens the way to the Romantic construal of taste as *Erlebnis*.

Gadamer agrees with Kant that judgments of taste point toward the existence of a *sensus communis*, which he construes, with Vico, as "the sense that founds community," something that is "less a gift than . . . [a] constant task" (TM 21, 26). If we think of the history of culture as an extended Kantian "quarrel" – not necessarily about what is and is not beautiful, but about meanings – then Gadamer's point is that this history – what we call "tradition" – has no proper telos outside itself. Thus in contrast to the natural sciences, for which reflective judging serves as a mere ancillary to determining judging, the dialogue with tradition involves a perpetual work of reflection.

Gadamer criticizes Kant's conception of genius for preparing the way for the Romantic view of artworks as the mere expression of subjective *Erlebnis*. Kant seems to be aware of the subjectivistic danger when he maintains that taste is obliged to "clip the wings" of genius. But because taste itself lacks any cognitive content, the way is open to an account of aesthetic experience that puts genius in the role of both creator and spectator. According to Gadamer, this was the step taken by Schiller and the Romantics, for whom aesthetic experience (*Erlebnis*) – not the *sensus communis* – became both the ground and destiny of works of art. In this view, the task of the reader or spectator was to achieve a direct intimation of the private subjective experience of the creator. What especially concerns Gadamer about Romantic aesthetics is its influence on hermeneutics. Beginning with Friedrich Schleiermacher (1768–1834), the task of interpretation came to be equated with the task of having an aesthetic *Erlebnis*. Gadamer claims that this conception had two unfortunate consequences. First, it gave rise to psychologism, the doctrine that the meaning of a product of the human mind is to be found in the psychological (as well as biographical and historical) processes by which the product was originally created. Following Husserl's critique of psychologism, Gadamer criticizes the "historical school" of the nineteenth century for reducing the hermeneutical concern for content to a psychologistic or historicist desire for some sort of "mysterious communion" with the past (TM 292). Second, by generalizing the Kantian account of genius, Schleiermacher encouraged the human sciences to treat all artistic production as non-cognitive. By conceding this point, they were forced to rely on the only conception of truth still available, namely, that which pertains to the natural sciences. As a result they found themselves in a paradoxical situation, namely, that insofar as they relied on aesthetic experience (*Erlebnis*) to guide their method of inquiry, they had to forsake the very sense of truth that was proper not only to the experience (*Erfahrung*) of art but to human experience in general.

Originally, the term "hermeneutics" referred to the art of interpreting texts that for one reason or another resisted interpretation. Problems of interpretation were faced by philologists who had to interpret manuscripts written in ancient languages, by theologians who had to interpret scripture, and by judges who had to interpret the law. But, in the nineteenth century, hermeneutics came to be conceived as the method of inquiry appropriate to the so-called *Geisteswissenschaften*. The very concept of the *Geisteswissenschaften* – a term first used by the German translator of John Stuart Mill's *Logic* to render the expression "moral sciences" and which roughly corresponds to what we would call the humanities and social sciences – reflects the rise of the scientistic paradigm (TM 3–4). For Wilhelm Dilthey (1833–1911), the aim of a hermeneutical engagement with texts was not to participate in a substantive dialogue about their content but simply to reconstruct the psychological processes that gave rise to them in the first place. This subjectivistic construal of hermeneutics completed the ascension of the natural sciences to their hegemonic position as exclusive arbiters of truth. In order to reverse this trend and reclaim a sense of truth that began to be eclipsed with Kant, it is necessary to develop a philosophical hermeneutics that is sensitive to the difference between scientific understanding and the understanding of "traditionary" texts such as works of art. Insofar as all human understanding is hermeneutical in character (as Heidegger observed in *Being and Time*), the task of philosophical hermeneutics is not so much to demonstrate the cognitive import of hermeneutics as it is to reveal the hermeneutical import of cognition in general.

Gadamer's attempt to contrast hermeneutical *Erfahrung* with aesthetic *Erlebnis* is not only a way of providing the human sciences with a new understanding of their mission. More profoundly, it is intended to revise our understanding of human existence. Along with Husserl, Gadamer argues that it is a mistake to think of ourselves merely as natural beings who have acquired cultural capacities. To recognize ourselves as belonging to a culture (*Bildung*) is to see that our identities are formed (*gebildet*) by historical traditions whose contours are never fully accessible to critical reflection. Thus to exist in nature is first and foremost to belong to a lifeworld. To bring this out, Gadamer appeals to Heidegger's conception of "facticity," the ontological condition of "thrownness" that casts us as inescapably belonging to a "world" whose very essence lies in its linguisticality.

Because we are unable to "get behind the facticity" of our being-in-the-world, it is an illusion to think that our belonging to history can be ontologically reduced to our existence in temporal nature (TM 264). Ultimately, the claims of natural science are "relative to a particular world orientation and cannot at all claim to be the whole" (TM 449). The great danger of modernity – and here one can hear an echo of not only Heidegger's but also Adorno's worry – is that the scientific conception of objectivity threatens to occlude the ontologically significant fact that scientific practice is itself but one of the dimensions of our hermeneutical experience of the world itself (TM 559). Although he chides Horkheimer and Adorno for anachronistically treating Odysseus as a bourgeois subject, Gadamer accepts "their analysis of the 'dialectic of the Enlightenment,'" tracing the roots of the scientistic illusion to the Enlightenment dichotomy between science and myth (TM 274n). According to Gadamer, this dichotomy presupposes an ideal of presuppositionlessness. Where Adorno claimed that the fundamental myth of the Enlightenment was the myth that it had escaped myth, Gadamer holds that "the fundamental prejudice of the Enlightenment is the prejudice against prejudice itself." Not only is it impossible to uncover all of the prejudices that inform our cognitive activity, but the very ideal of prejudice-free cognition is misplaced. Commenting on Heidegger's construal of the hermeneutic circle, Gadamer notes that every act of judgment (*Urteil*) necessarily takes place within a context of pre-judgments (*Vor-urteile*) – i.e., prejudices – without which understanding would be impossible (TM 270). Perhaps the ideal of prejudice-free cognition would be appropriate for a being with intellectual intuition, but not for beings whose intellects are discursive.

This is not to say that we should renounce the Enlightenment demand for critique. Though all knowing rests on cultural prejudices, we must still ask "what distinguishes legitimate prejudices from the countless others which it is the undeniable task of critical reason to overcome" (TM 277). Thus in contrast to Marcuse, who criticized Heidegger for valorizing irrational pre-givens, Gadamer suggests that to recognize that we are always working within a horizon of prejudices is not to preclude the possibility for engaging in critical reflection. Just as Adorno and Marcuse blamed the natural sciences for contributing to the "total administration" of social life, so Gadamer argues that "science can fulfill its social function only when it acknowledges its own limits. . . . Philosophy must make this clear to an age credulous about science to the point of superstition" (TM 552). Gadamer also agrees with the critical theorists that works of art can fulfill a socially critical function, and that "art documents a social reality only when it is really art, and not when it is used as an instrument" (TM 579). What the members of the Frankfurt School decried in art's commodification, Gadamer deplores in the aesthetic differentiation promoted by museums (TM 87). His analysis of the genesis of aesthetic *Erlebnis* purports to explain how art first became invested with its utopian vocation and why this was doomed to failure: "The romantic demand for a new mythology . . . gives the artist and his task in the world the consciousness of a new consecration . . . his creations are expected to achieve on a small scale the propitiation of disaster for which an unsaved world hopes. This claim has since defined the tragedy of the artist in the world, for any fulfillment of it is always only a local one, and in fact that means it is refuted" (TM 88).

Gadamer's appeal to the authority of tradition is less a prescriptive claim about how we should comport ourselves than a descriptive claim about the nature of any understanding whatsoever, for even the ability to disagree with someone about something rests on a willingness to consider that what the other person is saying might be true.[28] Thus to recognize the authority of a text or another person's speech is just to see that something purportedly true has been articulated in it. This is something we can see only by co-attending to the subject matter about which it speaks. Accordingly, to enter into dialogue is to acknowledge the possibility that one could be wrong: "Openness to the other . . . involves recognizing that I myself must accept some things that are against me, even though no one else forces me to do so" (TM 361). Because tradition has no epistemic telos outside of its own continuous historical transformation, to recognize its normative force is not to accept a ready-made doctrine. On the contrary, tradition only acquires its meaning through interpreters' critical engagement with it; no text contains a fixed "meaning-in-itself" (TM 473). Thus hermeneutics is opposed to all forms of dogmatism, both the dogmatism that ascribes absolute authority to the text and the dogmatism that ascribes absolute authority to the interpreter (TM 355).

To treat another person's utterances merely as expressions of his or her personality – that is, as psychological phenomena rather than as cognitive claims – is to fail to be in a true dialogue at all (TM 303–4). Put otherwise, it is only by adopting an attitude of hermeneutic openness that we treat another person as another person with something to say. Thus the demand for hermeneutic openness can be regarded as a special case of the moral duty to treat others as ends rather than merely as means. Gadamer readily acknowledges the ethical import of hermeneutics, but he shies away from developing its political significance, insisting on the separability of the vocations of philosopher and statesman. Yet just as Arendt took political deliberation to be oriented toward a *sensus communis*, so Gadamer claims that all genuine dialogue aims at a "fusion" of its participants' hermeneutical "horizons," the interpretive perspectives that inform their understanding of themselves and the world (TM 306). Just as Arendt's judge was never entirely removed from the scene of action, so Gadamer's participant in hermeneutic dialogue belongs to the tradition that he or she interprets. But whereas Arendt maintains that judgment cannot be guided by any predetermined transcendent truths, Gadamer suggests that judgment is always guided not by transcendent truths per se, but by texts that symbolically represent such truths to us. This is the function not only of religious texts, but also of works of art.

Thus, just as Kant took beauty to be a symbol of the morally good, so in "The Relevance of the Beautiful" (*Die Aktualität des Schönen*, 1977), Gadamer characterizes beauty as a symbol of truth: "beauty . . . gives us an assurance that the truth does not lie far off and inaccessible to us, but can be encountered in the disorder of reality" (RBOE 15). Following Heidegger, Gadamer suggests that the essence of the symbolic lies in the "interplay of showing and concealing" (RBOE 33). So long as art remained within a religious horizon of meaning, its symbolic function was readily manifest. Modern art disturbs us because it renounces its symbolic function. But just as Adorno took art's renunciation of mimesis to attest to a higher mimetic vocation, so Gadamer suggests that art fulfills its symbolic function precisely insofar as it repudiates symbolism, for in this way it mimetically represents the "unfamiliarity and impersonality of the world about us" (RBOE 74). Like Adorno, Gadamer criticizes "the understanding and practice of art in the age of the culture industry" on the grounds that it offers mere "escapism" and "the enjoyment of a spurious freedom" rather than a meaningful engagement with something that speaks to us (RBOE 129–30). Lyric poetry has responded to this crisis by becoming increasingly "hermetic," as if retracting its feelers from a hostile world (RBOE 135). Gadamer suggests that of all manifestations of language, a poem is unique in that it stands on its own, apart from any animating intentions on the part of the poet. Thus to interpret a poem is not to seek a fusion of horizons with the poet but to attend to the work itself (RBOE 106–7). Like the Christian proclamation of the "good news" or the promulgation of a law, a poem "stands written," but in a different way, because it neither "promises" nor "pledges" anything other than itself (RBOE 114). Thus despite Gadamer's critique of aesthetic differentiation, he does not seek to undo the distinction between art and religion. Yet, at the same time, he does maintain that all art is essentially tied to the "festive" celebration of the divine. Though modern art is no longer explicitly allegorical in the way that Christian art once was, its symbolism continues to point in the direction of the divine, even if only to bear witness to the flight of the gods (RBOE 32; cf. 71). Conversely, since even poetic allegory exhibits the ambiguity of symbolism (and therefore requires interpretation), the distinction between allegory and symbolism is somewhat arbitrary (GOC 163). To respond to any work of art thoughtfully is to approach it not from the standpoint of aesthetic taste but rather from the standpoint of an interpellated subject who has been called to interpret an enigma.

Insofar as art is symbolic, it represents an immanent manifestation of the transcendent. Gadamer suggests that the essence of play lies in "immanent transcendence," but by this I take him to mean what I have been calling "transcendent immanence" because, like Heidegger, he treats the work of art less as a stand-in for the unsayable (as Adorno did) than as a sensuous embodiment of its meaning (RBOE 46). The difference between Adorno and Gadamer on this point – the difference, that is, between beautiful sublimity and sublime beauty – can be characterized as the aesthetic equivalent of the religious distinction between the Judaic prohibition against graven images and the Christian acceptance of symbols of the divine. Gadamer explicitly connects his own profession of Christian faith with his conception of the nature of art:

> As a Protestant, . . . I share with Luther the conviction that Jesus' words "This is my body and this is my blood" do not mean that the bread and wine signify his body and blood. I believe that . . . the bread and wine of the sacrament *are* the flesh and blood of Christ . . . if we really want to think about the experience of art, we can, indeed must, think along these lines: the work of art does not simply refer to something, because what it refers to is actually there.
>
> (RBOE 35)

Significantly, Gadamer also claims that it is only with Christianity that philosophical hermeneutics became necessary, because in contrast to Judaic law (which, despite its sublimity, merely demands obedience), "the Christian proclamation" requires interpretation (RBOE 149; cf. 141).

In "Intuition and Vividness" (*Anschauung und Anschaulichkeit*, 1980), Gadamer criticizes Adorno for adhering to a fundamentally Kantian conception of taste instead of accepting the Hegelian conception of art as a sensible expression of meaning (RBOE 161). Though earlier he had blamed Kant's conception of genius for opening the way to aesthetic differentiation, he now emphasizes the fact that this conception points away from an aesthetics of taste to the genuinely hermeneutical point of view that makes it possible to prize works of art above natural beauty (RBOE 165). To "surpass" the standpoint of taste is to open oneself to the enigmatic message which the work of art expresses and thus to pass from an encounter with *mere* beauty to an encounter with *sublime* beauty: "Is not the intuition, to which the imagination seeks to elevate itself in the act of intuiting the work of art, of a similar immensity (and a similar overwhelming power) insofar as it cannot be expounded by concepts?" (RBOE 168–9). By tracing the experience of the mathematically and dynamically sublime not to the aesthetic encounter with the work's form but to the hermeneutic encounter with its meaning – what Kant called its "aesthetic idea" – Gadamer implies that art exhibits sublime beauty only insofar as it represents an aesthetic analogue of the Christian proclamation. This comes through in his reading of the poetry of Paul Celan (1920–1970). Gadamer acknowledges – citing "Adorno's related comments" – that "Celan's poetry . . . constitutes a single confession and expression of horror about the Holocaust" (GOC 161). But rather than read Celan as a poet who writes about what it means to write poetry after Auschwitz – thereby, perhaps, taking up the theme of beautiful sublimity – he instead reads Celan as a poet who conjures "a theology of the *Deus absconditus*," that is, a theology of the god who has departed. Thus Gadamer reads Celan in the same way that Heidegger read Hölderlin, namely, as a poet who attests to "the most extreme estrangement from God" (GOC 80). Like the despairing flip side of the "good news" of the Gospels, Celan's poems attest to "the distance of the hidden God, or the remoteness of the one nearest to us" (GOC 89). Yet because they are poems, and not religious texts, the despairing proclamation that the poetic "I" (*ich*) repeatedly addresses to an unnamed "you" (*du*) ultimately concerns the poem's own being: "'You' are what it testifies to ('Your' witness) – the intimate, unknown You which, for the I that here is the I of the poet as well as the reader, is its You, 'wholly, wholly real'" (GOC 126).

3.10   Ricoeur's dialectic of rival hermeneutics

> *Gloucester.*   But shall I live in hope?
> *Anne.*   All men, I hope, live so.
>   (*The Tragedy of Richard the Third*,
>   I, ii, 199–200)

Like Gadamer, the French philosopher Paul Ricoeur (1913–2005) derives his conception of hermeneutics from Heidegger's substitution of "an *ontology of understanding*" for a theory of knowledge (CI 6). But Ricoeur regards Heidegger's "short route" from epistemology to hermeneutics as too hasty because it bypasses the *ratio cognoscendi* of hermeneutics for its *ratio essendi*. That is, instead of working patiently from what is first "for us," Heidegger plunges immediately into what is first "in itself" without showing how we get access to it. This is not just a heuristic shortcoming but a substantive one. Just as Hegel criticized Schelling's conception of intellectual intuition on the grounds that it impossible to have unmediated access to the absolute, so Ricoeur criticizes Heidegger for undervaluing the mediating role played by symbols in posing the question concerning being. He proposes to "follow a more roundabout, more arduous path" (CI 6) that will lead *toward* an ontology of understanding. This path must start from what is most salient about human understanding, namely, the fact that there is a conflict – perhaps irreducible – among competing interpretations of ourselves and the world. We are thereby forced to confront not merely the question of the meaning of being but the question of whether there is a univocal meaning of being: "it is only in a conflict of rival hermeneutics that we perceive something of the being to be interpreted: a unified ontology is as inaccessible to our method as a separate ontology" (CI 19). The lesson to be drawn from philosophical reflection upon the conflict of rival interpretations is that all understanding is rooted in our relationship to symbols: "the very possibility of divergent and rival hermeneutics . . . is related to a fundamental condition . . . that symbolics is the means of expressing an extralinguistic reality" (CI 65). Unlike mere signs, which within certain limits can be regarded as univocal, symbols possess a double significance – a primary literal meaning and a secondary, figurative meaning that is intended by the first. By virtue of the symbol's relation to this secondary meaning – a semantic property Ricoeur later thematizes through an analysis of metaphor – it possesses an inexhaustible semantic richness that attests to "the equivocalness of being" itself (CI 67).

Ricoeur's strategy is to attempt to take a pre-hermeneutic transcendental philosophy of reflection as far as it can go, namely, to the point where it encounters the fact of symbolism as that which requires it to become hermeneutics. Thus rather than attempt to deepen philosophical reflection through a series of ever more stringent reductions, as Husserl does, he proposes to go in the opposite direction, namely, from the abstract plane of transcendental inquiry to the richness of lived experience. Such is the enterprise he undertakes in his multi-volume *Philosophy of the Will* (*Philosophie de la volonté*), a project that he eventually abandoned. The aim of this ambitious work is to show exactly where and why philosophical reflection on the nature of evil must give way to an interpretation of religious symbols. For Kant, the need for symbols was a function of the unrepresentability of ideas in general and of the idea of the good in particular; the beautiful served as a symbol of the morally good. In a sense Ricoeur reverses this argument, according a privileged status to the symbolism of evil. Of the three published volumes of the *Philosophy of the Will*, the first and third stand at opposite poles: *Freedom and Nature: the Voluntary and the Involuntary* (*Philosophie de la volonté: I. Le volontaire et l'involontaire*, 1950) is an eidetic analysis which starts from a bracketing of the phenomena of fallibility and evil, while the third volume, *The Symbolism of Evil* (*Philosophie de la volonté: Finitude et Culpabilité: II. La symbolique du mal*, 1960), begins from the manifold ways in which the confession of evil has been symbolized throughout the Judeo-Christian tradition. It is the second volume, *Fallible Man* (*Philosophie de la volonté: Finitude et Culpabilité: I. L'homme fallible*, 1960), that provides the crucial hinge between these two, that is, between pure reflection and concrete hermeneutical reflection.

The phenomenon of fallibility stands at the crossroads between two distinct dimensions of human experience, that which is accessible to conscious reflection and that which is not. Whatever is so accessible can be articulated in concepts; whatever is not can only be expressed in symbols. If fallibility is to serve as the hinge between an eidetics of the will and a symbolics of evil, it must itself be of a double nature, part concept and part symbol. So, on the one hand, Ricoeur must make the case that fallibility is a concept: "In maintaining that fallibility is a concept, I am presupposing at the outset that pure reflection ... can reach a certain threshold of intelligibility where the possibility of evil appears inscribed in the innermost structure of human reality" (FM-R 1). At the same time he must show that fallibility is the conceptual apprehension of something that cannot be expressed in concepts, namely evil or fault: "Fault remains a foreign body in the eidetics of man" (FM-R xlii). Thus fallibility plays the role of a schema in the Kantian sense; it bridges two domains while attesting to their irreducibility to each other. The analogy with Kant goes much further, for Ricoeur defines fallibility itself as a "'disproportion of self to self'" (FM-R 1) structured around the gap separating sensibility from understanding. In a series of chapters that more or less recapitulate the path traversed by Kant's three *Critiques* (though not without expressed reservations here and there), Ricoeur attempts to develop a philosophical anthropology that would identify the different ways in which man experiences himself as a disproportion or "non-coincidence" between rival aspects of his being. In each case this disproportion will be mediated by an avatar of the transcendental imagination. Thus in the domain of knowledge, imagination mediates the relationship between the finitude of sensible, perspectival adumbrations and the infinitude of judgment (figured for Ricoeur in "the Verb"); in the domain of ethics, respect will play a mediating role between the finitude of character and the infinitude of happiness conceived as Kant's "highest good"; and finally in the domain of affect, Plato's *thymos*, or heart, mediates between a finite self-love and an infinite beatitude. Ricoeur emphasizes two features of these analyses. The first is that they bear not only upon the finitude of man but upon the relationship between what is finite and what is infinite in him. The second is that the mediating avatars of the Kantian imagination attest in each case to a disproportion between the finite and the infinite. Both of these points distinguish Ricoeur's appropriation of Kant from that of Heidegger. Thus while he fully accepts the Kantian thesis that "Time is ... that mediating order, homogeneous both with the sensible ... and with the intelligible" (FM-R 42), he objects to Heidegger's "pious wish" to make time the common root of the two poles of man's disproportionate being. In particular, he objects to Heidegger's tendency to reduce the distinct pole of conceptual determination to the sensible manifestation of phenomena, thereby providing "a genesis of the categories from the schemata": "No one has ever shown how, from the consideration of time alone, one can educe a well-formed notional order. . . . That is why a philosophy of finitude, even interpreted as transcending finitude, is not sufficient to the problem" (FM-R 43).

At the end of *Fallible Man*, Ricoeur is able to measure the distance between the abstract account of fallibility that his transcendental analysis has provided and the concrete experience of what in the first chapter he had called "the *pathétique* of 'misery,'" the lived experience of suffering which, short of transcendental reflection, had been unable to separate the two poles of man's disproportion sufficiently to understand itself. In place of a Platonic "myth of 'melange'" or a Pascalian "rhetoric of 'misery'" we have achieved a precise conceptual understanding of that which makes the experience of misery possible (FM-R 17). Using the categories that Kant subsumed under the heading of quality to present a phenomenological account of the structure of appearance in general, Ricoeur's philosophical anthropology concludes that man is an "intermediate" being (limitation) stretched not "between angel and animal" (FM-R 3) but between an "originating affirmation" (reality) and an "existential difference" (negation) (FM-R 135). In measuring the distance between transcendental reflection and concrete experience we have discovered the gulf that separates fallibility as a mere condition for the possibility of evil from evil itself. The latter eludes transcendental inquiry altogether. Hence we find ourselves faced with what can only be described conceptually as an "enigma." But evil is enigmatic not merely because of the gap that separates a condition for the possibility of a phenomenon from the given phenomenon itself. More radically, Ricoeur's contention is that, while fallibility is the condition for the possibility of evil, the act of committing evil is never given as such. What is given, in place of the act, is the symbolic attestation of evil already committed. Thus although transcendental inquiry takes us to the threshold of evil, we do not find ourselves in a position to confront it directly. All that we can do is to make a leap from one threshold to another, from "before" to "after" the act of consenting to evil: "The enigma thenceforward is the 'leap' itself from fallibility to the already fallen. Our anthropological reflection remained short of this leap, but ethics arrives too late" (FM-R 143). Elsewhere Ricoeur will look to Kant's account of radical evil as the exemplary presentation of the experience of "the servile will," that is, the paradoxical experience of finding oneself responsible for an evil that eludes – because it is the very ground of – voluntary choice itself (CI 434). Precisely because of its paradoxical character, such an experience can only be expressed in symbols, the Kantian account of radical evil essentially being the most rarefied of philosophical attempts to present a concept for that to which the symbol of "original sin" attests (CI 308).

This leads us to Ricoeur's second conclusion, one that will play a decisive role in showing where hermeneutics must supplant transcendental reflection: "fallibility is the *condition* of evil, although evil is the revealer of fallibility" (FM-R 144). This is to say that our experience of evil – or more precisely our experience of the symbolic avowal of evil already committed – must serve as the existential support for a transcendental account of fallibility. Only by way of fallenness can we retroactively glimpse the possibility of an "innocent" condition prior to evil, of unfallen fallibility – a condition in which a certain harmony or "proportion" among man's disproportionate faculties might be attained. But if this is so, then transcendental inquiry is itself always already mediated by a prior hermeneutic encounter with symbols that express man's fallenness. This suggests that it is necessary to reverse the methodological order that Ricoeur himself follows in *The Philosophy of the Will*; "concrete" reflection must come before "abstract" reflection. In this sense it is only in the third volume, *The Symbolism of Evil*, that we encounter the true point of departure for Ricoeur's entire enterprise. This work concludes with a chapter which, in the preface to *Fallible Man*, Ricoeur had characterized as "the pivotal point of the whole work" (FM-R xliv).

Under the title *"Le symbole donne à penser,"* – "the symbol gives rise to thought" – Ricoeur proposes "rules for transposing the symbolics of evil into a new type of philosophic discourse" (FM-R xliv). At issue is a certain beholdenness of thought to symbols. To say that thinking begins from symbols is to subordinate the activity of determining judgment to that of aesthetic reflective judgment. Like a beautiful form, a symbol provokes potentially endless reflection. Ricoeur suggests that such reflection is guided by the hermeneutic circle, which he interprets as the double precept that "We must understand in order to believe, but we must believe in order to understand" (SOE 351; cf. CI 298, 389). To start exclusively from the demand for understanding would be to engage in a merely logically reflective judgment, one that would reduce what is enigmatic in the symbol to the merely indeterminate. By contrast, to start exclusively from the side of belief would be to succumb to the temptation of elevating the symbol to the status of a fully determinate allegorical representation of a purely conceptual truth. To avoid both of these extremes, each of which misses what is proper to the symbol qua symbol, Ricoeur suggests that it is necessary to "demythologize" the symbol (so as to avoid the allegorizing temptation) without stripping the symbol of its evocative power to provoke thought. Neither indeterminate nor determinate, the symbol presents itself as indefinitely determinable. For this reason Ricoeur frequently speaks of the symbol as an "enigma" (FM-R 143; CI 78, 192, 207) in what it is tempting to say is Adorno's sense of this term – particularly given the fact that in his later writings Ricoeur shifts the emphasis from the idea of the symbol as revealer of evil to that of the symbol or metaphor as attesting to the "excessive suffering that overwhelms the world" (CC 29). Ricoeur is also close to Adorno when he writes, "we should not be fooled about the nature of *mimesis* – and I shall maintain this paradox: it is in the twentieth century when painting ceased to be figurative that the full measure of this *mimesis* could be taken, namely, that its function is not to help us recognize objects but to discover dimensions of experience that did not exist prior to the work" (CC 173). As for Adorno's problem concerning the possibility of poetry after Auschwitz, Ricoeur focuses instead on the commemorative duty of thought: "After Auschwitz there is a duty to convey Jewish thought before Auschwitz, in opposition to those who say that after Auschwitz thought is no longer possible" (CC 166).

True to the Kantian thrust of his larger project, Ricoeur once proposed to provide, in a volume of *The Philosophy of the Will* that he eventually abandoned, something like "a 'transcendental deduction' of symbols," one that would involve "a qualitative transformation of reflexive consciousness" (SOE 355–6). Although it leaves behind the plane of transcendental analysis, such a project can still be called transcendental insofar as it represents the sublation of transcendental inquiry; put otherwise, it is the very attempt to carry out a purely transcendental analysis that calls forth a hermeneutics of symbols. A transcendental deduction of symbols would not merely indicate the place where concepts end and symbols begin; rather, it would provide something like an existential analytic of Dasein on the basis of those specific symbols through which evil is confessed: "The task, then, is, starting from the symbols, to elaborate existential concepts – that is to say, not only structures of reflection but structures of existence, insofar as existence is the being of man" (SOE 356–7). Thus, by a "transcendental deduction of symbols" Ricoeur envisions an ontology of understanding that would complete the "roundabout" return to Heidegger's starting-point. The fact that he did not carry out this undertaking suggests that he came to regard the detour through symbols as interminable – not simply because of their inexhaustible depth of meaning, but because of the irreducibility of the conflict between rival hermeneutical attitudes toward them. It is this conflict that Heidegger avoided by hastening to put forth an ontology of understanding.

Ricoeur suggests that so long as the conflict between rival interpretations is sidestepped, there is nothing in the concept of the hermeneutical circle as Heidegger develops it in *Being and Time* that could not be accounted for phenomenologically in terms of Husserl's analysis of the reanimation of texts with sedimented meanings. The real shock to the phenomenological enterprise comes not from fundamental ontology but from psychoanalysis. In *Freud and Philosophy* (*De l'interprétation: Essai sur Freud*, 1965), Ricoeur argues (contra Sartre) that Freud's distinction between consciousness and the unconscious cannot be reduced to the phenomenological distinction between reflective and prereflective experience. The latter distinction corresponds to the relatively superficial contrast between consciousness and the preconscious; to disclose the sedimentations of past lived experience – to reflect on the unreflected – is to make conscious what had been preconscious. But the unconscious is something completely different. It concerns a level of our being that is not at all accessible to mere conscious reflection and which manifests itself in a kind of language that we produce without our being aware of what that language says. Only the manifest meaning of our dreams and symptoms is accessible to the cogito through phenomenological reflection. The unconscious meaning can be approached only if we are prepared to abandon the self-assurance of consciousness – the presumption that by mere reflection I can know what I mean by what I say – for the obscure and alienating task of an interpretation which starts from the assumption that whatever in speech is accessible to conscious reflection is "false" or insufficient. Thus psychoanalysis does not merely repeat the decentering gesture by which phenomenological description gives way to hermeneutics; more profoundly it calls forth a "hermeneutics of suspicion," that is, an interpretation predicated upon "the novel problem of the lie of consciousness and consciousness as a lie" (CI 99).

Ricoeur characterizes psychoanalysis as "an antiphenomenology which requires, not the reduction *to* consciousness, but the reduction *of* consciousness" (CI 237). This is the deep significance of Freud's remark that psychoanalysis delivers a blow to man's narcissism, one that is psychologically equivalent to the blows delivered by Copernicus and Darwin (FAP 277, 426; CI 152). In this respect Freud is also close, and in a hermeneutically more profound way, to Marx and Nietzsche (FAP 33). All three of these modern "masters" (FAP 32) or "protagonists" (CI 99) of suspicion reduce the consciousness of meaning to a problem concerning the meaning of consciousness, whether it be ideology, will to power, or the libido that is at stake: "Henceforth, seeking meaning no longer means spelling out the consciousness of meaning but, rather, *deciphering its expressions*. We are therefore faced not with three types of suspicion but with three types of deception" (CI 149). Though qua consciousness I can assert with apodictic certainty that I am, I can no longer presume to know on the basis of mere self-consciousness what I am: "*What* I am is just as problematical as *that* I am is apodictic" (CI 242). Thus the shift from Husserlian phenomenology to hermeneutics is made not by way of an ontology of Dasein but by way of the dispossession of the cogito through a specific kind of hermeneutics, namely, one of suspicion. Because of his emphasis on the fact "that one does not know oneself, that one has to go by way of the detour of others, always valuing the detour of critique," Ricoeur regards his own conception of hermeneutics as more nuanced than Gadamer's "hermeneutics of appropriation" (CC 33).

Ricoeur's intention is not to abandon the work of reflection but to displace it in the direction of a meta-reflection upon conflicting hermeneutics. For Marx, Nietzsche, and Freud, conscious appropriation of that which escapes consciousness remains the telos of suspicion: "All three,... far from being detractors of 'consciousness,' aim at extending it" (CI 150). Understood in this way, the suspicion that manifest meanings are false or illusory is a first step toward the recovery of hidden meanings that are true or authentic. Though complete self-consciousness must remain a mere regulative ideal, it is one that we can hope to approach asymptotically.

To treat the hermeneutics of suspicion as a means to the end of the recovery of authentic meanings is to incorporate it within a larger hermeneutic project, one that involves not merely the destruction of false idols but the reconstruction of authentic symbols. It is here that Ricoeur begins to supplement – and even subordinate – the work of suspicion to the work of a "restoration" of meaning. Suspicion works retroactively; it seeks to uncover archaic meanings that, through various disguises, have found their way into present speech (construing this term broadly so as to cover all forms of human signification). Running counter to suspicion is the prospective work of a "dialectic of figures" that seeks the significance of symbols not in what is archaically buried in them but in what comes to overtake them. In contrast to Freud's "archaeology of the subject" (CI 21) – a phrase Ricoeur borrows from Merleau-Ponty (CI 243) – Hegel's *Phenomenology of Spirit* presents us with a "teleology of the subject" (CI 22). Here it is a question not of that which "pushes" language from behind, so to speak, but of that which "pulls" language toward it. Freud tried to capture this double movement with his conception of sublimation. Unlike repression, the psychic attempt to thwart archaic meanings which then manifest themselves through a "return of the repressed" in distorted language, sublimation is supposed to involve a genuinely creative transformation of archaic meanings. But if the distinction between repression and sublimation is to have any significance, it must point to the difference between the "pushing" and "pulling" poles of human expression. Unfortunately Freud reneges on this implication, typically seeing only the repressed in even the highest forms of human expression; in this sense "Sublimation ... is as much the title of a problem as the name of a solution" (CI 207). Like Bachelard, who raised the same objection, Ricoeur thinks that Hegel shows us how to recognize the properly transcending – or sublating – character of sublimation. This is not to say that psychoanalysis can be reduced to a mere chapter of an Hegelian-style phenomenology of spirit, however. Just as Freud reduces teleology to archaeology, so Hegel tends to reduce archaeology to teleology. Both are one-sided gestures that obscure precisely what is significant about the conflict among rival hermeneutics, namely, that it is the very same symbols that are subject to competing interpretations. What interests Ricoeur is the confrontation between Freud and Hegel, though he also dreams of a new phenomenology of spirit, a "dialectical philosophy" that would be in a position to take up the relationship among competing hermeneutics (CI 497). Such a dialectic would not culminate in a determinate telos like that of absolute knowing. Along with Levinas and so many other post-Hegelians, Ricoeur resists the gesture of totalization, arguing, with Kant, that totality is both an inescapable aim of human reason and something that necessarily eludes it. To bring out this double aspect of man's relationship to totality requires a third kind of hermeneutics that is reducible to neither Freudian archaeology nor Hegelian teleology: a phenomenology of the sacred.

For Ricoeur the sacred is radically different in kind from an anthropological arche or telos; more originary than such an arche and more final than such a telos, the sacred is that which manifests itself in symbols of religious transcendence: "An archaeology and a teleology still unveil an *arche* and a *telos* which the subject, while understanding them, can command. It is not the same in the case of the sacred, which manifests itself in a phenomenology of religion." Through the encounter with the sacred the subject experiences itself "as effort and as desire to be" (CI 22), that is, as a longing for totality, for a belonging to being. To experience such longing is to persist in the disproportion that is the stretching of the finite toward the infinite. As a Christian, Ricoeur draws here upon the kerygmatic nature of symbols of redemption through Christ. But so as to remain true to their symbolic character, he regards them through the lens of a religion of hope rather than a religion of revealed truth: "The 'already' of his Resurrection orients the 'not yet' of the final recapitulation" (CI 406). Whence the messianic character of Ricoeur's Christianity, which, like Benjamin's Judaism, not only respects the merely promissory character of the promise but also construes redemption as a fulfillment of the hopes of the past: "every period is surrounded by an aura of hopes that were not fulfilled; it is this aura that permits renewals in the future, and perhaps this is how utopia could be cured of its congenital illness – believing that one can start over from zero: utopia is instead a rebirth" (CC 125).

Just as consciousness must renounce itself through a hermeneutics of suspicion if it is to reclaim itself through a hermeneutics of restoration, so it is necessary for a phenomenology of the sacred to pass through the death of God: "The 'timid' hope must cross the desert of the path of mourning" (CI 176). In neither case would it suffice to carry out the first gesture from the standpoint of prospective confidence in the second; on the contrary, it is only by genuinely risking the despair of endless deferral – the interminability of the roundabout approach – that we authentically enter on the path of religious hope. Ricoeur regards Kant's critique of the dialectical illusions of reason as an exemplary instance of what it means to run such a risk: "the critique of . . . transcendental illusion . . . plays . . . the role of a speculative 'death of God'" (CI 418). Only insofar as the problems concerning the immortality of the soul and the existence of God are exposed as illusions can they be regained as objects of hope: "I hope, there where I necessarily deceive myself, by forming absolute objects: self, freedom, God" (CI 415). In other words, Kant opened up the possibility of a "religion within the limits of hope alone" precisely by enduring the full force of the question, "Must we despair?"

Kant was able to preserve the possibility of a religion of hope because he distinguished between the intuition of appearances and the thought of things in themselves. In "Kant and Husserl" ("*Kant et Husserl*," 1954),

Ricoeur interprets this as the distinction between the givenness of beings and the transcendence of the being of beings (KAH 192).[29] Husserl blurred this distinction by reducing intentionality to intuition, or rather by treating signifying acts as "empty" intuitions rather than as indications of the non-givenness of things in themselves (KAH 189). Ricoeur interprets non-givenness as the mark of alterity, and he suggests that Kant's conception of respect for rational beings is grounded in the relation to alterity (thereby anticipating Levinas). But Ricoeur also criticizes Kant's insistence that salvation is conditional upon moral worth. With Freud, he objects to the "accusatory" character of the categorical imperative, detecting in it the severity of superegoic cruelty; with Hegel, he denounces the formalism of Kantian ethics from the perspective of a richer conception of social life; and with St. Paul, he locates evil not in the failure to act from duty but, on the contrary, in the "premature" appeal to the sublimity of the moral law (CI 345). Thus, evil is to be found not in man's falling short of holiness of will (the crime of Claudio in *Measure for Measure*), but in moral fanaticism (the sin of Angelo, which Kant does not entirely escape): "evil . . . consists less in a transgression of a law than in a *pretension* of man to be master of his life . . . worse than injustice is one's own justice" (CI 438). Characterizing man as "a being sick with the sublime," Ricoeur implies that the virtue of symbols lies precisely in their ability to ground the relation to the sublime in beautiful forms (CI 338). In this sense, symbols exhibit sublime beauty.

Just as Benjamin located genuine violence in the founding of laws rather than in their transgression, so Ricoeur suggests that evil manifests itself in any human institution that aspires to the totalization of human experience: "the true malice of man appears only in the state and in the church, as institutions of gathering together, of recapitulation, of totalization" (CI 423). Like Arendt, Ricoeur distinguishes between violence — the evil of totalization — and power, which is predicated on relations of mutual recognition (FM-R 120). Accepting Arendt's critique of totalitarianism, he suggests that "we become human" only insofar as we come together as citizens motivated by a "wish to live within just institutions" (TJ xvi). Perhaps the only significant difference between Ricoeur and Arendt is that, whereas she looks to Kant's account of aesthetic judgment to articulate her conception of the democratic polis, he turns to Kant's conception of teleological judgment in order to inscribe the concern for justice within the horizon of hope. Without an appeal to teleology, Benjamin's messianic hope on behalf of the past remains incomplete: "How apart from some underlying teleology can the regard directed to the past turn back in expectation toward the future?" Hence, whereas Arendt stressed Kant's separation of the standpoints of the actor and the spectator, Ricoeur highlights Kant's attempt to bridge the perspectives of the spectator and the prophet: "Hope, for Kant, appears as a bridge between the regard of the witness and the expectation of the prophet" (TJ 106).

3.11 Habermas's defense of the project of modernity

Good reasons must of force give place to the better
(*The Tragedy of Julius Caesar*, IV, iii, 203)

The "theory of communicative action" developed in the work of the German philosopher Jürgen Habermas (1929–) represents a critical continuation of the legacy of the Frankfurt School. On the one hand, Habermas is sympathetic with the charge that Horkheimer and Adorno level against the direction taken by economic and political institutions in modernity. On the other hand, he objects to their conflation of processes of rationalization with processes of domination. Not only does this conflation force Horkheimer and Adorno to push the birth of capitalism and political bureaucracy back as far as the origins of civilization itself (TCA I 379), but it leaves them unable to articulate the normative sense of rationality in terms of which the *so-called* rationalization of society can be judged as irrational. This tension is in keeping with the dialectical character of their analyses. But the critique of modernity can be made fruitful only by carefully distinguishing between the rational and irrational aspects of the Enlightenment. Horkheimer and Adorno were unable to make such distinctions because their critical theory relied on the very model of subject-centered instrumental reason that they condemned. As a result, they could only call attention to the futility of their own arguments, allowing the normative claim implied in the judgment that rationalization is irrational to rest, paradoxically, on an *irrational* appeal to a lost experience of nature that human beings had to forsake at the beginning of civilization. Despite his aversion to Heidegger's mytho-poetics of remembrance, Adorno succumbs to the same temptation by treating works of art not merely as standing in for rational claims about justice and injustice that we are not yet fully prepared to articulate, but as enigmas that respond mimetically to the domination of humanity and nature (TCA I 385).

In *Knowledge and Human Interests* (*Erkenntnis und Interesse*, 1968), Habermas seeks to explain how the Kantian critical project degenerated into that positivistic self-understanding of the sciences which the members of the Frankfurt School rightly rebelled against. The aim of Kant's critical project was to submit all validity claims to the tribunal of pure reason. But Kant was unable to demonstrate the competence of pure reason to judge itself. His immediate successors called attention to the need for a "metacritique," which in Hegel took the form of a phenomenology of spirit. In phenomenological reflection, claims to knowledge are subjected to critical scrutiny in such a way as to revise the very standards guiding critical reflection itself. Habermas agrees with Hegel on the need for this type of self-reflection, but he criticizes him for thinking that phenomenological reflection could be guided by the presumption of the attainability of absolute knowledge (KHI 12).

For Marx, the telos of reconciliation becomes a task to be achieved. Marx provides an account of human history as a succession of social practices, each of which has been "irrational" not only in the sense that forces of production have been in contradiction with relations of production, but in the normative sense that each has proved itself unable to satisfy human interests that are inherently rational. From Marx, by way of Fichte and (to a lesser extent) Kant, Habermas develops his own conception of knowledge-constitutive interests, interests *in* rationality that are both anchored in our animal existence in nature and yet still intrinsically rational. Working on the assumption that all knowledge claims – and validity claims in general – are *epistemically* linked to a human interest in emancipation, he seeks to undermine the positivistic pretension to a purely disinterested conception of science. Marx failed to develop such an approach, succumbing instead to an instrumental construal of labor and hence a naturalistic interpretation of human interests, thereby encouraging a positivistic tendency within the Marxist tradition itself (KHI 42). Even Dilthey, whose hermeneutics emphasizes the difference between the natural sciences and the social sciences, was unable to avoid the positivistic temptation to view meanings as objective facts (KHI 181).

Because it believes only in a world of facts, positivism denigrates as "psychologistic" any attempt to ground our orientation to facts on underlying human interests. In so doing it blocks the work of critical reflection; indeed, for Habermas, positivism *is* this refusal of reflection (KHI vii). In order to renew the work of reflection, a transcendental assessment of the boundaries of science is no longer feasible. Instead, the sciences must themselves become self-reflective so as to overcome the positivistic "illusion of objectivism" (KHI 69).

Habermas suggests that psychoanalysis provides an exemplary model for such a work of reflection: "Psychoanalysis is . . . the only tangible example of a science incorporating methical self-reflection" (KHI 214). Underlying psychoanalytic practice is an "emancipatory cognitive interest," for the patient who comes to see his or her analyst wishes to be freed from unpleasant symptoms (KHI 198). The analyst helps the patient reflect upon a lived history that was not originally lived through reflectively (KHI 242). On this interpretation, which closely resembles that of Ricoeur, repression is the obverse of reflection, the work of psychoanalysis being essentially equivalent to the reflective activity of the Hegelian phenomenologist. In attempting to work through that which the patient has repressed, both analyst and patient together engage in a resumption of a process of reflection whose interruption was the cause of symptom-formation in the first place. Though Freud himself ultimately fell back on a positivistic construal of his own method – "he did not comprehend metapsychology as the only thing it can be in the system of reference of self-reflection: a *general interpretation of self-formative processes*" – Habermas regards psychoanalytic technique as a model for what it would mean to work through that which has been collectively repressed in the interrupted project of Enlightenment. If hermeneutics provides an account of what it means to "come to an understanding" with tradition, psychoanalysis offers the necessary supplement of a "metahermeneutics" capable of disclosing those "split-off symbols" that give rise to speech pathologies (KHI 254). Though Habermas criticizes Gadamer for succumbing to a "hermeneutic idealism" that is unable to go beyond the retrieval of surface meanings, he also credits him with clarifying the anti-positivistic point that one can understand the meaning of normative and expressive speech only by adopting the stance of a self who participates as a member – even if only vicariously – of the speaker's speech community (TCA I 134).

In his two-volume *Theory of Communicative Action* (*Theorie des kommunikativen Handelns*, 1981), Habermas develops his systematic account of what exactly has gone wrong in modernity. In their *Dialectic of Enlightenment*, Horkheimer and Adorno assimilated two different accounts of the rise of capitalism and political bureaucracy, namely, those presented by Marx and Weber. Unlike Marx, who treats modern political institutions as an extension of a capitalist economy whose origins lie exclusively in the history of the class struggle, Weber treats both capitalism and the modern state as twin expressions of a process of rationalization that began with the Reformation. Marx predicted that a proletarian revolution would lead to the dissolution of both the capitalist mode of production and the modern state. For Weber, by contrast, these institutions represent an "iron cage" whose very rationality makes them resistant to change despite the fact that they have given rise to a prevailing sense of purposelessness and meaninglessness. However, Weber does not conclude from this that societal rationalization is irrational; on the contrary, he simply notes that processes of rationalization inevitably produce a "disenchantment of the world." So long as we remain in a society whose world-view is essentially mythical in nature, we live in an "enchanted" world that is inhabited by gods, full of meaning, and manipulable by means of magic. In such a world, no rigorous distinction can be drawn between the values of truth, goodness, and beauty. Rationalization takes place when we come to demarcate the boundaries that separate truth claims, normative claims, and aesthetic claims. As a result, we can no longer treat the world – that is, the true world, the world of "all that is the case" – as if it were intrinsically good or beautiful. Rational scientific inquiry becomes possible only once we have purged the world of moral and aesthetic values – as Descartes did when he separated scientific concern with natural laws from theological concern with final causes. The separation between truth, goodness, and beauty culminates in Kant's distinction between scientific claims of the understanding, practical claims of reason, and aesthetic claims of reflective judgment.

The members of the Frankfurt School situated Weber's account of rationalization within a Marxist account of the history of class struggle (TAC I 144). As a result, they tended to identify liberation from domination with the re-enchantment of the world. But according to Habermas, such longing for a premodern world-view cannot but renege on those achievements of rationalization that depend on the "decentration of the world," that is, on the division of the mythical world into separable regions or "worlds" which pertain, respectively, to claims to truth, goodness, and beauty. Drawing on the work of Jean Piaget (1896–1980) and George Herbert Mead (1863–1931), whose "ontogenetic" accounts of a child's acquisition of rational capacities he applies to a "phylogenetic" account of the evolution of society, Habermas treats world decentration not merely as a contingent historical event but as an intrinsically rational stage of human development. Provided we are operating in a linguistic community for which world-decentration has taken place, we each recognize that it is rationally incumbent upon us to distinguish between (1) "the" objective world of facts to which we refer when we make truth claims; (2) "our" shared social world of recognized norms to which we appeal when we make moral claims; and (3) for each of us, "my" subjective world of private experiences which I express when I make aesthetic or expressive claims (TCA I 100). To each of these worlds there corresponds a particular class of speech acts: (1) assertions that purport to be true from a third-person perspective; (2) promises or commands that claim to be normatively binding from a second-person perspective; and (3) avowals that purport to be sincere from a first-person perspective.

While defending the process of rationalization that corresponds to world-decentration, Habermas traces the ills of modernization to an institutional failure to develop cultural, societal, and personal "systems" and "subsystems" that would be fully adequate to what is rational in world-decentration itself. More precisely, his analysis turns on an account of the relationship between the action systems that have developed in modernity and the lifeworld which they have come to colonize. The lifeworld comprises the indeterminate set of unthematized (but, in principle, thematizable) background practices and assumptions that inform a shared orientation toward each of the three worlds (or, in the case of a mythical society for whom world-decentration has not taken place, toward the enchanted world) (TCA I 13, 335). Just as there is a kind of rationality proper to each of the three decentered worlds – cognitive-instrumental, normative, and aesthetic – so communicative rationality pertains to the lifeworld (TCA I 70). Communicative rationality represents the shared capacity of members of a speech community to reach consensus through the force of reasons alone. As such, it points toward the limit case of an "ideal speech situation," the regulative ideal of unconstrained rational inquiry in which all members of a community collectively seek agreement without any threat of coercion. Habermas draws in this connection on the American pragmatist Charles Peirce (1839–1914), for whom truth is what would be agreed upon by the members of such a community at the (factually unattainable) end of inquiry. He applies this idea not only to our orientation toward the objective world of facts but toward the social and subjective worlds as well. Thus the three cognitive values of truth, goodness or moral rightness, and beauty or authenticity can all be defined as regulative ideals that would guide processes of consensus-seeking in an ideal speech situation. Conceived in this way, the idea of communicative rationality provides an over-arching framework in terms of which we can conceive the relationship between the lifeworld and the three validity spheres.

As the lifeworld becomes rationalized, it becomes divided into the separable domains of culture, society, and personality (TCA II 138). Such differentiation – the correlate of world decentration – makes it possible to develop separate action systems some of which acquire semi-autonomy. To each action system there corresponds a "steering mechanism" or "steering medium" that, for reasons of efficiency, is capable of coordinating action directly, that is, without having to pass through the normal channels of lifeworld communication (TCA I 342). Such steering media as money (which governs economic action) and power (which governs administrative political action) are intrinsically non-rational, not in the sense that they necessarily by-pass communicative rationality altogether, but in the potentially innocuous sense that they serve as potentially redeemable "proxies" for reasons. However, once they are granted this power, steering media become capable of acquiring a life of their own, increasing the distance of the systems they govern from the lifeworld. The danger is that, instead of merely "mediatizing" the lifeworld, action systems will end up "colonizing" it (TCA II 196). This is what has happened in modernity: communicative interaction has become subordinate to the semi-autonomous demands of system maintenance. For Weber, such "loss of freedom" was an inevitable off-shoot of the rise of capitalism and a bureaucratic political administration. But for Habermas – and here he is closer to Marx – it is a contingent consequence of *"the uncoupling of system and lifeworld"* (TCA II 318). The task of a "critical theory of society" is to diagnose both the systemic "crises" that result from the colonizaton of the lifeworld and the "pathologies" that such crises give rise to in the lifeworld (TCA II 385).

Habermas's assessment of the colonization of the lifeworld implies that the development of semi-independent action systems is not itself intrinsically irrational. Put otherwise, "reification" in the normatively pejorative sense of this term occurs not with the mediatization of the lifeworld but only with its colonization – a distinction that the Marxist tradition has failed to make. Thus in contrast to Horkheimer and Adorno, for whom the ills of modernity were to be blamed on the unchecked triumph of instrumental rationality, Habermas argues that the real problem is that communicative rationality has been subordinated to a "functionalist" rationality whose aim is mere system-maintenance (TCA I 398–9). Corresponding to this circumstance is a tendency to reduce interpersonal relations among agents who ought to coordinate their interests through communicative action to relations among merely self-interested agents who manipulate one another in accordance with the demands of strategic rationality. The goal of consensus is thereby reduced to that of coercion.

An effective critical theory – that is, one capable of reclaiming the entitlement of reasons to guide steering media – must reassert the primacy of communicative rationality over functional reason. This does not mean that all cooperative action should be directly governed by processes of consensus-formation. Such an ideal is neither necessary nor feasible in an age of increased system complexity. Moreover, it is impossible for communicative action to be completely autonomous and self-transparent. The hermeneutic interaction of the members of a shared lifeworld always takes place under conditions of material reproduction that cannot be reduced to communicative interaction. To understand the systemic mechanisms by which the differentiated aspects of the lifeworld – culture, society, and personality – are sustained, it is necessary to supplement an internal, communicative model of understanding the lifeworld with an external, systemic model of the sort developed by the sociologists Talcott Parsons (1902–1979) and Niklas Luhmann (1927–1998) (TCA II 150–1). But, while a merely communicative model of society is guilty of succumbing to "hermeneutic idealism," the one-sided model developed by Parsons and Luhmann is guilty of its inverse, a kind of systemic realism that ends up ignoring the phenomenon of reification altogether. The exaggerated emphasis that systems theory places on functionalist reason is itself an expression of the colonization of the lifeworld.

So long as consensus is achieved by way of rational agreement among the members of a speech community, it remains within the horizon of the lifeworld. But once money and power replace reasons as steering media, consensus tends to be achieved on the basis of mere self-interest or force. Habermas's distinction between these two types of consensus can be likened to Rousseau's distinction between the normatively binding general will and the contingently forged will of all. For an authentic expression of the general will to be achieved, speakers must be able to communicate with each other with a sincere commitment to accepting the force of reasons. If they come to regard one another merely as means to their own selfish ends, communicative interaction is no longer possible; at that point, utterances that invoke norms and express values become mere rhetorical devices for achieving strategic ends. Drawing on the speech act theory of Austin and John Searle (1932–), Habermas contrasts "perlocutionary" acts – utterances made with the strategic intent of manipulating hearers – and "illocutionary" acts in which we make our intentions explicit (TCA I 289).[30] Communicative rationality requires that all speech acts be illocutionary rather than perlocutionary. This principle can be thought of as Habermas's version of Kant's "*transcendental formula* of public right" (a weaker version of the one mentioned above), according to which an action is wrong if its performance is inconsistent with the announcement of its maxim (PW 126).

In many respects, Habermas's attempt to reclaim the communicative integrity of the lifeworld echoes Arendt's call for a reclamation of the public sphere. But unlike Arendt, who equates political emancipation with the liberation of the public sphere from economic action systems, Habermas thinks that it is necessary to incorporate the concern for social welfare within the purview of the public realm. He also thinks that Arendt, like Gadamer, underestimates the need for a critique of ideology. By placing her faith entirely in the public contest of clashing opinions, she overlooks the fact that a genuinely reflective critique of prevailing opinions must itself be informed by robust knowledge claims (P-PP 184). Neither money nor power (in the Arendtian sense of violence) can be excluded from the purview of critical theory, not only because of their tendency to distort speech – to replace reasons as steering media – but because the action systems to which they belong must be regulated from the perspective of the lifeworld. In appealing to the Greek polis as her model, Arendt reverts to a premodern point of view as if the colonization of the lifeworld could be corrected by a repudiation of the economic, juridical, and political subsystems that have developed in modernity. In this respect she succumbs, as did the Marxist tradition from which she otherwise distinguished herself, to a nostalgia for a *less* rational society.

With his theory of the colonization of the lifeworld, Habermas is able to unite a Marxist account of reification with a Weberian appreciation of the intrinsically rational character of modernization, and to substitute for the radical pessimism of Horkheimer and Adorno a vision of how to reactivate the stalled process of Enlightenment. In carrying out this project, he sees himself as returning to the interdisciplinary model of critical theory that was first spelled out by the members of the Frankfurt School in the 1930s. The theory of communicative action is philosophical insofar as it is concerned with rationality in the normative sense, and sociological insofar as it seeks to identify the ways in which structures of rationality have come to be – or failed to be – embodied in concrete cultural, social, and personal practices (TCA I 385–6).

For Habermas, a genuinely critical sociology must dispense with a positivistic conception of social "facts." Positivism, the scientistic view that there are nothing but facts, purports to leave behind the mythical view of the world while at the same time refusing to recognize the force of world-decentration. In so doing, it grants hegemony to the cognitive orientation toward truth and relegates moral and aesthetic claims to pre-rational aspects of the mythical view of the world. Such a point of view is exemplified in behaviorism, which attempts to explain human action exclusively in terms of the observable movements of human bodies, thereby obfuscating the very nature of communicative acts. Because of its narrow point of view, positivism is unable to adopt those hermeneutical and metahermeneutical perspectives that are crucial for diagnosing the communicative pathologies of the lifeworld.

Any attempt either to de-differentiate the three validity spheres or to collapse the distinction between lifeworld and system is regressive (TCA I 240). Positivism represents a quasi-mythical point of view because it reduces the social and subjective worlds to the world of facts. As such it is only one of three structurally possible forms of regression. Another is the quasi-myth of aestheticism, exemplified in the attempt to reduce truth claims and normative claims to expressive claims. This is the error to which Nietzsche and those influenced by him succumb. Nietzsche saw that claims to truth and justice rest on interests that are rooted in the lifeworld. But instead of using this insight as the basis for a critical reflection upon the epistemic and normative import of interests, he accepts the positivistic charge that such interests undermine the cognitive import of truth claims and moral claims (KHI 298). Positivism wielded the specter of psychologism as a way of both preserving truth from contamination and relegating morality and aesthetics to the level of prerationality. Nietzsche turns the tables on positivism by calling attention to its own underlying – and supposedly vitiating – life-interests. He concludes that all purportedly cognitive claims (in the narrow sense of being oriented toward truth) are merely expressive claims, and that all expressive claims rest on underlying interests (KHI 290ff.). This two-fold assessment underwrites his attempt to view science through the lens of art and art through the lens of life. All cognitive claims turn out to be expressions of will to power, that is, expressions of life itself. Thus in place of the scientistic reduction that positivism represents, Nietzsche opts for an aestheticist reduction, one that strips aesthetic claims themselves of all genuine cognitive import. Habermas resists such an aestheticist reduction – which, like Gadamer and Rorty, he traces back to Schiller and the Romantics – on the grounds that it is both irrational and dangerous (PDOM 45ff.).

In "What is Orientation in Thinking?," Kant warned that to forsake the difficult path of critique for the supposedly free inspiration of genius is to court despotism. For although genius "captivates . . . with its authoritative pronouncements and great expectations, and now appears to have set itself up on a throne on which slow and ponderous reason looked so out of place," it leads directly to fanaticism, superstition, unbelief, and a libertinism that threatens civil order, at which point "the authorities intervene" and a despotic form of government arises (PW 248–9). This passage can be read as a prophetic anticipation of the path that German politics actually took from Romanticism to Nazism. Rather than attempting to distinguish a political aesthetics from an aesthetic politics, Habermas cuts the link between the two altogether, returning to a Kantian conception of reason, construed now in terms of his own theory of communicative rationality. Like Kant, he takes the heterogeneity of disparate cognitive spheres to be irreducible – though, unlike Kant, he regards these not as faculties belonging to individual conscious subjects but rather as the differentiated linguistic capacities belonging to the members of a shared lifeworld.

Weber thought that there was an inherent antagonism between the three modern cultural domains of (1) science, (2) law and morality, and (3) art. But Habermas thinks that it is only with the colonization of the lifeworld that the mode of rationality proper to a particular domain threatens to displace the others. There are various ways in which linguistic, cultural, and social links can be forged between the three worlds, giving rise to "complexes" of interwoven validity claims. Moreover, though every validity claim is primarily oriented toward a single world insofar as it is either assertoric or predictive, norm-invoking, or expressive, it implicitly makes reference to all three. Thus, a speaker making a normative claim is both tacitly invoking factual claims that are relevant and expressing her own subjective point of view. Habermas also suggests that any sentence can be converted into an assertoric sentence without loss of meaning, though this convertibility must not be taken as evidence against the specificity of normative or expressive claims. Though it is possible for one of the three validity spheres to gain hegemony over the others – this is what has happened with the rise of positivism in modernity – a fully rational lifeworld will be able to allow for non-pathological translations from one to another.

3.12 Lyotard's assessment of postmodernity

'Tis rigor and not law.
(*The Winter's Tale*, III, ii, 114)

From 1954–1966, the French philosopher Jean-François Lyotard (1924–1998) was a member of *Socialisme ou barbarie*, a group of intellectuals which, like the Frankfurt School, "preserved and refined" the Marxist critique of capitalism (PC 13). When theoretical disagreements within the group led to a schism, Lyotard decided to resign. He had become suspicious of any discourse – be it Marxist or otherwise – that purported to be able to translate all disagreements into its own terms (Per 47ff.). Lyotard's sense of the need to challenge all claims to conceptual hegemony was further strengthened by the apparent insufficiency of orthodox Marxist interpretations of the student and worker protests that took place in France in May 1968. Like many others, he regarded the "events of May" as marking an important historical break: "The crisis that began in May 1968 is not a 'crisis'; it ushers us into a new period of history" (PW-L 41).

In *Libidinal Economy* (*Économie libidinale*, 1974), Lyotard attempts to give expression to the feeling of enthusiasm that the events of May aroused in both spectators and participants. "Give expression" is the right way to put it, because the task of the "libidinal economist" is to record the felt "intensities" or "affects" that circulate on the "ephemeral skin" of the body politic. Marx failed to see that domination is essentially libidinal in character. In order to accommodate this new insight, Lyotard suggests that the critique of political economy must give way to a critique of libidinal economy. Such a critique cannot conform to classical models because the very idea of a critical *theory* is complicitous with social domination: "It is the place of theory that must be vanquished" (LE 105). Thus Lyotard finds himself faced with the paradoxical task of critiquing critique: "the *critique* of religion we rebegin is no longer a critique at all" (LE 6); "we laugh at critique" (LE 95); "May this

supreme effort of thought die, such is our wish as libidinal economists"
(LE 14).

The double bind faced by such an anti-critical critique was thematized by
Kristeva in *Revolution and Poetic Language* – also published in 1974 and
inspired by the events of May – as the textual problem of simultaneously
adopting and subverting the thetic standpoint. But while Kristeva contented herself with a scholarly examination of such revolutionary forms of
writing, Lyotard tries to write an anti-theoretical treatise about his own
writing. Instead of communicating ideas through the use of linguistic signs,
he hopes to convey affects through "tensors": "we quit signs, we enter the
extra-semiotic order of tensors" (LE 50). In 1988, Lyotard characterized the
style of *Libidinal Economy* as "an expression of boisterous despair" akin to
that found in Denis Diderot's (1713–1784) *Rameau's Nephew* – a work that
Kristeva characterizes as refusing "to settle down" (Per 13; STO 135). His
approach was doomed to failure, because "inscribing the passage of intensities directly in the prose itself without any mediation . . . does not allow us
to separate the wheat from the chaff" (Per 13, 15). Separating the wheat
from the chaff is, of course, the critical ideal par excellence. Thus the challenge that Lyotard faced after writing *Libidinal Economy* was to figure out
how to revive the Kantian and Marxist critical heritage while preserving his
own insight into the essentially affective character of the critical enterprise
itself.

The idea that a critique of affects must itself be rooted in the affect of
critique leads Lyotard to reflect on Kant's account of the experience of the
sublime. For Kant, all aesthetic judgments are based on feelings of a certain
kind – specifically, on the pleasurable feelings that attend acts of reflective
judging – rather than on concepts. An aesthetic judgment is both an expression of a feeling and a justification of that feeling, a justification that ultimately rests on the imputation of a shared affective capacity – the *sensus
communis* – to all human beings. Though Kant characterizes all aesthetic
judgments in this way, Lyotard notes that there is an important difference
between the judgment that an object is beautiful and the judgment that an
idea is sublime. Only in aesthetic quarrels about the beautiful does the *sensus
communis* function as a principle of consensus. In the case of the judgment of
the sublime, the more complex feeling of discord between the faculties
attests to a principle of dissensus. Thus if the aim of critique is to resist the
forces by which affects are made to conform to a dominant consensus, the
feeling of the sublime must function as the affect proper to the critical
impulse itself.

In *The Postmodern Condition: a Report on Knowledge* (*La Condition postmoderne:
rapport sur le savoir*, 1979), Lyotard agrees with Habermas that a systems-
theoretic understanding of society is repressive in the sense that it subordinates all human ends to the technocratic demand for performative efficiency,
but he rejects Habermas's proposed solution, namely, a theory of communicative praxis geared toward the legitimation of norms through consensus

(PC 66). Maintaining against Habermas that "consensus does violence to the heterogeneity of language games," Lyotard tries to do justice to such heterogeneity by conceiving of legitimation on the model of "paralogy" (PC xxv, 61). In modernity, scientific discourses were legitimated in one of two ways – either by linking knowledge to the liberation of humanity (a trope associated with the French Revolution) or by raising it to the meta-perspective of speculative spirit (the path taken by Hegel) (PC 31). By contrast, postmodernity is characterized by a skeptical "incredulity" toward these "grand narratives" (PC xxiv). Rather than "mourning" this situation, Lyotard seeks to draw out its practical implications (PC 26). In one way, the failure of the grand narratives plays into the hands of those who would subordinate the heterogeneity of language games to the overarching demand for systemic performativity. But it also opens up the possibility of a proliferation of language games, which Lyotard conceives as "agonistic" in the sense that they promote dissensus rather than consensus (PC 11). Thus, rather than return to a Marxist narrative about the fate of capitalism – a narrative that in its Frankfurt School and Stalinist forms "wavered" between the emancipatory and speculative models – Lyotard wants to accentuate the postmodern tendency toward fragmentation and legitimation by paralogy (PC 36–7). The mistake made by Habermas is to cling instead to "the narrative of emancipation" (PC 60). Habermas's fidelity to the ideal of consensus is rooted in his failure to appreciate "the Kantian sublime," which Lyotard suggests is due to his reactionary "aesthetics . . . of the beautiful" (PC 79). Thus Habermas is implicitly criticized for conceiving of consensus in the same way that Arendt represents the telos of a politics of the beautiful.

In *The Differend: Phrases in Dispute* (*Le différend*, 1983), Lyotard develops his conception of the heterogeneity of language games in terms of the category of "genres of discourse." Every discursive genre has various subject positions, such as addressor, addressee, and referent. By treating subjectivity as a function of such genres, Lyotard wants "to refute the prejudice . . . that there is 'man,' that there is 'language,' that the former makes use of the latter for his own ends" (DPID xiii). What enables heterogeneous genres to enter into conflict with one another is their ability to appropriate individual "sentences" or "phrases." An isolated sentence such as "Open the door" – a prescriptive utterance – can be "linked" onto by sentences belonging to any of an indefinite number of genres, each of which thereby subjects it to its own juridical regime (DPID 42). When two sentences belonging to the same genre dispute each other, a "litigation" arises, with each of two parties claiming "damages" (DPID xi). In such cases, it is in principle possible to "render justice" to both claimants. By contrast, when two sentences belonging to different genres dispute each other, a "differend" results (DPID xi). In such cases, it is impossible to do justice to both sides. The best – or worst – we can do is to settle the dispute in accordance with the legitimation criteria of one of the two genres. The "party" represented by a sentence belonging to the excluded genre is then said to suffer a "wrong." Though differends are "symmetrical" to the extent that each party is equally unable to express its claim in the other's language, they become essentially "asymmetrical" when a dominant language decides the issue: "I would like to call a *differend* . . . the case where the plaintiff is divested of the means to argue and becomes for that reason a victim" (DPID 9).

Because differends are incapable of being resolved without committing a wrong against one of the two parties, there is no overarching Kantian-style tribunal that could adjudicate them. Even when conceived only as a regulative ideal (as in Arendt's conception of the public sphere or Habermas's conception of the ideal speech situation) such a tribunal will inevitably reduce differends – which cut across discursive genres – to internal disagreements within a single genre. Thus it is not because we fall short of an ideal speech situation that differends exist, but because of the irreducible heterogeneity of discursive genres.

Kant introduced the concept of reflective judgments as a way of overcoming the heterogeneity between two different types of determining judgments, namely, the cognitive and the moral. Following Levinas, Lyotard argues that descriptive statements about the world are not only different in kind from morally obliging prescriptives, but that it is impossible to translate the one into the other. To "hear" the categorical imperative is to be constituted as the addressee of a "You ought" (DPID 121). Such a subject position is completely different from that of the addressor of the statement "I am obliged" or "I am able to" (DPID 122). Though my awareness of being obliged seems to sanction the shift from the first statement to the second, Lyotard points out that cognitive statements can pertain only to the realm of phenomena, in which it is impossible for a subject to be morally obliged. This is why Kant insists on the difference between membership in the kingdom of nature and membership in the kingdom of ends. But Lyotard goes one step further than Kant, namely, by insisting that any attempt to thematize one's condition as a morally obliged subject – that is, to "translate" the "You ought" into the cognitive "I am obliged" – cannot but undermine the force of the moral prescriptive.

Kant's inability to "bridge the gulf" separating the subject of cognition from the subject of moral obligation is attested to in his account of the feeling of the sublime, which for Lyotard bears witness to the radical incompatibility of the cognitive and moral points of view. The subject who says of a moral idea, "This is sublime," indicates thereby the impossibility of exhibiting the "You ought" in a sensible (i.e., cognizable) intuition. Both the pain that arises from the fact that reason requires the imagination to do something that it cannot, and the pleasure that results from the awareness of the impossibility of effecting this "passage," bear witness to a differend between the faculties. In characterizing as sublime the biblical prohibition against graven images, Kant attests to this differend, resisting not only the idolatry of graven images but the fanaticism that would result from "sacrificing" the imagination on the alter of "holy law" (LOAS 189). Thus, in contrast to Deleuze, for whom Kant subordinated the felt discord between the faculties to the harmonious feeling of accord as this is experienced in the feeling of the beautiful, Lyotard suggests, in *Lessons on the Analytic of the Sublime* (*Leçons sur l'analytique du sublime*, 1991), that Kant remains faithful to a facultative heterogeneity which only "promises a subject," and that for this reason "it is very difficult to classify Kantism among philosophies of the subject" (LOAS 20, 146).

Each of the Kantian faculties can be thought of as a distinct "genre" that gives voice to a unique kind of sentence or phrase. Sensibility is the faculty of receiving "sentences" that are "spoken" in the quasi-language of "matter"; it responds to these by giving utterance to sentences – the "syntheses of apprehension" – in the quasi-language of "space-time" (DPID 62). By characterizing both the raw sensible manifold and synthesized intuitions as sentences, Lyotard deliberately extends the concept of a sentence or phrase to refer to any sort of event whatsoever, allowing the heterogeneity of faculties to provide a paradigm of the incommensurability of discursive genres. Thus the conflict between descriptives uttered by the understanding and prescriptives uttered by practical reason represents only one of an indefinite number of conflicts. In addition to descriptives and prescriptives, Lyotard calls attention to interrogative, rhetorical, poetic, and other genres, each of which defines its own stakes and legitimation criteria. The "ineffability" of "sentences" belonging to non-discursive genres – notably those expressing affects – is itself a sign of the radical incompatibility of genres.

Marx detected a differend in the conflict between those who benefit from a capitalist mode of production and those who are exploited by it. Those capable of buying wage labor and of extracting its surplus value "speak" the language of capital in that they describe the contractual relations between buyers and sellers of wage labor as ones freely entered into by both parties. By contrast, those forced to sell their wage labor "speak" the language of exploitation, defining the relation between buyers and sellers as one that is based on coercion. It is impossible for those who speak the language of the exploited to express their claim in the language of capital, because the latter translates statements about exploitation into statements about contractual exchange. The "alienation" of wage-labor can therefore be characterized as the differend that condemns workers not only to suffering but to silence. Marx's insistence on the need for praxis rather than mere theory – and for revolutionary struggle rather than piecemeal reform – reflects his awareness that the differend between workers and capitalists can only be resolved through conflict, through a "resolution" that will inevitably appear to be "violent" and "unjust" to one of the two sides.

While Lyotard accepts Marx's critique of the language of wage labor, he rejects the idea of the proletariat as a universal historical subject capable of resolving all differends. Like Arendt, he suggests that Marx overlooked the importance of political conflict. Arendt also criticized Hegelian-style metanarratives, emphasizing instead the irreducible plurality and open-endedness of the narratives that we live. Analogously, Lyotard calls attention to the multiplicity and incompletability of "little narratives": "The history of the world cannot pass a last judgment. It is made out of judged judgments" (PC 60; DPID 8). But Lyotard disagrees with Arendt about the nature of political conflict. For Arendt, political discourse remains oriented toward the *sensus communis*. But differends are conflicts that can only be sustained in light of an irreducible element of "dissensus" (Per 44). Arendt's reduction of politics to the clash of opinions would reduce differends to mere litigations. Moreover, her account of the Kantian *sensus communis* is "sociologizing and anthropologizing" (LOAS 18). For Lyotard, politics is not a particular genre of discourse but the underlying condition of heterogeneity among conflicting genres: "Politics . . . is the threat of the differend. It is not a genre, it is the multiplicity of genres" (DPID 138). In contrast to Arendt, he regards founding acts not as utterances made by autonomous subjects who commit themselves to mutual promises, but as "sentences" that constitute their addressors and addressees *as* mutually promising subjects. Benjamin is right to see an irreducible element of violence in founding acts, though this is less a function of the arbitrariness of a new "beginning" than of the heterogeneity of the "phrase regimens" or genres that the "We" attempts to fuse. As an attempt to forge a "dynamic synthesis" (in the Kantian sense) between the empirical reality of the French nation (the rights of citizens) and the rational idea of humanity (the rights of man), the Declaration of the Rights of Man represents an act of "subreption" by which the collective addressee of a prescriptive ("You ought") identifies itself with the "We" qua addressor of prescriptives ("We can") (DPID 145ff.).

For Kant, revolutionary acts were unjust because they had to be judged from the standpoint of the regime that they would seek to overthrow – despite the fact that these same deeds would appear just from the standpoint of the new regime if they were to succeed. Thus he resolved a differend by interpreting the utterances of one party in terms of that of the other. Arendt notes the limited character of Kant's experience with political action, and criticizes him for confusing a revolution with a coup-d'état (LKPP 60). Kant's peculiar response to the French Revolution – that of disinterested enthusiasm – is echoed in one of Lyotard's examples of the different ways in which it is possible to link on to a phrase: "the officer cries *Avanti!* and leaps up out of the trench; moved, the soldiers cry *Bravo!* but don't budge" (DPID 30). Like the soldiers, Kant cries *Bravo!* to the French Revolutionaries' *Avanti!* In effect, he remains bound to the mast like Adorno's Odysseus, a mere spectator without the "least intention" of budging. Though Lyotard shares Kant's desire to distinguish enthusiasm from fanaticism, what he affirms in the feeling of the sublime is not the difference between the standpoints of spectator and actor but the affective (or libidinal) correlate of a moral respect for differends.

At the very beginning of *The Differend*, Lyotard calls attention to the impossibility of convincing a Holocaust-denier that the Holocaust ever happened. If only a witness actually killed in a gas chamber could testify to the fact that the Nazis killed Jews in gas chambers, then the event to which the name "Auschwitz" refers is one that can never be attested to. The "case" of "Auschwitz" is not a mere example for Lyotard (DPID 88). Like Adorno, whose analysis of the problem of thinking "after Auschwitz" he invokes, Lyotard treats the name "Auschwitz" as referring to an entirely unprecedented event: "with Auschwitz, something new has happened in history (which can only be a sign and not a fact)" (DPID 57). By referring to Auschwitz as a "sign," Lyotard deliberately borrows the very word that Kant had used in referring to the enthusiasm felt by those who witnessed the French Revolution. For Kant, this "unforgettable" enthusiasm provided a kind of affective proof of the moral progress of humanity. Lyotard asks whether it is possible for "we who hardly hope in the Kantian sense" to treat a very different sort of sublime feeling – the feeling of despair in the face of another sort of unforgettable event – as if it were itself, paradoxically, the basis for something like hope (LOAS 55). This is a question very close to one raised by Adorno, who in effect had asked if a despairing poetry could speak the language of hope. Echoing Adorno, Lyotard asks, "Would a vigorously melancholic humanity be sufficient thereby to supply the proof that it is 'progressing toward the better?'" (DPID 179).

If "Auschwitz" is the name of an unspeakable event, it is in a certain sense a non-name, or at any rate a name to which no definite description could attach itself, but only an affect: "It is not a concept that results from 'Auschwitz,' but a feeling . . ., an impossible phrase, one that would link the SS phrase onto the deportee's phrase, or vice-versa" (DPID 104). So radically heterogeneous is the language of the SS and the language of those killed in the gas chambers that "there is not even a differend. . . . There is no *Is it happening?* It happened" (DPID 106). Thus in the name "Auschwitz" Lyotard asks us to hear an appeal so ineffable that it could not even be voiced. Something comparable is at work in the experience of obligation in general, that is, in the experience of being summoned by a prescriptive phrase. If the obliging phrase is, so to speak, "minimal" – almost ineffable or even "empty" in the sense that the categorical imperative is without content – then the experience of obligation will be a feeling of something that cannot be conceptualized. Like Kant, Lyotard associates this feeling with the Judaic experience of being summoned by an unpresentable divine Law, and he suggests that the Nazi "Final Solution" can be thought of as an attempt to eradicate precisely this feeling: "The Final Solution was the project of exterminating the (involuntary) witnesses to this forgotten event and of having done with the unpresentable affect once and for all" (PW-L 143).

After the war, Heidegger publicly referred to the Holocaust only once, likening the production of corpses in gas chambers to the production of food in agribusiness. Perhaps Heidegger thought that his silence could be explained by a statement in *Being and Time*, that "the person who keeps silent can 'make one understand' . . . more authentically than the person who is never short of words" (BAT 208). But Lyotard suggests that Heidegger's silence represents an attempt to forget the feeling proper to the experience of the sublime, serving thereby as a kind of anaesthetic: "the Forgotten is not (only) Being, but the Law" (PW-L 147). This suggests that wonder at the sheer fact of being is paid for by an obliviousness to the fact of trauma.[31] In siding with Levinas against Heidegger, Lyotard is not trying to speak on behalf of those who cannot – such, he believes with Deleuze and Foucault, would be another kind of violence – but to give voice to the inexpressibility of that which cannot express itself. Only by attesting to the inexpressible might it still – after Auschwitz – be morally permissible to hope on behalf of humanity. To represent political discourse on the model of quarrels about taste is to construe obligation in terms of the free exchange of opinions, and hope as the community's shared orientation toward the future. By contrast, to represent political discourse on the model of the experience of the sublime is to construe obligation as the paradoxical gift of heteronomy, and hope as predicated upon the commemoration of an unsharable past. Lyotard detects "an anticipation of the postmodern" in Adorno insofar as he attests to an experience of the incommensurable, that is, an experience of whatever resists being transformed into exchange value (PW-L 28).

Each of Habermas's three validity spheres – cognitive, moral, and aesthetic – represents a distinct discursive genre with its own criteria of legitimation. For Habermas, it was possible to negotiate between these different domains from the meta-level perspective of a shared lifeworld. But for Lyotard, the impossibility of translating claims that belong to one genre into those that belong to another attests to the fact that no such common ground exists. World-decentration – or genre decentration – leaves us with an unremitting competition between domains that can only be crossed through the use of force. Put otherwise, world-decentration does not only make world conflation *possible*; it makes it *unavoidable*, for there is no "critical" point of view that would exist outside one of the competing genres. On the contrary, there are as many critical projects as there are types of rationality. This is why Kant found it necessary to carry out three separate critiques, one cognitive-instrumental, one normative, and one aesthetic. However, Kant – like Habermas – still thought that it was possible to reconcile these several points of view. The task of Kant's third *Critique* – his critique of aesthetic rationality – is to "bridge" the other two. But according to Lyotard, there is no non-violent way of accomplishing this task – a fact that is attested to in the feeling of the sublime. To the extent that Kant remains true to this feeling, the third *Critique* can be read not as bridging the cognitive–instrumental and normative points of view but rather as sustaining the differend between them. Only in this way is it possible to resist (two different kinds of) world conflation.

Like Kant, Habermas also tries to avoid the temptation of world conflation. On the one hand, he criticizes the positivists for reducing everything to the cognitive–instrumental point of view; on the other, he criticizes thinkers such as Nietzsche and Adorno for reducing everything to an aesthetic point of view. But the question that Lyotard poses is whether either Kant or Habermas can prevent world conflation from a neutral point of view, or whether they can only do so from the perspective of another validity sphere. Kant only manages to keep the cognitive–instrumental and normative worlds apart by adopting an aesthetic point of view. Analogously, Habermas avoids the positivistic and aestheticist conflations only insofar as he tacitly adopts a normative point of view. In other words, the entire theory of communicative action – though it claims to be articulated from the perspective of the shared lifeworld – is arguably carried out from the perspective of one of the three world-perspectives. To be sure, Habermas insists on the integrity of each of the three validity spheres. But he is articulating this defense from the perspective of the world of norms. That this is so can be seen from the fact that he finds it necessary to trade off two apparently distinct senses of normativity. On the one hand, he reserves the term "norm" to refer to the object of a validity claim in the second (moral–juridical) world. Yet at the same time, he treats *all* validity claims – including both the factual/predictive and the expressive – as normative in the sense that they rest on reasons.

This double sense of normativity plagues all post-Kantian attempts to revive the critical project. But this is just to raise the possibility – with Nietzsche – that the Socratic conception of rationality *as* normative is an intrinsically moral notion. Habermas's fundamental distinction between consensus based on mere force and consensus achieved through the force of reasons is the topic of the first book of Plato's *Republic*. According to Thrasymachus, justice is the advantage of the stronger. This implies that any consensus is ultimately based on force. Socrates tries to show Thrasymachus that he is wrong by reaching rational consensus with him, that is, by allowing the force of reasons alone to guide their dialogue. But it is noteworthy that, at a certain point in the dialogue, Thrasymachus explicitly says that henceforth his "yes/no" responses to Socrates's questions will not be sincere. He agrees to play along with Socrates so as to give the impression of reaching consensus and not spoil the party. In announcing this strategy, Thrasymachus does something that Habermas claims is self-contradictory: he makes public his perlocutionary intent. Such an announcement violates Habermas's equivalent of Kant's "*transcendental formula* of public right" according to which "All actions affecting the rights of other human beings are wrong if their maxim is not compatible with their being made public" (PW 126). By sincerely confessing that he will merely give the appearance of reaching consensus with Socrates, Thrasymachus seeks to show that Socratic consensus is not the opposite of the advantage of the stronger but an example of it. The supposed force of better reasons cannot be extricated from an effect of domination.

The usual reading of Thrasymachus – that is, the Platonic reading – accuses him of repudiating all norms and of not reasoning in good faith. But a Lyotardian restatement of Thrasymachus' position could construe the assertion that justice is the advantage of the stronger as a way of bearing witness to the violence done to the weaker party. At a certain point in every argument the process of justifying claims must eventually trail off. It is at this point that the arbitrariness of claim-making is revealed. What Habermas wants to hold out for is the idea that the activity of reason-giving, even if it can be continued indefinitely, must be guided by the regulative idea of a first principle that would not itself stand in need of justification. The question is whether we should regard the idea of first principles as a rhetorical device or as a legitimate presumption.

This question can be framed as an antinomy. The thesis would say that chains of arguments can be traced back to first principles, while the antithesis would deny this. This is not the debate between Habermas and Lyotard. Rather, their debate is whether this antinomy is like Kant's mathematical antinomies in that both sides are false, or like the dynamical antinomies in that both sides can be true. That is, for Lyotard, it is false to say that we must presuppose first principles, even though it is also false to think that we can do without them. But for Habermas, it is true that we must presuppose first principles even though it is also true that we will never reach them. The difference is that Lyotard's solution leaves us with an irreducibly agonistic conception of discourse, while Habermas's solution serves as the basis for a moral conception of discourse because it allows the scales to tip in favor of the thesis – that is, for the presumption that there are first principles – just as Kant allowed the interests of practical reason to tip the scales in favor of the existence of freedom and a necessary being.

To take seriously Thrasymachus or Nietzsche's critique of Socrates is to ask if normativity in the broad sense is an expression of normativity in the narrow sense. If so, then the Socratic conception of rational discourse presupposes a third kind of reductionism that Habermas does not explicitly thematize, one that stands between the scientistic and the aestheticist. The same reduction is made by Kant, who despite his separation of the respective claims of speculative reason, practical reason, and reflective judgment, subordinates all of reason's interests to the moral. Lyotard suggests that to the extent that Habermas implicitly follows Kant in this regard, he does not take world decentration far enough. A truly radical critical theory must forsake the moral search for consensus and instead attest to the political fact of dissensus. But since the force of this "must" – even if only felt – remains for Lyotard no less ethical than it does for Levinas and Kant, his critique of Habermas cannot escape the very problem to which he himself calls attention. Like Rameau's nephew, he refuses to settle down in the very moral discourse that continues to motivate his own writing.

3.13   Žižek's fidelity to the messianic promise of the Russian Revolution

I'll so offend, to make offense a skill,
Redeeming time when men think least I will.
(*The First Part of Henry the Fourth*,
I, ii, 216–17)

Instead of merely bearing witness to the irreducibility of differends, the Slovenian philosopher, Slavoj Žižek (1949–), shares Benjamin's hope for a revolutionary act capable of retroactively redeeming past wrongs. Like Habermas, Žižek emphasizes the continuity between psychoanalysis and critical theory, but instead of characterizing psychoanalysis as a meta-hermeneutics whose aim is to disclose the speech pathologies that distort the lifeworld, he takes it to reveal the ineliminable "fundamental antagonisms" that make the ideal speech situation unattainable in principle. Žižek agrees with Habermas that human beings only become subjects by being introduced into a speech community, but he interprets this fact not in terms of Habermas's account of the priority of communicative rationality over subject-centered rationality, but in terms of Lacan's view of the subject as irremediably wedded to a symptomatic object of enjoyment.

In *The Sublime Object of Ideology* (1989), Žižek criticizes Habermas for misconstruing Freud's account of symptom-formation in general and of the dreamwork in particular (SOI 13). For Freud, there are two levels of dream interpretation. The first consists in laying bare the latent (preconscious) thought that is expressed in the manifest content of a dream. This dimension of interpretation is hermeneutical (or metahermeneutical) in character. But discerning the latent dream thought is only a preliminary step. The second, more crucial, work of analysis consists in attempting to identify the unconscious "kernel" that determines the form in which the dreamwork has translated the latent thought into the dream's manifest content. This kernel is a strictly meaningless element that, as such, resists hermeneutical (or even metahermeneutical) interpretation. And yet it is precisely this non-semantic element around which everything in the dream ultimately turns. By overlooking it, Habermas reduces the work of analysis to that of simply fathoming the symbolic meaning of imaginary symptoms (MOE 26–7). Žižek objects that this represents a misunderstanding of the nature of symptoms. Lacan defined the subject as what one signifier represents for another signifier. But according to Žižek, this is only a preliminary thesis, one that corresponds to Althusser's conception of interpellation. Understood in these terms, a symptom is just an imaginary and symbolic formation that could be dissolved through its interpretation. But the fact that mere interpretation fails to make symptoms disappear is a sign that there is something more in them, that subjects are unwilling or unable to "give up" their symptoms (SOI 74). In his late work, Lacan equated the subject with its symptom (or "sinthome") (SOI 75). Understood in these terms, a subject is not simply what one signifier *represents* for another; it is what one signifier (the imaginary "ideal ego") *enjoys* for another (the symbolic "ego ideal").

For Žižek, the properly ideological level of experience is to be located not in a subject's symptom per se but in the underlying "fundamental fantasy" that structures it. Fantasy is to a symptom what the dream-work is to a dream: it structures the subject's enjoyment. For Freud, psychoanalysis was first and foremost a way of interpreting the psychic lives of individual subjects; only later did he try to expand its purview to account for social phenomena such as group formation and the development of culture. Taking his cue from Lacan's suggestion that it was Marx and not Freud who first discovered the psychoanalytic conception of a symptom, Žižek inverts this relationship: for him, psychoanalysis is first and foremost a way of critiquing ideology – and only for this reason is it useful in making sense of the psychic lives of individuals (SOI 11). The members of the Frankfurt School failed to carry out this inversion, basing their critique of fascism on "the personality structure" of fascists rather than on an analysis of fascist ideology (MOE 21). In correcting for this shortcoming, Žižek fulfills Althusser's prediction that psychoanalysis would eventually be absorbed by Marxism – though he claims that Althusser failed to appreciate the role played by fantasy in ideological formations.

For Žižek, as for Althusser, ideology is not a set of subjectively held beliefs that obscure an underlying factual reality, but something that is embodied in reality itself. In support of this idea, Althusser drew on the Pascalian idea that to acquire faith one must act as if one already had faith (LAP 168–9). For Žižek, the point is that ideological beliefs are located not "in the heads" of agents but in their practices, in what they actually *do* rather than in what they subjectively *think* they do (SOI 36ff.). To act "as if" one subjectively believed is to act on the basis of an unconscious belief. For Lacan the unconscious is "extimate" in the sense that it exists outside of consciousness but exhibits the form of thought.

In commodity fetishism, everyone subjectively "knows" that money is just an arbitrary symbolic medium for representing value, but objectively we act as if we did not know this. Thus the ideological fantasy lies in our (objective) belief that money is intrinsically valuable. Marx discovered the symptom precisely here. To say that the apparently meaningless value of a commodity is to be explained by its being an embodiment of surplus value is equivalent to discerning the latent thought that finds expression in the manifest content of a dream. But the real mystery, according to Marx, lies with the commodity form itself, that is, with the manner in which surplus value finds expression in the commodity (SOI 14–15). In a feudalist economy, the underlying fantasy is based on a fetishization of social relations. Subjectively, everyone is well aware that a king is a king only insofar as he is recognized as such, but "objectively," in their practices, they act as if he were a king because of some intrinsic property. Žižek argues that there is an important structural relationship between these two forms of fetishism. In one, we fetishize commodities but not persons; in the other we fetishize persons rather than commodities (SOI 25–6). Either way, our experience of the world is ideological at the level of practice rather than at the level of subjective attitudes.

Žižek distinguishes between two different levels of the process by which we become interpellated in ideology. The first level is that recognized by Althusser. Every ideology is grounded in a single, meaningless "master signifier" in relation to which all other signifiers "retroactively" find their meaning. In the ideology of anti-Semitism, for example, the signifier "Jew" functions as a point of (negative) identification that gives meaning to an otherwise meaningless social world. To be interpellated into an ideology such as anti-Semitism is to undergo both imaginary and symbolic identification. At the imaginary level, one acquires an ideal ego that stands in relation to the ego ideal that serves as the point of symbolic identification. In effect, the interpellated subject succumbs to two dialectical illusions, one pertaining to its supposed existence as a substantial subject and the other to the supposed existence of the Other (such as God or Nation) from whom the interpellating call seems to come. The second dimension of interpellation involves the subject's traumatic encounter with the unfathomable desire of the interpellating Other. To the question, *"Che vuoi?"* or "What do you want?," the subject experiences an anxiety that can be likened to the pain felt in the experience of the sublime. Through fantasy, the subject protects itself from the abyss of the Other's desire (SOI 110ff.).

Once again Žižek appeals to the example of anti-Semitism, but this time with a twist. In order to understand its deep structure, it is necessary to recognize that anti-Semitism is not merely one of many examples of an ideological fantasy; it is the exemplary form of an ideological fantasy in general. This is because Judaism represents the purest experience of the *"Che vuoi?"* itself. Not only does the Jewish people take itself to be interpellated by God as "the chosen people," but they do so with the added proviso that they are prohibited from constructing a fantasy – a graven image – that would explain what it means to be chosen, that would protect them from this traumatic experience (SOI 115). The exemplary figure here is that of Abraham, summoned to sacrifice Isaac on Mount Moriah. Abraham is implicitly prohibited from asking, "Why?" or, worse, from imagining a fantasy that would justify this demand. The fact that he cannot ask why he should do what God commands can be explained by the fact that the imperative is categorical rather than hypothetical. Kant claimed that there is nothing more sublime in Jewish law than its prohibition against graven images. In this respect there is a close homology between Abraham and Kant. But it was Kierkegaard who called attention to another dimension of Abraham's situation. To accept the mandate that God has given him, Abraham must carry out a "teleological suspension of the ethical." In other words, he must perform an act that from the standpoint of the moral law can only appear as "diabolically evil." For Žižek, Abraham's gesture is equivalent to that of Antigone, who defies Creon not because of some "pathological" inclination such as affection for her brother but because of her allegiance to an unspeakable command that comes from the very place of the sublime itself, the place of the Kantian Thing. He concludes that just as the beautiful is a symbol of the good, so the sublime is a symbol of evil (TWTN 47).[32] In the hubris of Abraham and Antigone we encounter the purest possible response to the "*Che vuoi?*" of the Other.

What then is anti-Semitism? For Žižek, it is a way in which those who are not interpellated as Jews protect themselves from being interpellated as Jews; in other words, anti-Semitism protects anti-Semites from the traumatic force of the encounter with the transcendent voice of the Other. In this way, they protect themselves from a direct experience of the sublime (much as Lyotard thought that Heidegger protected himself). By building a fantasy around the figure of the Jew, the anti-Semite puts the "empirical" body of the Jew in the place of the Other. The Jew thereby functions as a "sublime body," an empirical object raised (here negatively) to what Lacan called the "dignity of the Thing." Every ideology is structured around such a sublime object, which can function as the target of either negative or positive transference. But anti-Semitism is an "exemplary" ideology in that it puts the figure of the Jew – that is, of the one who, prima facie, resists ideological fantasy – in this place.

Given this analysis – which seems to divide the entire world into Jews and anti-Semites – the Judaic prohibition of graven images would appear to be the anti-ideological stance par excellence. But Žižek suggests that ideology can only be resisted not by lingering in the encounter with the traumatic "*Che vuoi?*" – this is arguably the stance taken by Lyotard – but by recognizing the existence of a "lack" in the interpellating Other itself. The dialectical movement whereby the subject progresses from an encounter with the terrifying "*Che vuoi?*" to a fantasy and then to its traversal corresponds for Žižek to the passage from Judaism to Christianity as Hegel conceived it. For Hegel, the first stage of Christian belief is the properly "fantasmatic" level at which one accepts that Christ is God, but this must be superceded through the traversal by which one accepts the death of Christ as the mark of the "incompleteness" of God. Just as Dorothy must discover not that there is no Wizard of Oz but that he is himself a profoundly needy being, so for Žižek the ultimate lesson of Christianity is that the enigmatic God of Abraham is an enigma to Himself (DSST 56–7).

Just as Žižek's construal of Christianity owes much to his reading of Schelling, so his analysis of the relationship between Judaism and Christianity is guided by his understanding of the difference between Kant and Hegel. Following Hegel, Žižek suggests that, although Kant rejects the ethical stance of Abraham, he adheres to a fundamentally Judaic construal of the relationship between the human and the divine. This can be seen not only in his account of the sublimity of the moral law, but in his allegorical construal of the incarnation of Christ. These views attest to the gap separating the phenomenal realm of appearances from the hidden realm of things in themselves. For Hegel, the very idea of the thing in itself is an empty concept that thought arrives at by abstracting from all of the phenomenal properties of a thing. But according to Žižek, Hegel accepts the Kantian distinction between the receptivity of sensibility and the spontaneity of the understanding. On this reading, absolute knowing, the unity of being and thought, represents not the elimination of the intuition/concept dualism but the identification of the subject with the very gap separating the two. Žižek takes this to be the gap separating the Lacanian real from symbolized reality. Thus Hegel's *Phenomenology* culminates not in the apotheosis of a narcissistic subject but in the utter destitution of a subject who has "traversed" all possible fantasies. This is why Hegel's text culminates with its reference to the Golgotha of spirit. For Žižek, to accept the crucifixion of Christ is to accept the fact of castration. This implies three things: first, that there is no soul (the subject is "split"); second, that there is no God ("the big Other does not exist," or exists only as "split"); third, that there *is* freedom, but only for the split (rather than the noumenal) subject.

Having "traversed" the fantasies of dogmatic metaphysics, Kant should have concluded that the very idea of the thing in itself was a fantasmatic way of "filling out" the problematic concept of the transcendental object = x, that which remains inassimilable to symbolically structured reality. Žižek emphasizes the Lacanian claim that there is an inassimilable real only insofar as there is a symbolic structuring of reality. This idea can be illustrated in terms of the history of philosophical idealism. In the metaphysical idealism of George Berkeley (1685–1753), the only things that exist are God, created souls or minds, and the messages (ideas) that minds receive from God. In Kant's transcendental idealism, by contrast, the only things that we can be certain of are the "messages" (i.e., appearances), but the existence of the soul and God is no longer certain. Finally, in the "absolute idealism" of Hegel – at least as Žižek interprets it – there is nothing but the "gap" that results from the discovery that any messages which the subject "receives" in the real are those which it has sent itself. To reach the standpoint of absolute knowing is to suspend all of the imaginary fantasies that suture the real to the symbolic.

For Habermas, world-decentration was rooted in the communicative experience of the lifeworld, which served as a quasi-transcendental frame through which subjects smoothly interrelate to objective reality, social norms, and private experiences. For Žižek, the three radically decentered "worlds" or regions discerned by Lacan – the real, the symbolic, and the imaginary – function as conditions for the possibility of the lifeworld itself. The communicative experience of the lifeworld is always structured by an ideological fantasy through whose lens we encounter facts, norms, and private experiences. Hence to complete the project of modernity it is not enough to reclaim the lifeworld; one must "traverse" its underlying fantasy.

Like Habermas, Žižek likens psychoanalysis to Hegelian reflection, but for entirely different reasons. For Habermas, the aim of analysis is not absolute knowing but the self-fulfillment and self-realization of subjects who thereby acquire social (symbolic) and personal (imaginary) identities. But for Žižek, the aim of analysis is, precisely, absolute knowing conceived as the completion of world decentration. This situation leaves the subject not comfortably situated within a fantasmatically structured lifeworld that mediates its triple relationship to reality, a symbolic identity and an imaginary personality, but face to face with the gap separating reality from the real. By stripping the subject of its customary fantasmatic support, analysis disrupts its social identity and challenges its personality.

Žižek claims that Habermas overlooks the crucial dimension of the Lacanian real, the unfathomable Thing confronted by Abraham and Antigone: "if there is no Thing to underpin our everyday symbolically regulated exchange with others, we find ourselves in a Habermasian 'flat' aseptic universe in which subjects are deprived of their *hubris* of excessive passion, reduced to lifeless pawns in the regulated game of communication" (DSST 165). This passage recalls Nietzsche's critique of the "pale" bourgeois subject who "seeks only honesty, truth, freedom from illusions, and protection from the onslaughts of things which might distract him" (OTL 153). But Žižek is ambivalent about the diabolical evil at work in the ethical act of Abraham and Antigone. Though the act of hubris can represent the "highest" ethical stance, it can also give rise to "the very worst." (Imagine an Adolf Eichmann who instead of claiming to have done his duty remained silent on the witness stand, thereby implying that his actions were morally equivalent to those of Abraham and Antigone.) Žižek notes that Antigone – "the anti-Habermasian *par excellence*" – succumbs to another kind of world conflation (DSST 158). Whereas Habermas occludes the dimension of the real, she eliminates the symbolic order. The third type of foreclosure, characterized by the occlusion of the imaginary, is represented for Žižek in the psychosis of Schreber (DSST 165). But it is also evidenced in Schelling, whose account of creation – God created the world because of a fundamental lack that "caused" him to do it – is central to Žižek's conception of the "Christian legacy." Just as Žižek reads Hegel as radicalizing Kant's transcendental philosophy, so Žižek can be read as radicalizing Habermas's theory of communicative action by calling attention to the "fundamental 'alienation'" to which world-decentration attests (LA 142). Like Althusser, Habermas fails to capture the role played by enjoyment in the subject's interpellation into ideological fantasy. To borrow a term from John McDowell, subjectivization is reduced for Habermas to a "frictionless" process by which individuals merely acquire a social (symbolic) identity and a private (imaginary) personality. The encounter with the "real" of enjoyment never takes place.

In *Looking Awry: an Introduction to Jacques Lacan through Popular Culture* (1991), Žižek credits Benjamin with the "theoretically productive and subversive procedure" of "reading . . . the highest spiritual products of a culture alongside its common, prosaic, worldly products" (LA vii). In keeping with Žižek's penchant for finding critical theoretical insights in products of the culture industry, his response to Habermas can be approached by considering Tom Shadyac's 1997 Hollywood film, *Liar Liar*. Jim Carrey plays a lawyer named Fletcher Reede who represents the epitome of what for Habermas has gone wrong in modernity, notably in the failure of legal institutions to fill the void created by the retreat of traditional conceptions of justice and in the rise of strategic rationality in interpersonal relations. Fletcher manipulates the law to help criminals escape conviction – Habermas, following Hegel, views the conviction and punishment of criminals as a way of achieving "reconciliation" of the violated social order (KHI 56–7) – and in so doing he is forced to lie constantly, treating everyone else, including his ex-wife Audrey and his son Max, as mere means to instrumental ends. When Fletcher skips Max's birthday party because he is having sex with one of his firm's partners – significantly not because he enjoys it, but solely to try to make partner himself – we know that he has reached the Weberian nadir represented by the loss of an "ethic of conviction." Deeply hurt by his father's absence, Max makes a wish that Fletcher will be unable to tell a single lie for an entire day. Predictably, the wish comes true, and most of the film is devoted to showing how Fletcher is affected by suddenly being forced to act as if he inhabited Habermas's ideal speech situation. At first this causes him tremendous inconvenience and embarrassment; in his capacity as a cynical lawyer he desperately needs to dissemble in court but suddenly cannot. But eventually he discovers that it is better not to lie, that his family is more important than his career, that money can't buy happiness, and so on. He can now *voluntarily* assume the principled and authentic persona that Max's magical wish had temporarily forced upon him. At the end of the film Fletcher is reunited with Audrey and Max not because the world has become "re-enchanted" – the second time Max makes a birthday wish it is only for a consumer good (roller blades), not for the "utopian" reconciliation of his parents – but because the disenchanted world has become more rational.

At the level of its "manifest content," *Liar Liar* could be said to exemplify Habermas's account of the need to critique the distorted speech of a pathological lifeworld. Fletcher gives expression to this distortion when he tells Max, "I have to lie. Everybody lies." We can detect the key moment of his ethical awakening in the transition between two different speech acts. First, after cutting off another driver, who asks him, "What's your problem, schmuck?" Fletcher responds, "I'm an inconsiderate prick!" This statement is true, but since Fletcher has only said it because he has been forced to tell the truth, it has no real significance for him. Later, however, after realizing that, by helping a client win an unjust verdict, he has inadvertently harmed her children, Fletcher responds to Judge Marshall Stevens' warning that he is about to hold him in contempt, "I hold myself in contempt!" In this eminently Habermasian form of self-disclosure, Fletcher sees through the pathological distortions of his lifeworld.

It is tempting to say that the latent thought that is both repressed and expressed in *Liar Liar* is that it is in fact necessary to lie, that "normal" life depends upon lying. As Fletcher explains to Max, "When your mother was pregnant and she asked how she looked, it was better to lie and say she looked beautiful." Here Fletcher gives voice to the classic "consequentialist" objection to Kant's strict prohibition against lying under any circumstances: if it would cause more harm to tell the truth than to lie, do we not have an obligation to lie? Should we not do the "wrong" thing for the "right" reason?

In response to this line of argument, Kant and Habermas insist that one should always act as if one were in the kingdom of ends or ideal speech situation. According to Kant's "publicity maxim," the political analogue of the categorical imperative, it is impossible to conceive of a world in which everyone announced, sincerely, that they were lying. But is such a world really inconceivable? In *Jokes and their Relation to the Unconscious* (*Der Witz und seine Beziehung zum Unbewussten*, 1905), Freud tells a joke that Žižek frequently cites (SOI 197; LA 73; FA 81; cf. S III 37). Two acquaintances meet on a train and one says to the other that he is going to Warsaw. To this, his friend replies, "Why are you telling me you're going to Warsaw so I'll think you're going to Lemberg when you're really going to Warsaw?" This joke gives a perfect description of what it would mean to "lie" in a world in which everyone always lied, namely, by "telling the truth." It also shows that, contra Kant, it *is* possible to imagine a world in which everyone always lied, for such a world turns out to be formally indistinguishable from a world in which everyone always tells the truth: you tell me that you are going to Warsaw, so I conclude that you are not. In a precisely analogous way, Kant himself acknowledges that there are some untruths, such as compliments, which everyone knows to be mere formalities; such gestures of politeness "are not always the *truth* . . . but this still does not make them *deception*, because everyone knows how to take them" (AFPPV 31). Thus a Kantian analogue of Freud's joke would be, "Why are you complimenting me when you really mean it?"

In contrast to obscene, aggressive, or cynical jokes, Freud characterizes jokes of the "Why are you telling me. . .?" variety as "skeptical" in that they challenge "the certainty of our knowledge itself" (JRU 115). A good way to regard Žižek's critique of Habermas would be to say that it expresses skepticism about the ideal speech situation. For Habermas, the exemplary task of psychoanalysis is to "explain" the tics and grimaces that are a mark of inauthentic speech. But, in *Liar Liar*, Fletcher's tics and grimaces appear *only when he finds himself in the so-called ideal speech situation*. It is here that we can find the equivalent of the dream-work in this film. Thus instead of focusing on the latent thought – the idea that, in normal life, it is necessary to lie – what is really significant is the way in which this thesis is expressed, namely, in the tics and grimaces that distort Fletcher's face as he finds himself unable to say anything other than the truth. One might object that these symptoms appear only because Fletcher is being coerced into telling the truth, and that were he to adopt the Kantian publicity maxim of his own free will (as he arguably does at the end of the film) the tics and grimaces would disappear. But this is to consider the film's message at the level of its ideological (manifest) content. What Fletcher's tics and grimaces reveal is nothing less than the ideological character of Habermas's theory of communicative action, the fact that every speech situation is constructed around the meaningless elements that are its ideological core. In other words, there is a distorting "form of understanding" in the ideal speech situation itself.

This conclusion seems to entail the "tragic" Althusserian point that it is impossible to escape ideology altogether. But according to Žižek, the fact that there is always a "fundamental deadlock" in society does not mean that we are always necessarily in ideology. On the contrary, through what Lacan calls "separation" – freeing ourselves from fantasy by recognizing that the big Other is itself "incomplete" – it is possible to work through one's interpellation as an ideological subject. Thus to be skeptical of the ideological speech situation is not the same as cynically confessing that one is caught in ideology. Following the German social theorist, Peter Sloterdijk (1947–), Žižek suggests that such a cynical attitude is ideological because it merely confirms the gap between the subject's self-consciousness and its objectively embodied beliefs; when I "cynically" distance myself from my behavior, I am all the more caught in ideology (SOI 28–30). By contrast, skepticism is *behavior* that challenges the subject's pretension to knowledge. In this respect it can be likened to ancient Cynicism. Instead of trying to change people's minds, the Cynics attacked objective beliefs by doing things like urinating and masturbating in public.

According to Žižek, a truly revolutionary intervention would require not an authentic speech act but an excessive "hysterical" act that would not merely interpret the world but change it (WTDOR 88). Along with Lacan, he appeals in this context to Antigone, the significance of whose act lies not in any of the justificatory arguments that she presents for it in her dialogues with Ismene and Creon but in the moment of ethical and political hubris that adheres to it. Perhaps it is possible to distinguish between an "enthusiastic" Antigone whose "diabolical evil" would retroactively constitute itself as justified – a revolutionary "founding" act of the sort that Arendt defended against Kant – and a "fanatical" Antigone whose act represents "the worst." At any rate, Žižek can be read not so much as rejecting the theory of communicative action as extending it. For the real lesson of world-decentration is that neither Antigone nor Habermas alone can present us with a satisfactory critical theory. What we need is Habermas *avec* Antigone (in the manner of Lacan's Kant *avec* Sade), that is, a politics of the symbolic *and* the real, respectively.[33] A fully decentered critical theory would also require a politics of the imaginary as well. Such a politics is arguably exemplified in

Adorno's insistence that art alone can bear witness to suffering. Thus instead of accusing Adorno of succumbing to an aestheticist reductionism – as Habermas does – Žižek implicitly invites us to think of Adorno and Habermas as offering two facets of a three-sided critical theory.

In contrast to Habermas, for whom communicative action replaces the Marxist conception of a redemptive revolutionary act, Žižek characterizes Lenin as the exemplary political agent. Instead of waiting for the right moment to act, Lenin acted in such a way as to create thereby the "right moment." In *Welcome to the Desert of the Real*, Žižek characterizes his fellow East Europeans' *Ostalgie* not as nostalgia for communism as it actually existed – Stalin's "really existing socialism" – but rather "for what *might have happened* there, for the missed opportunity" (WTDOR 23–4). Benjamin's messianism involves the hope for a redemption of a past failure, the longing for an act that would deliver the past from its inability to achieve a possible future that never materialized. In his fidelity to the messianic moment of the Russian Revolution, Žižek resists Arendt's tendency to lump Nazism and communism together under the single heading of "totalitarianism." He distinguishes between the revolutionary "hysteria" of Lenin and the "obsessional neurosis" of Stalin, attempting to link the former to a genuinely ethical project that would be free from "the 'Stalinist' obscene underside of the Law" (WTDOR 89, 29): "the revolutionary political counterpoint to Lacan's *Kant avec Sade* is undoubtedly *Lenin avec Stalin* – it is only with Stalin that the Leninist revolutionary subject turns into the perverse object-instrument of the big Other's *jouissance*" (DSST 113).

Thus, unlike Lacan, who more or less equated the ethical stances of Kant and Sade on the grounds that both experience tremendous – albeit apathetic, non-pathological – enjoyment as a consequence of their sacrifice of all pathological pleasures, Žižek insists on *separating* Kant from Sade: "at its most radical, Kantian ethics is *not* 'sadistic,' but precisely what prohibits assuming the position of a Sadeian executioner" (DSST 112–13). Ironically, this separation requires that we impute to Kant the other side of his disavowal of the diabolical evil that is "formally indistinguishable from the Good" (DSST 172). If there is a kind of Sadeian violence today it is, as Bataille recognized, the violence of capitalism. Consumers do not so much "enjoy" themselves – as Marcuse's analysis of repressive desublimation would have us think – as they make themselves instruments of enjoyment for Capital (the big Other) itself. For Marx, Capital is not a mere fiction but the exact opposite – a "real abstraction" that sadistically enjoys for us (FA 15). We can break out of our subservience to it only by traversing the consumerist fantasy that raises commodities to the level of the sublime Thing. In calling for such a traversal, Žižek invokes the paradoxical figure of a fundamentally Kantian Stalinist – as opposed to a *Stalinist* Kantian (in keeping with Kant's contrast between the moral politician and the political moralist) – that is, an actor capable of performing, and not merely witnessing, a revolutionary act in the Benjaminian sense (SOI 141–2; FA 89). A condition for the possibility of rekindling such hope is that we fully accept the moment of subjective destitution, the fact that there is no support, immanent or transcendent, for the abyssal project that still resonates in the Marxist imperative.

In holding out hope for a redemptive revolutionary act, Žižek resists the idea – emphasized in the work of Claude Lefort (1924–), a founding member of *Socialisme ou barbarie* – that the "place of power" should be left unoccupied. In Freudian terms, this would be the place of the primal father, deliberately kept empty by the brothers who killed and devoured him. In *Group Psychology*, Freud called attention to the atavistic tendency of anti-social groups to identify with a leader who takes the place of the primal father. Freud located the elementary structure of interpellation in the phenomenon of "suggestion," the process by which individuals acquire beliefs that are immune to reality-testing because they are based upon a libidinal tie. Though written in 1921, Freud's book is often taken to explain the rise of fascism in the 1930s. But according to Žižek, it is a mistake to characterize all "anti-social" groups as "proto-Fascist" – a concept he takes to be both ill-defined and ideologically motivated (WTDOR 76). On the contrary, any effective transformation of existing social conditions requires an absolute fidelity to a dogma of some sort (WTDOR 3). Such a faith differs from that of Kant in that its object is incarnated in some particular pathological object which "stands in" for the universal, "heteronomously" determining the will. But according to Žižek, no effective resistance to the hegemony of Capital is possible without something or someone assuming the absent place of the leader – i.e., without a (temporary) suspension of democracy (WTDOR 153). Though such an absolute faith could take a "fascist" turn at any time, Žižek insists on the necessity of accepting this risk:

> The democratic political order is of its very nature susceptible to corruption. The ultimate choice is: do we accept and endorse this corruption in a spirit of realistic resigned wisdom, or can we summon up the courage to formulate a Leftist alternative to democracy . . .?
>
> (WTDOR 79)

When the Marxist revolutionary Rosa Luxemburg (1870–1919) accused the Bolsheviks of "'fetishizing' formal democracy, instead of treating it as one of the possible strategies to be endorsed or rejected with regard to the demands of a concrete revolutionary situation," Lukács responded that the Soviet dictatorship of the proletariat was justified in suspending democracy: *"Freedom must serve the rule of the proletariat, not the other way around"* (GLAPL 153; HACC 292). Žižek acknowledges that Lukács might be criticized for accommodating himself to Stalinism, but he regards this failure as rooted in a laudable fidelity to the messianic promise of the Russian Revolution. As for the members of the Frankfurt School, "if they had been really cornered as to where they stood in the Cold War, they would have chosen Western liberal democracy" (GLAPL 158). In siding with Lukács as "the philosopher

of Leninism," Žižek attempts to separate the Leninist revolutionary event
from its subsequent (and contingent) betrayal. Toward this end he distinguishes the Stalinist fetishism of "sublime beauty" from the Leninist fidelity
to the unrepresentable Cause:

> the Stalinist sublime body of the Leader (with mausoleums and all the
> accompanying theatrics) is unthinkable within the strict Leninist horizon:
> the Leader can be elevated into a figure of Sublime Beauty only when the
> "people" whom he represents is no longer the thoroughly dislocated prole-
> tariat, but the positively existing substantial entity, the "working masses."
>
> (GLAPL 170)

In other words, while we can no longer accept a conception of the proletariat as the embodiment of the big Other, it is possible to conceive the
Lukácsian proletariat as a split subject for whom the cause of communism is
beautifully sublime. Thus rather than mourning, with Adorno, the missed
opportunity to which the work of Lukács still bears witness, Žižek echoes
Benjamin's messianic hope for a second chance.

Notes

1 Presumably the wig-maker is independent because he produces something that
   he can sell, whereas the barber merely offers his services without appropriating
   any product of his labor. But given Kant's extended use of the word "property,"
   one could suppose that it is the wig-maker's skill, rather than his ownership of
   wigs, that gives him his independence. In the third *Critique*, Kant tells a joke
   about a "merchant who, returning from India to Europe with all his fortune in
   merchandise, was forced to throw it all overboard in a terrible storm, and was so
   upset that in the very same night his **wig** turned gray" (CPJ 210). The context
   of colonialism aside, Kant presumably finds this joke funny because while we
   can imagine a person's hair turning gray from grief, it is absurd to think that his
   wig could express his grief – for although the wig is "his," it does not belong to
   him (and so cannot express his essence) in the same way that a natural property
   might. Yet if it is absurd to think that mere ownership could magically endow a
   wig with the power to express a person's grief, is it not equally absurd to make
   the right of citizenship depend on the ownership of wigs? This "absurdity" is
   precisely that of commodity fetishism (though obviously it would be no less
   absurd to make rights dependent on the color of one's hair or skin). The fact
   that the merchant's wig turns gray could be said to symbolize the loss of citizenship that he might very well incur by the loss of his property. To his credit,
   Kant concedes "that it is somewhat difficult to define the qualifications which
   entitle anyone to claim the status of being his own master" (PW 78n).
2 Cf. Hans Reiss's comments at PW 279 n17 and 261–2.
3 Though Guyer and Matthews translate *streiten* as "argue," I prefer J.H. Bernard's
   older rendering of this term as "quarrel." In Chapter 5 I will characterize "disputes" and "quarrels" as two different models of philosophical arguments.
4 Cf. Lévi-Strauss's critique of Freud.
5 For Marx's conception of epic as a form of art specific to the social world of the
   ancient Greeks, cf. KMAR 19–20.
6 See Arpad Kadarkay's introductory comments at TLR 213.

7 But see Lukács's recently discovered manuscript from the mid-1920s, *A Defence of History and Class Consciousness: Tailism and the Dialectic (Chvostismus und Dialektik*, 1996).

8 Cf. Lucien Goldmann, *Lukács and Heidegger*, pp. 27–8, and Žižek's comments at GLAPL 151–2.

9 Cf. GLAPL 157, where Žižek offers a Lukácsian rejoinder to this claim.

10 Benjamin does not refer to Frege, but he does mention Carnap's *The Logical Syntax of Language (Logische Syntax der Sprache*, 1934), noting that Carnap is concerned only with "the formal aspects of language" and not with those of "a genuine language" (SW III 77).

11 The two branches of this hyperbola could be said to represent Hölderlin's "double flight" of mortals and gods, to which both Heidegger and Blanchot refer.

12 The experience of linear time also begins to break down in the judgment of taste, insofar as we desire to "linger" with beautiful forms. Cf. Rudolf Makkreel, *Imagination and Interpretation in Kant*: "In the case of the instantaneous comprehension involved in the sublime, the time flow is suspended, as it were; in the case of the lingering inherent in the contemplation of beauty, the passage of time is slowed" (p. 93).

13 Cf. Derrida's discussion of this passage at SOM 114ff.

14 Cf. TCC 105, 115, 119.

15 Cf. the queen's words – worthy of Horkheimer – at II, ii, 68–72.

16 In analyzing one of the founding "myths" of Western culture, Horkheimer and Adorno do precisely what Lévi-Strauss said Freud *should* have done in *Totem and Taboo*.

17 Juliette is not a hedonistic libertine like the Lotus-eaters; on the contrary, her relentless pursuit of cruelty is carried out in the name of an indifferent apathy. For Lacan, this feeling of apathy was equivalent to the Kantian feeling of respect for the moral law, an experience of enjoyment different in kind from all pathological forms of gratification. But for Horkheimer and Adorno it is not Kant's moral philosophy per se that puts him in proximity to Sade; rather, it is the inability of his critique of pure speculative reason to give meaningful expression to the force of the categorical imperative itself. Closer to Horkheimer and Adorno is Deleuze, for whom Sade's "alliance" between the father and the daughter against the mother represents an extreme expression of reason's domination of the claims of sensuousness. Analogously, Masoch's alliance of mother and son against the father could be read as a protest against domination in the name of repressed sensuousness. Adorno's later conception of art's willful ugliness, its becoming-painful in protest against a painful society, implies that the more sadistic society gets, the more masochistic art becomes (I owe this elegant formulation to Darin McGinnis.).

18 In a 1938 letter to Adorno, Benjamin suggests that "the launching of the sound film must be regarded as an operation of the film industry designed to break the revolutionary primacy of the silent film, which had produced reactions that were difficult to control and hence dangerous politically. An analysis of the sound film would constitute a critique of contemporary art, which would provide a dialectical mediation between your views and mine" (TCC 295).

19 Benjamin is also scolded by Adorno for the insufficiently dialectical character of his analyses (TCC 107, 282).

20 Cf. LOAS 141.

21 Freud called attention to an analogous double bind concerning the superego, which simultaneously demands that the ego be and not be like the father.

22 In the second part of this quotation, Lukács cites his book, *The Destruction of Reason (Die Zerstörung der Vernunft*, 1962).

23 Cf. Kant's reference to ambivalent feelings such as *"bitter joy"* and *"sweet sorrow"* (AFPPV 105; CPJ 208).

24 Drawing upon Giorgio Agamben's *Remnants of Auschwitz*, Žižek characterizes such an apotropaic work of mourning as a melancholic relationship to something not yet lost (DSST 146; cf. 87 for his reading of Adorno's question concerning the possibility of poetry after Auschwitz).

25 Pseudo-Ammonius, cited in David Ross, *Aristotle*, p. 7.

26 To this Marcuse might have added that neither Quine's nor Sellars's repudiation of the category of givenness took the form of a critique of ideology (as Althusser's did).

27 Marcuse's suggestion that analytic philosophers believe in more ghosts than Marxists do bears comparison with Derrida's discernment (in *Specters of Marx*) of a comparable rhetorical strategy in Marx's polemic with Stirner.

28 In this respect Gadamer's conception of hermeneutic openness resembles Davidson's "principle of charity" (as both philosophers acknowledge).

29 Cf. Horkheimer and Adorno's characterization of Kant's "oracular wisdom": "There is no being in the world that knowledge cannot penetrate, but what can be penetrated by knowledge is not being" (DOE 19).

30 In response to criticisms of his construal of the perlocutionary/illocutionary dichotomy, Habermas later acknowledges that not all perlocutionary acts in Austin's sense of this term need be strategic in their intent, but he claims that this terminological concession does not affect "the distinction between *communicative* and *strategic* action" (Habermas, "A Reply," p. 240). My thanks to Tom McCarthy and David Ingram for calling this passage to my attention.

31 Thus Ed Casey has distinguished between being "thaumatized" and being "traumatized."

32 Likewise, one could say that what the beautiful is to the agreeable, the sublime is to jouissance.

33 Here I assume that what Žižek takes to be Habermas's foreclosure of the real can better be characterized as a reduction of both the real and the imaginary to the symbolic, and that likewise Antigone's foreclosure of the symbolic amounts to a reduction of both the symbolic and the imaginary to the order of the real (The same would hold, mutatis mutandis, for Žižek's characterization of Schreber as foreclosing the realm of the imaginary.).

4   The problem of the relationship between the empirical and the transcendental: what is the meaning of philosophical humanism?

Kant's fourth question – "What is man?" – has a special status not only because it is omitted from the list of questions presented in the first *Critique*, but because it is singled out in Kant's lectures on logic as somehow encompassing the other three (L 29). Insofar as it is an empirical science, anthropology falls outside the purview of transcendental philosophy. But Kant suggests that there is a "higher" anthropology that has as its object not empirically existing "men" but "man" (PW 119; cf. 91). This suggests that, in contrast to the empirical question, "What are *men* like?," the question, "What is *man*?" is a properly transcendental one. By abandoning Kant's distinction between the transcendental and empirical dimensions of human experience, his successors were forced to rethink the relationship between an anthropology of man and an anthropology of men. Hegel resolved this difficulty by treating individuals as accidental shapes that spirit happens to take throughout human history. The first thinker to rebel against this idea was Kierkegaard, who insisted on the irreducibility of individuals to any overarching universal category. For Kierkegaard, only individuals exist; "man" as such does not. Therefore, instead of addressing Kant's question about the being of man, he urges his readers to ask themselves the existentially personal question, "Who am I?" Like Kierkegaard, Nietzsche also abandons transcendental reflections about the nature of man in favor of psychological analyses of individuals, emphasizing the importance of becoming oneself. But unlike Kierkegaard – for whom becoming oneself ultimately means relating to oneself in such a way as to rest in a relation to God – Nietzsche insists that overcoming man and overcoming God are one and the same thing. The existential humanism of Sartre and Beauvoir has its roots in this Nietzschean idea, while Heidegger's call for a more authentic humanism represents a retrieval of Kierkegaard's position. A different approach to the question of humanism is opened up by thinkers such as Fanon, Lévi-Strauss, and Foucault, for whom the peculiarly European sense of the category of man comes into question. By connecting the advent of the "sciences of man" with the problem concerning the transcendental and the empirical, Foucault is able to clarify the complicity of humanism with power. This assessment leads him to criticize psychoanalytic accounts of sexuality. Irigaray shares these concerns, but she suggests that the problems concerning "man and his doubles" bear first and foremost on the repression of sexual difference.

Habermas attempts to circumvent Foucault's empirico-transcendental doublet through a more encompassing reflection on the "betweenness" of relations between the members of a shared lifeworld.

4.1   Kant's pragmatic anthropology

> O, that way madness lies, let me shun that!
> (*The Tragedy of King Lear*, III, iv, 21)[1]

In his *Anthropology From a Pragmatic Point of View* (*Anthropologie in pragmatischer Hinsicht*, 1798), Kant contrasts "physiological" anthropology, which considers man as a product of "what *nature* makes of him," with "pragmatic" anthropology, which is concerned with what man "makes, or can and should make, of himself" (AFPPV 3). Physiological anthropology is of little interest, not only because we are ignorant about how the human body works – "we can speculate to and fro (as Descartes did) about traces, remaining in the brain, of impressions left by sensations we have experienced" (AFPPV 3) – but, more fundamentally, because such an investigation, even if successful, would be useless to us. The physiological anthropologist studies human beings as a spectator of man's first nature rather than from the engaged standpoint of an actor acquiring a second nature. In contrast to the neutral observations of the physiological anthropologist, those of the pragmatic anthropologist have prescriptive and not merely descriptive value.

For Kant, the term "pragmatic" refers to all goal-directed human activities. As such, it bears equally on what in the *Groundwork* he calls "*rules* of skill," "*counsels* of prudence," and "*commands (laws)* of morality," that is, principles pertaining to problematic, assertoric, and categorical imperatives (G 69).[2] He also distinguishes between the technical, pragmatic, and moral points of view, the first pertaining to skill, the second to prudence in our relations with other human beings, and the third to moral principles (AFPPV 183ff.).[3] As a "popular" treatise intended "for the reading public," Kant's *Anthropology* has the character of a self-help book whose aim is to distinguish between morally edifying and morally degenerating uses of our faculties (AFPPV 5).

Kant notes that the study of human nature poses "serious difficulties" (AFPPV 4). We cannot rely exclusively on inner sense for several reasons. All natural science requires something permanent in experience to serve as a "substratum grounding the transitory determinations" (CPR A381), but there is nothing permanent in the flux of inner sense (cf. MFNS 186; AFPPV 15). Moreover, because there is a fundamental difference between the standpoints of the actor and the spectator, it is impossible to observe ourselves at the very moment when we act. Finally, even if we could know ourselves through introspection, we would have no way of knowing to what extent our own character differs from that of other people (AFPPV 4). This suggests that an anthropological science must rely on the observation of others. But here too there are difficulties. In his review of Herder's *Ideas on the Philosophy of the History of Mankind*, Kant claims that anthropology should be grounded in observations of human action: "the basic materials of anthropology . . . are to be found only in human *actions*, in which the human character is revealed" (PW 211–12). But in the *Anthropology* he notes that we cannot observe other people without making them "self-conscious" and so causing them to "dissemble" (AFPPV 4). Likewise, "physiognomic" observations – which Kant takes up under the heading of an "Anthropological Characterization: on How to Discern Man's Inner Self from His Exterior" – are insufficient because they attend primarily to what nature makes of men rather than to what they make of themselves (though it is also concerned with acquired features such as facial expressions).

To these difficulties Kant adds another that pertains to the relationship between "general" and "local" knowledge. On the one hand, "if we want to know what we should look for abroad . . . we must first have acquired knowledge of men at home" (AFPPV 4). On the other hand, "Circumstances of place and time, if they are stable, produce *habits* which, as we say, are second nature and make it hard for us to decide what view to take of ourselves, but much harder to know what to think of our associates" (AFPPV 4). We thus seem to be faced with a dilemma: we cannot understand foreigners unless we understand ourselves, yet we cannot recognize what is idiosyncratic in our own habits unless we know something about others. Kant resolves this hermeneutical dilemma by regarding it as a double methodological requirement: we must regard others from our own standpoint, and ourselves from the standpoint of others. We can accomplish these two things by engaging in dialogue and by reading what Gadamer would call "traditionary" texts (under the heading of such "auxiliary means," Kant mentions "world history, biography, and even plays and novels") (AFPPV 5). To accept this version of the hermeneutic circle is to consider "man as a *citizen of the world*" (AFPPV 3). The two maxims governing such a cosmopolitan attitude are "Think for yourself" and "Think from the standpoint of others" (AFPPV 72, 96; CPJ 174). By conversing with as many different people as possible – members of both sexes, representatives of different races, and citizens of different nations – we transcend our own provincial point of view.

Engaging in dialogue not only enables us to compare our own inner states with those of others, but it offers us our only means of access to our own mental life. We cannot rely on inner sense, not only because introspection alters what it would apprehend, but because self-observation "easily leads to fanaticism and madness." The reason for this is that when we introspect, we invert the proper relationship between the faculties of imagination and understanding: "to try to eavesdrop on ourselves . . . is to overturn the natural order of the cognitive powers, because then the principles of thinking do not come first . . . but follow after" (AFPPV 15). In the second edition of the first *Critique*, Kant emphasizes the fact that our cognitive faculties are properly oriented toward objects of outer sense: "the representations **of outer sense** make up the proper material with which we occupy our mind" (CPR B67; cf. B154, B276–7). So long as we attend to objects of outer sense, the subjective play of the imagination trails behind the understanding. Fanaticism occurs when an "unruly" imagination takes the lead, determining the course taken by the understanding. Thus to turn our attention inward is to risk succumbing to fanaticism, the situation in which we "regard inner sense as laying down the law on its own" (AFPPV 25). Unlike the genius, in whom "originality of imagination . . . harmonizes with concepts," the fanatic's imagination runs amok, allowing mere figments of inner sense to be treated as genuine objects of outer sense (AFPPV 48). No appeal to rational ideas can cure such a person, "for what power have they against supposed intuitions?" (AFPPV 40).[4]

To illustrate the risk associated with introspection, Kant refers to the case of Albrecht Haller (1708–1777), who suffered such torment from keeping "a diary of his state of soul" that he found it necessary to ask one of his colleagues, a Dr. Less, for professional help (AFPPV 15).[5] To avert this danger, Kant issues a "strict *warning* . . . against occupying ourselves with spying out the *involuntary* course of our thoughts and feelings, and, so to speak, carefully recording its interior history" (AFPPV 14). Similarly, "it is dangerous to experiment on the mind and to make it ill to a certain degree so that we can observe it and investigate its nature by the appearances that may be found there. . . . Madness artificially induced can easily become genuine" (AFPPV 86).

In order to avoid this danger, we should only observe our own mental states indirectly. One way to do this is to engage in dialogue with another person, from whose perspective we learn something about ourselves. This is the role that Freud ascribed to the analyst. Instead of performing a self-analysis, the analysand's job is to free-associate without observing, while the analyst's job is to observe without free-associating. Through the mechanism of transference, the analysand can then engage in self-observation *from the point of view of another*. Lacan observes that like an anamorphically represented object – which looked upon directly cannot be seen for what it is – the unconscious can only be observed by "looking awry" at it – a phrase that Žižek borrows from Bushy's reference to anamorphosis in Shakespeare's *Richard II* (S XI 88). Similarly, Kant notes that "we can be *mediately* conscious of having an idea even if we are not immediately conscious of it." So great is the field of the unconscious that "our mind is like an immense *map* with only a few places *illuminated*" (AFPPV 16). For this reason, conversing with other people can tell us many things that we would otherwise not know about ourselves. It also enables us to distinguish between the idiosyncratic contribution that the play of our own inner sense makes to our thoughts and the genuine insights that can only be achieved through the understanding. This is one reason why Kant insists on the right to free speech; scholars can know if they have judged correctly only by submitting their results to the public for scrutiny (AFPPV 10–11; cf. PW 247). One way in which we distinguish between the idiosyncratic and universal dimensions of our own judgments is by quarreling about matters of taste. Another is by comparing our private likes and dislikes. In all these ways, dialogue is the vehicle by which we cultivate a cosmopolitan point of view.[6]

Cosmopolitanism is not only a means but an end for pragmatic anthropology, for the highest vocation of man is to live (morally) as a citizen of the world. In a footnote to his pre-critical *Observations on the Feeling of the Beautiful and Sublime* (*Beobachtungen über das Gefühl des Schönen und Erhabenen*, 1764) – a work whose post-critical counterpart is less the third *Critique* than the second part of the *Anthropology* – Kant recounts the first-person report of a dream by a "wealthy miser" named Carazan who had long shunned the company of other human beings. In his dream, Carazan is reproached by the Angel of Death for having "closed your heart to the love of man." He is then "swept away by an unseen power" into "the boundless void" for all eternity. Filled with horror, Carazan says:

> I thrust out my hands with such force toward the objects of reality that I awoke. And now I have been taught to esteem mankind; for in that terrifying solitude I would have preferred even the least of those whom in the pride of my fortune I had turned from my door to all the treasures of Golconda –

> (OFBS 48–9)

Arendt suggests that Kant placed such emphasis on man's sociability because, like Carazan, he too had to learn "to esteem mankind" (LKPP 10–11; cf. 28–9). In the *Anthropology*, Kant reports a dream that he had when he was a child:

> I remember very well how once, when I was a boy, I went to bed tired out from play and, just as I was falling asleep, was suddenly awakened by a dream that I had fallen into water and was being carried around in a whirlpool, almost drowning.

> (AFPPV 63)

Kant interprets his dream as a response to the fact that he had temporarily stopped breathing; by startling him, the dream restored his normal respiration. This explanation resembles the one that Freud gives of a dream to which he attaches special importance. A man whose son had just died dreamt that his son came up to his bed and reproached him with the words, *"Father, don't you see I'm burning?"* He then awoke to find that in fact his son's corpse was being burned by a candle that had fallen over. Freud suggests that the man must have been aware of what was happening and that his dream enabled him to sleep a little longer (IOD 547–8). But Lacan interprets the man's awakening to "reality" as a way of avoiding an encounter with the terrifying "real" kernel of his dream (S XI 58).

Kant regards dreaming as a kind of temporary fanaticism – "involuntary invention in a state of health" (AFPPV 63). Both the dreamer and the fanatic inhabit a private world cut off from other people: "if different people have each of them their own world, then we may suppose that they are dreaming" (DOSS 329). The only difference between the dreamer and the fanatic is that the dreamer is able to wake up, thereby becoming once again a citizen of the world (DOSS 329). In the dreams of both Carazan and Kant there is a recoiling from the void which "arouses horror (*horror vacui*) and, as it were, the presentiment of a slow death" (AFPPV 102) or the "horror at the thought of *having died*" (AFPPV 44). To be horrified at the thought of having died is to imagine that one has forfeited one's citizenship in the world, something that Kant thinks can only be attained with other people in civil society. One reason why Kant regards revolutionary acts with such horror is that, by reverting to a state of nature, we forfeit our citizenship in the world. What makes the very thought of the execution (as opposed to the mere murder) of a monarch "arouse dread" in us is not merely that such an act is wrong but that it is an *inexpiable* crime. To execute a monarch is to will never to return to civil society. Hence even to contemplate such a crime is to encounter "an abyss which engulfs everything beyond hope of return" (PW 145–6n). It is possible to experience "a kind of holy thrill at seeing the abyss of the supersensible opening at our feet" (AFPPV 128). But the revolutionary fanatic is like a Carazan who actively wills his own banishment from the world. Kant notes that "Deep loneliness is sublime, but in a way that stirs terror" (OFBS 48).

The distinctive trait of all forms of mental derangement (not only fanaticism) is "loss of *common sense* (*sensus communis*) and substitution of *logical private sense* (*sensus privatus*)" (AFPPV 88). Common sense is that by virtue of which all citizens of the world recognize a shared world of experience. As such, it is oriented to objects of outer sense. But the *sensus communis* to which Kant refers in his account of the judgment of taste pertains to a shared awareness of something in inner sense, namely, the felt accord of the harmony of the faculties. Quarreling about matters of taste is important because it enables us to form the *sensus communis*, thereby becoming more fully the members of a shared world. This explains the importance that Kant ascribes to "laws of refined humanity," which, though seemingly "insignificant . . . in comparison with pure moral laws," are of genuine importance for promoting human sociability, a necessary though not sufficient condition for a virtuous life (AFPPV 147). Though "interest" in society is in one sense merely empirical, in another it is part of our vocation as rational (moral) beings (CPJ 177; AFPPV 186). Likewise, there is a prudential interest in society that everyone "ought" to have only in a qualified sense, but overriding this is a moral interest in society that everyone "ought" to have in the categorical sense.

Insofar as it provides us with an opportunity to cultivate our cosmopolitan vocation, Kant regards a good dinner party – i.e., one conducive to good conversation – as "the kind of good living that seems to harmonize best with humanity." Such an occasion makes use of our sensuous need for nourishment as an "instrument" for "companionable enjoyment." Though private rather than public, it should provide an open forum in which each person speaks to the entire assembled group rather than just to his or her neighbors. To meet this condition, it is important that the number of guests be just right and that the company be "varied" (AFPPV 144). Just as the judgment of taste reflects an attempt to communicate a felt harmonizing of the faculties, so "a good meal in good company is unsurpassed as a situation in which sensibility and understanding unite in one enjoyment that lasts a long time and can be repeated with pleasure so frequently" (AFPPV 110).

Not only does a good dinner party serve reason's interest by enabling us to adopt a cosmopolitan point of view, but it also provides the ideal forum for the pragmatic anthropologist – and the philosopher – to engage in research:

> *Dining alone* ... is unhealthy for a scholar who *philosophizes*. ... A man who, while dining, gnaws at himself intellectually during his solitary meal gradually loses his sprightliness; on the other hand he increases it if a table companion, by presenting the alternative of his own ideas, offers him new material to stimulate him, without his having to track it down himself.
>
> (AFPPV 145)

Thus the ideal meal – exemplified for Kant in Plato's *Symposium* – serves not only as an occasion for rest and restoration of powers but for prompting us to reflect (AFPPV 144n). Kant did not regard the philosopher as a solitary thinker like Descartes but as a public intellectual like Socrates. To remind himself of this fact, he kept a portrait of Rousseau – who Kant says taught him to esteem mankind – in his study.

Like Rousseau, Kant claims that "by nature" man is a "solitary" animal "who shies away from his neighbors," but that nature has also given him the task of making himself a social animal (AFPPV 184–5). To promote its end of making man give himself ends, nature has divided the species into two sexes each of which has a different task. The traits that nature has assigned to women serve two purposes: "the preservation of the species" and "the cultivation of society and its refinement" (AFPPV 169). Men have been given the physical strength to control women. But since women elicit men's desire, they have the ability to solicit their attentiveness. This ability of women to tame men is the first step toward civilization. Thus sexual difference plays a crucial role in leading *men* to make the transition from "the crude state of nature" to civilization, while civilization enables the "feminine qualities" of women to develop (AFPPV 167).

Insofar as women exert a civilizing influence over men, they promote the progress of the species as a whole. But this civilizing influence has its limits.

In effect, it corresponds only to the non-moral pragmatic interest in human sociability. A civilization that allowed itself to be run by women would remain at a stunted level of moral growth. In order to fulfill humanity's moral predisposition, it is necessary for men to exercise their capacity for acting from rational principles, a capacity that Kant thinks women do not possess (OFBS 81). By associating women with inclination and men with understanding and reason, Kant adheres to a patriarchal point of view that accords genuine citizenship only to men: "just as it is not woman's role to go to war, so she cannot personally defend her rights and engage in civil affairs for herself, but only through her representative" (AFPPV 80). This is not to say that women should accept a merely subordinate status, either in society at large or in marriage. In the case of marriage, Kant proposes that "the woman should *reign* and the man *govern*; for inclination reigns and understanding governs" (AFPPV 172).

The fact that inclination is allowed to reign is in keeping with Kant's condemnation of moral asceticism. Happiness retains a legitimate, if subordinate, place in his conception of the highest good. In the *Anthropology*, Kant connects the idea of the highest good with that of humanity: "The way of thinking that unites well-being with virtue in our social intercourse is *humanity*" (AFPPV 143). By associating men with reason and women with inclination, Kant suggests that a genuine union of virtue and happiness can only be achieved in the mutual relations between the sexes. What it means for the woman to reign and the man to govern is that "he will be like a minister to his monarch who thinks only of amusement ... so that the monarch can do all that he wills, but on one condition: that his minister lets him know what his will is" (AFPPV 173). In putting the woman rather than the man in the position of monarch, Kant implicitly highlights the eudaimonistic dimension of his moral philosophy. Moreover, even if it is the minister who ultimately makes all the decisions, these must be formally ratified by the monarch herself.[7]

Kant associates a feeling for the beautiful with women and a feeling for the sublime with men. Though "one expects that a person of either sex brings both together" – Kant's analogue of Freud's theory of constitutional bisexuality – the tendencies of both sexes should contribute to the beauty of women and the nobility of men (OFBS 76). Thus the ideal marriage – insofar as it represents the highest good for humanity – can be thought of as embodying sublime beauty or beautiful sublimity, depending on whether the accent is placed on the woman who reigns or the man who governs.

Kant's estimation of the different propensities of the two sexes guides his assessment of the characteristic differences among national types. At one extreme are the French, a people said to embody the feminine traits of affability, courteousness, and lovableness. At the other extreme are the English, who exemplify the masculine traits of solitary self-reliance and acting on principles (AFPPV 175–8). Each of these national types has its strengths but is one-sided, an assessment that reflects Kant's view that each of the two sexes has traits that need to be checked by those of the other. The rest of the European nations can be thought of as combining the extreme elements of the English and French temperaments. For example, the typical German has "a feeling mixed from that of an Englishman and that of a Frenchman. . . . He has a fortunate combination of feeling, both in that of the sublime and in that of the beautiful; and if in the first he does not equal an Englishman, nor in the second a Frenchman, he yet surpasses both so far as he unites them" (OFBS 104). Though such a balance between feminine and masculine tendencies would seem to be a good thing, Kant suggests "that a mixture of races . . . which gradually extinguishes their characters, is not beneficial to the human race." Intermarriage yields bad admixtures, as in "the fickle and obsequious character of the modern Greek," whose racial purity has been compromised over time (AFPPV 182).

Kant goes out of his way to suggest that no one should be offended by such stereotypes because they are said of peoples rather than individuals, so that "each one can hit it like a ball to his neighbor" (OFBS 97n). But even if this is true for his distinction between different national types, it does not seem to carry over to his distinction between the races, as is evidenced by his casual reference to "a Negro carpenter" who "was quite black from head to foot, a clear proof that what he said was stupid" (OFBS 113). In his 1775 essay, "On the Different Races of Man" (*Von den verschiedenen Rassen der Menschen*), Kant argues that all human beings belong to a single species that geography and climate have differentiated into four basic racial groups. In this way, he sanctions racial judgments, but without providing a criterion for criticizing *racist* judgments. Likewise, he allows for judgments about the differences between the sexes without developing the concept of *sexist* judgments. These shortcomings attest to a dilemma concerning the very idea of cosmopolitan anthropology. On the one hand, Kant wants to provide an anthropology of *man* rather than of *men*, and this requires that he emphasize what all human beings have in common. On the other hand, he wants to provide an anthropology of men (and women), and this requires that he call attention to what he perceives to be genuine differences. The fact that he is unable to develop a critique of racism and sexism shows that Kant has not entirely resolved the problem of how to reconcile these two projects. This dilemma survives in post-Kantian debates about race and gender. Nietzsche argues that there are significant sexual and racial differences and that these can be ranked in terms of their intrinsic worth. Lévi-Strauss and Irigaray agree that there are genuine differences but they deny that these can be ranked in any meaningful way. Fanon and Beauvoir deny the significance of such differences as there are by emphasizing what is universal in human nature.

Turning his attention from the differences between people to what we have in common, Kant asks whether ours is "a *good* race or an *evil* one." To this question he gives two complementary answers. On the one hand, man is evil because he persists in being motivated by pathological inclinations despite being summoned by the moral law to act from rational principles. Hence if we consider the overall course of human history, "we are often tempted to take the part of *Timon* the misanthropist in our judgments" (AFPPV 192). But just as enthusiasm for a good cause (such as the French Revolution) can attest to man's innate propensity for moral improvement, so can aversion to the evil that men do: "our very judgment of condemnation reveals a moral predisposition in us" by virtue of which man must be considered to be good (AFPPV 192–3). Thus a morally justifiable misanthropy (toward men) can attest to a fundamental principle of philanthropy (toward man); by condemning men for their factual wickedness, we bear witness to man's counterfactual vocation for goodness. The difficulty is to reconcile esteem for man with revulsion toward men. In the *Observations*, Kant laments, "If I examine alternatively the noble and the weak side of men, I reprimand myself that I am unable to take that standpoint from which these contrasts present the great portrait of the whole of human nature in a stirring form" (OFBS 73).

Kant says that Rousseau taught him to *esteem* mankind. But esteem and love are two very different feelings. In the third *Critique*, Kant suggests that, while the experience of the sublime both fosters and depends upon our ability to esteem man's vocation as a moral being, the experience of the beautiful teaches us to love nature – presumably both the nature that is outside us as well as the nature that is in ourselves in the form of talents and inclinations. For men to appear not merely as worthy of respect but as lovable, the nature that is in them must be represented as beautiful. But man's nature is evil. As such its aesthetic analogue is not the beautiful (the symbol of the morally good) but the ugly – and just as the beautiful prepares us to love, so the ugly prepares us to hate. Hence the difficulty with learning to love men is that they are not lovable. Indeed, Kant's comment about taking the part of Timon suggests that it is only by *detesting* men that can one bear witness to one's esteem for the humanity *in* them: "I hate men – therefore I esteem man." Nietzsche's Zarathustra implicitly inverts this formula: "I love men – therefore I have contempt for man."

4.2   Nietzsche's overman

> Is man no more than this?
> (*The Tragedy of King Lear*,
>   III, iv, 102–3)

In *Thus Spoke Zarathustra: a Book for All and None* (*Also Sprach Zarathustra: Ein Buch für Alle und Keinen*, 1883–1884, 1892), Nietzsche characterizes man as "a rope, tied between beast and overman – a rope over an abyss" (Z 14). For Kant, man was a rope stretched between beast and what the Christian Gospels refer to as the "new man" (RWBMR 92). To overcome man in this sense is to overcome his evil: "virtue consists precisely in *self-overcoming*"

(RRT 409). Zarathustra also says that "Man is something that shall be over-come," but he laments the fact that man's evil – not his virtue – is "still so small" (Z 12; cf. NAP 163). Kant said that man was only radically and not diabolically evil, for despite his innate propensity to violate the moral law, he always has respect for it (RWBMR 70). For Zarathustra, man's respect for the moral law is like a burden carried by a camel. In his description of "the three metamorphoses" of the spirit, he contends that it is necessary for the spirit of the camel to give way to that of a lion who must slay "the great dragon" that bears the name "'Thou shalt.'" By making "resistance to the [moral] law" itself into a principle, the lion is diabolically evil (RWBMR 82). But the spirit of the lion must in turn give way to the innocent spirit of the child whose "sacred 'Yes'" is *beyond good and evil* (Z 25–7).

The distinction between the lion and the child suggests that man must become "more" evil, not so that he can transgress the moral law, but so that he can transcend it. Zarathustra says that his "higher men" would be amazed at the "kindness" of the overman. This implies that the child might well act "in accordance with" duty but not "from" duty. It also implies that even when the child acts "contrary to duty," she acts not out of hatred but out of love. What Nietzsche calls "the great contempt" is the misanthropic hatred that man directs at everything that is still animal in him: "On the way to becoming an 'angel' . . . man has upset his stomach and developed a furry tongue so that he finds not only that the joy and innocence of animals is dis-gusting, but that life itself is distasteful" (OGOM 47). This attitude is exemplified in Kant, for whom a merely animal existence for man would be worth "less than zero" (CPJ 301n; G 51).

When Zarathustra first comes down from his mountain, the first person he meets is a saintly hermit who asks him why he is abandoning his solitude to rejoin humanity. When Zarathustra responds with the simple words, "I love man," the saint warns him: "Do not go to man. . . . Go rather even to the animals!" (Z 11). The misanthropic attitude of the hermit suggests that he is like a Carazan who has repented from his greed but who still sees no reason to seek the company of others. More precisely, he is what Kant feared he would have become if Rousseau had not taught him to esteem mankind. By contrast, Zarathustra's attitude is philanthropic. He does not seek human companions because he fears eternal solitude, but because he wants to bring men a gift.

At one point, Zarathustra recounts to his followers a series of dreams, the first of which has a striking resemblance to the dream of Carazan:

> I had turned my back on all life, thus I dreamed. I had become a night watchman and a guardian of tombs upon the lonely mountain castle of death. . . . Thus time passed and crawled, if time still existed – how should I know? But eventually that happened which awakened me. Thrice, strokes struck at the gate like thunder. . . . Then a roaring wind . . . cast up a black coffin before me . . . the coffin burst and spewed out a

thousandfold laughter. . . . I cried in horror as I have never cried. And my own cry awakened me – and I came to my senses.

(Z 134–5)

One of his disciples interprets Zarathustra's dream as a symbol of his struggle with those who preach death rather than life; in awakening from the dream he triumphs over his enemies. Zarathustra listens patiently to this interpretation but rejects it as inadequate. He recognizes that the dream represents his confrontation with his "most abysmal thought," the thought of the eternal return. The fact that he awakens from the dream is a sign that – like the father who dreamt that his son was burning – he is not yet ready to confront his abysmal thought. Awakening to human company – i.e., prematurely rejoining the *sensus communis* – is construed as a symptom, a sign that it is necessary for him to retreat into the solitude of his own *sensus privatus* (Z 218).

The second dream that Zarathustra reports is of stillness: "Yesterday, in the stillest hour, the ground gave under me, the dream began. The hand moved, the clock of my life drew a breath; never had I heard such stillness around me: my heart took fright." This time, he does not immediately awaken. Instead, the stillness speaks to him: "You know it, Zarathustra?" (Z 145). Once again, he is confronted by his most abysmal thought, but he is not yet ready to speak it – not even to himself. For this reason, he tells his friends, "I must return to my solitude" (Z 147).

Zarathustra's third dream, the one in which he is finally able not merely to confront his most abysmal thought but to affirm it as his most blissful thought, is a dream during which he remains fully conscious. This time, instead of being frightened by eternal stillness he embraces it, admonishing his soul, "Still! Still! Did not the world become perfect just now?" (Z 276). Having affirmed his most abysmal thought, Zarathustra is ready to convene a convivial gathering ("The Last Supper") of "higher men," that is, to bring *his* taste to the table.

Why is the thought of the eternal return an object of horror that Zarathustra must confront? For Freud, the object of a traumatic experience is something that in a sense "eternally recurs," resisting all efforts of assimilation. In this sense, eternal return is like an accidental property that a contingent object of horror acquires. But for Zarathustra the object of horror is the thought of eternal return itself. What recurs qua symptom is recurrence itself. An object does not recur because it is horrifying; on the contrary, it is horrifying because it recurs. Thus when first the dwarf and later Zarathustra's animals present the doctrine of the eternal return as a simple fact, Zarathustra chides them for making things too easy. So long as one fails to grasp what is horrifying in the thought of the return, one fails to grasp it at all.

For Kant, time is not only linear but straight, so that it is impossible for the past to recur; only madmen see ghosts. But how exactly can one orient oneself in time so as to be able to distinguish the direction of the past from the direction of the future? Kant provides a clue to this question in his essay, "What is orientation in thinking?" (*Was heisst: Sich im Denken orientiren*, 1786):

> To *orientate* oneself, in the proper sense of the word, means to use a given direction – and we divide the horizon into four of these – in order to find the others, and in particular that of *sunrise*. If I see the sun in the sky and know that it is not midday, I know how to find south, west, north, and east.
>
> (PW 238)

Here orientation is conceived (in accordance with what Heidegger will call the "vulgar" conception of time) as a problem of locating ourselves in space. Our ability to orient ourselves rests upon a subjective feeling of the difference between the right and left sides of our bodies. But suppose it is a question not of spatial orientation but of orientation in thought. Metaphysics is reason's attempt to get its bearings beyond the confines of possible experience. But since there are no objectively given transcendent coordinates to which reason can appeal, we must rely on the subjectively felt "needs" of reason. Though we cannot see God as we see the sun (contra Plato), we feel reason's subjective need to posit God's existence as a transcendent analogue of the sun.

To be oriented in *time* is to have a will that directs us toward the future. But only respect for the moral law can orient us toward a noumenal "future" of the soul's continued existence after death. It is here that the attitudes of fear and hope take on their properly transcendent meanings. Were I to know that no afterlife awaited me upon death, the experience would be morally disorienting in the specific sense that I would lose my temporal pole star, the ultimate object of fear and hope. "Whither are we plunging?" asked Nietzsche's madman in the marketplace to those who failed to appreciate what it meant to pronounce the death of God. Yet far worse, for Kant, would be to discover not only that there is no afterlife but that *this* life eternally recurs. For apart from the prospect of an afterlife, the value of life is "less than zero." Thus to discover that my life eternally recurs would truly be an occasion for rational despair.

Such is the conclusion reached by the soothsayer who confronts Zarathustra with his most abysmal thought. But there is a difference between the absolute despair experienced by the soothsayer and the temporary despair to which Zarathustra succumbs. In Zarathustra's case it is not despair over the fact that we never attain an afterlife but despair that "the small man," the despairing Kantian, eternally recurs. In a sense, Zarathustra's despair is pity on behalf of those who eternally recur as despairers-of-the-afterworldly. What enables him to overcome his pity is his discovery that such despair rests upon a clandestine hatred of humanity. The teaching of the eternal return is a joyous teaching, but only for those who love humanity "both in themselves and in others."

Zarathustra's teaching therefore turns on a new conception of orientation in time, that is, on a new conception of hope. For Kant, it is religion, not politics, that is charged with the question, "For what may I hope?" For Nietzsche, a new hope is born with the teaching that God is dead, and it is with Kant's substitution of religion for politics in mind that we should read his pronouncement, in *Ecce Homo*, "It is only beginning with me that the earth knows *great politics*" (EH 327). To accept the fact that God is dead is to forsake the transcendent analogue of spatial orientation, while to affirm the eternal return is to forsake the transcendent analogue of temporal orientation. This is not – as the soothsayer thinks – to forsake orientation altogether. On the contrary, Zarathustra's other teaching, the doctrine of the will to power, is an account of what it means to orient oneself in space and time. "Distant seas" and "blessed isles" are metaphors for an object of spatial orientation. But it is the sun that functions as the sole object of temporal orientation. From the Prologue, where he apostrophizes the sun ("You great star"), to the closing sentence in which he is himself described as "glowing and strong as a morning sun that comes out of dark mountains," – virtually every event in Zarathustra's narrative is oriented with respect to the sun (Z 9, 327). What is perhaps most significant is that each of these purely immanent indices of time – "before sunrise," "dawn," "at noon," "sunset," and "midnight" – are times that recur.

Replacing God and the afterlife as transcendent objects of orientation is the overman: "Once one said God when one looked upon distant seas; but now I have taught you to say: overman" (Z 85). The overman represents man's future not as enduring – i.e., as the lasting of the "last man" – but as that toward which his perishing is directed. In this respect, the overman represents not a transcendent point of temporal orientation like the Other in Levinas – this is arguably the stance of Nietzsche's "last pope" – but an immanent beyond, "the meaning of the earth" toward which man's most authentic "arrow of longing" is directed. It is in this sense that Zarathustra teaches not "love of the neighbor" but "love of the farthest," or rather love of what is farthest *in* the neighbor. In effect, the overman can only be "approached" by protentions and retentions – what Žižek characterizes as a kind of "temporal anamorphosis" (FA 171).

Understood in terms of the teaching of the return, to orient oneself in time is not merely to act with regard to the future but to overcome the present for the sake of both past and future: "I love him who justifies future and redeems past generations: for he wants to perish of the present" (Z 16). For Heidegger, Zarathustra's conception of redemption represents "the will's ill will against time and its 'it was'" (Z 140; N IV 223). On this interpretation, redemption frees the will from the need for revenge, that is, from resentment toward the transiency of all that is. But this construal overlooks the positive statement that Zarathustra makes about willing backward: "To redeem those who lived in the past and to recreate all 'it was' into a 'thus I willed it' – that alone should I call redemption" (Z 139). Though Nietzsche denies that Zarathustra is a "world-redeemer" in the Christian sense, this passage suggests that his conception of redemption is not so far removed from that of Benjamin.

In *The Fragile Absolute, Or Why the Christian Legacy is Worth Fighting For* (2000), Žižek suggests that the real message of Christianity is that love in the form of *agape* provides us with a way of renouncing the moral law without ending up endorsing its obscene, superegoic flip side. By contrast, in *The Antichrist* (*Der Antichrist*, 1895, written in 1888), Nietzsche suggests that something like superegoic cruelty is at the heart of St. Paul's teaching: "In Paul was embodied the antithetical type to the 'bringer of glad tidings,' the genius of hatred, of the vision of hatred, of the inexorable logic of hatred" (AC 164).[8] Likewise, Zarathustra calls attention to an obscene underside of the contemplative stance that is embodied in Pauline Christianity: "now your emasculated leers wish to be called 'contemplation'" (Z 123). In effect, both Žižek and Nietzsche defend the possibility of a diabolically evil act that would retroactively redeem the past. But diabolical evil in this sense must be conceived as acting from love rather than hatred. To act from love would require what Žižek characterizes as a "traversal of the fantasy," the acceptance of subjective destitution. For Nietzsche it would involve the "passage from beast to overman" and the acceptance of Zarathustra's "most abysmal thought." Žižek characterizes the absolute as "fragile" in the sense that it appears only fleetingly; an act of love represents a "magic moment when *the Absolute appears* in all its fragility" (FA 159). Sartre characterized acts of freedom this way: "By the sole fact that our choice is absolute, it is *fragile*" (BN 598). But in contrast to the figure of the fragile absolute – the evanescent moment when the absolute becomes incarnate – Nietzsche invokes a moment of *absolute fragility*, not the evanescence of the eternal but the eternality of the evanescent: "*For I love you, O eternity!*" (Z 228ff.). Thus Zarathustra speaks of the world's "just now" becoming perfect – something necessarily missed by the blinking last man – and affirms that "Thoughts that come on doves' feet guide the world" (Z 146; cf. EH 219). If the figure of the fragile absolute holds out the promise of transcendence, that of absolute fragility represents an affirmation of temporal immanence: "Precisely the least, the softest, lightest, a lizard's rustling, a breath, a breeze, a moment's glance – it is *little* that makes the *best* happiness" (Z 277).

Much as Kant treated Platonic banquets as ideal occasions for thematizing the nature of man, so Zarathustra uses his "Last Supper" to characterize the "higher man" as a "bridge" to the overman, rather than as an "end" in itself (Z 283, 198; cf. OGOM 62). For Kant, the aim of a good dinner conversation was to strive to achieve a *sensus communis*. By contrast, at his dinner party, Zarathustra emphasizes the idiosyncratic character of his own taste: "I am a law only for my kind, I am no law for all" (Z 285; cf. 209). In *Ecce Homo* – the book in which he announces "*who I am*" – Nietzsche quotes

Zarathustra: "You say you believe in Zarathustra? But what matters Zarathustra? . . . You had not yet sought yourselves: and you found me. . . . Now I bid you lose me and find yourselves; and only when you have all denied me will I return to you" (EH 217, 220; Z 78). Like Nietzsche himself, Zarathustra stresses the difficulty of becoming who one is: "Man is hard to discover – hardest of all for himself. . . . He, however, has discovered himself who says, 'This is *my* good and evil'. . . . Deep yellow and hot red: thus *my* taste wants it" (Z 194). Likewise, in *Beyond Good and Evil*, Nietzsche insists: "'My judgment is *my* judgment': no one else is easily entitled to it" (BGE 53). In affirming the unique character of his own taste, Nietzsche is not defending the thesis of Kant's antinomy according to which there is no *disputing* about matters of taste. On the contrary, "all of life is a dispute over taste and tasting" (Z 117). Zarathustra does not shun human company as the solitary hermit does. Instead he seeks it, as the Greeks did, for the sake of conflict. Whereas the peace-loving life of the hermit bespeaks asceticism and *ressentiment* toward humanity "both in oneself and in others," Zarathustra bids his higher men to affirm their *sensus privatus* – and to value peace only as a means to new wars.

4.3 Sartre's resolve for man's freedom

> Men at some time are masters of their fates;
> The fault, dear Brutus, is not in our stars,
> But in ourselves, that we are underlings.
> (*The Tragedy of Julius Caesar*, I, ii, 139–41)

At the end of *Being and Nothingness*, Sartre alluded to a work in progress in which he would address the question of whether there was "another fundamental attitude" besides that of bad faith (BN 798). Though this work was never completed, Sartre takes up this possibility in his 1946 lecture, "Existentialism is a Humanism" (*L'Existentialism est un humanisme*).[9] Whereas earlier he had characterized man as a "useless passion" who could not forsake the desire to be God – i.e., the desire for the freedom of the for-itself to coincide with the facticity of the in-itself – he now suggests that it is possible to make sheer freedom the object of one's aspiration (BN 784). This project is paradoxical in that the for-itself is always ineluctably free. But to be in bad faith is to be in flight from one's freedom, so that the choice would be between bad faith – the project of becoming God – and the project of embracing one's freedom. If the desire to be God represents man's "fundamental fantasy," then to "traverse" this fantasy is to accept the irreducible fissure that prevents the for-itself from coinciding with an imaginary or symbolic identity. This was the aim of Lacanian analysis, which Žižek identified with Hegel's construal of the death of Christ. By contrast, Sartre equates the goal of existential analysis with Nietzsche's atheism. Thus, although he distinguishes the "necessity of choosing" from "the will to power," Sartre explicitly echoes Zarathustra's view that man's principal nemesis is the "spirit of seriousness," i.e., the belief in the existence of transcendent values (BN 607, 796; Z 41). Just as Nietzsche's madman chided the "atheists in the marketplace" for still believing in God, so Sartre criticizes those who think that, despite the death of God, "values exist all the same" (EHE 22). To deny the existence of transcendent values is not to embrace nihilism but to acknowledge that we ourselves are the source of all values: "if I've discarded God the Father, there has to be someone to invent values" (EHE 49).

The central tenet of Sartre's "atheistic existentialism" is that "if God does not exist, there is at least one being in whom existence precedes essence, a being who exists before he can be defined by any concept ... this being is man" (EHE 15). In contrast to something whose existence is exhausted by its facticity, a being that is free cannot be completely subsumed under any pre-existing concept. Only through existing does it acquire an essence. Just as Zarathustra characterized man as an "arrow and longing," so Sartre characterizes man as a "passing-beyond": "The existentialist will never consider man as an end because he is always in the making ... it is by pursuing transcendent goals that he is able to exist" (EHE 50). To exist is not merely to determine the relationship between my for-itself and my in-itself but to determine my existence with respect to others. In *Being and Nothingness*, Sartre left open the abstract possibility that there could be an isolated human being for whom others would not exist, but he also claimed that such a possibility is meaningless for us: "It would perhaps not be impossible to conceive of a For-itself which would be wholly free from all For-others. . . . But this For-itself simply would not be 'man'" (BN 376). Just as the for-itself stands in a relation of "internal negation" to the in-itself, so it stands in a comparable relation to the Other. Insofar as it discloses the existence of another person, this second negation has a radically alienating effect on the for-itself. Drawing on Hegel's account of the master/slave dialectic, Sartre characterizes the relationship of the for-itself to the Other as one of irreducible conflict (BN 475). The relationship is conflictual because it is seemingly impossible for each of the two to recognize the other *as* a for-itself at the same time. Either I subject the body of the Other to my gaze, in which case the Other is alienated in the sense of being what he or she is as something in-itself for me, or else I am alienated in the sense of being subject to the gaze of the Other. Each of us, as a for-itself, is a transcendence of the in-itself. But to gaze at the Other is to transcend the Other's transcendence. Sartre describes various strategies by which the for-itself and the Other attempt to negotiate their mutual alienation. Love, masochism, indifference, hate, and sadism are all so many attempts to accomplish on the plane of the relationship between the for-itself and the Other the same impossible coincidence that we desire at the level of the relationship between the for-itself and the in-itself. Indeed, the relationship to the Other becomes the vehicle through which we attempt to achieve the coincidence of for-itself and in-itself, for in the eyes of the Other I am my in-itself; were I able to look at myself through the eyes of the Other while miraculously retaining my own standpoint, I would thereby attain a coincidence of my for-itself and in-itself. In this way the desire to be God takes on its properly social dimension.

Just as it is impossible for the individual for-itself to coincide with its in-itself, so it is impossible for the for-itself to coincide with the Other. For Hegel, the master/slave dialectic could be overcome through "mutual recognition," by which each individual becomes capable of identifying itself with spirit – that is, with God. But for Sartre, to presume that we can take the point of view of the totality is to accept the very fantasy that must be traversed if the for-itself is to affirm its condition of irreducible alienation. To renounce the desire to be God is to renounce the possibility of any totalizing point of view. Because my in-itself is "in the hands of the Other," I cannot extricate myself from other human beings. Thus human interaction is a perpetual attempt to achieve a totality that can never be fully attained. In choosing myself I not only choose what I am for others and what others are for me; more radically, I choose what it is to be a human being in general: "when we say that a man is responsible for himself, we do not only mean that he is responsible for his own individuality, but that he is responsible for all men" (EHE 16). By making explicit this aspect of human existence, existentialism represents a kind of "humanism." On one construal, humanism is the view that the value of human existence is determined by an essence that does precede it in some way – as in Kant's view that the a priori nature of humanity is determined by the categorical imperative. But if man is that being who has to create an essence for himself, then existentialism is the only authentic humanism.

To affirm one's freedom is to take responsibility for all of humanity. The experience of freedom is an occasion for anxiety precisely because each of us must act as a "lawmaker who is, at the same time, choosing all mankind as well as himself" (EHE 18). This principle resembles Kant's categorical imperative, according to which I must act as if the maxim of my action were to be adopted by all rational beings. In Sartre's version, I must act as if by my action I were choosing an essence for all of humanity. The difference between these two formulas turns on the force of the word "must." The categorical imperative tells me what I "ought" to do, thereby providing me with a transcendent moral norm with which the maxim of my action may or may not accord. Its existential analogue tells me that, whatever I do, I "cannot but" choose for humanity as a whole. Paradoxically, it is the very failure of my freedom to escape the force of this existential "must" that marks my condition as radically free – i.e., as "condemned" to be free. Even if I were to attempt to shirk my responsibility by relying on the categorical imperative, it would always be by way of a choice – and even then I would have to choose how to apply the categorical imperative to concrete situations (EHE 47).

The fact that I cannot *not* choose an essence for all of humanity shows that, if there is such a thing as an existentialist imperative, it is to be found not in the statement, "I must act as if I were choosing for all of humanity," but rather in the meta-level demand that I acknowledge the compelling force of this very statement. This is equivalent to the demand that one be sincere by renouncing bad faith. But what exactly is the nature of this demand? It cannot be a categorical imperative, for that would vitiate Sartre's repudiation of the spirit of seriousness. But neither can it be a hypothetical imperative since it bids me to accept responsibility for the very objects of my desire. Sartre calls attention to a similar paradox apropos our relationship to the past:

> Logically the requirements of the past are hypothetical imperatives: "If you wish to have such and such a past, act in such and such a way." But as the first term is a concrete and categorical choice, the imperative also is transformed into a categorical imperative.
>
> (BN 646)

Thus the form of Sartre's existential imperative is itself categorical; essentially it says, "Accept your responsibility!" rather than "If you want such-and-such, then you ought to accept your responsibility." But can the imperative to be responsible escape the bad faith that Sartre detected in the demand for sincerity: "a task impossible to achieve"? (BN 105; cf. 112).

To resolve this difficulty, Sartre suggests that I cannot choose freedom for myself without choosing freedom for everyone: "in wanting freedom we discover that it depends entirely on the freedom of others" (EHE 46). That is, only the choice of freedom can justify the choice of freedom. Were I to choose bad faith, my choice would be a justification of bad faith. Although there is no transcendent value in terms of which the choice between freedom and bad faith could be adjudicated, Sartre characterizes it as the choice between courage and cowardice, where "courage" and "cowardice" refer not to objects of choice but to our willingness or unwillingness to accept responsibility for what we choose. When Sartre says that "even the red-hot pincers of the torturer do not exempt us from being free," he does not mean that the choice between holding out and confessing is itself a choice between courage and cowardice. Rather, everything points to the conclusion that courage consists in recognizing that whatever I do will have been freely chosen. At first Sartre claims that it is always possible for the torture victim to refuse to confess, since any limitation on possibility would entail the possibility of an unfree consciousness. But later he acknowledges that the omnipresence of freedom "does not mean that it is always *possible*" to resist the red-hot pincers "but simply that the *very impossibility* ... must be freely constituted" (BN 649). In constituting myself as no longer capable of resisting the red-hot pincers, I am in effect reduced to my being-toward-death – i.e., toward the possibility of no longer having possibilities.

Being-toward-death remains a way of comporting myself with respect to my living possibilities, but insofar as my facticity narrows the range of what is possible for me – ultimately to the limit of a single possibility – it reveals the gap that separates the omnipresent freedom of a constituting consciousness from the factical conditions for what might be called "real" freedom.

The example of the torture victim points toward a more general problem concerning the relationship between facticity and freedom. Sartre's heroic existential imperative seems to pertain solely to the constituting freedom of consciousness. Though it thereby points toward the ever-present possibility of resistance to facticity – and so to the project of transforming one's situation – it risks placing so high a value on the constituting freedom of consciousness that it overlooks those elements of facticity that exercise a constraint on the scope of the real freedom of situated individuals. To resolve this difficulty, Sartre abandons his existentialist ethics in favor of an attempt to incorporate an existentialist account of the human predicament within a more encompassing analysis of the relationship between freedom and facticity, one that would take into account those elements of situations that prevent a complete identification of freedom with possibility. Such a more encompassing framework had already been developed by Marx, who, like Sartre, stressed the irreducibly social character of freedom: "my *own* existence *is* social activity, and therefore that which I make of myself, I make of myself for society and with the consciousness of myself as a social being" (EAPM 137). Though the Marxist tradition had given rise to an ossified set of a priori dogmas, Marx's own theory of history provides precisely the sort of broader anthropological framework in terms of which the limited insights of existentialism can be situated (SFM 27).

In his *Critique of Dialectical Reason* (*Critique de la raison dialectique, précédé de questions de méthode, I. Théorie des ensembles pratiques*, 1960), Sartre attempts to put historical materialism on existentially secure foundations and to rework his own "pre-critical" accounts of the relationship between freedom and facticity from an explicitly Marxist point of view. The first task requires that Marxist concepts be derived from the concrete existential situations in which individual human beings find themselves. But the second requires a transformation of the theoretical concepts employed in *Being and Nothingness*. There it was a question of beginning with the concrete individual who had to identify with his or her facticity in the mode of fleeing from it, forever alienated from others. But now it is necessary to regard this individual not merely from the standpoint of the constituting freedom of consciousness but from that of the realizing freedom of praxis. Praxis is an engagement not merely with what *Being and Nothingness* called the in-itself but with the "practico-inert," the totality of constraining factors on real freedom, whether these belong to the in-itself proper or to the condition of being-for-others. The ultimate aim of the *Critique* is to analyze the various forms that being-for-others can take over the course of history, with an eye toward envisioning a conception of History as a dialectical totalizing that has as its regulative ideal the realization of human freedom. Marxism represents a provisional anthropology that will have outlived its usefulness when this ideal is achieved. Only at that point – that is, the point at which the bare constituting freedom of consciousness and real possibility coincide – will humanity have attained the standpoint at which a new philosophy of freedom will spontaneously arise:

> As soon as there will exist *for everyone* a margin of *real* freedom beyond the production of life, Marxism will have lived out its span; a philosophy of freedom will take its place. But we have no means, no intellectual instrument, no concrete experience which allows us to conceive of this freedom or of this philosophy.
>
> (SFM 34)

4.4   Heidegger's reproach against man's hubris

> But wherefore did you so much tempt the heavens?
> It is the part of men to fear and tremble
> When the most mighty gods by tokens send
> Such dreadful heralds to astonish us.
> (*The Tragedy of Julius Caesar*, I, iii, 53–6)

In his "Letter on Humanism" – a response to a series of questions raised by the Catholic philosopher Jean Beaufret (1907–1982) apropos Sartre's "Existentialism is a Humanism" – Heidegger expresses serious reservations about the concept of humanism, particularly insofar as it is founded upon the traditional definition of man as "rational animal" (BW 226). Insofar as this definition belongs to metaphysics – that is, to the oblivion of being – it fails to question man's relation to being and so cannot say what or who man "is." In *Being and Time*, Heidegger deliberately avoided the expressions "man" and "rational animal," using the word "Dasein" to refer to the unique kind of existence by which we stand in a relation to being. In later works, Heidegger attempts to rekindle a sense of the ontological import of Kant's question, "What is man?" The history of metaphysics represents the coming to presence of man's hubris, notably in the fateful Cartesian conception of man as subject – a definition which is consolidated in the subsequent history of metaphysics that extends from Leibniz's conception of the appetite through Kant's definition of the will to Nietzsche's construal of the will to power (QCT 82, 90ff.). This trajectory culminates in the transformation of ontology itself into anthropology (QCT 133). Despite the fact that anthropology puts man at the foundation of being – or rather, precisely because it does this – it is unable even to hear what is being asked in the question, "What is man?: "Anthropology is that interpretation of man that already knows fundamentally what man is and hence can never ask who he may be" (QCT 153; cf. N IV 138–9).

From this point of view, Sartre's conception of man as that being who must decide his own fate represents an unthinking continuation of the nihilism that Nietzsche diagnosed but could not circumvent. Only by renouncing the arrogance of his will can man hope to regain his proper relation to being: "the concealed essence of Being ... will be given over to man when he has overcome himself as subject" (QCT 154). Sartre's conception of man's fundamental nothingness is so lost in the darkening of nihilism that he is unable to recognize his own destitution. In effect, he is like one of the "atheists in the marketplace" whom Nietzsche's madman chided for not understanding what it means to seek God: "these men are not unbelievers because God as God has to them become unworthy of belief, but rather because they themselves have given up the possibility of belief, inasmuch as they are no longer able to seek God" (QCT 112). The only way in which man can regain his essence as man – thereby opening up the possibility of an authentic humanism – is for him to recognize himself as *claimed* by being: "man essentially occurs only in his essence, where he is claimed by Being" (BW 227).

In *Kant and the Problem of Metaphysics*, Heidegger tried to overcome modern anthropology by construing Kant's question, "What is man?," as a way of asking about "the *Dasein* in man" (KAPOM 242). This expression reappears in the "Letter on Humanism." To say that Dasein is "in" man cannot mean that it belongs to man as one of his properties; on the contrary, the being of Dasein – Dasein's being-*in*-the-world – is fundamentally a belonging to being. To speak of the Dasein that is in man is to speak of that by virtue of which man has "dignity." For Kant, man had dignity because of the presence of the moral law within him. Insofar as he is radically evil, man must strive to recover his dignity by striving for purity of the will. Kant characterizes the moral law as a "holy treasure" that man is charged with safekeeping. Analogously, Heidegger suggests that man's dignity lies with that belonging-to-being within him which he is called to preserve. However, whereas Kant identified the safekeeping of the moral law with the purity of man's will, Heidegger instead characterizes man's "shepherding of being" as depending on his renunciation of willing: "Man is not the lord of beings. Man is the shepherd of Being. He gains the essential poverty of the shepherd, whose dignity consists in being called by Being itself into the preservation of Being's truth" (BW 245; cf. QCT 42). To accord dignity to man's will is to degrade that which is alone truly worthy of dignity. Insofar as "humanists" such as Sartre fail to grasp this insight, they degrade man in the very moment that they exalt him: "the highest determinations of the essence of man in humanism still do not realize the proper dignity of man" (BW 233).

According to Heidegger, Nietzsche misconstrued nihilism as a sign of man's need to create new values, when in fact valuing is itself a symptom of nihilism: "precisely through the characterization of something as 'a value' what is so valued is robbed of its worth" (BW 251). Despite the fact that

Nietzsche denounces the Cartesian cogito as a fiction generated by man's need to impose a semblance of fixity on restless becoming, Heidegger regards his conception of the will to power as an extension of the Cartesian subject. By defining man as that being who creates an essence for himself, Sartre makes this connection explicit, while unwittingly extending the reign of nihilism.

The ontological hubris of Sartre's existential humanism is evidenced in his attempt to recast Heidegger's distinction between Dasein's preontological and ontological understanding of being as that between the prereflective and reflective cogitos, and in his view that it is man who brings nothingness into the world. Against this point of view, Heidegger insists that nothingness is brought forth by being itself: "Nihilation unfolds essentially in Being itself, and not at all in the existence of man – so far as this is thought as the subjectivity of the *ego cogito*" (BW 261). Here nihilation is to be understood as the "clearing" of the opening [*Da*] by which man "is there" [*Da-sein*] in the world. As the unpublished third division of part one of *Being and Time* was to have shown, it is not man but being itself that is essential in man's being-in-the-world: "in the determination of the humanity of man as ek-sistence what is essential is not man but Being" (BW 237).

For Sartre, Heidegger's attempt to think man's presencing as an event that takes place within the plenitude of being is an expression of the desire to be God. Sartre concedes that everything happens *as if* the in-itself negated itself so that the for-itself might affirm it, but he regards this as a kind of dialectical illusion. For Heidegger, however, this argument begs the question. Only if we had already accepted the metaphysical interpretation of "being-in-itself" as inert objectness would it follow that it is man rather than being that brings forth the clearing through which beings show themselves. Thus in contrast to Sartre, for whom "The in-itself has nothing secret," Heidegger insists on the fact that "Being remains mysterious" (BN 28; BW 236). Heidegger's criticism of Sartre's atheism does not derive from a prior commitment to theism – "no one dominated by an attitude – whether approving or disapproving – inspired by theology, can enter the dimension of the problem of a metaphysics of *Dasein*" – but rather from a conception of piety as the duty of thought to seek God: "For questioning is the piety of thought" (KAPOM 245; QCT 35).

In Plato's *Euthyphro*, Socrates interrogates Euthyphro about the nature of piety after learning that Euthyphro is bringing a charge of impiety against his father for inadvertently causing the death of a slave. The discussion reaches an impasse when Euthyphro finds himself unable to say whether the pious is pious because the gods love it or whether the gods love it because it is pious. Perhaps the pious is a transcendent value. Or perhaps there is no such thing as the pious apart from the arbitrary whim of those who value something as pious. Interpreted in either of these two ways, Plato's dialogue would represent for Heidegger a symptom of nihilism, of the fact that "the highest values must eventually lose their value." But the aporia could be taken instead as a sign that the question has not yet been properly posed. For Heidegger, we obscure what is at stake in the question – namely, man's comportment with respect to the Dasein that is in him – whether we accept the existence of transcendent values or regard man as the creator of values.

Upon agreeing that the pious cannot be defined as that which is pleasing to all of the gods, Socrates and Euthyphro go on to consider whether it might consist in a certain kind of service to the gods. Though inconclusive, their discussion of this question suggests that piety might have something to do with the activity of questioning. In this view, impiety would mean neglecting the question of piety. We neglect the question not only when we fail to raise it explicitly, but whenever we believe ourselves entitled to determine what is or is not pious. Euthyphro's father did not know what would be the pious thing to do with the man who had committed murder, and so he left him in a ditch until the authorities could arrive. There the man died.

Should Euthyphro's father be convicted of impiety? For Kant, to be pious is simply to do what we ought to do; this is what it means to confine religion within the bounds of reason. But for Heidegger, we can only be pious "if, *before* considering the question that is seemingly always the most immediate one and the only urgent one, What shall we do? we ponder this: *How must we think?*" (QCT 40). If questioning is the piety of thought, then to "do" the pious thing is not to perform "works" but to allow oneself to be claimed by the grace of being. Since Euthyphro does not know the essence of the pious, it is presumptuous for him to accuse his father, who in any event did not kill the man who died. In 1946, Heidegger had a number of reasons to identify with Euthyphro's father, having just been suspended from his teaching position even though he did not kill anyone during the Nazi era. But Heidegger did choose to join the Nazi Party. Sartre would have said that, just as Euthyphro was in bad faith insofar as he tried to justify his actions by appealing to a transcendent value, so Euthyphro's father would be in bad faith were he to shirk his responsibility for the death of the slave. Sartre's question was whether repudiating the spirit of seriousness necessarily entails nihilism (BN 796). This is to ask if it is possible to conceive of human dignity once we admit that man is claimed not by being but by nothing.

4.5 Beauvoir's project of solidarity and her analysis of the lived experience of gender

And since you know you cannot see yourself
So well as by reflection, I, your glass,
Will modestly discover to yourself
That of yourself which you yet know not of.
    (*The Tragedy of Julius Caesar*, I, ii, 67–70)

In 1947, Simone de Beauvoir (1908–1986), Sartre's life-long companion, defended existential humanism in her book, *The Ethics of Ambiguity (Pour une morale de l'ambiguïté*). Beauvoir suggests that, although Heidegger is right to characterize man as a being who "belongs to being," Sartre is right to insist that man belongs to being in the mode of not belonging to it. This is what it means to be free. Because we are free, there is a kind of ontological hubris that is irreducible in human existence. Sartre captures this condition in his characterization of man as a "useless passion." If the "metaphysics of the will" can be characterized as the project of becoming God, then Sartre opens up the possibility of a critique of such a metaphysics by asking if it is possible to forsake this project. To do so would be to make freedom – rather than the impossible ideal of a coincidence of freedom and facticity – the object of man's passion.

Beauvoir suggests that, while one cannot renounce the project of becoming God altogether, one can bracket it. Doing so amounts to bringing about a radical shift in one's fundamental project. Without ceasing to exist as a "wanting to be," the suspension of this mode of being manifests itself as a "wanting to be free." To want to be free is not to want to be freed from the human predicament – that would be to desire suicide, itself another form of the desire to be God – but to affirm the predicament itself. To say that man belongs to being in the mode of not belonging to it is to say that man is both an ineluctable disclosure of being and the frustrated alienation from it. To affirm the human predicament would accordingly be to want to disclose that very being from which one is alienated. If the desire to be God must necessarily fail, the desire to disclose that very failure cannot but succeed. Thus we find in the suspension of man's ontological hubris an affirmation of that hubris as hubris. Put otherwise, in "wanting to disclose being" (EOA 12) we have what Heidegger would have regarded as a horrifying contradiction in terms: not the *will to power* but, as it were, a kind of *will to shepherd*.

Beauvoir is thus able to offer a precise answer to Sartre's question concerning the possibility of an existential ethics: "Ethics is the triumph of freedom over facticity" (EOA 44). In this account, existentialism is not merely compatible with ethics; it alone entails a genuine ethics, what Beauvoir calls an "ethics of ambiguity." The human condition is ambiguous in precisely the manner described by Sartre: man is torn between freedom and facticity, the for-itself and the in-itself. To say that it is in one sense impossible to forsake the desire to be God is not, however, to conclude that existence is absurd. Existence would be absurd only if it were impossible to give it any meaning. But, in fact, man is constantly giving existence meaning; his every choice is a determination of the meaning that existence will have. The problem is that this meaning can never be fixed once and for all. Thus existence is not absurd but ambiguous (EOA 129). If existence were absurd, no ethics would be possible. But insofar as it is ambiguous, ethics is on the contrary unavoidable. Existentialism teaches that ethics is nothing other than the demand that we take responsibility for whatever meaning existence will have. As such, it is simply the explicit acknowledgement of our ethical responsibility.

Despite the fact that "every man is originally free," flight is possible. For although "it would be contradictory deliberately to will oneself not free . . . one can choose not to will himself free" (EOA 25). Here Beauvoir assumes that we can distinguish, as it were, between prereflective freedom and reflective freedom. Thus at the most basic level there are only two possible ways of comporting oneself with respect to one's freedom: flight (bad faith) and perseverance (authenticity). To persevere in freedom is to will not the object of one's will but the will itself: "To will is to engage myself to persevere in my will" (EOA 27). In order to rise to the level of a properly ethical point of view, it is both necessary and sufficient reflectively to affirm one's freedom. But since there is no over-arching moral law that calls an individual to persevere, the injunction to persevere can only take the form of a hypothetical imperative: "If man wishes to save his existence, as only he himself can do, his original spontaneity must be raised to the height of moral freedom by taking itself as an end through the disclosure of a particular content" (EOA 32). It is possible not to want to save one's existence, in which case one will live one's freedom in flight. The choice between flight and perseverance is thus an irreducible either/or. What Beauvoir nevertheless wishes to demonstrate is that we can attain genuine dignity only through perseverance. In order to support this claim, she develops a typology of forms of flight.

In some sense prior to the distinction between flight and perseverance is the condition of childhood. An infant necessarily begins its life within the spirit of seriousness, regarding the world around it, including other people, as given compass points of practical orientation. Whether a very young child is happy or unhappy, she is in principle spared the anxiety of freedom. This condition of existential immaturity disappears the moment that the child recognizes itself as responsible for its own actions. Now for the first time she is faced with the choice of flight or perseverance, a choice that she will be perpetually confronted with from then on. Crucial to the experience of freedom is the recognition of one's character as a "useless passion." Either we are frustrated in our attempt to achieve something or we are disappointed in what we succeed in accomplishing. This is due not to a contingent psychological failure to be content with what we have but to our essential condition as lacks that are ever in vain seeking being. Nonetheless it is possible to respond to this condition in different ways. At one extreme is the attitude of the "sub-man." Instead of affirming his fundamental lack by throwing himself into his projects, the sub-man cultivates an attitude of indifference or apathy toward the world. In effect he pretends not to exist: "The sub-man rejects this 'passion' which is his human condition, the laceration and the failure of that drive toward being which always misses its goal, but which thereby is the very existence which he rejects" (EOA 42). Whether intended to represent the antithesis to Nietzsche's overman or not, the sub-man adopts an attitude that is diametrically opposed to that of the existentialist: the one attempts to identify itself with sheer facticity, the other with freedom.

Although the sub-man is in a condition of flight, he nonetheless remains free. His project of being pure facticity is therefore frustrated by his transcendence. For this reason the sub-man's fundamental project is unstable and can give way to that of the "serious man." Instead of attempting in vain to be apathetic toward the world, the serious man either reaffirms those transcendent social values that had guided him in childhood or adopts a new, but equally stable, fixed set of ready-made reference points. Socially conservative, the serious man lives in a condition akin to what Kant called "man's self-incurred immaturity," that is, his willful but futile attempt to return to the existentially comforting condition of childhood. Since a return to childhood is in fact impossible, the project of the serious man is once again unstable and liable to be forsaken in favor of the attitude of the nihilist.

Nihilism is the result of "disappointed seriousness" (EOA 52). Aware of the futility of the attempt to take refuge in transcendent values, the nihilist swings to the diametrically opposed position of pure freedom. Critical of all customary values, the nihilist attempts to deny facticity altogether. But for this very reason, her position is just as untenable as that of the sub-man, though for opposite reasons. If she does not commit suicide, the nihilist must acknowledge the very facticity from which she flees. If she then becomes capable of actively throwing herself back into her practical engagements, the nihilist thereby forsakes her project for that of the "adventurer."

The adventurer is someone who affirms her engaged freedom. As such hers is a project that could be entered into immediately after childhood. But even the adventurer remains in flight – not with respect to the being-for-itself/being-in-itself dyad, but with respect to the being-for-itself/being-for-others dyad. The adventurer attempts to be indifferent toward others, but her efforts to accomplish her freedom depend upon others' recognition. Hence the indifference of the adventurer is liable to give way to the sadism of the tyrant. Complementary to the attitude of the adventurer is that of the passionate man. Whereas the adventurer attempts to reduce others to the status of mere objects, the passionate man becomes an object for another into whose freedom he flees his own. Just as the spirit of adventure can give way to sadism, so masochism is one of the fundamental forms of passion.

In contrast to the symmetrical failures of the adventurer and the man of passion, the "genuinely free man" (EOA 61) is an individual who realizes that he cannot affirm his own freedom without affirming that of others (and vice versa): "To will oneself free is also to will others free" (EOA 73). By seeking solidarity with others, the authentically free individual attains a "genuine seriousness" that can be thought of as the negation of the negation of the spirit of seriousness (in that it contrasts not only with the spurious seriousness of the serious man but also with the nonseriousness of the nihilist) (EOA 60). Genuine seriousness is the attitude in which we find ourselves forced to make value judgments, knowing in advance that we are thereby condemned to the errancy of ontological hubris. Only through such an attitude can the project of solidarity be taken up in a meaningful way. Like Sartre, Beauvoir criticizes Heidegger's apparent reduction of the dialectical complexities of being-for-others to *Mitsein*.

In *The Second Sex* (*Le Deuxième Sexe*, 1949), Beauvoir suggests that the problem of solidarity can be properly posed only by taking into account the "fundamental hostility" that every consciousness initially feels toward every other consciousness (SS xxiii). This theme had already been explored in her first published novel, *She Came to Stay* (*L'Invitée*, 1943), for which Beauvoir chose as an epigram a passage from Hegel's account of the struggle for recognition: "Each consciousness seeks the death of the other."[10] Beauvoir's novel prefigures many of the analyses to be found in both *Being and Nothingness* and *The Ethics of Ambiguity*. Set just before the German invasion of France, Françoise and Pierre have a relationship not unlike that between Beauvoir and Sartre, a relationship based on the ideal of granting each other total freedom. Then a young woman named Xavière enters their lives, and Françoise finds herself torn between trying to welcome her into their lives and trying to avoid being smothered by her. Unable to resolve this tension in a satisfactory way, Françoise finally decides to kill her rival for Pierre's attention.

Throughout her writings, Beauvoir acknowledges the "absolute fragility" of solidarity. Unlike Hegel's absolute spirit, in which the fundamental ambiguities of existence are overcome, the project of solidarity is something that must be risked by concrete individual existing in the midst of others:

> I remember having experienced a great feeling of calm on reading Hegel in the impersonal framework of the Bibliothèque Nationale in August 1940. But once I got into the street again, into my life, out of the system, beneath a real sky, the system was no longer of any use to me: what it had offered me, under a show of the infinite, was the consolations of death; and I again wanted to live in the midst of living men.
>
> (EOA 158)

In August 1940, Beauvoir saw in the nascent Resistance movement more than the project of liberating France, for the Resistance "did not aspire to a positive effectiveness; it was a negation, a revolt, a martyrdom; and in this negative movement freedom was positively and absolutely confirmed" (EOA 131).

For Beauvoir, someone who is genuinely free makes every struggle against oppression her own. But it is possible for an individual or group of persons to be oppressed without actively rebelling against their condition. The objective situation can be such that those oppressed are forcibly kept in a state of passivity analogous to that of childhood. Beauvoir suggests that this was the case with black slaves in the United States who "respected the world of the whites" because they were in a situation of compulsory immaturity (EOA 37). There are also cases of "self-incurred" immaturity, that is, of willful acceptance of oppression as a way of fleeing one's freedom. In such a situation it would be necessary first to rouse a desire for freedom in those who are oppressed. Beauvoir regards both compulsory and self-incurred forms of immaturity as factors in the oppression of women. Thus, on the one hand, men continue to assert their sovereignty as subjects by actively subjugating women; yet, unlike the child or the slave, whose childlike condition is either natural or enforced, "the woman (I mean the western woman of today) chooses it or at least consents to it" (EOA 38). In order to combat the oppression of women, it is therefore necessary not only to resist the socially subordinate status to which women have been consigned but at the same time to foster a sense of ethical solidarity in those women who willingly accept their condition as a way of fleeing from their freedom.

Whereas *She Came to Stay* depicts the tragic consequences that can arise out of the struggle for recognition, *The Second Sex* tries to articulate the conditions under which such a struggle could culminate neither in death nor in slavery but in solidarity. For Beauvoir, the relationship between men and women cannot be understood in exclusively biological terms. Drawing on Lévi-Strauss's *Elementary Structures of Kinship*, she observes that social relations between men and women are based upon an interpretation of biological differences. One sign of this is the fact that the male/female dyad is treated not merely as an opposition between two "species" of humanity but simultaneously as the difference between genus and species: "the relation of the two sexes is not quite like that of two electrical poles, for man represents both the positive and the neutral" (SS xxi). In order to make sense of this eminently Hegelian phenomenon, according to which one side of an opposition has privilege over the other, it is necessary to view it through the lens of Hegel's account of the master/slave dialectic. A subject taking part in a struggle for recognition can acquire a sense of self only by subordinating his adversary to the position of the "inessential" or "other" (SS xxiii). This is precisely what men have done in order to establish their identity as "men" — in both the generic and specific senses of this term. Hence the salient feature of the social predicament of women is that they are identified by men as "the other," a condition that (male) philosophers from Aristotle to Levinas have insisted upon (SS xxii). Here, "other" must once again be understood not as that which is to be excluded but as an otherness immanent to humanity, an essential inessentiality by virtue of which man retains his status as "master" in relation to his "slave": "she is the Other in a totality of which the two components are necessary to one another" (SS xxvi).

Both men and women suffer from this predicament since neither can achieve that sense of genuine freedom which could arise only through mutual recognition. But since men nonetheless benefit from the situation, it is incumbent upon women themselves to overcome their oppression. In order for this to be possible, it is first necessary that women recognize themselves as a collective subject. Hitherto this has not been the case for two reasons. First, women recognize themselves not as a collective subject but as a collective object: "women do not say 'We,' . . .; men say 'women,' and women use the same word in referring to themselves" (SS xxv). Second, insofar as individual women have a sense of group identity, it is determined not on the basis of gender but on that of class or race: "If they belong to the bourgeoisie, they feel solidarity with men of that class, not with proletarian women; if they are white, their allegiance is to white men, not to Negro women" (SS xxv). In *The Ethics of Ambiguity*, Beauvoir acknowledges that in a world in which oppression takes many forms there are situations in which one must make difficult choices between competing group loyalties. Yet she also insists that the genuinely free individual is someone who, in principle, identifies with every oppressed group. Thus the formation of a sense of solidarity among women is not necessarily in competition with a sense of solidarity along class or race lines. Indeed, there is an affinity among every struggle against oppression, one that suggests the possibility of a broader conception of solidarity among all of those who are oppressed (SS xxix).

Beauvoir's conceptions of solidarity and mutual recognition as the telos of struggle are in marked contrast to the ethical position advanced by Levinas. Not only does she reject Levinas's equation of otherness with femininity, but she repudiates the conception of generosity as exclusively other-regarding: "generosity seems to us to be better grounded and therefore more valid the less distinction there is between the other and oneself and the more we fulfill ourself in taking the other as an end" (EOA 144). This implies that what is objectionable in Levinas's ethics is not so much its presumption in favor of masculinity as its fetishization of femininity. Insofar as he thinks the ethical relation as a way of being claimed by the wholly other, that is, by the feminine, Levinas succumbs to another version of the spirit of seriousness — not the blatantly patriarchal seriousness of the master but its perverse obverse, the celebration of the "eternal feminine." Thus he replaces the sadism of the master with the masochism of the slave. By seeking another way of identifying with the standpoint of the slave, Beauvoir is able to defend the Hegelian conception of mutual recognition as the proper telos of ethics.

Wherever there is oppression, time is out of joint. In relationships between men and women, "the time they spend together — which fallaciously seems to be the same time — does not have the same value for both partners . . . for a man normally integrated in society, time is a positive value . . . when she succeeds in killing time, it is a benefit to her" (SS 722). The struggle for recognition between Françoise and Xavière takes the form of a conflict between rival temporalities. What eventually becomes unbearable for Françoise is the fact that in the eyes of Xavière, her own future is reduced to the status of a mere past: "There was no longer any future. The past alone was real, and it was in Xavière that the past was incarnate" (SCTS 388). Even more unbearable is Françoise's realization that she is forced to choose between reducing the other's future to a past and allowing her own future to be reduced to a past. She does not want to reduce Xavière's future to a mere past; on the contrary, she implores her rival: "Spare me the remorse of having ruined your future" (SCTS 403). But when Xavière refuses this request, Françoise takes herself to be faced with the sole alternatives of suicide or murder. After turning on the gas in Xavière's room, she thinks, *"Tomorrow morning she will be dead"*: that is, Xavière's future *will have been* reduced to the past. The last sentence of the novel, "She had chosen herself" (*Elle s'était choisie*), suggests that Françoise's decision to have a future – "Tomorrow morning..." – is already something past, a sign that murdering Xavière has not given her back an authentic future.

Although Beauvoir does not condemn Françoise's act in the name of any transcendent value – ironically, Françoise is the only member of her circle of friends who is known for her sense of morality – she suggests that the polar alternatives of suicide and murder are both "failures" because they cannot accomplish that genuine experience of "shared time" which would require mutual recognition. In *The Ethics of Ambiguity*, she suggests, in terms that cannot but remind us of Benjamin, that every struggle against oppression must be fought on behalf of the past: "The past is an appeal; it is an appeal toward the future which sometimes can save it only by destroying it.... But a genuine ethics does not teach us either to sacrifice it or deny it: we must assume it" (EOA 95). For this very reason, the futurity of the future – the formal object of hope – must be conceived not merely as the horizon of the projects of Dasein but as the messianic promise for redemption: "When I envisage my future, I consider that movement which, prolonging my exist-ence of today, will fulfill my present projects and will surpass them toward new ends ... this is the future which Heidegger considered.... But through the centuries men have dreamed of another future...; this future did not prolong the present; it came down upon the world like a cataclysm announced by signs which cut the continuity of time" (EOA 116). In murdering Xavière, Françoise achieves only the first kind of future; the second cannot be achieved apart from the project of solidarity and mutual recognition. Beauvoir acknowledges the danger of accepting an Hegelian conception of unified time according to which "the Future appears as both the infinite and as Totality" (EOA 116). But whereas Levinas cleaves to infinity in opposition to totality, Beauvoir – following Sartre – invokes the idea of a "detotalized totality," of a shared time of History that would not engulf within it the separate existence of each individual: "mutually recognizing each other as subject, each will yet remain for the other an *other*" (SS 731).

Just as *She Came to Stay* restages Hegel's master/slave dialectic, con-fronting the problem of how to forge a sense of solidarity between two or more people, so Beauvoir's novel, *All Men are Mortal* (*Tous les hommes sont mortels*, 1946), personifies Hegel's "world-historical spirit," asking whether finite individuals can meaningfully adopt a world-historical point of view. Born in the thirteenth century, Fosca, the ruler of a small Italian city-state, achieves immortality by drinking a special elixir. He recounts the story of his life to Regina, an actress living in modern Paris. From helping to unite the Holy Roman Empire through being present at Luther's condemnation before the Diet of Worms to exploring the New World, participating in the early modern scientific revolution, and playing an active role in the French Revolution, Fosca personifies the course of history itself. But unlike Hegel's world-historical spirit, he is still a particular individual, the only difference being that he is unable to die. This difference proves to have devastating consequences, not only for Fosca himself but for all those who come to love or befriend him on a personal level. Unable to die in a world of mortals, Fosca cannot give meaning to any of the projects that he listlessly undertakes. Ironically, as Regina observes, he is already dead precisely because he cannot die: "'At least when I die, *I'll* have lived.... You, you're already a corpse'" (AMAM 24). Likewise, Fosca himself reflects, "And I, too, was dead, but I was still here, a witness to my absence" (AMAM 177).

In *She Came to Stay*, everything moved inexorably toward the murder of Xavière, whose death seems, however falsely, to promise Françoise the hope of liberation from an oppressive other. In *All Men are Mortal*, everything remains mired within the timeless – because everlasting – stagnant pool of Fosca's immortality. Regina is initially drawn to him because she hopes to achieve a vicarious immortality through his memory of her performances on the stage. But in listening to his story she realizes that this fantasy is untenable, not only because she herself will never be immortal, but because Fosca will forget her. From his world-historical perspective, individual human lives are as interchangeable as those of ants: "And the ants came and went, thousands of ants, thousands of times the same ant" (AMAM 333). He understands that finite, mortal human beings think differently; they risk their lives precisely to distinguish themselves from ants: "They gave their lives to prove to themselves that they were living men and not ants, or flies, or blocks of stone" (AMAM 307). By accepting their own mortality, human beings become capable of mutual recognition: "because they looked at each other and spoke to each other, they knew they were neither gnats, nor ants, nor stones, but men" (AMAM 339). Unable to share in this experience, Fosca is not reduced to the level of an ant – as he would be if he were mortal but capable of a merely animal death; on the contrary, he reduces others to this level. Such is the unbearable weight of the standpoint of world history. Whereas in principle Françoise could have achieved genuine mutual recognition with Xavière, Regina can never be anything but an interchangeable ant for Fosca: "He had disappeared, but she remained the same as he had made her – a blade of grass, a gnat, an ant, a bit of foam.... In horror, in terror, she accepted the metamorphosis – gnat, foam, ant, until death" (AMAM 344–5). Unable to kill this intolerable presence – as Françoise killed Xavière – Regina can only scream in frustration at the end of the novel.

Françoise's belief that she must choose between killing her friend and losing her own freedom is shared by Brutus in Shakespeare's *The Tragedy of Julius Caesar*. At the beginning of Beauvoir's novel, this play is in production, with Pierre in the title role. The possibility that Françoise's life-and-death struggle with Xavière represents a displacement of her aggression toward Pierre/Caesar attests to the difficulty that women have of forging genuine friendships. At the beginning of *All Men are Mortal*, Regina is playing the part of Rosalind in a production of *As You Like It*, but she is unable to feel a sense of solidarity with Florence, presumably cast in the role of Celia. In Shakespeare's play, Rosalind – who must dress up like a man in order to achieve her freedom as a woman – has been banished from the court by Celia's father; but out of an act of solidarity, Celia leaves with her for the Forest of Arden. Significantly, Regina leaves the city not with Florence but with Fosca, with whom it is impossible to achieve genuine solidarity. Yet whereas *She Came to Stay* ends with something that looks like hope but is actually closer to despair, Regina's lonely scream at the end of *All Men are Mortal* – the polar opposite of Rosalind's idyllic wedding to Orlando – suggests less despair than a cathartic condition for the possibility of hope (a situation akin to what Hegel calls "unhappy consciousness"). Perhaps with Fosca's departure, Regina will be able to accept her finitude and achieve a meaningful friendship with Florence, as well as a satisfying sexual relationship with her spurned lover, Roger.

That on some level it is impossible to accept the fact of our mortality is suggested in Beauvoir's *A Very Easy Death* (*Une mort très douce*, 1964), a memoir of the death of her mother:

> Maman loved life as I love it and in the face of death she had the same feeling of rebellion that I have.... Religion could do no more for my mother than the hope of posthumous success could do for me. Whether you think of it as heavenly or as earthly, if you love life immortality is no consolation for death.
>
> (VED 91–2)

Neither an other who must be killed (like Xavière) nor an other who cannot be killed (like Fosca), Beauvoir's mother is someone whose dying can only be endured – with all the emotional difficulties that a work of mourning involves: "It was so expected and so unimaginable, that dead body lying on the bed in Maman's place" (VED 86). Beauvoir suggests that in mourning the death of another person, we mourn our own as well. Her epigram from the poet Dylan Thomas (1914–1953) – "Do not go gentle into that good night" – suggests that we are all to some extent in the predicament of Regina: "All men must die: but for every man his death is an accident and, even if he knows it and consents to it, an unjustifiable violation" (VED 106).

Although we die as individuals, we can meaningfully engage in world-historical projects. Participants in the French Revolution tell Fosca that they accept the fact that, after they die, the people on whose behalf they fight are likely to have entirely different concerns. Armand blames Fosca for looking at things through the lens of a world-historical spirit:

"You're already far off in the future," he said. "And you look upon these moments as if they were part of the past. And all past enterprises appear derisive when they're seen only as dead, embalmed, and buried. . . . In my opinion, we should concern ourselves only with that part of the future on which we have a hold. But we should try our best to enlarge our hold on it as much as possible."

(AMAM 328)

In this respect Fosca's problem is the same as Regina's; indeed, he could be regarded as her fantasmatic double. What she needs to discover is that she cannot look at her life from the standpoint of world history – i.e., of *man* – because she, like all other "men," is mortal. Somehow we must balance our own finitude with an orientation toward the collective future of humanity. Just as Sartre claimed that only with the accomplishment of the Marxist struggle would it be possible to realize a genuine philosophy of freedom, so Beauvoir suggests that we cannot know what human relations will be like in a world that no longer knows oppression: "New relations of flesh and sentiment of which we have no conception will arise between the sexes; already, indeed, there have appeared between men and women friendships, rivalries, complicities, comradeships – chaste or sensual – which past centuries could not have conceived" (SS 730). The same, Beauvoir notes, can be hoped for relations between the different races.

4.6   Fanon's indictment of colonialism and his analysis of the lived experience of race

Not I; I must be found.
My parts, my title, and my perfect soul
Shall manifest me rightly.
                    (*The Tragedy of Othello, the*
                    Moor of Venice, I, ii, 30–2)

The work of Frantz Fanon (1925–1961) – a native Martinican (and therefore a French citizen) who fought in defense of France during the Second World War but against his country of citizenship in the Algerian war of liberation – is inextricably bound to his experience of, and resistance to, colonialism. In *Black Skin, White Masks* (*Peau noire, masques blancs*, 1952), Fanon calls attention to the unique psychic traumas faced by colonized subjects. In contrast to Hegel, for whom the master/slave dialectic revolved around the fact that the slave recognizes the master without the master recognizing the slave, Fanon suggests that in the colonial context, the identity of the colonized subject is determined from the beginning by the gaze of the colonizer. To be identified in this way is to be recognized not as an independent self-consciousness but as something less than fully human. The colonizer accomplishes this act of dehumanization by treating the consciousness of the colonized subject as an accidental feature of an essentially animal identity defined by race. The practice of treating skin pigment as a mark of race – and of whiteness and blackness as the respective emblems of humanity and animality – has its origin in the attempt of Europeans to justify colonial practices both to themselves and to those whom they colonized. Just as Beauvoir observed that "man" denotes both a genus and one of two "species" of humanity, so Fanon calls attention to the double status that the term "white" enjoys under European colonialism. To be recognized as black in a society in which whiteness is equated with humanity is to face a dilemma not envisaged by Hegel: either to prove that one is "really" white, notwithstanding the manner in which one's skin pigment appears to others, or else to renounce the equation of humanity with whiteness altogether.

Fanon sympathetically describes but also denounces the first strategy, the attempt of colonized blacks to achieve recognition of their whiteness. In some colonial contexts – particularly those in which racial discriminations are fine-tuned and elaborated along a graded hierarchy from black to white – certain individuals may grow up thinking of themselves as white, refusing to accept the fact that others regard them as black. Such individuals typically aspire to a social status that would supposedly render their "whiteness" definitive. Here gender relations play a crucial role. A woman who disavows her social status as black is likely to believe that she can guarantee her whiteness by marrying a white man and taking up residence with him in a white part of town, thereby effectively attaining the status of a free self-consciousness: "A house in Didier . . . there you have Hegel's subjective certainty made flesh" (BSWM 44). Conversely, a man who wishes to repudiate his blackness will seek recognition from a white woman:

> I wish to be acknowledged not as *black* but as *white*. Now – and this is a form of recognition that Hegel had not envisaged – who but a white woman can do this for me? By loving me she proves that I am worthy of white love. I am loved like a white man. I am a white man.
>
> (BSWM 63; paragraph breaks omitted)

A psychiatrist by training, Fanon's analysis of these and other efforts at "a hallucinatory whitening" (BSWM 100) is strictly therapeutic: "What I want to do is help the black man to free himself of the arsenal of complexes that has been developed by the colonial environment" (BSWM 30). In the end, the only way for colonized subjects to achieve genuine human dignity is to overthrow the entire racist colonial framework.

Even in its more attenuated forms the relationship between colonizer and colonized is that between master and slave. But, in contrast to the Hegelian master/slave dialectic, which is predicated on the slave's recognition of the master, colonial domination rests upon an inverted structure of recognition: "For Hegel there is reciprocity; here the master laughs at the consciousness of the slave. What he wants from the slave is not recognition but work"

(BSWM 220n). The Hegelian slave is forced to work too, but his condition as slave is the result of a struggle for recognition won by the master. Under colonialism it is the master who recognizes the slave rather than the other way around, and this recognition paradoxically precedes and undercuts the possibility of struggle altogether: "One day the White Master, *without conflict*, recognized the Negro slave" (BSWM 217). To be "recognized" *as* a Negro – and "therefore" as a slave – is in Sartrean terms to be identified with an aspect of one's facticity; more precisely, it is to be equated with what one is for others. Even if the inference were not automatically made from "being black" to "being a slave," to be recognized *as* black is to find oneself in an existentially ambiguous situation. In *Anti-Semite and Jew* (*Réflexions sur la question juive*, 1946), Sartre had argued that to be a Jew is first and foremost to be a Jew for others. The individual who is recognized by others "as" a Jew is condemned to the double-bind of bad faith: if I cling to my consciousness of myself as free I will deny that I "am" a Jew, but this is to deny what I actually am, since my being lies exclusively in my being-for-others; yet if I identify with my Jewishness then I thereby flee my freedom by taking refuge in sheer facticity. For Sartre, a Jew is someone who is forced to live this ambiguous relationship to Jewishness. Fanon accepts and extends this analysis: "A Malagasy is a Malagasy; or, rather, no, not he *is* a Malagasy but, rather, in an absolute sense he 'lives' his Malagasyhood. If he is a Malagasy, it is because the white man has come" (BSWM 98).

At first glance it might seem as if whites are subjected to the same existential predicament as blacks, but Fanon insists upon the asymmetrical character of racial relations in a colonized society: "For not only must the black man be black; he must be black in relation to the white man. Some critics will take it on themselves to remind us that this proposition has a converse. I say that this is false" (BSWM 110). Elsewhere Fanon does call attention to the double mimetic character of this fundamental asymmetry. Commenting on Lacan's conception of the mirror stage he observes, "When one has grasped the mechanism described by Lacan, one can have no further doubt that the real Other for the white man is and will continue to be the black man. And conversely" (BSWM 161). In the collective unconscious of colonial society, the black man represents unbridled sexuality: "In relation to the Negro, everything takes place on the genital level" (BSWM 157). Thus the imaginary representation of the black man plays a privileged role in the psychic life of the white man, serving as a kind of block to his own bodily integrity, just as "in the white world the man of color encounters difficulties in the development of his bodily schema" (BSWM 110). But once again the relationship remains asymmetrical, as it is the white man whose body serves as the archetype of a man; in contrast to it, the body of a black man is always already a racialized body: "the corporeal schema crumbled, its place taken by a racial epidermal schema" (BSWM 112).

Fanon thus regards the "lived experience of the black man" as an existential predicament that in form, if not in content, is equivalent to the "lived experience" of a woman as Beauvoir analyzes it. Ironically, both of their English translators elide these key phrases, H.M. Parshley preferring "Woman's Life Today" for *L'Expérience vécue* and Charles Lam Markmann opting for "The Fact of Blackness" as a translation of *L'Expérience vécue de l'homme noir*. Both renderings downplay the crucial element of ambiguity in the experience of having to "live" a gendered or racialized identity as if it were a simple identity.[11] Sartre's principle that the for-itself only ever "is" what it is in the mode of not being it underpins the analyses of both Beauvoir and Fanon. All three remain committed to the humanistic ideal of "man" as a being who transcends his gendered and racialized facticity. As Sartre puts it in *Being and Nothingness*, "face, sense organs, presence – all that is nothing but the contingent form of the Other's necessity to *exist himself* as belonging to a race, a class, an environment, *etc*" (BN 451). "Each for-itself ... is a for-itself only by choosing itself beyond nationality and race" (BN 666). Fanon shares Sartre and Beauvoir's commitment to a humanistic ethic of solidarity. If oppression can be defined as any practice that reduces human beings to their facticity, then every struggle against oppression is a struggle for humanity as a whole: "All forms of exploitation are identical because all of them are applied against the same 'object': man. . . . Colonial racism is no different from any other racism" (BSWM 88). Against the false "recognition" by which blacks have been recognized as blacks – or Jews as Jews or women as women – must be opposed a demand for genuine recognition of the humanity of all individuals: "All I wanted was to be a man among other men" (BSWM 112).

At the same time, Fanon resists an overhasty universalization of particular struggles. In "Black Orpheus" (*Orphée Noir*), his introduction to a 1949 collection of works by the so-called poets of negritude, Sartre drew the conclusion that the racialized struggle of blacks against their colonial oppressors must eventually be construed otherwise than as a revolt carried out in the name of negritude; specifically, it will belong to that universal struggle of humanity against its own degradation: "Thus negritude is the root of its own destruction, it is a transition and not a conclusion, a means and not an ultimate end" (quoted in BSWM 133).[12] Perhaps it is true, Fanon concedes, that when all is said and done the racialized struggle for recognition that is taking place throughout the world will be viewed from a perspective that transcends race altogether. But to adopt the standpoint of "when all is said and done" is to do an injustice to those who must live the struggle that may eventually lead to that standpoint: "For once, that born Hegelian had forgotten that consciousness has to lose itself in the night of the absolute" (BSWM 133). Alternatively, one might hazard that Sartre's proleptic humanism is too Hegelian in the sense that it prematurely projects the realization of an end of history that would absorb all particular struggles within it: "What? I have barely opened eyes that had been blindfolded, and someone already wants to drown me in the universal?" (BSWM 186). It is not Sartre's humanism but the proleptic character of his characterization of the future of negritude that makes Fanon hesitate; in order to make history, one must bracket the eternal perspective of the end of history: "I do not come with timeless truths" (BSWM 7). "Every human problem must be considered from the standpoint of time. Ideally, the present will always contribute to the building of the future. . . . In no fashion should I undertake to prepare the world that will come later. I belong irreducibly to my time" (BSWM 12–13).

For the colonized subject, to belong to one's time is to belong to a time of struggle on behalf of the future: "Was my freedom not given to me then in order to build the world of the *You?*" (BSWM 232). Colonialism interrupted the native's history, consigning him to a mythical past. This is why it is so important to situate the racialized neuroses caused by colonialism in their proper historical context. Taking issue with an attempt on the part of the psychoanalyst Octave Mannoni (1899–1989) to glean a transhistorical inferiority complex from a patient's dream, Fanon bitingly observes, "What must be done is to restore this dream *to its proper time,* . . . the period during which eighty thousand natives were killed" (BSWM 104). In order to resume history, to have a future, the native must put an end to the history of colonialism: "The immobility to which the native is condemned can only be called in question if the native decides to put an end to the history of colonization . . . and to bring into existence the history of the nation – the history of decolonization" (WOE 51). To accomplish this movement it is necessary to initiate the struggle for recognition which was foreclosed at the beginning of colonialism. Such is the impetus behind Third World struggles for liberation. Fanon addresses the vicissitudes of these struggles in *The Wretched of the Earth* (*Les Damnés de la terre*, 1961), a book that is informed by his own participation in the Algerian war.

Under colonialism, the struggle for recognition is deflected. Instead of directing his aggression toward the settler, the native vents it by engaging in ersatz conflicts with his fellow colonized subjects: "In the colonial context, . . . the natives fight among themselves. They tend to use each other as a screen, and each hides from his neighbor the national enemy" (WOE 306–7). So long as violence is deflected in this way, the struggle against oppression is deferred: "It is as if plunging into a fraternal bloodbath allowed them to ignore the obstacle, and to put off till later the choice, nevertheless inevitable, which opens up the question of armed resistance to colonialism" (WOE 54). Precisely because it puts off the struggle against oppression, this fraternal combat among the natives falls short of being an authentic struggle for recognition. Indeed, Fanon goes so far as to suggest that there can be no genuine experience of being-for-others among the natives themselves until they decide to throw off their chains and *exact* recognition through armed rebellion against their colonial oppressors:

As long as the black man is among his own, he will have no occasion, except in minor internal conflicts, to experience his being through others.

There is of course the moment of "being for others," of which Hegel speaks, but every ontology is made unattainable in a colonized and civilized society.

(BSWM 109; cf. 115, 217)

One of the principal theses of *The Wretched of the Earth* – and one that is emphasized in Sartre's preface to the book – is that decolonization can succeed only through violence. It would be useless for the native to seek redress for the evils of colonialism through the colonial system itself. For one thing, "colonialism never gives anything away for nothing" (WOE 142). For another, the native is not subject to colonial rule in the same way that a citizen in a European state is subject to state law; if "the native . . . hardly ever seeks for justice in the colonial framework" it is because colonial law is not the expression of a general will but the imposition of violence on a people treated not as citizens but as children (WOE 85; cf. BSWM 26–7). Hence colonialism represents not a state of civil society but a state of nature: "colonialism . . . is violence in its natural state, and it will only yield when confronted with greater violence" (WOE 61). To say that colonial rule is equivalent to a state of nature is to imply that Kant's strictures against the right of subjects to rebel against the sovereign do not apply. For if it is only by violence that the natives are subject to the settlers' rule, there can be no colonial sovereign in the proper sense of the term: "The colonial regime owes its legitimacy to force and at no time tries to hide this aspect of things" (WOE 84). It is therefore on the colonizers' own terms that the natives take up arms against them: "by an ironic turning of the tables it is the native who now affirms that the colonialist understands nothing but force" (WOE 84). If "the colonized man finds his freedom in and through violence" (WOE 86), it is because this is the only way of emerging from his enforced – not self-incurred – immaturity: "the Algerian people is today an adult people, responsible and fully conscious of its responsibilities" (WOE 193).

Despite Fanon's strong claim that colonialism "at no time" masks its inherently violent character, he does take note of the many reforms that are introduced by colonizing powers once a full-blooded anti-colonial movement emerges. Natives formerly treated as slaves are officially recognized as citizens and may even assume positions of power in the colonial government. But such token gestures leave the condition of the masses relatively unchanged; oppressed as much from economic exploitation as from political disenfranchisement, the peasants and *lumpenproletariat* who typically suffer the effects of colonial domination much more than workers in the major cities are the main protagonists in the struggle against colonialism. Fanon emphasizes the need for an alliance between these masses, who are quick to mobilize, and the anti-colonial intellectuals who can both educate and learn from them. It is through this alliance that channeled violence emerges as the crucial tactic of decolonization: "Violence alone, violence committed by the people, violence organized and educated by its leaders, makes it possible for the masses to understand social truths and gives the key to them" (WOE 147).

In "On Violence," Arendt criticized both Fanon and – especially – Sartre for advocating violence as a means toward the attainment of political power (COTR 114–15). Arendt agrees that any oppressed people has a right to revolt – it was on this point that she departed from Kant – but she reiterates her thesis that a genuine revolution depends upon the assertion of power rather than violence. Fanon, who died shortly after the publication of *The Wretched of the Earth*, would perhaps have reminded Arendt that there is a difference between a revolution and a war of liberation; from the standpoint of the Algerians, French rule represented not a form of government to be peacefully overthrown but an occupying force to be expelled. Far from ignoring the distinction between violence and power, Fanon's analyses presuppose it, for colonial rule is founded – as was that of the Nazis – on a racist distinction between those who, as citizens, are subject to power and those who, as non-citizens, are subjected to sheer violence. He also draws a sharp distinction between the violence that needs to be brought to bear against colonialism and the cooperative power upon which both rebellion and the post-colonial future of a liberated nation depends. Arendt's position rests on the assumption that war can be entirely replaced by politics. Fanon shares this ideal, but he is not willing to stake the future of the Third World upon the eventual promise of perpetual peace. Like the *Aufhebung* of negritude, such a gesture would be premature. Moreover, as Kant himself argued, history must first prepare the way for perpetual peace through the wars by which nations establish their sovereignty.

Fanon thus shares the Kantian assumption that civil society proper can exist only in an autonomous nation-state, and much of *The Wretched of the Earth* is geared toward addressing the problems posed by the struggle for national sovereignty. Although he does not specify a criterion by virtue of which nations should be distinguished from international leagues, on the one hand, or from subnational factions, on the other, he does insist upon the integrity of the nation as the first aim of decolonization. It is, however, only a first aim; a typical mistake of anti-colonial movements throughout the Third World is to give too little thought ahead of time to the political, economic, and social challenges that will face their newly independent nations. As a result of such neglect, many retain the old economic, social, and political structures, thereby replicating colonial domination. Popular discontent with the new regime is once again quelled by violence:

> The state, which by its strength and discretion ought to inspire confidence and disarm and lull everybody to sleep, on the contrary seeks to impose itself in spectacular fashion. It makes a display, it jostles people and bullies them, thus intimating to the citizen that he is in continual danger.[13]

> (WOE 165)

Despite the somewhat misleading reference to the state's vocation to "lull everybody to sleep," Fanon takes the empowerment of the people to be the proper telos of nationalist movements. Unlike Arendt, who regards tyranny as the predictable result of political recourse to violence, he presumes that it is in principle possible to forestall this particular chapter of post-colonial history.

The greatest challenge facing the Third World is to avoid the temptation to emulate Europe. Emulation is tempting not only for economic reasons but because there is something compelling in the European ideal of man as a being with dignity. Yet however noble in intent, the purportedly universal idea of man as a being with dignity is betrayed by the realities of European practices. Fanon accordingly urges his Third World readers to "Leave this Europe where they are never done talking of Man, yet murder men everywhere they find them" (WOE 311). In "Philosophy and the Crisis of European Humanity," Husserl characterized the idea of Europe as a universal spiritual ideal to which all nations might aspire (CES 273ff.). Though no one would dream of, say, the Eskimoization of humanity – since the Eskimo is merely an empirical example of man – it is meaningful to speak of the *Europeanization* of humanity provided that this is interpreted as a genuinely universal ideal. Once again we find a term – in this case "European" – functioning as both an overarching genus and as a particular species. But although Fanon repudiates the dangerous ideal of *European* man, he does not forsake the idea of *man*; on the contrary, "It is a question of the Third World starting a new history of Man" (WOE 315). Whether this new history would amount to an *Aufhebung* or not, *The Wretched of the Earth* can be read as an attempt to chart the continuation of the history of man after Hegel had consigned Africa to the timeless past of Europe's end of history: "For Europe, for ourselves, and for humanity, comrades,... we must work out new concepts, and try to set afoot a new man" (WOE 316). Perhaps, out of this plunge back in to the "night of the absolute," a new humanism will emerge: "As a man, I undertake to face the possibility of annihilation in order that two or three truths may cast their eternal brilliance over the world" (BSWM 228).[14]

4.7   Lévi-Strauss's repudiation of the category of man

> We'll set thee to school to an ant
> > (*The Tragedy of King Lear*,
> > II, iv, 67)

In the same year that Fanon's *Black Skin, White Masks* first appeared in French (1952), Lévi-Strauss published an article entitled "Race and History" (*Race et histoire*) that had been commissioned by UNESCO. Unlike Fanon, who wrote from the perspective of a colonized subject whose education had steeped him in the culture of the colonial power, Lévi-Strauss's point of view was that of an ethnographer whose study of other cultures enabled him to "look from afar" at his own (SM 247; the phrase, from Rousseau, is one that Lévi-Strauss is fond of citing; cf. SA II 35 and *The View from Afar*, [*Le Regard éloigné*, 1983]). The history of the relationship between ethnography and colonialism is a complicated one. For Kant, who never left his native Königsberg, ethnographies played an important role in forming his belief that the various races spread out in space could be regarded as if they were temporal stages in the progress of humanity from infancy to adulthood; colonial stewardship could be justified on the grounds that some races were relatively immature in comparison to the European. Like Fanon, Lévi-Strauss dismisses this Eurocentric prejudice, noting that there is no demonstrable link between the various cultures and whatever surface physical differences happen to distinguish those who belong to them:

> anthropology's original sin lies in the confusion between the purely biological notion of race (supposing that even in this limited field such a notion might pretend to a measure of objectivity, which modern genetics denies) and the sociological and psychological products of human cultures.
>
> (SA II 324)

If anthropology is to repent of its original sin, it must assist in the decoupling of the concepts of race and culture, with an eye toward both explaining and ameliorating the history of colonial domination.

Europeans are not alone in their sense of cultural superiority. Every culture tends to regard itself as the norm in contrast to which others appear to be immature. The very idea of progress is an ethnocentric concept since it is always with respect to a chosen criterion that one looks for progress, regress, or stasis over time: "progress is nothing but the maximum of progress, predetermined, in a sense, by everyone's taste" (SA II 354). To ask, with Kant, if the human race is constantly progressing is thus to give in to a "false evolutionism," that is, "an attempt at suppressing the diversity of cultures while pretending to recognize it fully" (SA II 330). The lesson to be learned from comparative ethnography is that particular cultures tend to flourish when they are in close contact with cultures other than their own: "Diversity is less a function of the isolation of groups than of the relationships which unite them" (SA II 328). Accordingly, not progress with respect to an ethnocentric standard but the maintenance of cultural diversity ought to be the goal of a genuinely cosmopolitan subject: "World civilization could not be anything on the world scale except the coalition of cultures, each preserving its originality" (SA II 358). This is not to say that we should fetishize "original" cultural forms, artificially preserving them at all costs against outside influence; on the contrary, it is precisely the contact among a multiplicity of cultures that spurs each to develop on its own terms: "It is the fact of diversity which must be saved, not the historical content given to it by each era" (SA II 362). Lévi-Strauss concludes that humanity is best served by what we might call an aesthetic "quarrel" among cultures in the Kantian sense of this term, in contrast to the strife that a colonizing power instigates. The perpetuation of this quarrel between cultures is in the interest of humanity as a whole, for it is "this state of disequilibrium on which the biological and cultural survival of mankind depend" (SA II 360).

Thus Lévi-Strauss, like Fanon, can be said to adopt a humanistic ideal that is based on both the repudiation of all forms of racism and the maintenance of cultural diversity, and in the *Introduction to the Work of Marcel Mauss* he explicitly invokes such "a new humanism" (IWMM 32). But unlike Fanon, who despite his reservations concerning "Black Orpheus" seems to accept Sartre's basic conception of humanism, Lévi-Strauss rejects a number of Sartre's central theses. In the *Critique of Dialectical Reason*, Sartre attempted to appropriate Lévi-Strauss's analysis of kinship relations, situating it within his own account of the relationship between praxis and the practico-inert. Correctly understood, a set of kinship rules does not predestine individuals to their fate but is fully compatible with – and even presupposes – the existentialist claim that man is free. To be "constrained" to choose a wife in accordance with a fixed structure is to find oneself obliged by a pledge that may have preceded one's own existence. But as soon as the individual acts in accordance with such constraints he thereby renews the pledge, effectively *taking up a norm*: "From birth onwards, the arrival of the child in the milieu of the pledge is the equivalent for him of making a pledge" (CDR 485). In terms that resonate with Arendt's account of what it means to initiate a political act, Sartre concludes, "What is certain is that birth is a pledge to precisely the extent that the pledge is a birth" (CDR 486). Naturally this account must be situated within the Marxist framework of Sartre's *Critique*. Man's "real" freedom can be realized only at the end of an historical process that will liberate all human beings from the problem of scarcity that has been at the basis of all social structures hitherto, be it the scarcity of wives in a primitive society or the scarcity that conditions the class struggle in modern societies. Thus rather than repudiate the point of view of a universal history of man, Sartre attempts to rehabilitate it. In place of a Eurocentric history of "man" per se – which he concedes is "an abstraction which never occurs in concrete intuition" – he defends a Marxist history of "men." This is justified methodologically by the ideal of an ethnographer who, instead of regarding others "as ants (as the aesthete does) or as robots (as the neurotic does)," attempts to determine simultaneously the respective projects of both himself and those whom he observes (CDR 101).

In distinguishing between ants and men, Sartre was perhaps thinking of a passage from the 1844 Manuscripts in which Marx explicitly distinguishes the products of "bees, beavers, ants, etc." from the products of "man" (EAPM 113). But, like Althusser, Lévi-Strauss was more interested in the structuralist Marx than in the humanistic Marx. In the last chapter of *The Savage Mind*, he defends the idea of studying men as if they were ants:

apart from the fact that this seems to me just the attitude of any scientist who is an agnostic, there is nothing very compromising about it, for ants with their artificial tunnels, their social life and their chemical messages, already present a sufficiently tough resistance to the enterprises of analytical reason . . . So I accept the characterization of aesthete in so far as I believe the ultimate goal of the human sciences to be not to constitute, but to dissolve man.

(SM 246–7; Lévi-Strauss's ellipsis)

Thus for Lévi-Strauss the differences between ants and men are differences in degree (of complexity) rather than differences in kind – as they were for both Sartre and Beauvoir (as evidenced in the passages cited above from *All Men are Mortal*).[15]

Though Sartre acknowledges that the concept of man is a mere abstraction, his construal of Marxism succumbs to the very totalizing temptation that informs Eurocentric conceptions of progress, while his construal of the history of class struggle is no less mythical than was Freud's speculations about the killing of the totemic father. For Lévi-Strauss, Marx was not a philosopher of history but an analyst of economic structures – as well as the first ethnographer to provide a cogent account of colonialism (SA II 314–15). Unlike Heidegger, Lévi-Strauss shares Sartre's enthusiasm for Marx's dictum that "men make their own history," but he disagrees with Sartre about the nature of the human sciences. The idea that everything is ultimately rooted in man's fundamental historicity represents "the last refuge of a transcendental humanism," an unavowed metaphysical bulwark against a properly scientific point of view (SM 262). The task of structural anthropology is not to insist on man's uniqueness in nature – this was the mistake that Lévi-Strauss himself made when he initially "attached [too] much importance" to the nature/culture dichotomy (SM 247n; my brackets) – but to prepare the way for a reduction of anthropology to "the exact natural sciences": "the reintegration of culture in nature and finally of life within the whole of its physico-chemical conditions" (SM 247). Thus Lévi-Strauss is to be taken quite literally when he claims that man is something to be dissolved rather than constituted.

To break with a transcendental theory of constitution is not to deny the existence of practices in which human beings do create their own identities. In his *Introduction to the Work of Marcel Mauss*, Lévi-Strauss called attention to the great variety of ways in which different cultures shape human bodies through discipline and training. Since the idea that biology is the sole determinant of culture is the racialist idea par excellence, an anthropological study of "body techniques" could combat racism by showing "that it is the other way around: man has, at all times and in all places, been able to turn his body into a product of his techniques and his representations" (IWMM 8–9).

4.8   Foucault's genealogy of power

What studied torments, tyrant, hast for me?
What wheels? racks? fires? What flaying? boiling
In leads or oils?
                              (*The Winter's Tale*, III, ii, 175–7)

Your friends, sir, the hangman. You must be so good, sir, to rise,
   and be put to death.
                              (*Measure for Measure*, IV, iii, 26–7)

In *The Order of Things*, Foucault had effectively presented a vertical (i.e., historical) analogue of the horizontal (i.e., ethnological) analyses developed in Lévi-Strauss's *The Savage Mind*. Just as Lévi-Strauss characterized "savage thought" as an attempt to view the world as "a room of mirrors fixed on opposite walls, which reflect each other (as well as objects in the intervening space) although without being strictly parallel," so Foucault describes the Renaissance conception of the world as "an endless zigzag course from resemblance to what resembles it" (SM 263; OT 30). By implicitly equating Renaissance thought with savage thought, Foucault locates modernity's "Other" not just outside the West but within it. Like Lévi-Strauss, Foucault regards the category of man with suspicion, crediting the various structuralist "counter-sciences" with rousing modernity from the "anthropological sleep" in which it had languished ever since Kant raised the question, "What is man?" (OT 340–1; cf. PTAFM 57). Although he consistently refused the label of structuralist, Foucault also shared Lévi-Strauss's (and Althusser's) suspicions about Sartre's existential humanism. In an interview from 1966, he characterizes humanism as a failed attempt to reconcile the figure of man with a structuralist account of signification (AME 265). In contrast to Sartre's theorization of the "practico-inert," the sedimented in-itself of human praxis, Foucault defines archaeology as an attempt to disclose the "theoretico-active," that is, the "knowledge" that is capable of exerting power over human bodies (AME 262). A few years later, he introduces the expression "power-knowledge" to refer to the theoretico-active, characterizing its investigation not as "archaeological" but as "genealogical" in character.

In "Nietzsche, Genealogy, History" (*Nietzsche, la généalogie, l'histoire*, 1971), Foucault contrasts Nietzsche's conception of a genealogy of bodies with that of an ideal historical search for origins. In the *Genealogy*, Nietzsche briefly contrasts *Ursprung* and *Herkunft*, two German words that can be translated, respectively, as "origin" and "descent" (AME 371). On Foucault's interpretation, to inquire into a thing's origin – as Husserl does when he inquires into the origin of geometry – is to treat the object of investigation as if it had an essence that was already present at its birth. Like Althusser, Foucault repudiates such an approach. By contrast, to trace a thing's descent

— as the genealogist does — is to treat it as the accidental product of a conflu-
ence of "myriad events" (AME 374). Thus instead of presuming to reconstruct the pure history of an ideal essence, the genealogist investigates the
ignoble and inglorious "details and accidents that accompany every beginning" (AME 373). More precisely, the genealogist is interested in the
history of what Lévi-Strauss called "body techniques": "The body — and
everything that touches it: diet, climate, and soil — is the domain of the
Herkunft" (AME 375).

By adopting a genealogical point of view, Foucault is able to rearticulate
his principled resistance to phenomenology while abandoning his earlier
quasi-structuralist concept of a unified "historical a priori" supposedly governing all forms of thinking in a particular cultural period — an idea from
which he was already retreating in the foreword to the English translation of
The Order of Things (OT x). Though genealogy remains a way of approaching
written documents — Nietzsche said the most important color for a genealogist was grey (OGOM 8) — it is especially concerned with the ways in which
bodies of knowledge are used to exert power over corporeal human bodies.
As such, it attends less to the history of institutions such as the state than to
the seemingly marginal details of everyday practice — or rather, it accords
equal value to everything pertaining to the formation of human bodies.

In the second essay of the *Genealogy*, Nietzsche claimed that, far from
having had a single purpose throughout its history, punishment had been
adapted to innumerable ends (OGOM 57–8). In *Discipline and Punish: the Birth
of the Prison* (*Surveiller et punir: Naissance de la prison*, 1975), Foucault traces the
multiple lines of descent that have culminated not only in the modern prison
system but in the distinctively modern way in which power is exercised on
human bodies throughout the body politic. He begins by contrasting an eye-
witness report of the horrific public execution of Robert-François Damiens
(1714–1757), who attempted to kill King Louis XV (1710–1774) in 1757,
with an 1838 timetable describing the minute regimentation of the daily lives
of prisoners in a Parisian house of correction (DP 3–7). Damiens was not
merely executed; his body was subjected to a violence so extravagant that it
could not but leave the spectators dazzled by the display of the power of the
sovereign. Conversely, the timetable did not merely propose an external
mechanism for structuring the time spent by the prisoners; it aspired to
nothing less than an implantation of a quasi-Kantian schematism: "Time pen-
etrates the body" (DP 152). Just as the idealized limit of the torture and execution of Damiens would have been the visible annihilation of the last traces of
his body, so the idealized limit of the application of the timetable would have
been a schedule with no gaps between specified activities. The question that
Foucault asks is, how did we get from there to here?

Instead of relying as he did in his earlier works on the division between
the Renaissance, classical, and modern periods, Foucault identifies two key
breaks in the history of punishment from the *Ancien Régime* to the birth of
the modern "carceral system" in the first half of the nineteenth century. The

first concerns the advent of a reform movement in the late eighteenth century, an effort to replace the spectacular punishment of the bodies of criminals with a method of inculcating representations in the souls of the citizens (DP 94). Its ideal was to make of punishment not an overwhelming spectacle but a didactic "theatre" that would educate the public (a formulation that recalls Nietzsche's characterization of the shift from Aeschylean tragedy to Euripidean drama) (DP 106). Kant shared the reform movement's idea that punishments should fit their crimes in such a way that the mere thought of the crime would immediately suggest the thought of the punishment: "If you slander him, you slander yourself; if you rob him, you rob yourself; if you strike him, you strike yourself; and if you kill him, you kill yourself" (PW 155).

The second break pertains to the apparent failure of the reform movement, for no sooner had its ideals been articulated than an entirely different program was carried out. Before the French Revolution, prison was only one of an array of punitive techniques. The reformers regarded prison sentences as an especially egregious example of the arbitrary use of sovereign power. But within a few years, confinement in prison became the standard mechanism for the punishment of all crimes: "The theatre of punishment . . . which would have acted essentially on the minds of the general public was replaced by the great uniform machinery of the prisons" (DP 116).

Prior to the French Revolution, punishment was the prerogative of the king. In punishing a criminal, the king was in a sense avenging himself on someone who had challenged his sole entitlement to the exercise of power. Thus Damiens's attempted regicide was only an extreme manifestation of what was implied in criminality in general, just as the extreme measure of punishment which he received differed only in degree, not kind, from the punishment meted out to minor offenders (DP 47). Crucial to all punishment was that it be a spectacle, a visible manifestation of the king's power. By contrast, the carceral system that emerged in the first half of the nineteenth century was based on an inverted relationship: instead of functioning as a visible spectacle to be observed by a public that remained outside the eye of power, power now began to function as an invisible observation of the public itself (DP 201–2).[16] To meet this requirement, Jeremy Bentham (1748–1832) drew up a plan for an ideal prison called the "panopticon," which Foucault takes to exemplify the new form of power. The panopticon grew out of a number of historical antecedents, including the rules governing life in monasteries, disciplinary procedures in the military, and practices of confinement during an epidemic of the plague. "Panopticism" is not merely a prison model. On the contrary, as Bentham himself emphasized, the architectural design of the panopticon could lend itself to an indefinite number of social institutions whose aim was to organize an unwieldy mass of human bodies into a unified and differentiated whole (DP 205). As such, panopticism represents a "diffuse" form of power that permeates the entire body politic, so that even supposedly non-carceral social spaces have the feel of prisons: "Is it surprising that prisons resemble factories, schools, barracks, hospitals, which all resemble prisons?" (DP 228).

In *The Order of Things* Foucault called attention to the classical episteme's obsession with the figure of the table, the representational grid that was to have served simultaneously as an ordering of signs and an ordering of beings. He now observes that "the table was both a technique of power and a procedure of knowledge," and that side-by-side with the attempt made in natural history to construct a table of living beings – institutionalized in the design of several "panoptical" zoos – was a military dream of arranging human bodies in a table (DP 148). In both cases it was not just a question of assigning each individual to a particular compartment but of arranging – and rearranging – so that at the limit the exact character of an individual could be determined by its place within the classificatory grid. Originally a military tactic, this mania for order became the principal feature of panopticism in general. In each of the great panoptical domains – schools, hospitals, factories, barracks, and prisons – individuals were studied so that they could be properly located in a space that was half-physical and half-ideal: "They are mixed spaces: real because they govern the disposition of buildings, rooms, furniture, but also ideal, because they are projected over this arrangement of characterizations, assessments, hierarchies" (DP 148). These arrangements were made not simply for their own sake but for the use that could be made of bodies that were properly classified. Thus the gathering of knowledge about individuals functioned as a means of exerting power which was, in turn, exercised as a means of observing and classifying – that is, of gaining further knowledge about – individuals. It is here that Foucault locates the "ignoble" beginnings of the human sciences (DP 191; cf. 23).

Panopticism corresponds to a new form of power that Foucault calls "discipline" (DP 137). Bentham noted that the possibility of constant surveillance was itself a mechanism of correction, for knowing that they could be observed at any moment would incline individuals to alter their own behavior. Thus the panopticon was designed to train individuals to train themselves. Disciplinary power is not negative but positive – i.e., it does not prohibit or repress but instead produces specific effects. In contrast to the spectacular punishment of the bodies of criminals during the Ancien Régime, it "touches" the individual only obliquely. Though modern forms of punishment are touted as more "humane," Foucault argues that they simply reflect a different "economy of power" (DP 304). Like the human sciences, humanism itself is rooted in the history of petty disciplinary practices (DP 141).

Foucault identifies four distinct characteristics of disciplinary power: it is "cellular," "organic," "genetic," and combinatory" (DP 167). As the example of the timetable illustrates, these four aspects of "the panoptic schema" represent so many forms of "time-determination" in the Kantian sense (DP 205). In the first place, discipline determines a time-series in the extensive magnitudes of bodies (that is, it is cellular); it specifies a time-content in the form of an intensive magnitude "by the coding of activities;" it governs a time-order (the properly dynamical element in the genetic training of bodies); and it pertains to the sum total of time (its combinatory character) (DP 167). Foucault notes that in the modern prison system "the length of the penalty" functions not as a "time-measure" commensurate with the nature of the crime committed but as "a time finalized" – i.e., as an open-ended duration whose term coincides with the criminal's moral conversion (DP 244). If the first function corresponds to the image of a prisoner using hash marks to determine the number of days left in his or her sentence, the second corresponds to Kant's characterization of time as the form in which we represent the infinite duration of the soul's aspiration toward holiness of will. It is in this sense that "the soul is the prison of the body" (DP 30).

Insofar as the modern prison serves as the model of all of the other panoptical spaces, it functions as a kind of Lacanian *point-de-capiton* or suturing point of the "carceral archipelago" (DP 297). The aim of the prison itself is to isolate the phenomenon of "delinquency" (DP 251ff.). Like the leper of the Middle Ages and the madman of the classical period, the delinquent is the Other who cannot simply be excluded but must be incorporated within the body politic: "the delinquent is not outside the law; he is, from the very outset, in the law, at the very heart of the law" (DP 301). Thus the prison exists not to eliminate delinquency but to produce and confine it. This is evidenced in the fact that

> For a century and a half the prison had always been offered as its own remedy.... One must not, therefore, regard the prison, its "failure" and its more or less successful reform as three successive stages. One should think rather of a simultaneous system that historically has been superimposed on the juridical deprivation of liberty.
>
> (DP 268)

Thus there is no genuine conflict between those who advocate sending delinquents to prison and those who call for prison reform. On the contrary, these two positions function as the reciprocally determining disjuncts of an episteme. In contrast to the merely juridical subject who is punished for committing an offense, the delinquent classified as "abnormal" is the target of an entire network of power-knowledge. Whether initially sentenced to prison or to a psychiatric clinic, the delinquent is routinely shuttled back and forth from one part of the "carceral system" to another. For Foucault, all of the sciences that have "the root 'psycho-'" as their prefix are parasitic on the carceral system because the axis of normality and abnormality upon which they situate individuals is first and foremost a tactic of power and only secondarily a category of knowledge (DP 193).

In *The History of Sexuality, Volume I: an Introduction* (*Histoire de la sexualité 1: la volonté de savoir*, 1976), Foucault contrasts the classical sovereign's power to take life with the modern power to "*foster* life or *disallow* it"

(HS 138; cf. BPAF 150). Just as disciplinary power is exercised over individual bodies (i.e., over *men*), so "bio-power" is exercised on "the species body" (i.e., on *man*) (HS 139). By targeting all of the biological processes that pertain to human existence, bio-power infiltrates bodies in a fundamentally new way. Foucault argues that psychoanalysis is itself a manifestation of bio-power. Though it allegedly aims at the "liberation" of a repressed human sexuality, it is in fact just a new technique for policing "bodies and pleasures" (HS 159). Like the eye at the center of the panopticon, the ear of the analyst functions as the suturing-point of a power-knowledge network. As Foucault already put it in *Folie et déraison*: "psychoanalysis doubled the absolute observation of the watcher with the endless monologue of the person watched" (MC 250–1). In his final writings on "practices of the self," Foucault tried to articulate an alternative to the modern conception of subjectivity, turning to antiquity and to early Christian practices of confession. Foucault finds one model for what it means to "tell the truth to power" in the Socratic conception of *parrhesia*, or "frank speech." Another he finds in Kant's conception of Enlightenment. The task of the critic should be not to put forth a "theory" or "permanent body of knowledge" (as Kant did in his three *Critiques*) but to practice "an ethos, a philosophical life in which the critique of what we are is at one and the same time the historical analysis of the limits that are imposed on us and an experiment with the possibility of going beyond them" (POT 132).

4.9   Irigaray's sensible transcendental

> My way is to conjure you, and I'll begin with the women.
> (*As You Like It*, Epilogue, 11–12)

For the Belgian-born French philosopher, Luce Irigaray (1930?–), the problem concerning man and his doubles bears first and foremost on the phenomenon of sexual difference. Irigaray's first book, *Speculum of the Other Woman* (*Speculum de l'autre femme*, 1974), got her "excommunicated" from Lacan's Ecole Freudienne. Her heresy was to challenge Freud's belief that everything pertaining to feminine sexuality revolves around penis envy. Like Deleuze and Guattari, Irigaray regards the theory and practice of Oedipalization as complicitous with capitalism. But whereas they trace Oedipalization back to the vicissitudes of a desiring-production that is not yet sexually differentiated, she explains it in terms of a primordial subordination of femininity to masculinity. In this view, Oedipalization is the process by which a child's awareness of sexual difference is repressed or foreclosed, replaced by the ideological "recognition" (in Althusser's sense of misrecognition) of "obvious" differences between men and women. Though we pay "lip service" to the idea that women's bodies are different from those of men, we do so through a phallocentric lens, reducing sexual difference to the having or not having of a penis. In "discovering" that all subjects are either always-already castrated or merely perpetually threatened with castration, we repress sexual difference by forgetting femininity. Because not only boys but also girls are subjected to this regimen, it is no wonder that adult women seem to suffer from something like penis envy. But this situation has to be understood as the consequence of a specific form of social domination rather than as the inevitable outcome of biological constitution. The problem with Freud's account of feminine sexuality is that, while he correctly diagnoses the manner in which a phallocentric society reproduces itself by subjecting children to Oedipalization, he does so with an eye toward reinforcing rather than undermining this state of affairs: "Obviously Freud is right insofar as he is describing the status quo. But his statements are not mere descriptions. They establish rules intended to be put into practice" (SOW 123).

The forgetting of sexual difference is not merely the result of a failure to attend to empirical differences between male and female bodies, though it is that too. At a deeper level, sexual difference is that by virtue of which any empirical differences between the sexes can be given as such – much as, for Deleuze, difference is not empirical diversity but that through which diversity is given. By reducing sexual difference to the polar alternatives of having or not having a penis, difference as such is reduced to the mere opposition between supposedly self-identical terms – or rather it is reduced to the opposition between one self-identical term (the masculine) and its negative, privative double: "woman's lack of penis and her envy of the penis *ensure the function of the negative*" (SOW 52). In this sense, phallocentrism represents the rule of the Same, the reduction of heterogeneity to a principle of homogeneity: "Here the two has already been reduced to the one, even in the various modes of its difference" (SOW 236). For this reason, phallocentrism cannot be overcome merely by inverting the existing order. Just as Heidegger claimed that Nietzsche's inversion of the Platonic hierarchy between the intelligible and the sensible remained within the ambit of metaphysics, so Irigaray suggests that an inverted patriarchy – i.e., a matriarchy – would be just another form of phallocentrism. Unlike Bataille, however, Irigaray does not celebrate sheer heterogeneity either. Her ideal of a rapturous union between the sexes involves not the obliteration of differences but a new experience of the couple, of the two qua two. As she puts it in *To Be Two* (*Essere Due*, 1994): "This two does not allow the submission of one to the other, if it is not to suffer the loss of the two. It does not even correspond to a juxtaposition of one + one subjects. It has to do with a relationship *between*" (TBT 35).

Another insufficient response to phallocentrism would be for women to seek recognition as masculine subjects (SOW 118–19). This would be a mistake not only because patriarchy is predicated upon the treatment of women as commodities rather than as persons – a thesis that Irigaray attributes to Engels but which is also crucial in the work of Lévi-Strauss and Lacan – but because even if women were to be recognized as the equivalent of masculine subjects, this would merely perpetuate the occlusion of sexed subjectivity in general and feminine subjectivity in particular. Irigaray thinks that Beauvoir succumbs to this temptation when instead of attending to the genuine differences between the sexes she rejects any conception of women as "other" than men: "Rather than refusing, as Simone de Beauvoir does, to be the other gender, the other sex, I am asking to be recognized as really an other, irreducible to the masculine subject" (DBBT 125; cf. JTN 9–14). Like Sartre, Beauvoir regards all subjects as bare empty consciousnesses whose bodily facticity – including their sexual identity – pertains to the order of the in-itself rather than that of the for-itself. By contrast, Irigaray argues that these two orders are essentially intertwined: "In so far as I belong to a gender, my body . . . already involves a for-itself" (TBT 30).

Insofar as the forgetting of sexual difference can be characterized as a forgetting of the difference between sexual difference and sexual diversity – Irigaray's version of the forgetting of the ontological difference between being and beings – *Speculum* can be read as an attempt to carry out a "destruction" of the history of (sexual) metaphysics from Freud to Plato. Irigaray locates the founding gesture of phallocentric metaphysics in Plato's metaphor of the cave, or *hystera*, the Greek word for "womb." What for Plato is the process by which a prisoner is liberated from the shadowy realm of untruth and brought out to the light of truth is, for Irigaray, a metaphor for the violent process by which a child is forced to renounce its primordial relation to the maternal in favor of a supposedly self-engendering relation to the paternal law. All of the hierarchical oppositions of Western metaphysics are condensed in this metaphor, which Irigaray reads (like Derrida) as a metaphor of metaphorization as such. The elemental ground of the maternal body of the earth serves as the necessary place of inscription for a paternal logos that claims to be autochthonous. As such, it functions as a concave mirror, reflecting back to the intelligible masculine soul an image of itself. This mirror – the wall of Plato's cave upon which the shadows of the simulacra are cast – must be fetishistically disavowed in the name of a phallic God who denies that he needs anything other than himself to reflect himself. Man is then made in the image of this god.

Thus everything operates in this "photological" primal scene to allow man to represent himself to himself as coming to presence without mirrors – when in fact he exists only as his mirror's focus imaginarius. Like the Hegelian negation of the negation, this specular "reflection of the reflection" yields a speculative profit for a subject who believes that he is immediately identical with himself without having to pass through a relation to alterity. By highlighting the role played by sexual difference in this specular scene, Irigaray complicates the Lacanian (and Althusserian) account of the mirror stage as the process by which a narcissistic subject (mis-)recognizes himself in another. In the very act by which the prisoner is supposedly freed from the illusions of the cave he – and she – are surreptitiously subjected to a metaphysical sleight of hand. Allegedly, we leave behind a place of illusion for the secure path of truth, a feminine art of the sensible for a masculine science of the intelligible. But, in fact, we are still in the funhouse of man and his doubles, subject to what Foucault called "that other form of madness," the madness of pure reason.

Irigaray's reading of the cave analogy recalls Nietzsche's account of the birth of Socratism. Like the Greek spectator whom Socrates forced to renounce the spectacle of tragedy, the prisoner from the cave is wrested from a nocturnal theater and forced to tread the path to clarity and distinctness. Irigaray suggests that the shadows projected at the back of the cave are not just Apollonian images but expressions of an unutterable Dionysian ecstasy that must be renounced (SOW 198, 335). The mute regret that Irigaray associates with the renunciation of the maternal also recalls Adorno and Horkheimer's characterization of the heavy hearts with which Odysseus and his men left the land of the lotus-eaters, just as her overall assessment – "From the trickery of magic we move on to the trickery of authority" – encapsulates their assessment of the dialectic of enlightenment (SOW 274). Like each of these thinkers, Irigaray is trying to awaken her readers to a sense of what we have lost, not only in forsaking the maternal but in forgetting the very act of forsaking. With Heidegger she locates the stakes of this forgetting in Kant's subordination of the imagination to the faculty of understanding: "For the most sophisticated faculty of the senses, the imaginary, will remain the slave of understanding" (SOW 204; cf. 44 n28). Heidegger thought that Kant recoiled from the imagination because he wanted to preserve the autonomous pretensions of pure practical reason. Irigaray implicitly agrees with this assessment, but following Freud and Lacan she traces the moral law back to the prohibition of incest: "The principle 'noli tangere matrem' locates its economy of reason and desire in the *categorical imperative*" (SOW 210). Once we leave the cave we are never to return: such is the first rule of Oedipalization.

In *The Forgetting of Air in Martin Heidegger* (L'Oubli de l'air chez Martin Heidegger, 1983), Irigaray suggests that Heidegger himself "recoiled" from the feminine and hence from the question of sexual difference. This is evidenced in the fact that in his elemental thinking he attends to the earth but not to the air (FAMH 12–13). Analogously, Irigaray argues in *The Marine Lover of Friedrich Nietzsche* (Amante marine de Friedrich Nietzsche, 1980) that, while Zarathustra teaches fidelity to the earth, he keeps his distance from the unfathomable depths of the maternal sea from which life first originated: "Why leave the sea? To carry a gift – of life. But it is to the earth that you preach fidelity. And forgetfulness of your birth" (ML 12). Zarathustra is accompanied by an eagle (whose medium is the air) and a snake (an inhabitant of the earth), but "as companion you never choose a sea creature" (ML 13). As this passage indicates, it is as his "marine lover" that Irigaray addresses Nietzsche in the first section of her book. In the final sections, she summons female companions for the male gods Dionysus, Apollo, and Christ.[17]

Like Bachelard – who also wrote about the elements (including air imagery in Nietzsche) – Irigaray suggests that it is necessary to free scientific thought from rigid (i.e., phallic) categories. For example, she wonders whether fluid mechanics might need to be looked at through a different kind of lens than the speculum through which classical mechanics observes elemental flows. In contrast to Beauvoir, for whom it was impossible to be "born" a woman, Irigaray speculates that biological – or at least morphological – differences between the sexes may be essential to gender identities. Thus, rather than treating patriarchy as a mere social construct, she considers the possibility that there is something inherent in the morphological differences between the sexes that predisposes men to assume the status of ontological touchstone (SOW 119; cf. 103 n107). This conjecture lends credence to Kant's association of women with beauty and men with sublimity. Presumably Irigaray would object to many of Kant's "observations" – such as "A woman who has a head full of Greek, like Mme Dacier, or carries on fundamental controversies about mechanics, like the Marquise de Châtelet, might as well even have a beard; for perhaps that would express more obviously the mien of profundity for which she strives" – but because of her views about morphological differences, there is no *a priori* basis on which she could do so (particularly if the "mechanics" in question are not fluid) (OFBS 78). Certainly Irigaray does not accept Kant's view that "just as it is not woman's role to go to war, so she cannot personally defend her rights and engage in civil affairs for herself, but only through her representative" (AFPPV 80). But instead of arguing for political equality, Irigaray instead tries to develop a conception of *sexed* rights.

Throughout the history of patriarchy, women have been faced with the "choice" of either becoming man's double – thereby losing their own subjectivity – or being labeled hysterics. Irigaray seeks to undermine the supposedly transcendental character of this forced choice (akin to Lacan's "Your money or your life!") by showing that there is a genuine alternative (S XI 212). Kant characterized man as an end in himself, while Nietzsche suggested that he was something that had to be overcome. Irigaray offers a middle way: man is something that must be complemented, for he is an end not "in himself" but only through his relationship to an other. Foucault characterized man as an empirico-transcendental doublet, a living contradiction about to disappear "like a face drawn in sand at the edge of the sea" (OT 387). But instead of waiting for man (or men) to *disappear*, Irigaray tries to help woman (or women) *appear*, so that a genuine sexual relationship might occur where before only sexual panopticism had prevailed. Together, in the very betweenness of their relationship to one another, a man and a woman have the potential to achieve what Irigaray calls in *An Ethics of Sexual Difference* (*Éthique de la différence sexuelle*, 1984) the "sensible transcendental," something that she associates with the experience of "sublime beauty" that Diotima describes in Plato's *Symposium* (EOSD 32).

In Irigaray's view, Kant's Copernican turn represents a classically patriarchal attempt on the part of a masculine subject to give birth to himself by turning away from the maternal (SOW 204). Though Kant denies that we can leave the cave behind and gaze upon the intelligible sun, he nonetheless maintains that we must orient ourselves (in thought) away from the body and toward the intelligible Good. In this way he privileges spontaneity over receptivity, autonomy over heteronomy, transcendence over immanence, the transcendental over the empirical. By contrast, Irigaray's ideal of a sensible transcendental represents an attempt to think spontaneity in the receptivity of the senses, autonomy in the relation to alterity, and transcendence in immanence – i.e., sublimity in beauty – "in the tranquil rising of the sun" rather than "in the tempest" (TBT 71). To locate the sublime in the tranquil rising of the sensible sun is not the same as finding it in the intelligible sun from which we must shield our eyes. On the contrary, it suggests a completely different way of thinking about fire.

Everything in Kant's critique of dogmatic metaphysics attests to both the allure and the danger of fire. We yearn to see the sun, and this yearning is like an internal fire or "zealous heat" that inspires us to soar higher (CPR A465/B493). But when the fire burns too much, we risk being consumed by it: enthusiasm gives way to fanaticism; the fire becomes a conflagration. Irigaray suggests that Kant conceived of God as "a sort of ultimate foundation, an imaginary fire" whose capacity for intellectual intuition must be set apart from the subject's own finitude (TBT 87). Everything depends upon keeping a respectful distance: "*Modesty* forbids us to speak of providence as something we can recognise, for this would mean donning the wings of Icarus and presuming to approach the mystery of its inscrutable intentions" (PW 109). To avoid this Icarian temptation, taste must temper genius by "clipping its wings" (CPJ 197).[18] The passage through the conduit leading out of Plato's cave can be likened to the search for the unconditioned condition for every empirical series of conditions. In the case of the two dynamical antinomies, concerning freedom and the existence of a necessary being, reason posits the existence of something at the end of the conduit, but *speculation* will never lead us there. No matter how far we go, the object keeps receding, for it is in fact nothing but a specular illusion (*focus imaginarius*). Kant takes this fact to be "reason's hint that we should turn our self-knowledge away from fruitless and extravagant speculation toward fruitful practical uses" (CPR B421). In this respect he teaches a kind of fidelity to the earth, one that curbs the aspiration of the soul to fly:

> The light dove, in free flight cutting through the air the resistance of which it feels, could get the idea that it could do even better in airless space. Likewise, Plato abandoned the world of the senses because it set such narrow limits for the understanding, and dared to go beyond it on the wings of the ideas, in the empty space of pure understanding.
>
> (CPR A5/B8–9)

In leaving room for faith, Kant suggests that it is possible to remain earth-bound without having to forsake our aspiration for flight. We find ourselves on an island surrounded by a vast sea, and although we would like to set sail for more distant lands – or blessed isles – the way is fraught with peril, for "many a fog bank and rapidly melting iceberg pretend to be new lands" (CPR A235–6/B295). To be sure, every transcendental illusion "dissolves into mere haze when put to the fiery test of critique" (CPR A406/B433; cf. A746/B774). But it is safer to stand upon the shore and gaze upon the horizon, remaining this side of the Pillars of Hercules (CPR A395). Kant's fear of the watery depths and dissimulating fog banks echoes the apprehensiveness that Irigaray detected in Nietzsche and Heidegger. But the water that surrounds the island of human cognition also serves as a uterine moat protecting us from the father, for if we actually had an immediate intuition of God our every action would become heteronomous (CPrR 258).

Confined to a fireplace, a fire is charming – but not beautiful, as its flickering nature prevents it from assuming a definite form (CPJ 127). Conversely, a raging out-of-control fire can provide the occasion for a feeling of sublimity – but only if we keep our distance. The great danger is always that of fanaticism, the desire to burn everything. As Lucetta cautions Julia in *The Two Gentlemen of Verona*: "I do not seek to quench your love's hot fire,/But qualify the fire's extreme rage,/Lest it should burn above the bounds of reason" (II, vii, 21–3). Irigaray says almost exactly the same thing about the "vision of the Flaming Heart" of Saint Teresa of Avila (1515–1582), namely, that she admires her ecstasy but worries when all boundaries begin to disappear (SOW 201). In contrast to Bataille – who linked mystical experience to sexual union, but in such a way that the twoness of the couple was reduced to sheer heterogeneity – Irigaray envisions a shared passion that would not ignite everything: "Your irreducible alterity gives me the present, presence: the possibility of being in myself, of attempting to cultivate the in-stasy and not only the ex-stasy" (TBT 37).[19] This is not altogether different from Kant's ideal of a marriage based on mutual love and respect (OFBS 65). The problem with Kant is that he does not enter into a genuine dialogue *with* women; instead he talks *about* women *to* men. To Nietzsche, who did the same thing, Irigaray responded from the perspective of his marine lover. Likewise, she implicitly responds to Kant as his secret "muse of fire."[20]

4.10   Habermas's evasion of the dilemmas concerning man and his doubles

> Harp not on that; nor do not banish reason
> For inequality
> (*Measure for Measure*, V, i, 64–5)

Like Irigaray, Habermas responds to the problem concerning man and his doubles by seeking to replace a one-sided conception of human subjectivity with an account that is rooted in relations between first and second persons.

In his view, the patriarchal oppression of women is one of a number of ill effects that have resulted from the dominance of the subject-centered conception of rationality. Only through communicative interaction can men and women begin to repair a distorted lifeworld (TCA II 393–4).

In *The Philosophical Discourse of Modernity: Twelve Lectures* (*Der philosophische Diskurs der Moderne: Zwölf Vorlesungen*, 1985), Habermas reads Foucault as convincingly revealing the costs that have been incurred with the rise in modernity of the subject-centered conception of reason. These include the reduction of "dialogical relationships" between the members of a shared lifeworld to the various instrumental relations of supervision that Foucault detects in the advent of the clinic (PDOM 246). At the theoretical level, they also include the "aporias" pertaining to the category of man. Habermas agrees with Foucault that, insofar as the human sciences remain caught within these aporias, they are "pseudo-sciences" clandestinely motivated by a will to power. Such a critique presupposes the possibility of a discourse that would not be motivated by power. But instead of endorsing this implication – and seeking an alternative to the subject-centered conception of rationality in a communicative conception of the sort that Habermas himself develops – Foucault ends up making the sweeping claim that "*all* discourses . . . can be shown to have the character of hidden power and derive from practices of power" (PDOM 265). For Habermas, this neo-Nietzschean totalizing reduction of the "will to knowledge" to the "will to power" undercuts the force of Foucault's critique of the human sciences, for it implies that they are no more or less implicated in power relations than any other discourse, including Foucault's own.

Like the category of man, Foucault's conception of power is itself an empirico-transcendental doublet in that it functions both as the object of empirical descriptions (the various ways in which power is exercised on bodies) and as the constituting ground of all discursive practices (PDOM 270). According to Habermas, Foucault was well aware of the fact that genealogy thereby inherits the very aporias that he had earlier attributed to the human sciences, but he does not pursue any way around them (PDOM 276, 309). Instead, he contents himself with pursuing a critique of specific practices of power without pretending to be able to legitimate this critique in any way. Unlike the members of the Frankfurt School, for whom the Hegelian–Marxist ideal of reconciliation could serve as a criterion for the denunciation of instrumental reason, Foucault follows Nietzsche in repudiating the ideal of reconciliation as the aim of his critique of modernity (PDOM 251). As a result, his genealogical analyses commit all the sins that he had rightly denounced in the human sciences, namely, "presentism," "relativism," and "cryptonormativism." For Habermas, these relapses are debilitating because they make it impossible to assess "the internal aspects of *meaning*, of *truth-validity*, and of *evaluating*" which "do not go without remainder into the externally grasped aspects of practices of power" (PDOM 276). In other words, by reducing all discursive operations to mere expressions of power, Foucault collapses the distinction between the force of sheer power and the force of reasons.

According to Habermas, only a theory that sees "subject-centered reason" as "the *product of division and usurpation*" can provide a genuine solution to the problems surrounding man and his doubles (PDOM 315). Foucault was right in thinking that the Hegelian–Marxist tradition could not provide such a solution, but he failed to see the possibility of a communications–theoretic solution. Instead of being forced to construe oneself as both the subject and the object of one's own reflective activity, an individual subject is always already engaged in a dialogical situation with others from whom one learns how to engage in critical self-reflection (PDOM 297). This means that it is not the individual subject but the members of a shared lifeworld who collectively serve as the ground of their discursive practices. Though it might seem as if the group thereby inherits all of the aporias that Foucault detected in connection with the category of man, Habermas argues that this is not so, because there is nothing at the level of the shared lifeworld that would correspond to the concept of the subject – as was the case with Hegel's conception of spirit and Marx's conception of the victorious proletariat. The theory of communicative action avoids the dilemmas of subjectivity by abandoning its transcendental pretensions in favor of a "here and now" ground for the here-and-now-*transcending* claims of reason (PDOM 323).

In support of this re-orientation, Habermas offers two correctives to Foucault's specific genealogical analyses. First, he criticizes Foucault for being unable to account for the genuine gains that have been made in modern legal institutions that have not *merely* served the interests of disciplinary power but have also secured rights of individuals not to be coerced (PDOM 290). Second, he argues that psychoanalysis has not *merely* contributed to the proliferation of bio-power; it has also opened up genuinely liberatory possibilities that Foucault ignores (PDOM 292–3). Construed from the standpoint of a communicative theory of action – as Habermas does in his earlier works – psychoanalysis presents an exemplary model for how "the two procedures of reconstruction and self-critique can still be brought together" (PDOM 300).

Though Habermas thinks that it is possible to avoid the dilemma concerning the relation between the empirical and transcendental dimensions of human experience, in *The Future of Human Nature* (*Die Zukunft der menschlichen Natur: Auf dem Weg zu einer liberalen Eugenik?*, 2001) he acknowledges the possibility that specific manifestations of bio-power may open it up in a new way. So long as eugenics was restricted to traditional breeding techniques, it fell under the heading of instrumental relations between human beings and nature (FOHN 45). But now that developments in biotechnology have enabled us to alter the future course of the human species, a completely different kind of intervention has become possible, one that threatens to "uproot the categorical distinction between the subjective and the objective, the naturally grown and the made" (FOHN 42). Non-therapeutic eugenic interventions ought to be resisted, not only because they are wrong in a conventional sense but because they *may* undermine the conditions for the possibility of engaging in communicative action at all (FOHN 39). Paradoxically, our very capacity to reinvent ourselves requires that each of us inherit a natural condition that has not been selected by someone else for us. Put otherwise, it is important to preserve the distinction that Kant thought could be drawn a priori between physiological and pragmatic anthropology. In conceding the possibility that the new biotechnologies might erase such a distinction by enabling us to change human nature, Habermas acknowledges that there *is* a kind of power capable of functioning as an empirico-transcendental doublet, one that should be resisted for this very reason. The question would be whether he can concede this possibility while continuing to insist that the theory of communicative action is exempt from this threat in principle. For, as he admits:

> It is not so simple to counter the suspicion that with the concept of action oriented to validity claims the idealism of a pure, nonsituated reason slips in again, and the dichotomies between the realms of the transcendental and the empirical are given new life in another form.
>
> (PDOM 322)

Though he maintains that "the communications–theoretic concept of the lifeworld has been freed from the mortgages of transcendental philosophy," his insistence that men not tamper with the nature of man suggests otherwise (PDOM 358).

Notes

1 Deleuze, apropos "The Last Days of Emmanuel Kant," by Thomas De Quincey (1785–1859), detects "a Shakespearian side of Kant, a kind of *King Lear*" (KCP xiii).
2 Cf. Mary Gregor's translator's introduction to AFPPV, pp. xviii–xix.
3 But cf. the merely two-fold distinction between the pragmatic and moral points of view at AFPPV 103.
4 Cf. Žižek's characterization of the Lacanian conception of the "sinthome," a symptom that persists even after analysis (SOI 75).
5 Foucault refers to Haller in passing at MC 127, 155.
6 Kant considered himself to be a cosmopolitan thinker even though he never left his native Königsberg – as the title of an essay by T.J. Reed, "The Stay-at-Home Man of the World," brings out (cited at PW 253n). Interestingly, Kant characterizes the smoking of tobacco as a substitute for conversing with another person (AFPPV 39, 101). Perhaps Freud was able to psychoanalyze himself because his cigars "listened" to him. Adorno suggests another relationship between smoking and listening:

> The gesture of smoking is rather the opposite of that involved in listening to a concert: for it is directed against the aura of the work of art, and it blows smoke in the face of sound . . . the person who smokes is experiencing himself.
>
> (TCC 238)

7   Žižek characterizes the Hegelian "absolute subject" as precisely such a monarch who reigns only by "'choosing what is already given' . . . pretending that the given reality is already his work" (SOI 220).

8   Cf. Kant: "If Christianity should ever come to the point where it ceased to be worthy of love (which could very well transpire if instead of its gentle spirit it were armed with commanding authority), then . . . the *Antichrist* . . . would begin his – albeit short – regime" (EOAT 231).

9   Cf. his *Notebooks for an Ethics* (*Cahiers pour une morale*) written in 1947–1948 and published in 1983.

10 Here and throughout the novel, the French *conscience* is rendered as "conscience" rather than as "consciousness."

11 As David Macey observes in *Frantz Fanon: a Biography*: "The mistranslation obliterates Fanon's philosophical frame of reference, which is supplied by a phenomenological theory of experience, but it also perverts his whole argument; for Fanon, there is no 'fact of blackness'" (p. 26).

12 In John MacCombie's translation: "Thus, negritude is *for* destroying itself; it is a 'crossing to' and not an 'arrival at,' a means and not an end" (WIL 327).

13 The idea that spectacular displays of state violence threaten the legitimacy of the state serves as the basis of Foucault's explanation for the disappearance of public displays of punishment in modern Europe.

14 Cf. Heidegger: "To think is to confine yourself to a single thought that one day stands still like a star in the world's sky" (PLT 4).

15 For passing references to ants in Sartre's own fiction, cf. Nau 59, 62; WAOS 34, 41, 108; AOR 255; R 307; TS 19, 197, 202, 224, 353. For other references to ants in Beauvoir, cf. SCTS 25; SS 17–18.

16 This reversal of the gaze is anticipated in Fanon's analysis of the way that colonial power works, not by exacting the recognition of the oppressed (as in Hegel's master/slave dialectic) but by subjecting the oppressed to a form of recognition.

17 In *The Conflict of the Faculties*, Kant notes that the sixteenth-century mystic, Guillaume Postel (1510–1581), believed that since Jesus was a man with specifically "masculine frailties," there must also have been a female Christ as well:

> since the frailties as well as the transgressions of the other sex are specifically different from those of the male, we are, not without reason, tempted to suppose that the female sex will also have its special representative (a divine daughter, as it were) as its expiatress.

Though conceding that this idea is "not without reason," Kant nonetheless characterizes Postel as a fanatic whose idea is "an excellent example of the sort of aberration" that "raving people can fall into if they transform the perceptible rendering of a pure idea of reason into the representation of an object of the senses." But it is not entirely clear from the context whether it is the mere idea of a female Christ that Kant regards as fanatical, or the fact that Postel "thought he had found her, in the person of a pious Venetian maiden" (COF 265).

18 Cf. Kant's wish that Herder would "curb his lively genius somewhat" (PW 211).

19 Of the dangers of sexual desire, Kant writes: "it is only to be regretted that easier than another it degenerates into dissoluteness. For as any other can extinguish the fire one person has lighted, there are not enough obstacles that can confine an intractable inclination" (OFBS 86n). Freud suggests that patriarchy has its roots in man's ability to control this fire:

> It is as though primal man had the habit, when he came in contact with fire, of satisfying an infantile desire connected with it, by putting it out with a

stream of his urine. . . . The first person to renounce this desire and spare the fire was able to carry it off with him and subdue it to his own use. By damping down the fire of his own sexual excitation, he had tamed the natural force of fire. . . . Further, it is as though woman had been appointed guardian of the fire which was held captive on the domestic hearth, because her anatomy made it impossible for her to yield to the temptation of this desire.

(CAID 42–3n)

20 In his "Succinct Exposition of Some Meditations on Fire" (*Meditationum quarundam de igne succincta delineatio*, 1755), Kant suggests that fire is "nothing but the elastic matter . . . which holds together the elements of bodies with which it is intermixed; its undulatory or vibratory motion is that which is called heat" (SESMF 32). As for flame, it "is nothing but vapor brought to that degree of fire that it flashes with light and goes out only when there is insufficient fuel" (SESMF 42). Though untenable from the standpoint of modern chemistry, it is interesting to note that Kant's explanation situates fire with respect to fluid rather than static mechanics.

5   Conclusion: what is philosophy?

Now that various claims to the Kantian legacy have been recounted on behalf of the House of Continental, it is time to consider what corresponding claims can be made on behalf of the House of Analytic. In the Introduction I suggested that, by responding to Kant's dualisms in divergent ways, continental and analytic philosophers had prioritized different philosophical questions. In this concluding chapter I will first present an extremely brief synopsis of how the analytic variants have been pursued. I will then try to show that the division between the two houses can be represented as a meta-antinomy about the nature of antinomies. Finally, I will suggest that the analytic/continental distinction attests to a shared anxiety that all post-Kantian thinkers have had to face about the philosopher's cosmopolitan vocation.

5.1   Kant's questions as taken up in the House of Analytic

> I durst go no further than the Lie Circumstantial, nor he durst not give
> me the Lie Direct; and so we measur'd swords and parted.
> > (*As You Like It*, V, iv, 85–7)

i   Just as the continental question concerning the aesthetic disclosure of truth was taken up in an exemplary way in Nietzsche's *The Birth of Tragedy*, so the analytic question, "What can be known on the basis of logical analysis alone?," received its first canonical formulation in Frege's *Foundations of Arithmetic* (*Die Grundlagen der Arithmetik, eine logisch mathematische Untersuchung über den Begriff der Zahl*, 1884).[1] Against the empiricist strain of the prevailing neo-Kantian orthodoxy, Frege rejects psychologistic explanations about how we acquire knowledge of the laws of arithmetic, maintaining that arithmetical truths are analytic rather than synthetic, and thus that they can be known (and *only* can be known) on the basis of the logical analysis of concepts (rather than by appeal to sensible intuitions of any sort). In his late essay, "Thought" (*Der Gedanke*, 1918–1919), Frege characterizes truth not as a function of judgments (as it was for Kant), nor as that which is both disclosed and concealed in givenness (as it was for Nietzsche and the phenomenologists), but as an eternal property of mind-independent thoughts that can only be apprehended through "a special mental capacity, the power of thinking" (FR 341). This capacity consists not in sheer spontaneity, as if by thinking we created the thoughts that we think; rather, it is a spontaneity that is *receptive* to true thoughts: "In thinking we do not produce thoughts, we grasp them" (FR 341–2). By representing human cognition as a kind of receptive spontaneity, Frege is able to extend the reach of logical analysis beyond the bounds that Kant set to it when he claimed that, without the aid of intuition, it was useless to "reflect on the triangle philosophically, i.e., discursively" (CPR A718/B746).

Frege's logicist program was taken one step further by Bertrand Russell (1872–1970). Not only does Russell try to complete Frege's project of reducing arithmetic to logic (which, however, he takes to be synthetic rather than analytic), but he claims that "*every* philosophical problem, when it is subjected to the necessary analysis and purification, is found either to be not really philosophical at all, or else to be . . . logical" (OKEW 42; my italics). While acknowledging that there may be "mystical" truths that can only be intuited, Russell dismisses mystical *claims* from philosophical consideration on the grounds that they cannot be defended with logical arguments. Ludwig Wittgenstein (1889–1951) concedes in his *Tractatus Logico-Philosophicus* (*Logisch-Philosophische Abhandlung*, 1921) that mystical truths are ineffable, but he attempts to restore their philosophical dignity by distinguishing the world – the totality of facts in logical space – from its inexpressible givenness. This doctrine (minus the caveat about givenness) became the credo of the logical positivists, who, instead of asking about givenness, asked what role "the given" should play in logical constructions of the world. In *Our Knowledge of the External World* (1914), Russell had showed how the world could be "logically constructed" on the sole basis of the individual's private acquaintance with "sense-data." But in *The Logical Structure of the World* (*Der logische Aufbau der Welt*, 1928), Carnap claims that the choice of primitive givens for such constructions is completely arbitrary. However it is constructed, the world is no longer the indefinite totality of phenomena (Kant), or that which is disclosed and concealed in works of art (Nietzsche and Heidegger), but that which can be logically analyzed.

W.V.O. Quine (1908–2000) and Wilfrid Sellars (1912–1989) took Carnap's conventionalist idea one step further, denying that there is any such thing as "the given" at all. To abandon "the entire framework of givenness," as Sellars recommends in his 1956 essay, "Empiricism and the Philosophy of Mind," is not to deny that we make non-inferential reports about appearances; but it is to say that any non-inferential appeal to phenomena qua phenomena (the way things "seem") is only meaningful insofar as it is possible to provide an inferential justification of such an appeal (EPM 14). This construal of phenomenological descriptions of the world represents an attempt to eliminate the last traces of the intuition/concept dichotomy. Thus John McDowell (1942–) goes so far as to claim in his book, *Mind and World* (1994), that "receptivity does not make an *even notionally* separable contribution to the co-operation" between sensibility and understanding in cognition.[2] As McDowell notes, the main problem faced by those, like he and Donald Davidson (1917–2003), who reject what Sellars calls the "myth of the given" is to show how, in the absence of separable intuitions, human understanding makes contact with a mind-independent world. But according to McDowell, those who persist in retaining the given are faced with an even more difficult problem, namely, of showing how something without intrinsic conceptual content can play a role in justifying or falsifying beliefs. In posing the dilemma in these terms, McDowell makes explicit the problem that Frege opened up when he claimed that truth could only be accessed by a faculty of receptive spontaneity. In effect, he is looking for the exact inverse of Husserl's conception of categorial intuition, for the only difference between categorial intuition and conceptually informed intuitions lies in what order receptivity and spontaneity are put back together. As Kant says (of the relationship between morality and statutory religion), "So much depends, when we wish to join two good things, on the order in which we combine them!" (RRT 197).

ii   In the Introduction I suggested that analytic ethicists have been concerned with the force of moral prescriptives rather than with the genealogy of the moral feelings of humiliation and respect. Just as Frege argued that truth could only be grasped through a special faculty of thinking, so G.E. Moore (1873–1958) claims in his *Principia Ethica* (1903) that goodness can only be apprehended through a special kind of non-sensible intuition. Whereas Frege argued for the analyticity of arithmetical truths, Moore argues that all propositions about the good must be synthetic because the predicate "good" is indefinable (PE 58). Accordingly, he rejects the "naturalistic fallacy," i.e., the view that goodness can be identified with one of its properties (PE 62). Maintaining that the primary object of ethical inquiry is not "assertions about human conduct" but "assertions about that property of things which is denoted by the term 'good,'" Moore criticizes Kant not for succumbing to the naturalistic fallacy but for attempting to derive true ethical propositions from an analysis of "the essential nature of will" (PE 87, 181). By subordinating the question, "What should I do?," to the question, "What is good?," Moore inverts Kant's understanding of the relationship between the concept of duty and the concept of goodness, asserting that moral duties must be derived from appraisals of goodness rather than the other way around. Kant claimed that to derive the concept of duty from an independently given conception of the good would make the will heteronomous. But Moore argues that it is perfectly legitimate for the will to be motivated both by sensuous inclinations such as pity and by insight into the nature of the good (PE 228). Thus instead of taking heteronomy of the will to be incompatible with moral autonomy, he implicitly characterizes a will that promotes the good as *heteronomously autonomous*, that is, as pathologically motivated to obey self-imposed duties. To be heteronomously autonomous is to be subject to moral prescriptives – "ought" claims – for which one is answerable (the practical analogue of Sellars's account of being answerable for one's non-inferential reports about how things seem). The central debate to which Moore's work gave rise in the early analytic tradition was whether moral prescriptives should be thought of as "objective" (as

Kant claims the categorical imperative is) or as "subjective" (in the manner of arbitrarily chosen maxims). This controversy differs from the continental debate between an ethics of transgression and an ethics of fidelity to the law, for the former concerns the status of moral principles, while the latter concerns incentives that arise prior to the obliged subject's capacity either to acknowledge or take on moral principles. The difference between the analytic conception of heteronomous autonomy and the continental conception of autonomous heteronomy can be likened to the difference between Odysseus consciously deciding to bind himself to the mast and Gulliver waking up to find himself bound by the Lilliputians. Once again, it is a question of how to put two things back together; but as Kant says in connection with the difference between Epicurean and Stoic construals of the highest good: "two wholes can . . . be specifically different from each other although they consist of the same material, if, namely, the two parts are combined into a whole in quite different ways" (CPrR 230).

    iii In Chapter 3 I tried to show how continental philosophers have responded to the problem of the relationship between immanence and transcendence by reflecting on Kant's distinction between the beautiful and the sublime. Analytic philosophers have focused not on the "aesthetic" dimension of this problem but rather on its "teleological" dimension. The reason for this is that Kant's critique of teleological judgment inherits problems that arise in connection with his Transcendental Logic (as opposed to the Transcendental Aesthetic). By conceiving of cognition as receptive spontaneity, analytic philosophers have been led to ask what ontological implications the collapse of the immanence/transcendence distinction has for natural science and metaphysics. In the Introduction I suggested that the difference between sublime beauty and beautiful sublimity as aesthetic indicators of transcendent immanence and immanent transcendence corresponds to the difference between empirical facts and metaphysical problems. The two-fold question posed by analytic philosophers has been, first, whether empirical facts have metaphysical significance, and, second, whether it is still meaningful to pose metaphysical questions concerning the soul, freedom, and God. In his *Language, Truth and Logic* (1936), A.J. Ayer (1910–1989) defends the logical positivist credo that metaphysical questions are completely meaningless because they violate the so-called "verifiability criterion" of meaning, the requirement that all meaningful assertions be empirically testable in some way. This early analytic orthodoxy eventually gave way to the view that metaphysical questions are, in fact, meaningful, but it remains controversial as to whether logic and natural science can provide an exhaustive account of "what there is." In increasingly technical terms, analytic philosophers have tackled the problem of "general metaphysics" in philosophy of science (notably in the debate between "realists" and "antirealists"), as well as the problems pertaining to "special metaphysis" (under the rubrics of the mind/body problem, the problem of free will, and the problem of the existence of God). Each of these problems can be situated with respect to Kant's critique of teleological judgment because they all bear on the concept of objective purposiveness. Analytic philosophers have also taken up the problems that Kant ascribed to the metaphysics of *morals*, and it is here that a relevant contrast with critical theory and hermeneutics emerges.

In *A Theory of Justice* (1971), John Rawls (1921–2002) attempts, as Kant did in *The Metaphysics of Morals*, to specify universal duties of right. Toward this end, he defends, against Moore, the Kantian view that the concept of justice must be determined independently of particular agents' intuitions about the good. Critics of Rawls, such as Alasdair MacIntyre (1929–), Michael Walzer (1935–), and Michael Sandel (1953–) claim that it is impossible to divorce conceptions of justice from substantive conceptions of the good. This debate between "liberal" and "communitarian" conceptions of justice can be likened to the continental debate concerning the relative priority that should be accorded to the sublime (i.e., the idea of law considered aesthetically) and the beautiful (the symbol of the morally good). Kant sought to maintain a precarious balance between the need for aesthetic representations of the good and the moral prohibition of graven images. Following the lead of Schiller, Marx brought these two principles together by representing the telos of human history as an aesthetic ideal. In effect, this was to treat the beautiful not merely as a symbol of morality but as its sensible manifestation. The central question over which critical theory and hermeneutics divided was whether to preserve the possibility of hope through beautiful sublimity or sublime beauty.[3] Analogously, the point of contention between Rawls and his critics is whether to affirm *just* goods (the analogue of beautiful sublimity) or *good* laws (the analogue of sublime beauty). Elaine Scarry has noted that Rawls's conception of fairness "as a 'symmetry of everyone's relations to each other'" implicitly connects the idea of justice to the idea of beauty.[4] This observation suggests that, despite the unrepresentability of the Rawlsian idea of justice (it can only be determined behind a "veil of ignorance"), it is not merely sublime but *beautifully* sublime (i.e., it is akin to the critical theorists' conception of beautiful sublimity). Conversely, the communitarian emphasis on traditional conceptions of the good is of a piece with hermeneutical conceptions of sublime beauty. However, in contrast to both critical theory and hermeneutics, reflections on art have not been central to analytic debates about the nature of justice. One reason for aligning Habermas with the analytic tradition rather than the continental is the fact that he draws a sharp distinction between "norm-conformative" and "expressive" attitudes (TCA I 237). In recent works such as *Between Facts and Norms: Contributions to a Discourse Theory of Law and Democracy* (*Beiträge zur Diskurstheorie des Rechts und des demokratischen Rechtsstaats*, 1992), his main interlocutors have been liberal theorists of justice such as Rawls and Ronald Dworkin (1931–).

iv In Chapter 4 I suggested that, in contrast to Kant, who tried to sustain the tension between empirically existing men and the transcendental essence of man, the existentialists characterized human existence as empirically transcendental. As a result, they rejected Kant's conception of transcendental philosophy in favor of a conception of philosophical humanism. By contrast, analytic philosophers (at least since Quine) have embraced philosophical naturalism, and with it a conception of human existence as transcendentally empirical.[5] To regard ourselves as transcendentally empirical is to accept the natural attitude while recognizing that for some unknown (but possibly knowable) reason, we possess the anomalous ability to enter a "space of reasons" through which we relate to the world. From this point of view, the world's existence *as a world* may depend upon us in the trivial sense that nothing can exist "as" something without there being someone who takes it as being that way, but the *being* of the natural world would not in any way depend upon us. If it did, we would inhabit not a space of reasons but what Blanchot calls "the space of literature." Just as Sartre and Heidegger disagreed about the meaning of humanism, so analytic philosophers have argued about the exact meaning of philosophical naturalism. On one side are those whom McDowell characterizes as "bald naturalists," philosophers who deny that there is anything distinctive about human existence at all. On the other side are those, like McDowell himself, who defend the irreducibility of some particular feature of human existence to a merely physicalistic description of the natural world. Just as the concept of transcendental freedom enabled Kant to limit the reach of an otherwise thorough-going naturalism, so "weak" naturalists have appealed either to the phenomenon of consciousness or to the human capacity to justify our beliefs and actions with reasons.

Kant claimed that his fourth question had a certain privilege in that it somehow subsumed the other three. Likewise, of all the points of heresy that divide the House of Continental from the House of Analytic, it is perhaps this fourth, methodological, division that is most fundamental.

Keeping in mind that the overview of analytic philosophy that I have just sketched is highly schematic (throughout this book we have inhabited the space of literature), the division between the two houses can be represented as a series of divergent variations on Kant's four questions (the first in each pair representing the continental alternative):

I "How is truth disclosed aesthetically?"
    "What can be known on the basis of logical analysis alone?"
II "To what does the feeling of respect attest?"
    "What is the force of moral prescriptives?"
III "Must we despair, or may we still hope?"
    "Are metaphysical questions still meaningful?"
IV "What is the meaning of philosophical humanism?"
    "What is the meaning of philosophical naturalism?"

If it is true that these questions derive from divergent resolutions of the four Kantian dualisms that I have identified — receptivity/spontaneity, heteronomy/autonomy, immanence/transcendence, empirical/transcendental —

then the analytic/continental division should be representable as a series of conflicts between continental theses and analytic antitheses. If so, we could ask whether these post-critical controversies can be settled in the same manner in which Kant resolved the pre-critical controversies that he identified as antinomies. Perhaps by setting up a new tribunal before which the two houses could plead their respective cases, a civil war could be transformed into a litigable civil suit. But what if the competing ordered conflations advocated by the two houses gave rise to a conflict about the very nature of philosophical controversies? In that case, civil war might turn out to be perpetual. In the remaining pages of this book, I will suggest that this is, in fact, the predicament that we are in.

5.2   The conflict of the philosophy faculty with itself

> O madness of discourse,
> That cause sets up with and against itself!
> *(The History of Troilus and Cressida,*
> V, ii, 142–3)

> Smile heaven upon this fair conjunction,
> That long have frown'd upon their enmity!
> *(The Tragedy of Richard the Third,*
> V, v, 20–1)

In the preface to the first edition of the *Critique of Pure Reason*, Kant bemoans the "battlefield of ... endless controversies" and "internal wars" that had plagued metaphysics throughout its history (CPR Aviii–ix). In order to avoid the danger of indifferentism – the ennui that arises from the belief that philosophical controversies are unresolvable and therefore pointless – it is necessary to establish a "court of justice" before which all such controversies can be legally settled. Until such a court is established, "reason is as it were in the state of nature, and it cannot make its assertions and claims valid or secure them except through **war**" (CPR A751/B779).

Kant told Garve that it was his discovery of the antinomies which first prompted his critical investigations. In the second *Critique*, he characterizes the antinomy of pure reason as "the most beneficial error into which human reason could ever have fallen, inasmuch as it finally drives us to search for the key to escape from this labyrinth" (CPrR 226). Likewise, in the first *Critique* he claims that the antinomy "guards reason against the slumber of an imagined conviction" (CPR A407/B434). Just as nature uses war to prompt us to make peace, so it uses the antinomies to provoke philosophers to institute "a state of law" in order to "secure a perpetual peace" in metaphysics (CPR A751–2/B779–80; cf. A777/B805, PTPPP 453). Yet despite their ultimately salutary character, the antinomies are no less "worrisome and depressing" than war itself is (CPR A740/B768). There is a real danger that in learning of its "natural antithetic," reason will succumb to either despair or denial, that is, to "the temptation either to surrender itself to a skeptical hopelessness or else to assume an attitude of dogmatic stubbornness" (CPR A407/B433–4). In this sense, the antinomical has the character of what Plato refers to in the *Phaedrus* as a *pharmakon*, something that can either poison or cure. The resolve to seek out a solution to the antinomies represents an attempt on the part of reason to cure itself of what threatens to poison it. To engage in critique – to rouse oneself from a "dogmatic slumber" – is to respond to a trauma not by repressing it but by working through it (PTAFM 57). Kant thought that, by completing his self-analysis of human reason, he had fully dealt with the "shock" of the antinomical (CPR A757/B785). But what if the analytic/continental division represented a "return of the repressed," an antinomy – or meta-antinomy – that had come back to haunt the critical project itself?

A clue to the nature of such a meta-antinomy can be found in Kant's account of the antinomy of taste. According to its thesis, "The judgment of taste is not based on concepts, for otherwise it would be possible to dispute about it (decide by means of proofs)." By contrast, the antithesis states, "The judgment of taste is based on concepts, for otherwise, despite its variety, it would not even be possible to quarrel about it (to lay claim to the necessary assent of others to this judgment)" (CPJ 215; translation slightly modified). Kant resolved this antinomy by claiming that the judgment of taste is based upon an "**indeterminate** concept" that makes quarreling but not disputing possible (CPJ 216). Genuine disputes arise only where determining judgments are at stake; mere quarrels when we disagree about reflective judgments of taste. By relegating these two different kinds of controversies to the separable domains of metaphysics (of nature and morals) and art, Kant was able to forestall a conflict between disputing and quarreling as paradigms of *philosophical* argumentation. More precisely, he forestalled this conflict by putting forth *transcendental* arguments that enabled him to resolve the antinomies without having to decide whether they should be treated as disputes or quarrels. Kant's successors could no longer avail themselves of this solution after they had rejected both the transcendental ideality thesis and with it the transcendental/empirical dichotomy. Depending on whether they conceived of human cognition as receptive spontaneity or spontaneous receptivity, they were led to conceive of philosophical arguments on the model of either disputes or aesthetic quarrels. As a result, they were led to put forth competing assessments about what an antinomy is.

Consider how two diametrically opposed representatives of the rival houses have responded to the encounter with the antinomical: Russell and Derrida. In 1902, Russell wrote to Frege about a paradox he had discovered about self-reference. Suppose there is a town barber who shaves everyone in the town who does not shave himself. To the question, "Does the barber shave himself?," there appears to be no correct answer: for if he does, then he does not; and if he does not, then he does. In keeping with Kant's description of the antinomies as "shocking," Russell was dismayed by his discovery of this paradox, because for technical reasons it threatened to undermine his attempt to reduce mathematics to logic. Kant noted that in the face of the antinomical it was possible either to be driven to despair or to rouse oneself to new efforts. After grasping the implications of Russell's paradox, Frege gave in to despair, abandoning his own attempt to reduce arithmetic to logic. By contrast, Russell tried to resolve the paradox by supposing that self-reference must be impossible. This led to the development of his so-called "theory of types," a technical device for eliminating apparently self-referring expressions from mathematical logic. Buoyed by the fruitfulness of his solution, Russell thereafter preached the virtue of persevering in the face of the antinomical:

> Failure to think of the right possibility leaves insoluble difficulties, balanced arguments pro and con, utter bewilderment and despair. But the right possibility, as a rule, when once conceived, justifies itself swiftly by its astonishing power of absorbing apparently conflicting facts.
>
> (OKEW 245)

Just as Kant dismissed both the theses and antitheses of the mathematical antinomies on the grounds that they were based upon contradictory concepts, so the theory of types implies that it is meaningless to assert either that the barber shaves himself or that he does not. Yet despite this surface similarity, Russell's approach to the antinomical is entirely different from that of Kant — as can be seen by Russell's criticisms of Kant's treatment of the mathematical antinomies. Kant argued that if we assume the world to have a determinate magnitude, it could be shown to be both infinite and finite. Hence the only solution to the first antinomy is to deny that the world has any determinate magnitude and hence that objects in space and time are appearances rather than things in themselves. Likewise, Kant argued that if we assume that all of the possible subdivisions of a given appearance are already given, then it could be proven that every composite object both is and is not comprised of simple parts. Thus we must conclude that, although there is no limit to the subdivision of an appearance into its parts, those parts are not already given (as they would have to be if appearances were things in themselves).

In *The Principles of Mathematics* (1903), Russell rejects both of these analyses, maintaining that the mathematical antinomies can be resolved without denying the transcendental reality of space and time. In support of the thesis of the first antinomy — that the world is finite — Kant argued that if the world had no beginning in time, an infinite series of events would have occurred before the present moment had been reached, but since "the infinity of a series consists precisely in the fact that it can never be completed through a successive synthesis," this is impossible (CPR A426/B454). In response to this argument, Russell concedes that it is impossible to reach the final element of an infinite series by enumerating its terms one at a time, but he observes that from the standpoint of set theory, there is nothing contradictory in the idea of an infinite series that has a terminal member. Thus it is conceivable that the present moment of the world's history might have been preceded by an infinite past. A contradiction would only arise if we had to assume — as Kant does — that the present had been reached by successively enumerating past moments (POM 459). In *Our Knowledge of the External World*, Russell criticizes Kant for thinking that an infinite past could only exist if it were possible for a transcendental subject to traverse its moments through a retroactive act of synthesis (OKEW 161). Replacing Kant's transcendental point of view with a strictly logical point of view, Russell concludes that the thesis of the first antinomy should be rejected in favor of the antithesis.

As for the second antinomy, Russell claims that in this case it is Kant's argument on behalf of the antithesis that is flawed, for there is no basis for the claim that space is comprised only of spaces and not of points. Russell conjectures that Kant's position on this question was motivated by his assumption that a collection of points must be finite. But developments in mathematical logic have definitively shown that this assumption is false. Likewise, there is no reason to conclude that a physical collection of material points must be finite, which is to say that there is no sound argument disproving the thesis of the second antinomy (POM 460–1; OKEW 162–3).

Thus, for Russell, the two mathematical antinomies are not pseudo-disputes that can only be resolved by recognizing the transcendental ideality of space and time. On the contrary, they are genuine disputes that can be decided in favor of one of the two disputing parties. This is why the surface similarity between Kant's dismissal of their theses and antitheses and Russell's solution to the barber paradox is misleading. To the extent that Russell's paradox involves an antinomy, it lies not in the disagreement as to whether the barber does or does not shave himself, but rather in the conflict between the seemingly self-evident thesis that self-reference is possible and the antithesis that it is not. As with Kant's mathematical antinomies, Russell treats *this* antinomy as a dispute, arguing in favor of the antithesis. One reason why Frege despaired of overcoming Russell's paradox was that he regarded Russell's solution to it (the theory of types) as an arbitrary stipulation. As Hamlet says to Ophelia: "This was sometime a paradox, but now the time gives it proof" (III, i, 113–14).

The word "paradox" comes from the Greek *para-doxos*, or contrary to opinion. Zeno's arguments against the reality of motion were considered paradoxical by the Greeks because their conclusions went against common sense. Kant credited Zeno with realizing that the assumption of the transcendental reality of space and time led to conflicts that could only be resolved by denying that things in themselves were in space and time (CPR A502/B530). By contrast, Russell praises Zeno for calling attention to genuine logical paradoxes that could only be resolved after satisfactory accounts of infinity and continuity had been developed by nineteenth-century logicians (OKEW 175). Aristotle, who offers his own solutions to Zeno's paradoxes, claims in his *Metaphysics* that "men began to philosophize" when they encountered not paradoxes but *aporias*, conundra that seem at first to admit of no solution whatsoever. The word *a-poria* means "impasse" or "dead end." According to Aristotle, the task of the philosopher is to resolve aporias by juxtaposing and assessing the contrary arguments that give rise to them. Philosophy, like poetry, begins in the wonder to which the encounter with the aporetic gives rise. The poet responds to this experience by making something, the philosopher by seeking to know. Thus rather than lingering in the encounter with the aporetic, the philosopher is, for Aristotle, a path-breaker, someone who tries to find a way out of an aporia. This description of what it means to philosophize perfectly captures Russell's response to both the Kantian antinomies and the paradoxes of self-reference.

Derrida's response is completely different. Instead of reducing aporias to resolvable antinomies or paradoxes, he invokes a "duty" to persist in "an interminable experience" of them (A 16). To persist in the encounter with the aporetic is to endure the shock of the antinomical, succumbing neither to despair nor to a triumphalist solution. Thus in his essay, "Plato's Pharmacy" (*La pharmacie de Platon*, 1972), Derrida emphasizes the impossibility of reducing the *pharmakon* to *either* a poison *or* a cure. Likewise, in *Given Time*, he affirms *both* the necessity *and* the impossibility of thinking the gift. By insisting upon the aporetic nature of the gift or *pharmakon*, Derrida is not trying to prove something – as he would be if he were engaged in a dispute – but quarreling on behalf of an experience to which he feels compelled to bear witness – as if by the possession of an indeterminate concept. In other words, his arguments are akin to aesthetic quarrels. Just as Kant claimed that we feel compelled to "linger" in the encounter with the beautiful, so Derrida feels compelled to linger in the encounter with the aporetic (CPJ 107). Rather than finding a "way out" of an impasse, as Aristotle would have the philosopher do, Derrida seeks to confirm that there really is "no exit." The key difference between Derrida and Heidegger in this respect is that, instead of encouraging philosophers to become thinkers who write or read poetry, Derrida bids us to attend to an obscure ethical duty to which the shock of wonder calls us.

Kant claimed that it was possible to affirm both the theses and antitheses of the third and fourth antinomies. In an analogous way, Derrida affirms both the "thesis" that the gift is necessary and the "antithesis" that it is impossible. Hence just as we detected a surface similarity between Russell's paradox of self-reference and the mathematical antinomies (in that both seemed to require false/false solutions), so there is a surface similarity between Derrida's aporias and the dynamical antinomies (in that both seem to call for double affirmations). But once again there is a crucial difference. Kant could only affirm the two sides of the dynamical antinomies by distinguishing between the phenomenal and noumenal orders to which they respectively pertained. For Derrida, to affirm both the necessity and the impossibility of the gift is not to reconcile apparently opposed claims by showing that there is really no conflict between them; on the contrary, it is to accentuate the conflict by thinking the necessity *of* the impossible itself. To affirm the gift *despite* its impossibility is to quarrel – not dispute – on behalf of an insupportable claim. Thus we could say that just as Russell reduced the mathematical antinomies to resolvable disputes about paradoxes, so Derrida construes dynamical antinomies as quarrels about unresolvable aporias.

Assuming that this contrast between Russell and Derrida is broadly representative of analytic and continental approaches to the antinomical, the meta-antinomy that we have been seeking can be stated like this:

Thesis: Antinomies are logical paradoxes that can be resolved through disputing.

Antithesis: Antinomies are aporias that can only be attested to through quarreling.[6]

This characterization of the division highlights the fact that each of the two houses has its own conception of what it means to put forth a philosophical argument. In the House of Analytic, to advance a philosophical claim is to provide an argument that purports to prove that its conclusion is true. Conversely, in the House of Continental, to make a philosophical claim is to respond, thoughtfully, to an aesthetic provocation of a certain sort. This contrast in philosophical "styles" is reflected in the different ways in which analytic and continental philosophers read Plato. Because they are trained to think of philosophical arguments as disputes, analytic philosophers are especially attentive to the logical structure of the dialogues, while continental philosophers are more interested in what is conveyed through their literary form. Throughout the dialogues, Socrates prompts his interlocutors to confront hitherto unexpected aporias. Meno refers to the sense of shock to which this experience invariably gives rise, characterizing Socrates as a stingray who numbs his prey. In the *Parmenides*, Plato shows how the young Socrates was himself benumbed by bewildering dialectical arguments about the one and the many. In the *Theaetetus*, Socrates anticipates Aristotle, suggesting that philosophy begins in wonder. But unlike Aristotle, who specifically states that the task of the philosopher is to find a way out of aporias, Plato leaves us uncertain as to whether Socrates is prompting us to resolve logical paradoxes or to linger in the encounter with the aporetic. To the extent that this remains an open question, the analytic/continental division can be characterized as a struggle over the *Socratic* legacy and not simply as a struggle over the Kantian legacy.

Kant side-stepped the meta-antinomy between disputing and quarreling by dismissing both the theses and antitheses of the mathematical antinomies and by showing that there was no genuine conflict between the theses and antitheses of the dynamical antinomies. In other words, he treated all four of the antinomies neither as disputes nor as quarrels but as simple misunderstandings. To adopt the transcendental point of view of the critical philosopher is to distinguish the various cognitive faculties we possess and to demarcate their respective domains of employment. Because this task amounts only to taking stock of the materials at hand, no genuine controversy can arise in the domain of transcendental inquiry (CPR A707/B735). To underscore this point, Kant issued a "Proclamation of the Imminent Conclusion of a Treaty of Perpetual Peace in Philosophy" (*Verkündigung des nahen Abschlusses eines Traktats zum ewigen Frieden in der Philosophie*, 1796), in which he argues that the only reason why philosophical controversies still persist fifteen years after the publication of the first edition of the *Critique of Pure Reason* is that the critical philosophy has not yet been fully understood (PTPPP 457). There are no properly critical conflicts the resolution of which would require a metacritical perspective, because the stance of the critic is already neutral and hence peaceful. In confronting the antinomies, the critic adopts the method of the skeptic, observing philosophical controversies from the disinterested standpoint of the spectator (CPR A423–4/B450–1). A philosophical controversy could only arise at this level of reflection if the antinomical threatened to intrude within the critical project itself, that is, if the nature and possibility of transcendental arguments came to be questioned. Kant did not countenance such a possibility. Yet this is precisely what the meta-antinomy separating analytic and continental conceptions of the philosophical enterprise amounts to. Both parties reject Kant's conception of transcendental arguments, but they disagree as to whether philosophical arguments should be thought of as disputes or quarrels.

It might seem possible to split the difference by acknowledging that there simply are two distinct but compatible kinds of philosophical arguments. This was Rorty's strategy in pleading for a live-and-let-live attitude, one that would allow systematic and edifying philosophers to co-exist peacefully in the same philosophy departments. But Rorty underestimates the force of the meta-antinomy, which, insofar as it concerns diametrically opposed conceptions of *all* philosophical arguments, cannot be reduced to either a dispute or a quarrel without begging the question and so doing violence to one of the two parties. This is to say that the analytic/continental division has the form of a Lyotardian differend – which is why it can be neither resolved before a Kantian-style tribunal nor dissolved by Rorty's good intentions. Like all differends, it manifests itself as a struggle for institutional hegemony, specifically for control over philosophy departments. Though rarely made explicit, the question that obscurely sustains this institutional struggle is yet another Kantian question, namely, "What is philosophizing good for and what is its ultimate end?" (L 27).

In a chapter of the first *Critique* entitled, "The Architectonic of Pure Reason," Kant distinguishes between the "scholastic" conception of the philosopher as a mere "artist of reason" and the "cosmopolitan" conception of the philosopher as a "legislator of human reason." He defines cosmopolitan philosophy as "the science of the relation of all cognition to the essential ends of human reason." By contrast, scholastic (or academic) philosophy is "a system of cognition that is sought only as a science without having as its end anything more than the systematic unity of this knowledge, thus the **logical** perfection of cognition." Thus the scholastic artist of reason is someone who falls short of the philosopher's true vocation, which is "personified and represented as an archetype in the ideal of the **philosopher**." All philosophers ought to aspire to this cosmopolitan ideal, but because it is an ideal, it would be presumptuous for anyone to claim to have succeeded in realizing it: "It would be very boastful to call oneself a philosopher in this sense and to pretend to have equaled the archetype, which lies only in the idea" (CPR A838–9/B866–7). Kant elaborates on this point in the second *Critique*, equating the ideal of the philosopher with "a *master in the knowledge of wisdom*, which says more than a modest man would himself claim" (CPrR 227). Thus there are two complementary ways in which an individual might fail to be a philosopher: either by *falling short* of the ideal (remaining content with mere artistry of reason), or by *going too far* (pretending to embody the ideal). Kant claimed that the antinomies arise because the cosmological ideas of reason are always "either **too big** or **too small** for every **concept of the understanding**" (CPR A486/B514). In a precisely analogous way, the cosmopolitan ideal of the philosopher as lawgiver is *too big* for us, but the idea of the philosopher as a mere artist of reason is *too small*.[7] Hence the question concerning the philosopher's vocation gives rise to an antinomy, which can be stated like this:

> Thesis: Philosophers should be legislators because this is in keeping with the cosmopolitan ideal of the philosopher.

> Antithesis: Philosophers should not be legislators because no one can pretend to embody the ideal.

Another way to frame this antinomy would be to pit Plato's thesis (in the *Republic*) that philosophers should be kings against Aristotle's antithesis (in the *Politics*) that they should not. Kant implicitly resolves this conflict in the same way that he did the dynamical antinomies, namely, by distinguishing between two separate realms: in this case, the public realm of government and the private realm of the university. Concerning the former, Aristotle is right: "It is not to be expected that kings will philosophise or that philosophers will become kings; nor is it to be desired, however, since the possession of power inevitably corrupts the free judgment of reason" (PW 115). However, within the university, Plato is right, for there the sole duty of the philosopher is to follow "laws given by reason, not by the government" (COF 255). At first glance, this dynamical solution seems to reiterate the double principle that Kant commended in "An Answer to the Question: 'What is Enlightenment?,'", namely, "*Argue* as much as you like and about whatever you like, *but obey!*" (PW 55). But, in fact, Kant's construal of the philosopher's vocation runs counter to this credo. In the essay on enlightenment, he claims that, while the private use of reason may be legitimately restricted by the government, the public use of reason should be kept free. But since the private use of reason pertains to one's "particular *civil* post or office," and the public use only to the situation of "*a man of learning* addressing the entire *reading public*," this distinction implies that, insofar as the philosopher has a private university function to perform, the government may legitimately restrict his or her academic freedom (PW 55). But in *The Conflict of the Faculties*, Kant argues to the contrary.

The overall aim of *The Conflict of the Faculties* is to specify the institutional position and professional responsibilities of the members of a department of philosophy in the modern university. Toward this end, Kant distinguishes between "higher" and "lower" academic disciplines or "faculties." The higher faculties of theology, law, and medicine are those whose teachings "interest the government itself." Hence it is appropriate that the members of these faculties be obliged to espouse whatever teachings the sovereign decrees. By contrast, the members of the lower faculty of philosophy – which Kant takes to comprise most of what we would call the humanities and natural sciences – should be exempt from government supervision because their teachings concern "the interests of science" rather than the interests of the government (COF 248). Accordingly, the faculty of philosophy should be granted *complete academic freedom*: "So the philosophy faculty, because it must answer for the truth of the teachings it is to adopt or even allow, must be conceived as free and subject only to laws given by reason, not by the government" (COF 255).

By according the right of academic freedom to the philosophy faculty, Kant implies that there is no relevant distinction between the philosopher's public and private vocations. This distinction only pertains to the members of the higher faculties, whose private use of reason the government is entitled to restrict. Thus we could say that Kant resolves the antinomy concerning the philosopher's vocation by situating the academic freedom of the philosopher at the nexus of the public and private realms – just as he situated transcendental freedom at the nexus of the sensible and intelligible worlds. As a powerless critic with academic freedom – i.e., as a privately situated public intellectual – the philosopher both is and is not a legislator. This double role can only be fulfilled by throwing off the merely scholastic conception of the philosopher as a private university functionary in favor of the cosmopolitan conception of the philosopher as a citizen of the world.

The fact that the teachings of the philosophy faculty do not bear on the interests of the government does not mean that the members of the philosophy faculty should remain silent on matters of concern to it. On the contrary, the parrhesiastic duty of philosophers to tell the truth requires that they enter into conflict with the government's representatives in the higher faculties: "the lower faculty has not only the title but also the duty, if not to state the *whole* truth in public, at least to see to it that *everything* put forward in public as a principle is true" (COF 259). This duty obliges philosophers not only to defend themselves against attacks, but to *initiate* – in perpetuity – conflicts with the members of the higher faculties, for the latter will inevitably abuse their power:

> This conflict can never end, and it is the philosophy faculty that must always be prepared to keep it going ... the philosophy faculty can never lay aside its arms in the face of the danger that threatens the truth entrusted to its protection, because the higher faculties will never give up their desire to rule.
>
> (COF 260)

Thus, although Kant envisions perpetual peace within philosophy, he also envisions perpetual war between philosophy and the other faculties. Like Socrates as he is represented in the *Apology*, Kant's cosmopolitan philosopher has the obligation to subject existing institutions, practices, and discourses to perpetual critical examination. Just as Socrates compared himself to an irritating gadfly who kept the Athenians from becoming too complacent, so Kant suggests that the relationship between the philosophy faculty and the higher faculties is like that between "an opposition party" and a dominant power:

> The rank of the higher faculties (as the right side of the parliament of learning) supports the government's statutes; but in as free a system of government as must exist when it is a question of truth, there must also be an opposition party (the left side), and this is the philosophy faculty's bench.
>
> (COF 261)

The only restriction that Kant places on philosophers is the very one that Socrates placed upon himself in the *Crito*, namely, the obligation not to usurp the laws of the state.[8] By confining the polemical use of reason within the constraints of obedience to civil laws, Kant seeks to avoid the danger of "too big" a conception of the philosopher's cosmopolitan vocation. Conversely, by making the public exercise of reason both a right and a duty, he avoids the extreme of a *merely* obedient subject or an apolitical artist of reason. Neither aspiring to be a public sovereign who makes the laws, nor settling for the status of a passive subject (or private ironist), the Kantian philosopher is a citizen (i.e., an active subject) with the right to advise the sovereign from an institutional position that straddles the public and private realms.

Thus Kant resolves the antinomy concerning the philosopher's vocation by clarifying what exactly it means to be a member of a philosophy department.

By exercising the academic freedom to "speak the truth to power"[9] while at the same time refraining from any act of rebellion, the philosophy professor is able to steer a middle course between self-conceptions that are "too small" and "too big." The question that arises is whether this solution is truly adequate to the dilemma (or aporia or paradox) in question. Arendt criticized Kant for failing to see that there are occasions in which the philosopher might legitimately advocate revolution. Might it not be argued that Kant's conception of the obedient philosopher remains too small insofar as it prohibits us even from advocating, or engaging in, an act of principled civil disobedience against an unjust law? Certainly Socrates had a significantly bigger construal of the cosmopolitan vocation of the philosopher than Kant did, for although he declined to break the law by escaping from prison, he also refused to obey the Thirty Tyrants' unjust order that he arrest Leon of Salamis.

Marx was the first philosopher to criticize not only Kant but all of his predecessors for having too small a conception of the philosopher's vocation. Like his fellow Young Hegelians, Marx did not have a university appointment, and so he was able to perceive the shortcomings of an institutional arrangement that relegated the supposedly cosmopolitan philosopher to an academic position that was still too "scholastic." Habermas notes that after the death of Hegel the scholastic and cosmopolitan vocations of the philosopher became separated, with genuinely cosmopolitan thinkers such as Marx, Kierkegaard, and Nietzsche working outside the university, and academic philosophers – notably the neo-Kantians – hunkering down into sterile, scholastic pursuits (PDOM 52). In the twentieth century, Heidegger and the critical theorists tried to transform the scholastic conception of philosophy into a cosmopolitan "diagnosis of the times," but as Habermas observes, there remains a widespread feeling that academic – i.e., scholastic – philosophy has become irrelevant (PDOM 53). This view is held not only by the public, but by academics, as literary critics, on the one hand, and natural and social scientists, on the other, have supplanted continental and analytic philosophers as purveyors, respectively, of the art of quarreling and the skill of disputing. The fact that philosophy – especially in the USA and UK – finds itself in such "critical" condition suggests that *both* analytic *and* continental philosophers have fallen short of their cosmopolitan vocation.

In his controversial book, *Time in the Ditch: American Philosophy and the McCarthy Era* (2000), John McCumber suggests that by failing to raise the question, "What is philosophy?," in an explicit way, American philosophers have settled into mere scholasticism (TITD xxi, 133, 84).[10] McCumber claims that this is especially true of analytic philosophers, whose "exclusive focus on the truth of sentences rigorously *suppresses* philosophical discussion of philosophy itself" (TITD 128). By restricting their activity to the construction and evaluation of arguments, analytic philosophers have neglected the "cultivation of language," that is, the care and feeding of the words that we use to make arguments (TITD 101). According to McCumber, this emphasis is misplaced, in part because the nature of philosophical argumentation is relatively non-controversial (TITD 137–8). Although he does not put it this way, McCumber's point is that analytic philosophers are good at framing arguments as disputes, but that in neglecting the cultivation of words they have overlooked the cosmopolitan virtues of quarreling. This characterization implies that analytic philosophers are mere "artists of reason" whose undeniable skill at constructing and evaluating arguments is never put to any ultimate purpose that would lend the enterprise its dignity. McCumber suggests that the reason why American analytic philosophers have such a "small" construal of their vocation is that the analytic paradigm achieved hegemony in the United States in the early 1950s as a response to the threat of McCarthyism. By adopting a conception of philosophy as the "pursuit of timeless truths," philosophy professors managed to stay under the radar of the House Committee on Un-American Activities, but in so doing they effectively abdicated their responsibility to address cosmopolitan questions. But American "continental" philosophers have not done much better. They too have succumbed to mere artistry of reason, in their case by failing to relate their quarrels about the historicity of language to present cosmopolitan concerns. In order to remedy the shortcomings of both houses, McCumber advocates a conception of philosophy that involves both disputing and quarreling – or, as he puts it, both arguing about sentences and cultivating language (TITD 163ff.).

The fact that neither of the two houses has been able to overcome the shortcomings associated with Kant's resolution of the antinomy concerning the philosopher's vocation suggests that it would be a mistake to *identify* the analytic/continental division with the antinomy itself, as if one of the two houses advocated the thesis and the other the antithesis. On the contrary, each side has been faced with the same difficulty. In keeping with my characterization of the division as a meta-antinomy about what it means to respond philosophically to antinomies, it is tempting to say that analytic philosophers have decided in favor of the antithesis – that philosophers should not be kings, period – while continental philosophers have tried to affirm both the antithesis and the thesis simultaneously without distinguishing (as Kant did) the public realm of government from the private realm of the university. Whether this is so or not, the analytic/continental division could be said to represent a displacement of a problem that all philosophers have had to face since Kant first articulated their new institutional position as members of modern university philosophy departments. Žižek observes that "horizontal" conflicts between opposed factions typically serve as screens masking "vertical" antagonisms that everyone faces: "any notion of a 'vertical' *antagonism* that cuts through the social body is strictly censored, substituted by and/or translated into the wholly different notion of 'horizontal' differences" (WTDOR 65).[11] In keeping with this logic, the analytic/continental division could be said to attest to a shared sense of trauma to which no response – whether that of disputing or quarreling – could ever be fully adequate.

What makes the antinomy concerning the philosopher's vocation so formidable is that, while the ideal of the cosmopolitan philosopher is always too big, it remains the ideal to which we ought to aspire. Just as reason does violence to the imagination in the experience of the sublime, so in the experience of the antinomical, reason does violence to the understanding, prompting it to keep "going further." At the crucial moment when the understanding finds itself unable to keep up with reason, the subject experiences a cognitive analogue of the mathematically sublime, the idea being "too big" for us to represent. Kant tried to avoid this problem by distinguishing between the enthusiasm of the cosmopolitan philosopher and the fanaticism of the revolutionary. But perhaps the deadlock between the demand posed in the cosmopolitan ideal and the inadequacy of every attempt to realize it can be resolved only through an attempt to think or act "excessively." It is true that we risk a certain philosophical fanaticism at the moment when we attempt to think or do something that we no longer understand. But the only other alternative is to settle for something that can only be too small. Perhaps the only way of remaining faithful to the cosmopolitan ideal is to accept a certain risk that arises when we make a "fanatical" leap of some sort. This is the point that Žižek is getting at when he insists on the moral necessity of an act that could only be retroactively justified. In defending Leninist enthusiasm against Stalinist fanaticism, Žižek does not say that Stalin had too big a conception of the cosmopolitan philosopher whereas Lenin's was "just right"; on the contrary, he claims that Lenin's conception was "just right" precisely insofar as it was *too big*:

> The basic attitude of a Stalinist Communist is that of following the correct Party line against the "Rightist" or "Leftist" deviation – in short, steering a safe middle course; for authentic Leninism, in clear contrast, there is ultimately only one deviation, the Centrist one – that of "playing it safe," of opportunistically avoiding the risk of clearly and excessively "taking sides."
>
> (WTDOR 89)

Perhaps in an analogous way, the task represented in the cosmopolitan ideal of the philosopher is not that of steering a middle course between the extremes of "too small" and "too big" (the Goldilocks model) but rather of finding a measure between the "too too big" and the "not too big enough," between the "too fanatical" and the "not fanatical enough."

Derrida makes a similar point in *Given Time* when he speaks of the necessity and impossibility of finding a proper measure between measure itself and the immeasurable. To respond to the encounter with the aporetic – whether by lingering or by attempting to find a way out – is to be torn between an excessive, hysterical response and an insufficiently fanatical, obsessional caution. But if the choice between the "too fanatical" and the "insufficiently fanatical" is faced by all philosophers, then the "lateral" antagonism between analytic and continental philosophers should be recognized as a displacement of this "fundamental antagonism." The fact that the analytic/continental division concerns the relationship between spontaneity and receptivity (and their practical analogues, autonomy and heteronomy) attests to this fact, for the cosmopolitan ideal of the philosopher as king or lawgiver is ultimately just the idea of a fully spontaneous and autonomous thinker in the manner of a kind of primal philosophical father, while the passive stance of the artist of reason would be that of a merely receptive and heteronomous thinker. Thus at stake in the twin oppositions between "spontaneous receptivity"/"receptive spontaneity" and "autonomous heteronomy"/"heteronomous autonomy" would be alternative ways of negotiating the "too fanatical"/"insufficiently fanatical" problem that is posed in the antinomy concerning the philosopher's cosmopolitan vocation.

Rorty suggested that the conflict between analytic and continental philosophers could be resolved by thinking of it as a division of labor: analytic philosophers make systematic claims which continental (or "conversational") philosophers go about ironically challenging. Unlike Kant, who tried to unite the private and public roles of the philosopher, Rorty limits the philosopher's public role to the defense of moderate liberal causes, restricting the excessive hubris of the "strong poet" to the philosopher's private life. The problem with this solution is that it uses the public/private dichotomy to settle for a comfortable stance between excessive extremes instead of accepting the risk that comes with having to negotiate the "too extreme"/"not extreme enough" dilemma *in public*. Not only does Rorty restrict risk-taking to the private realm, but instead of identifying the private realm with one's workplace (as Kant did) he equates it with what one does as an asocial subject behind closed doors.

Just as Kant claimed that the problem of achieving a perfect constitution could be solved only at the end of the entirety of human history, so it is tempting to say that the problem of determining the philosopher's cosmopolitan vocation is one that could only be solved by the entire history of philosophy. But how we conceive of the philosopher's vocation is determined in part by how we understand the history of philosophy. Rorty's reminder of Kant's role in constituting our current conception of the history of philosophy is important, because one of the main points of contention between analytic and continental philosophers has been the question of who does and who does not belong to this history.

Kant knew that it would be unjust to bind future generations to our current beliefs about what is best:

> One age cannot enter into an alliance on oath to put the next age in a position where it would be impossible for it to extend and correct its knowledge ... or to make any progress whatsoever in enlightenment. This would be a crime against human nature.
>
> (PW 57)

In keeping with this principle, he acknowledges his own responsibility to submit the fruit of his critical reflections to public scrutiny. Thus in the preface to the first edition of the *Critique of Pure Reason* he writes: "Whether I have performed what I have just pledged . . . remains wholly to the judgment of the reader, since it is appropriate for an author only to present the grounds, but not to judge about their effect on his judges" (CPR Axv). However, in response to the actual criticisms of readers of the first edition, he writes in the second edition preface: "the danger is not that I will be refuted, but that I will not be understood . . . from now on I cannot let myself become involved in controversies" (CPR Bxliii). Kant goes on to insist that such philosophical disagreements as will arise in the future cannot affect the principles of the critique itself: "I hope this system will henceforth maintain itself in this unalterability. It is not self-conceit that justifies my trust in this, but rather merely the evidence" (CPR Bxxxviii). Thus Kant really did come to think of himself as a sovereign lawgiver whose dynasty, like that of Edward III, was supposed to have been perpetual. This expectation comes through in his characterization of the Socratic vocation: "critique puts an end *for all future time* to objections against morality and religion in a **Socratic** way" (CPR Bxxxi; translation slightly modified; my italics).

The problem with this conception – which is too big for us insofar as it puts Kant in the position of lawgiver – is that it fails to recognize that a certain kind of strife, rather than peace, may be the most desirable condition in philosophy. The trouble with the analytic/continental division is not that the two houses are in conflict with each other but that despite their mutual hostility they have been unable to *argue* about their respective conceptions of the philosophical enterprise. Kant claimed that, as "the *doctrine of wisdom*," philosophy ought to be "a *doctrine of the highest good*" (CPrR 227). But just as the ancient schools of Epicureanism and Stoicism could not agree about the exact nature of the highest good – did it consist in virtuous happiness or happy virtue? – so today analytic and continental philosophers have been unable to agree about the nature of the highest philosophical good. Each of the two houses remains convinced that it is the true inheritor of the Socratic and Kantian legacies, but neither has been able to confront the fundamental deadlock to which the encounter with the cosmopolitan ideal attests. To renew the conflict of the philosophy faculty with itself – and to try to live up to our cosmopolitan vocations – both houses must take up – in public – Kant's *fifth* question, namely, "What is philosophizing good for and what is its ultimate end?" Otherwise, any attempt to "overcome" the division will be doomed to repeat the mistake that King Edward IV made when he proclaimed – *falsely* – that the Wars of the Roses had finally come to an end:

> Farewell sour annoy!
> For here I hope begins our lasting joy.
> (*The Third Part of Henry the Sixth*,
> V, vii, 45–6)

Notes

1 In his *Origins of Analytical Philosophy*, Michael Dummett suggests that Frege advocated what Dummett takes to be the distinctive feature of analytic philosophy, namely, its commitment to the view that the only to way to acquire a "comprehensive account" of the structure of thought is to analyze the structure of language (p. 4). But it seems to me that some version of this thesis was shared by Nietzsche, who, like Frege, attributed to language the function that Kant ascribed to the schematism. Cf. my "Nietzsche, Frege, and the Origins of the Analytic/Continental Polemic."

2 John McDowell, *Mind and World*, p. 9; my italics.

3 As the art critic Jeremy Gilbert-Rolfe has observed, the very idea of beautiful sublimity seems paradoxical in a way that the idea of sublime beauty does not:

> The sublime and the beautiful coexist in a differential relationship. The one does what the other does not, but they also partake of one another, although not, as their interdependence would otherwise imply, symmetrically, because they are not traditionally seen as equal: One may have the sublimely beautiful, but I'm not sure that things can be beautifully sublime.
> (Jeremy Gilbert-Rolfe, *Beauty and the Contemporary Sublime*, p. 1)

4 Elaine Scarry, *On Beauty and Being Just*, p. 93.

5 I take it that Deleuze's "transcendental empiricism" is in keeping with the broadly continental conception of the empirically transcendental. Like Bergson and Merleau-Ponty, Deleuze narrows the gap between the transcendental and the empirical by abandoning the search for conditions of the possibility of experience to the search for conditions of actuality.

6 In his book, *Paradoxes from A to Z* – which, significantly, does not mention a single continental philosopher – Michael Clark writes: "Pick up a recent issue of a philosophical journal like *Mind* or *Analysis* and it is surprising how many of the papers you see there are about philosophical paradoxes. Philosophy thrives on them, and many have borne abundant fruit" (p. ix). Just as striking is the plethora of philosophical aporias in continental philosophy. Examples would include Heidegger's attempt to make sense of the sentence, "The nothing itself nihilates," *despite* the fact that it violates the laws of formal logic, Levinas's account of the relationship between the "saying" that attests to skepticism and the ontological "said" that refutes it, Adorno's approach to the question of whether or not it is possible to write poetry after Auschwitz, etc. Perhaps the main reason why Bergson had so much trouble with the physicists was that he tried to resolve the twin paradox (which they had already done) instead of insisting on the aporetic character of lived duration. According to Deleuze, paradox is "the pathos or the passion of philosophy," but it "cannot be equalised or cancelled at the direction of a good sense" (DR 227). In this respect, he too seeks not the resolution of a paradox but the persistence in an aporia. Of course, not all continental philosophers have treated antinomies as unresolvable aporias. Arendt suggests that "paradoxes always indicate perplexities, they do not solve them and hence are never convincing" (HC 229). For Marx and Lukács, antinomies can only be resolved through practice:

> the resolution of the *theoretical* antitheses is *only* possible *in a practical way*. . . . Their resolution is therefore by no means merely a problem of understanding, but a *real* problem of life, which *philosophy* could not solve precisely because it conceived this problem as *merely* a theoretical one.
> (EAPM 141–2)

Cf. Marx's deflationary response to Kant's fourth antinomy (concerning the existence or non-existence of a necessary being): "Who begot the first man, and nature as a whole? I can only answer you: Your question is itself a product of abstraction" (EAPM 145).

When George Bush was arguing with the French and Germans about whether or not an invasion of Iraq was justified, everything transpired as if he felt that the matter were a readily resolvable dispute, whereas they seemed to realize that, whatever decision would eventually be made, one could only quarrel on its behalf. Though many (if not most) American analytic philosophers were against the invasion, was there not a strange affinity between the Bush administration's sneering attitude toward "the French" and the contemptuousness with which so many analytic philosophers have dismissed the likes of Derrida?

7 Cf. Lukács's claim that in the bourgeois novel the soul of the protagonist is always either "too narrow" or "too broad" for the world (TOTN 13, 97).

8 It is noteworthy that the charges which Friedrich Wilhelm II and his Minister of Education and Religious Affairs, J.C. Wöllner, brought against Kant are strikingly reminiscent of the ones that the Athenians leveled against Socrates, namely, teaching false gods and corrupting the youth:

> Our most high person has long observed with great displeasure how you misuse your philosophy to distort and disparage many of the cardinal and basic teachings of the Holy Scriptures and of Christianity. . . . We expected better things of you, as you yourself must realize how irresponsibly you have acted against your duty as a teacher of youth and against our paternal purpose, which you know very well.
>
> (RRT 240)

In *Who's Afraid of Philosophy?*, Derrida asks: "In one form or another, has impiety not, from time immemorial, and thus still today, been the indictment against every disturbing thinker?" (WAOP 25).

9 Edward W. Said, *Representations of the Intellectual*, p. xvi.

10 But see the essays collected in *What is Philosophy?*, edited by C.P. Ragland and Sarah Heidt.

11 Lévi-Strauss calls attention to a similar logic: "the Jivaro . . . change the cosmic conflict between the celestial and chthonian powers into a political conflict, in which the tribes become the opponents" (JP 77).

References

Note: All page references to Kant's *Critique of Pure Reason* are to the standard A/B pagination of the first and second editions. All quotations from Shakespeare are from *The Riverside Shakespeare*.

Abraham, Nicolas and Maria Torok, *The Wolf Man's Magic Word: a Cryptonymy*, trans. Nicholas Rand with a foreword by Jacques Derrida, (Minneapolis: University of Minnesota Press, 1986).
—— *The Shell and the Kernel Volume I*, ed. and trans. Nicholas T. Rand, (Chicago: The University of Chicago Press, 1994).
—— *The Jargon of Authenticity*, trans. Knut Tarnowski and Frederic Will (Evanston: Northwestern University Press, 1973).
—— *Negative Dialectics*, trans. E.B. Ashton (New York: Continuum Publishing Company, 1973).
—— *Prisms*, trans. Samuel and Shierry Weber (Cambridge: The MIT Press, 1981).
—— *Against Epistemology: a Metacritique: Studies in Husserl and the Phenomenological Antinomies*, trans. Willis Domingo (Cambridge: The MIT Press, 1983).
—— *Notes to Literature Volume One*, ed. Rolf Tiedemann, trans. Shierry Weber Nicholsen (New York: Columbia University Press, 1991).
—— *Notes to Literature Volume Two*, ed. Rolf Tiedemann, trans. Shierry Weber Nicholsen (New York: Columbia University Press, 1992).
Adorno, Theodor W., *Aesthetic Theory*, eds Gretel Adorno and Rolf Tiedemann, trans. Robert Hullot-Kentor (Minneapolis: University of Minnesota Press, 1997).
—— *Essays on Music*, trans. Susan H. Gillespie, selected, with introduction, commentary and notes, Richard Leppert (Berkeley: University of California Press, 2002).
Adorno, Theodor W. and Walter Benjamin, *The Complete Correspondence 1928–1940*, ed. Henri Lonitz, trans. Nicholas Walker (Cambridge: Polity Press, 1999).
Adorno, Theodor W. and Max Horkheimer, *Dialectic of Enlightenment: Philosophical Fragments*, ed. Gunzelin Schmid Noerr, trans. Edmund Jephcott (Stanford: Stanford University Press, 2002).
Agamben, Giorgio, *Remnants of Auschwitz: the Witness and the Archive*, trans. Daniel Heller-Roazen (New York: Zone Books, 1999).
Althusser, Louis, *For Marx*, trans. Ben Brewster (New York: Vintage Books, 1970).
—— *Lenin and Philosophy and Other Essays*, trans. Ben Brewster (New York: Monthly Review Press, 1971).
—— *The Future Lasts Forever: a Memoir*, eds Olivier Corpet and Yann Moulier Boutang, trans. Richard Veasey (New York: The New Press, 1993).
—— *Writings on Psychoanalysis: Freud and Lacan*, eds Olivier Corpet and François Matheron, trans. Jeffrey Mehlman (New York: Columbia University Press, 1996).
—— *The Humanist Controversy and Other Writings*, ed. François Matheron, trans. G.M. Goshgarian (New York: Verso, 2003).
Althusser, Louis and Étienne Balibar, *Reading Capital*, trans. Ben Brewster (London: New Left Books, 1977).

Arendt, Hannah, *On Revolution* (New York: Penguin Books, 1965).
—— *Crises of the Republic* (New York: Harcourt Brace Jovanovich, 1972).
—— "On Violence," in *Crises of the Republic*, op. cit., pp. 103–98.
—— *The Origins of Totalitarianism*, new edition with added prefaces (New York: Harcourt Brace Jovanovich, 1979).
—— *The Life of the Mind: One/Thinking, Two/Willing* (New York: Harcourt Brace Jovanovich, 1981).
—— *Lectures on Kant's Political Philosophy*, ed. Ronald Beiner (Chicago: The University of Chicago Press, 1989).
—— *Between Past and Future* (New York, Penguin, 1993).
—— *Eichmann in Jerusalem: a Report on the Banality of Evil*, revised and enlarged edition (New York: Penguin Books, 1994).
—— *The Human Condition*, second edn (Chicago: The University of Chicago Press, 1998).
Aristotle, *The Complete Works of Aristotle: the Revised Oxford Translation*, two volumes, ed. Jonathan Barnes (Princeton: Princeton University Press, 1984).
Armstrong, D.M. *The Mind–Body Problem: an Opinionated Introduction* (Boulder: Westview Press, 1999).
Ayer, Alfred Jules, *Language, Truth and Logic* (New York: Dover Publications, Inc., 1952).
Bachelard, Gaston, *The Psychoanalysis of Fire*, trans. Alan C.M. Ross (Boston: Beacon Press, 1964).
—— *The Philosophy of No: a Philosophy of the New Scientific Mind*, trans. G.C. Waterston (New York: The Orion Press, 1968).
—— *The Poetics of Reverie: Childhood, Language, and the Cosmos*, trans. Daniel Russell (Boston: Beacon Press, 1969).
—— *Water and Dreams: an Essay on Imagination and Matter*, trans. Edith R. Farrell (Dallas: The Dallas Institute of Humanities and Culture, 1983).
—— *The New Scientific Spirit*, trans. Arthur Goldhammer (Boston: Beacon Press, 1984).
—— *Fragments of a Poetics of Fire*, ed. Suzanne Bachelard, trans. Kenneth Haltman (Dallas: The Dallas Institute of Humanities and Culture, 1990).
—— *The Dialectic of Duration*, trans. Mary McAllester Jones (Manchester: Clinamen Press, 2000).
Bataille, Georges, *Visions of Excess: Selected Writings, 1927–1939*, ed. Allan Stoekl, trans. Allan Stoekl with Carl R. Lovitt and Donald M. Leslie Jr. (Minneapolis: University of Minnesota Press, 1985).
—— *L'Abbé C*, trans. Philip A. Facey (New York: Marion Boyars, 1988).
—— *The Accursed Share: an Essay on General Economy Volume I: Consumption*, trans. Robert Hurley (New York: Zone Books, 1988).
—— *On Nietzsche*, trans. Bruce Boone (New York: Paragon House, 1992).
—— *The Accursed Share: an Essay on General Economy Volume II: The History of Eroticism, Volume III: Sovereignty*, trans. Robert Hurley (New York: Zone Books, 1993).
—— *Literature and Evil*, trans. Alastair Hamilton (New York: Marion Boyars, 1997).
Benjamin, Walter, *Illuminations*, ed. and with an introduction by Hannah Arendt, trans. Harry Zohn (New York: Schocken Books, 1969).
—— *Selected Writings, Volume 1: 1913–1926*, eds Marcus Bullock and Michael W. Jennings (Cambridge: Harvard University Press, 1996).

—— *The Origin of German Tragic Drama*, trans. John Osborne (New York: Verso, 1998).

—— *Selected Writings, Volume 2: 1927–1934*, eds Michael W. Jennings, Howard Eiland, and Gary Smith (Cambridge: Harvard University Press, 1999).

—— *The Arcades Project*, ed. Rolf Tiedemann, trans. Howard Eiland and Kevin McLaughlin (Cambridge: Harvard University Press, 1999).

—— *Selected Writings, Volume 3: 1935–1938*, eds Howard Eiland and Michael W. Jennings, trans. Edmund Jephcott, Howard Eiland, and others (Cambridge: Harvard University Press, 2002).

—— *Selected Writings, Volume 4: 1938–1940*, eds Howard Eiland and Michael W. Jennings (Cambridge: Harvard University Press, 2003).

Bergson, Henri, *Time and Free Will: an Essay on the Immediate Data of Consciousness*, trans. F.L. Pogson (New York: Harper & Brothers, 1960).

—— *Matter and Memory*, trans. N.M. Paul and W.S. Palmer (New York: Zone Books, 1991).

—— *Creative Evolution*, trans. Arthur Mitchell (Mineola: Dover Publications, Inc., 1998).

—— *Duration and Simultaneity: Bergson and the Einsteinian Universe*, ed. Robin Durie, trans. Leon Jacobson, Mark Lewis, and Robin Durie (Manchester: Clinamen Press, 1999).

—— *The Creative Mind: an Introduction to Metaphysics*, trans. Mabelle L. Andison (New York: Citadel Press, 2002).

Blanchot, Maurice, *Death Sentence*, trans. Lydia Davis (Barrytown: Station Hill Press, 1978).

—— *The Unavowable Community*, trans. Pierre Joris (Barrytown: Station Hill Press, 1988).

—— *The Space of Literature*, trans. Ann Smock (Lincoln: University of Nebraska Press, 1989).

—— *The Step Not Beyond*, trans. Lycette Nelson (Albany: State University of New York Press, 1992).

—— *The Infinite Conversation*, trans. Susan Hanson (Minneapolis: University of Minnesota Press, 1993).

—— *Friendship*, trans. Elizabeth Rottenberg (Stanford: Stanford University Press, 1997).

—— "The Instant of My Death," published together with Jacques Derrida, "Demeure: Fiction and Testimony," trans. Elizabeth Rottenberg (Stanford: Stanford University Press, 2000).

Brentano, Franz, *Psychology From an Empirical Standpoint*, trans. Antos C. Rancurello, D.B. Terrell, and Linda L. McAlister (New York: Humanities Press, 1973).

—— *On the Several Senses of Being in Aristotle*, ed. and trans. Rolf George (Berkeley: University of California Press, 1981).

Carnap, Rudolf, "The Elimination of Metaphysics through Logical Analysis of Language," trans. A. Pap, in *Logical Positivism*, ed. A.J. Ayer (Glencoe: The Free Press, 1959), pp. 60–81.

—— *The Logical Structure of the World and Pseudoproblems in Philosophy*, trans. Rolf A. George (Berkeley: University of California Press, 1969).

—— *The Logical Syntax of Language*, trans. Amethe Smeaton (Peru: Open Court, 2002).

Clark, Michael, *Paradoxes from A to Z* (New York: Routledge, 2002).

Coffa, J. Alberto, *The Semantic Tradition from Kant to Carnap: to the Vienna Station* (New York: Cambridge University Press, 1991).

Cutrofello, Andrew, "Nietzsche, Frege, and the Origins of the Analytic/Continental Polemic," *Philosophy Today* 46:5, 2002: Selected Studies in Phenomenology and Existential Philosophy Volume 28, eds Stephen Crowell and Margaret A. Simons, pp. 42–51.

De Beauvoir, Simone, *A Very Easy Death*, trans. Patrick O'Brian (New York: Pantheon Books, 1965).

—— *The Ethics of Ambiguity*, trans. Bernard Frechtman (New York: Citadel Press, 1976).

—— *The Second Sex*, ed. and trans. H.M. Parshley (New York: Vintage Books, 1989).

—— *She Came to Stay*, unattributed translation (New York: W.W. Norton & Company, 1990).

—— *All Men are Mortal*, trans. Leonard M. Friedman (New York: W.W. Norton & Company, 1992).

Deleuze, Gilles, *Nietzsche and Philosophy*, trans. Hugh Tomlinson (New York: Columbia University Press, 1983).

—— *Kant's Critical Philosophy: the Doctrine of the Faculties*, trans. Hugh Tomlinson and Barbara Habberjam (Minneapolis: University of Minnesota Press, 1984).

—— *Foucault*, trans. Seán Hand (Minneapolis: University of Minnesota Press, 1988).

—— *The Logic of Sense*, ed. Constantin V. Boundas, trans. Mark Lester with Charles Stivale (New York: Columbia University Press, 1990).

—— *Bergsonism*, trans. Hugh Tomlinson and Barbara Habberjam (New York: Zone Books, 1991).

—— "Coldness and Cruelty," trans. Jean McNeil, published in *Masochism* together with *Venus in Furs*, Leopold von Sacher-Masoch (New York: Zone Books, 1991).

—— *Difference and Repetition*, trans. Paul Patton (New York: Columbia University Press, 1994).

—— "How Do We Recognize Structuralism?," trans. Melissa McMahon and Charles J. Stivale, in Charles J. Stivale, *The Two-Fold Thought of Deleuze and Guattari* (New York: The Guilford Press, 1998), pp. 251–82.

—— "Bergson's Conception of Difference," in *The New Bergson*, ed. John Mullarkey (New York: Manchester University Press, 1999), pp. 42–65.

—— *Pure Immanence: Essays on a Life*, trans. Anne Boyman (Cambridge: Zone Books, 2001).

—— *Francis Bacon: the Logic of Sensation*, trans. Daniel W. Smith (Minneapolis: University of Minnesota Press, 2003).

Deleuze, Gilles and Félix Guattari, *Anti-Oedipus: Capitalism and Schizophrenia*, trans. Robert Hurley, Mark Seem, and Helen R. Lane (Minneapolis: University of Minnesota Press, 1983).

Derrida, Jacques, *Speech and Phenomena and Other Essays on Husserl's Theory of Signs*, trans. David B. Allison (Evanston: Northwestern University Press, 1973).

—— *Writing and Difference*, trans. Alan Bass (Chicago: The University of Chicago Press, 1978).

—— *Dissemination*, trans. Barbara Johnson (Chicago: The University of Chicago Press, 1981).

—— "Plato's Pharmacy," in *Dissemination*, op. cit., pp. 61–171.

—— *Margins of Philosophy*, trans. Alan Bass (Chicago: The University of Chicago Press, 1982).

—— "Foreword: *Fors*: The Anglish Words of Nicholas Abraham and Maria Torok," in Abraham and Torok, *The Wolf Man's Magic Word*, op. cit., pp. xi–xlviii.

—— *The Post Card: From Socrates to Freud and Beyond*, trans. Alan Bass (Chicago: The University of Chicago Press, 1987).

—— *Edmund Husserl's Origin of Geometry: an Introduction*, trans. John P. Leavey, Jr. (Lincoln: University of Nebraska Press, 1989).

—— *Given Time: I. Counterfeit Money*, trans. Peggy Kamuf (Chicago, The University of Chicago Press, 1992).

—— *Aporias*, trans. Thomas Dutoit (Stanford: Stanford University Press, 1993).

—— "Text Read at Louis Althusser's Funeral," trans. Robert Harvey, in *The Althusserian Legacy*, eds E. Ann Kaplan and Michael Sprinker (New York: Verso, 1993), pp. 241–5.

—— *Specters of Marx: the State of the Debt, the Work of Mourning, and the New International*, trans. Peggy Kamuf (New York: Routledge, 1994).

—— *Who's Afraid of Philosophy? Right to Philosophy I*, trans. Jan Plug (Stanford: Stanford University Press, 2002).

Descartes, *Meditations on First Philosophy*, trans. Donald A. Cress (Indianapolis: Hackett Press, 1979).

Dummett, Michael, *Origins of Analytical Philosophy* (Cambridge: Harvard University Press, 1993).

Fanon, Frantz, *Black Skin, White Masks*, trans. Charles Lam Markmann (New York: Grove Press, 1967).

—— *The Wretched of the Earth*, with a preface by Jean-Paul Sartre, trans. Constance Farrington (New York: Grove Weidenfeld, 1991).

Foucault, Michel, *The Archaeology of Knowledge and the Discourse on Language*, trans. A.M. Sheridan Smith (New York: Pantheon Books, 1972).

—— *Madness and Civilization: a History of Insanity in the Age of Reason*, trans. Richard Howard (New York: Vintage Books, 1973).

—— *The Order of Things: an Archaeology of the Human Sciences*, unattributed translation (New York: Vintage Books, 1973).

—— *Language, Counter-Memory, Practice: Selected Essays and Interviews*, ed. Donald F. Bouchard, trans. Donald F. Bouchard and Sherry Simon (Ithaca: Cornell University Press, 1977).

—— *Discipline and Punish: the Birth of the Prison*, trans. Alan Sheridan (New York: Vintage Books, 1979).

—— *This is not a Pipe*, ed. and trans. James Harkness (Berkeley: University of California Press, 1983).

—— "Dream, Imagination, and Existence: an Introduction to Ludwig Binswanger's 'Dream and Existence,'" trans. Forrest Williams, in *Review of Existential Psychology and Psychiatry*, XIX:1, 1985, pp. 31–78.

—— *The Care of the Self: Volume 3 of The History of Sexuality*, trans. Robert Hurley (New York: Vintage Books, 1988).

—— *The History of Sexuality Volume I: an Introduction*, trans. Robert Hurley (New York: Vintage Books, 1990).

—— *The Use of Pleasure: Volume 2 of The History of Sexuality*, trans. Robert Hurley (New York: Vintage Books, 1990).

—— *The Politics of Truth*, ed. Sylvère Lotringer and Lysa Hochroth (New York: Semtiotext(e), 1997).

—— *Aesthetics, Method, and Epistemology: Essential Works of Foucault 1954–1984 Volume Two*, ed. James D. Faubion, trans. Robert Hurley and others (New York: The New Press, 1998).

Frege, Gottlob, *The Foundations of Arithmetic*, trans. J.L. Austin (Evanston: Northwestern University Press, 1980).

—— *The Frege Reader*, ed. Michael Beaney (Oxford: Blackwell Publishers, 1997).

Freud, Sigmund, *Jokes and their Relation to the Unconscious*, ed. and trans. James Strachey (New York: W.W. Norton & Company, 1963).

—— *The Interpretation of Dreams*, ed. and trans. James Strachey (New York: Avon Books, 1965).

—— *Beyond the Pleasure Principle*, ed. and trans. James Strachey (New York: W.W. Norton & Company, 1989).

—— *Civilization and its Discontents*, ed. and trans. James Strachey (New York: W.W. Norton & Company, 1989).

—— *The Ego and the Id*, trans. Joan Riviere, rev. trans. and ed. James Strachey (New York: W.W. Norton & Company, 1989).

—— *Group Psychology and the Analysis of the Ego*, ed. and trans. James Strachey (New York: W.W. Norton & Company, 1989).

—— *New Introductory Lectures on Psycho-Analysis*, ed. and trans. James Strachey (New York: W.W. Norton & Company, 1989).

—— *Totem and Taboo: Some Points of Agreement between the Mental Lives of Savages and Neurotics*, ed. and trans. James Strachey (New York: W.W. Norton & Company, 1989).

—— *General Psychological Theory: Papers on Metapsychology*, ed. Philip Rieff (New York: Simon & Schuster, 1997).

Friedman, Michael, *A Parting of the Ways: Carnap, Cassirer, and Heidegger* (Chicago: Open Court, 2000).

Gadamer, Hans-Georg, *The Relevance of the Beautiful and Other Essays*, ed. Robert Bernasconi, trans. Nicholas Walker (New York: Cambridge University Press, 1986).

—— *Truth and Method*, second rev. edn, trans. Joel Weinsheimer and Donald G. Marshall (New York: Continuum, 1989).

—— *Gadamer on Celan: "Who Am I and Who are You?" and Other Essays*, ed. and trans. Richard Heinemann and Bruce Krajewski (Albany: State University of New York Press, 1997).

Gilbert-Rolfe, Jeremy, *Beauty and the Contemporary Sublime* (New York: Allworth Press, 1999).

Goldmann, Lucien, *Lukács and Heidegger: Towards a New Philosophy*, trans. William Q. Boelhower (London: Routledge & Kegan Paul, 1977).

Habermas, Jürgen, *Knowledge and Human Interests*, trans. Jeremy J. Shapiro (Boston: Beacon Press, 1971).

—— *Philosophical–Political Profiles*, trans. Frederick G. Lawrence (Cambridge: The MIT Press, 1983).

—— *The Theory of Communicative Action Volume One: Reason and the Rationalization of Society*, trans. Thomas McCarthy (Boston: Beacon Press, 1984).

—— *The Philosophical Discourse of Modernity: Twelve Lectures*, trans. Frederick Lawrence (Cambridge: The MIT Press, 1987).

—— *The Theory of Communicative Action Volume Two: Lifeworld and System: a Critique of Functionalist Reason*, trans. Thomas McCarthy (Boston: Beacon Press, 1987).

—— *On the Logic of the Social Sciences*, trans. Shierry Weber Nicholsen and Jerry A. Stark (Cambridge: The MIT Press, 1988).

—— "A Reply," in *Communicative Action: Essays on Jürgen Habermas's The Theory of Communicative Action*, eds Axel Honneth and Hans Joas, trans. Jeremy Gaines and Doris L. Jones (Cambridge: The MIT Press, 1991), pp. 214–64.

—— *Between Facts and Norms: Contributions to a Discourse Theory of Law and Democracy*, trans. William Rehg (Cambridge: The MIT Press, 1996).

—— *The Future of Human Nature*, trans. William Rehg, Max Pensky, and Hella Beister (Cambridge: Polity Press, 2003).

Hahn, Lewis Edwin, ed., *The Philosophy of Hans-Georg Gadamer* (Chicago: Open Court, 1997).

Hanna, Robert, *Kant and the Foundations of Analytic Philosophy* (New York: Oxford University Press, 2001).

Hegel, G.W.F., *Faith and Knowledge*, trans. Walter Cerf and H.S. Harris (Albany: State University of New York Press, 1977).

—— *Phenomenology of Spirit*, trans. A.V. Miller (New York: Oxford University Press, 1977).

Heidegger, Martin, *Being and Time*, trans. John Macquarrie and Edward Robinson (New York: Harper & Row, 1962).

—— *Kant and the Problem of Metaphysics*, trans. James S. Churchill (Bloomington: Indiana University Press, 1962).

—— *Discourse on Thinking*, trans. John M. Anderson and E. Hans Freund (New York: Harper Colophon, 1969).

—— "My Way to Phenomenology," in *On Time and Being*, op. cit., pp. 74–82.

—— *On Time and Being*, trans. Joan Stambaugh (New York: Harper & Row, 1972).

—— *Poetry, Language, Thought*, trans. Albert Hofstadter (New York: Harper & Row, 1975).

—— *The Question Concerning Technology and Other Essays*, trans. William Lovitt (New York: Harper & Row Publishers, 1977).

—— *Nietzsche*, Volumes I and II, trans. David Farrell Krell (New York: Harper-Collins, 1991).

—— *Nietzsche*, Volumes III and IV, ed. David Farrell Krell, trans. Joan Stambaugh, David Farrell Krell, and Frank A. Capuzzi (New York: HarperCollins, 1991).

—— *Basic Writings*, rev. edn, ed. David Farrell Krell (New York: HarperCollins, 1993).

—— *Kant and the Problem of Metaphysics*, fifth edn, trans. Richard Taft (Bloomington: Indiana University Press, 1997).

—— *Pathmarks*, ed. William McNeill (New York: Cambridge University Press, 1998).

—— *Elucidations of Hölderlin's Poetry*, trans. Keith Hoeller (New York: Humanity Books, 2000).

—— *Introduction to Metaphysics*, trans. Gregory Fried and Richard Polt (New Haven: Yale University Press, 2000).

Husserl, Edmund, *Cartesian Meditations: an Introduction to Phenomenology*, trans. Dorion Cairns (Boston: Martinus Nijhoff Publishers, 1960).

—— "Philosophy as Rigorous Science," in *Phenomenology and the Crisis of Philosophy*, ed. Quentin Lauer (New York: Harper & Row, 1965), pp. 71–147.

—— *The Crisis of European Sciences and Transcendental Phenomenology: an Introduction to Phenomenological Philosophy*, trans. David Carr (Evanston: Northwestern University Press, 1970).

—— "The Origin of Geometry," in *The Crisis of European Sciences and Transcendental Phenomenology*, op. cit., pp. 353–78.

—— "Philosophy and the Crisis of European Humanity," in *The Crisis of European Sciences and Transcendental Phenomenology*, op. cit., pp. 269–99.

—— *Ideas Pertaining to a Pure Phenomenology and to a Phenomenological Philosophy, First Book: General Introduction to a Pure Phenomenology*, trans. F. Kersten (Dordrecht: Kluwer Academic Publishers, 1983).

—— *On the Phenomenology of the Consciousness of Internal Time (1893–1917)*, trans. John Barnett Brough (Boston: Kluwer Academic Publishers, 1991).

—— *Logical Investigations*, 2 vols., ed. Dermot Moran, trans. J.N. Findlay (New York: Routledge, 2001).

—— *Philosophy of Arithmetic*, trans. Dallas Willard (Dordrecht: Kluwer, 2003).

Irigaray, Luce, *Speculum of the Other Woman*, trans. Gillian C. Gill (Ithaca: Cornell University Press, 1985).

—— *Marine Lover of Friedrich Nietzsche*, trans. Gillian C. Gill (New York: Columbia University Press, 1991).

—— *An Ethics of Sexual Difference*, trans. Carolyn Burke and Gillian C. Gill (Ithaca: Cornell University Press, 1993).

—— *Je, Tu, Nous: Toward a Culture of Difference*, trans. Alison Martin (New York: Routledge, 1993).

—— *The Forgetting of Air in Martin Heidegger*, trans. Mary Beth Mader (Austin: University of Texas Press, 1999).

—— *Democracy Begins Between Two*, trans. Kirsteen Anderson (London: The Athlone Press, 2000).

—— *To Be Two*, trans. Monique M. Rhodes and Marco F. Cocito-Monoc (London: The Athlone Press, 2000).

Kant, Immanuel, *Kant's Critique of Judgement*, trans. J.H. Bernard, rev. edn (London: Macmillan and Co., 1931).

—— *Observations on the Feeling of the Beautiful and Sublime*, trans. John T. Goldthwait (Berkeley: University of California Press, 1960).

—— *Anthropology From a Pragmatic Point of View*, trans. Mary. J. Gregor (The Hague: Martinus Nijhoff, 1974).

—— *Philosophical Correspondence, 1759–99*, ed. and trans. Arnulf Zweig (Chicago: The University of Chicago Press, 1986).

—— "Succinct Exposition of Some Meditations on Fire," trans. Lewis White Beck, in *Kant's Latin Writings: Translations, Commentaries, and Notes*, eds Lewis White Beck in collaboration with Mary J. Gregor, Ralf Meerbote, and John A. Reuscher (New York: Peter Lang, 1986), pp. 23–46.

—— *Logic*, trans. Robert S. Hartman and Wolfgang Schwarz (New York: Dover Publications, Inc., 1988).

—— *Political Writings*, second, enlarged edn, ed. Hans Reiss, trans. H.B. Nisbet (New York: Cambridge University Press, 1991).

—— "What is Orientation in Thinking?," in *Political Writings*, op. cit., pp. 237–49.

—— "Concerning the Ultimate Ground of the Differentiation of Directions in Space," in *Theoretical Philosophy 1755–1770*, op. cit., pp. 361–72.

—— "Dreams of a Spirit-Seer Elucidated by Dreams of Metaphysics," in *Theoretical Philosophy 1755–1770*, op. cit., pp. 301–59.

—— *Theoretical Philosophy 1755–1770*, ed. and trans. David Walford in collaboration with Ralf Meerbote (New York: Cambridge University Press, 1992).

—— *The Conflict of the Faculties*, in *Religion and Rational Theology*, op. cit., pp. 237–327.

—— *Critique of Practical Reason*, in *Practical Philosophy*, op. cit., pp. 137–271.

—— "The End of All Things," in *Religion and Rational Theology*, op. cit., pp. 221–31.

—— *Groundwork of the Metaphysics of Morals*, trans. Mary J. Gregor, in *Practical Philosophy*, op. cit., pp. 41–108.

—— *Lectures on the Philosophical Doctrine of Religion*, in *Religion and Rational Theology*, op. cit., pp. 339–451.

—— *Metaphysics of Morals*, in *Practical Philosophy*, op. cit., pp. 353–603.

—— *Practical Philosophy*, ed. and trans. Mary J. Gregor (New York: Cambridge University Press, 1996).

—— *Religion and Rational Theology*, ed. and trans. Allen W. Wood and George Di Giovanni (New York: Cambridge University Press, 1996).

—— *Critique of Pure Reason*, trans. Paul Guyer and Allen W. Wood (New York: Cambridge University Press, 1997).

—— *Lectures on Metaphysics*, ed. and trans. Karl Ameriks and Steve Naragon (New York: Cambridge University Press, 1997).

—— "On the Different Races of Man," in *Race and the Enlightenment: a Reader*, ed. Emmanuel Chukwudi Eze (Cambridge: Blackwell Publishers, 1997), pp. 38–48.

—— *Critique of the Power of Judgment*, ed. Paul Guyer, trans. Paul Guyer and Eric Matthews (New York: Cambridge University Press, 2000).

—— *Metaphysical Foundations of Natural Science*, trans. Michael Friedman, in *Theoretical Philosophy After 1781*, op. cit., pp. 181–270.

—— "Proclamation of the Imminent Conclusion of a Treaty of Perpetual Peace in Philosophy," in *Theoretical Philosophy After 1781*, op. cit., pp. 451–60.

—— *Prolegomena to any Future Metaphysics that will be able to come forth as Science*, trans. Gary Hatfield, in *Theoretical Philosophy After 1781*, op. cit., pp. 49–169.

—— *Theoretical Philosophy After 1781*, eds Henry Allison and Peter Heath, trans. Gary Hatfield, Michael Friedman, Henry Allison, and Peter Heath (New York: Cambridge University Press, 2002).

Klossowski, Pierre, *Nietzsche and the Vicious Circle*, trans. Daniel W. Smith (Chicago: The University of Chicago Press, 1997).

Kristeva, Julia, *Powers of Horror: an Essay on Abjection*, trans. Leon S. Roudiez (New York: Columbia University Press, 1982).

—— *Revolution in Poetic Language*, trans. Margaret Waller (New York: Columbia University Press, 1984).

—— *Black Sun: Depression and Melancholia*, trans. Leon S. Roudiez (New York: Columbia University Press, 1989).

—— *Strangers to Ourselves*, trans. Leon S. Roudiez (New York: Columbia University Press, 1991).

—— *Julia Kristeva Interviews*, ed. Ross Mitchell Guberman (New York: Columbia University Press, 1996).

Lacan, Jacques, *Écrits: A Selection*, trans. Alan Sheridan (New York: W.W. Norton & Company, 1977).

——— *The Four Fundamental Concepts of Psycho-Analysis*, trans. Alan Sheridan (New York: W.W. Norton & Company, 1978).

——— *The Seminar of Jacques Lacan Book I: Freud's Papers on Technique 1953–1954*, ed. Jacques-Alain Miller, trans. John Forrester (New York: W.W. Norton & Company, 1988).

——— *The Seminar of Jacques Lacan Book II: the Ego in Freud's Theory and in the Technique of Psychoanalysis 1954–1955*, ed. Jacques-Alain Miller, trans. Sylvana Tomaselli, with notes by John Forrester (New York: W.W. Norton & Company, 1988).

——— "Seminar on 'The Purloined Letter,'" in *The Purloined Poe: Lacan, Derrida, and Psychoanalytic Reading*, eds John P. Muller and William J. Richardson (Baltimore: The Johns Hopkins University Press, 1988), pp. 28–54.

——— *The Seminar of Jacques Lacan Book VII: The Ethics of Psychoanalysis 1959–1960*, ed. Jacques-Alain Miller, trans. Dennis Porter (New York: W.W. Norton & Company, 1992).

——— *The Seminar of Jacques Lacan Book III: The Psychoses 1955–1956*, ed. Jacques-Alain Miller, trans. Russell Grigg (New York: W.W. Norton & Company, 1993).

——— *The Seminar of Jacques Lacan Book XX: Encore 1972–1973: On Feminine Sexuality, the Limits of Love and Knowledge*, ed. Jacques-Alain Miller, trans. Bruce Fink (New York: W.W. Norton & Company, 1998).

Levinas, Emmanuel, *Totality and Infinity: an Essay on Exteriority*, trans. Alphonso Lingis (Pittsburgh: Duquesne University Press, 1969).

——— *Time and the Other*, trans. Richard A. Cohen (Pittsburgh: Duquesne University Press, 1987).

——— *Existence and Existents*, trans. Alphonso Lingis, foreword by Robert Bernasconi (Pittsburgh: Duquesne University Press, 2001).

——— *Otherwise than Being, or, Beyond Essence*, trans. Alphonso Lingis (Pittsburgh: Duquesne University Press, 1998).

——— *The Theory of Intuition in Husserl's Phenomenology*, second edn, trans. André Orianne (Evanston: Northwestern University Press, 1998).

Lévi-Strauss, Claude, *Structural Anthropology*, trans. Claire Jacobson and Brooke Grundfest Schoepf (BasicBooks, 1963).

——— *Totemism*, trans. Rodney Needham (Boston: Beacon Press, 1963).

——— *The Savage Mind*, unattributed translation (Chicago: The University of Chicago Press, 1966).

——— *The Elementary Structures of Kinship*, rev. edn, trans. James Harle Bell, John Richard von Sturmer, and Rodney Needham (Boston: Beacon Press, 1969).

——— *Structural Anthropology Volume II*, trans. Monique Layton (Chicago: The University of Chicago Press, 1983).

——— *Introduction to the Work of Marcel Mauss*, trans. Felicity Baker (London: Routledge, 1987).

——— *The Jealous Potter*, trans. Bénédicte Chorier (Chicago: The University of Chicago Press, 1988).

Lukács, Georg, *History and Class Consciousness: Studies in Marxist Dialectics*, trans. Rodney Livingstone (Cambridge: The MIT Press, 1971).

——— *The Theory of the Novel: a Historico-Philosophical Essay on the Forms of Great Epic Literature*, trans. Anna Bostock (Cambridge: The MIT Press, 1971).

——— *Soul and Form*, trans. Anna Bostock (Cambridge: The MIT Press, 1974).

—— *The Destruction of Reason*, trans. Peter Palmer (London: Merlin, 1980).

—— *The Historical Novel*, trans. Hannah Mitchell and Stanley Mitchell (Lincoln: University of Nebraska Press, 1983).

—— *The Lukács Reader*, ed. Arpad Kadarkay (Cambridge: Blackwell Publishers, 1995).

—— *A Defence of History and Class Consciousness: Tailism and the Dialectic*, trans. Esther Leslie (New York: Verso, 2000).

Lyotard, Jean-François, *The Postmodern Condition: a Report on Knowledge*, trans. Geoff Bennington and Brian Massumi (Minneapolis: University of Minnesota Press, 1984).

—— *The Differend: Phrases in Dispute*, trans. Georges Van Den Abbeele (Minneapolis: University of Minnesota Press, 1988).

—— *Peregrinations: Law, Form, Event* (New York: Columbia University Press, 1988).

—— *Libidinal Economy*, trans. Iain Hamilton Grant (Bloomington: Indiana University Press, 1993).

—— *Political Writings*, trans. Bill Readings and Kevin Paul Geiman (Minneapolis: University of Minnesota Press, 1993).

—— *Lessons on the Analytic of the Sublime*, trans. Elizabeth Rottenberg (Stanford: Stanford University Press, 1994).

McCumber, John, *Time in the Ditch: American Philosophy and the McCarthy Era* (Evanston: Northwestern University Press, 2001).

McDowell, John, *Mind and World*, with a new introduction (Cambridge: Harvard University Press, 1996).

Macey, David, *Frantz Fanon: a Biography* (New York: Picador, 2002).

Makkreel, Rudolf A., *Imagination and Interpretation in Kant: the Hermeneutical Import of the Critique of Judgment* (Chicago: The University of Chicago Press, 1990).

Marcuse, Herbert, *Eros and Civilization: a Philosophical Inquiry into Freud*, with a new preface (Boston: Beacon Press, 1966).

—— *Negations: Essays in Critical Theory*, trans. Jeremy J. Shapiro (Boston: Beacon Press, 1969).

—— *One-Dimensional Man: Studies in the Ideology of Advanced Industrial Society*, with a new introduction by Douglas Kellner (Boston: Beacon Press, 1991).

Marx, Karl, *The Economic and Philosophic Manuscripts of 1844*, ed. Dirk J. Struik, trans. Martin Milligan (New York: International Publishers, 1964).

—— *Capital: a Critique of Political Economy Volume One*, trans. Ben Fowkes (New York: Vintage Books, 1977).

—— *Karl Marx: a Reader*, ed. Jon Elster (New York: Cambridge University Press, 1986).

—— *Later Political Writings*, ed. Terrell Carver (New York: Cambridge University Press, 1996).

Marx, Karl and Friedrich Engels, *The German Ideology*, in Marx and Engels, *Collected Works* Volume 5 (London: Lawrence & Wishart, 1976), pp. 19–539.

Mauss, Marcel, *The Gift: the Form and Reason for Exchange in Archaic Societies*, trans. W.D. Halls, foreword by Mary Douglas (New York: W.W. Norton & Company, 1990).

Merleau-Ponty, Maurice, *Phenomenology of Perception*, trans. Colin Smith (New York: Routledge & Kegan Paul, 1962).

—— *The Primacy of Perception and Other Essays on Phenomenological Psychology, the*

Philosophy of Art, History and Politics, ed. James M. Edie (Evanston: Northwestern University Press, 1964).

——— *Sense and Non-Sense*, trans. Hubert L. Dreyfus and Patricia Allen Dreyfus (Evanston: Northwestern University Press, 1964).

——— *Signs*, trans. Richard C. McCleary (Evanston: Northwestern University Press, 1964).

——— *The Visible and the Invisible Followed by Working Notes*, ed. Claude Lefort, trans. Alphonso Lingis (Evanston: Northwestern University Press, 1968).

——— *In Praise of Philosophy and Other Essays*, trans. John Wild, James Edie, and John O'Neill (Evanston: Northwestern University Press, 1988).

Moore, G.E., *Principia Ethica*, rev. edn, ed. Thomas Baldwin (New York: Cambridge University Press, 1993).

Nancy, Jean-Luc, *The Inoperative Community*, trans. Peter Connor, Lisa Garbus, Michael Holland, and Simona Sawhney (Minneapolis: University of Minnesota Press, 1991).

Nietzsche, Friedrich, *The Case of Wagner*, published together with *The Birth of Tragedy*, trans. Walter Kaufmann (New York: Vintage Books, 1967).

——— *Ecce Homo*, trans. Walter Kaufmann, published together with *On the Genealogy of Morals* (New York: Vintage Books, 1969).

——— *The Gay Science with a Prelude in Rhymes and an Appendix of Songs*, trans. Walter Kaufmann (New York: Vintage Books, 1974).

——— *Thus Spoke Zarathustra: a Book for None and All*, trans. Walter Kaufmann (New York: Penguin Books, 1978).

——— *Daybreak: Thoughts on the Prejudices of Morality*, trans. R.J. Hollingdale (New York: Cambridge University Press, 1982).

——— *Beyond Good and Evil: Prelude to a Philosophy of the Future*, trans. Walter Kaufmann (New York: Vintage Books, 1989).

——— *The Anti-Christ*, published together with *Twilight of the Idols*, trans. R.J. Hollingdale (New York: Penguin Books, 1990).

——— *On the Genealogy of Morality*, ed. Keith Ansell-Pearson, trans. Carol Diethe (New York: Cambridge University Press, 1994).

——— "Homer on Competition," in *On the Genealogy of Morality*, op. cit., pp. 187–94.

——— *Twilight of the Idols: or, How to Philosophize with the Hammer*, trans. Richard Polt (Indianapolis: Hackett Publishing Company, 1997).

——— *The Birth of Tragedy and Other Writings*, trans. Ronald Speirs, eds Raymond Geuss and Ronald Speirs (New York: Cambridge University Press, 1999).

——— "On Truth and Lying in a Non-Moral Sense," in *The Birth of Tragedy and Other Writings*, op. cit., pp. 139–53.

Plato, *The Collected Dialogues including the Letters*, eds Edith Hamilton and Huntington Cairns (Princeton: Princeton University Press, 1961).

Ragland, C.P. and Sarah Heidt, eds, *What is Philosophy?* (New Haven: Yale University Press, 2001).

Ricoeur, Paul, "Kant and Husserl," in *Husserl: an Analysis of his Phenomenology*, trans. Edward G. Ballard and Lester E. Embree (Evanston: Northwestern University Press, 1967), pp. 175–201.

——— *The Symbolism of Evil*, trans. Emerson Buchanan (Boston: Beacon Press, 1969).

——— *Freud and Philosophy: an Essay on Interpretation*, trans. Denis Savage (New Haven: Yale University Press, 1970).

—— *The Conflict of Interpretations: Essays in Hermeneutics*, ed. Don Ihde (Evanston: Northwestern University Press, 1974).

—— *Fallible Man*, rev. trans. Charles A. Kelbley (New York: Fordham University Press, 1986).

—— *Critique and Conviction: Conversations with François Azouvi and Marc de Launay*, trans. Kathleen Blamey (New York: Columbia University Press, 1998).

—— *The Just*, trans. David Pellauer (Chicago: The University of Chicago Press, 2000).

Rorty, Richard, *Philosophy and the Mirror of Nature* (Princeton: Princeton University Press, 1979).

—— *Consequences of Pragmatism (Essays: 1972–1980)* (Minneapolis: University of Minnesota Press, 1982).

—— *Contingency, Irony, and Solidarity* (New York: Cambridge University Press, 1989).

Ross, David, *Aristotle* (London: Methuen & Co. Ltd., 1964).

Russell, Bertand, *The Principles of Mathematics*, second edn (New York: W.W. Norton & Company, 1938).

—— *A History of Western Philosophy* (New York: Simon and Schuster, 1945).

—— *Our Knowledge of the External World as a Field for Scientific Method in Philosophy* (New York: Routledge, 1993).

Said, Edward W., *Representations of the Intellectual* (New York: Vintage Books, 1996).

Sartre, Jean-Paul, *Nausea*, trans. Lloyd Alexander, in *Nausea/The Wall and Other Stories: Two Volumes in One* (New York: MJF Books, n.d.).

—— *The Wall and Other Stories*, trans. Lloyd Alexander, in *Nausea/The Wall and Other Stories: Two Volumes in One*, op. cit.

—— *The Transcendence of the Ego: an Existentialist Theory of Consciousness*, trans. Forrest Williams and Robert Kirkpatrick (New York: Farrar, Straus and Giroux, n.d.).

—— *Search for a Method*, trans. Hazel E. Barnes (New York: Vintage Books, 1968).

—— *Critique of Dialectical Reason: I. Theory of Practical Ensembles*, ed. Jonathan Rée, trans. Alan Sheridan-Smith (London: Verso, 1982).

—— *"What is Literature?" and Other Essays* (Cambridge: Harvard University Press, 1988).

—— *No Exit and Three Other Plays*, trans. S. Gilbert and L. Abel (New York: Vintage Books, 1989).

—— *Existentialism and Human Emotions*, trans. Bernard Frechtman and Hazel E. Barnes (New York: Carol Publishing Group, 1990).

—— *The Age of Reason*, trans. Eric Sutton (New York: Vintage Books, 1992).

—— *Being and Nothingness: a Phenomenological Essay on Ontology*, trans. Hazel E. Barnes (New York: Washington Square Press, 1992).

—— *The Reprieve*, trans. Eric Sutton (New York: Vintage Books, 1992).

—— *Troubled Sleep*, trans. Gerard Hopkins (New York: Vintage Books, 1992).

—— *Anti-Semite and Jew*, trans. George J. Becker, preface by Michael Walzer (New York: Schocken Books, 1995).

—— *The Imaginary: a Phenomenological Psychology of the Imagination*, revisions and historical introduction by Arlette Elkaïm-Sartre, trans. Jonathan Webber (New York: Routledge, 2004).

Scarry, Elaine, *On Beauty and Being Just* (Princeton: Princeton University Press, 1999).

Schiller, Friedrich, *On the Aesthetic Education of Man in a Series of Letters*, ed. and trans. Elizabeth M. Wilkinson and L.A. Willoughby (New York: Oxford University Press, 1982).

Sellars, Wilfrid, *Empiricism and the Philosophy of Mind*, with an introduction by Richard Rorty and a study guide by Robert Brandom (Cambridge: Harvard University Press, 1997).

Shakespeare, William, *The Riverside Shakespeare*, second edn (New York: Houghton Mifflin Company, 1997).

Weil, Simone, *Gravity and Grace*, trans. Emma Crawford and Mario von der Ruhr (New York: Routledge, 2002).

Wittgenstein, Ludwig, *Tractatus Logico-Philosophicus*, trans. D.F. Pears and B.F. McGuinness (Atlantic Highlands: Humanities Press, 1974).

Žižek, Slavoj, *Looking Awry: an Introduction to Jacques Lacan Through Popular Culture* (Cambridge: The MIT Press, 1992).

—— *Tarrying with the Negative: Kant, Hegel, and the Critique of Ideology* (Durham: Duke University Press, 1993).

—— *The Metastases of Enjoyment: Six Essays on Woman and Causality* (New York: Verso, 1994).

—— *The Fragile Absolute or, Why is the Christian Legacy Worth Fighting For?* (New York: Verso, 2000).

—— "Postface: Georg Lukács as the Philosopher of Leninism," in Georg Lukács, *A Defence of History and Class Consciousness*, op. cit., pp. 151–82.

—— *Did Somebody Say Totalitarianism? Five Interventions in the (Mis)use of a Notion* (New York: Verso, 2001).

—— *Welcome to the Desert of the Real! Five Essays on September 11 and Related Dates* (New York: Verso, 2002).

Index

Printed in Great Britain
by Amazon